FRENCH LITERATURE

HISTORY

OF

FRENCH LITERATURE

IN

THE EIGHTEENTH CENTURY.

BY ALEXANDER VINET

TRANSLATED FROM THE FRENCH

BY THE

REV. JAMES BRYCE.

KENNIKAT PRESS
Port Washington, N. Y./London

HISTORY OF FRENCH LITERATURE

First published in 1854
Reissued in 1970 by Kennikat Press
Library of Congress Catalog Card No: 70-103237
SBN 8046-0873-3

Manufactured by Taylor Publishing Company   Dallas, Texas

TRANSLATOR'S PREFACE.

THE work, of which a translation is here presented to the Public, has some of the disadvantages of a posthumous publication. It is the substance of a course of Lectures prepared for delivery during the summer of 1846; however, when the author was about the middle of his Lectures on the character and writings of J. J. Rousseau, he was arrested by a mortal distemper, under which he sunk, after a few months' illness. In these circumstances, the final revision of the author was impossible; but it must also be added, that M. Vinet did not write his Lectures. He seems to have had great power in extempore address, and usually spoke from notes, suggesting the progress of thought, felicitous epithets, and passages for quotation. These notes form the basis of this work, and the French editors carefully compared them with the note-books of four of the pupils, who attended this course so far as it was continued.

91895

From these sources the contents of this volume have
been collected, and I cannot help paying a tribute of
admiration to the fidelity and success with which the
French editors have performed their very difficult task.
M. Vinet's style and forms of expression are wonderfully
preserved; and, in the circumstances of the case, the
work could not have been brought before the public
under more favourable auspices.

There are other very distinguished works on this
subject, which may appear to render this publication
altogether unnecessary. Villemain and de Barante have
written the history of French literature with a brilliancy
that might seem to defy competition. On this point,
a difference of opinion may be justly entertained. Every
subject must be improved by new and independent
thought; and, in the present case, the young and inex-
perienced will derive singular benefit from the sound
religious principles of the author, which are a tacit refutation of the unsound opinions entertained by some
even of the best writers in France during the eighteenth
century. Vinet had collected materials for a complete
history of French literature, and had he lived to publish
it, few will deny that it would have been a great boon
conferred on his country.

This work will be found occasionally very unequal.
Some of the writers are little known, and their writings
appear to us in these days extremely uninteresting. No
critic can render them attractive, and yet as they were

famous in their day, they could not be passed over in silence. Mademoiselle de Launay, Marivaux, Houdard de la Motte, and even La Chaussée, are names which are now almost forgotten, even in France, and would never have reached Britain, unless in a history of French literature. On the other hand, the Duke de Saint-Simon, Fontenelle, Montesquieu, Voltaire, and Rousseau, are brought before the reader with a graphical power, which shows the author to have been very highly fitted for the delineation of character, and for critical analysis.

The attention of the reader is especially claimed in behalf of the writings of the Duke de Saint-Simon. He is, perhaps, the most extraordinary writer of his own, or of any other age. He is a Christian of the Jansenist school, but withal he is a peer of France, and his Christianity was not allowed to impinge on any of his dignities or privileges. His high notions of the importance of the peerage would lead us to question the soundness and sincerity of the Christian profession, which appears to hold only the second place in his mind; but all this passes with the Duke for a species of eccentricity, and we are rather disposed to smile at the absurdity of his expressions than doubt the correctness of his principles. The very exalted opinion which he entertained of the dignity of the French peerage, would probably be a part of the *wood, hay,* and *stubble,* which was to be burnt up.

His writings consist of memoirs of his own times, and present to us a series of portraits of the distinguished

men of that age, delineated with a degree of fidelity,
which must in general have given very little satisfaction
to the originals.   It was the fashion to flatter Louis
XIV., and call him great; the Duke de Saint-Simon
does nothing of the kind, but he brings out facts and
anecdotes illustrative of his tyranny, oppression, dishonesty, and petty revenge, till the reader begins to
wonder whether the opposite epithet might not have
been, in all the circumstances of the case, the more
appropriate.   He strips him of all the trappings of
royalty, and convinces us that his character would
hardly have been held respectable in the middle classes
of society.   If any one be charmed with the stately
elegance of the French Court at that time, the Duke de
Saint-Simon will show what it is really worth.   Other
characters he dissects with anatomical precision, and lays
bare their weaknesses with unsparing severity.   The
Marshall de Villars, the great antagonist of the Duke of
Marlborough, he treats with indignant contempt.   By
far the finest part of his memoirs is the portrait of the
Duke of Burgundy, which is found in this volume at full
length.   He was the grandson of Louis XIV., the presumptive heir of the throne of France, gifted with talents
of the highest order, and fitted by nature for fathoming
the depths of abstract science, but his natural temper
was that of a demon, and its workings rendered him an
object of terror to all around him.   A change, however,
took place, which the Spirit of God alone can accomplish;

and in his eighteenth year he became an humble and devoted Christian. The whole of this portrait is especially recommended to the notice of the reader, as it is believed that a narrative of the life and death of this remarkable prince, so faithful and minute, is nowhere else to be found.

The writings of the Duke de St Simon are by no means attractive in their style, for it often requires some thought to discover his meaning. He occasionally feels himself entangled with an unwieldy sentiment, which he will not reject ; and the French language is bent to the purpose of expressing it, while the rules of syntax and established idiom are entirely disregarded. But, amid the ruggedness and carelessness of his style, the freshness and vividness of the pictures, keep up the reader's attention. It is no small matter to find an independent writer in the age of Louis XIV.

On the whole, this work of Vinet appears to be worthy of public approbation ; and the translation, which only aims at fidelity, will enable the mere English reader to become acquainted with French literature in an interesting age.

CONTENTS.

THE

HISTORY OF FRENCH LITERATURE

IN THE

EIGHTEENTH CENTURY.

INTRODUCTION.

GENTLEMEN,

The subject of investigation in this place is chiefly a history, a history rather than a series of notices, opinions, and analyses. These two modes of inquiry are very closely connected, and are often confounded. The seventeenth and eighteenth centuries, in relation to us, take already the place of antiquity. The authors who belong to these two eras, seem to be little more than the ornaments of a literature whose sun is set, and those who enjoyed the least disputed popularity, are, in the present day, generally speaking, little read.

We shall begin by taking a rapid and final view of the seventeenth century, and shall attempt to give a summary of its peculiar characteristics before we enter upon the examination of the period which succeeded it.

The seventeenth century, taken as a whole, but especially considered during its second half, has been represented more than once as a resting-place, an intermediate space between two ages of criticism and infidelity. The sixteenth century was the age of Montaigne and Charron. In the eighteenth, the tendencies of Montaigne and Charron found new representatives in Voltaire, Diderot, d'Alembert and Rousseau. Between the two, the river had stopped its course, and had become a vast transparent lake, but at its outlet, amid rocks and precipices, the current regained its strength. After a time of repose, the human mind set out again in its career of improvement; not that this repose was a time of inactivity, on the contrary, there was regular and uninterrupted exertion, which had for its object to fix the attention of mankind on certain doctrines. The torrent of doubt and denial was stemmed by a work of construction. In the sixteenth century, men deny and interrogate; in the seventeenth, they answer and affirm; in the eighteenth, they begin anew to put questions.

Let us not consider as mere chance, gentlemen, a state of mind, which is easily explained. The seventeenth century is the logical sequence, the natural production of the sixteenth. In reference to philosophy and thought in general, the human mind always proceeds in this manner: it makes progress by antithesis and reaction, and resembles the pendulum, which unceasingly oscillates from right to left and from left to right. But the pendulum moves in a fixed space, and the value of one of its oscillations is constantly compensated by that of the other, while the action and reaction of the human mind do not entirely destroy each other, some quantity remains, and these quantities, added together, make up the sum of its progress. At the first glance, man seems to us to undo to the same extent what he has already done; but if we extend the field of our observation, we shall be convinced of the real and gradual advancement of human nature. Whether this advancement is for good or evil, is a different question.

The seventeenth century is, indeed, a resting-place between two periods of denial or unbelief,[1] and whatever variety the nature of its intellectual acquirements may present, it is evident that a certain satisfaction is commonly derived from the aspect of an era, during which the human mind has sought rest in affirmation. But we must not deceive ourselves; the human mind affirms but little, its certainties are seldom full and satis-

---

[1] French *Negation*.

factory; and when an age or even a man affirms, it always remains to be seen whether this age or this man be sincere and consistent. In the bosom of that clear but deep basin, in which the mind of the seventeenth century is settled, we catch a glimpse of the form of the monster that must in after times be brought to light.

The general and primary character of the seventeenth century is authority; but is *authority* identical with *affirmation?* This is an important question. Yes, although the terms are not synonymous, at this point the two facts meet. It is not the same with an age or a people as with an individual. A man may affirm from his own individual conviction; when a nation affirms, it is under the persuasion of its authority.

However this may be, the seventeenth century bears the impress of authority in religion, politics, and literature.

As to religion, we see the religious troubles allayed, at the same time as the civil commotions, of which they were the principal cause. Calvinism has retired within limits beyond which it will no more be found, men no longer attempt its extermination, but they trace for it a boundary beyond which it cannot pass. Scepticism, the other enemy of catholicism, is reduced to silence, but it gnaws its bit and secretly cherishes daring thoughts; nor is it satisfied with loosely rejecting the doctrines of revelation, it treats in the same manner the principles of natural religion. The unbelief of the seventeenth century is atheism, and to atheists the arguments of the defenders of religion are addressed. We do not find at that time religious rationalism, because little was done for France, and therefore rationalism was then impossible—there was no middle place between orthodox catholicism and downright atheism. But this unbelief avoids the light, it goes deep, so to speak, into the earth, from which it will come forth in the most hideous form another day.

On the other hand, the dispute between Jansenism and Molinism is public and important. Jansenism produces a reaction in two ways; in the way of piety in opposition to the worldly spirit of Molinism, and also, but without knowing it, in the way of freedom of thought in opposition to the constraint of laws and institutions. It is at once the representative of a more fervent Christianity and of the rights and privileges of the human mind. Nevertheless this movement, which animates catholicism, does not reach the authority of its principle, on the contrary, it shows its extent. What must have been the strength of a unity, which Jansenism, supported by its high privilege and by its genius, was unable to shake? It was because the seventeenth century had, above all, need of repose; happily that repose was glorious. The catholic religion at that time possessed so great men, that they made its authority loved, or at least honoured. Politics found their account in it.

As to politics, authority reigns uncontrolled. The parliaments are mute. The Fronde is only a movement without ability. Political questions are generally kept out of view. No man of talent during that time directed his attention to such points, with the exception of Fenelon and Massillon toward the end of the century. Every where else silence is maintained. Perhaps La Bruyère deserves also to be excepted.

In regard to literature, in it more than in anything else, if possible, the same need of authority makes itself be felt. At that time conventional forms were established, of which some may be defended and others were adopted without examination. It is a kind of literary religion, mingled no doubt with superstition, but not with superstition in itself, because it is founded on true principles. It is connected with the worship of antiquity, imperfectly comprehended indeed, but approved, felt, and honoured. Here and there, however, we perceive some feeble wishes for independence; some men of talent complain, that literature is not sufficiently national, and they would go back to the middle ages, our own antiquity : they would free style from certain laws and restraints; but these are only powerless desires, the attempts of some men of second-rate ability, and weak aspirations at what we in the present day term *romantisme*. No man of eminence adopts the creed of such ordinary persons, who are consigned to contempt by the oracles of the classical religion, of which Boileau is high priest.

If there be any department in which liberty has made progress, it is philosophy. This century, to which the epithet philosophical has been refused, is in reality more philosophical than the succeeding period, in which philosophy will only be found to consist of analysis and criticism, and no longer to possess that speculative and disinterested character which distinguishes the writings of Descartes and Malebranche.

It may be asked, how this liberty of thinking could have existed in an age that bowed to authority. The extraordinary abundance of intellectual productions during that time was undoubtedly one of its causes. An age quite literary cannot be anti-philosophical. Between literature and philosophy, there naturally exists a very close connection; we cannot exclusively cultivate one of these domains and entirely neglect the other, for a great literary epoch will be remarkable for the exercise of thinking. Thought will not always assume the form of philosophy, but it will have it for its foundation, and even the poets themselves may be philosophers. While philosophy presented itself under the form of literature, it excited no jealousy. When it was not disguised under this covering, it prevented all suspicion by coming to the conflict in the armour of religion. It took its seat at the foot of the cross, or rather at the foot of the apostolic see. Descartes, Malebranche, Bossuet, used great liberty of thinking under the shelter of the orthodoxy of the church. In that position they were beyond all suspicion; and, in short, the philosophers of the seventeenth century were as bold thinkers as those who succeeded them. This statement might furnish a subject for discussion. Authority envelopes everything, but destroys nothing. Universal activity is the guarantee of liberty, inactivity alone is its destruction.

We come now to this literature in itself. In the seventeenth century, what was its object? The proper ground of its activity is the second characteristic by which it must be distinguished. It is confined within a narrow circle, but we must draw a line of distinction; two kinds of literature simultaneously exist, the literature of action, or that which is practical, and the literature of taste, which may be considered as including every species of fine writing.

The first appears as merely a vehicle. The form alone of this kind of writing belongs to literature; the end in view is plainly separated from it. The authors of these writings are anxious by their means to bring about changes, to produce results—in a word, to influence the conduct. The practical literature of the seventeenth century is marvellously rich; almost all the prose belongs to it. Bossuet, Bourdaloue, all the great preachers, Pascal, Arnauld, Nicole, fill up its ranks. La Bruyère does not come in here. This species of literature is exclusively practical; its form agrees with its end, but mere form is never substituted for the end. Here may be discovered the admirable superiority of such men as Fenelon and Bossuet. They did not write a work for a purely literary purpose—they consecrated their talents to their own official duties, and especially to the development and defence of the truths of their religion. Such were the objects to which practical literature was principally directed. The literature of taste makes itself its own object and end ; its single aim is fine writing. The things of the real world and its circumstances only furnish occasion for its exercise. In the seventeenth century, it is as purely confined to matters of taste, as the other is purely practical—a real contrast to the following age, in which practical literature will be found to be too much occupied with matters of taste and esthetic literature—too much devoted to matters of practice.

Having laid down this distinction, it appears to us that the circle of literary operation in the seventeenth century is far too confined, when compared with the space which it comprehended in the sixteenth. We must not, however, deceive ourselves. At every period this circle will seem to us incomplete. The literature of all past ages will appear to us to have neglected certain subjects, and a certain class of interests and thoughts, to which the present time attaches great importance. We may be astonished at what we have, and not at what we want. No time has completely embraced the sphere of all the ideas, which may be called literary, and every age has had a gap different from that which has gone before it. We fancy that we comprehend within the narrow space that we occupy almost every thing capable of affording food to the mind, and this pretension is one of the characteristics of the nineteenth century. Perhaps we are not absolutely wrong; perhaps, in this way, we have, indeed, surpassed our predecessors, but we must not give way too much to flattery, our age has also its limits, and the eighteenth century imagined, like ours, that it had embraced every thing.

We may, nevertheless, agree to this, that the seventeenth century, the age of grandeur, presents singular gaps. The social world such as it was at that time, the passions of private life, man as he really is, but independent of the conditions of age, fortune, and nationality, in a word, social abstract man—these form the mine, from which this literature has derived its materials. It carefully avoids many things which we cultivate with delight, such as national memorials and the history of our country, to which it does not willingly even allude. It no longer occupies its attention with views of nature; it might even be said, that it does not look at nature at all; only in the way of imitation, it makes still use of some hackneyed expressions, and it has cultivated or rather parodied the ancient idyl. Truly, the seventeenth century appears devoid of the capacity of perceiving nature. The people, too, with their pleasures, their instincts, and their sorrows, are entirely unknown to it. It knows nothing of the citizens but on the side of ridicule. It remains indifferent to the inner recesses of a family, which are always sacrificed to the way in which society views them. It, no doubt, represents private, but not domestic life. This remark is not universally applicable, and we may satisfy ourselves by referring to *Andromaché*.[1]

The literature which now engages our attention, concentrated on man such as society presents him to our view, no longer contemplates him in his retirement, holding converse with himself, with the mysteries of life and of human nature, in a word, with the Infinite. It is with the Infinite that the solitude of the inner man holds intercourse. Man in this aspect has entirely escaped the observation of the seventeenth century. It produced many serious writings, but in none of them do the relations of mankind to religion suppose an anterior relation of the individual to the mysteries of God. Perhaps we must attribute this defect to Christianity, which was much more generally spread at that period. In our times, men take the indefinite for the sublime, and it is natural for us readily to suppose that to be immense of which we do not see the end. A false appearance of greatness is a peculiar characteristic of an age of scepticism. The seventeenth century had not much to ask from the mysterious, the vague, and the indefinite—it affirmed. Its mode of thinking was limited by precision, and in one sense by the definite. We may, therefore, say openly, but without exaggeration, man in his most extended and most elementary relations, and in his more general destiny, has not occupied the attention of the seventeenth century, unless it be under the religious point of view.

The object of this literature being thus determined, let us now see what were its peculiar features.

[1] One of Racine's plays.—T.

In the first place, its morality presents itself for our consideration.   The literature of the seventeenth century has the credit
of being more moral than that of the eighteenth.   It is really
so in the most part of its serious writings, but this remark
must be greatly restricted.   Morality is far from being perfect
in the works of Corneille, Racine, and La Rochefoucauld.
Lighter literature is, in this respect, to say the least, indifferent.
Molière, without perhaps acknowledging it to himself, has given
to morality the hardest blows, and made the deepest wounds.
The tales of La Fontaine are positively immoral, and his fables
are filled with a subtle and dangerous poison.   What favours the
repeated assertion regarding the superior morality of the literature of the seventeenth century is the fact, that preaching formed
a part of it.   This fact eludes inquiry ; we do not at first reflect
that the preachers of that time discharged the duty of their office
like those in all ages.   So soon as they were put aside, the general
spirit will appear to us sensibly changed.   But yet, in spite of
what is wanting to others in point of morality, and in spite of
numerous exceptions, we shall find that the mass of writers, in
this respect, have shown a little more reverence for it than had
been done in the sixteenth, and was done at a later period, in
the eighteenth century.

Next to morality comes the esthetic point of view.   The seventeenth century is distinguished by its diligent inquiry into the
ideal ; but although the true ideal of life was at that time the end
of this inquiry, the point of view adopted was erroneous ; the ideal
rested on incomplete data ; and consequently also poetry, which
endeavoured to reproduce it.   The prevailing idea of this period
was the separation of two essential elements of human life,—the
noble and the familiar.   Literature, indeed, admitted them both,
but separately.   A prejudice, or, to call it by its right name, an
error of such importance, deserves our attention.   On what could
it rest ?

The literature of the seventeenth century expressed and imitated the effort of society, which especially brought about the separation of the classes, according to the degree of their mental improvement.   A class was formed, in which the manners, without
doubt, became more polished, but in which the politeness of the
language far surpassed the polish of the manners.   This politeness of language became the ideal of poetry, and the authors took

as their rule the conventional phraseology, in which the artificial elegance of the manners of the time consisted. Above all, they wished to respect propriety, and this respect forms a singular contrast to the remaining grossness in the manners, and even in the expressions in constant use. They made the language of the court the type of poetical language in general. The court and the city formed two separate worlds—the city was coarse and barbarous compared with the court—noble manners belonged only to the nobility, and the citizens merely followed them with a servile and imperfect imitation. The court ruled over letters with absolute sway, and at one time it was the sole judge of the productions of the mind.

As to the esthetic powers, which were developed in the literature of the seventeenth century, we may remark, as in every golden age of literature, and now more than ever perhaps, the equal balance of the imagination and the powers of reflection. The imagination, powerful and fertile, is then directed, not restrained, by reflection. Wisdom, moderation, good sense, and taste, characterise their compositions. The preference granted to the whole in detail is a distinctive trait of a classical epoch.

This literature is also distinguished by what might be called the purity of the beautiful. The writings possess, in relation to beauty, a certain innocence and ingenuousness, which at a later period entirely vanish; and this is a third characteristic, and a distinguished feature, of truly classical periods. In general, authors are preserved by it from anticipating the effect which leads to times of decay. If they attend to what they say, it is especially for the purpose of expressing their thoughts; in their case beauty is only a part of truth,—not that they are indifferent to beauty, for they produce sublime passages, but they do not show any pretension to be sublime. A great number of beauties in Corneille and Racine have passed without observation—men, no doubt, felt them, but they found them natural, and they did not value them, as we do at present. Synthesis prevailed, that is to say, instinct—at a later period, it will be analysis. Instead of taking a work, a being, an idea as a whole, an artist, who analyzes, decompounds it, and draws to the surface all its elements. In this sense it may be said, that each century is more ingenious than its predecessor; inferior in synthesis, it is superior in analysis, and producing less, it exercises the judgment more. Synthesis is the inspiration, the powerful creation, the distinctive sign of periods essentially literary.

But a doubt arises in many minds; as we have already mentioned, there is, in the seventeenth century, a proportion between the imagination and reflection, the imagination is discreet, and this equilibrium appears to them timidity. Racine does not show the boldness of Victor Hugo, but the more we study the writers of that elegant period, the more will we find their literature original and varied, filled with novelties, and entirely independent. Perhaps the pernicious savour of the writings of the eighteenth century is more alluring; perhaps the scepticism of Voltaire and Rousseau appears to us literary courage. Jean Jacques and his contemporaries assume the appearance of creators, because they destroy; but in itself, affirmation is not more timid than denial. In short, the literature of the seventeenth century is truly national. It has bound itself, indeed, to imitate the ancients, but it is French, because it does not come in contact with any other literature. The tints which the Spanish school spread over it, are very weak and superficial. At a later period, the special character of French literature was entirely destroyed; in our times, it welcomes all modes and all associations—it is universal. It is so much so, that the writers who remain eminently French, such as Beranger and Chateaubriand, become, in this respect, the object of particular notice. The seventeenth century would never have thought of distinguishing among the number of its writers those who might be found more French than the rest.

The language of the seventeenth century, like everything else, came under the yoke of authority. It is purified, but at the same time, impoverished—that is to say, it has been reduced to terms and turns necessary to express the ideas peculiar to the civilization of the period. It ceases to be the language of the people and of the citizens, and becomes the language of the court. The court itself is raised, so far as thought and expression are concerned, to a degree of politeness, which claims a new language. The rich and picturesque language of Rabelais, Montaigne, and Amyot has passed away, even that of Mathurin Regnier is referred to the sixteenth century. Thus, the change begun with the names of Malherbe and Balzac is accomplished. Pascal afterwards comes forward to consecrate the new language, to fix it and to stamp it with the seal of his genius. From that time, the revolution is complete.

Here, then, in the seventeenth century, we have a language entirely distinct from that of the sixteenth. Never did a difference more decided separate two contiguous ages. This youthful language is pure, elegant, flexible, and kept within the limits of its true genius. It has acquired harmony, but it is by no means vigorous or analytic, but quite suitable for the minds of that time. All that I have said of the characteristics of the mind of that age may be applied to the characteristics of the language, and might lead us to anticipate them. The character of a people and that of their language ought to go together. I have spoken of authority, and this change in the language was in some measure decided by personal authority. About the middle of the seventeenth century Richelieu founded the French Academy. He imagined that he could rule the language, as he ruled the nation, by force. This authority, however, although it was admitted, produced little effect. The *Dictionary of the Academy,* of a later date, is only, in point of fact, *a register* of all which the language has acquired, and which is consecrated by usage. It has obtained a kind of authority, and is appealed to in certain cases, as, for example, in judicial disputes; but it is on usage that the empire of language ultimately rests.

In every age languages borrowed terms from the different spheres of human life, but, at that time, the French language borrowed little. It did not so much create, as select, among the mingled elements which the past furnished. In former times there had been introduced a number of proverbial or metaphysical expressions obtained from feudal manners. The sports of the nobility, the chase, and war, are the principal sources of those figures, which, by long use, have ceased to be figurative expressions. We must join to these religion ; religion and war are the two great features by which the middle ages are distinguished.

The seventeenth century did not pursue this plan of borrowing. The religious writers, however, have left distinct traces in the language of Louis XIV. The greater part of the eminent prose writers belong to the church, and they borrowed from religion new terms and phrases, very sublime, and expressive of the inmost feelings of the soul, of which the meaning was afterwards extended and applied to other objects. The eighteenth century invented still less; and when it did so, it was not certainly in the department of religion.   The nineteenth has begun again to invent.   We are enriched with a number of terms formerly unknown, but less happily borrowed from politics, science, and industry, and hence the language is enlarging its boundaries, but losing its purity.   Undoubtedly this is necessary; a language takes its character from the manners of its age; but the spoils of the middle ages are more abundant, and their phraseology more felicitous, than the expressions taken from the scientific and industrial tendency.

We come now, gentlemen, to the republic of letters, or to literary men collectively considered.   Certain relations necessarily exist, more or less intimate, among men who are engaged together in literary pursuits, but these relations vary according to the spirit of different ages.   In the seventeenth century there was a great resemblance in the life, feelings, and doctrines, and an absolute monarch, who was the centre of universal attraction— circumstances which contributed to strengthen the union among writers of the first class.   A real division only existed between these and authors of the second rank; and even that was not owing to the superiority of the one party, and the inferiority of the other; it arose from this, that the former were attached to one school, while the latter followed or tried to find another. The revolution was accomplished, the new era overcame the middle ages, but only by appealing to the authority of the ancients.

In revolutionary periods, authority generally has a time of repose; as in youth we begin with denying the authority of antiquity, then we pass to the new authority, which our riper years require in their turn.   Thus the most part of moral and intellectual, as well as of political revolutions occur; for instance, the Revival of Letters and the Reformation.   But what characterizes the literary revolution of the seventeenth century is the fact, that it was decided by authority.   Some men accomplished it ostensibly, we ought to say officially, among others Boileau, the legislator of this new Parnassus.   All the great authors were devoted to the classics, and this love of classical learning met every where with opposition in the ranks of second-rate writers, but the band of insurgents was speedily dispersed by means of the study of antiquity, by public taste and by politeness of manners. The middle ages were extinguished, and the feeble desire of independence vanished, to appear again at a later period.

In regard to the position of men of letters in the state and in society, we observe that it differs from what it was afterwards. They aspire at no political influence, and we see them only active in the exclusive sphere of literature, or in the discharge of their peculiar duties. When they approach the throne, they prostrate themselves before it; their sentiments of respect and gratitude assume the character of worship; their requests only refer to personal rewards, and no participation of power, and no direct influence on society ever mingle with their hopes.

No period presents so many writers of the first class, and so few of the second. I said writers of the second class, I should have said inferior writers, for in themselves writers of the second class may be greatly distinguished, and the eighteenth century reckons several of this description. But in the seventeenth century there were none of that kind, and if among those of the lowest rank some names have survived, such as Chapelain, they owe it rather to the ridicule with which they were assailed. The saying which Boileau has applied to poetry, is true in regard to literature, generally speaking, in the seventeenth century: "There are no degrees between mediocrity and utter drivelling;[1] and he who does not fly to the summit, falls to the bottom."[2]

A review of the principal authors of the seventeenth century would be out of place here, but we may give their names, grouping them according to the nature and form of their writings:—

PHILOSOPHERS AND PROSE MORALISTS.—Pascal (*Thoughts*), Nicole (*Moral Essays*), Malebranche (*Inquiry after Truth*), Bossuet, Fenelon (in a great majority of his works), La Rochefoucauld, La Bruyère.

ORATORS AND CONTROVERSIALISTS.—The controversial writer is an orator with the pen in his hand. Bossuet appears in both characters—Bourdaloue, Mascaron, Flechier, Massillon, Fenelon, Pascal (*Provincial Letters*).

HISTORIANS.—Bossuet in this department also by his *Universal History*. Mezeray, too much neglected in the present day

---

[1] Boileau, L'Art Poetique, chant iv.
[2] Boileau, Satire ix.

but worthy of particular notice. Saint Réal, who has written little, and whose histories are more or less romances, but who possesses in the highest degree the manner of the writers of antiquity.

WRITERS OF MEMOIRS.—The Cardinal de Retz, Hamilton (*Memoirs of the Chevalier de Grammont*), the Duke de Saint Simon.

ROMANCE WRITERS.—Madame de La Fayette, Hamilton (*Tales*), Fenelon (*Telemachus*), Scarron (*Comic Romances*).

Epistolary writing, cultivated without lasting success by Balzac and Voiture, was perfected by Madame de Sevigné and Madame de Maintenon.

TRANSLATIONS.—The seventeenth century translated much, but translation was badly understood. In translating, they were guided by their own particular views, but in reference to the style, the translations of that period, even those that possess least excellence, are still remarkable. We have always the language, whose secret is lost, and the style, which cannot and ought not to be copied, but there is great inaccuracy in regard to the precise sense of the original. Look, for example, at the translation of *Don Quixotte* by Filleau de Saint Martin. What renders these books defective translations, although agreeably written, but the plan, which was adopted, of adapting everything to the French manners of the time, of making Greek and Latin antiquity contemporaneous with Louis XIV., of allowing nothing in point of language but what the dignity and politeness of the period authorised, and of keeping out of view all the familiarities of the ancient authors?

Energy kept under due restraint is a characteristic of the seventeenth century. At a later period writers were afraid lest they should not always appear sufficiently strong and ready to surprise their readers; it was their aim to make the muscles quiver under the skin. But at that time they studied to soften sallies of wit, to smooth what was rough, and to blunt the edge of what was keen and cutting. Then such phrases as these were common: *if I may be permitted, if I may so express myself.* Bossuet is the boldest and most romantic of the authors of that period. Bossuet and perhaps Pascal. But how prudent is the boldness of Bossuet! In his severest thrusts, how frequently does he reach the boundary of propriety without ever passing beyond it! Racine no doubt abounds in strong expressions to one who understands him, but all his boldness is veiled. It is this delicate taste, this somewhat exclusive system, which has injured and vitiated translation. In addressing the Athenians, the Demosthenes of Father Boulhours calls them, *Gentlemen.*

POETRY.

DRAMATIC POETRY.—Corneille and Racine are the two great names in tragedy. I may mention Thomas Corneille, but after the two masters of the art. Among their inferiors, Lafosse is the only tragic writer whom I am disposed to name. He is no doubt far below them, but his Manlius is a play of some value.

COMEDY possesses Molière, Reynard, Dancourt, and Quinault.

SATIRE, EPIC, AND DIDACTIC POETRY, have for all the three only a single representative, Boileau; and in the second we find merely a parody, *Le Lutrin.*

FABLES AND TALES.—La Fontaine.

PASTORAL POETRY.—Madame Deshoulières, but the pastoral in her hands is only the garb in which moral poetry is dressed—her works are nothing more than those of La Rochefoucauld versified.

ELEGY only reckons a single work worthy of that name, the epistle of La Fontaine to the *Nymphs of Vaux.* We may mention, however, Madame de La Suze.

LYRIC POETRY languishes every where, with the exception of the splendour which it casts in the choruses of *Esther* and *Athalie.* Chaulieu and J. B. Rousseau belong rather to the eighteenth century.

We thus see that the kind of writing which prevails in the literature of the seventeenth century is the drama, and eloquence, which itself is a drama. This great period supports in an eminent degree the dramatic character.

Such in our view are the character and summary of the literature during the age of Louis XIV. So far as we are concerned, it is entirely comprehended in the *Provincial Letters,* and in the series of sermons by Massillon, entitled *Le Petit Câreme.*

This age is divided into two periods quite distinct, of which the one commences about 1660 and ends about 1690; it was remarkable for warmth of imagination and great energy. The second period begins about 1680, and ends with Louis XIV. in 1715. Some of the writers of this period, such as Regnard and Fenelon, belong entirely to the time of the great king ; others, such as J. B. Rousseau and Massillon partake of both divisions, and should perhaps form an intermediate period.

In like manner the eighteenth century should be divided into two periods.[1]

The first begins at the death of Louis XIV., or some years before, and ends nearly in 1746, the year of the death of Vauvenargues, and of the publication of his writings.

The second extends from 1746 to 1780, the year in which the work of the Abbé Raynal appeared.—*History of the Establishment of the French in the East and West Indies.*

There remain, as a third period, the years comprehended between 1780 and the Consulship (18th Brumaire, 9th November 1799) ; but the Revolution is not favourable to literature.

These divisions are natural, they are founded on facts, and hence they are of real importance. But for the present we shall make an abstract of them, and take the eighteenth century in the mass, and in its general character.

We have already remarked, gentlemen, that the seventeenth century was in some respects a resting place between two periods, of which we are now to see the last take up the work formerly begun. This century dissolves the continuity between the sixteenth and the eighteenth. In reference to its predecessor, the eighteenth century is at once a continuation, a development and a reaction.

A continuation. This should not be understood without restriction. On certain points it copies its predecessor, at the same time that it modifies and weakens it. Every continuation which is neither a development nor reaction, is necessarily feeble. This continuation especially appears in three forms—tragedy, comedy, and preaching. The tragedy of Voltaire has in it an element of development, it is not entirely a copy ; but as to comedy, and, above all, preaching, we find in them nothing else than feebleness.

A development. Whatever may have been the inferiority of the eighteenth century compared with the seventeenth, and when we even look at it as a period of corruption and death in reference

[1] See on that subject M. Villemain.

to the elements of society, still it must bring to its predecessor some development. Death even is productive, and putrefaction is fruitful ; from the decomposed trunk of the old tree, new buds are put forth in spring. Thus, towards its termination, and when worn out with analysis, the eighteenth century saw the poetry of nature send forth its blossoms.

Finally, this age is particularly a reaction. This is the prevailing characteristic of the eighteenth century, and it is thus with people of a great intellectual development, ages succeed each other, and the human mind accomplishes its destiny. "Nothing," says M. Villemain, "can be more opposite and yet nothing more closely united than these two periods."[1] There is, in fact, a connection, a continuity between action and reaction, which is itself the consequence of action. And yet let us not deceive ourselves in this matter, the elements of the eighteenth century were found already in the seventeenth, not dead, but concealed under the mass of opposite elements. They could not be openly exhibited, and they therefore continued without producing any actual effect in the hands of the best known authors of that age, and especially in the hands of many secondary writers. Saint-Evremond, who died in 1709, at nearly a hundred years of age, bears the exclusive impress of the eighteenth century. These were the remains of which the sixteenth century, investigating the same principles, and so boldly sceptical, had deposited the germs under the splendid edifice of the seventeenth. Thus, when those who are proscribed, take to flight, they bury their treasures in the earth, that they may find them at a future day, and thus a rag, concealed in a hole, retains the germ of the plague.

All reaction is vindictive and partial, and resembles a system of reprisals. That of the eighteenth century is excessive. Three things of great interest and authority were denied or doubted— the ancients, religion, and social institutions.

The ancients were abandoned and even rejected. Men set up theories, which overturned their throne ; very soon they do not use them, and neither imitate nor study them. In spite of itself, however, the eighteenth century continues to be more devoted to the classics than it is aware. It is at once incredulous and superstitious, it honours from habit the gods that,

---

[1] Villemain, Cours de Literature Française, Dix-huitième siécle, Ire Leçon.

it thinks, have been abandoned from reason, and goes on uninterruptedly in the track of mythological allusion.

Religion, often attacked with as much ability as injustice, was only defended with timidity, and with that awkwardness which springs from weakness of conviction, and from a secret connivance with what was refuted.

Finally, in politics there was a reaction declared against authorities and institutions—a reaction no doubt purely theoretical, and only in writing. Absolute monarchy seemed to remain unscathed, and social authority maintained its position; but two things were wanting, high reputation and full confidence in connection with existing institutions. These in themselves too much abounded in abuses, for men to be contented with the mere pretence of high reputation ; their glory vanished, and the institutions must necessarily be subjected to a strict examination. This examination was not always conducted with the intention of overturning them, the attacks at first presented a scientific and conservative aspect. Thus Montesquieu wrote his book " On the Spirit of Laws," with a view to preserve and consolidate, but at length all questions are found in it distinctly put, and this could not have been done in the preceding century.

Things were not attacked in front, but they nibbled at them all around. Some had only a friendly feeling to the religion established by law, but catholicism was incrusted on the whole social body like the portrait of Phidias which could not be detached from the statue of Jupiter without breaking it in pieces. By calling in question a part of the past, the whole was shaken, and the foundation gave way. Those who derived benefit from prejudices and abuses, took pains to render their claims ridiculous ; the glory of showing their wit prevailed over everything else. This is what precisely characterizes the French mind. " Intellect, or ability, is a dignity in the world," says Madame de La Fayette—a bold saying for the seventeenth century. In France, intellect is so much the more necessary, as you occupy there a more conspicuous position. The man who has merely intellect is superior to him who merely possesses rank and fortune. There was then some blunder in the saying of Madame de La Fayette. By not improving her position, she prepared its ruin. In the eighteenth century the greater part of men of quality preferred their intellectual endowments to their rank. In some cases, however, there was something better than that, there were found among them intelligence, a sincere desire to see abuses corrected, and the love of what began to be called *the public good.* But power, which, when wanting in glory, might have been supported by honour, of which glory is only the excess, conspired to its own ruin by becoming contemptible. Literature at length precipitated all these elements in one direction, or at least accelerated their course. Literature is never the expression of society established by law, it represents moral and intellectual society, the condition of manners and of minds.

Antiquity, religion, and social institutions were the three points on which the reaction of the eighteenth century bore. We may now pass on to other characteristics.

And first let us direct our attention to that of which that age was proud, and of which the name still remains. It is entitled *the philosophic age,* and this pretension in itself, is its most accurate characteristic. Every scribbler called himself a philosopher. A man became a philosopher first and a writer afterwards; the writer only appeared to express the ideas of the philosopher. The epigram and the pastoral song were reckoned a kind of philosophy. But what was this philosophy of the century which preceded ours ?

It was composed of three elements. First, an affectation of independence with regard to tradition and prejudice. Among the *prejudices* against which this age directed their battery, religion was the most hated, and was considered the most hateful.

Secondly, the spirit of analysis and the necessity of decompounding, dividing, and discovering the elements of things. The seventeenth century had been the age of synthesis; the philosophic error of the eighteenth century was in not allowing to synthesis its own place. Without it we only philosophize to destroy.

Lastly, sensualism or the sensational philosophy. A man was reckoned to be more philosophical the more he became a sensationalist, and completely rejected the doctrines of the thinkers of the former age. The eighteenth century had its philosophical pedantry, which degraded man and pretended to reduce him to the condition of a mere machine. This pedantry, strange to say, succeeded in heating the imagination ; they were supposed to be elevated by what debased them; contempt for everything immaterial, and freedom from every rule of conduct.

We may add to these characteristics the increasing taste for the exact sciences, and especially for the science of nature. No doubt these sciences may be, cultivated in an age opposed to materialism; but yet there exists a relation between the tendencies of the materialists of the eighteenth century, and the taste for the science of nature, the spirit of analysis, and the exercise of observation which began to prevail. Men observe better than formerly, and the method of Bacon hastens the development of knowledge. Observation proceeds from ourselves; it leads us to dispute with the objective element; speculation is properly an idea operating upon itself. To be a good philosopher a man must be able both to observe and to speculate; but the seventeenth century, turned to observation, obtained a high rank in speculation. In the eighteenth it was the reverse.

As another characteristic, literature became utilitarian. In the course of the seventeenth century, we have seen practical literature continue bold, and without any secret intention, and the literary perfection of its form derived from the superior excellence of the men of genius, by whom it was cultivated. Esthetic literature, on its part, maintained its nature without mixture. But, in the eighteenth century, the two branches are confounded. Strictly speaking, literature . no longer exists in a state of purity; even poetry is devoted to practical objects, and seeks to exercise its influence in the way of external advantage. This tendency has marred many things in the writings of Voltaire, who has made of his tragedies real sermons upon texts. He preaches on toleration, which afforded an excellent subject for preaching, but it is out of place. On the other hand, science becomes literary and worldly. It is not necessary to quote the coquettish book of Fontenelle *on the Plurality of Worlds;* Buffon himself is a literary naturalist.

One feature more : the literature of the eighteenth century is no longer exclusively French. Truly, under Louis XIV., they were not ignorant either of Italy or Spain, but the literature of these two countries only furnished to France a variety of expressions. Spain afforded pomp, Italy the play of wit. These were blemishes of which they soon got rid, and there was nothing more French, on the whole, than the literature of the seventeenth century. At a later period this character changed. They turned to the north at the commencement of the century, namely, to England. Germany only comes in at the end, and even then its influence is weak. England furnishes more, and Voltaire is the first to reveal it. He profits by Shakspeare, and becomes familiar with Newton. Milton was translated by Louis Racine. But they do not so much borrow forms as ideas, of which they avail themselves. English influence is more philosophical than literary. In general, however, there is no balance remaining in this commerce between Europe and France—the latter gives more than she receives. She indemnifies herself for the thought of what she loses in reference to conquest; and, if her arms number more reverses than successes, the Europe of the eighteenth century submitted to the yoke of the French mind, more than that of the seventeenth had submitted to the ascendancy of the French arms.

The republic of letters, or the society of literary men, has increased since the seventeenth century, and the number of writers of the second class is greatly multiplied. Great literary success may still be found, but there are far more who enjoy it in a moderate degree. It is the time of the golden mediocrity, both in the literal and metaphorical sense; pecuniary ease, more widely spread, increases according to the degree of talent displayed by authors of the second and third rank. Improvement in every department is more general, and men perceive that they are on the eve of a great epoch.

This mass of writers has more personal relations to the world and to the business of life. Those of the seventeenth century mixed much less with the world, but were gathered more around the king. Now the court is no longer the centre of regard and ambition, it is the suffrage of the public which is sought. The public contains in itself more elevated points, and more exalted spheres, for which men of talent show their preference.

Women play a particular part in this literary society. In the full splendour of the reign of Louis XIV., we observe, no doubt, Madame de Sevigné, Madame de La Fayette, Madame Deshoulières in connection with men of wit, but this connection was not attended with such important consequences as to entitle it to the character of a general fact. After the hôtel de Rambouillet, which belongs to a period a little anterior, women did not dare to put themselves at the head of a lettered society; they saw the presidency, which had been conceded to them for a moment, vanish away. In the eighteenth century this part began anew, and the saloons of ladies became the general resort of authors.

Under Louis XIV., among men of letters, we observe nothing which bears any resemblance to a confederacy, a league, or even a party. The theological wars take their course, but literary men differ about esthetics and taste. It was the only civil war permitted during the second half of the seventeenth century. On one side were drawn up the men of genius of the time, with Boileau at their head, the great Justice-General of Parnassus; on the other, the band of secondary writers, the only satisfaction which could be granted to the turbulent restlessness of that lively people, which had received their last pleasure from the quarrels of the Fronde.[1]

In the eighteenth century, literary quarrels no doubt existed, but their noise was lost amid the interest felt for social and philosophical questions. The most numerous party were honoured with the name of *philosopher;* it had an organization or discipline, and a plan of campaigning; in a word, it was a faction which aimed at the overthrow of what existed. In religion, in philosophy, and in certain departments of politics, it represented the absence of actual order. It had found a chief—Voltaire. His eminent talent, the astonishing variety of his natural abilities, his activity of mind, boldness of will, and even absence, contribute to his ascendancy. Resentment for his exile, and the consciousness of disgrace, sharpened an opposition which free permission to remain in his native land might perhaps have blunted; and, besides, in excepting him from every alleviation, exile became in his case power. Under the sceptre of Voltaire, the republic of letters was transformed into a monarchy, and although it was restrained by talents, special circumstances, rivalships and enmities frankly confessed, yet never was literature subjected to such royalty. The general tone was given to it by Voltaire. The only parallel to this influence is that which Bossuet exercised in the seventeenth century.

---

[1] During the minority of Louis XIV., and the misgovernment of Mazarin, a party was formed against the court and the minister, which was called the Fronde, from the French word, which signifies *a sling.* The Cardinal de Retz was at its head, but the imprudence of the other leaders prevented it from accomplishing anything for the benefit of the country. It existed from 1648 to 1654.—(*Translator*).

Bossuet, so attractive by his genius, is still more so by the number of writings which have proceeded from his pen. Among authors of great name, Voltaire alone surpasses him in the multitude of his productions. This fertility of mind, when it is united to original thinking and a highly polished style, implies great power and possesses great merit. All the writers of the highest order have been endowed with this quality, and although a poet has said somewhere—"Believe me, no one who rides on Pegasus reaches posterity with such heavy luggage,"[1] we are very sure that the number of works which a man of genius has produced, instead of retarding, facilitates his progress to posterity. To speak merely of the present and not of the future, the *multa* is of no less importance than the *multum*, the quantity is not less necessary than the quality, with a view of exercising influence over his contemporaries by means of eloquence, an influence at once decisive, vast, and profound. It has been often said, that there are individuals raised up by Providence, who are distinguished by comprehensive thought, by whom the tendencies and necessities of their age are represented, and of whom each personifies an entire century. Without determining whether their age forces them out, as a plant forces out the bud, by internal power and spontaneous movement; or whether from without, that is to say, from on high, a sovereign will by turns bestows, refuses, imposes them on the period, which without them would find no expression of its thoughts and feelings, and would not even be known; beyond all question, certain times have seen such persons raised up. Sometimes great captains, sometimes great politicians, sometimes great writers, and in all cases great minds, whose particular form is of no consequence. But if such a one appears as a great writer, then he only discharges his duty, and can merely personify and govern his age by multiplying himself; by going rapidly through every kind of business; by occupying space and improving time. In certain circumstances, a single great work is sufficient, but in general popularity and immediate and universal influence are only secured by continued labours and constant writing. If a man would reign everywhere, he must be everywhere, he must have intellectually the gift of ubiquity.

[1] Ou ne va point, crois-moi, sur Pegase monté
Avec ce lourd bagage á la posterité.

By the immense number of their works, Bossuet and Voltaire have each exercised dominion over their age. It is this circumstance which obliges me in some measure to mention these two names together. Between their two destinies, and the two parts they acted, there is presented more than one contrast, and one relation.

Both by birth belonged to the order of citizens, and both were born under the shade of the sanctuary of the laws, but the family of Bossuet was ancient and considerable, that of the young Arouet was without distinction, and the legal condition of its chief was no doubt greatly inferior to that of the dignified man to whom Bossuet owes his birth. In Bossuet's family, there were historical traditions, in Voltaire's there were probably none. The latter was born at Paris, in the centre of agitation, and in the bosom of a population fickle and always desirous of novelties; it was in old Burgundy, and amid the calm dignity of a parliamentary city, that the future Bishop of Meaux opened his eyes to the light. When Bossuet came into the world all things stood firm, when Voltaire was born all things were shaken; the great age was in the wane, and a dull but powerful and irresistible reaction in public opinion had begun. If we contemplate these two writers personally, nothing appears less equivocal or more prompt than the vocation of Bossuet, it might be called the highest inspiration. Nothing so much resembles a vocation as the first impulses of Voltaire; everything in the heir of the library of Ninon seems to have been a preparation from his infancy for the priesthood of impiety. Yet from the time that Bossuet knew anything, he knew what he aimed at, he experienced neither hesitation at the beginning nor doubt at a later period. Voltaire, drawn on when very young towards art and pleasure, towards fortune and glory, did not at first attribute to himself any mission, but soon instructed by his instincts and the aspects of society, and guided by hatred, and, in order to be just, we must add, by indignation, the poet gradually became chief of a party, and pursued with all the earnestness of an apostle the annihilation of the same traditions, to the establishment of which Bossuet had consecrated an admirable genius and a zeal perhaps more admirable still.

Although a thousand different objects seem to have contended for the attention and time of Voltaire, while Bossuet has not written a page in which catholicism and episcopacy have not left their impressions, I doubt whether Voltaire, with regard to the end in view, had an impression less fixed or less earnest. As to activity, it was equal in these two men, so distinguished in their own age. Their life and their writings prove it beyond dispute. Both of them have made of their time and their faculties all that a man can do, the one sedentary and collected, the other pressed with the necessity of change of place as well as of occupation; the one gifted with robust health, and dying at the age of seventy-seven of his first and very short illness; the other pitiful in appearance, and incommoded with a thousand diseases, of which he was continually speaking, and of which his devouring activity seemed to take no account. Neither allows a moment's relaxation of the public attention, and from the remembrance of one work to the expectation of another there was no interval and no respite. Bossuet wrote less, but at each of the blows which he dealt, a long rebound, a vast uproar succeeds; in the life of Voltaire scarcely a month passes without a new work giving notice, like the cries uttered by the sentinels of a camp or the guards placed on watch towers, that the champion of the new doctrines had not allowed himself to be surprised by sleep. Shut up in the citadel of the church, which covers and guards the whole political and social system, Bossuet appears, at the proper time, at all the points of attack. Voltaire, the invader, spreads himself, if I may say so, in all directions, occupies every post, or twenty times abandoning each position, twenty times attacks and retakes it. Both augment their forces by the extent and number of their relations. Voltaire has them of all sorts, Bossuet has only some of importance and dignity; but however this may be, neither is merely a writer. They take their part in business, they use their influence by personal intercourse, the one, indeed, always under the pretence of duty and with the character of authority, the other as a simple individual and in the way of insinuation and allurement.

Notwithstanding, in the case of Voltaire, the artist, very often compromised by party feeling, always reappears; letters are one of his objects, literary reputation one of his ends; letters and literary reputation are for Bossuet simply means, and it only is incidentally that he became the first prose writer of his day. But by a contrast well worthy of remark, Voltaire, more an artist in intention, is less so in reality, except in his fugitive poetry. Bossuet, who wishes only to be a man of business, prevails as an artist. The literary man by profession is more impassioned; the literary man for the occasion, the practical man, the prose writer rises to enthusiasm. He who has written so many verses, has not perhaps made a single lyric verse; lyric poetry shines forth in the pages of him who has only written in vile prose. If eloquence be merely the art of affecting the mind and of mastering the will, then both were eloquent; but if eloquence, as we delight to believe, be the power of making eternal truth, the consciousness of justice and the feeling of what is divine re-echo in the human heart, Voltaire, the prince of irony and the priest of common sense, is rarely eloquent.

In pronouncing here the phrase *common sense* or good sense, I indicate between Bossuet and Voltaire a relation as well as an opposition. Good sense, the use of good sense as a controversial weapon, characterizes these two great adversaries, whom their works, presented at once to our view, render so far as we are concerned, contemporaneous. With the double intention of praise and blame, we may make good sense the attribute common to the author of the *History of the Variations*, and to that of the *Essay on Manners*. Merely considering the controversial part of their work, both of them have appealed to good sense by reserving further, the one for his poetical productions, and the other for the development of his religious thoughts, that supreme intuition which is the true good sense of the soul, and which shows to the good sense of the understanding such decided falsehoods. The catholicism of Bossuet, contemplated in opposition to everything which is not itself, is habitually armed with common sense against the most part of its adversaries—and observe well that unbelief or atheism is not among the number of the adversaries which Bossuet encountered; against these good sense would not have been sufficient; but against quietism, against the ultramontane doctrines, and even, or perhaps especially, against Protestantism, no weapon was better chosen, at least if a man wished to be popular, and in a certain sense Bossuet wished to be so. This same weapon, passing from the hands of the bishop into those of the philosopher, dealt terrible blows against Christianity and against all religion. Voltaire, in another point of view, and with other intentions than Bossuet, is the apostle of good sense, with this difference only, that good sense is not for Bossuet what it is for Voltaire, the measure of everything. You must not be astonished at this coincidence; it has nothing fortuitous and nothing personal. Catholicism, not in so far as it is Christian, but in so far as it is catholic, is the church of common sense; it is by common sense that it triumphs; whereas Protestantism, which has the appearance of it, but only the appearance, has a more ideal basis, and has placed itself in the perilous and sublime position either of perishing, if it does not wish to go back, as Protestantism, beyond common sense, or of casting its anchor within the veil, if it does not wish to perish.

Good sense, besides, is not analysis. Thus, whatever difference or opposition there may be between Voltaire and Bossuet, neither essentially possesses an analytic spirit.

Between the work accomplished by the one and that completed by the other, there is undoubtedly a great gulf. No relation can be perceived, and no reconciliation can be attempted between the ideas of which Voltaire is the organ, and those which Bossuet represents. They are two worlds; but this is mere commonplace, sheer trifling; it is necessary to be particular.

The world of Bossuet is the theocracy, which is the entire subjection, or at least the subordination of all human affairs to the empire of a religious tradition; it is the hierarchy pretending to the direction of general society. This pretension, during the course of the sixteenth century, had encountered terrible dangers. The empire of mind and the government of human nature were at that time disputed by more than two competitors. After a very long period, in which politics, morality and religion, had taken their own course, without inquiring about one another, the impossibility of going on in this way began to be felt, and the necessity of some sort of union became evident. Religion, such as pharisaism had made it, was nothing more than an excrescence and an encumbrance, and philosophy, which at that time could scarcely be anything else than atheism, simply voted the suppression of this element in the problem. As to morality, it was very much left to itself; almost nobody inquired about it. This being the state of the question, religion and philosophy were brought together, and philosophy, for the time at least, was to gain the ascendancy. A third element unexpectedly appeared and made a change. Reform, or shall we rather say

morality, for reform is the renewal of the moral element in religion, of which it is the substance, and to which it gives all its
weight.   Yes, under the name of Protestantism, this third term
morality, neglected and despised—morality came in and entered
again into religion; the flame of religion, almost extinguished,
was rekindled, and ages, nay centuries, were added to catholicism, which, without a reform, would have perished along with
religion itself.   Catholicism was reformed, as far as possible,
without renouncing its principles, and without ceasing to be
catholicism.   In this struggle it was reanimated, its parts were
brought together, and it was endowed with new energy.   There
was more than this.   For the first time it showed what it was,
and rendered an account of itself.   The church was strengthened
at its foundation, it brought to a fixed condition a thousand
wavering and doubtful elements, it regulated, as well as it could,
its relation to the state and to society.   It settled better the
meaning of all its institutions, it marked carefully the boundary
of all its powers, and in short, in the domains of learning and
philosophy, it provided its vindication and learned its system of
defence.   In behalf of France, Bossuet is the personification of
this work, whose aim is consolidation and internal perfection.
Between the threatenings of the sixteenth century and their accomplishment in the eighteenth, the seventeenth century was
given to the church, and Bossuet was given to the seventeenth
century.   The religion of the theocracy, confined within limits,
but within limits which the harmony between the priesthood
and the monarchy concealed, appeared calm and majestic during
the splendid years in the reign of Louis XIV., and it gained
for itself not only approbation, but also general interest.   This
century is eminently ecclesiastical, as ours perhaps is eminently social and political.   In the time of Louis XIV., religion was the preoccupation, the conversation, and, shall I say,
the amusement of everybody; and the assemblies of the clergy
at that time excited a curiosity as lively and as general, as at
the present day the deliberations of the Chambers, the strug-
gling of the Tribune and the clashing of parties.   Some will
say, it was for want of anything better, others, it was for
want of something worse, that all this was at that time popular,
and Bossuet was in his own age not only illustrious but celebrated.   When I speak of popularity, I attach to this word a

relative sense; the people in the most extended sense of the term, escape our notice in this refined and unfortunate period. La Bruyère alone gives us a glimpse of them half buried in the trenches which he dug, and a passing and powerless commotion makes us see them for a moment in some frivolous and unfeeling lines of Madame de Sevigné. The people of that age, and even those whose advancement Colbert hastened in the sea-ports and large cities of the provinces were not the class among whom Bossuet was popular. The people of Bossuet was merely a public. But all, which could then be called the *public* hung on the lips of Bossuet, while in the eighteenth century a whole people walked, as if they had been chained to the triumphal chariot of Voltaire. Bossuet was with respect to his public, in point of sympathy, curiosity, and even popularity, what at a later period Voltaire was in regard to his; or if you only look at the fact of general prejudice, Voltaire was the Bossuet of his age, Bossuet was the Voltaire of his.

But in this triumph, or in this success of the theocracy in the seventeenth century, there was something artificial or accidental, although the constancy and combination of effort, the mass of labour and the real seriousness of the inspiration, give us a different idea of it. The seventeenth century (others have already observed it), was a resting-place by which the theocracy knew admirably how to profit. Encamped for a short time on ground prepared for it, instead of setting up tents, it built palaces and erected monuments. Time moved on in its course, and the theocracy, without being aware, by imposing itself on generations, in which a mere material civilization made the necessity of emancipation ferment, called forth this imperious necessity, and by weighing down the spring of human liberty, prepared it for rebounding with so much greater force. From that time we might have told its members, as we showed to them human nature determined to make use entirely of its own resources, and only to reckon upon itself, " Go not into its arms to provoke the victory." The theocracy believed itself, and was generally believed, to be all-powerful, although it was now losing ground.

Between the birth of Voltaire, in 1694, and the death of Bossuet, ten years later, " a great destiny begins, a great destiny is accomplished." The empire of the theocratic religion was for ever at an end, if not in fact, at least in opinion. What succeeded it? Impiety, undoubtedly, for the human mind never takes vengeance by halves, nor exercises moderate reaction. But without refusing to this fact that just and terrible qualification, we may say, that it has still a different aspect. The theocratic religion, so far as man had a part in it, disregarded him, and the gospel very fully acknowledged him—man maintains his own position, and should not be slow in showing self-respect. How severely soever the eighteenth century may be judged, the fact which characterizes it is the advancement, in the bosom of modern history, of the purely human element. What shall we say of Bossuet? In him the condition of the priest suppressed the feelings of the man—that *universal quality*, which Pascal thought so important, and which, towards the end of the seventeenth century, shines with so much sweetness and purity in the person of another bishop, the disciple of Bossuet, and the author of Telemachus. Ah, well! Fenelon has connected this idea with the eighteenth century, which was scarcely worthy perhaps to give it effect, but which, notwithstanding, did take it up and exhibit it. The eighteenth century entwined it with unbelief, for, after an interval of a hundred years, Montaigne and Charron again appeared on the stage of time, but ardent, passionate, and envenomed. Nevertheless, the eighteenth century is truly the age of humanity, as the seventeenth was of catholicism. Man begins to seek his own law in the nature of things, and even in his own nature, badly observed, no doubt, for divine light was wanting. The revolution was complete and rapid. Books give assurance of it. The tomb of Bossuet is the boundary between two kinds of literature, of public opinion and of philosophy. On the one hand the *Treatise on Universal History ;* on the other, the *Essay on Manners ;* on one side, the *Politics of Holy Scripture ;* on the other, the *Spirit of Laws ;* there the *Treatise on the Knowledge of God and of ourselves ;* here, the book of Helvetius. Each of these books belongs to its own age, and represents it. It may be added that Voltaire, in the midst of the philosophers, like Bossuet in the midst of the doctors, affects that true middle course, which constitutes in catholicism the character and authority of Bossuet. The deism of Voltaire comes rather from common sense than from the heart, but in truth he is a deist among atheists. Violent in religion, but only to destroy, he is moderate in politics, and in that department he satisfies himself with claiming reasonable privileges and humane laws. But the destiny of these two celebrated men differs in this : Bossuet was to end in being denied, Voltaire was to have the precedence. The regency danced upon the ashes of the great bishop—those of the author of *La Henriade*, less patriotic perhaps than Bossuet, but not less a supporter of the monarchy, were in 1792 transferred with great solemnity to the republican Pantheon.

Which of the two possessed greater authority? "It was," said Bossuet, speaking of Cromwell, "it was given to this man to deceive the people and prevail over kings." These words applied to Voltaire are found true, if it be not that Voltaire deceived even kings. Bossuet no doubt reigned, and his reign was not disputed; but he was to consecrate his authority by the dignity of his life and manners, from which the following age excused its prophet, for a faction does not impose on its leader the same moral rules as a church upon its guide. Bossuet had respectful disciples, Voltaire devoted partisans. Bossuet was associated with fellow-labourers, Voltaire with agents and almost with accomplices—the one governed, the other conspired. It may appear at the first glance that the one was popular and not the other; but when we look at the matter narrowly, Bossuet had all the popularity which a serious writer could enjoy in the seventeenth century, and indeed that alone which he could have. The great difference is, that he had a public, and Voltaire had a people. This people Voltaire created, or rather his writings called them forth. The instructions of Bossuet could not reach so far nor so low as the sarcasms of Voltaire, and then, at certain times, negation is more extensively popular than assertion or affirmation can be. The people in the fifteenth and sixteenth centuries had their place at the banquet of literature; Voltaire made them sit there again, only it was not, as the Scripture expresses it, "a feast of things purified." [1] Both died in full possession of their fame, but the one with gravity and holiness, as it becomes a man to die; the other in haste and violently, if I may be allowed to say so; the one amid universal veneration, the other amid the loud explosions of enthusiasm, with which respect was certainly not mingled. To the defender of the national worship, seventy-seven years were granted that he might rear to that worship immortal monuments; to the other eighty-four

[1] Isaiah xxv. 6.

years, that he might· efface from the minds of the people, that which, whether true or false, had only been engraved upon them by the hand of tradition.

In spite, however, of his vast popularity, Voltaire as a writer is not more secure of the future than Bossuet. In some respects he is more out of date than his attractive rival. Many things written by Voltaire will continue to be read, and many also by Bossuet. Not only the rare perfection of the style and his inimitable eloquence will make a great number of the works of the illustrious bishop live for ever, and that too with a real and energetic life, but the substance, not less than the form, will render many of them immortal. Truth never dies, and what responds with so much power to the profound necessities of the soul and to its inmost wishes, is so precious in itself, and clothed by Bossuet with such incomparable beauty, that men of cultivated minds in all ages will incessantly repeat such magnificent language, and will find in it a perpetual source of delight. Nobody had ever so much talent as Voltaire, or more good sense, but, "after the Scriptures, which have been inspired by the Holy Ghost, there is nothing so great as Bossuet." The writer of whom we have been able to speak thus, will live for ever by his writings, in the memory and in the thoughts of mankind.

We have seen that the French Academy was founded in the seventeenth century by Richelieu, with the design, at once frivolous and ambitious, of perfecting and directing the language. In this respect it exercised, at the time of its foundation, a very harmless influence. But soon it became the means of exciting emulation among literary men; it was a sort of prytaneum; above all, it served as a point of contact between the nobility and men of letters—it taught them to fraternize. The former attended at first with the intention of doing honour to the latter, but they came at last to discover that in going thither they did honour to themselves. Among all earthly dignities, mind or talent is the first. Men of letters felt this, and profited by it; but, in their turn, they submitted to it, by bending under the ascendancy of a strong individuality.

In the seventeenth century we see the influence of the Academy extended. The mere statement of the questions discussed at their successive meetings gives the measure of this increase. " Among all the virtues of the king, which is the greatest?"

was the question put at the commencement. Now, real philosophical and social interests are debated there; the discourses delivered at the admission of members are treatises, manifestoes, confessions of faith; they inaugurate not only the thought of him who delivers them, but they are an indication of the minds before whom they are delivered. There is nothing more important than these discourses, as a proof of the opinions, the general tendency, and the end at which they aim.

What became of the language in the eighteenth century—a matter so important as an instrument and a symptom? It gained and it lost, but it lost more than it gained. It was perfected in precision, exactness, and regularity. The distinction of synonymous terms was studied, and the first book on that subject was then published. The idea of such a work had previously occurred to Fenelon. In point of language, this is a sign of the times, but some authors complain of the introduction of neologisms. Voltaire, in prose, the faithful heir of the traditions of the seventeenth century, utters a cry of alarm, and this cry finds an echo. At present we no longer comprehend it; the purity of the language of Louis XIV. does not appear to us to have undergone any perceptible alteration in the writings of the time of Louis XV. What is their hardihood compared with ours? Some gold spangles laid on the blue-and-white robe of the seventeenth century. With respect to us, we have loaded our language with brass, copper, and glass. Diderot is the most disorderly writer of his time—nay, he has something impudent in the style, as well as in the thought—and yet he has written pages, whose purity excites our envy. *The Danger of putting one's-self above the laws* is a masterpiece of all that is simple, natural, and true in language.

It must be acknowledged, however, that the style of the eighteenth century has not the frankness, freshness, modesty, grace, and noble ease of its predecessor. Towards the middle of the period, we see the use and abuse of general terms introduced. This abstract character does not exist in the great age: in it the language never became incorporeal; and, even in treating of Metaphysics, it preserves its forms of expression plain and simple. Descartes, Malebranche, Fenelon, and Bossuet, have always a charm and a grace, which contrast with the stiffness and emphasis which the philosophy of the eighteenth century, mixing itself with everything, introduced into the language. There still remains, however, a fine language, precise, clear, natural, energetic, and true.

The style, consisting of long and rounded sentences, gradually disappeared. Traces of it remain, indeed ; the period of Balzac and Flechier appears at a great distance. It may be easily discovered in the writings of the Chancellor d'Aguesseau, who belongs certainly to the end of the seventeenth century ; it appears again in the works of Buffon, La Condamine, and J. J. Rousseau. The beautiful period still finds a place, but the long and round period is not, in general, the style of the eighteenth century. It had ceased to be a reality. This is the style of a period settled, peaceful, and at rest, when the opinion prevails, that the future will be like the present. The form of the phraseology is thus expressive of the sentiments of society. An age, in which the period opens up the long folds of its floating robe, is a time of stability, authority, and confidence. But, when literature has become a means of action, instead of continuing to be used for its own sake, we no longer amuse ourselves with the turning of periods. The period is contemporary with the peruke—the period is the peruke of style. The eighteenth century has shortened the one as much as the other. The peruke, reaching the middle of the loins, could neither be suitable to the courtiers of Madame de Pompadour, nor to men in haste to accomplish a work of destruction. When was J. J. Rousseau himself given to the turning of periods ? Assuredly it was not in his pamphlets.

We may add, that the prose of the seventeenth century had imitators very late in the succeeding age. It had even a defender, who, with the exception of the rounded period, remained faithful to it to the very last. Voltaire has preserved as much of this fine prose as could be transferred to the eighteenth century, but we are speaking of Voltaire as a prose writer, and not as a poet.

In reference to poetry and eloquence, these two distinguished esthetic elements of literature, it may be said that both came forth ; that is to say, they spontaneously made their escape from the trammels with which the preceding age had encumbered them. " Rome is no more in Rome," said Sertorius. Poetry is no more in poetry, nor eloquence in eloquence, in the sense which the seventeenth century attached to these terms. Poetry at that time was verse ; Telemachus would never have passed for a poem. But, in the following age, poetry languished under its official form ; it quitted the domain of verse to go into the territory of prose. This remark is only completely true of the second half of the century. In the first half Voltaire keeps up poetry, but, about 1750, we observe J. J. Rousseau preparing poetical prose. He and Bernardin de Saint Pierre were the true poets of that age.

It is the same with eloquence. It is no longer in the pulpit, sometimes we find it at the bar, but it is especially displayed in the pamphlet. It is no more presented to the public by the living mouth—they obtain it from the bookseller's shop. The advertisement is issued, and the faithful come to them. The orators are Rousseau, Voltaire, Diderot, in a cloud of tracts and pamphlets—pamphlets become large books. This period deserves to be called an age of pamphlets. When Voltaire himself attempts the style of the orator, his eloquence abandons him, of which we have a proof in the *Eulogium on the Officers who died during the campaign of* 1752. He is affecting, however, when he speaks of Vauvenargues, whom he really loved, but open his pamphlets, and read among others that one which he has entitled *Il faut prendre un parti* (we must take a side) along with what is detestable—what fancy, and what power !

Two acquisitions quite new, enrich the French literature of the eighteenth century—nature and politics. In an age of faith in every sense of the term, of stability, power, glory and security, there was no place for nature ; so long as society is sufficient for man, he merely casts upon nature a wandering look, and the more active his employment the less does the place where it is carried on attract his attention. We do not give this as an absolute rule, but we in this manner succeed in explaining to ourselves the total absence of the poetry of nature in the seventeenth century.

I have said that the eighteenth century, like that of which it takes the place, comprehends two periods. It is necessary to distinguish them, for Voltaire alone is common to both ; and yet the Voltaire of the one, and the Voltaire of the other, are two different men.

There is in the age, which now engages our attention, a

remarkable coincidence between the historical and the literary dates. A glance at the political history of the thirty years between the death of Louis XIV. (1715), and the treaty of Aix-la-Chapelle will be sufficient to convince us of this : 1746 is our literary date, and 1748 saw this treaty concluded, one hundred years after the peace of Westphalia. With what were these years filled, whether in the political or literary point of view ?

They began with the disorders of the regency. The boldness of men's ideas was not at that time on a level with the boldness of their actions ; the new literature was not commensurate with the licentiousness of manners. These troublesome years have for their principal episode the system of Law—a desolating eruption, which brought ruin on a multitude of families. These fatal troubles were not, as some pretend, without compensation ; they produced some advantageous results—an improvement in the system of finance, the sudden but merely momentary mixture of all classes, and the abasement of the privileged ranks. Later, from 1726 to 1743, France had a breathing time under the ministry of Cardinal de Fleury. Within, the disputes relating to the bull *Unigenitus*, which became the law of the state in 1730, were continued. By the side of this theological war, another was prosecuted in Italy, which ended in the acquisition of Lorraine. A year before his death, Fleury allowed himself to take part in the struggle against Maria Theresa. The disasters which befell the French armies in Bohemia are well known, but they were repaired at Fontenoy in 1745, an advantage which led to the peace of Aix-la-Chapelle. The seven years' war did not commence till a later period.

On the whole, during these thirty years peace prevailed, France was tranquil within, and consequently prosperous. But the moral effects of a long calm are not always analogous to physical effects. Peace is good when it is united to justice and morality. Peace may be transformed into a calamity, when it heats the exhalations of which war would have favoured the evaporation. Peace during this period was not salutary either to morals or to national character. At the end of the reign of Louis XIV. there was left on the shore a quantity of mud, which a new wave might have carried away, but with which the atmosphere continued to be infected. The ideas which physical force had suppressed, but of which the suppression had redoubled the energy, broke loose in fearful reprisals, and found a ready welcome from a public weary of the past. Liberty cannot subsist alone, it must have, as an auxiliary, either action or danger, or the principles which render it respectable. By the force of the weight used in suppression, the hand of despotism became benumbed, lost its hold, and the human mind only continued to appearance in its subserviency. During the eighteenth century, power appeared to be sovereign, at the same time it felt that it was no longer master; the despotism of this period was despotism asleep, which only awoke by starts, and liberty was involved neither in action nor in danger.

With respect to literature it may be said, that during this first period, the seventeenth century is exhausted, comes to an end, and is prolonged in its echo; we have somehow a posthumous seventeenth century, yet two parallel currents, whose source is not common, are easily distinguished in it. The one is very evidently a prolongation and a termination of the age of Louis XIV., of which it reproduces the tendencies, and cultivates, though with a weary hand, the traditions, and to which at least it neither adds nor supplies almost anything of what constitutes the character of the eighteenth century.

This first current is that which brings forward Massillon (1663–1742), d'Aguesseau (1668–1751), Cochin (1687–1747), Saint Simon (1675–1755), Rollin (1661–1741), Vertot (1655–1735), Madame de Lambert (1667–1748), Louis Racine (1692–1763), Dubos (1670–1742), Mademoiselle de Launay (1693–1750), Crebillon (1674–1752), J. B. Rousseau (1671–1741), Le Sage (1668–1748), Destouches (1680–1754), Prévost (1697–1773).

The other current is confined within a narrower bed, but between its high banks it rushes with much greater force. It brings forward Fontenelle (1657–1757), he belongs equally to the seventeenth and eighteenth centuries, for as long as he lived he continued in the exercise of all his faculties; La Motte (1672–1742), Marivaux (1688–1763), Henault (1685–1770), Vauvenargues (1715–1747), Montesquieu (1689–1755), Voltaire (1694–1778).

These two currents have run together without mingling their waters, without troubling each other, and without the somewhat insipid sweetness of the first having been changed by the bitterness of the second. The former reminds us of Arethusa going pure from the bosom of the sea. These are two kinds of contemporaneous literature which have not been derived the one from the other, which subsist the one by the side of the other, and which have no knowledge of one another. It is remarkable that the first of these currents has held its course so far through so many passions and novelties under the regency, and greatly beyond it. *The Ancient History* of Rollin was published from 1730 to 1738; the poem on *Religion* in 1742; several of the *Odes* of J. B. Rousseau, from 1716 to 1741,[1] the *Roman Revolutions* of Vertot, in 1719; and his *History of Malta* in 1726; the masterpiece of Prévost, *Manon Lescaut,* in 1732; the last volume of *Gil Blas,* in 1735. The *Glorieux* of Destouches, in 1732. Now, if all these works differ in any thing from the seventeenth century, they have very little or almost nothing at all of the character peculiar to the eighteenth.

With respect to literature in the other countries of Europe, Great Britain stands alone at that period. The reign of Queen Anne (1702–1714), was a great epoch in an intellectual and literary view. England possessed Pope (1688–1744), Swift (1667–1745), Addison (1672–1719), Steele (1675–1729), Prior (1664–1721), Gay (1688–1743), Bolingbroke 1672–1751), Savage (1698–1743).

We must not forget to inquire whether the literary manners had more or less dignity in the eighteenth than in the seventeenth century? At the first glance we might be tempted to accuse the seventeenth century of more servility; but although in this respect we cannot acquit such men as Bossuet, Flechier, Racine, and Boileau, we must admit that, on the whole, the literary manners of this epoch were more estimable than those of the following age. Adulation at least had its source in real feeling. In point of baseness, pitiful intrigues, and dishonourable acts, the eighteenth century has certainly the superiority. There are, however, honourable exceptions. No charge can be brought against Buffon and Montesquieu, nor even in this respect against J. J. Rousseau; but, notwithstanding this admission, it must not be forgotten that the Abbé de Saint Pierre was expelled from the Academy by his colleagues for raising the question whether Louis

---

[1] It does not appear, however, that any of the principal works of J. B. Rousseau are posterior to 1716.

XIV. really deserved to be called *Great.* Fontenelle was the sycophant of Cardinal Dubois, and lavished on him his eulogies in that same academy, shamefully giving the lie to the public conscience.

Now, if we study in its general aspect the intellectual movement and the peculiar character of the thirty years of this first period, we are struck with the contrast. Certain branches of knowledge are developed and others decline.

We may consider, in the first place, those which have made improvement—every modification which has brought with it profit·

The exact sciences and natural philosophy were cultivated with a success entirely new. For example, Réaumur (1683–1757), Antoine de Jussieu, Bernard de Jussieu (1686–1777), men so eminent in the history of science. But science does not merely belong to particular men who make discoveries; it is also the property of persons of secondary talents, who propagate and put within the reach of the many that which was only the privilege of the few. Thus Fontenelle, who simply reports the discoveries of others, has rendered real service to science by giving a short summary of the labours of his brethren—see the *Memoirs of the Academy of Science.* Voltaire wrote the *Philosophy of Newton;* the Marchioness du Chatelet was no stranger to this species of study; Montesquieu himself composed a *Treatise on the Glands.* Among works of this kind, the *Spectacle of Nature,* by the Abbé Pluche (1688 1761), is remarkable for its religious character.

Works of erudition are numerous. We may quote among those which have been devoted to this subject, Fréret (1688–1749), Dom Calmet (1672–1757), Father Brumoy (1688–1742), who made known the Greek theatre by a translation which, indeed, possesses little excellence, but which first introduced us to this unknown world. M. and Madame Dacier (1651–1722) are still celebrated. The Abbé Gedoyn (1667–1744), translated Quintilian in 1718; d'Olivet (1682–1748), published the *Orations* of Cicero in French, and valuable remarks on French prosody. In 1718 the Abbé Girard (1677–1748), published his book on *French synonymes.* Restaut's grammar appeared in 1730. After this enumeration, and with the addition of Du Cange, the Academy of Inscriptions, and the Collection of Montfaucon, many gaps are still left in the field of erudition.

History was subjected to important modifications. National

history especially is more accurately traced to its sources. This is the peculiar excellence of Father Daniel (1649–1728), whose history otherwise is written with a view to class and party. Mezeray, on the contrary, cared little for the original documents ; he substituted genius for learning, and Father Daniel learning for genius—so much for learned history.

Another species of history then arose—critical history. The first work of this sort is due to the Abbé Dubos (1670–1742). It is a *History of the Establishment of Monarchy in France.* The book is systematic, and opens the way to the works which M, Thierry and M. de Barante have published in our times.

Other historians are famous for the elegance of the narrative, and recall the manner of the ancients. The Abbé de Vertot published in succession the *Revolutions of Sweden and of Portugal, the Roman Revolutions, and the History of the Order of Malta.* Rollin falls under this category. His *Ancient History* is an immortal work, notwithstanding its defects, its tediousness, its idle reflections, its deficiency in general views, in criticism and philosophy. The book, however, is still in repute for its representation of antiquity, for its simplicity, kindly feeling, and the inimitably fine tone in which it is written, and for the unction which is spread over every subject. The *Roman History* is of less value. Montesquieu applies to Rollin what is said of Xenophon with respect to Attica,—he calls him the bee of France.

Philosophical history begins to peep out in the *Reflections on History* by the President Henault ; it is better characterised in Montesquieu's book on the *Grandeur and Decline of the Romans.* Voltaire, who at a later period attached himself to this kind of history, belongs, for the moment, to the class of epic writers. His *History of Charles XII.* is a true epic poem, which he has bound himself to relate with picturesque rapidity.

We must not forget the writers of Memoirs, Saint Simon, Mademoiselle de Launay, Madame de Caylus, and Louis Racine.

Political science now comes to light. *The Spirit of Laws* enlarges the circle within which we are confined ; we shall fall in with this important work afterwards. But the social questions are cursorily referred to in the *Persian Letters* (1721), and in the *Sethos* of Terrasson (1731). The works of Saint Pierre are only important for their number ; he was not a man of genius. We owe to him, however, in this department, the first manifestation of liberty of thought; he did what could not have been done under Louis XIV., he dared distinctly to point out the nature of wickedness. A similar boldness had cost Fenelon dear, and yet he only expressed his ideas through a veil in the Utopia of *Telemachus*. *Telemachus* is the political work of the seventeenth century. But the Duke of Orleans was indulgent and good-natured, he did not love liberty from principle, he tolerated it from his natural disposition, and his curious mind made him enjoy every species of invention. The most important work of that age, for the boldness and novelty of its views, is the *Letters on the English*, by Voltaire (1725). Although this book was not printed in France, it produced there such an effect that Voltaire was subjected to a severe punishment for having published it. This work, which appears to us now not remarkable for boldness, was so much so at the time as to excite our astonishment, that we owe it to the pen of Voltaire, who was conservative in all things but religion. But he aimed at something new; he was in quest of fame; he came from England, and took upon him to reveal to France that land as little known as America was before the time of Christopher Columbus.

In all these branches the eighteenth century made great improvement, and nowhere in this department at least have we to show any decline, but in every quarter the inquiry was about things, not about mankind. The inner, the abstract man, whom the seventeenth century so much delighted to investigate, was by no means the object of research in the eighteenth, and it is in the literary branches, which refer to man, that any declension is perceptible. Philosophy had fallen asleep—it was, as it were, suspended; there was no original production; foreign systems were studied, especially the system of Locke. Nothing at this time shows philosophical activity—we wait for Condillac.

It is the same with religious morality; men scarcely make any inquiry about it. Duguet (1649–1733), so substantial, and more a moralist than a theologian, belongs partly to this age, but entered on his course in the preceding. He stands alone, and is out of date. We have only Madame de Lambert, Vauvenargues, and Fontenelle, in whose writings morality is quite detached from religion.

The Fine Arts are on the decline; we meet with no great name, and no popular fame.

Eloquence is subject to the same observation. Massillon was still alive, but his principal works were connected with a former period. D'Aguesseau, Cochin, Normaud (1687–1745), made themselves remarkable by their pleadings. At the French bar they are perhaps the most distinguished, but are far from rising to the height which the orators of the seventeenth century had reached.

Finally, what would Poetry be without Voltaire? Take away Voltaire, and what remains to the poetry of this period? Lyric poetry has no existence. J. B. Rousseau was still alive, and his reputation also, but, in a literary point of view, it is with him as with Massillon—he is dead. Epic poetry is honoured by the *Henriade* (1723), a brilliant production.

Tragedy was held up by Voltaire, it was the age of *Œdipus, Brutus, Zaire, Alzire*, and *Merope*. In some respects it is a new kind of tragedy, the domain of tragic poetry was really extended. Crebillon was still alive, but his best tragedies preceded the death of Louis XIV. We shall take him up in the eighteenth century. La Motte, another writer, had a day of inspiration in *Ines de Castro* (1723). The *Dido* of Lefranc de Pompignan (1734), and the *Mahomet II.* of Lanoue (1737), may still be quoted.

Comedy without doubt declined, as it had no longer Molière, but a revolution here was manifest. The spirit of Molière is found again in Le Sage (see *Turcaret*, 1709), and in the *School of Citizens* of d'Allainval (1728). Molière and the writers of his school, Le Sage, d'Allainval, Dancourt, Regnard, are unanimous in banishing from comedy the element of interest and sympathy. But in the eighteenth century this interest begins to appear; Destouches approaches the tragi-comic without falling into it; it is still comedy, although the tragi-comic allows itself to be seen. His *Glorieux* (1732) contains scenes of the true pathetic. The revolution is accomplished in the works of La Chaussée (1692–1756). He is properly the inventor of the *interesting*[1] comedy, which takes possession of the heart more than of the understanding. The author is of the second order, but on that account, is his style of writing of the second order too?

Analytic comedy was framed by Marivaux. It is a microscopic

---

[1] This term is literally translated from the French, and seems to correspond to what is known in English as sentimental comedy.—*Translator.*

study of the secrets of the human heart, and especially of the female heart. Marivaux shows women to themselves. He does not seek to represent characters that are most prominent and most widely spread, but those delicate mysteries which are only discovered in the profound secrecy of the heart. It is romance brought upon the stage. It is the stage transformed into romance. Was this the right place for romance? and may we not say that it was wrong?

Didactic poetry was cultivated by Louis Racine. We owe to him the poem on *Religion* and on *Grace*.

Translation in verse, feeble in the seventeenth century, furnished, in the eighteenth, very fine works. The Abbé du Resnel (1692-1761) successfully translated the *Essay on Criticism* and the *Essay on Man*, by Pope. Father Porée, tutor of Voltaire, Vanière, and Cardinal Polignac (1661-1741), wrote Latin poems.

The Romance has not declined. *The Princess of Cleves* is, beyond all doubt, unrivalled; but the eighteenth century gives, in *Gil Blas* (1735), one of the best romances in the world. The Abbé Prèvost produced a kind of romance, written, so to speak, at the gallop, irreproachable in respect of morals—the romance of adventures, the romance of romances. *Manon Lescaut* is more than that, but it is his masterpiece. Marivaux has made very interesting romances; among others, *Marianne*, a work in which the eloquence of passion is admirable.

In literary criticism, Rollin and Louis Racine are the interpreters of classical learning; they render pure homage to the seventeenth century, and maintain the highest reverence for antiquity. But elsewhere there is a revolution. La Motte and Voltaire form a second school, which allows innovations. La Motte especially criticises the ancients with boldness. The Abbé Dubos, in short, without going very far, introduces philosophy into the domain of criticism. In his *Essay on Taste*, Montesquieu follows the same path. These two authors have inaugurated esthetics in France, and hence there are three distinct schools.

We now come, gentlemen, to the literary lives of the principal writers of this period. They are, no doubt, interesting, but all the writers have not a history. There are some who have not advanced, and who have only turned upon themselves. Others, on the contrary, have undergone developments, and accomplished great changes. In a literary history, we must take account of writers of the second class. They frequently characterize better than those that are first, the spirit of the age. M. Lerminier has made this remark,—the writer of the first rank especially lives in the thought of the future, while an inferior genius is satisfied with the present.

I.

THE CHANCELLOR D'AGUESSEAU.

1668–1751.

D'AGUESSEAU belonged to a family of distinction in the magistracy. At a very early period he was made king's advocate, afterwards he became attorney-general, and at length, in 1718, chancellor. His life was not without storms, on account of his opinions and political events, but in his works we perceive the remarkable print of inward peace. Already, under Louis XIV., he was subjected to a sort of disgrace, occasioned by the bull *Unigenitus.* Brought up among the magistrates of France, he inherited their spirit. The parliaments maintained, with the greatest firmness, their opposition to ultra-montane tendencies. Afterwards, under the regency, he was obliged to give up the seals, because he was opposed to the system of Law. He was recalled, disgraced a second time, again recalled, and died chancellor. Obliged to take a part in politics, he was not, however, a politician like the Chancellor de L'Hopital. D'Aguesseau was more learned, a better writer, and possessed of more extensive accomplishments than L'Hopital, but he was deficient in the qualities which constitute the statesman. He was in other respects an excellent magistrate. He was distinguished for his integrity, his dignity of manners and his vast and profound knowledge. He wrote much on law, religion, and philosophy, but none of his works bears the stamp of originality. Although sincerely religious, he exhibits in his philosophy something of the age to which he belonged. His style, clear and pure, but without ornament, has little real force. He was not a man of genius. His writings, though worthy of esteem, are not, when taken together, works of great value; they have not the power of exercising any remarkable influence over the understanding or the imagination; we have some difficulty in getting through them. They consist of *speeches* and *charges*—the reproofs, instructions, and exhortations, delivered by the representative of the public minister at the opening of the sittings of parliament. D'Aguesseau generally chose excellent subjects, such as love of one's condition, a scientific spirit, love of country, the conduct of magistrates, firmness, true and false justice, knowledge of mankind indispensable to the lawyer. It is a style of writing analogous to preaching, analogous to the synodal addresses of a bishop, and to the conferences of Massillon. The whole constitutes a true exhibition of the theory of *judicial wisdom*.[1] It should contain a theory of the duties of the judicial as well as of the apostolic minister.

We fully understand that subjects so didactic do not tend to produce much animation in the speaker. In his discourses, d'Aguesseau is dignified, noble, elegant, and harmonious; he has an elevation of thought which inspires us with interest, both in the subject and the orator; we cannot read his writings without feeling the better for them, at least for the time. His eloquence, however, is not without preparation, and not without stiffness; his dignity is solemn; his sentences are symmetrical; his phraseology rises and falls like the two ends of a balance; it is ingeniously weighed, and we think we hear the rustling of the magistrate's silken robe. His taste for antithesis is too obvious; the author allows himself to fall into witticisms, which, if you choose, are not frivolous, but are merely jests. The whole is deficient in ease and simplicity. L'Hopital is much more uncultivated; he composes badly, but he is much more eloquent; he has much more force and originality; there is that in him which makes the heart beat. No such thing appears in the writings of d'Aguesseau, yet the address on the *Knowledge of Mankind* as well as the seventh charge, should be read. *On the mind and on science*, the following are some passages worthy of notice :—

"The study of morality and eloquence began at the same time, and their union in the world is as ancient as thought and language.

"Men did not formerly separate two sciences, which are in their nature inseparable. The philosopher and the orator possessed

---

[1] The French phrase is *prudence judiciaire*. The French Editors have the following note :—It is an allusion to *prudence pastorale*, an expression which implies the theory of duties performed by the pastor in a part of French Switzerland.

in common the empire of wisdom; they maintained a happy intercourse and a perfect understanding between the art of thinking and speaking well, and they had not yet imagined that distinction injurious to orators, that divorce fatal to eloquence of the imagination and the reason, of sentiment and expression, of the orator and the philosopher."

" Whence have proceeded those surprising effects of an eloquence more than human? What is the source of so many wonders, of which the simple reading, after so many ages, is still the object of our admiration?

" These arms were not framed in the school of a declaimer; the thunders and the lightnings which made kings tremble on their thrones were forged in a higher region. From the bosom of wisdom Demosthenes derived that bold and generous policy, that firm and intrepid liberty, that invincible love of country; in the study of morality he received, from the hands of reason, that absolute empire and that sovereign power, which he exercised over the minds of his hearers. A Plato was required to form a Demosthenes, that the greatest of orators might pay homage with all his reputation to the greatest of philosophers."

" Ye masters in the art of speaking to the heart, be not afraid of ever wanting figures, ornaments, and everything which composes that innocent pleasure of which the orator should be the artist.

" Those who only bring to the profession of eloquence an imperfect knowledge, not to say an entire ignorance of the science of morals, may be afraid of falling into this defect. Unassisted by their acquaintance with things, they ambitiously seek the aid of expressions as a magnificent veil, under whose covering they hope to conceal their want of talent, and to appear to say more than they think.

" But the very words which fly from those who seek nothing but them, present themselves in great numbers to an orator who has been fed for a long time on the substance of the things themselves. Readiness of thought produces readiness of expression; the agreeable is found in the useful; and the arms, which are only given to the soldier to conquer, become his most beautiful ornament." [1]

[1] *The Knowledge of Mankind.* The three preceding quotations are taken from this discourse.

" To think little, to speak on every subject, to doubt nothing, to dwell apart from the soul, merely to cultivate the surface of the understanding; to use happy expressions, to have an agreeable imagination, light and delicate conversation, and to know how to please without knowing how to acquire esteem; to be born with the equivocal talent of a ready conception, and on that account to consider reflection quite useless ; to fly from object to object, without deeply investigating any one; to cull rapidly all flowers, and never to give to the fruits time to come to maturity, —this is a feeble picture of what it pleases our age to honour with the name of wit.

" Attention is fatiguing, reason is a constraint, and authority is revolting to the man possessed of a mind more brilliant than solid, and of knowledge often erroneous and inaccurate; incapable of perseverance in his inquiries after truth, it escapes him more from instability than idleness." [1]

Although this manner is not simple, we cannot charge it with affectation. Imperturbable reason is the characteristic of d'Aguesseau; but to be an orator, reason must be empassioned. Cicero says, *Orator, ut ita dicam, tragicus.* [2] It is because the tragic is the true name of the serious. D'Aguesseau was once tragical, or at least eloquent. The spirit of liberty, maintained by the reading of the ancients and by parliamentary traditions, was stirred up in the passage on the *Love of Country*, delivered two months after the death of Louis XIV. Two months before, he could not have given utterance to such words. The term *country* does not occur twice in the writers of the seventeenth century. When Racine uses it, it is under cover of a subject taken from the Greek theatre; perhaps it is found also in Boileau. By crushing parliament, the great king had, as it were, stifled the patriotic spirit; but this spirit lived in d'Aguesseau, and to him the king was not the state :—

" Sacred tie of the authority of kings, and of the obedience of the people, the love of country should unite all their desires. But does this love, almost natural to man, does this virtue, which we know by feeling, praise by reason, and should follow from interest, cast its roots deep into our heart? and should we not say, that it is like a strange plant in monarchies, and that it

---

[1] Septienne Mercuriale : De l'Esprit et de la Science.
[2] An orator, so to speak, is a tragedian.

only grows luxuriantly and makes its precious fruits be tasted in republics?

"In these, each citizen is accustomed early, nay, almost at his birth, to regard the fortune of the state as identified with his own. That perfect equality, and that species of civic fraternity, which makes all the citizens only, as it were, a single family, gives to them all an equal interest in the good and evil of their country. The fate of the vessel, of which every one thinks himself the pilot, could not be a matter of indifference. The love of country becomes a species of self-love. They truly love themselves in the love of the republic, and they come at last to love it more than themselves.

"The inflexible Roman sacrifices his children to the safety of the republic. He orders their punishment—he does more, he sees it executed. The father is absorbed, and, as it were, annihilated in the consul. Nature shudders at it, but country, stronger than nature, bestows upon him as many children as the citizens, whom he preserves by the loss of his own offspring.

"Shall we, then, be reduced to seek the love of country in popular states, and perhaps in the ruins of ancient Rome? Is the safety of the state, then, less the safety of each citizen in the countries which only know a single master? Will it be necessary to teach men in them to love a country which gives or preserves to them all which they love in their other benefits? But shall we be surprised at this? How many are there who live and die without even knowing whether there is such a thing as country?

"Freed from the care, and deprived of the honour of government, they regard the fortune of the state as a vessel that floats at the will of its master, and for him alone is saved or lost. If the voyage be fortunate, we sleep, with full confidence in the pilot who guides us. If any unexpected storm awakes us, it only rouses us to make powerless vows and rash complaints, which merely annoy him who holds the helm; and sometimes even, when we stand as idle spectators of the shipwreck of our country, so great is our folly, that we console ourselves with the pleasure of reviling those by whom it was occasioned. A brilliant stroke of satire, whose severity gratifies us by its novelty, or delights us by its malignity, is an indemnification for all public misfortunes, and it might be said that we sought rather to avenge our country by our criticisms than to defend it by our services."[1]

We may read, on this subject, what Du Vair says on the principal causes of the decline of eloquence.

II.

COCHIN.

1687—1747.

THE works of Cochin were collected in 1751, and form six volumes in quarto. The respectability of a lawyer has a date in France. The magistracy there was always respected, but the respect which the profession of the bar inspires does not go back so far. The fifteenth and sixteenth centuries present to us some traces of the consideration with which lawyers began to be treated. Towards the end of the sixteenth only, this profession was elevated, and the dignity of parliament was conferred upon the advocate, who at last became a kind of magistrate. In the seventeenth century, rhetoric invaded the bar, which lost a little of its dignity. Le Maître, for example, celebrated for his retreat to Port Royal, in the midst of his brilliant success is, after all, a rhetorician. But the eighteenth century sees the value of rhetoric lowered, and the high dignity of the bar restored. The best days of the lawyer are those which we are now considering. Gresset does not give a just idea of them in those verses of *La Chartreuse*, in which, after having passed in review all the professions, he concludes that it is his part to have none. But, if the unfaithful representation does not correspond with the spirit of his time, the verses are charming :—

" Wandering in the dark labyrinth where the ghost of Themis, lying on purple and lilies, inclines her unequal balance, and draws from a venal urn decrees dictated by Venus, shall I go, a

mercenary orator of falsehood and truth, charged with a hatred
of strangers, to sell to the quarrels of the vulgar my voice and my
peace of mind, and, in the grotto of chicanery, bend to the laws
of a profane tribunal the law of the Eternal, and, by an English
eloquence, sap the foundations both of the throne and the
altar ?"

Cochin contributed to make his profession honoured. His
remarkable integrity originated in a deep sentiment of piety.
Disinterestedness, indefatigable devotedness, wonderful modesty,
vast and profound knowledge—these were the distinctions that
he possessed. He was the first advocate of his time.

But is his talent precisely that of the orator? Obliged to
keep close to his pleadings, such as they have come down to us,
we cannot maintain the affirmative. Let us not forget that he
did not write them as they were delivered. They are rather
memoirs : in putting them in order, he withdrew the passages
that were really oratorical; it is not the picture, but the simple
engraving that we possess.

In what remains of Cochin's works, his qualities are rather
solid than brilliant, but he pushes them to the point at which
they become brilliant. The most prominent characteristic of his
mind is the force and simplicity of his logic ; he excels in dialectics without showing it. There was no want of able logicians,
but those who could refrain from the exhibition of their logic *in
sapientia retinere moduum*,[1] were rare. His unity of thought
has been much and justly praised. " What is truly his invention," says the editor of his works, " is the reduction of any
cause whatever to a single point of dispute. No other before
his time had made this rule. A faithful observer of the unity
of his subject, so much recommended by the poets, he always
maintains a single proposition, and hence arises the admirable
clearness of his reasoning. After he had reduced his cause to
two, or at most to three, arguments, he began with the most
conclusive, and afterwards introduced it into the discussion of
the second and the third. Thus, without leaving the judges in
any uncertainty, the proof went on, always increasing. No one
part of his reasoning was more conclusive than another, because
the prevailing argument communicated its strength throughout."

---

[1] Preserve moderation in their wisdom.

Cochin was accomplished in narration ; the clearness of his narratives produced at the bar a surprising effect. When Cochin related, he proved. " Did ever any one tell a story so well ?" is a question put by the writer now quoted. " He may serve as a model in any kind of narrative whatever, grave or playful, historical or fabulous. A man of letters, who could not pardon in French writers their indifference for the history of their country, had come to hear one of his great causes. As he listened to the statement of the facts, he could not help exclaiming, as loud as respect for the place permitted,—What ! will not M. de Thou find there a continuator capable of writing history with clearness, precision, and grace ?"

Farther, the perfect propriety of his language is worthy of observation : and, first of all, moral propriety, and then propriety in all the details—a delicate observation of all that is suitable to the subject, to places, and to circumstances. No one has better practised the *apte dicere* without cold reserve. An internal heat makes itself always felt, and hence he attains to eloquence.

The causes which Cochin pleaded are in general more interesting to professional men than to the public, especially to the public of our times—questions respecting ecclesiastical jurisdiction or feudal privileges ; more civil causes than any others ; and a very great number of questions about condition—that is to say, genealogy, or, to speak more accurately, descent. Such questions are rare at present, thanks to the good management of the public registers. The only one of this kind, among those managed by Cochin, which excites any interest at present, is the case of Mademoiselle Ferrand, which is one of his masterpieces. She was a person forty-five years of age, disowned by her mother.

I repeat here what I have often said to those who study eloquence, do not satisfy yourselves with the authors in your own particular profession. Let the orator study his art in the writings of historians, the preacher in those of lawyers, all, among those who are neither orators nor writers. It is a principle, found in no treatise on the subject, and yet it occupies a principal place. Whoever wishes to be an advocate, or preacher, must study the language of common life. It is by going among the peasantry, and by keeping away from people of your own class, that you will rise to general ideas on the nature of eloquence.

III.

DUKE DE SAINT-SIMON.

1675–1755.

THE fame of the Duke de Saint-Simon is merely posthumous. He has left memoirs, of which some fragments were published in 1788, and a complete and authentic edition in 1829.

Descended from an illustrious race, he was, according to custom, destined to the profession of arms. But dissatisfied with an unfair promotion, he early quitted the service, before he had acquired any reputation in it. At a later period he was engaged in diplomacy, and in the administration under the regent, whom he loved, notwithstanding the difference of their characters. No remarkable event distinguished his career; his name is scarcely found in history, and his literary genius has alone preserved his memory from oblivion. A single passion seems to have ruled his life—a superstitious regard for birth and rank. He has the utmost reverence for the peerage, and the highest respect for precedency. He was duke and peer, and if any feeling can vie with that which he has respecting the importance of his dignity, it is the hatred that he bears to the natural children of Louis XIV., who were made legitimate princes. In religion he belongs to the Jansenist party. He adopts not only its controversial element, but its religion, serious and sincere. His most intimate intercourse was with men of piety; so we see him closely connected with the Duke de Beauvillieres on the one side, and on the other with the Abbé de Rancé, the celebrated restorer of La Trappe.

The Duke de Saint-Simon presents a singular mixture of elements apparently contradictory. We are accustomed to meet with contrasts, and especially in men of strong minds and eminent talents, but in him the anthithesis is more brought out, and deserves signal observation. He possesses in a rare degree the power of rising to vast and noble thoughts, and he continues subject to narrow prejudices. It is he who calls that maxim sublime—" that kings are made for the people, and not the people for kings." He is among the few men of his time who have noticed the people and pitied their sufferings, but it is always from the height of his peerage. He wishes for liberty, but as a duke and a peer. "He is," says M. de Barante, "a severe judge of a government, whom no one knew better how to judge, but his independence belongs neither to the philosopher, the lawyer, nor the citizen."[1]

He was a Christian, but still without prejudice to the peerage; in the details of his life, he is incessantly smitten with the privileges of the nobles, and the sincerity of his religion does not prevent him from allowing himself to go to excess in the exercise of an insupportable pride without ever reflecting on the matter. In this relation he still belonged to that conventional and representative age, in which religion, very true for him who professed it, preserved above all its character of propriety. Men intend to spend some weeks at La Trappe with the Abbé de Rancé, and begin by delaying their visit till they are gratified with all the vanities of the world.

Saint-Simon, if it be true that he was of an implacable disposition, and of a bitter, caustic and acrimonious temper, and that he was a severe censor, had still a heart susceptible of tender impressions. Any accidental display of virtuous conduct, or the remembrance of a virtuous man, makes his heart beat, and communicates to his style a pathos which no one has surpassed, because no one has been more deeply affected.

As to the qualities of his mind, none had quicker discernment or more profound sagacity. Two causes produced this sagacity, sympathy and antipathy, benevolence and ill-will, all that was amiable in the soul, and all that was atrabilarious in the character. But sagacity connected with charity is perhaps the most profound. Hatred is no doubt sagacious, but it is blind; not only does it prevent us from seeing what is before us, but it makes us see still more what is not. Saint-Simon drew from both sources, and we must not trust him too far,—for he is frequently unjust, nor be too hasty in condemning him. The glory of the time of Louis XIV. is frequently conventional; it has a prejudice in its favour. We feel indignant at reading the character of Fenelon, and yet in his life we meet with circumstances which confirm the judgment that Saint-Simon has pronounced.

[1] De Barante, Melanges Literaires, tome ii., De l'Histoire.

Above all, we owe to Saint-Simon the picture of a reign. This book is the true *Age of Louis XIV.* Voltaire has only made a flattering portrait of it; he pardons everything in an epoch favourable to literature and the arts. We cannot but be astonished that the illusion still continues. This age, after all that has been said, although we cannot help charging it with hypocrisy, must have been great. The Memoirs of Saint-Simon produce in this respect a strange and painful impression. He treats this memorable period nearly in the same way as the herald-at-arms of La Marck is treated in Quentin Durward. This brilliant court, distinguished for propriety, mental refinement, and politeness of language, is stripped naked, lashed and torn to pieces by one of those who formed a part of it. He, himself eminently aristocratical, does not perceive how much contempt he brings upon his order; but royalty especially is rendered contemptible by this species of reading. In some things it becomes ridiculous, in others hateful. See the history of Fargues :—

"There was a great hunting-match at Saint-Germain. At that time dogs, not men, caught the deer, and we cannot tell the number of dogs, horses, mounted huntsmen, relays and routes across the country. The chase took the direction of Dourdan, and continued so long that the king turned away at a very late hour and left the field. The Count de Guiche, the Count, afterwards Duke de Lude, Vardes, M. de Lauzun, who told me the story, and I know not who more, lost their way, and when it grew dark, knew not where they were. By pushing forward their weary horses, they at length saw a light; they went towards it, and at last arrived at the gate of a kind of castle. They knocked, cried, told their names, and requested hospitality. It was about the end of autumn, and between ten and eleven o'clock at night. The gate was opened to them, and the master came and made them put off their boots and warm themselves; he ordered the horses to be put into the stable, and supper to be made ready, of which they had great need. The repast was speedily placed on the table—it was excellent, and they had various kinds of wine. The host was polished, respectful, neither ceremonious nor forward, with all the air and manners of superior society. They learned that he was called Fargues, and the house Courson; that he had retired to it; that he had not gone out of it for several years; that he sometimes received his friends there, and that he had neither wife nor children. The household seemed to be well regulated, and the house had an air of comfort. After they had made a good supper, Fargues did not detain them from their beds. Each of them found one perfectly good, each had his chamber, and the men-servants of Fargues waited upon them with great propriety. They were very weary, and slept long. So soon as they were dressed, an excellent breakfast was served up, and when they rose from table, their horses were ready, as much refreshed as they were themselves. Charmed with the manners and politeness of Fargues, and pleased with his kind entertainment, they made him many offers of service, and set out for Saint-Germain. Their losing their way was one piece of news, their return and where they had been during the night was another.

"These gentlemen were the flower of the court and the pink of gallantry, and they were all at the time in close intimacy with the king. They related to him their adventure and their extraordinary reception, and praised in a very high degree the host— his cheer and his house. The king asked his name, and so soon as he heard it, said, *How, Fargues, is he so near this?* The gentlemen redoubled their praises, and the king made no farther remark. He went directly to the apartments of the queen-mother and told what had occurred; both felt that Fargues was very bold to dwell so near the court, and thought it very extraordinary that they had only learned by this hunting adventure of his having lived there so long.

"Fargues had greatly distinguished himself in all the commotions of Paris against the court and Cardinal Mazarin. If he had not been executed, it was not from any want of will to take special vengeance upon him, but he had been protected by his party, and was formally comprehended in the amnesty. The hatred which he had incurred, and to which he thought he must yield, made him resolve to quit Paris for ever, to avoid all strife, and to withdraw to his own house without observation, and till that time he had remained unknown. Cardinal Mazarin was dead, and no one was questioned about past events, but as he had been quite notorious, he was afraid lest some new action might be raised against him, and on that account he lived very retired, at peace with all his neighbours, and quite at ease about former troubles, trusting to the amnesty and to the length of time that had elapsed. The king and the queen-mother, who had only pardoned him from necessity, sent for the first president, Lamoignon, and charged him secretly to sift the life and conduct of Fargues, to examine carefully whether or not means might be found to punish his former insolence, and to make him repent of bearding the court in the enjoyment of wealth and tranquillity. They told him of the hunting adventure which had made them acquainted with his place of abode, and showed to Lamoignon extreme anxiety that he might find legal means to ruin him.

"Lamoignon, avaricious and a good courtier, resolved to gratify them, and to make his own advantage of the transaction. He made his inquiries, gave an account of them, and was so successful as to discover a way of implicating Fargues in a murder committed at Paris, when the disturbances were at their height, upon which he gave a decree privately, and one morning sent tipstaffs to apprehend him and bring him into the prison of the Conciergerie. Fargues, who, from the time that the amnesty was passed, felt sure of having done nothing blameworthy, was quite astonished, but he was much more so when he learned from the examination the nature of the crime, of which he was accused. He met his accusation with a very powerful defence, and farther alleged that the murder in question having been committed in the heat of the disturbances and of the revolt of Paris in Paris itself, the amnesty, which had followed them, effaced the remembrance of every thing which had passed in these times of confusion, and covered every circumstance which could not have been expressed in detail regarding each individual according to the spirit, privilege, custom, and effect of amnesties, not called in question till the present moment. The distinguished courtiers, who had been so well entertained at the unhappy man's house, made every effort with the judges, and the king in his favour, but all in vain. Fargues was immediately beheaded, and his confiscated estate was given as a reward to the first president. It was very suitable for him, and became the portion of his second son. It was scarcely a league between Basville and Courson. Thus the father-in-law and the son-in-law were successively enriched in the same office, the one with the blood of the innocent, the other with the deposit which his friend had entrusted to him to keep, which he afterwards declared to the king that he gave it to him, and which he knew very well how to use as if it had been his own."[1]

As to what remains, the picture of this great reign is not only sketched with rare sagacity, but also with genius. These memoirs are truly a history. Saint-Simon is a narrator accomplished, lively, copious, ornamental, and picturesque, when he tells of battles, or relates anecdotes. In this last style of writing nobody succeeded better than he. He is still more an eloquent reasoner, on account of others, as well as on his own. It is impossible to report with more interest the discussion of the king's council. We may follow, as an example, the statement of the affair regarding the Spanish succession.

The most striking part of Saint-Simon's writings is his portraits. People made much of them in the society of the seventeenth century. They applied to them their whole mind; the style was conventional, and somewhat artificial, and there was less said about what the original was than what it should have been; antithesis and play of wit were not wanting.—See Madame de La Fayette, M. de La Rochefoucauld, and Cardinal de Retz. There is nothing in common with Saint-Simon and his portraits. He does not draw them for the mere purpose of drawing them. He is full of his subject; he gives himself up to the vivacity of his remembrances, and to the force of his impressions; he is entirely occupied with the objects of his aversion or friendship; he proceeds without order, throws out the first ideas that occur to his mind, accumulates the features of the character, mixes the general with the particular, inserts, in the form of a parenthesis, a whole history in consequence of a single word, takes up what he has left, is again interrupted, returns once more to his purpose, and only stops when he has exhausted his subject. There is nothing analytical in his mode of proceeding—it is synthesis, life quite pure. He throws himself on the character represented; he pursues it without relaxation—it is the central point, which constitutes the individuality, and which is only the supreme effort by which he gains his end. This is the manner peculiar to his genius; but, in reference to us, these preliminaries are the portrait. The personage moves, walks, and speaks before us. There is some relation between this method, which, in the case of Saint-

[1] Memoires complets de Saint-Simon, tome iv., pp. 416-420.

Simon, is no method, and that of M. Sainte-Beuve. The latter also admits us to intimacy with his originals.

Among so many portraits, so admirably brought out, we shall notice some, and first that of Fenelon. We have already mentioned it, and may add, that no one has judged Fenelon with so much severity, or praised him to such excess. Next, that of Marshal de Villars, to a certain extent unjust perhaps; we find in it these harsh expressions :—" Such was Villars, generally speaking, whose successes in war and at court will acquire in the sequel a great name in history, when time shall have lost sight of the man himself, and when oblivion shall have effaced what is scarcely known but to his contemporaries. . . . The name which an unwearied good luck has procured for him for the time to come, has frequently disgusted me with history, and I have found a great number of people of this opinion." Saint-Simon concludes thus :—" The mother of Villars always said to him, *My son, speak always of yourself to the king, and never speak of yourself to others.* He profited well by the first part of this great lesson, but not by the last, for he never ceased to stun and wear out every body with himself." [1]

The portrait of the Princess d'Harcourt is quite different :—

" This Princess d'Harcourt was a sort of personage whom it is good to make known, with a view to make known more particularly a court which did not hesitate to receive such persons. She was then a large fat creature, very active, her colour resembling milk soup, with thick filthy lips and flaxen hair, always escaping and trailing about, like all the rest of her dress. Slovenly, nasty, always intriguing, designing, encroaching, ever quarrelling, and ever humbled to the dust or exalted to the skies, according to the condition of the parties with whom she had to do—she was a fair-haired fury, and, what is more, a harpy. She had that animal's effrontery, wickedness, deceit, and violence— she had its covetousness and greed. . . . She transacted business on all hands, and ran as far for a hundred livres as for a hundred thousand. The comptrollers-general did not easily get rid of her, and, so far as she could, she deceived men of business, to get more out of them. Her boldness in cheating at play was inconceivable, and that, too, openly. You surprised her in the very act; she railed at you, and put it in her pocket; as the result

[1] Memoires complets de Saint-Simon, tome iv., pp. 372-376.

was never different, she was regarded as a fish-woman, with whom no one wished to commit himself, and that, too, in the full saloon at Marly, at the game of lansquenet, in presence of Monseigneur and of Madame Duchess of Burgundy.   At other games, as ombre, etc., she was avoided, but that was not always possible; as she cheated there also as much as possible, she never failed to say, at the end of the rounds, that she allowed what might not have been fair play, and she asked that it might also be allowed to her, and assured herself of it without receiving an answer.   She was a great devotee by profession, and thus reckoned on putting her conscience in security, because, added she, in play there is always some mistake.   She went to all the religious services, and constantly communicated, very often after having been engaged in play till four o'clock in the morning." [1]

We have further the portrait of the Duke of Burgundy :—

" This prince, the indubitable and afterwards the presumptive heir of the crown, was born an object of terror, and his early youth made people tremble; hard-hearted, and giving way to the highest transports of passion, even against inanimate objects; impetuous with rage, incapable of bearing the slightest resistance, even from time and the elements, without getting into a fury, so as to produce alarm lest he should do to himself some great bodily injury; excessively obstinate, and to the last degree eager in the pursuit of every kind of pleasure.   He loved wine and good living, was passionately devoted to hunting, was ravished with music, and given to play, at which he could not bear to be vanquished, and hence the danger of engaging in any game with him was extreme.   In short, he was the slave of every passion, and transported with all kinds of pleasure; he was often savage, and naturally disposed to cruelty; he was barbarous in his jests, and in turning people into ridicule with an accuracy that was overwhelming.   From the height of heaven, he looked upon men as atoms, to whom he bore no resemblance, whatever they might be.   His brothers scarcely appeared to him to occupy an intermediate place between him and the human race, although it had been always intended to educate all the three together, on the principle of perfect equality.   His wit and sagacity were uniformly brilliant; and, even in the midst of his rage, his answers

---

[1] Memoires complets de Saint-Simon, tome iii., p. 397.

were astonishing. His reasonings were always directed to the exact and the profound, even in the transports of his passion. He sported with the most abstract knowledge, and the extent and vivacity of his understanding were prodigious, and prevented him from applying himself to one thing at a time, till he became incapable of doing so. The necessity of allowing him to sketch, as he studied, in which he had great taste and dexterity, and without which his study was fruitless, perhaps injured his shape.

" He was rather little than tall, his countenance long and brown, the upper part perfect, with the finest eyes in the world; his look was lively, touching, striking, admirable, very commonly pleasant, and always piercing; and the expression of his face agreeable, lofty, refined, and intellectual, so much so as to be suggestive of genius. The lower part of the visage very pointed, with a nose long and elevated, but not fine, did not produce such an agreeable effect. His hair was of a chesnut colour, so curled and in such quantity as to be blown about by the wind; the lips and the mouth agreeable, when he did not speak; but although his teeth were not bad, the upper jaw came too far forward, and almost shut up the lower, which, when he spoke and laughed, produced a disagreeable effect. He had the finest legs and feet that, next to the king, I have ever seen in any one; but these, as well as his thighs, were too long in proportion to his body. He came quite straight from the hands of his female attendants. It was soon perceived that his form began to be crooked. Immediately, and for a long time, the collar and iron cross were employed, which he wore so long as he was in his apartment, and even before company, and none of the games and exercises calculated to restore his figure were neglected. Nature remained the stronger : he became deformed, and particularly so in one shoulder, that he was at last lame; not that his thighs and legs were not perfectly equal, but because, in proportion as that shoulder enlarged, there was no longer the same distance from the two haunches to the two feet, and, instead of being straight, he inclined to one side. He walked neither with less ease nor for a shorter time, nor with less speed nor less willingly, and he was not less disposed for exercise on foot or on horseback, although he was very bad at it. What must surprise us is, that this prince, with his eyes, and with a mind so elevated, and which had attained to the most extraordinary virtue, and to the most eminent and solid piety, should never have seen himself, such as he was, with respect to his shape, or should never have accustomed himself to it. It was a weakness, which put men on their guard against absence of mind and any indiscretion, and which occasioned trouble to such of his people as, in his dress, and in the arrangement of his hair, concealed that natural defect as much as they possibly could, but they were on their guard, lest they should let him perceive what was so apparent. We must conclude, from this fact, that it is not granted to man here below to be quite perfect.

" So great a mind, and such a kind of mind, joined to such vivacity, sensibility, and passions, and all so ardent, was not easily trained. The Duke de Beauvilliers, who equally felt its difficulties and its consequences, went beyond himself in his application, patience, and in the variety of his resources. Deriving little help from the under-governors, he availed himself of every one who was at hand. Fenelon, Fleury under-teacher, who published a beautiful *History of the Church;* some gentlemen ushers; Moreau, first valet-de-chambre, a man very much above his condition, without forgetting himself; some rare men-servants of the household ; the Duke de Chevreuse alone from without,—all set to work, and all in the same spirit laboured, each under the direction of the governor, whose skill, unfolded in a narrative, would form a suitable work, equally curious and instructive. But God, who is the master of all hearts, and whose divine Spirit breathes where He wills, performed on this prince a work of conversion, and between the eighteenth and twentieth year of his age his work was accomplished. From this abyss went forth a prince affable, pleasant, humane, moderate, patient, modest, penitent, and, as far as was suitable to his condition, and even beyond it, humble and severe to himself. Quite devoted to his duties, and understanding them to be immense, he thought no more but how he should unite the duties of son and subject with those to which he saw himself destined. The shortness of the day was all his regret. He placed all his strength and all his consolation in prayer, and sought his preservatives in the reading of pious books. His taste for abstract science, and his readiness in apprehending it, robbed him at first of time, which he perceived must be devoted to the obtaining of information about things connected with his condition, and to the propriety due to that rank, which led to the throne, and which required him in the meantime to hold a court.

" Being a novice in the exercises of devotion, and apprehensive of his weakness in regard to pleasure, he was inclined at first to seek solitude. Watchfulness over himself—for in his case he allowed nothing to pass, and thought that nothing should be passed over —shut him up in his closet as in an asylum, not to be entered on any pretence whatever. How strange is the world! It had treated him with abhorrence in his first condition, and it was tempted to despise the second. The prince felt it, bore it, and attached with joy this species of opprobrium to the cross of his Saviour, that he might feel ashamed at the bitter remembrance of his former pride. He met with what was still more painful— the dull and heavy looks of his nearest relations. The king, with his external devotion and regularity, soon saw, with secret indignation, a prince of that age censuring, unintentionally, his life by his conduct, refusing to himself a new chest of drawers, with a view to give to the poor the price that was destined for it, and thanking him modestly for a new gilding, with which some wished to renew his little apartment. It was observed how much piqued he was at his too obstinate refusal to be present at a ball at Marly, on the day of the Kings. Truly, it was the fault of a novice. He owed this respect, nay, to speak plainly, this chari- table compliance, to the king, his grandfather, not to provoke him by this strange contrast; but, in the main, when we look at it in itself, it was a very great action, which exposed him to all the consequences of the disgust for himself, that he produced in the king, and to the talk of a court of which the king was the idol, and which turned into ridicule such singularity.

" Monseigneur [1] was in his side a thorn not less sharp, quite given up to material objects, and to the direction of others, whose politics already frightened this young prince; he only perceived his out- ward appearance and his rudeness, and alienated himself from him as from an accuser. The Duchess of Burgundy, alarmed at the austerity of her husband, omitted nothing calculated to soften his manners. Her charms, with which he was deeply smitten, the policy and unrestrained importunities of the young ladies of her suite, disguised in a hundred different forms, the allurement of pleasure and of parties, of which he was by no means insensible, were every day displayed. There followed him into the inner closet

---

[1] This title belonged to the king's son, who was the father of the Duke of Burgundy.

remonstrances from·the devoted fairy, and the pointed expression of the king's face, the alienation of Monseigneur, which was the subject of coarse remarks, the mischievous preference of his household, and his own, all too natural, for the Duke de Berry, whom his elder brother, treated there as a troublesome stranger, saw cherished and welcomed with applause. One must have a very strong mind to support such trials, and that, too, every day, without being shaken; one must be powerfully upheld by an invisible hand, when every external prop was withheld, and when a prince of that rank sees that he is disliked by his own relations, before whom every one bows, and experiences almost the contempt of a court, which was no longer under restraint, and which had a secret fear of being one day under his laws. As he, however, reflected more with himself respecting the scruple of displeasing the king, of repulsing Monseigneur, and of occasioning to others any estrangement from virtue, the rude and hard bark is gradually softened, but without injury to the solidity of the trunk. He at length comprehended what it is to leave God for God, and how the faithful performance of the duties peculiar to the state in which God had placed him, is the solid piety, which is most agreeable to him. He set himself forthwith to apply his mind to what might teach him how to rule; he appeared more in the world; he did so with so much grace, and an air so natural, that his reason for withdrawing from it, and his difficulty in only lending himself to it, were soon perceived, and the world, which is so much delighted with being loved, began to be reconciled to him.

"It was believed that his presence was necessary to revive the spirit of the army, and to restore in it the discipline that had been lost. This was in 1708. The horoscope has been seen, which the knowledge of the interests and intrigues induced me to make of them to the Duke de Beauvilliers in the gardens of Marly before the declaration was made public, and we have seen its incredible success, and by what rapid degrees of falsehood, cunning, unmeasured boldness of impudence in betraying the king, the state, the truth even then unknown, an infernal cabal, the most efficient, that ever was organized, made this prince be eclipsed in the kingdom, whose crown he was to wear, and in his father's house, so as to render it odious and dangerous to speak a word there in his favour. A trial so strangely new and cruel, was very severe to a prince, who saw all united against him, and who had, only for himself, the truth stifled by all the tricks of the magicians of Pharaoh. He felt it in all its weight, in all its extent, and in all its sharpness. He also bore it with all the patience, firmness, and especially with all the charity of an elect one, who wishes only to see God in every thing, who is humbled under his hand, who is purified in the crucible which this divine hand presents to him, who renders thanks to Him for every thing, who carries his magnanimity so far, as only to wish to speak or do precisely what he owes to the state and to truth, and who is so much on his guard against human nature, that he keeps far within the boundaries of justice and holiness.

" So much virtue obtained at length its reward from the world, and with so much more purity, that the prince, very far from contributing to it, kept very much out of view. At that time he, more than ever, redoubled his application to the affairs of government, and sought information about every thing calculated to render him more capable of exercising it. He banished all amusement from science, with a view to divide his retirement for study between prayer, which he abridged, and information, which he increased; and without, he devoted his time and attention to the king, to the care of Madame Maintenon, to the conveniency and enjoyments of his wife, and to the holding of a court, in which it was his aim to render himself accessible and amiable. The more the king raised him, the more he desired to keep himself submissive in his hand; the more he showed him consideration and confidence, the more could he answer it by sentiment, wisdom, knowledge, and, above all, by a moderation removed from all desire and all complaisance in himself, and far less did he betray the slightest presumption. His own secret and that of others was in his case impenetrable. His confidence in his confessor did not extend to business.

. . . " This prince's discernment was under no restraint, but, like the bee, he collected the most excellent substance from the best and finest flowers. He endeavoured to become acquainted with men, and to draw from them such knowledge and information as he had reason to expect. With some individuals he conversed sometimes, but rarely, and as he walked backwards and forwards, on particular subjects ; more seldom in private, on some explanations which he judged necessary, but this was not his uniform practice. . . . Beyond this number, I was the only person who had free and frequent access to his private apartments, whether on his side or mine. There he laid open to me his intentions respecting the present and the future with confidence, and yet with wisdom, moderation, and discretion. He expatiated on the plans which he thought necessary; he spoke freely on general topics, and was reserved on what referred to particular matters; but as he wished, on this subject, also to draw from me all that could be of use to him, I cunningly led him on to open his mind freely, and often not without success.

" A volume would not sufficiently describe the various conversations between this prince and me. What love of virtue! What self-denial! What researches! What results! What purity in the end proposed, and if I may presume to say it, what reflection of the divinity in that candid, simple, and brave soul, which, as far as it is permitted here below, had preserved its image! We perceived in him the brilliant marks of an education at once laborious and ingenious, equally learned, wise, and Christian, and the reflections of an enlightened disciple born to command. There the scruples which swayed him in public were kept out of view. He wished to know with whom he had and should have to do; he brought into play the first of these parties in order to profit by a pointless and uninteresting conversation. But how vast this private conference, and how much the charms that were felt, were diversified by the variety which the prince put in regular order by his skill, by leading on curiosity and by his thirst for knowledge. He led the man from one thing to another on so many subjects, topics, people, and facts, that whosoever was not ready with the requisite information would go away displeased with himself and would leave him discontented. . . . . . In this way a person who usually reckoned on discussing a subject with him for a quarter or half an hour would spend two hours or more, according as the time of the prince left him more or less liberty. He brought him always back to the point which he had determined chiefly to discuss, but through parentheses, which he set before him and handled as a master, and some of these were often his principal aim. There was no waste of words, no compliment, no praise, nothing unprofitable, no preface, no idle story, not the slightest joke, every object and design, nay, every particular was brought in and rendered important to the point in hand and to the end in view; there was nothing without a reason or without a cause, nothing for amusement or for pleasure; there, general prevailed over particular charity, and what each one should bestow was accurately discussed; there, plans, arrangements, changes, and preferences were formed, matured, unfolded, and often prepared without appearing to be so.

"With so many and so great accomplishments, this distinguished prince did not fail to show some remains of humanity, that is to say, some defects, and these occasionally by no means decent; and this is what, in the midst of so much that is solid and great, we have difficulty in comprehending; because there was no wish to recal his former vices and faults, nor to reflect on the prodigious change, and what it must have cost, which had made of him a prince so near all perfection, that in looking closely at him we are astonished at his not having reached its summit. I have referred elsewhere to some of his slight faults, which, in spite of his age, were still the errors of childhood, and which were sufficiently corrected every day to enable us accurately to conjecture that they would soon entirely disappear.

"The grand and sublime maxim, that kings are made for the people, and not the people for kings, was so strongly impressed on his mind that it rendered luxury and war hateful to him. This circumstance made him sometimes express his feelings too sharply on this last point, carried away by a truth too hard for the ears of the world, and this unfortunately made it be said on some occasions, that he did not love war. His justice was furnished with that impenetrable bond, which constituted all its security.

"His conversation was amiable, so long as it was solid and in good taste, and it was always suited to those with whom he was speaking. He willingly diverted himself with walking, and it was then that he conversed most. If he fell in there with any man with whom he could talk on science, it was his pleasure, but a modest pleasure, and merely for amusement and information, by saying a little and listening more. But he sought, above all, in such conversations, what was useful, and was eager to get people to speak on war and the fortresses, about naval and commercial affairs, about courts and foreign countries, sometimes about facts relating to individuals, but made public, and about points of history and wars long past. These walks, which

afforded to him much information, procured for him the minds of
the people, their hearts, their admiration, and their highest hopes.
He had substituted for the public shows, which he had for a long
time dispensed with, a small game which the most moderate
purses might easily reach. . . . . So long as Monseigneur
lived, he carefully performed every duty which was due to him.
. . . . He loved the princes, his brothers, with tenderness,
and his wife passionately. Grief for her loss penetrated his
inmost soul. Piety raised him above it, but it was by the
most prodigious efforts. The sacrifice was complete, but it was
a bloody one. In this terrible affliction there was nothing
mean, little, or unbecoming. There was the man in violent
agitation, laying hold by violence of a smooth surface, but he
finally sunk.

"The days of this affliction were speedily abridged. He was
the same under his disease; he did not think he would recover,
and under this impression he reasoned upon it with his physicians,
and did not conceal the foundation on which his opinion rested.
It was told to him not long before, and all that he felt from the
first day to the last, confirmed him in it more and more. What
a fearful persuasion of his wife's death and of his own! But,
great God! what a spectacle didst Thou give us in him, and
why is 'it not permitted to reveal still farther qualities at once
secret and so sublime, that it is only Thou who canst bestow
them and know their full value! What imitation of Jesus
Christ upon the cross! We speak not merely in regard to the
death and sufferings, it was elevated far above them. What
tender but calm views! What lively transports of thanksgiving,
because he had been prevented from wielding the sceptre, and
from the account of it which he must have rendered! What
submission, and how perfect! What ardent love of God! What
an acute perception of his own nothingness and sins! What a
magnificent idea of infinite mercy! What religious and humble
fear! What sober confidence! What wise peace! What
readings! What continual prayers! What an ardent desire
for the last sacraments! What profound recollection! What
invincible patience! What gentleness, and what constant goodness to every one who came near him! What pure love, which
urged him to go to God! France fell at length under this last
punishment. God showed her a prince whom she did not

deserve. The earth was not worthy of him, he was already ripe for the happiness of eternity." [1]

The French language is a courser less fiery than restive, which each writer in his turn has subjected to the bit and spur, but the Duke de Saint-Simon has been its most astonishing conqueror. No one has darted across the fields as he has done, no one with more authority has made it break its habits and vary its paces. No writer has better shown with how many articulations it is provided, which had not been suspected, and of how many changes it is capable, which it seemed to reject. The proportion of the conventional and the determined appears weak in this extraordinary dialect, at the expense of what is free and flexible. We do not profess to deny or palliate the fact, that incorrectness and obscurity are frequent in a language so adventurous. But to be removed from the classical style, it is not less the style of a man of genius.

Always sure of his end, but not at all careful about the road which leads to it, Saint-Simon throws out his phraseology in every direction, resolved not to change it and not to turn back. If for any reason connected with the style, the form of the beginning does not suit what remains of his thought, he forces the rule, or checks it, or extends it, or makes it ingeniously enter into his design; this first design in the face of all difficulties, assimilates to itself whatever follows; hence faults more or less shocking, but from the same source we have fortunate discoveries and true graces of style.

Abounding in recollections, assailed by the numerous circumstances in the facts which he relates, eager to tell them all and wanting leisure to arrange them, Saint-Simon gives them in charge to his phraseology, hanging them, so to speak, on each projecting angle of the period, under the form of incident, epithet, or parenthesis, and finding, in the double necessity of saying everything and of going forward, a conciseness often surprising, which makes each circumstance fly out like a spark. The phraseology of Saint-Simon, full, lively, and copious from abundance of matter is a real phenomenon, in which the ideas seem to multiply, to cross each other, and to move backward and forward

---

[1] Memoires complets de Saint-Simon, tome x. pp. 197-217. See this passage commented upon by M. Vinet, and the reflections which follow in the Chrestomathie Française, troisième edition, tome iii. pp. 42-53.

like a crowd in some public place. It is not the beauty of the oratorical period, its large proportions, and its skilful and noble arrangement; it is sometimes a turn painfully strong, but very frequently also a model of energy and dexterity, and for a genius of the stamp of Saint-Simon, an opportunity of conquest over the language, and of astonishing exhibitions of style.

The choice of materials for the phraseology is not less remarkable than its construction. Here is the same liberty as in all the rest. I do not speak of metaphors so extraordinary that their analogies would be found with difficulty elsewhere. In this mode of writing, liberty has no limits traced out and previously known. Every metaphor is a substitution founded on a relation; the rules are that this relation may be true, and that the term substituted may suit the nature of the subject, but to know them belongs to taste and reason, not to custom. The liberty of custom shows itself farther in modifying the usual acceptation of words, and the mode of using them, for here the rule is as much more inflexible as it is arbitrary. This is the peculiarity of Saint-Simon, as he makes the words slip softly off their base and obliges them to cover more space; and he often does it with much tact and good fortune, so that it may be asked if he has done anything else than avail himself of a neglected but incontestable privilege. And whether he restrains custom or respects it, his expressions, even the shortest, cast the richest light upon the whole idea. In this exceptionable language, the Duke of Burgundy is *un disciple lumineux*, although *lumineux* is not applied to persons, but you may try to say it otherwise. The charms of a conversation are agités par la varieté où le prince s'espace par art. " *Des charmes agités!* This expression takes analysis at a disadvantage; but the imagination adopts it with eagerness. "The duchess alarmed at a spouse so austere," *L'austèrité de son époux*—more regular would have been less graceful—" Which caused to be said *sinistrement*, that he did not love war." The application of this adverb is unusual but very expressive. " Il s'extorquait une surface unie." Taste trembles before such expressions; but we see with pleasure this verb *extorquer* going beyond the limits of its traditional acceptation. We must, however, confess, in such a liberty the abuse comes very near the use. The use is almost an abuse. This liberty threatens the foundations of language. Language, as well as civil society, rests on respect for property ; in grammar, as in politics, there are acquired rights—each word claims its idea, as each individual claims his property. That these privileges may be given up to the good pleasure of all or of one, language is shaken as well as civil society ; but, on the other hand, by the immovable power of propriety, language and society stand still. The French language owes its life and its improvement to the constant change which innovations, if not equal, at least similar to those which we have just observed, have impressed upon it. But this change in the language should operate slowly and without violence, the more insensible it is the more sure—it is so much the more legitimate the less we know its origin—it should be as much as possible anonymous. In our times it is very far from remaining in this condition. In respect to language property is threatened on all sides—the individual arbitrator is substituted for the legal —convention, the basis of language, is swept away, and consequently confusion will be introduced.

IV.

ROLLIN.

1661—1741.

To pass from Saint-Simon to Rollin is to pass from wormwood to honey, and yet, notwithstanding this natural opposition, and every thing that separates the great lord from the cutler's son, certain relations unite these two men. They were of the same age, and their most cherished opinions were common to both. We find ourselves here in the very centre of Jansenism ; Saint-Simon and Rollin belonged both to this honest and illustrious party.

Rollin was indebted to the benevolence of a friar who frequented his father's house, for the advantage of an accurate education and of a learned career. At a later period, a rich farmer of the taxes, or a lawyer, whose sons were his school-fellows, furnished him with the means of prosecuting his classical studies.

Rollin was not a man to forget this, and in his *Treatise on Study*,
we meet with allusions to the liberality of which his youth was
the object:—

"I know not if there be for a man of letters, and for a virtuous
man, a purer joy than that which is derived from contributing,
by his care and liberality, to the training of young persons, who
afterwards become able professors, and by their rare talents do
honour to the University. This joy, it appears to me, is more
sensibly felt when, under the pretext of gratitude, they render
these services, with a view to acknowledge and repay in some
degree, those which they themselves received when they were in
a similar situation." [1]

For some time he studied theology, but he did not take orders.
His inclination led him to the education of youth. He at first
taught the belles lettres in a college at Paris; afterwards, when
he had acquired a moderate income, about six or seven hundred
livres, he withdrew to devote himself to sedentary studies, only
reserving certain functions in the College of France. His reputation was already great. In 1694 he was appointed Rector of
the University—a temporary office granted to eminent men—of
this rectorship he left the most honourable memorials. In 1699
we find him quite devoted to teaching; he was made Principal
of the College of Beauvais, at that time almost ruined by bad
management. He restored it and rendered it prosperous by the
wisdom and gentleness of his government. He wrote the history
of his peaceful reign in the part of the *Treatise on Study*, which
is appropriated to the government of colleges.

Such a career, concentrated on the labours of schools, one
would think, should have been sheltered from storms; but Rollin was a Jansenist; he was also a friend of Duguet. At this
period Jansenism was the object of persecution on account of the
bull *Unigenitus*, and ill-will even extended to laymen. Rollin
was gentle but firm. He had settled convictions, and without
any bitterness of expression. He could at heart remain un-
shaken. Gentleness did not exclude firmness; there is gentleness in characters really strong,—and in the case of Rollin, tenderness did not banish energy. The formulary of the Jansenist
is no where laid down in his works; but his Catholicism savours

[1] Traité des Etudes. Livre viii., partie ii., chap. i., art. ii.

of Jansenism. He belonged to the class that were nearest to the gospel, and you have only to read his writings to feel that he belonged to *that party ;* his language reveals it. Farther, the actions of his life marked him out as a Jansenist. In consequence he was deprived of his office of Principal in 1712, and retired to private life. The account of his life should be read in the Picture of the Eighteenth Century by M. Villemain.[1] " Rollin," he says, " was the true saint of teaching, as Pestalozzi was the Vincent de Paul of education."

This saying is very just. The name of Rollin awakens the most respectful and the most tender feelings, and it makes us involuntarily think of Fenelon. We feel ourselves gently attracted towards both, towards the son of the tradesman as well as towards the Archbishop, and we would have wished to have known them both. There are two kinds of temper belonging to the same family, energy of conviction and concealed strength, tenderness of heart and gentleness of character. But although Rollin is equal at least in virtue, piety, and moral elevation to the author of Telemachus, his glory is less intimidating, and we get more familiar with the *good* rector than we dare to be with the illustrious prelate.

Rollin may have had equals, but he possessed the most difficult of the virtues connected with instruction—humility. Germany and England have produced obscure Rollins, but the great distinction of ours, besides his virtue, is, that he was eminently French. A Christian sagacious and fervent, Christianity, which is so comprehensive, did not blunt in him the graces of the French mind. His goodness was universal. We think we have said all when we call him the *good* Rollin; but, in fact, he possesses as much grace of mind as of character.

Antiquity and Christianity, these springs of public education in France, are the elements which appear to be combined in Rollin. He is equally imbued with these two qualities, which have between them marvellous affinities, and always form the perfection of education. Antiquity and Christianity are the two primitive ages of human nature. Antiquity is man in the fulness and simplicity of his human development, Christianity is the fulness and simplicity of man made divine. There are relations

---

[1] Villemain, Cours de Literature Française. Dix-huitième siècle, Ire Leçon.

between these terms, which no doubt an abyss separates, antiquity finishes, in the esthetic sense, a development, whose basis, entirely moral, is enlarged and corrected by Christianity. The human development will only be complete by these two means, improvement of the soul by Christianity, and the cultivation of the mind and taste by the study of antiquity. Rollin is devoted to antiquity in two ways, for Christianity is also ancient.

Rollin was the object of universal admiration. Notwithstanding differences of opinion, no one thought of refusing to him a heartfelt homage. That same Rollin, who would converse on study in his youth, " on the winter evenings with Racine,"[1] received in mature age the praises of Voltaire. In 1731, when the *Treatise on Study* was the only work of Rollin then known, Voltaire in his *Temple of Taste* consecrates some lines to the *good* rector : " Not far from this Rollin dictated lessons to youth, and though in the teacher's robe they listened to him." Frederic the Great, the other hero of the eighteenth century, cultivated Rollin's acquaintance, and was particularly anxious to attract his attention. Their correspondence is extant.

The works of Rollin are voluminous, but not numerous. They are, besides an edition of Quintilian, with Latin notes (1725), the *Treatise on Study, or on the manner of teaching and studying the belles lettres, with a view to form the mind and the heart* (1726–1728). *Ancient History* (1730–1738), and the *Roman History* (1738). This was the work of his last years.

In the *Treatise on Study*, after an introduction on the studies of childhood, and on the education of daughters, Rollin treats of six points—Of *languages,* that is, French, Greek, and Latin ; *poetry ; eloquence ; history ;* and *philosophy*, a title under which he introduces everything which belongs neither to philology nor history ; and *the government of colleges.*

What especially deserves to be praised in this work is its moral excellence. Every thing is brought into it subordinate to the education of the heart, but subordinate and not sacrificed. Next, uprightness of judgment, and this prevails over every thing else. Every upright mind is independent, and candour produces originality of thought. Rollin, whom we willingly accept as the docile pupil of tradition, has made more new remarks than one

---

[1] Sainte Beuve Consolations. Les larmes de Racine.

would suppose, and some of them are new still. He first showed the importance of the study of history in education, and especially of national history, and first recommended, for teaching the mother tongue, method and exercises. Study, for example, the analysis, which he gives of the account of Ambrose's election to the bishopric of Milan, taken from the *History of Theodosius* by Flechier. The conclusion of it is as follows : —

" After these grammatical observations, you will read a second time the same narrative, and at the end of each paragraph you will ask your pupils what they find remarkable either in the expression, the thoughts, or the moral conduct. This mode of questioning them renders them more attentive, obliges them to make use of their understanding, furnishes them with the means of forming their taste and judgment, gives them a more lively interest in understanding the author by the secret delight which they feel at the discovery of all his beauties by their own exertions, and gradually puts them in a condition to become independent of the master's assistance, and this is the end to which the trouble that he takes to instruct them ought to tend."[1]

And again : " There is a way of questioning which contributes much to draw out him who is to answer, and on it, we may say, that all the success of an exercise depends. The object in view for the time is not to give the pupil information, still less to puzzle him with far-fetched and difficult questions, but to give him an opportunity of bringing out what he knows. You should ascertain the depth of his understanding and his power, you should propose to him no question which is beyond his capacity, and which you ought not reasonably to presume that he will be able to answer, and you should choose the fine passages in an author on which you can be sure that he is better prepared than on any other ; when he tells a story, you should not unseasonably interrupt him, but let him continue till he has quite finished, you should then put forth its difficulties with so much clearness and skill that the pupil, if he has no great talents, may discover the solution that he should give ; you should make a rule to speak little, and make him that is examined speak much ; in short, you should only think of drawing him out by forgetting yourself, and in consequence you will never fail to please the audience, and to gain their esteem.

[1] Traité des Etudes. Livre ii., chap. i., art. ii.

" A young man is examined on the Greek gospel of St Luke. In order to give proofs of his attainments, after he has explained, as I have said, some lines here and there at the opening of the book, he turns to the most remarkable histories, for example, to that of Lazarus and the bad rich man. He tells the story, introducing into it Latin and even Greek passages from the gospel which contain some fine maxim. You ask the pupil which he would have preferred to be, the rich man or Lazarus ; he makes no hesitation in his choice. You next ask him his reasons for it ; the very passage that he explains furnishes them. By this you put him in the way, and afford to him the means of drawing on his own attainments, or at least on the book which he has in his hand, for some very solid reflections on the principal circumstances of this story. On this occasion you make him bring forward every thing that is said in that same gospel respecting poverty and riches. It is easy to comprehend how many excellent principles may be instilled into the mind of a young man under the pretence of teaching him the Greek language." [1]

At present the analytic reading of authors recommended by Rollin is unhappily neglected. In his case there is nothing distrustful, nothing exclusive. He does not pretend to be large and liberal in his advices, but he is so without knowing it, and to an extent which might astonish us. The innocence of his character shut his eyes to certain things, as well as to the fables of Fontaine, which he points out without selection or exception.[2] La Fontaine's innocence is malice.

Rollin had an exquisite perception of all that is beautiful and good, and he communicated it not by precept and inference, but because he knew how to make the things of which he was speaking, loved and enjoyed. There is nothing fine, subtile or systematic, he loves virtue in every shape, he loves nature, he loves antiquity, he spreads in every direction the delicious savour of his excellent literature, we profit by him because we delight in him. There are books more methodical and more learned than his *Treatise on Study*, there is none of this kind capable of doing greater good. It is a work which every one should read and which nobody does.

It may be imagined, perhaps, that Rollin was attached to scho-

---

[1] Traité des Etudes. Livre viii., partie ii., art. ii.
[2] Ib. livre i., chap. iv.

lastic traditions. This was not the case. With Fenelon, he was the restorer of literary instruction. Both had the merit of appealing to nature and of going back to first principles. Fenelon had greater intelligence, superior penetration, in a word, more genius, but Rollin delivered the same instructions with as much taste and correctness, and kept quite as far from the beaten track.

The form of the *Treatise on Study* is singularly unconstrained and graceful. The author has no fear to open his heart overflowing with Christian feelings and classic elegance, and hence the book acquires the character of being somewhat sagacious. It is written with so much tenderness, and we readily perceive that it is overspread with the love of youth, that we cannot help liking it. The author fears no digressions, and introduces precepts into his narratives with a charming kindness of heart. Take, among other examples, the description of the friendship of Basil and Gregory :—

" They were both descended from families very noble in the eye of the world, and still more so in the eye of God. They were born nearly at the same time, and their birth was the fruit of the prayers and piety of their mothers, who from that very moment offered them to God, from whom they had received them. The mother of St Gregory presented him to God in the church, and sanctified his hands by the sacred books which she made him touch.

" They had every thing which renders children amiable—personal beauty, an agreeable temper, and gentle and polite manners.

" The happy disposition which God had bestowed, was cultivated with all possible care. After studying at home, they were separately sent to the cities of Greece, which had the greatest reputation for science, and there they received instructions from the most excellent masters.

" At last they met at Athens. This city was distinguished as the theatre and the centre of fine writing and of every kind of learning. It was also, as it were, the cradle of the celebrated friendship of our two saints, or at least it was of great use in tying the knot more closely. It originated in a very extraordinary occurrence. There was at Athens an extremely whimsical custom in reference to the arrival of new scholars, who came from different provinces. They began by introducing them to a numerous assembly of young men like themselves, and there they were made the butt of a thousand taunts, jests, and insults; after this they were conducted to the public baths with great ceremony, through the city, escorted and preceded by all these young men marching two and two. When they came to the baths the whole company stopped, uttered loud cries, and pretended to break up the doors as if the people refused to open them. When the stranger was admitted, he then recovered his liberty. Gregory, who had arrived at Athens first, and who felt how inconsistent this ridiculous ceremony was with the grave and serious character of Basil, and how painful it would be to him, had sufficient credit with his companions to get them to dispense with it. It was there, said Gregory Nazianzen, in his admirable account of this occurrence, that our holy friendship originated, that the flame began to be kindled in us which was never extinguished, and that our hearts were pierced with an arrow which always remained in them. Happy Athens! he exclaims, source of all my happiness. I had only gone thither to acquire knowledge, and discovered there the most precious of all treasures, a tender and faithful friend; more fortunate in this than Saul, who, going in quest of asses, found a kingdom.

" This connection, formed and begun, as I have now mentioned, was always more and more strengthened, particularly when these two friends, who had no secret from each other, opened their hearts to one another, and discovered that they had both the same end in view, and were seeking the same treasures—I mean wisdom and virtue. They lived under the same roof, eat at the same table, engaged in the same exercises and pleasures, and had only, properly speaking, one soul—a marvellous union, says St Gregory, which, in all its reality, can only be produced by a chaste and Christian friendship.

" We both equally aspired at knowledge, an object the most likely to stir up feelings of envy and jealousy, and yet absolutely exempted from this subtile and malignant passion; we only knew and experienced between ourselves a noble emulation. Each of us feeling more tenderness for the glory of his friend than for his own, sought not to gain the superiority over him, but to yield to him, and to imitate his conduct.

" Our principal study and our only end was virtue. We thought of rendering our friendship eternal by preparing ourselves for a happy immortality, and by detaching ourselves more and more from the love of earthly things. We took for our leader and our guide the word of God. We used one another as masters and inspectors, by mutual exhortation to the practice of godliness; and I might say, if there was not some sort of vanity in so expressing myself, that .we held to each other the place of a rule, to discern falsehood from truth and good from evil.

" These two saints, and it cannot be too often repeated to young people, always shone among their companions by the excellence and vivacity of their temper, by their persevering exertions, by extraordinary success in their studies, and by the ease and readiness with which they acquired all the sciences taught at Athens, belles lettres, poetry, eloquence, and philosophy; but they distinguished themselves still more by the innocence of their behaviour, which was alarmed at the sight of the least danger, and which was afraid of the very shadow of evil. A dream which Gregory had in his early youth, and of which he has left us an elegant description in verse, contributed much to inspire him with such sentiments. While he slept, he thought he saw two virgins, of the same age and of equal beauty, modestly dressed, and without any of those ornaments which people of the world earnestly seek. Their eyes were cast upon the ground, and their faces were covered with a veil, which did not prevent one from getting a glimpse of the blush which virgin modesty spread over their cheeks. The sight of them, adds the saint, filled me with joy, for they appeared to me to be something more than human. They, on their side, embraced and caressed me as a child, whom they tenderly loved; and when I asked them who they were, they told me, the one that she was Purity, and the other Chastity, but both the companions of Jesus Christ, and the friends of those who renounce marriage to lead a heavenly life. They exhorted me to unite my heart and spirit with theirs, that, having filled me with the splendour of virginity, they might present me before the brightness of the eternal Trinity. After these words, they flew up to heaven, and my eyes followed them as far as they could. All this was but a dream, yet it produced a real effect on the heart of the saint. He never forgot this pleasant image of chastity.

" He and Basil had great need of such virtue to support them

amid the perils of Athens, a city the most dangerous in the world
to morals; but, says St Gregory, we had the good fortune to
experience in this corrupted city something similar to what the
poets say of a river, which preserves the sweetness of its waters
amid the bitterness of the ocean, and of an animal which subsists
in the midst of the fire.

" One would think that young people of this character, who
kept away from all society, who took no part in the pleasures
and diversions of persons of their age, and whose pure and innocent life was a perpetual censure on the irregularity of others,
must have been a butt to all their companions, and must have
become the object of their hatred, or at least of their contempt
and raillery. It was quite the contrary; and nothing is more
glorious to the memory of these illustrious friends, and, I must say,
does more honour to piety itself than such an event. In truth,
their virtue must have been very pure, and their conduct very
wise and moderate, to have been able not only to avoid envy and
hatred, but generally to attract the esteem, love and respect of
all their companions."[1]

The language of Rollin is very much the pure language of the
seventeenth century, sweet, harmonious, flexible, without softness
and without laxity. His diction is melodious. He uses sometimes the period, without falling into the formal periodic style;
in short, he is not devoid of originality. Originality is the literary virtue, without which all the rest come to nothing. We
find in this book a mind and an individuality; we feel that one
man alone, Rollin and no other, was able to form the conception
of it, and write it. " It is," says M. Villemain, " one of the best
books in our language, next to books of genius."[2]

The *Ancient History*, in thirteen volumes, was published from
1730 to 1738. It was, like the other works of the author, written
for the education of youth. Rollin never addressed himself to
the public, which has, however, enjoyed his writings. It is good
to remember this; by losing sight of this part of his character,
we would run the risk of being unjust. This end partly excuses
any failure in point of criticism—the absence of that philosophical
sagacity, which divines causes, which binds together events, and
which makes the history of a nation the development of an idea.

[1] Traité des Etudes. Livre viii., partie ii., chap. v.
[2] Villemain, Cours de Literature Française. Dix-huitième siècle, Ire Leçon.

We may further confess that his reflections may at times appear idle, and that his mode of writing is not exempt from puerility. He assumes from time to time the manner of a tender nurse, and he descends as low as his nature allows him. Sometimes he jests, but his jests smell of the college or the child's-maid. Voltaire takes notice of this circumstance in one of the notes on the *Temple of Taste.* " He is reproached with being too minute. He scarcely ever departed from good taste, but when he wished to joke." Rollin rarely takes this tone—he smiles, but does not laugh.

We have exaggerated the weakness and defects of his book. Rollin had a much stronger judgment than is generally believed. He cultivated the faculty of reasoning, and, without having much criticism, he was not devoid of it; he examined and knew on occasions to refute fables and conventional opinions. Observe how he takes up the judgment of Titus Livius on the subject of Annibal's sojourn at Capua :—

" I know not, if all that Titus Livius has said about the fatal consequences, which the winter quarters taken up by the Carthaginian army in that voluptuous city produced, is quite accurate and well founded. When we carefully examine all the circumstances of this history, we have some difficulty in persuading ourselves that it is necessary to attribute the little progress, made by the arms of Annibal afterwards, to the sojourn at Capua. It is in some degree a cause of it, but the least considerable; and the bravery with which the Carthaginians after that time beat consuls and pretors, took cities in the face of the Romans, maintained their conquests, and remained still fourteen years in Italy, without it being possible to drive them out of it—all this is a sufficient proof that Titus Livius exaggerates the pernicious effects of the luxury of Capua. The true cause of the decline of Annibal's affairs was the withholding of assistance and recruits on the part of his country."[1]

We do not indeed find in Rollin what we in the present day principally require in history. But his moral and religious tendency does not prevent him from having much more liberality than his contemporaries. This excellent teacher had breathed in the writings of the ancients the fragrant atmosphere of liberty.

[1] Histoire Romaine. Livre xv., § ii. See, further, the history of Tigranes, eldest son of the king of Armenia, and the reflections with which Rollin has accompanied it. Livre xxxvi., § i.

Throughout his works he casts disgrace on tyranny, he censures conquests, ambition, and despotism; everywhere he expresses his attachment to humanity and justice, and he plainly loves liberty and equality, the Christian and moral republic. It is curious to hear him speaking about the laws of Sparta, and showing himself favourable to the community of goods :—

" The design formed by Lycurgus, of making an equal division of the lands among the citizens, and of entirely banishing from Sparta all luxury, avarice, lawsuits, and dissensions, by abolishing the use of gold and silver, would appear to us the scheme of a commonwealth, finely conceived in speculation, but utterly impracticable in execution, did not history assure us that Sparta actually subsisted in that condition for many ages.

" When I place the transaction I am now speaking of among the laudable parts of Lycurgus' laws, I do not pretend it to be absolutely unexceptionable, for I think it can scarcely be reconciled with that general law of nature which forbids the taking away of one man's property to give it to another; and yet this is what was really done on this occasion. Therefore, in this affair of dividing the lands, I consider only so much of it as was truly good in itself and worthy of admiration.

" Can we possibly conceive, that a man could persuade the richest and most opulent inhabitants of a city to resign all their revenues and estates, to level and confound themselves with the poorest of the people; to subject themselves to a new way of living—severe and full of restraint ; in a word, to debar themselves from the use of every thing in which the comfort and happiness of life is thought to consist? And yet this is what Lycurgus effected in Sparta." [1]

Rollin declares himself in favour of the ancient philosophy, on this ground, that he regarded it as a providential means of preparing for the Gospel :—

" The sovereign Arbiter of the universe has not permitted mankind, though abandoned to the utmost corruptions, to degenerate into absolute barbarity, and brutalize themselves, in a manner, by the extinction of the first principles of the law of nature, as is seen in several savage nations. Such an obstacle would have too much retarded the rapid progress promised by Him to the first preachers of the doctrine of His Son.

[1] Histoire Ancienne. Livre v., art. vii.

" He darted from far, into the minds of men, the rays of several great truths, to dispose them for the reception of others more important. He prepared them for the instructions of the Gospel, by those of philosophers; and it was with this view that God permitted the heathen professors to examine, in their schools, several questions, and establish several principles, which are nearly allied to religion ; and to engage the attention of mankind by the brilliancy of their disputations. It is well known that the philosophers inculcate, in every part of their writings, the existence of a God, the necessity of a Providence that presides over the government of the world, the immortality of the soul, the ultimate end of man, the reward of the good and punishment of the wicked, the nature of those duties which constitute the band of society, the character of virtues that are the basis of morality, as prudence, justice, fortitude, temperance, and other similar truths, which, though incapable of guiding men to righteousness, were yet of use to scatter certain clouds, and to dispel certain obscurities." [1]

With respect to his ideas taken together, Rollin may be compared with the liberal men of the most enlarged minds in our times. What forms, even at present, the charm of his book, is the abundance of its details, the happy mixture of the original references with his own text, and his admirable perception of antiquity. An interesting scene is presented to him; he never thinks of its disproportion to his subject; he brings it before us with all the strokes that enliven it and engrave it on the memory. An opportunity for digression falls in his way, he has no difficulty in following it out. You will see this exemplified in the character of Scipio Emilianus,[2] and, a little farther on, in the reflections on the surrender of Carthage.[3]

No doubt, he is mistaken on many points : he did not understand antiquity in the same way as modern authors make it understood ; but his fame will remain, for he is sagacious. No other history has taken its place ; it is in the same condition as the translation of Homer by Madame Dacier. She and Rollin are the two authors who have best felt antiquity, and who have made it be best felt.

Unction is the chief characteristic of Rollin's style, in his

[1] Histoire Ancienne. Preface, § 1.   [2] Histoire Romaine. Livre xxvi., § 2.
[3] Histoire Romaine. Livre xxvi., § 3.

History as well as in his *Treatise on Study*. We breathe in it something familiar and paternal. There is never effort or pretension; everywhere he keeps himself out of view. He is a Christian Nestor, with more humility, for he never speaks of himself; his discourses communicate grace to those who listen to them.

In our days Rollin is rather unknown than forgotten. The memory of the excellent man, and accomplished teacher, often makes the excellent writer be overlooked.

Montesquieu, speaking of him, says: " M. Rollin, an honest man, has enchanted the public by his works on History. It is the heart which speaks to the heart : there is a secret satisfaction felt in hearing virtue speak; he is the bee of France."[1] And M. de Chateaubriand, in the *Genius of Christianity*—" Rollin is the Fenelon of history, and, like him, he has embellished Egypt and Greece. The first volumes of the *Ancient History* breathe the genius of antiquity; the narrative of the virtuous Rector is full, simple, and calm ; and Christianity makes his pen tender, and furnishes him with something to move the feelings. His writings reveal *the good man, whose heart is a continual feast,* according to the remarkable expression of Scripture. We know no works on which the soul reposes more pleasantly. Rollin has spread over the crimes of men the calmness of a conscience without reproach, and the pious charity of an apostle of Jesus Christ."[2]

V.

LOUIS RACINE.

1692–1763.

HERE again we are in the Jansenist school. Louis Racine was a contemporary of Rollin, and one of the persons affording the

---

[1] Montesquieu Pensées diverses : Des modernes.
[2] Chateaubriand Le Genie du Christianisme. Livre iii., chap. vii.

best characteristic of that class of writers who, in the eighteenth, in fact belong to the seventeenth century. Louis Racine had family reasons for attaching himself to this grand epoch. *Vestigia semper adoremus*.[1]

An orphan when he was six years of age, in 1699, he was educated under the direction of Rollin, and of Boileau the best friend of his father. The latter, however, did not foster his rising genius, since he was anxious to turn his attention from poetry. Besides, Louis Racine attached to the doctrines of Port Royal, could not permit to his talent the same exalted flight which his father, in the time of his worldly vanity, had allowed to his fine genius. It must be confessed, serious Christianity in some respects hampers literary genius. He was tempted by the theatre; his friends and his piety kept him from it. He remembered that his father had repented of having written tragedies. Nothing in him, however, shows a natural fitness for dramatic compositions.

He deprived himself of the public favour, which would have been willingly granted to his real talent, and to the influence of his father's name. As he was a Jansenist, no favour was shown to him by the court, and he mingled little with the world. He was a member of the Academy of Inscriptions and Belles Lettres, but not of the French Academy. Cardinal Fleury was opposed to his election, as being a Jansenist, and, after the death of that minister, no one thought of bringing him in. He was old, and sought no distinctions. His noble modesty has been justly praised; but we must not forget that it is rather an easy thing for the son of an illustrious father to be humble—the paternal glory is a bright halo around his head. When a man is crowned with it, there are, as it were, the distinctions of a hereditary aristocracy, and he is quite contented to be nothing in himself. And yet, Louis Racine lived little in the world; circumstances connected with his fortune obliged him to accept in the provinces appointments of little importance, and quite inconsistent with his tastes. Afterwards he returned to Paris, but there he was like one lost. He lived till 1763, always a man of the age which preceded him. We may judge of him by a single trait. He frequently speaks of the theatre; and there are names, such as Voltaire's, which not more than once or twice drop from his

---

[1] Let us always respect its footsteps.

pen. The eighteenth century is entirely, so to speak, absent from his mind. And yet, in two points, he fell in with the spirit of his age—he read Pope in the original, and translated Milton. Besides, he attempted a new subject—the philosophy of art and of taste.

His life, spent in obscurity, presents few events. The only considerable one is also the most distressing—the loss of his only son. It might be said, that a bitter presentiment dictated to him the verses which he wrote in 1730, two years after his marriage : " Impatient mortals, when you presume to complain of a barren marriage-bed, have you forgotten that Hymen is to be feared, even when he brings gifts ?" [1]

Some had been anxious to turn Louis Racine from the pursuit of poetry. In like manner, he was anxious to prevent his son from engaging in that study, and he made him adopt the career of commerce. The young man perished in the earthquake at Lisbon in 1755. He was born for letters, if we may believe his friend Lefranc de Pompignan, who consecrated to his memory some beautiful and tender verses : " He is no more ; and his tenderness in the last days of old age will not support thy feeble steps. My friend, neither his virtues nor thine,.nor his pleasant and Christian manners, were able to save him from death. This object of the most tender prayers will not go to lay thy ashes under that marble, corroded by time, where his grandfather and thy model awaits the corpse of the heir of his talents. Far from thy sight, far from his mother, in a foreign land, his body is the sport of the waves, but his soul, cherished by heaven, beyond a doubt enjoys, in its native land, eternal rest. O holy laws ! O Providence ! it is often on the innocent that thy fearful blows fall. A child of the world prospers ; the man who has only God for his father groans under the burden of adversity."

Le Brun, in his *Ode on the Disaster at Lisbon*,[2] deplores also the loss of Louis Racine's son, and alludes to his poetical leanings.

However this may be, the life of Louis Racine was from that time only a long period of mourning. He gave up writing ; his last work was dated the night his son perished. We know nothing more of him, but that his existence was consecrated to

---

[1] Ode iii.   [2] Le Brun, Odes. Livre ii., Ode xviii.

the domestic virtues. He was not mixed up with the literary quarrels which disgraced the eighteenth century, and, though a Jansenist, he was spared by those men who spared nothing. With him was extinguished a great name.

Louis Racine has left well-written odes, such as show a real talent for versification, which may be called *pleasing*, but nothing more. They are scarcely lyric. We must, however, make some exceptions. Among the *Sacred Odes*, the xix.—the imitation of Isaiah xiv. 4–21—is worthy of notice :—

" How has the merciless tyrant passed away, and how are we relieved from the tribute with which we were oppressed! The Lord has broken the formidable sceptre, whose weight overwhelmed a languishing race—that sceptre which struck with an incurable wound the groaning nations. Cruel king! thy look made the kingdom of darkness tremble; all hell was troubled; the haughtiest spirits of the dead ran to get a sight of thee; the kings of the nations descended from their thrones, and went forward to receive thee. ' King of Babylon,' they say, ' art thou there thyself, ruined as we are ? Cast down to the dust, art thou become the food of worms, and is thy bed the filthy mud ? How art thou fallen from heaven, bright star, son of the morning! Powerful, audacious prince, the earth now devours thee. How art thou fallen from heaven, bright star, son of the morning!' In thy heart thou saidst, ' Like God himself, I will establish my throne above the sun; and northward, on the holy mountain I will fearlessly take my seat; at my feet the world will be dismayed and tremble.' Such was thy boast, and thou art no more. Passers by, who will see thy carcase cast forth, will exclaim, as they stoop down to see thee better, ' Is this the man, the terror of the universe, by whom so many captives sighed in chains! Is this the man, whose arm destroyed so many cities, and under whose sway the most fertile fields became a barren wilderness! All the kings of the earth have obtained the honour of burial; thou alone art deprived of that privilege.' Everywhere rejected, the horror of nature, the murderer of a people entrusted to thy care, now, by this people, thou seest thyself consigned to oblivion. Let his wretched children be prepared for death—the race of the wicked will not continue. Run and announce to all his sons that their hour i come. Let them perish; the author of their unhappy life ha

filled them with his iniquity. Strike! drain from their guilty
veins all the unhappy blood which they have inherited!"

We should also notice an *Ode on Harmony,* in which Louis
Racine endeavours to characterize the harmony peculiar to the
most celebrated poets:—

" By what art does the poet, who sings of Achilles, produce
sounds so varied? If he places before me the criminal, who, in
the empire of darkness, rolls a large stone to the summit of a
rugged mountain, his trembling knees, which bend under him,
and his brawny arms, which grow stiff, make me pale with terror
on his account. The unhappy man at length fails, and the noise
of the tumbling stone resounds in my ears. In the flow of
Virgil's verse, a courser outstrips the lightning. Often, when I
am ready to follow Camilla, like her I think I am treading on
the wind. Sometimes I urge on the slowness of the tardy ox,
which nothing astonishes, and which his master goads in vain,
and the heavy, horrid, and shapeless mass of an enormous giant
overwhelms me by his weight. At the slightest zephyr, whose
breath wrinkles the surface of the water, the amiable and tender
La Fontaine excites my interest for a reed. But if he calls in
the tempest against the proud head, that endeavours to brave its
efforts. What a fall! what ruin! the oak which it roots up
reached the empire of the dead."[1]

In 1722, or 1726, the poem on *Grace* was published, divided
into four cantos. In the fifth century St Prosper versified the
doctrine of his master Augustine in a poem, whose title is more
poetical than its contents—*Against the Graceless (Ingrats).* He
wished to vindicate predestination and free grace, and he must
therefore assail the graceless. But to be instructive on such a
point of doctrine in a poem, is to attempt to connect two things,
of which the union is impossible—theology, properly so called,
and poetry.

Now the poem *on Grace* is the development and proof of the
Jansenist doctrines. Jansenism is moderate Calvinism; with
Louis Racine it is so, particularly on two points—he admits free-
will, and declares that grace is not inconsistent with it, and
maintains that Jesus Christ loved all men and died for all.
Racine wishes to put in a clear light the sovereignty of divine

---

[1] Poésies sur differents sujets. Ode vii.

grace, and the perfect liberty of God's decree relative to the salvation of some and to the loss of others—a subject disagreeable to poetry, and not easily brought under its authority, of which the author has not taken all possible advantage, but which a great poet would never have chosen.

As it is, originality is wanting to the poem *on Grace*. Perhaps this gift was not bestowed on Louis Racine, who besides considered it of far more importance to be orthodox than original. He did little more than put in verse the writings of St Augustine, Pascal, and Bossuet.

" Formed by their writings, full of their maxims, I follow their track, only lending my rhymes." [1]

Here and there, however, we meet with fine verses thrown off with some degree of boldness. Louis Racine was skilful in fine versification, and has done much in this way. He has more fine verses than fine pieces, yet we reckon two or three, in which poetry takes its proper place in the poem *on Grace*:—

" This God with a single look confounds all greatness, the brightness of the stars is eclipsed in His presence, the cherubim, prostrate before the throne, where His glory dazzles them, tremble and cover their faces with their wings. Be annihilated, audacious mortals ! He flies on the winds, He sits on the heavens, He says to the sea, Dash thyself against thy shore, and in its narrow bed the sea remains captive." [2]

What follows is a much longer piece. Racine wishing to teach us, " That which man is without God, and that power which God exercises over him," makes St Augustine speak thus :—

" My fiery youth, eager in the pursuit of crimes, made me run from one abyss to another. O Lord, I fled from Thee, but Thou didst not abandon me, and with the rod in thy hand, and following me step by step, by producing profitable disgust, Thou renderedst those same pleasures, so agreeable to many others, bitter to me. Thy thunders rolled over my head, and by thy urgent advice, my mother joined in weeping over her son. At that time I only heard the rattling of my chain—the chain of passion, which I wretchedly dragged along. My mother by her tears could not move me, and thy thunders, great God, failed to make

---

[1] La Grace, Chant ii. [2] La Grace, Chant iv.

me tremble. At length my ardour for pleasure was deadened. I returned to myself and detested my life. I saw the road in which I wished to walk, but a fatal weight made me pause. I found this beautiful pearl and loved it, without the power of resolving to sell all to obtain it. Drawn in turn by two powerful rivals, I was inwardly distracted by their contentions. My God loved me still, and His supreme goodness in my sad looks presented me to myself. Alas, how frightful I appeared at that moment! but I soon forgot my unhappy condition. A lethargic slumber weighed down my eyelids, I sometimes awoke and sought the light, and so soon as the feeble dawn appeared, I shut my eyes lest I should perceive it. A voice cried to me, ' Get away from this abode,' and my answer was, ' A moment, immediately!' But this fatal moment had no end, and this hour was put off till to-morrow. The enchanting troop of my first pleasures fluttered around and constantly repeated, We offer to thee all the good we have, and wilt thou leave us? Who can be satisfied without us and without our delights? The wise man seeks us and finds a ready relaxation; his body is satisfied and his mind tranquil. Mortals, live happy and improve your time; intoxicate yourselves with the tumultuous stream of joy. Avoid the troublesome sternness of virtue. Lie down on the flowers —sleep in luxury. And thou, whom our favours have so long charmed, dost thou think, that thy heart, accustomed to us, will be able to tear itself from the delights which it loves. Alas! by avoiding us thou wilt lose thyself! But before me sweet and lovely chastity, with a pure and calm air full of majesty, showed me her friends of both sexes and of all ages, and with a scornful smile spoke to me thus : Thou lovest me ; I call thee, but thou darest not come—weak and cowardly Augustine, who can keep thee back? Uncertain, vacillating, and inconsistent with thyself, thou wishest to break thy chains ; thou art willing and again thou art unwilling. Wilt thou not fix thy irresolute steps? Look at these faithful doves by my side, God gave them wings to fly to me; that God opens to thee His bosom, cast thyself into His arms. Alas! I knew Him, but I did not run to Him. At length one day, weary with this sharp warfare, I wept, cried, and rolled myself on the ground, when all at once struck with a sound that came from heaven, and with the words of the Holy Bible, on which I cast my eyes—the storm was calmed, my troubles were appeased, by thy hand, Lord, my chains were broken, my spirit was no longer bent towards the earth, I escaped from the mud in which I was engulphed. My will changed, what was opposed to thy nature was displeasing to me, and I loved every thing in which Thou delightest. My mother, whom Thou sawest so often at thy feet weeping over a graceless child, and a rebel against Thee—my tender mother at last was delivered from her apprehensions, and found alive the son of so many tears. I knew well at the time that thy yoke was pleasant. No, Lord, there is nothing like Thee. Here below, my voice, united with the angels, will not cease to sing thy praise. I will love only Thee; thou wilt be henceforth my glory, my salvation, my refuge, my peace. Holy and beloved law, eternal sweetness, ineffable greatness, beauty ever new, truth which was able to charm me too late, alas! what time have I lost in not loving you?"[1]

We farther quote the following verses:—" The church at length triumphs, and, shining with glory, makes heaven re-echo with the songs of her victory. She sings, while we, enslaved, desolate, and exiled, still groan on the earth. We sit and weep on the banks of the Euphrates, a reasonable grief keeps our tongues captive, and how could we, O heavenly Zion, in the midst of the wicked make thy songs be heard! Alas, we are silent! our harps unstrung and hung on the willows send forth no sound. How tedious is my exile! O tranquil city, O holy Jerusalem, O beloved eternity, when shall I go to the stream of thy pure pleasure and drink the happy oblivion of the pains which I endure? When shall I taste of thy adorable peace? When shall I see the day, which has no end?"[2]

The poem on Religion is more celebrated than that on Grace. Consisting of six cantos, it was published in 1742. The title points out its subject. It is in truth religion in its widest sense. The author argues in favour of natural religion against the atheists, of revealed religion against the deists, and of evangelical morality against loose Christians. Truly pious, he could not apply to himself what he says in his Discourse on Paradise Lost. " A poet who, in expectation of the reward of his labour from men, sings of religion, has made a bad choice of his subject."

Louis Racine argues very well; he has taken the cream of the

---

[1] La Grace, Chant iii.   [2] La Grace, Chant ii.

argument from the greatest apologists of Christianity, but after all, he almost always argues; his mode and form of proceeding are essentially didactic, the epic and dramatic element is wanting. There are exceptions, however, as in the passage, where he relates the miracles of Jesus Christ, and that on the first preaching of the Gospel:—

"Notwithstanding, there appears to that astonished people a man, if that name can be given to Him, who, coming all at once from an obscure retreat, as Lord and as God, commanded nature. At His voice, eyes long shut are opened, dazzled, and charmed with the sun, which strikes upon them. By a word He makes the invincible barrier fall which rendered the ear inaccessible to sound, and the tongue which escapes from captivity, blesses its liberty with cheerful songs. Unhappy men dragged along their useless limbs, but at His command, they on the instant find them serviceable. The dying man laid on a bed of pain, runs to wipe away the tears of his desolate children. Death himself is no longer certain of his prey. An object at once of fear and joy he, whom a powerful cry recals from the grave, rises up, and his sister becomes pale as she embraces him. He does not force back the rivers to their source, He does not interfere with the stars in their courses, He is asked in vain for signs from heaven. Does He come to satisfy the minds of the curious? Whatever splendid work He does, it is on us that He performs it, and for us gives forth His salutary virtue, He cures our diseases and recals us to life, His power is always the harbinger of His love. But it is a small thing to enchant the eyes by these miracles. He speaks, His discourses ravish our ears. By Him are announced terrible decrees, and by Him sublime secrets are revealed. He alone is not moved by the secrets which He reveals. He speaks calmly of eternal glory. He astonishes the world and is not astonished. In this same glory He seems to have been born, and appears here below with His glory veiled."

Here follows our second quotation:—"The prophecy is fulfilled. The righteous One is sacrificed. All is in commotion, and from the banks of the desolate Jordan to the Tiber, in a moment the sound makes itself be heard. Intrepid men hasten to spread it—they fly; the universe is filled with their voice. Repent, weep and go to His cross, whatever be the offence the victim expiates it; you have put to death the Lord of Life. He whom your executioners dragged as a criminal, is the image, the brightness, the Son of the eternal God. That God, whose word brought forth light, was laid in a tomb and slept in the dust. But death is vanquished and hell is spoiled. Nature cried out, her God has awoke, He lives, our eyes have seen Him, believe, strange word! They command men to believe—they believe, and every thing is changed!"[1]

And farther on we have the following piece :—" Inconceivable prodigy, an instrument of horror, the cross, becomes the ornament of an emperor's brow. Constantine in his triumph, rendered triumphant the glory of the luminous sign, which promised him the victory. Ceres at Eleusis, sees those initiated into her mysteries tread under their feet the robe, the crown, and the basket. Diana, thou art no more, thy goldsmiths at Ephesus, the supporters of thy power, have lost their hope. The temples are deserted, and the priest at a loss, throws down the censer of his God no longer esteemed, and abandons an altar at which no offerings are presented. Delphi, formerly so ready to answer questions, is now shamefully silenced by a stern law. In short, all the gods, like Apollo, have lost their voice. At the tombs of the martyrs abounding in miracles, people and kings seek for true oracles—they present their prayers to a man, whom they had murdered, and break the god whom they had adored."[2]

The first canto of this poem has also in itself a character more worthy of observation; in it the author gives the proofs of the existence of God, from the wonders of creation and the consciousness of mankind. The heart and the imagination can take greater interest in it. But on the whole, we desire more philosophical and poetical invention. Reasoning always ends without spirit, when dramatic talent is not brought in to give it animation. Is it respect, which stops Louis Racine? Is it weakness? What is chiefly wanting is subjectivity. His poem is purely objective. The author does justice to the subject, which it is his duty to discuss, but he does not mix himself with it. Now, every great writer, every poet should be the incarnation of an idea. There must be a fusion of the author and his subject, and they must be identified, that the two may be only one, that the author may communicate to the subject the character of his mind, and

---

[1] La Religion, Chant iv.   [2] La Religion, Chant iv.

that he may be completely imbued with his subject. One would wish to be able to say more frequently of Louis Racine, what should be said of a poet: "These verses are only his, he alone could make them." Montesquieu has in his *Essay on Taste*, a chapter entitled, *on I Know not What*. This *I Know not What*, I am persuaded is the *proprie communia* of Horace, originality, and this is the reason, why this pure and elegant author, this excellent versifier, this poet abounding in fine verses, does not leave that ineffaceable impression, which is the seal of superior talents; sometimes, indeed, we meet in his writings with verses, which we remember, but they are very few.

Easy negligence and frankness are also wanting in this poem. Its versification is too rigid. Louis Racine is timid: he is anxious to do good, not to be applauded, but for having done good. He writes poetry as if he were performing a duty. He is a Jansenist even in point of verse. There are, however, moments of expansive sensibility; a concealed vein of John Racine's genius may be seen, and you would call it an echo of Esther. John Racine is a bright flame, which shines at times in his son, as it were, through an unpolished glass. The ray is quenched, but the light is not obstructed. We find it in several passages. That on the migration of birds is an example of it:—

" Those that fear the rigour of our winters, and wish to take refuge in a milder climate, will never permit the severe season to surprise, in our land, their lazy band. In a wise council assembled by their chiefs, the great day for the general movement is appointed. It comes. On every side the youngest perhaps ask, as they look at the place of their birth, when will that spring come, by which so many exiles will be recalled to their paternal fields?"[1]

In the sixth canto, Louis Racine makes the Christian speak thus: " Greatness, O my God, spreads not its enchantments before me, and I am never tormented with the thirst of gold. My sole ambition is to be entirely thine; my pleasure, my greatness, my riches are thy law. I sigh not for renown. May my glory, unknown to men, but hidden in Thee alone, have always thine eyes for its witnesses. It is in Thee that I find rest in the midst of my cares. Thou holdest to me the place of day in this

---

[1] La Religion, Chant i.

night of profound darkness. In the midst of a desert, Thou art to me all the world. Men would in vain offer to me all their good things; men could not separate me from thine. Thy law lets those understand, that love Thee not, that they must all expect the greatest misfortunes. O my God, this threatening cannot alarm me! The greatest of misfortunes is not to love Thee. May thy cross be in my hands at my last hour, and, with my eyes fixed on Thee, let me embrace Thee and die!' '

With more genius, Louis Racine might have lessened the influence of Voltaire's somewhat careless versification, sometimes too feebly jointed, sometimes redundant, in a way that prevailed in the eighteenth century, till the time of Delille. Racine joined to it, what was then new, technical skill. The latter arose at the very time when all care about detail disappeared. The splendour of Voltaire's abilities conceals, in his case, what is wanting in his method of versification, but the defects become prominent in his imitators. The pliant, strong, harmonious verse, which gracefully bends to all the emotions of the soul, the Racinian verse is forgotten. Louis Racine, almost alone, remains faithful to the traditions of the previous age : he ably cultivates the rhythm, pure diction, melodious and skilful versification ; in a word, the method of his father. Yet he has at times great verses, bold in form and touch, which make us enjoy beforehand the verses of Voltaire. Indeed, Voltaire abounds in those verses, thrown off altogether with the happiest indifference and ease. From this circumstance they have received the epithet *Voltairian*. Corneille has many of this kind; and certainly Louis Racine has some of them : " Nous allons tous penser, Descartes va paraître," etc.

We have the same measure in a very long piece :—

> " Je la vois cette Rome, oú d'augustes vieillards
> Heritiers d'un apôtre et vainqueurs des Césars," etc.

This happy form may be thrown out here and there in the piece, but it cannot form its texture. Louis Racine has furnished the first examples of picturesque and descriptive poetry—applied, indeed, to particular and isolated subjects, rather than to one entire. The seventeenth century had not attempted this species

---

[1] La Religion, Chant iv.

of poetry : the external world interested them little ; it furnished them with images and expressions, but they only employed them with moderation ; their poetry, entirely humane and moral, was eminently intellectual.   The eighteenth century did the reverse, and Louis Racine was found to have made concessions to his age, but without the spirit of system.   His subject led him to it, and induced him to bring under poetry certain technical details, which it had not yet reached.   " The criminal father of a proscribed race, peopled with unfortunate men, a cursed land," etc.[1]

The judgment of Voltaire on Louis Racine is well known— " The good versifier Racine, son of the great poet Racine." The saying is severe, but not altogether unjust.   In short, Louis Racine is rather a versifier than a poet.   He has the poetry of detail and of isolated verse ; but, in his compositions, taken as a whole, he is little of a poet—invention is wanting.   And yet, the humble Racine might be contented with the slender eulogium of Voltaire.   He made his portrait be taken, holding the works of his father open at the place, where may be read this verse of Phèdre :—

> " And I the unknown son of so glorious a father ! " [2]

The Memoirs, containing some Particulars respecting the Life and Works of John Racine of the French Academy, were published in 1748.   Louis Racine addressed them to his son, as Marmontel addressed his to his children half a century later. What a contrast between these Memoirs, with so little morality, and those of Racine, so pure and so Christian !

He had scarcely known his father. " I was hardly born when he died, and my memory can only recal caresses." [3]   But besides family papers, he had his mother, who died only in 1732, his elder brother, and Boileau, who lived till 1711.

These memoirs are precious on account of many details, which would have been lost, but for the care which Louis Racine took in collecting them.   They furnish lively information respecting the court, the life and manners of men of letters at that time,

---

[1] La Religion, Chant iii.—The passages which Vinet quotes to illustrate the versification are not translated, because the object is not to show the sentiments of the writer, but the peculiar form of his poetry.

[2] Phèdre, Acti iii., scène v.

[3] Memoires sur la vie de Jean Racine.   Introduction.

and Port-Royal, and the religion of an age eminently religious. As a form especially, religion plays an immense part, it explains many events, and characterises many personages. Thus Jansenism, which in another place, and at another time, would have been only a sect, becomes an important part of the national history.

But the spirit which animates these memoirs renders them particularly worthy of commendation. We find in them a noble candour, a pious, but chastened tenderness and filial prepossessions, which, however, are not obtrusive. He is a son who writes, but he is also a man and a Christian, and boasts less of the genius than of the domestic virtues of his father:—

"Plutarch has already informed you that the elder Cato preferred the glory of being a good husband to that of being a great senator; and that he left the most important business to go to see his wife dress and undress her child. Is this ancient sensibility no longer a part of our manners, and are we ashamed to have a heart? Human nature, always delicate, takes particular pleasure in delicate minds, and things which appear puerile weakness in the eyes of a wit, are the true pleasures of a great man. He who has been so often, perhaps too often, mentioned to you as one whose name you ought to revive, was never so happy as when at liberty to quit the court, where in his early years he found so many charms, and to come and spend a few days with us. Even in presence of strangers, he showed himself a father. He took part in all our sports, and I remember (I may write it, since I am writing to you)—I remember processions, in which my sisters were the clergy, I was the rector, and the author of Athalie, singing along with us, bore the cross.

"There is a simplicity of manners so admirable in a man all feeling and all heart, which is the reason that in copying to you his letters, I constantly shed tears, because he communicates to me the tenderness with which he was filled.

"Yes, my son, he was tender-hearted from his birth, and you will hear it much spoken of; but when he was converted, he felt tender love to God, and from the day that he returned to those who had taught him to know Him in his childhood, he showed a tender feeling towards them without reserve, he did so to the king, whose history he had so great pleasure in writing, he did so all his life to his friends, he did so, from his marriage and till the end of his life, to his wife and to his children without any predilection."[1]

He makes an excuse for speaking of his father's tragedies :— "I cannot pass without notice, at least in a few words, the history of the theatrical pieces of my father."[2] What a healthful and enlivening perfume exhales from these pages, and with what eagerness should the young welcome them !

Under the title of *Reflections on Poetry*, Louis Racine has published a series of discourses read at the Academy of Inscriptions, in which he treats of general questions, such as poetic language, observations on manners in reference to poetry. It is quite a treatise on the art of poetry, in which, like Rollin, Louis Racine shows himself the disciple of two antiquities, the Homeric and the Biblical, the two breasts, so to speak, of true poetry.

These *Reflections* give proof of a very pure taste, and of extensive literary information, but the author does not appear profound. This criticism is very important; without depth, there is only the appearance of clearness. We are really clear by merely returning to primary reason, and to the idea at once simple and complete. There is a profound, as well as a superficial simplicity. So Condillac, for example, who appears clear to superficial minds, remains obscure to those who require profound investigation—throughout they find enigmas to be solved. We may experience satisfaction in seeing the relation of an effect to its immediate cause; but though this may be quite clear, the instruction derived from it is not good. At times, however, Louis Racine goes back to principles, but in general he does not give sufficient information. For instance, when he treats of the essence of poetry, he makes poetry consist in enthusiasm, and confounds enthusiasm with passion.

The *Remarks on the Tragedies of John Racine, followed by a Treatise on Dramatic Poetry, Ancient and Modern,* form three volumes, which were published in 1752. It is an excellent introduction to the study of dramatic literature. Its ideas are just, but not vigorous ; as a whole, it is valuable, though not equal to Rollin, nor especially to Fenelon. It wants the freshness, the life, and the indescribable individuality, whose absence

---

[1] Memoires sur la vie de J. Racine. Introduction. [2] Ibid.

in the writings of Louis Racine, we have already remarked. The observations on his father's works possess little ability—they are minute, and too frequently expressive of approbation.

In conclusion, it does not appear to me that the dissertations of Louis Racine, although instructive and judicious, have made the philosophy of art advance a single step. They have not even the merit of anticipating the new method. The Abbé Dubos had pointed it out, and entered upon it in his *Critical Reflections on Poetry and Painting*, published in 1719, which appear to me to be more new, and to possess greater philosophical ability than the treatises of Racine. Without depth, the philosophy of Dubos has some originality. He enters upon questions at that time little studied—the nature of esthetic enjoyment, the different conditions of the different arts, and their respective power; the part which physical causes may have in the development of genius, in the character of its works, and in the literary splendour of certain epochs; the art of judging on an esthetic subject; and the competency of criticism. It is a curious work even at present; its diction is not remarkable, but easy and natural. It will be right to look at Voltaire's judgment respecting Dubos in the catalogue of the writers in the age of Louis XIV.

By his prose translation of *Paradise Lost*, 1755, Louis Racine entered doubly into the spirit of his age. Milton had been already translated by Dupré de Saint Maur; and this first translation had met with great success. It is interesting to study the system of translation in the seventeenth century, it characterizes better than anything else the spirit of the time. To soften and weaken bold expressions—to prefer abstract truth—to diminish the reality of style—to yield much to propriety and conventional dignity—to transfer to the ancients and to foreigners the modern French language, instead of bending the modern language to the exigence of the subject—all this was the spirit of translation at that period. This age, however, had so much taste, and even candour, that, notwithstanding the faults of the system, it was able to give, by means of beautiful translations, an idea of antiquity; for example, the *Homer* of Madame Dacier. But this is not the system of Louis Racine. In the seventeenth century, the ancient writers only were translated; he translates a modern—an Englishman, one whom

Boileau describes as a *barbarian*. He is most anxious to be accurate, but is not sufficiently so—

" 'Tis wisdom by turns to fear or to dare."

For a long time, Dupré de Saint Maur was preferred as being more elegant. He has the elegance of the eighteenth century; Racine has that of the preceding century, and is much more exact. He has translated in verse, but feebly, some pieces of the same poem. Delille has taken from him, without acknowledgment, some happy verses, such as that in the invocation to Light.

Tout revient, mais le jour ne revient pas pour moi.
Seasons return, but not to me returns—day, etc.

VI.

CREBILLON.

1674–1762.

CREBILLON really belongs to the period, which forms the subject of our present study. His dramatic career was interrupted for twenty years, but it was of uncommon length. *Idomenée*, his first tragedy, appeared in 1703; his last, *le Triumvirat*, in 1754; he was eighty years of age.

He was born far from the capital, of an honourable family connected with the law; he was destined for the bar, and was placed in an attorney's office, after a very superficial course of study, during which he had shown more quickness than application. What is a rare occurrence, the attorney himself urged Crebillon to try the theatre, and the success of *Idomenée* decided his future pursuits. His life, in other respects, presents few events worthy of remark; his works alone form its epoch. An excessive feeling of independence rendered his existence wild and solitary. He continued a stranger to the spirit of his age. A great enthusiast for the ancient republicanism, he would have readily found his part in a revolutionary era; but in monarchical France, there was no place for him. The circle of his ideas was by no means extensive; he lived more by imagination than by thought, and it may be said, that his life was only a long dream. He stayed at home, enveloped in tobacco smoke, surrounded with animals, for which he had a singular taste, and composing romantic adventures, without committing them to paper. The philosophical movement of the eighteenth century never reached him; out of the theatre, he is nothing, and understands nothing. A man has not sufficient understanding when it is confined to one species of objects; it should be comprehensive.

Crebillon had only a mind suited to tragedy, and even for tragedy that is not enough. Philosophy is necessary, of which we have none in the writings of Crebillon. There is a want of breadth and perspective, he only gives us his first sketch. He excelled, it is said, in terrific poetry; it is meant that in this style of writing he surpassed Racine and Corneille, but this is far from being proved. Poetry implies active intelligence; when it merely produces emotion, it confounds the means with the end. Sensation ought to be considered the way by which an idea is obtained; poetry, no doubt, is not negligent of the sensible impression, but it passes through it to arrive at something higher. It must enlarge the horizon of thought, and procure the noble pleasure of contemplation. Crebillon expends very little thought, and never exercises the mind in its most exalted sense. We have a sensible and an intellectual soul; of the latter, Crebillon knew nothing. His unquestionable energy gives occasion to blame as much as to praise. When we speak of him, we can scarcely separate the one from the other. If Crebillon stops at sensible impressions, we must admit that he knew how to direct them to the noble affections of man, and that he is not less remarkable for the expression of generous sentiments than for the practice of exciting terror.

The romantic element prevails in the structure of Crebillon's plays; and it may be even said of him, that he has countenanced romance in tragedy. The romantic spirit is the grand defect of French tragedy, a defect which is connected with the very origin of that tragedy, and with the nature and education of him who gave to it its form. Corneille was romantic, and France has

long confounded romance and poetry. Racine had nearly cured
tragedy of this wrong tendency; *Phédre, Esther, Athalie,* are
certainly not romances, but Crebillon made it undergo a relapse.
The romantic is a pure illusion in human life, it is the avoiding
of what is real and possible—the dream of a world, which does
not and cannot exist, a sort of convention in which certain spirits
and epochs pass before us. Poetry, on the contrary, is the
liveliest comprehension of things, and their most intimate as
well as their highest truth.

Crebillon has the twofold romance of sentiments and *situation.*
He paints passion more than character, and *situation*[1] more than
passion. Now, passion, which is an accident in life, has something more particular than character, and *situation* is still more
particular than passion. Crebillon is profound without
breadth, a great defect, for depth without breadth is really not
depth.

He has been justly reproached for having mixed love, or,
rather, a soft and languishing gallantry, with the bloody horrors
of his tragedies. Corneille had already committed this fault,
but how much better did he know the mode of redeeming it?
Besides, the charm of style is almost entirely wanting in Crebillon. His language is rude, uncultivated, incorrect, and almost
barbarous; and, when it has no important defect, it has scarcely
any better quality. It wants ornament and originality; it is
dull, and might be called a bare mountain, from which all ver-
dure has disappeared, and nothing remains but the naked rock.
What it has of wildness may, however, on rare occasions, become
beauty. We may apply to the style of Crebillon what he himself has put in the mouth of Pharasmenes in *Rhadamiste* :
" Nature, a step-mother, in these rough climates instead of gold,
produces only iron and soldiers; her rugged bosom offers to the
desires of man nothing which can tempt the avarice of
Rome."[2]

The tragedies of Crebillon are *Idomenée, Atrée et Thyeste,
Electre, Rhadamiste et Zenobie, Xerxes, Semiramis, Pyrrhus,*

---

[1] *Situation* is a French word applied to the drama, and signifies that part in the
action of the play, at which the feelings of the audience are most highly excited. The
translator could not find a single English word to express the idea, and hence he has
given the French word in italics.

[2] Rhadamiste et Zenobie, acte ii., scène ii.

Catalina, le Triumvirat. Three are especially worthy of notice
—*Electre, Rhadamiste,* and *Pyrrhus.*

Electre appeared in 1708. This play has undoubtedly great
defects; the author did not keep by the ancient simplicity; he
introduces false and insipid elements—the double love of the
children of Ægistheus and Agamemnon—into the most tragic
subject in the world. But *Electre* has also great beauties; for
instance, the dream of Clytemnestra :—

" Twice I awoke from distressing slumber—for the third time
my senses sunk in sleep—when I thought that I felt myself
dragged, amid terrible and mournful cries, into the horror of
darkness. I followed, in spite of myself, these doleful shrieks.
I cannot tell what remorse agitated my mind. A thousand
thunders roared in a thick cloud, which, however, appeared to
yield to me a passage. Under my wavering steps a gulf was
opened, and the frightful abode of the dead was presented to my
eyes. Across Acheron the unhappy Electra, at a great pace,
seemed to guide a spectre to the place where I was. I fled—it
followed me. Ah! my lord, at that name my blood freezes.
Alas! it was Agamemnon. ' Stop,' he said to me with a fearful voice, ' this is the dreadful termination of thy crimes! stop,
unworthy spouse, and shudder at that blood which the cruel
Ægistheus drew from my side!' That blood, which streamed
from a large wound, appeared, as it flowed, to send forth a long
murmur. On the instant I thought I saw mine run also ; but,
wretch that I am, scarcely did it touch his, when I saw spring
from it a pitiless monster, which first darted at me a frightful
look. Twice the Styx, struck by its bellowings, answered with
prolonged groans."[1]

The meeting of Orestes and Electra is full of fire; the part
of Palamedes, entirely the invention of Crebillon, is nobly conceived, and as nobly executed. In short, the remorse of Orestes
forms an admirable passage : nearly in the style of Racine, in
Andromaque, it is almost superior to it. We meet there with a
stroke of genius : Orestes lets his own name escape his lips, and,
in his fearful trouble, he takes it for a voice that came from
hell :—

" But how! what vapour now obscures the air? Thanks to

[1] Electre, acte i., scène viii.

heaven, the road to hell is open, let us descend ; hell has nothing to frighten me ; let us follow the dark path which destiny presents to me ; let us conceal ourselves in the horrors of eternal night ! What a mournful brightness at this moment lights my way ! Who brings day into these gloomy retreats ? What do I see—my look frightens the spirits of the dead ! What groanings ! what doleful cries ! Orestes ! Who calls me in this horrid abode—Ægistheus ? Ah ! it is too much ; I must, in my wrath . . . . What do I see ? in his hands my mother's head ! What looks ! whither shall I flee ? Ah ! furious monster, what a spectacle dost thou dare present to my eyes ! I only suffer too much. Cruel monster, stop ! take this head away from my eyes, overwhelmed with terror ! Ah ! my mother, spare your unhappy son ! Shade of Agamemnon, listen to my cries ! I implore thy aid, dear shade of my father ! Come, defend thy son from his mother's fury ! Take pity on the condition to which thou seest me reduced ! What ! the barbarous woman follows me, even into thy arms ! It is done ; I yield to this frightful punishment." [1]

Rhadamiste, 1711, is much superior to *Electre*, and to all the other works of Crebillon. Had this tragedy been better written, it would have occupied the first rank on the French stage. Yet something would always be wanting to it—good sense—not precisely on the stage, but in the distribution of the piece. Aristotle allows absurdity in the events previous to the action of the play ; Crebillon has made large use of this permission. Nothing can be more absurd than the facts related in the explanation, which is made twice over, in the first and second acts, always in a dull, complicated, and confused manner. The points of interest which result from these painful antecedents are fine. In the scene between Rhadamistus and his confidant Hieron, these verses ought to be noticed :—

" And what do I know, Hieron ? Furious, wavering, a criminal without inclination, and virtuous without intention— unfortunate sport of my extreme grief—in my present condition do I know myself ? My heart, incessantly assailed by different cares, and an enemy of crime, without loving virtue—deplorable victim of an unfortunate love—is abandoned to remorse without

---

[1] Electre, acte v., scène ix.

renouncing the crime. I yield to repentance, but without pro-
fiting by it, and my self-knowledge leads me only to detest myself. Do I know what draws me into this cruel abode—is it
despair, or love, or hatred? I have lost Zenobia : after that
horrid blow, can you still ask me what I wish? Desperate,
proscribed, abhorring the light, I would wish to avenge myself
on all nature ! I know not what poison pervades my heart, but,
even in my remorse, every thing there becomes fury !" [1]

The dialogue between Pharasmenes and his son Rhadamistus,
who, without making himself known, is presented as ambassador
of the Romans, is admirable. Here the energy of the style and
the power of fancy are on a level with the thought.

What is still superior, is the meeting of Rhadamistus and of
his wife Zenobia, whom he thought he had sacrificed. Nothing
surpasses, not even the characters of Corneille, the noble sentiments and expressions of Zenobia :—

" Ah cruel one! would that thy hostile hand had never attempted any other life than that of Zenobia! With my heart
divested of anger by thy look, I would make it my happiness to see
my husband again, and love, honoured by thy jealous fury, would
have placed thy wife in thy arms. Think not, however, that I
can look on thee with enmity or without pity."

And again—" Go, it is not to us that the gods have committed
the power of punishing enemies so dear. Mention to me the
country where thou wishest to live. Speak! from this moment I
am ready to follow thee, assured that the remorse, which has taken
possession of thy heart, springs from thy virtue more than from
thy misfortune. Happy, if the cares of Zenobia for thee might
one day serve as an example to Armenia—to render the people
like me submissive to thee, and, at least, to instruct them how to
discharge their duty. . . . . Calm the vain suspicions which
have arisen in thy mind, or conceal at least from me thy unworthy jealousy—remember that a heart which can pardon thee
cannot be suspected without a crime."

Rhadamistus affected with so much generosity, exclaims:—
" Ye gods, who have restored her to me, fulfil my desires, and
condescend to make my heart worthy of your benefits." [2]

In the fourth act, forced by the jealousy of Rhadamistus,

---

[1] Rhadamiste et Zenobie, acte ii., scène i.   [2] Rhadamiste, acte iii., scène v.

Zenobia, in the presence of his brother Arsames, confesses her feelings in favour of the latter, which she had concealed till then : —"But since thou wishest to give thyself up to thy suspicions, know then all in this heart, which thou canst suspect; I am about by a single stroke, to make thee acquainted with it, and afterwards leave thee master of my destiny. Thy brother was dear to me, I cannot deny it, nay, I do not even seek to justify it, but in spite of his love, that prince, who was ignorant of my partiality, would not yet have known it, but for thy ungenerous suspicions." She ends as she goes out, with these famous verses:— " I know the rage of thy jealous suspicions, but I have too much virtue to be afraid of my husband." [1]

Pyrrhus (1726) is not esteemed according to its value. The subject of this tragedy is interesting and extremely probable, its structure is at once skilful and simple, the characters are noble and engaging. Here we find some traces of Corneille—the exhibition of generosity in youthful hearts—a trait of nature, which both poets knew how to represent. Besides, this play is better written than the rest, but notwithstanding this comparative superiority, it still wants the charm, which might have secured to it a theatrical reputation.

Some persons wished to place Crebillon in opposition to Voltaire. A cabal was organized for that purpose, much less unjust, certainly, than that which placed Pradon in opposition to Racine. In certain respects, indeed, Crebillon deserved to contend against Voltaire, but his poetical talents taken together generally exhibited his inferiority. Voltaire felt the opposition too keenly. He was irritated, he showed some littleness of mind, and set himself to prove that, on all subjects, he was superior to Crebillon. He placed *Oreste* against *Electre, Semiramis* and *Rome Sauvée* against the *Semiramis* and the *Catalina* of Crebillon. The date of Voltaire's *Semiramis* is 1748, and of his *Rome Sauvée* 1750. His superiority in these two pieces is indisputable, but we cannot say quite so much for *Oreste*. Besides, Crebillon was personally a stranger to the exertions of the anti-Voltairian cabal in his favour, and was only the instrument of the enemies of his rival. His reputation evidently suffered from their endeavours, by which they pretended to make him equal to Voltaire. The

---

[1] Rhadamiste, acte iv., scène v.

usurpation of the place which they assigned to him, made him fall below his real merit. At present he is more highly valued. There has hitherto been no attempt to bring his tragedies again upon the stage, but their turn will perhaps come.

<hr>

VII.

LE SAGE.

1668–1747.

LE SAGE spent a life of obscurity, labour and poverty. He wrote much for the little theatres, especially for that of La Foire, to which he left a hundred and one comedies, or rather farces. It is sad to contemplate such degradation of talent. Forgotten by the great and by the government, Le Sage fell early into second childhood, and was taken care of by a son, an ecclesiastic, at whose house he lingered and died.

The romances of Le Sage are of a new kind, he has written several, but, after *Gil Blas, the Devil on Two Sticks* is the only one generally known. At the time when some were attempting to put romance into comedy, Le Sage put comedy into romance. His is the true *comic romance;* that of Scarron, which bears its title, is only a series of burlesque scenes pleasantly related; *Gil Blas* is " an ample comedy with a hundred different acts." In general, the romance is a little epic poem—the history of a short period in a man's life, but here the epic embraces a whole life, it is a romance defective in unity, a series of episodes, the memoirs of an adventurer. Le Sage did not apply himself to any other mode of writing, this kind was sufficient for his success, and perhaps the romance reduced to unity and with an intricate plot was not suited to his natural talent.

Some are disposed to see in *Gil Blas* the description of a particular class, or of a short time spent in society. This is true to a certain extent. *Gil Blas* should necessarily represent the man-

ners of his time, but here the picture of man generally far exceeds
that of a certain period, and of certain conditions in life. This
admirable painting is one of the plainest and most profound that
exist. After Molière there is nothing equal to it. Sir Walter
Scott's enthusiasm for Le Sage is easily understood; their genius
was of the same stamp, both younger brothers of Molière, and
both endowed with the power of representing human nature in
all its reality. *Gil Blas* presents a series of perfect and immortal
types—a magazine perpetually open to the allusions of social wit.
Who is unacquainted with Dr Sangrado, the Archbishop of
Grenada's homilies, the parasite and the gluttonous canon. The
plot has indeed nothing remarkable, it is frequently childish, and
amuses children, or what remains of the child in every one. But
what should more reasonably amuse us is the episodes, which
may be compared to the scenes of Molière and are the result of
invention, the extreme variety and the comic in incident as well
as the comic in character.

The style is on a level with all the rest, natural, pure, perfectly correct, and astonishingly circumspect. Le Sage is not
one of those writers who always say every thing, and whose
expressions go beyond the thought. He restrains himself, and
leaves something to be conjectured, or rather he gives the reader
something to do. It is a delicate artifice of good writers; they
know that the reader delights in taking his share with the
author. The writers of the present day break up the door; *Gil
Blas* opens it to you gently.

Besides, the subjects treated by Le Sage, require caution; his
pen is as chaste as his subjects are unfortunately the reverse.
At present, the more dangerous the subject, the more is the
danger increased by the mode of expression. Le Sage, on the
contrary, remains cool, where he might have attempted to be
vehement. He treats grave subjects with irony, and makes you
laugh at wickedness, which is certainly not right, but it is better
than to make you sympathize with it. He may use a pernicious
influence over your mind—over your senses, never.

This romance ought not, however, to be put into every body's
hands. It does not contain a single honest character, nothing
but knaves and weaklings, and even the very weaklings are far
from being honest. This is a mere abstraction; happily the
real world is not so constituted. The result is, that Le Sage

does not interest us in any one, not even in his hero; we could
have no pleasure in such bad company. Even when he winds
up the story, and when Gil Blas is happy as he advances in age,
we would be delighted to think that the author is to leave us
under an impression somewhat pleasant and serious; at that
moment, and in the last expression in the book, he is pleased
to throw us into irony and scepticism. In a word, *Gil Blas*
is the paraphrase of the celebrated maxim of Rochefoucauld:—
" Virtue is only a word, it is nowhere found on the earth, and
we must be resigned."

Le Sage does not excel less in dialogue than in narrative.
Gil Blas belongs to the style of comedy, not merely in the
main subject of the book, but still more in its form; several
chapters of this romance are real scenes, in which nothing would
be found wanting for theatrical success. Thus, no one is surprised that Le Sage has written comedies, and excellent
comedies too, such as *Turcaret*, and *Crispin his Master's Rival.*

Crispin is a farce exceedingly immoral. This style of writing
was scarcely otherwise understood; applause uniformly followed
the triumph of audacious knavery. For comic fancy, animated
action, and originality, this play deserves to be classed among
the best of the kind.

Turcaret (1709) is at the head of the comedies of the second
order. A severe satire on the baseness, cupidity, stupid pride,
and moral disorder of the farmers of the revenues, the financiers
of the time, that play might seem to be contemporaneous with
Law, whom, however, it preceded by several years. *Turcaret*
is a financier, a weak knave, duped and robbed by a baroness,
who was an ingenious cheat. The valet and chambermaid are
worse than those whom they serve. There is not an honest
person in it—they are all the very dregs of society. It cannot,
therefore, produce much interest; but the originality of the
thoughts, and the fidelity of the characters, make this comedy
the best in the eighteenth century, and a work worthy of
Molière. This brings me, gentlemen, to some more general
observations.

The spirit of the comedy of the seventeenth century, finds
its last representatives in Le Sage, and in some contemporary
poets, d'Allainval especially, author of the *School of Citizens*
(1728). Beyond this period, comedy changes its character.

What, then, was its distinctive mark in the preceding century?

In the first place, the comedy of the seventeenth century takes away, and almost completely suppresses what is called *interest*, that is every thing calculated to excite the feelings. Interest may be of two kinds—that which is attached to the characters, and that which flows from principles. But these two interests are near akin, and are most frequently mixed and confounded; in all cases, there is a sympathy between them; we must say to the honour of our nature, degraded as it is, that the interest which we feel in any person whatever, has always for its motive the qualities which we think we perceive in him, and for its measure the amount of these qualities; and it is from this that the interest of the person is attached to the interest of the principle. Now, neither the one nor the other of these two interests prevails in the comedy of the seventeenth century.

Another character of this comedy is its making a good use of probability, not only of the probability of incidents, but also in a certain sense of the probability of characters. The latter, generally, set out from correct data, but in the execution, they pass the line of reality. As we read Molière, in reference to common life, we would feel ourselves no longer in our own country; as we read Shakspeare, our astonishment is redoubled. We ask ourselves, From what world has he taken those events, sometimes even those personages whose original we shall nowhere meet? Yet Shakspeare and Molière are the two greatest comic poets that the world has ever produced. The latter reveals to us a poetical spirit different from that which prevailed in the eighteenth century; the comedy of Shakspeare and, in an inferior degree, that of Molière are ideal.

In the eighteenth century, poetry declined; the forms remain but the poetical spirit is extinguished. Poetry is no longer its own end. The age in this relation may be of greater worth; perhaps, after all, it is to the honour of an age to labour to put back art to the second place, and to put in the first rank the moral end and the practical application, but certainly art itself is thus deteriorated. In the seventeenth century, comedy was written for the mere purpose of writing comedy. The wish was to make themselves and others merry. In this view, quite esthetic, Molière could make good use of common probability. The spectator, said he to himself, does not come hither to see a *fac simile* of his life. His public forbore to ask from him this pedantic probability. As to exciting the feelings, Molière was a comic poet, and what he had in view was the comic aspect of each character. Consequently, he did not go in the track of *interest*, but although he never sought it, he sometimes fell in with it as in the *Misanthrope*. Read the scene between Alcestes and Celimenes.[1] But Molière did not make for himself a system of this artistic form, nor was he the only inventor of it. We do not say that his individual impressions went for nothing in the conception of his comedies, but the origin of the ideas, which these represented falls back in a particular manner upon the age in which he lived. The French literature of the seventeenth century, strictly distinguished two worlds, the one that scoffed and derided, the other that was altogether serious. In reality, however, we see these two worlds susceptible of reconciliation, and even of fusion.

The same literature kept at a distance, and divided into two different classes, the noble and the familiar. It affected the noble in certain kinds of composition, and the familiar in others. The familiar only presents itself under the form of comedy, or rather the true familiar does not almost exist in French literature. You may be softened by the tragedies of Racine, you may have your soul elevated by those of Corneille, and afterwards you may go to the theatre of Molière, but it is only to laugh and not to experience emotion. How is this?

There are two kinds of people : those, in the first place, to whom the family forms an essential part of human life, who constantly turn towards the domestic hearth, who only leave it with the view of coming back to it, and to whom it is the centre of daily thought, and the great object of activity. Certain local and physical circumstances contribute to this importance. Men live in the chimney-corner in the north, and in the open air in the south; yet we meet with people in the south who possess the character of those in the north, and northern nations among whom southern manners prevail. Poland, for example, is in this condition. Besides, Christianity—and it is a farther proof of its

---

[1] Le Misanthrope, act iv., scène iii.

divine origin—has equalized to a certain extent the manners of
the people. But in order to judge of these influences in all their
purity, let us take Athens as an example—that city at once
pagan and southern, in which every one lived under the blue
sky, and in the light of the sun. How far did the political and
social life prevail over the domestic, the city over the family!

Among those modern people, where the social spirit essentially
surpasses the domestic, the separation of the serious and the
amusing, of the noble and the familiar, must naturally be produced. Vigilance in observing one's own conduct beyond the
family, necessarily gives rise to a distinction in language and
manners. That which is noble represents the conventional and
superficial relations of society; that which is familiar manifests
the family. Wherever private life is at the head of the interests
of existence, the mixture, or rather the unity, of the noble and
the familiar takes place of itself. This is shown in English and
German literature; these two nations do not separate two elements, which, in reference to them, are confounded in life. In
France, where social life prevails over the other, it is not the
same; and this is the reason why the comedy of the seventeenth
century so abounded in the feeling of this separation, that it
scarcely allowed any place for the element of interest—neither
for interest in the characters nor in the principles. Thus, without immoral intention, and from the single fact of an absolute
distinction, this comedy has excluded the interest of the mind,
or, in common language, morality; nay, it has gone so far as to
claim applause for crime, when it is agreeable and witty.

In the eighteenth century, this was no longer possible. This
age, no doubt in many respects deplorable, was, however, occupied with morality, as the end of art. It was even too much
occupied with it. A man must be good, must mean what is
really good, must be animated with noble and pure sentiments,
and then let himself go forth into the inspirations of art: "Love
and do what you please." On one side, the eighteenth century
was not very good; on the other, it was too much engaged with
the immediate end of art. Art was deteriorated by it, and the
morality of the age was, in fact, immoral. But our century is
worse than the eighteenth : instead of preaching an imperfect
morality, it is immorality, which some take pains to establish as
a doctrine, and pedantry is mixed up with the preaching of vice.

In the eighteenth century, comedy becomes interesting, or rather sentimental. We must say, however, philosophically speaking, it is less so than that of Molière. In the period which occupies our attention, some isolated works betray that revolution. *La Pupille* (1734), a pretty comedy of Fagan, made the transition. An orphan was attached to her guardian, and ends by marrying him, after having rejected different offers made through the generous guardian, who was ignorant of the affection of his charge. This was quite new.

Besides, comedy becomes more probable. It is less ideal, and therefore less poetical; we may add that it is less taken up with the classes of society. The comic writers of the seventeenth century particularly attacked these different classes; and whatever was peculiarly ridiculous in the members of whom they were constituted—physicians, citizens, courtiers, marquises, even those devoted to religion—for the *Tartuffe* is not only a satire on hypocrisy, but on a dominant party of the time. A little later, the nobility were ridiculed, the lawyers, the magistrates, and then the farmer of the revenues, who fattened on the substance of the people, and was white-washed by an alliance with some noble lady without fortune. But, in the eighteenth century, it is scarcely any longer classes which they take up—they aim at characters, and point at the ridicule connected with humanity itself, rather than at such and such a particular condition. The grand age, deprived of the liberty of the press, indemnified itself by the liberty of the pulpit, which was extensively used, and by the liberty of the comic theatre. It was the twofold refuge of French liberty. But under Louis XV. the press began to be emancipated, manners became quite free, and comedy laid down the office which it filled in the preceding ages. It is less political —it becomes more moral. We now come to the author by whom this change was accomplished.

VIII.

DESTOUCHES.

1680—1754.

DESTOUCHES accomplished the revolution of comedy, and at once introduced into it that new element of interest, to which Fagan led the way. Born at Tours, in the heart, and in the most French part of France, he was descended from an honourable and wealthy family. He appeared to be destined for a peaceful life, but thwarted in his affections, his career became difficult, and even stormy. By turns comedian, diplomatist, devotee, a youthful attachment made him leave the paternal roof. At first he joined a company of actors, who from city to city brought him to Soleure, where the French ambassador at that time resided. It was there that Destouches made his first work, *le Curieux impertinent*, be brought on the stage. The play was received with transport, but the author would have obtained but a moderate glory in the enthusiasm of the thirteen cantons, if their suffrage had not been confirmed by the very favourable reception of his work soon after on the French stage. This comedy of Destouches, besides one not quite so good, procured for him the notice of the ambassador, who perceived in him qualities far superior to the condition of a comedian, engaged him to quit the stage, and initiated him in diplomacy. The regent sent him to London, where he represented France for seven years, was married there, and on his return to his own country, lived in retirement, amusing his leisure hours with the composition of charming comedies, which procured for him merited reputation. Voltaire called him *his dear Terence, his illustrious friend*, and spoke of himself as his declared admirer. His verses on the *Glorieux* are well known :—" Solid and ingenious author, master of the theatre, it will be in your power, who wrote the *Glorieux*, to be yourself glorious." The theatrical writings of Destouches are voluminous. They consist of ten volumes of plays in prose and verse. The comedies in prose are generally of moderate merit ; among those in verse, the best are *Le Phi-*

losophe Marié (1727), *le Glorieux* (1732), and *le Dissipateur* (1753).

For the conduct of the action, knowledge of the stage, the nature and vivacity of the dialogue, the elegant purity of the style and talent for versification, Destouches has a claim to the first rank, after Molière and Regnard. More than either, he is interesting and moral; his morality, how imperfect soever it may be, has a relative value, which no one can dispute.

But a comic poet ought to be, above all, comic. Is Destouches really so? His comedy is much less profound and original than that of Molière, and much less lively and sparkling than that of Regnard: in his writings nothing recals that extravagant fancy of the author of the *Legataire*, which is irresistible. The comedy of Destouches is not very free, sometimes even it is a little forced. When he makes you laugh, it is scarcely the effect of humour, and to remedy this defect, he at times gives us a double portion, and then we have a kind of comedy which is rather debased. What we have of it is more in points of lively interest than in character. We are well aware that the nature of Destouches led him towards the serious, nay, towards the pathetic. Comedy with him had a strong tendency to the tragi-comic.

He has been especially blamed for the choice of his subjects, and this criticism, the strongest and best founded that has been made on the comedies of Destouches, is extended even to his masterpieces. *Le Philosophe Marié* is a charming play, but the subject is altogether exceptionable. The philosopher married for love, and concealed his marriage from false shame. Destouches himself felt the want of nature in his principal personage, since it is to a feeling of *false* shame, that is to say, to an artificial sentiment, that he attributes his repugnance to let the union be known which renders him happy.

Le Glorieux was criticised by Voltaire, who pretended that the principal character was a failure. Perhaps it is a little overcharged, but it is scarcely more so than *l'Avare* and *le Misanthrope*, and besides, in justification of Destouches, we find the name of Count de Tufière remaining in the language as a type, an excellent sign of the truth of the character. But the essential defect of the play is, that in spite of his pride, vanity, and ingratitude, the *Glorieux* is indeed its hero, so that the sympathy of the spectators is claimed for him, and in short he carries the day. This fault is palliated by the conduct of the action, and by an admirable scene between the count and his father. In it the true and deep pathos rises to the tone of tragedy.

Le Dissipateur is subject to the same observation. It is a play full of fancy, but the distribution of it is disagreeable. The betrothed of the spendthrift, a young and virtuous lady, is anxious to save her lover from ruin, and to succeed in this she lowers her character, and pretends to take her place among those who profit by plundering him. The detail, the order of the scenes, and the animation of the action, are admirable.

Upon the whole, the rank which criticism assigned to Destouches, third of French comic writers, appears to me to be perfectly just.

IX.

THE ABBÉ PREVOST.

1697-1773.

THE Abbé Prevost was one of the most laborious writers on different subjects in the eighteenth century. He translated ancient and modern works; he made compilations; in short, he composed several very voluminous romances. Necessity was the spring of so great activity; he was poor, and must live. He wrote with ease and grace, but with extreme haste, which too often rendered him quite insipid. His own romances must be excepted from this remark; he was born for this style of writing, and nature had endowed this writer of romance with the romantic character. His life was very stormy; it has been even pretended, but the charge appears to be groundless, that he had the dreadful misfortune of being the involuntary cause of his father's death, in consequence of a quarrel, in which he insulted the woman whom Prevost loved. His end was tragical. In a fainting fit he fell into a ditch; he was thought to be dead, and an ignorant surgeon, to whose house he was carried, killed him with a blow of his scalpel.

In his romances he is excessively romantic. He does not occupy himself either with making a satire on the human race, or searching deeply into character, or describing society, or rendering available some philosophical idea. Simplicity of intention could not go farther. His aim is to be interesting, and especially for the vulgar; but everybody is vulgar, in a certain point of view, and the Abbé Prevost knew the world. He was anxious to be moral. We have in what follows the manner in which he shows this pretension, in the beginning of the most celebrated of his romances, *Manon Lescaut,* which is certainly nothing less than a treatise on morality :—

" The public will see, in the conduct of M. Des Grieux, a terrible example of the strength of passion. . . . . . Persons of good sense will not consider a work of this nature a useless labour. Besides the pleasure of agreeable reading, few events will be found in it which may not serve for moral instruction ; and to instruct, while we amuse, is to render, in my opinion, a considerable service to the public. . . . . . Experience is not an advantage within everybody's reach, it depends on the different situations in which fortune has placed us. There only remains example to serve as a rule to many in the exercise of virtue. It is precisely for that class of readers that works such as this may be extremely useful, at least when they are written by a person of honour and good sense. Every fact which is related is a degree of light, a piece of information which supplies experience ; every adventure is a model, according to which men may form their character, ... The whole work is a treatise on morality, agreeably reduced to practice." [1]

The prevailing impression which the romances of Prevost leave on the mind, is by no means in favour of their morality ; we can draw no conclusion from them, either for good or evil, and this is all that can be said. We may apply to them the remark of Madame de Lambert on the tragedies of Corneille : " The best often give you lessons of virtue, and leave with you the impression of vice." [2]

Whatever may be in this observation, the Abbé Prevost is at least very chaste in the mode of expression, though we cannot say so much for his subjects. In his writings we never meet

---

[1] Manon Lescaut, Avis de l'auteur.
[2] Madame de Lambert, Avis d'une mère à sa fille.

with that kind of concealment, which is often worse than the
open display of vice ; and the most reprehensible of his romances,
as to its main subject, has not, perhaps, a single line, with which
any fault can be found in point of expression.

But his sensibility, the extreme good faith of his narrative,
his truth in the description of passion, and in the representation
of sentiment, and the genuine grace and ease of style, transparent
as the soul of the author, are found in Prevost to an extent
which has not been surpassed; and all these qualities, concentrated and reduced to the utmost simplicity of conception in
Manon Lescaut, make this episode one of the masterpieces in
our literature.   There are, so to speak, only one act and two
characters, but these constantly attract the attention, and never
let it flag.   The chevalier Des Grieux, a young man of good
family, falls into dissolute courses in consequence of his love for
Manon, a courtesan, and, urged by the distress of her whom he
loves, ends by becoming a sharper.   But, notwithstanding all
that is shameful in their life, the one has so much simplicity, and
the other so much grace, that the most serious man cannot avoid
taking an interest in them, not because they deserve it, but
because there is nothing more natural or more true than their
situation and character.   *Manon Lescaut* exercises over the
reader a real fascination, which is explained by the admirable
truth of the portrait.   Truth in works of art is the first quality.
Some are at great trouble to be striking or pathetic, but *Manon
Lescaut*, in a loose dress, eclipses beauties arrayed in the finest
attire.   " How very unjust is nature ! on whom is she going
to bestow beauty ?   It is an affront offered to people of condition !" [1]

It appears extraordinary, and even a little forced, to compare
Atala with *Manon Lescaut*—that story, so full of poetry, ornaments, and brilliant developments of passion ; but we cannot get
rid of the suspicion that, when M. de Chateaubriand described
the funeral of Atala, he had in his view the Abbé Prevost.   The
advantage is by no means on the side of the author of the Genius
of Christianity : —

" Taking a little dust in my hand, and keeping a frightful
silence, I fixed my eyes for the last time on the countenance of

[1] Voltaire, Nanène.

Atala. Afterwards I spread the earth of the grave over a fore-head of eighteen summers; I saw the features of my sister gradually disappear, and her graces concealed under the curtain of eternity."—(*Atala*).

" I opened in the sand a large grave, and put in it the idol of my heart, after I had wrapped her in all my clothes, to prevent the sand from touching her; but I did not place her there till I had embraced her a thousand times with all the ardour of perfect love. I sat down again near her, I looked at her for a long time, and could not come to the resolution of filling up her grave. At length my strength began to give way, and, afraid that it might entirely fail before the end of my undertaking, I buried for ever in the bosom of the earth all that it had borne of loveliness and perfection."—(*Manon Lescaut*).

There are some styles of writing which appear only once. No one will ever write like the Abbé Prevost or Madame de la Fayette. *Paul and Virginia* does not reach the simplicity of *Manon.* Bernardin de Saint-Pierre is simple, but his simplicity is studied and self-conscious; the simplicity of Prevost is pure. *Paul and Virginia*, as a whole, should be ranked above *Manon*, but the Abbé Prevost is the last example of a style that is lost.

Manon Lescaut and *Cléveland* are dated 1732. Cléveland is finely appreciated; and the sort of enjoyment which this work affords, is well characterized by Xavier de Maistre, in his *Journey Round my Chamber :* " How often have I cursed this Cléveland, who is every moment falling into new misfortunes, which he might avoid ! I cannot endure this book, and this series of calamities ; but if I open it for amusement, I must devour it to the end," etc.[1]

We may mention farther, among the romances of the Abbé Prevost, *Le Doyen de Killerine* (the Dean of Killerine), and *Les Memoires d'un homme de Qualité* (Memoirs of a Man of Quality), of which *Manon Lescaut* is an episode.

---

[1] Xavier de Maistre Voyage autour de ma chambre. Chapitre xxxvi.

X.

THE MARCHIONESS DE LAMBERT.

1647–1733.

THE Marchioness de Lambert was not a writer by profession, but a lady of quality, who spent her life in the midst of a select society. Her drawing-room served as a place of resort to men, such as Fontenelle, La Motte, Sacy, and in general, to any who supported the modern party in opposition to those around Madame Dacier, who brought together the worshippers of antiquity. Madame de Lambert, however, reckoned Fenelon among her friends, whose taste for antiquity was in the highest degree delicate.

She occupied her long life with some essays on morality not intended for publication, but some of them appeared in public contrary to her inclination. They are *The Advices of a Mother to her Son and Daughter*[1]; *A Treatise on Friendship*; another, *on Old Age; Reflections on Various Subjects and Letters*. These writings are bound up in a small volume, but they are exquisite pages, a real *little box of precious ointment.*[2]

Madame de Lambert is distinguished among those women who have emerged from obscurity without forgetting their sex, and whose writings unite to strength of judgment, to precision of thought, and to pointed conciseness of language, that charming reserve and modesty of which the profession of an author necessarily deprives a woman. Her ideas of morality are elevated and delicate, and far above those which, in some writings of imagination in the seventeenth century, appear to have inspired certain writers of her sex; but in writings on morality and education, the seventeenth century might perhaps have required, in a woman especially, something more positive respecting religion. We feel, in studying the *advices* of this mother, that

---

[1] See in the French *Chrestomathie*, tom. ii. p. 199, third edition, a long fragment of *Advices of a mother to her Daughter*, and some of the reflections of M. Vinet introduced here.

[2] Nardi parvus onyx.

the seventeenth century was already inclining towards the eighteenth, although in regard to the feeling of what is suitable and respectful to her sex, Madame de Lambert entirely belongs to the age of Louis XIV.

We remark in these counsels, a loftiness of mind, and a respect for herself, which, combined with a generous and sensible character, constitute all her morality. Her favourite notion, the word which most frequently comes to her pen, is *glory*. "If men rightly understood their own interests, they would neglect fortune, and in every profession, would have only glory for their object." It is true she takes care to distinguish glory from vanity. "Vanity seeks the approbation of others, true glory the secret testimony of conscience." She means that man should learn "to dispute for glory with himself," a fine saying, which shows that glory in the eyes of Madame de Lambert is a different thing from the noise and clapping of hands by the people. "The sentiment of glory is the greatest security that we have for virtue, but the question is, how to choose glory that is really good." Nevertheless, it is plain that, if she does not mean an unjust or frivolous glory, she still aims at glory. "The love of esteem is the soul of society, it unites us to one another. I have need of your approbation, and you have need of mine. If we withdraw from men, we withdraw from virtues, necessary to society, for when we are alone, we are neglected, and the world forces us to look to ourselves."

Fenelon said of *The Advices of a Mother to her Son*, from which the foregoing quotations are taken : "I would, perhaps, not quite agree with her about all the ambition which she requires from him, but we would soon come to an understanding about all the virtues, by which she means that this ambition should be maintained and regulated." [1]

In her *Advices to her Daughter*, the author speaks less of glory, for a very natural reason : "The virtues of women are difficult, because glory lends no aid in the practice of them." Still morality, in the second part, is a part of human nature, and as elevated as such a morality can be, but deficient in a fixed basis and a perceptible unity. A number of just and refined observations, and of judicious advices, give to these few

[1] Fenelon, Lettre à M. de Sacy.

pages an uncommon value ; we may say that Madame de Lambert has not a line that is vulgar, and not an expression that is far fetched.

Would Fenelon, who handles delicately the weak point of ambition, have been able to agree with this mother on religion ? She speaks of it with reverence, and recommends it to her children. She says : "The moral are in danger without the Christian virtues. . . . Religion is never attacked when men have no interest in attacking it."[1] But there is great difficulty in discovering what place religion, I mean Christianity, could hold in her system. Where religion enters, it fills all—it overspreads all. This is what Madame de Lambert says of it in her *Treatise on Old Age*, remarkable otherwise for the nobleness of the sentiment :—

"Devotion is a becoming feeling in women, and suitable to both sexes. Old age without religion, is a burden.' All external pleasures abandon us, we leave ourselves behind. The best advantages, health and youth, have vanished. The past furnishes us with regret, the present escapes our grasp, and the future makes us tremble. As to those who are sufficiently happy to be affected with religion, piety consoles them, it is also more easy to practise. All the ties which bind us to life, are almost broken ; it is more the work of nature than of reason to unbind us. We do not draw so much from the world as from devotion, it has many other resources."

You observe, that religion occupies her attention with a view to utility ; she does not perceive its necessity in the heart, its powerful attraction ; in short, its duty. She is less a Christian than a Stoic ; of a moderate and softened stoicism, such as that of a woman should be. The author who said, " Believe that we are as strong as we wish to be,"[2] and who does not immediately add, that the power over the will is that which fails us most, was not well acquainted with human nature. There has been formed in modern times, under the shelter of Christianity, a morality, which is not, however, Christian, but which borrows from Christianity some of its tenderness. A saying of Quintilian might serve to characterize this morality,—*Quod decet, what is becoming*. This is precisely the morality of Madame de Lambert—a lofty

[1] Avis d'une mère à son fils.   [2] Ibid.

propriety, a delicate respect ; in plain terms, a great adoration of one's-self. It is from respect to themselves that men grant to God any thing. At a later period, with Vauvenargues, there will be no longer question about God ; morality will become merely a habit of elevated sentiments. They will no longer ask how to please God, but how to please themselves. It is an exalted self-love, and well understood, which is supported by a foundation of justice, equity, and benevolence, but of which the feeling of personal dignity is the soul.

If Fenelon had looked more closely into this morality, he would have passed a more serious judgment upon it. Could he have approved of what Madame de Lambert says to her son about the duties of a man to the *woman who has entrusted to him her honour?* This phraseology, altogether French, expresses, with admirable delicacy, what was not easy to render. But is this all which a Christian mother could say? After all, the morality of the seventeenth century was not much better on this point ; but a woman at that time would not have spoken as Madame de Lambert has done here.

We have here some short passages, which we borrow from her :—

" Birth is not so honourable as it is a mere matter of arrangement, and to boast of one's race is to praise the merits of others." [1]

" Good hearts feel the obligation of doing good more than men feel the other necessities of life." [2]

" Raillery, which forms part of the amusement of conversation, is difficult to manage. From the most pleasant raillery to offence there is only a single step. Often the false friend abuses the right of jesting, and hurts your feelings, but the person whom you attack has the sole right of judging whether you are jesting ; so soon as you hurt his feelings, it is no longer raillery ; he is offended." [3]

" The object of raillery should fall upon slight defects, so that the person interested may joke about them himself. Delicate raillery is composed of praise and blame. It only touches defects lightly to lay a greater stress on great qualities. M. de la Rochefoucauld says that *dishonouring a man gives less offence than ridicule.* I am quite of his opinion, for this reason, that it is not in the power of any one to dishonour another ; it is our own con-

---

[1] Avis d'une mère à son fils.　　[2] Ibid.　　[3] Ibid.

duct, and not what others say, which dishonours us. The causes of dishonour are known and certain; ridicule is purely arbitrary, and depends on the way in which the objects are represented, and on the mode of thinking and feeling." [1]

" We must never reckon severely with any one. Exact honesty does not require every thing that is due to you. With your friends be not afraid to be in advance. If you wish to be an amiable friend, exact nothing too rigorously, but that your manners may not be inconsistent, as they express the dispositions of the mind, often reflect seriously on your own weaknesses, and lay bare, without disguise, your heart to yourself. From this examination you will become humble in your own eyes, and indulgent towards others." [2]

" In forming special judgments, we should imitate the equity of the courts of law. The judges never decide a case before they have examined and heard the witnesses, and confronted them with the persons interested; but we, without any commission, take upon ourselves the office of absolutely deciding on the reputation of others; every proof is sufficient, and every authority appears good, when it is necessary to condemn. Urged on by the malignity of our nature, we believe that we give to ourselves what we take from others." [3]

" Accustom yourself to treat your servants with kindness and humanity. One of the ancients said, *we should look upon them as unfortunate friends.* Consider that you owe only to chance the great difference that exists between you and them; do not make them feel their condition, and do not aggravate their trouble. Nothing is so low as to be haughty to one who is placed under you. Use no harsh expressions; that mode of speaking should be unknown to a person of a polished and delicate mind. As service is established contrary to the natural equality of mankind, it is our duty to sweeten it. Have we any right to wish our servants to be without faults, when we daily show them that we are not faultless?" [4]

" To live in a constant bustle, is to live fast; calm repose prolongs life. The world robs us of ourselves, but solitude restores us. The world is only a company endeavouring to flee from their own thoughts." [5]

---

[1] Avis d'une mère à son fils.   [2] Avis d'une mère à sa fille.   [3] Ibid.   [4] Ibid.
[5] Traité de la Vieillesse.

" When we are sound at heart we derive advantage from every thing that occurs, and every thing turns to pleasure. We engage in some pleasures with a sickly taste, and often think ourselves delicate, because we are merely disgusted. When the mind and heart are not spoiled by feelings which corrupt the imagination, nor by any ardent passion, joy is easily found; health and innocence are its true sources. But so soon as a person has the misfortune to become habituated to lively pleasures, he loses all taste for those of a more moderate description. We injure our tastes by amusements, and get accustomed to such an extent to ardent pleasures, that we cannot return to those that are simple." [1]

We shall only make one quotation more :—" Approve, but admire rarely; admiration is the inheritance of fools." [2] But, in the high road of thought, is it not necessary that the impulse should come to us from an enthusiastic character ? Must we not be favourable or unfavourable, praise or blame too much, and in short possess in ourselves a motive and a will sufficiently strong to communicate it to others ?

As to style, properly so called, there was no longer, in the time of Madame de Lambert, the phraseology which is harmonious, close, and softly flexible; the short and sententious turn began to prevail; the *Letter* of Fenelon to the *French Academy* is an example of it; and to an age in which literature had been pursued with great honesty, and quite at ease, succeeded that of a style less formal and more resembling public speaking. The *Advices* of Madame de Lambert are, as it were, a chaplet of maxims; but each grain of this chaplet is a pearl. There is, however, in spite of this mode of writing, neither affectation nor stiffness; and to this great precision of thought and expression, grace is by no means wanting. *The woman was evident by her gait.*

But the letters of Madame de Lambert form a contrast to all the rest. They have a precious and refined character; they betray some pretension, and show that this sort was not really written for their author.

[1] Avis d'une mère à sa fille.   [2] Ibid.

XI.

MADEMOISELLE DE LAUNAY
(MADAME DE STAÄL).

1693–1750.

AN obscure, perhaps an irregular birth, and an education exclusively received in a convent, while all her family was a sister,
her rival, and her enemy—these were the circumstances in which
Mademoiselle de Launay entered into the world.   This is perceived in her *Memoirs;* and it is observed that the family life,
a matter essential to a writer, was unknown to her.   Such previous occurrences contribute to determine the character of one's
style.   It is the same with marriage and celibacy; the manner
of a bachelor may always be perceived by what constitutes its
defect.

Mademoiselle de Launay, however, was educated with extreme
tenderness by the nuns of her convent; but a capricious love is
not the maternal feeling, and that artificial gentleness was but
of little use in relieving the bitterness of that which she afterwards experienced.

Her intelligence was lively and precocious.   She was distinguished, when quite a child, by her great desire for knowledge;
and agreeable reading had less attractions for her than books on
abstract subjects.   When she was still very young, she eagerly
read Malebranche's *Search after Truth.*   We have in the following extract what she says on this subject:—

" I was passionately fond of the author's system.   To ascertain whether I understood it, I set myself to determine beforehand the consequences of his principles, which I had no difficulty
in discovering.   This impressed me with the belief that I understood it.   It may happen that a head quite fresh and not imbued
with any opinion, receives more easily abstract ideas, than those
which are filled with different thoughts calculated to embarrass
one another."

At a very early period she manifested great strength of mind
and will, spoiled as she was by the nuns.   She not only exer-

cised it in manly studies, to which she applied herself, but also in habitual self-command :—

" Some boarders, of an age far more advanced than mine, lent me romances. Some one saw that I was engaged in dangerous reading, and told me that I must give it up. I did so at the moment; and although I stopped in the middle of an incident, which caused me great distress, yet I did not wish to see its end, and resisted all attempts to induce me to finish it; I have done few things which cost me so much."

And still farther :—" I resolved to suffer misery, and seek slavery, rather than belie my character, persuaded that it is only our own actions which can degrade us. I would not have known myself, if I had not gone through this experience; and it has taught me that we yield to necessity less by its power than by our own weakness."

Mademoiselle de Launay is truly distinguished by the uprightness of her mind and heart. " My temper and character are like my figure," she says; " there is nothing cross, but," she adds, " there is no charm." In truth there is nothing cross in her; what is unreasonable is foreign to her temper and character; but reason is without bitterness; and even becomes justice, when it is necessary to judge others, and especially those who most attacked her. With others, she made this species of reason of the greatest importance. " I never knew," speaking of a friend, " any other woman so perfectly reasonable, and whose reason had so little bitterness." And elsewhere—" I already understood that in morals, as in geometry, the whole is greater than a part."

But the love of truth is that which shines brightest in her writings, and in her character. She maintained truth in an eminent degree, and in very difficult circumstances. Mark what she says on a declaration that she was to make on the subject of the political intrigues of the Duchess du Maine : " I took care to put nothing into it but truth, persuaded that when we find it necessary to swerve from the truth, we must nevertheless abide by it as nearly as possible. It is the surest and most honourable part." And at a later period, after an examination : " I was quite satisfied with the way in which I had conducted myself on this first occasion, without appearing embarrassed or intimidated, having only said what I meant to say, and having scarcely swerved from the truth; to which, it appears to me, that the

mind, forced to any evasion, returns as naturally as the revolving
body returns to the straight line."

To this correctness of understanding and of judgment—in a
word, to the coolest head—she joined a very tender and inflam-
mable heart. This was the cause of the troubles and errors of
her life. " Every passion," says she, " is extinguished, when
one sees the object of it, as *he* really is." But passion is the very
thing which prevents a person from seeing its object, as he really
is. She had the misfortune almost always of attaching herself
to objects unworthy of her, and of rejecting the affection of persons who would have deserved hers.

After many difficulties, she had no other resource, in spite of
her understanding and talents, than to gain admittance into the
family of the Duchess du Maine, as a waiting maid. Nothing
was more opposite to her tastes, character, and abilities, than
such a position. Gradually, however, her distinguished talents
were observed, and attracted to her the confidence of the duchess.
She was mixed up with the intrigues of the Court of Seals during
the regency; and the discovery of the conspiracy framed between
the duchess and Alberoni, through the interference of the Spanish
ambassador, Cellamore, conducted her to the Bastille. She
passed two years in it, and was always faithful to the interests of
her mistress. During that time, which she calls the happiest
period of her life, she had an intrigue of another kind, of which
the account is given at length in her Memoirs.

When she came out of prison, she returned to the Duchess du
Maine. She had devoted herself to her, and good use was made
of her services ; but her reward was not in proportion to her
fidelity, and she had occasion to know that princes are ungrateful. At a later period, it was thought right to provide her with
a husband. M. de Staël, a native of Soleure, a captain in the
Swiss guards, was the man whom, now in the decline of life, she
married, almost without knowing him.

She died in 1750, very much regretted by the society in which
she lived, and leaving *Memoirs* written, without any pretension
to history, and without any object, but to give an account of her
own life. Sad in their general aspect, because they depict an
unhappy destiny, these Memoirs form one of the most agreeable
books, for its details, and for the manner in which it is written.
An animated narrative, striking portraits, just and lively reflec-

tions, delicacy of observation, and a style at once strong and light, unite in making this book a classical work. A number of the lively pieces have been given in different collections, such as her visit to the Duchess de La Ferté, her entrance into the house of the Duchess du Maine, and her arrival at the Bastille. They are too well known to render it necessary to give them here.

The following is an example of her taste for truth. She had been relating a story of her early youth, a preference and a jealousy that had so far remained unknown. She adds, immediately after, what she calls a *ridiculous adventure*, " I would have suppressed it, if I had been writing a romance. I know that the heroine ought only to have one taste, that it ought to be for some one quite perfect, and never to come to an end; but truth is as it may be, and has only merit in being what it is."

It is impossible to doubt that she is indeed devoted to truth, and this is the first charm of her story. We may apply to her, with good reason, what she says of the Duchess du Maine: " No one ever spoke with more correctness and neatness, and in a manner more noble and natural. Her mind did not use either turns of expression or figures, or anything which is called invention. Easily impressed by objects of sense, it reflected them, as the glass of a mirror reflects them, without addition, omission, or change."

Mademoiselle de Launay is contented with being exact, and we are satisfied that she is so, and that she uses *nothing of what is called invention*. She has not much imagination, or she makes little use of it. Her modes of speaking, the most picturesque and the most pointed, are borrowed, as we have already seen, from the mathematicians. Here is an example of it : " M. de Rey always showed to me great attachment. I discovered, by slight indications, some diminution of his passion. I went often to see Mesdemoiselles d'Epinay, at whose house he almost always was. As they lived very near my convent, I generally returned on foot, and he never failed to offer me his arm to conduct me home. We had to pass through a large square, and, at the beginning of our acquaintance, he took the road by the sides of the square. Then I saw that he crossed it in the middle, whence I concluded that his love had at least diminished by the difference between the diagonal and the two sides of the square."

There is a power and a charm in truth ; it is, perhaps, the first, but it is also the rarest, of literary qualifications. Perfect truth of thought and expression, when it is accompanied with grandeur in the idea and in the object, places the author in the first rank. Pascal rejected every kind of ornament, and put in its place the perfection of truth ; he is at once .true and grand. Mademoiselle de Launay has no grandeur of thought or of object, but she resembles Pascal in her regard for truth. When we read such authors, we might be tempted to believe that the recital of a real fact would be as attractive as a romance, if they put into it, or could put into it, as much truth as they put into fictions. Indeed, reality is very rich and very varied. You may study the character of M. de Maisonrouge, in the *Memoirs* of Mademoiselle de Launay. But, with equal talent, it is more difficult and more rare to put into the recital of events, of which we have been actual witnesses, as much truth as in a romance. This has the appearance of paradox, and yet it is quite correct. In the one case, we are preoccupied and interested ; in the other, we are at liberty as to the impression which we make. Generally speaking, art is more true than that which is not art. There are exceptions, perhaps, and Mademoiselle de Launay is one of them. Here follows the estimate which Grimm forms of Mademoiselle de Launay :—

" Apart from the prose of M. de Voltaire, I know none more agreeable than that of Madame de Staël. An astonishing rapidity, a fine and light touch, numberless strokes of the pencil, new, refined, and true reflections, a nature and a warmth always equally maintained, constitute the merit of these memoirs, to an extent so much the more remarkable, as the history, which is at the foundation of them, is by no means interesting in itself, and has no other charms than the light and tasteful graces which Madame de Staël scatters over every thing which she handles. They are a model to those who engage in writing memoirs, and they will be able confidently to judge of their merit, and of the degree of perfection to which their works have attained, in proportion as they are found to bear a greater or less resemblance to the work of Madame de Staël." [1]

<hr />

[1] Correspondance de Grimm, tome i. p. 421.

XII.

FONTENELLE.

1647–1747.

WE have spoken to you, gentlemen, of d'Aguesseau, Cochin, Saint-Simon, Rollin, Louis Racine, Crebillon, Le Sage, Destouches, Prevost, Madame de Lambert, and Mademoiselle de Launay. If we have said nothing of J. B. Rousseau, de Fleury, and M. Dubos, it is because they in fact belong to the seventeenth century. Those, who have so far occupied our attention, come near to one another; and although I do not maintain, from their writings, that they are entirely strangers to their age, or that they have gone astray, so to speak, in the eighteenth century, still I do not hesitate to affirm that they are separated from those whom it remains for us to bring under your consideration. I have also thought it my duty to bring together, in a distinct group, some writers, very unequal among themselves as to genius and influence, but resembling each other in one point, that of having manifestly borne, not only the impression of their age, but, farther, of having, each in his own measure and in his own sphere, contributed to give to it that impression. In this same group we make a division. We name together Fontenelle, La Motte, Marivaux, La Chaussée, Henault, and Vauvenargues. We keep apart Montesquieu and Voltaire.

It might be sometimes said that, in the disposal of men and of events, Providence is careful of our enjoyments as well as of the accomplishment of His own purposes. We see Him proceeding, so to speak, in the manner of artists, bringing about in history picturesque events, and forming for the eye of the beholder, groups, pictures, and contrasts. This idea has been more than once suggested to us by our subject. We shall see Voltaire gain the dominion, both by the variety of his gifts and the duration of his life, and the place which he occupies during the whole of the eighteenth century, and we shall find him its sole representative throughout its whole extent. There is Fontenelle who, though the contemporary and rival of the great

wits of the seventeenth century, belongs to the eighteenth by
some of his most important works, and by his personal influence.
Fontenelle, during a very long life, for he entered on his literary
career at fourteen years of age, formed the knot, the point of
transition, and the continuity of these two periods, of each of
which he was the representative to the other. It was a singular
circumstance that he lived a hundred years and did not outlive
himself; he continued to influence by his conversation, after he
had so long exercised an influence by his writings.

He had many other peculiarities, especially the contrasts of
his character, and the fusion of these contrasts. His intellectual
power is connected with this fusion; a man is only strong when
he bears within him some antitheses strongly marked. A faculty
without the opposite faculty, is not a power but a drag; there
is no power but that which restrains itself. We can only
restrain and regulate our conduct so far as one of our faculties
is balanced by its contrary, the counterpoise makes it complete.

Without being one of the great powers in the intellectual
world, Fontenelle exercised in the empire of literature an influence which did not belong to more illustrious men. Real
power is not measured by the noise which men make. That of
Fontenelle, especially, proceeded on the rare temper, which kept
in equilibrium his opposite faculties. Large and thin, geometrical and literary, philosopher and wit, frivolous and yet in the
main serious, a mind fond of paradoxes and yet just, a refined
mind without being weak or false,—which is worthy of remark,
as refinement, weakness, and falsehood generally go in company;
an ingenious understanding, but excluding invention, for Fontenelle did not invent; in his opinions at once bold and circumspect, full of misgivings and discretion, cool and sympathetic,
independent but not an opponent of the Government, respectable
and obliging, good-natured, very sociable, an egoist in theory
rather than in practice; he boasted of being worse than he was;
his actions always belied his words, and yet he has been judged
more by his words than by his conduct, as the former were better
known than the latter, a temperament such as is met with in
other men, but in none so marked as in him, and not set off
by so great superiority of intelligence.

On the whole, Fontenelle was a being by himself. Voltaire,
in his *Temple of Taste*, characterizes him by a just epithet; he

calls him " the discreet Fontenelle." *Discreet* marks a man who has at once discretion and discernment; now, in both senses, Fontenelle was discreet. He was called the Erasmus of the eighteenth century, but in spite of some relations, the differences are too marked,—let us keep by the epithet of Voltaire. We may add that Fontenelle was less discreet during the most reserved period, and that he became singularly so at the time when society threw off its reserve. Rash in the time of Louis XIV., and bearing then the character of the times which were coming, he became prudent as the eighteenth century proceeded in its development. As to this matter, we must reckon in Fontenelle the effect of age, and the progress of minds beyond himself; what but lately would have passed for boldness, had become reserve; but we must not mistake this mixture of boldness and circumspection for the peculiar character of Fontenelle.

He has also been called the *sage* Fontenelle. The philosphers of the eighteenth century regarded him as the model of wise men, because he had dared to think, and had only spoken out the half of his thoughts. It was a tractable wisdom and tolerably egoistic. He said, that " if he had his hand full of truths, he would take good care not to open it." He did, however, open this hand a little, but never entirely. Nowhere in his writings is there any very explicit explanation of morality or philosophy; nevertheless, from the whole of his life and writings, we may easily deduce a moral and philosophical system. It is nowhere and everywhere. This philosophy at bottom is mere scepticism. To affirm nothing, and to have no sure belief about anything, only there must be no question about the certainty of physical and mathematical truths, summed up the philosophy of an age, which regarded as wisdom the disbelief of philosophical truth. Fontenelle, a sceptic in history, as in every thing else, thought that he possessed this wisdom. Reserved as he was, he said he was unacquainted with any folly. Folly, indeed, as the age viewed it—that is to say, exaggeration and excess—was not in the nature of Fontenelle. His wisdom consisted in living morally and intellectually in a moderate temperature, it is a lukewarm existence, but pleasant, like every thing which is lukewarm. It may be said that his character itself was a system; the art of being happy was with him a talent, and in this respect his life deserves to be studied. At sixty years of age, he was placed in circumstances peculiarly favourable, but even then, though his nature prevented him from sharp suffering, he was exposed to a mass of contradiction. At war with the classical writers of the seventeenth century, he was on the point of being persecuted for having indulged in some writings by no means catholic, and he was attacked in libels, which, however, he made a rule not to read. These struggles were prolonged till the Regency ; at that period the prevailing opinion changed, and he had then only admirers. Fontenelle was a bachelor, and was really born for celibacy; he was afraid, above all, of lively impressions, and knew how to avoid them even to the end. In his last moments, when asked what he felt, he answered, " I feel only the difficulty of existing." Thus terminated a life singularly happy in a career which is scarcely so—that of men of letters.

We may now, if you please, consider his treatise *on Happiness* as his picture of a moralist. It is a little work of twenty pages, in which prevails a sort of mitigated epicurism, it might be called utilitarianism. Fontenelle, in truth, may be reckoned an epicurean, but temperate, reasonable, and full of moderation and delicacy, it is a becoming personality, which does not permit any impropriety. The saying is imputed to him, which lays down as an essential condition of happiness, having *the heart cold and the stomach warm.* Like others, he might think so, but certainly he did not say so. But to reconcile ourselves to this witty speaker, let us not forget the famous saying which he uttered on his death-bed : " I am a Frenchman ; I have lived a hundred years, and I have never cast the slightest ridicule on the smallest virtue."

Fontenelle remarks, that there are two opinions about happiness—the one that it entirely depends upon ourselves ; the other, that it does not depend upon ourselves at all, and that the latter is the more general. For himself, he thinks that " we can do something for our happiness, but only by our mode of thinking;" and few people care to get the mastery of fortune by thought.

In order to give happiness an entrance into, the soul, or at least that it may remain there, we must first of all expel from it all imaginary evils. " If we would only look at them for some time with a steady eye, they would be half vanquished. We should not be eager to afflict ourselves, let us wait till what appears so bad be developed." " We have for violent grief some indescribable complacency which sets remedy at defiance."

Besides, he attaches importance to negative happiness. "It is a great obstacle to our happiness to expect too great happiness." We should reflect on the great number of evils from which we have been preserved. "There is a man such, that all his desires would terminate in having two arms." Men disdain to think of a small good, and yet they have not the same contempt for moderate evils.

Here follow two reflections, which are, as it were, the conclusion of the treatise *on Happiness*:—

"Since there is so little good, we should not neglect any that falls to our share, yet we use it as if it were in great abundance, and as if we were sure of having as much of it as we please. We hold the present in our hands, but the future is a kind of juggler, who dazzles our eyes and filches it from us." "The greatest secret for obtaining happiness, is to be at peace with one's-self. Naturally all troublesome accidents, which come from without, throw us into ourselves, and it is well to have there an agreeable retreat, but it cannot be so, if it has not been prepared by the hands of virtue. All the indulgence of self-love does not prevent us from reproaching ourselves, at least in part with what we feel worthy of reproach; and how many are farther troubled with the humiliating care of concealing themselves from others, with the fear of being known, and with the inevitable vexation of being so. Men flee from themselves, and with good reason : it is only the virtuous who can see and know themselves. I do not say that he enters into his own heart for self-admiration and self-applause, and could he do so and yet be virtuous? but as men love themselves always very much, it is sufficient to be able to go into the heart without shame, that it may be entered with pleasure."

We readily agree with Fontenelle as to this conclusion, and all that we desire is a definition of what he means by the term *virtue*. We take it kindly of him that he has restored to their proper place small benefits, the pleasures of every moment, which, valued as paternal gifts, may enrich human life even in its most destitute form. This view is admirably brought out in a work, whose spirit is quite opposite to that of Fontenelle—*the Leper of Aosta*.[1]

---

[1] Le Lepreux de la cité d'Aosta.

Considered as a writer, Fontenelle is in the first place re-markable for his universality. Voltaire said, and justly too, that Fontenelle's was the only universal mind of the seventeenth century. Under Louis XIV., he was in truth what Voltaire himself was under Louis XV. In the seventeenth century, universality was rare. In one sense, this is always the case; besides, there is more than one kind of it, and there exists a certain universal capacity which might well be called a universal incapacity. In all cases, universality of talent is as much a chimera as universal monarchy. It would be in its full extent the creative faculty. It could not be conferred on any man, and history furnishes no example of it. Talent implies individuality, and the notion of individuality a limit; we are individuals by what we want as much as by what we possess. There is often a separation even between modes of writing that are most closely connected and most analogous, as a man may excel in satire, who is worthless in epigram. But we are here speaking of universality of intelligence, and of the gift of comprehending every subject, and of speaking about all things without becoming ridiculous. Men of exalted genius possess this universality; Leibnitz, Haller, Bacon, exercise their dominion in all the pro-vinces of thought. There is another universality less glorious, and yet rare and valuable, that of Fontenelle. He does not hold in his grasp all the faculties of man, but he possesses a clear and ready view of all things, and has cultivated knowledge in great variety.

The spirit of the eighteenth century displays more universality than that of the seventeenth, and in the nineteenth, every mind may be said to have become universal. It is no longer possible to know only one thing, and we cannot in fact know one thing at present and not know many others; this is the necessity of our age. Bossuet and Fenelon, the two greatest geniuses of the seventeenth century, did not exercise their talents on such a variety of topics, nor combine so many different elements of thought, as was done in the following age by a number of writers of much less value, and now almost every one surpasses them in this respect. In the seventeenth century there was only one sort of mental capacity; Fontenelle alone had several.

The part of Fontenelle, however, although analogous to that of Voltaire was certainly inferior to his, but although not so famous and less profound, his work was much more important than we have been led to believe. He laboured with little noise, and the sound that he made was lost amid a thousand others, yet he undoubtedly exercised over the spirit of his age a very sensible influence. Voltaire with more power and splendour continued the work of Fontenelle, and we continue it still, though it be only in the way of reaction. In the history of the human mind, is not reaction in reality perseverance?

The first efforts of Fontenelle were literary in an age devoted to literature. It was singular, that the mind of all others the least poetical made its first attempt in verse. He had for excuse that he was induced by example and relationship. A nephew of Corneille, his strongest passion was enthusiasm for the glory of his uncle. To say the truth, it stood alone, and for his happiness soon disappeared, for it would have rendered him ridiculous, and ridicule was that which was most contrary to the nature of Fontenelle. He was jealous of Racine, who as a rival had been preferred to his uncle, and he went so far as to write an epigram against *Athalie*. In this he was only the accomplice of his age, but it might be supposed that he would have judged better than it, if he had not been the nephew of Corneille.

It has been said, that Fontenelle was a poet by his natural abilities; it would have been better, if they had said that it was by his natural abilities he made it be forgotten that he was not a poet. Here a general observation presents itself, which refers to the history of letters. The age of Louis XIV. had great poets. Was it really poetical? We must see who are its poets, besides Corneille, Racine, La Fontaine, Boileau and Molière! We must see what by common consent was called poetry. In short, we must see what were theoretically the ideas of those who formed a theory. Why is it, that below these great names we only find verses and versifiers? Why is it that nowhere we can get small change for these large pieces of gold? Is it not that, notwithstanding these men of fine genius, the seventeenth century was not so poetical as it has been generally thought? In the present day, undoubtedly, we have no poets to place by the side of Corneille and Racine, but upon the whole there is more poetry in our age than in that, which could take Fontenelle for a poet.

Nevertheless, Fontenelle has too much wit for his verses to render him truly ridiculous. "Wit," says La Rochefoucauld, "helps us to do foolish things boldly." We may add, that it also serves to make foolish things appear less foolish. In France, wit possesses the power of rendering every thing admissible; one of the errors of the French mind is to mistake wit for talent and sometimes even for eloquence. It was by the force of wit that Fontenelle was able to succeed, at least in appearance, in various kinds of writing so remote from one another; in a word, it is to his wit that he owes the universality of which we have now spoken.

Besides some fugitive pieces, of which the most agreeable is the sonnet on *Daphne*, he composed operas. That of *Thetis* and *Peleus* was at the time very successful, but your professor does not consider himself a competent judge of an opera. If Quinault attains to beauty, it is because he rises above this mode of writing; the operas of Fontenelle as well as those of La Motte only produce utter weariness. He wrote pastorals, the privilege of a universal mind to attempt every thing, and that the antithesis might be complete. Pastoral poetry requires simplicity, frankness, and sincerity, so that you may judge whether of all writers he was not the least fitted for that department. The character of his mind is clearly manifested in this verse of one of his eclogues —"Though your heart be tender, you need not fall in love," [1] and in the expression addressed to the Cardinal Dubois:—"You are making yourself as useless as you can." [2]

He begins with a theory of pastoral poetry, in which he plainly regards it as a simple form. For him the pastoral life could have no charm, it must have appeared to him the dullest of all modes of living, but he discerns in it an element—tranquillity, which renders it fit to be used as the frame-work of an idea. The shepherd does not employ his time in thinking, which is all the worse for Fontenelle, and has nothing better to do than love —love, that is to say, metaphysical love. Fontenelle himself told Diderot, three years before his death, at the age of ninety-seven: "It is eighty-four years since I laid aside the sentiment contained in the eclogue." He who spoke thus must never have put much sentiment into the eclogue. In point of fact there is none, even in the eclogue of Ismene, the most agreeable of his pastorals, a

---

[1] Quatrieme eglogue.—*Delie.*
[2] Reponse au discours de reception du Cardinal Dubois à l'Academie Français.

piece, which is only ingenious, but this ingenuity has the effect of grace, and becomes charming.

Fontenelle also composed tragedies. In spite of the privileges of the mind, every thing has its limits, and when, with all the intelligence in the world, a man attempts tragedy with no sensibility nor warmth of heart, that intelligence would not prevent him from making himself ridiculous. Fontenelle had the good fortune to stop in time in this bad road; though still young, about thirty-five, he gave up writing verses. All that he wrote in this department, at all worthy of consideration, was, if I am not mistaken, before the end of the seventeenth century. At the age of ninety-seven, he wrote these verses—" Let men reason from this and from that, about my present existence, I am only a stomach; it is very little, but I am content with it." Perhaps the head was only wanting.

At a very early period, Fontenelle turned his attention to scientific and philosophical subjects. Science already reckoned him in the number of its adepts, when, in 1686, he published his *Conversations on the Plurality of Worlds*. Its title is more peculiar than its subject. This book contains a full exposition of the system of the universe, as it was conceived to be at that time. This had its scientific interest; and, with the exception of the doctrine of vortices, which ascribes the motion of the heavenly bodies to the motion of the ether, the work is really instructive. But, till his death, Fontenelle remained faithful to the system of Descartes.

It is, in truth, *conversations* of the author with a lady of quality, during the evening, in the country. This was the first time that science was introduced into the boudoir. Fontenelle says in his preface: " I have brought into these conversations a female as my pupil, who never heard me speak on these subjects at all. I thought that this fiction would be useful in making the work more agreeable, and in encouraging ladies by the example of a woman who did not go beyond the bounds of a person unacquainted with science, and did not hesitate to listen to what was said to her, and to arrange in her head without confusion vortices and worlds. Why should females yield to this imaginary marchioness, who only apprehends what she cannot help apprehending?" " I only ask of the ladies, for this whole system of philosophy, the same attention which they must give to the

Princess of Cleves, if they aim at following out its plot, and at knowing all its beauty."

Indeed—thanks to the admirable clearness of the exposition— the *Worlds* are as easily read as the *Princess of Cleves*. We are here very far from *Learned Women*, which was only published fifteen years before. Either Molière was deceived, or the times were changed, since a learned book for the use of ladies was received with great applause. The times were indeed changed; and we have only to convince ourselves of it by listening to this advice of Madame de Lambert: " Do not suppress the feeling of curiosity: you must only guide it, and give it a good object. But consider that young girls should have, respecting science, a modesty almost as delicate as respecting vice." [1]

But Fontenelle introduces to his female readers science a little adorned and somewhat like a coquette. Many of the details in his book smell of the boudoir. For example, we have a very curious comparison at the beginning of a work on astronomy :—

" Do you not feel, said I to her, that the day even is not so beautiful as a beautiful night? Yes, she answered; the beauty of the day is like a beauty with a fair complexion, who has more brilliancy; but the beauty of the night is a brunette, who is more striking. I agree, replied I; but, in return, a person of fair complexion, such as you, would make me enjoy a more pleasant dream than the finest night in the world, with all its beauty, resembling a brunette." [2]

And again : " A certain lady, who was seen in the moon with telescopes forty years ago, perhaps is considerably advanced in life. She had a very beautiful face; her cheeks are now sunk, her nose is lengthened, her forehead and chin stand out, so that all her charms have vanished, and we now feel some alarm for her life. What do you tell me? interrupted the marchioness. It is no joke, I replied. You observed in the moon a particular figure, which had the appearance of a woman's head coming forth from among the rocks; and some change has happened in that place, some portion of the mountain has fallen, and has left three points uncovered, which can only serve to form a forehead, a nose, and a chin to an old woman." [3]

What follows is agreeable trifling in better taste :—

Conseils d'une mère à sa fille.   [2] Premier soir.   [3] Sixième soir.

" I should like much to be able to guess at the bad reasonings which the philosophers of yonder world (the moon) employ about the apparent want of motion in our earth, when all the other heavenly bodies rise and set, going over their heads in fifteen days. They seemingly ascribe this want of motion to its size, for it is sixty times larger than the moon; and when the poets wish to praise indolent princes, I doubt not they take the example of this majestic repose—yet this repose is not perfect."[1]

These frivolities are redeemed by some philosophical passages, of which the following is an example :—

" It would appear, interrupted the marchioness, that your philosophy is a kind of mart, where those who offer to do things at least expense have the preference. It is true, I replied, and it is only in this way that we can apprehend the plan on which nature has performed her work. She displays extraordinary economy, and every thing which she can do, in a way that will cost a little less, when that would almost amount to nothing, be sure that is the way in which the work will be accomplished. This economy is, nevertheless, consistent with surprising magnificence, which shines in every thing that she has done. There is magnificence in the design, and economy in the execution. There is nothing finer than a great design, which is executed at little expense. We again are inclined in our ideas to reverse all this—we place economy in the design of nature, and magnificence in the execution."[2]

Besides, always when the subject leads to it, we meet with ingenious notions and agreeable relations, which are, considering the time, instructive. Thus, the history of bees during the third evening, the hypothesis of the saltpetre which might blow up the planet Mercury, and the following reflections on the diversity which must exist between the inhabitants and the productions of the different planets :—

" What nature does on a small scale among men, in regard to the distribution of happiness and of talents, she will have done on a large scale among the worlds ; and she will not have forgotten to bring out that marvellous secret which she possesses of diversifying all things, and of equalizing them at the same time, by means of compensations."[3]

---

[1] Troisième soir.   [2] Premier soir.   [3] Troisième soir.

But a distinctive characteristic of the *Conversations on the Plurality of Worlds* is the complete absence of religious sentiments. This magnificent subject has not been able to furnish to its author the smallest word or the slightest view of religious philosophy, or of the divine government of the world. Good taste alone might have introduced some of these things, instead of the puerilities with which the author thought he could not dispense. Notwithstanding this serious defect, the book was extremely popular.

It was in the following year, 1687, that Fontenelle published his *History of Oracles*, a spirited summary of the learned and dull work of the Dutchman, Van Dale. The avowed design of the book, with him, as with Fontenelle, was to establish the fact, " that oracles, whatever was their nature, were not delivered by devils, and that they did not cease at the coming of Jesus Christ. Each of these two points," says Fontenelle, " well deserves a dissertation." [1] He abridges the original work, by excluding from it certain details, and by giving to it an ingenious, concise, and simple form. It was only then that he was simple.

This work gave great scandal to the churchmen. Their penetration was not deficient. The book was a blow to them, not that it is essential to the truth of Christianity, to believe that oracles were delivered by devils, or that they did not cease at the coming of Jesus Christ; but this belief had been made an article of faith : to interfere with it therefore was to shake the faith; and the book appeared to be an attack on the doctrine respecting devils. In short, the circumstances of the times gave to this work a character, which it would not have had in the present day, and which it could only have had at that particular period. Certain shafts, shot at random, did not fail to hit the mark. For example, the history of the confession of the two Lacedemonians.

" Those who were initiated into the mysteries gave security for their discretion—they were obliged to confess to the priests the most secret actions of their life, and it became necessary for the poor men so admitted to entreat the priests to keep their secret. It was respecting this confession that a Lacedemonian, who was about to be initiated into the mysteries of Samothrace, told the priests bluntly,—*If I have committed crimes, it is a thing well known to the gods.* Another answered almost in the same manner,—*Is it to thee or to the god that a man must confess his*

[1] Histoire des Oracles. Introduction.

crimes? It is to the god, said the priest. *Ah! very well, with-draw then,* replied the Lacedemonian, *and I will confess them to the god.* These Lacedemonians had not very much of the spirit of devotion. But might it not have been possible to have fallen in with some impious fellow, who, with a false confession, might have been initiated into the mysteries, and then have discovered all their extravagance, and have published the trickery of the priests." [1]

In all the circumstances of the case, I should think it some-what imprudent to vouch for the innocence of Fontenelle's inten-tions : at least, for myself, I should not think it advisable. The book otherwise is very agreeable, for the great number of histo-rical facts and pointed anecdotes, for the elegance of the nar-rative, the refinement of the thoughts, and a great number of philosophical views.

The pretty story of the Golden Tooth is directed against those " who leap at once to the cause, and go beyond the truth of the fact."

" This misfortune," as Fontenelle relates, " happened so comi-cally, about the end of the last century, to some learned men in Germany, that I cannot resist mentioning it here. In 1593, the report was spread, that a child's teeth in Silesia had fallen out at the age of seven, and there had come in one of gold in the place of one of his large teeth. Horstius, professor of medicine in the university of Helmstadt, wrote, in 1595, the history of this tooth, and pretended that it was partly natural and partly miraculous, and that it had been sent by God to this child, to console the Christians, who had been oppressed by the Turks. Figure to yourselves the consolation and the relation of this tooth to the Christians or Turks. In the same year, that this golden tooth might not want historians, Rullandus wrote another history of it. Two years after, Ingolsteterus, another learned man, wrote against the opinion entertained by Rullandus on the golden tooth, and Rullandus instantly made a beautiful and learned reply. An-other great man, named Libarius, collected all that had been said about the tooth, and added to it his own opinion. One thing only was wanting in so great works, whether there was any truth in the tooth being of gold. When a goldsmith examined it, he found that it was a bit of gold leaf applied with great skill

[1] Première Dissertation, chapitre xiii.

to the tooth; but they began with making books, and then they consulted the goldsmith."

Here follow some sayings worthy of notice, on the respective authority of those who believe and do not believe a truth or an error long established.

" These two authorities are not equal. The testimony of those who believe a thing all but established, has no power to support it, but the testimony of those who do not believe it, has power to discredit it. Those who believe may be unacquainted with the reasons for disbelief, but it can scarcely happen that those who do not believe are ignorant of the reasons for believing.

" It is quite the contrary when the thing is established. The testimony of those who believe it is in itself stronger than the testimony of those who do not, for the former must have examined it, and the latter may not have done so.

" I do not mean to say, that either in the one case or the other, the authority of those who believe or do not believe is decisive : I mean merely to say, that if no respect is paid to the reasons on which both parties proceed, the authority of the one is sometimes rather to be admitted, sometimes that of the other. This is the general result, from giving up a common opinion or receiving a new one, that we must make some use of our reason, good or bad, but there is no need to use our reason in rejecting a new opinion, or taking up one that is common." [1]

Fontenelle forms this estimate of the pagan religion, in reference to the manner in which illustrious men, and Cicero among others, scoffed at the sacrifices.

" There is ground for believing that, with the pagans, religion was only a practice, about which the speculative opinions were matters of indifference. Do like others, and believe what you please. This principle is very extravagant; but the people, who did not discover its folly, were contented with it, and men of understanding readily submitted to it, because it placed them under no restraint. Thus, you see, the pagan religion only demanded ceremonies, but not the feelings of the heart. The gods are provoked, all their thunderbolts are ready to be launched— How will they be appeased ? Must we repent of the crimes that we have committed ? Must we return to the paths of natural justice, which should be among all men ? Not at all ; it is

---

[1] Première Dissertation, chapitre viii.

necessary merely to take a calf of a particular colour, calved at a particular time, and cut his throat with a particular knife, and that will appease the anger of all the gods; and then you may laugh at yourself for the sacrifice, if you choose, it will not be the worse."[1]

There are still some remarks on Plato, and on his doctrine of intermediate beings:—

" I admit that Plato has conjectured a thing which is true, and I reproach him, because it is a conjecture. Revelation assures us of the existence of angels and demons, but human reason has not been permitted to attain to certainty on the subject. We are perplexed with that infinite space which is between God and man, and fill it with spirits and demons; but with what are we to fill the infinite space between God and these spirits, or demons? For, from God to any creature whatever, the distance is infinite. As the action of God must traverse, so to speak, that infinite void to reach demons, it may well reach man also, since they are only more distant by a few degrees, which bear no proportion to the original distance. When God treats with men through the instrumentality of angels, it must not be said that angels are necessary for this communication, as Plato pretended; God employs them in it for reasons which philosophy will never discover, and which can never be perfectly known but by Him alone."[2]

These last ideas are just; but, in general, we perceive in this work the scepticism which Fontenelle carried into every thing, with the exception of the exact sciences and natural philosophy, and which is revealed in this saying, so well known : " History is a conventional fable." He believed neither the authority of testimony nor of feeling.

This double scepticism, combined with a cool contempt for the nature and condition of mankind, and seasoned with the smart quibbling of paradox, is the spirit which prevails in the *Dialogues of the Dead* (1686). If Fontenelle, in writing these *Dialogues*, had any serious intention, which I doubt, it was that of shaking every principle, and, still farther, of giving a blow to the respect which man owes to himself. Whether he did or did not mean it, he has done it. He sets out with the most insulting irony,

---

[1] Première dissertation, chapitre vii.　　[2] Première dissertation, chapitre vi.

and with the most cynical contempt for human nature, which abounds in the writings of Voltaire, and in the whole of the eighteenth century, for it seems to *aim at descending*. Fontenelle appears to me to have been, without fancy and without passion, what Voltaire was with passion and with eloquence. Besides, their philosophy was the same. In the *Dialogues* its proof is clear. The object is, above all, to surprise us, first, by the singular meeting between the parties (as Apicius and Galileo), and then by the conclusions to which we are forced to subscribe. All the ambition of the author is to make us say, at the end of each dialogue, That is extraordinary, that is strange, but that is nevertheless the case. There is no simplicity, little nature, and much wit. Fontenelle delights to arrive at truth by falsehood, and at seriousness by frivolity, of which we have a proof in *Alexander and Phryne*. She says to Alexander : " If you had only conquered Greece, the neighbouring islands, and perhaps some part of Asia Minor, and constituted them one state, nothing could have been better contrived, nor have been more reason-able ; but to be always running, without knowing whither, to be always taking cities, without knowing why, and to be always executing, without having any design, has displeased many sensible persons."

Man is attached to what he considers to be truth, and he be-lieves it to be made for him. But observe what Fontenelle puts in the mouth of Homer respecting the sympathy of human nature with falsehood :—

" You imagine that the human mind seeks only truth ; you are wrong, the human mind and falsehood have a strong sym-pathy with one another. If you have any truth to tell, you will do very well if you involve it in fables, it will give far greater pleasure. If you wish to tell what is fabulous, it will give much pleasure, if it contain not a grain of truth. Thus truth requires to borrow the figure of falsehood, to be agreeably received by the human mind ; but falsehood makes its way into it, under its own figure, for this is the place of its birth, and of its ordinary abode, and truth is a stranger there." [1]

In *Jeanne de Naples and Anselme*, Fontenelle undertakes to show the vanity of all our efforts. According to him, " man is

---

[1] Homère et Esope.

born to aspire at every thing, and enjoy nothing; to go always forward, but to arrive nowhere."

In *Parmenisque and Theocrite*, he sets himself to prove that thought prevents men from living : " Apparently the intention of nature was not that we should think with much refinement, for it sells that kind of thoughts very dear. You wish to make reflections, said she to us ; take care of that, I will be avenged by the sadness which they will cause to you. She put men in the world to live in it, and to live is not to know what is doing the most part of the time. When we discover the little importance of that which occupies and affects us, we snatch from nature her secret ; we become too wise, and are scarcely human ; we think and wish to do nothing else ; this is what nature finds not to be good."

As he proceeds, he makes the conversation turn upon the helplessness of man in his pursuit of knowledge : " If you merely wish to enjoy things, there is nothing wanting for your enjoyment ; but there is a universal deficiency when you wish to know them."[1]

Speaking of vanity, he makes Juliette de Gonzague say to Soliman : " At a certain point it is a vice ; a little short of that point, it is a virtue."

Thus the tendency of man to truth, his dignity of thought, his capacity for knowledge, and, still more, the distinction between vice and virtue, are all an illusion in the opinion of Fontenelle. It is the philosophy of a party, partial, exclusive, preoccupied with the misery of mankind, and blind to their greatness ; in his eyes man has need of nothing, and every thing. But is Fontenelle quite sincere when he degrades us ? I do not know. Voltaire is more sincere ; there is passion in his contempt for human nature. Fontenelle is cool in this, as in all that comes from him. Still, I repeat, this book should not be taken up seriously ; it is a piece of wit—a dexterous artifice well sustained.

" Lucian," says Voltaire, " never aims at wit. It is the fault of Fontenelle that he always wishes to be witty. It is he himself that you see, and never his heroes. He makes them say quite the reverse of what they ought to say ; he maintains both sides

---

[1] Apicius et Galileo.

of a question, and only desires to be brilliant. It is true that he succeeds in it; but he appears to me at length to become wearisome, because you know that there is nothing genuine in all that he sets before you. The quackery is perceived, and your ardour is cooled. Fontenelle in this work shows himself to be the most amusing juggler that I have ever known. This is always something, and it amuses."[1]

I willingly subscribe to the judgment of Voltaire respecting this witty and frivolous book. I may add, that among all the works of this first period, and I have not mentioned the most frivolous, Fontenelle produces in my mind the conviction that he is much better than we might suppose from his writings, and that he disparages himself for his own pleasure. Others are, as it were, suspended in a region which does not belong to them. There are two forms of falsehood: with the second I have no patience; with the first, which is that of Fontenelle, I am a little indignant.

However this may be, these works procured for Fontenelle an arm-chair in the French Academy in 1691. I think it was for them that he received it, and not for his literary opinions, which at that period were no longer orthodox. He was the prudent chief of the sect which had, as a double word of command, contempt for antiquity and poetry, a kind of literary atheism professed by barbarians in ruffles, who employed themselves in making verses. Then, what is astonishing, Fontenelle abandoned literature, and devoted himself to science. Once a man of science, he gained very much by it as a man of literature. This was natural; what was wanting to Fontenelle was a foundation. It was necessary to say something worth his pains—a new example of that great truth, that the value of the foundation is essential to that of the structure. He wanted materials, and was interested in nothing. He had sported with ideas—he could not sport with facts; besides the facts of natural order, the calculations of the exact sciences were to him a matter of real interest.

Appointed member and perpetual secretary of the Academy of Sciences in 1699, he wrote for forty years the *Memoirs* of that academy. It is his best title to honour. By this he rendered to science nearly as much service as the learned men whose studies

---

[1] Voltaire, Lettre au roi de Prusse.

he analyzed. Many researches, whose result without him would not have existed beyond the thoughts of their authors, who knew not how to make them be understood, received from the perfect clearness of his exposition their objective existence. Fontenelle, who invented nothing, so marvellously understood the discoveries of others, that he has almost effaced the distance between invention and intelligence. " Readers of the least application," says Duclos, " thought themselves learned, as they ran over his works ; and their ease in understanding him, was perhaps injurious to the feeling of gratitude, which they ought to entertain on that account."

We now come, gentlemen, to another work, which frequently excites our attention, and which we love to read again and again, in spite of its defects ; it is the *Panegyrics on the Members of the Royal Academy of Sciences who have died since the year* 1699. In a literary point of view, it is the first work of Fontenelle, the piece, which is a defence to all the rest.

They are not properly panegyrics, nor even intentionally eulogies. We must not inquire into the oratorical form—the author only praised what deserved to be praised. They are simple notices, and are so much the more valuable on that account. For the first time beyond subjects purely scientific, Fontenelle seems to have caught the beauty of his subject, and to have entered into it with his whole heart. Called to relate the events in the life of the noblest men, whose memory was preserved, he could speak in a manner worthy of the virtues of his heroes. He says somewhere : " We are almost weary of extolling the merit of the men of whom it is our duty to speak." This saying, which certainly wants simplicity, gives a moral picture, however, of the men of science of that age. With what pleasure the eye reposes on all these grave and serene figures ! How much do the heroes of Fontenelle belong to the contemplative age, and not to the contemptuous, of which he himself is the representative !

He who always treats men with contempt, is not far from being contemptible—the *nihil admirari* is on the very borders of folly. Madame de Lambert is quite in her age when she says, " Admiration is the inheritance of fools ;" but true admiration, the admiration which arises from reflection, belongs to great minds. The seventeenth century was contemplative ; the men of that age were men of faith—all rendered homage to the Creator. We may add, that dignity of manners is much more common among men of science than of literature, because their passions do not furnish the materials for their works. The latter class live in the world of mankind, the former in the world of God. The solitude of the literary man is not a real solitude : among his books he lives with the dead and the living ; he lives especially with himself, and often this is not too good company. Put the lives of sixty-nine literary men on a parallel with sixty-nine men of science, you will be indignant with the one and probably pleased with the other. Fontenelle did not pretend to write an edifying book ; but he describes the life of these men with truth, gravity, and comparative simplicity ; he makes us taste the peace of that life which is in general a stranger to vanity.

We must admire the conciseness and the ingenious and charming clearness with which he knows to sum up, not only the discoveries of these learned men, but their systems and ideas. He throws out a number of fine and judicious observations on human nature, on the singular qualities of the heart, and on the peculiarities of the social life. Take these examples :—

He says in the eulogy on Cassini : " In the last years of his life, he lost his sight, a misfortune, which was common to him with the great Galileo, and perhaps for the same reason, because nice observations require great exertion of the eyes. In the spirit of fable, these two great men who made so many discoveries in the heavens, resembled Tiresias, who became blind, because he saw some secret of the gods."

In the eulogy of Regis : " Although he was accustomed to instruction, his conversation was not more imperious on that account, but it was more easy and more simple, because he was in the habit of suiting himself to every one. His knowledge had not rendered him contemptuous to the ignorant, and indeed, we are commonly much less contemptuous to them, as we know more ; for we know better how much we still resemble them."

In speaking of Malebranche : " In the next edition of his *Christian Conversations*, Father Malebranche added meditations, in which, from philosophical *consideration*, he always obtains an *elevation* towards God. Perhaps he meant by this to answer some good people, who reproached him with his philosophy being abstract, and consequently dry, and with the impossibility of its producing emotions of piety sufficiently tender and affecting. It is, however, very probable that in this respect, metaphysical ideas will be always for the most part of the world, like the flame of the spirit of wine, which is too subtle to burn wood."

The following remark is met with in the eulogy on Littre : " A simple anatomist may do without eloquence, but a physician scarcely can. The one has only facts to open up, and place before the eyes, but the other, constantly obliged to form conjectures on very doubtful matters, must also support his conjectures by very solid reasoning, or which may, at least, encourage and flatter the terrified imagination,—he must sometimes speak almost without any other object than merely to speak, for he has the misfortune to deal with men only at the time when they are weaker and more childish than ever. If he has not the gift of speech, it is almost necessary that he should have, as a compensation, the power of working miracles."

He said of Newton : " He never spoke of himself or others, and never acted in such a way as to make the most malicious observers suspect the smallest feeling of vanity. It is true that he was spared the trouble of supporting his own dignity; but how many others would not have allowed any to take the trouble, which they so willingly undertake themselves, and which it is so difficult to trust to any one ?"

These sketches of manners are sometimes interwoven with some pointed anecdote : " Boerhaave was making a voyage in a vessel, and was led to take part in a conversation which turned on Spinosism. An individual unknown, more orthodox than able, made so bad an attack on this system, that Boerhaave asked him if he had read Spinosa. He was obliged to confess that he had not,-but he did not forgive Boerhaave. Nothing was easier than to denounce, as a zealous and ardent defender of Spinosa, the man who only requested that Spinosa should be known before he was attacked, so the bad reasoner in the vessel did not fail to do so, and the public, not only very susceptible, but eager to receive bad impressions, seconded him, and in a short time, Boerhaave was declared a Spinosist. This Spinosist, however, was all his life very regular in certain acts of piety, for example, in his prayers morning and evening. He never pronounced the name of God even on a physical subject without uncovering his head, a mark of respect, which, indeed, may appear little, but which a hypocrite would not have had the effrontery to affect."

At other times, the observations of Fontenelle are detached in short and neat sentences.

"A man of merit is not destined to be merely a critic, though a good one—that is to say, to be only able to point out faults in the productions of others, and to be unable to produce anything of his own."[1] "History ought to confess the faults of great men —they have themselves given the example of it."[2]

In spite of its undoubted qualities, this book is exposed to grave criticism. It wants that simplicity—that boldness of touch—that vigour of description—and that warmth, without which no one can be an eloquent writer. Every thing in it is secret or half concealed, even that which has the greatest truth and interest. Fontenelle employs the one-half of his mind in concealing the other half, not to bury it, but to make it be sought after. He assumes a simple and careless air, in proportion as he is really less so. This coquetry of language, by no means worthy of a masculine and serious mind, is astonishing in a work in which there are many views of a good and true morality, and, as it appears, some sympathy with it:—"Et fugit ad salices, et se cupit ante videri."[3] Fontenelle himself had said in the *Portrait de Clarice :* "What would be still very necessary, would be a mind which might think ingeniously, and yet believe itself to be an ordinary mind." The style of Fontenelle necessarily became the style of the eighteenth century. In this point of view, it requires on our part special attention. In the middle of the preceding century, the same danger presented itself. The *concetti*, mannerism, and affectation invaded the language, when Pascal, Molière, and Boileau put it right. The new style, which was introduced under the auspices of Fontenelle, and favoured by other writers, and whose allurements Montesquieu himself could not resist, would have at last been naturalized, if Voltaire, by the power of his fame and his genius, had not opposed this crude wit. Twice, then, we see affectation and fantastical notions banished from French literature.

The style peculiar to Fontenelle is as bad as it is charming. Under covert of the most ingenious imagination, there slips in a manner which would have been detestable in a more vulgar mind. He wishes to be found out, but although he is discovered without

---

[1] Eloge de Valincourt.   [2] Eloge du Czar Pierre.   [3] Virgili, Eglogue iii.

much difficulty, he has always, as if he feared to be so, something
crooked and a squint. This effort, although slight and almost imperceptible, does not fail to wear out the most sagacious, when
it is imposed upon them too frequently; a greater but more
serious labour would occasion less impatience. We must not
judge of it by some isolated strokes, of which each, taken apart,
gives pleasure; but we fall in with delicate or malicious in-
sinuations, as in the eulogy of Des Billettes :—

" A certain candour, which may not accompany great virtues,
but which greatly embellishes them, was one of his prevailing
qualities. The public good, order, or rather all the different
establishments set apart for maintaining the order which society
requires, always sacrificed without scruple, and violated even for
the love of mischief, were, in his case, objects of a lively and
delicate passion. He carried it so far (at the same time, this
sort of passion is so rare, that it is perhaps dangerous to put it
before the public), that, when he passed over the steps of the
Pont-Neuf, he kept by the ends of them, which were less used,
that the middle, which is always more used, might not be too
soon worn. But attention so trifling was ennobled by its principle; and how much should it be wished that the public good
were always loved with the same superstition !"

Here follows the conduct of the Archbishop of Rheims to the
Abbé de Louvois : " The late Archbishop of Rheims, his uncle,
gave him an office in his diocese, to train him to ecclesiastical
affairs. The school was good, but severe to such an extent,
that it might have corrected him of the very faults with which
the prelate, who was training him, was reproached. The Abbé
de Louvois had capacity, knowledge, the spirit of government;
in short, all the good qualities of his uncle, accompanied with
some others, which he might have learned from him, but which
he did not imitate."

Besides, there are some pointed, and even comical reticences :
" Sauveur was twice married. With respect to the first, he
rather took a novel precaution ; he did not wish to see her whom
he was to espouse till he had been with a notary, that he might
get the conditions drawn out in writing which he required ; he
feared lest he should be no longer master after he had seen her.
The second time he was used to discipline."[1]

---

[1] Eloge de Sauveur.

" In the middle of the twelfth century," observed Leibnitz, " men still distinguished truth from falsehood; but, afterwards, fables, formerly kept within cloisters, and contained in legends, violently burst their barriers, and spread over the world. These are nearly his own words. He ascribes the principal cause of the evil to men, whose institutions were poor, and who invented from necessity."[1]

But this mania for suppression, this twilight, this mode of writing, neither clear nor dark, went far to bring into question the gravity of his style, when he treats of important matters. Besides, he occasionally becomes quite enigmatic. When cunning prevails in the mind or in the style, it is less strength than weakness; it is, if not the source, at least the companion of many defects. In the first instance, a very cunning mind appears to be superior, and, in point of fact, there is a superiority of a certain kind. But, in the judgment of men of profound understanding, and of the public, how often do they end with the inevitable inference,—cunning is inferior to simplicity! How habitually cool, weak, frivolous, and often false, is the mind in which it prevails! Simple beauties are lasting, but cunning soon fades. Besides, there is naturally more intelligence in simplicity than in cunning. Simplicity and ingenuity are much more ingenious than ingenuity and cunning. " Only high-minded men know how much glory there is in being good," said Fenelon, in imitation of Sophocles. Only great minds know how much glory there is in being simple. Posterity always distinguishes this glory, but contemporaries may be deceived by it.

We must, however, confess that some great minds have been wanting in simplicity. We have mentioned Montesquieu; St Augustine and St Bernard are not simple. But we must make allowance for the false taste of their age, and for the lofty ideas by which they redeemed this want of simplicity.

And yet, Fontenelle has pages written in a style which the purest taste might acknowledge. Thus, in the eulogy on D'Argenson :—

" The inhabitants of a well regulated city enjoy the order which has been established there, without considering how much

[1] Eloge de Leibnitz.

trouble it costs those who arrange and maintain it—as almost all men enjoy the regularity of the motion of the heavenly bodies without knowing anything about it; and the more the order of a police resembles, by its uniformity, the order of the heavenly bodies, the more imperceptible it is, and consequently it is so much the more unknown, as it approaches perfection. But he who would wish to know and investigate it, would be terrified. To supply without interruption, in such a city as Paris, a vast consumption, when the available sources are always subject to be dried up by a multitude of accidents; to repress the tyranny of merchants in regard to the public, and at the same time to encourage their trade; to prevent mutual usurpations, often difficult to discover; to find out, in an immense crowd, all those who can so easily conceal a pernicious industry; to rid society of them, or only to tolerate them, as far as they may be useful to it by the performance of offices, which no other but they would undertake or discharge so well; to keep necessary abuses within the precise bounds of necessity, which they are always ready to overleap; to shut them up in obscurity, to which they ought to be condemned, and not to take them out of it by too public punishments; to be ignorant of what it is much better not to know, than to punish, and only to punish seldom and usefully; to penetrate secretly into the interior of families, and to keep their secrets, which they have not confided to any, so far as it is not necessary to make use of them; to be present everywhere without being seen; in short, to move or arrest at will a vast and tumultuous multitude, and to be always the acting and almost unknown soul of that great body—these are, in general, the functions of the magistrate of police. It does not appear that one man is sufficient for it, neither from the number of matters of which he must be informed, nor from the views that he must follow out, nor from the application which he must give, nor from the variety of ways that he must deal with the characters that it is necessary to bring before him; but the public voice will answer whether D'Argenson was fit for all this."

Among the sixty-nine eulogies composed by Fontenelle, I shall mention such illustrious men as Vauban, Newton, Ruysch, Malebranche, Leibnitz, the Czar Pierre, D'Argenson, Boerhaave; and men less known—Renau, Dodart, Des Billettes, Couplet, Morin.

XIII.

HOUDARD DE LA MOTTE.

1672–1742.

WE now pass, gentlemen, from Fontenelle to a friend—we may say an ally. La Motte, blind from his youth, was by this circumstance consigned exclusively to the domain of literature. In the early period of his life, he was mixed up with the affair of J. B. Rousseau, and of his infamous couplets, and very innocently became the object of that hateful attack. At a later period, he was entirely occupied with the controversy which he maintained against the pre-eminence of the ancients, and the superiority of poetry to prose. These agitations may be called storms; but what light breezes were close upon the tempests which fill up the life of so great writers! The first of these questions does not peculiarly belong to him; but the signal for the attack directed against poetry came from him. La Motte had at that time on his side numbers—the crowd which the dominant spirit urged on to prose. However this may be, in spite of this controversy he was generally beloved, contrary to the ordinary fortune of literary men. He deserved to be so, by the gentleness and amenity of his character. Some delightful traits are mentioned in connection with his name.

His mind was ingenious and natural; he was less cunning than Fontenelle, and not so concise; but he had a little more sensibility, though not much, for, if anything was wanting to make him a poet, it was sensibility; he has, however, some verses, which Fontenelle, with all his ability, would never have equalled.

What prevails in the writings of La Motte is good sense. His defect or weakness was not that he had too much of it, but that he ascribed too much to it, and believed that good sense held the place of every thing—that good sense, the basis of genius, was genius itself, and that it might be sufficient to make good and even beautiful verses. How does it happen that, with this good sense, at times a little tarnished, but which is all-powerful with

La Motte, he has been able to attain to modes of writing the most opposite to his nature, and the most contrary to the convictions which he avowed? He wrote in verse against poetry, he translated into prose the ode of La Faye, and translated himself into prose. J. B. Rousseau compared him, not unjustly, to the fox that had lost his tail. La Motte passed his life in self-contradiction, and thus presents us with some examples of the thousand contradictions of the human mind: with his thousands of verses he did not believe in poetry; he translated Homer, and did not believe in the ancients; he wanted imagination, and wrote odes. There were in him two men—the critic, or, if you choose, the man of literature, and the poet. In this last character he attempted all kinds of poetry—tragedies, comedies, operas, eclogues, odes, fables, and translations in verse.

The tragedies of La Motte are: *les Machabées, Romulus, Oedipe,* and *Inés de Castro.* All were very successful, but the last of these pieces more than the others. *Inés,* the masterpiece of La Motte, was more exposed to criticism than *les Machabées. Inés* belongs to the small number of tragedies, of the second order, which have not become old. This is rare; and we possess many tragedies of the second order which are still quoted, but no longer read. *Inés* has preserved all its freshness; and if it had the charm of fancy and vigour of style, it would be reckoned among the masterpieces of the stage. Its subject is admirable; and La Motte has altered the story of Camöens very happily, by introducing the generous character of Constance. The conduct of the action is easy; the characters are true, noble, natural, and without affectation: the subject is eminently tragical. There is nothing odious, but the character of the queen, who puts Inés to death by poison; but the author has banished her to the second place. Here La Motte has made use of his good sense—he has not a verse which smells of affectation. All is beautiful and simple; there are even some bold innovations, among others the introduction of the children of Inés, who succeed in persuading the king.

This play is not eloquently written, and that is its principal defect, but it abounds in admirable verses, which the heart alone can furnish, and which all the intellect in the world could not inspire. Thus Inés, poisoned without knowing it, exclaims, as she feels the first working of the poison: " Remove my children

—they irritate my pains." This saying has always called forth the applause of the theatre. Observe, also, the verses which she addresses to king Alphonso, as she presents to him her children : " Regard both with a compassionate eye; see in them not my blood, but only yours. Pour out on me alone the severity of your anger, but conceal for some time my fate from my husband." Don Pedro says to Inés : " Do not disown, Inés, that I love you." The dying Inés addresses Don Pedro : " Console your father, but do not forget how dear I was to you." She had formerly said to him : " What, alas ! is to be hoped from my weak reason ? I cannot without emotion hear your name !"

In scene second of the second act, Alphonso addresses his son with nobleness, truth, and a kind of eloquence : " Your rage is no rule for me ; you speak as a soldier—I must act as a king.[1] What is, then, the heir that I leave to my empire ? An audacious young man, whose heart is only eager for bloody battles and unjust schemes, and ready to count as nothing the blood of his subjects ! I pity Portugal for the evils which the barbarous ambition of this unbridled heart is preparing for her. Is it for conquests that Heaven made kings ? Would He, then, have only placed the people under our laws, that at our will foolish tyranny should dare with impunity to sport with their life. Ah ! judge better of the throne, and know, my son, by what sacred title we are seated there. Wise trustees of our subjects' blood, we are not so much their masters as their fathers. At the peril of our life we must render them happy, and neither conclude peace nor engage in war but for them, and know no honour but in their advantage ; and when in its excess our blind courage exposes their destiny for an unrighteous glory, we show ourselves less their kings than their assassins. Think of it when my death, every day drawing nearer, shall put in your hands the dignity of sovereign—remember these duties, and fulfil them. At present, Don Pedro, as my subject, obey." Let us not forget in les Machabées the following verse : " Rachel will follow Jacob without carrying away her gods !"

As to the operas of La Motte, the mode of writing once admitted, and we do not enter upon that discussion, Issé deserves

---

[1] This second verse is from Corneille, and La Motte has acknowledged it in his preface.

praise. It is the same with the comedy of the *Magnifique;* it is truly original, but the others are of little value.

What is worst in the works of La Motte is his odes. He had a mania for them, and we must confess that the bad taste of the times encouraged it. They took for poetry every thing which was regular and ingenious. La Motte is undoubtedly ingenious; he has ideas, and rhymes easily, yet he wants the feeling of harmony, and there is much prose less dry than his verses. His odes are in general little treatises on morality; he has one of them on *Self-love.* One would suppose himself reading La Rochefoucauld put into strophes. Another has for its subject *Enthusiasm.* He pretends at first to believe in enthusiasm, and addresses Polyhymnia, who answers him, that enthusiasm is nothing else than good sense. And all that is set forth in the garb of ancient lyric poetry. These odes are now forgotten. We remember no more than some epigrams of J. B. Rousseau :—" Old Ronsard having taken his spectacles, to furnish entertainment for assembled Parnassus, read aloud these odes, clause by clause, with which the public were lately regaled. Woes me! what is this? says Horace, immediately addressing the master of Parnassus; these odes come very near those of Perrault. Then Apollo, yawning, with his mouth shut, says, I only see one fault—the author should have written them in prose." [1] The most amusing thing is, that La Motte followed the ironical counsel of Rousseau, and put his odes into prose. He maintained the superiority of prose, and this time he was right.

After his tragedy of Inés, it is for his fables that La Motte is still esteemed. They are ingenious, and, to the merit of having invented their subjects, is added that of having treated them agreeably. It has been justly remarked, that the gift of invention, which has been wanting in very great men, has sometimes been the inheritance of talents of an inferior order. But when La Motte would have wished to imitate the simplicity of La Fontaine, he has completely failed. His animals neither speak the language of men, nor that which imagination might lend to brutes: they express themselves unnaturally, and with a pomp and monotony, which have made J. B. Rousseau, a good critic, although severe, say, that an ass expresses himself in these

---

[1] J. B. Rousseau. Epigrammes, livre ii., epig. xi.

fables like a member of the Academy. The fable of the *Two Sparrows*, the *Parrot*, and the *Watch and the Sun-dial*, may be considered as the best.

La Motte has translated Homer, by abridging and reducing to twelve the twenty-four books of the Iliad. We must observe how he has made the divisions. This parody, destitute of all poetry, and of the character of antiquity, was approved by the men of his time, and even the exquisite mind of Madame de Lambert was an accomplice in the general error. Thus shortened, the *Iliad* appeared longer; and Rousseau was right in saying,—
" The translator, who turned the Iliad into rhyme, pretended to abridge it by twelve books, but, by his style, equally dull and insipid, he has been able to lengthen it by twelve and upwards. Now, the reader who feels himself aggrieved, gives him to the devil, and says, losing his breath—Ha! come to an end of making rhymes by the dozen. Your abridgments are, to the last degree, tedious. Friendly reader, you are here in much trouble; let us make them short by not reading them at all." [1]
As a critic, La Motte has written many dissertations in support of his own works, and of his literary system. " He had made himself," says D'Alembert, " a poet according to his talents, as so many people make for themselves a morality according to their interests;" still he has many ideas and observations not profound, but good to pick up, and even new. One cannot be perfectly natural without being sometimes new; now, it is by the force of nature that La Motte falls in with novelty; he truly engages in the exercise of thought. Unhappily, two grave errors envelope the whole, ignorance of antiquity and denial of poetry; it was a double atheism.

Of his writings in prose, nothing is better than his *Reflections on Criticism*, in answer to Madame Dacier. It is a model of honest and ingenious controversy, but it has scarcely had imitators. Madame Dacier had translated Homer with a kind of instinct; she felt keenly its beauties, but she could give no reason for her admiration, and, in attacking La Motte, she reasoned to no purpose respecting the foundation, and was frequently wrong as to the form. She thought the ancient mode of controversy lawful, and allowed herself often to be bitter. La Motte, on the

---

[1] J. B. Rousseau. Epigrammes, livre ii., epig. xii.

contrary, only employed a little raillery, very delicate, and he always preserved a suitable tone.

" Alcibiades," said he, quoting himself a phrase from Madame Dacier, " reproached one day a rhetorician who had no knowledge of Homer. What would he do in the present day to a rhetorician who should read to him th e *Iliad* of M. de La Motte? Happily, when I read one of my books to Madame Dacier, she did not remember this circumstance."

" Ridicule, impertinence, blind rashness, gross mistakes, follies, a mass of ignorance—these are the words abounding in the book of Madame Dacier, like these charming Greek particles, which signify nothing, but, nevertheless, according to general opinion, support and adorn the verses of Homer."

We subjoin the judgment formed by Duclos respecting La Motte, who was nearly his contemporary :—

" Although he has written a number of beautiful verses, he is certainly inferior in this respect to Boileau, and to J. B. Rousseau, but he was superior to them in the extent of his accomplishments, and was not, like them, confined within the limits of this one talent. In his own time he passed for the best writer in prose. Voltaire had as yet only written in verse, and La Motte was deficient in vivacity of description ; but, on subjects susceptible of analysis and discussion, if Voltaire is more brilliant, La Motte is more lucid—the one dazzles, the other enlightens. I do not wish to institute a comparison between him and Voltaire in respect to genius, talents, and taste. I only speak here of what refers to reasoning. La Motte has lost much of his reputation since his death : he was in his time one of the most distinguished authors. Men of thought will always read with pleasure his discourses and his *Reflections on Criticism*. His odes, full of thought and acute reasoning, will give them more pleasure than those in which there prevails a pompous rhapsody of words, which is called enthusiasm, and which is equally cold and void of sense. *Inés de Castro* will remain in the theatre ; his operas are esteemed, and *l'Europe Galante* makes him be regarded as the inventor of the opera-ballet. We must forget that he wrote an Iliad. His fables, of which he invented almost all the subjects, would do him honour, were it not that the style is finical and affected, and therefore without taste in the expression."

XIV.

MARIVAUX.

1688–1763.

ALTHOUGH too much decried in the present day, we may still say that the character of Marivaux has been justly determined; all the critics are agreed about his excellencies and defects; those, however, who only know him from the opinions generally entertained, undervalue him, and if they become acquainted with his works, they will be agreeably surprised to find them much better than they expected.

Marivaux was a man of much wit, a delicate moralist and a very acute observer. We must add, that, in reference to morality, he was one of the purest writers of his age. He is not only irreproachable but exalted. In his literary opinions, he took part with the period in which he lived, but it was quite different in regard to his philosophical ideas, and he always showed respect for religion.

His taste for minute observation, which is nearly connected with the profession of a spy, injured, nay, ruined him as a writer. He is the spy of the human heart and the informer against it; he keeps always on its path, and has his ear constantly at the keyhole, and his accusations or indiscretions are a kind of unravelling of the web, which may appear sometimes trifling, but which destroys many threads of gold and silk.

From Marivaux, this has been termed *marivauder*, it is a prettier word than *ravauder*, but it is scarcely the same thing. It is to collect, to put aside grains of dust. Who knows, whether Marivaux was not flattered by seeing his name become a word in the language? Brilliant defects can alone procure for us this honour; still these defects must be entirely our own, and he who aims at this sort of thing does not attain it; too frequently our defects are borrowed. Voltaire said, " Marivaux weighed a fly's eggs in a spider's web," and a lady made this remark:—" He fatigues me and himself by making me travel twenty leagues on a piece of wood three feet square."

To this taste for minute analysis he unites the habit of keeping up the delicacy of the thought by the contrast of a vulgar expression. It is a kind of coquetry analogous to that of Fontenelle. The latter wished to appear simple, Marivaux to appear familiar.

Another fault of his was diffuseness. He scarcely knows when to stop, and his exuberance becomes mere babble; his psychology is a sort of gossip applied not to this and that individual, but to human nature.

He wrote several interesting comedies, full of the most amiable delicacy, but everybody there (*marivaudes*) has a taste for minute observation down to the footmen. I may mention *le Legs, les Jeux de l'Amour et du Hasard, les Fausses Confidences, l'Ecoles des Mères*. One of the best is entitled *la Surprise de l'Amour*. This title might suit almost the whole of them. We see in all a woman's heart *surprised* or insensibly assailed by a feeling, to which it appears at first quite averse. We observe with curiosity, provided we have a good magnifying glass, the successive transformations of this embryo, we discover a singular mixture of artlessness and hypocrisy in a tender heart, and see it contributing to the deception, which is attempted against it. It is a pleasure to the spectator, but not of a very esthetic character. Nothing of this kind is so valuable as the play of the False Confidence (*Fausses Confidences*). The principal personage, *Araminte*, is very noble, the action is interesting, and as to the description of the heart it is Racine in miniature, or as the prints of a fly's feet to those of a man.

Marivaux wrote romances, *le Paysan Parvenu*, and *la Vie de Marianne*. The characters of the first are frequently vulgar, and altogether it wants the tone of distinction, but the *Life of Marianne* is the masterpiece of its author. There is indeed little plan, little invention, numerous digressions and a disproportionate episode, a real romance inserted into the other, which occupies nearly the third part of the work. But the romances of Marivaux are not romantic in the ideas which they give of human nature. This praise is great, and of the first importance. The author is equal to Sir Walter Scott for the fidelity of his portraits. He evidently intends sincerely to represent man, and romance is only a suitable form for arriving at that end. Indeed, with reference to truth, Marivaux is not behind Molière. He

teaches us himself what is his aim, and we have an illustration
to the purpose in the story of the infidelity of Valville:—

"Valville is not such a monster as you represent him. No,
he is a very ordinary man, madam; the world is full of people
who resemble him, and it is only through mistake that you are
indignant with him—pure mistake. Instead of a true story you
thought you were reading a romance. You forgot that it was
my life I was relating to you, and this is the reason why you are
so much displeased with Valville, and in that view you were
right in telling me—say no more about it. An unfaithful hero
of romance! No one could ever have seen such a thing. It is
the rule, that they should all be constant—no one would interest
themselves in them but on this footing. Besides it is so easy
to render them so. It costs nature nothing, fiction makes it
expensive."[1]

Farther, the characters are happily conceived, clearly delineated,
and well supported. After the heroine, we must notice Madame
de Miran, Madame Dorsin, and especially M. de Climal, the
hypocrite, such as romance allows; the stage requires one quite
different. I say the stage, I might have said also, poetry.

In short, we observe many fine descriptions, and many just
and ingenious, nay, sometimes profound observations. But
Marivaux here exhibits his peculiar characteristic (*marivaudes*),
and occasionally to an immoderate extent :—

"Oh! it was at the time when he wished me to take that
beautiful linen, that I was informed of his sentiments. I was even
astonished that the dress, which was a very proper one, should
have still left me in any doubt, for charity is not gallant in her
gifts; even friendship, so disposed to help, confers a benefit,
and dreams not of magnificence. Virtuous men only perform their duty with great precision; they would more willingly
be niggardly than prodigal in the good that they do. It is
only the vicious who are not sparing."[2]

"She had eyes always moving, always occupied in looking,
and always seeking to provide for the amusement of an empty,
idle mind—a mind which has no resource in itself, for there
are people whose minds are active, purely for want of ideas; this
circumstance renders them extremely desirous of strange objects,

[1] Huitième Partie.   [2] Première Partie.

and so much the more that nothing remains to them, that every thing in them passes away, and that every thing goes from them; they are persons always looking and listening, but never thinking. I would compare them to a man who should pass his life sitting at his window; this is the image that I form of them, and of the functions of their mind."[1]

"The object which occupied me at first, you may believe, was the unfortunate situation in which I remained; no, this situation only regarded my life, and that which occupied my thoughts, regarded myself—me. You will say that I am in a dream, to make such a distinction. Not at all; our life, so to speak, is less dear to us than ourselves—than our passions. To see occasionally what is passing in our instinctive feelings on this subject, one would say that to be, it is not necessary to live, that it is only by accident that we live, but it is by nature that we exist. One would say that when a man kills himself, for example, he only quits life to make his escape, and to get rid of something disagreeable; it is not he, whom he no longer wishes, but rather the burden which he bears."[2]

"Suppose a woman to be a little ugly, it is no great misfortune, if she has a beautiful hand; there are a great number of men more affected with this beauty than with a lovely face, and shall I tell you the reason of it? I think I have felt it. Because it is not naked like a face, however lovely that face may be, and so our eyes do not attend to it; but a beautiful hand begins to be gradually seen; and to fix certain persons, it is quite as sure a way to tempt them as to please them."[3]

"You know that I was well dressed, and although she did not look at my face, there is an indescribable agility and lightness which is spread over a young and pretty figure, and which made her easily guess my age. My affliction, which appeared to her extreme, affected her, my youth, my good appearance, perhaps also my dress, softened her in my favour; when I speak of dress, it is because that did it no harm. Nothing assists us so much in being generous to people, nothing makes us so much taste the honour and pleasure of being so than to see them with the appearance of superior rank."[4] "Oh! this is what should have

---

[1] Cinquième Partie.   [2] Troisième Partie.
[3] Deuxième Partie.   [4] Ibid.

made me tremble, and not my shop; this was the real opprobrium which deserved my attention. I only perceived, however,
the last, and that is, according to order. We go at once to the
most urgent, and the most urgent for us is ourselves—that is to
say, our pride; for our pride and we are only one, while we and
our virtue are two. Is it not, madam? This virtue must be
bestowed upon us, and is partly a matter of acquirement. This
pride is not given to us, it is born with us; we possess it in such a
degree that it cannot be removed from us, and as it is the first in
date, so it is, as occasion requires, first used. Nature is superior
to education."[1]

"We often think that we have a delicate conscience, not on
account of the sacrifices which we make to it, but on account of
the trouble that we take to exempt ourselves from making to it
any sacrifice."[2]

In this manner Marivaux deals in minute observations, and
sometimes beyond all bounds. When once he enters into these
details, he is not always precise, and does not know how to
manage his advantages; in truth, he lavishes them with unsparing hand; yet he has not only fine thoughts, but some of them
are very noble :—

"These marks of goodness could not be repaid. Of all the
obligations which we can have to a person of accomplished mind,
these tender attentions, and that secret politeness of feeling are
the most affecting. I call it secret, because the heart, which en-
tertains such a feeling for you, does not place it to your account,
and has no wish to burden your gratitude with it. The impression is that this feeling is only known to itself, and hence it
is kept out of your view, and its merit is buried—that is most
praiseworthy. . . . I threw myself with transport, though
with respect, on the hand of this lady, which I for a long time
kissed, and moistened with the most tender and delicious tears
that I ever shed in my life; because our mind is elevated, and
every thing which has the appearance of respect for its dignity,
affects and enchants it, therefore our pride never led to ingratitude."[3]

Marivaux has much life, and often great eloquence in his discourses, with a flow of language, we must confess, which, if it

---

[1] Deuxième Partie.   [2] Ibid.   [3] Troisième Partie.

takes nothing from the truth, leaves us not a little fatigued. We may notice, as a specimen, the speech of Marianne to the minister.[1]

Farther, he is the only author who descended to the people, and who knew and made use of them. In the seventeenth century, La Bruyère alone was informed on this subject. Comedy made them a mere instrument of repulsion.

" The people in Paris," says Marivaux, " are not like those elsewhere. In other places, you will sometimes see them begin with being wicked, and end with being humane. When men quarrel, they excite and animate them ; when they wish to beat one another, they separate them. In other countries, they care not what is done, because they continue to be wicked. The populace of Paris are not so, they are less mere rabble and more people than those of other nations. When they meet together, it is not to amuse themselves with what is passing, nor to make merry with what is spoken : no, they have none of this malicious waggery ; they do not go to laugh—for they will perhaps weep, and that will be so much the better for them—they go to see, and to open their stupidly eager eyes ; they go to enjoy very seriously what they will see. In a word, then, they are neither waggish nor wicked, and this is the reason why I said they were less mere rabble. They are merely curious, and their curiosity is foolish and brutal, which intends neither good nor evil to any one, and which understands no other cunning than to come and be satisfied with what will happen. It is the emotions of the soul that this people require—the strongest are the best ; they are anxious to pity you, if any outrage has been committed against you ; to feel compassion for you if you are hurt, and to tremble for your life, if it be threatened. These are their delights ; and if your enemy had not sufficient room to beat you, they would make room for him themselves, without any bad intention, and would say to him, with all their heart—Hold, be quite at your ease, and do not diminish any of our pleasure in feeling a trembling interest in this unfortunate person. They, however, do not love cruelty ; on the contrary, they fear it, but they love the horror which cruelty produces ; that agitates their mind, which never knows anything, has never seen anything

---

[1] Septième Partie.

but this, and is quite unimpassioned. Such is the people of Paris, as I have had occasion to observe them."[1]

Marivaux is a man of understanding and of heart, but of uncertain taste. He has shown this by his contempt for antiquity. He took the side of La Motte, and even praised him to excess. He travestied the *Iliad*.

XV.

LA CHAUSSÉE.

1692–1754.

NIVELLE DE LA CHAUSSÉE, born in the midst of opulence, cultivated letters from taste. Late in life, he devoted himself to the theatre, and, when his first work appeared, he was nearly forty years of age.

Destouches had introduced the sentimental comedy; La Chaussée went a step farther, and published dramatic works, of which sentiment constituted all the interest. The plays of Destouches were still comedies; those of La Chaussée were not, they were tragi-comic. This innovation is not entirely the doing of La Chaussée, it belongs also to Voltaire. *L'Enfant Prodigue* appeared in 1736, and the principal works of La Chaussée are posterior to that date. Nevertheless, he is regarded as the founder of a style of writing very acceptable, and very much disputed, to which he has, beyond contradiction, given much consistency, by the number and success of his plays. People went to weep at *Melanide*, and they applauded the epigram of Piron on *the Homilies of the Reverend Father La Chaussée*.

Here, gentlemen, two questions are presented to us, the one respecting the fact, the other respecting the right. As to the first, Grimm, in 1776, spoke as follows: "There are two periods in the history of our manners in the eighteenth century—that which followed the follies of the regency, and that which com-

---

[1] Deuxième Partie.

menced with the misfortunes of the state—the tragi-comedies, and the great success of philosophy. The disorder of public affairs rendered us dull; we were more disposed to weep than to laugh. We found a kind of consolation for the injuries which the philosophers did by their writings to kings and gods, and our inability to be gay made us take up the part of sensible men and philosophers."[1] But the misfortunes of France came after the tragi-comedies of La Chaussée; the seven years' war continued from 1756 to 1763. And then, France had been much more unfortunate during the last years of Louis XIV., and that was still the age of Regnard, Dancourt, and Le Sage. The tragi-comedy, on the contrary, was begun amid the prosperity of France, and the greatest tranquillity which it had ever enjoyed. The beginning of the tragi-comedy, and its favourable reception, must, then, be differently explained.

It might be sufficient to answer, that this attempt must once be made; because it was natural, when the vein of comedy was exhausted, that another must be sought, and that writers should engage in the style near akin to it—the tragi-comic. And yet, an age less poetical, and more occupied with the reality than the ideal—an age in which the mind, struck with the vast importance of the social questions, is turned towards the citizens, must be essentially adapted to the tragi-comedy. On the stage, in the seventeenth century, the citizens were ridiculous, or held to be so. In the eighteenth century, they acquired there an avowed importance. If citizens are represented, it is no longer that, as citizens, they may be derided; the nobility would rather be the object of ridicule. This disposition must lead to the comedy or tragedy of the citizens, that is, to tragi-comedy.

Farther, poetry is in itself indifferent and disinterested, prose is less exempted from external influence. Poetry aspires at the ideal; it lives by contemplation, and is little compromised by the choice of its subjects. The poet looks high and far, and makes his choice, and scarcely inquires about the immediate end of his art. An age which becomes more prosaic, at once gains and loses by it; it loses by descending from the ideal, it gains by approaching the reality. Poetry falls back, and prose goes forward a step. The poetry of the seventeenth century has only

---

[1] Correspondance de Grimm, tome iii., p. 342.

itself in view ; the poetry, less poetical, of the eighteenth century aims at action. Comedy is the ideal of human nature contemplated on the ridiculous side. Tragedy is its ideal, viewed on the side of disaster and passion. The tragi-comedy, an intermediate style, has less poetry than either. It is the balloon forced to descend by the escape of the subtle fluid which raised it in the air.

So much for the question of fact. As to that of right, or the comparative value of the style of tragi-comedy, it must be admitted, that speaking according to the principles of literature, tragi-comedy is inferior. An objection is offered, it has not been cultivated by men of genius. But why has genius refused to cultivate this mode of writing? Why is a Molière wanting to it? It might be said here, as Don Diègue says in the Cid :— " It is no good sign of it to be refused." Yet tragi-comedy was cultivated by men of distinguished ability, Diderot, La Chaussée, and the ingenious Sedaine ; but, with the exception of Voltaire, none of the authors of the tragi-comedy can be called a man of genius. This style, besides, is at once the most easy and the most difficult ; and the romance more than the theatre appears to be its proper field. It is easy to make a romance interesting ; it is not even difficult to make a tragi-comedy interesting, but it is very difficult to idealise it, and to elevate it to the height of poetry. We cannot reject the *interest*, and yet after all the *interest* no more constitutes the essence of poetry than utility is the principle of morality, or persuasion the basis of eloquence.

La Chaussée was not a man of genius, although he was happy in invention, and combined with skill ; but he does not conceive powerfully, and does not search deeply into character. He wrote naturally. He has a great number of verses happily expressed, such as these : " When every body is wrong, every body is right." "When a man is like his neighbour, he is as he ought to be." (Bad morality in very good verses) : " The esteem of a husband ought to be love. Ah! I was respected and am no longer so." And yet his style has no power. It is soft like the mode of writing, which he cultivated, and very different from that of Destouches, who has a style singularly bold.

The best plays of La Chaussée are *Le Prejugé à la Mode*, *Melanide*, *La Gouvernante*. The two last are rather very highly wrought romances transferred to the stage. *Le Prejugé à la*

Mode comes nearer comedy; it is La Chaussée's masterpiece, although it is upon a subject which can no longer be very interesting. This *prejudice* is not now the *fashion*, and a man is no longer ashamed to be a good husband. Still there is more truth in this supposition than in that of the *Married Philosopher* of Destouches. There result some fine points of interest which La Chaussée has the merit of inventing, but which are not sufficiently set off by the style. Nevertheless in this play, there is great variety and interest; you may take the following verses :—
" I observe in the present day, that it has no longer a good appearance to love a companion with whom you associate. This practice is only found among the citizens. But, besides, conjugal love has been made perfectly ridiculous, an irregularity unequalled. A husband, at present, dares no longer appear so, he would be reproached with all that he should wish to be. He must sacrifice to cruel prejudice the pleasures of a lawful and mutual love. In vain is he attached to a wife who loves him; fashion subjects him in spite of himself, and soon reduces him to the necessity of passing from shame to unfaithfulness."[1]

This sort of tragi-comedy was cultivated, modified, and defended at a later period, by others, by Voltaire (*l'Enfant Prodigue*, 1736; *Nanine*, 1749), Saurin, Diderot, Sedaine, Beaumarchais, Fenouillot de Falbaire.

XVI.

LE PRESIDENT HENAULT.

1685–1770.

HENAULT, notwithstanding his title, was more a man of the world than a magistrate. Rich, and devoted to the literary and philosophical society of his time, he possessed solid merit, and was anxious to bring around him men of wit and talent.

[1] Le Préjugé à la Mode, acte i., scène iv.

Voltaire was very much with him, and addressed to him these verses in 1748 : " Henault, famous for your suppers, and chronology, for verses purely composed, full of sweetness and harmony ; you, who occupy in study the happy leisure of your life, condescend to teach me, I pray you, by what secret you escape the malignity of envy." Henault then made verses ; he was a fortunate amateur, who succeeded in some well-turned madrigals, which nobody remembers. We might quote the one, which begins thus : " These few words traced by a hand divine." He attempted also the historic drama, and composed in that style a play, entitled *Francis II.* The historic plays of Shakspeare might have furnished the idea of it. However this may be, it was for France a first attempt, which had certainly little value in itself, but it opened up a path, which, since that time, so many authors of our age have successfully pursued.

All this would not have preserved the memory of Henault, without his connections with the philosophical party, his intimacy with Madame de Deffand, and the pen of Voltaire. It is worthy of remark that, connected as he was with the philosophers, he did not adopt their opinions, and disapproved their schemes. But his name is deservedly distinguished for his *Chronological Abridgment of the History of France,* 1744. It is a mixture of chronology and history ; from time to time the author goes beyond the bounds allotted to him, and acts as the historian and the judge. The book obtained very great success, to which friends lent their aid, and it was justified, partly, at least, by the easy and agreeable novelty of its composition, and especially by a large amount of curious information respecting the proceedings of Parliaments, by the judicious estimate of men and of the times ; in short, by energetic passages, and expressive brevity.

For instance, in the article *Marie de Medicis,* we meet with these words : " A princess, whose end was to be pitied, but her spirit was too far below her ambition, and she was, perhaps, not sufficiently astonished and afflicted at the unfortunate death of one of our greatest kings."

We may notice the beautiful eulogy on the Chancellor de l'Hospital :—

" Who would not have thought that, at that time, all was lost? But the Chancellor de l'Hospital watched over his country. This great man, amid civil troubles, made the laws speak, which were usually silent in these times of storm and tempest; it never occurred to him to doubt their power, he did reason and justice the honour to think that they were stronger even than arms, and that their sacred majesty had rights in the human heart not to be annulled, when it was known how to render them available. Hence, these laws, whose noble simplicity may be compared to the laws of Rome—these laws, from which he banished, according to the precept of Seneca, every preamble, unworthy of the majesty with which they ought to be accompanied. Hence, those edicts, which by their wise foresight, embrace the future as the present, and have since become a fertile source, from which has been drawn the decision of cases, which they did not foresee; hence, those ordinances, whose united strength and wisdom make us forget the weakness of the reign in which they were passed; the immortal works of a magistrate, above all praise, who felt the extent of the duties which he performed, and the power of the high office which he filled; who knew how to sacrifice it so soon as he perceived it to be the general desire to restrain its functions, and by whom all those have been judged who dared to sit on that tribunal without his courage or his knowledge."

On the subject of Descartes, the parallel of the three last centuries deserves to be signally marked :—" The century to which he belonged was wrong, in as far as its erudition was entirely without the light of philosophy, and he put it right, so that out of an age merely scholastic he made one truly enlightened. To these two centuries a third succeeded, in which men, far from adopting others' opinions, have been rather too much disposed to rely on their own resources, and whose ambition for what is called *wit* has made truth be occasionally abused. Let us be on our guard lest the eighteenth century decry reason, as the sixteenth decried erudition."

Still farther, we have the portrait of Cardinal de Retz :—" We have difficulty in comprehending how a man, who passed his life in the midst of cabals, had never any real object. He loved intrigue for its own sake, and, with a mind bold, acute, enlarged, and somewhat romantic, knew how to take advantage of the authority which his condition gave him over the people, and to make his religion subservient to his politics. He sought at times to make a merit of what he owed to chance, and often, when too late, adapted the means to the events. He made war with the

king, but the character of rebel was the thing that most of all
flattered him in his rebellion. He was magnificent, witty, turbulent, and had more sallies of wit than order or connection, and
more idle fancies than designs; he was out of place in a monarchy, and was without all that was necessary to make him a
republican, because he was neither a faithful subject nor a good
citizen : he was a bolder and less honest man than Cicero, and
quite as vain; in short, with more judgment, he was not so great
nor so wicked a man as Cataline. His memoirs are very pleasant to read; but can any one conceive a man to have the courage, or rather the folly, to speak more evil of himself than would
have been spoken by his greatest enemy ? " [1]

Henault speaks of Colbert in the following terms :—" A man,
to be held in everlasting remembrance! His cares were divided
between economy and prodigality ; he economized in his closet,
from the spirit of order, by which he was characterized, what he
was obliged to lavish before all Europe, as much for the glory
of his master as from the necessity of obeying him. He was a
person of great sagacity, but had none of the extravagances of
genius. *Par negotiis neque supra erat.* He was only eight days
ill, and is said to have died out of favour—a great lesson for
ministers."

We shall quote the parallel between Augustus and Louis
XIV. :—" It has been justly remarked, that the reigns of Augustus and Louis XIV. resemble each other, by the multitude of
great men in all departments, who render them illustrious ; but
we ought not to think it merely the effect of chance, and if these
two reigns have a great resemblance, it is because they have been
accompanied with almost the same circumstances. These two
princes emerged from civil wars—from that time, in which the
people, always armed, constantly supported in the midst of dangers, and obstinate in carrying out the boldest designs, saw
nothing which they might not attain—from that time, in which
events, fortunate or unfortunate, a thousand times repeated,
enlarge the ideas, strengthen the mind by experience, increase its
resources, and give to it that desire of glory, which never fails to
produce great achievements.

" It was thus that Augustus and Louis XIV. found the world.

---

[1] Cf. Voltaire, les Lettres sur les Anglais reunies sous le titre de Lettres Philosophiques.

Cæsar had become its master, and had preceded Augustus; Henry IV. conquered his own kingdom, and was the grandfather of Louis XIV. There was the same agitation in the minds of men ; the people, in both cases, had been for the most part merely soldiers, and their captains heroes. To great commotions and intestine troubles succeeded the calm which restored authority; the pretensions of the republicans, and the foolish undertakings of the seditious, were overturned, and left the power in the hand of one individual, and these two princes became masters, and had nothing else to do than to render useful to their states that same heat, which hitherto had been only available for the public misfortune."

His judgment with respect to things is not less excellent than with respect to men. Henault understood well the importance which the triumph of royalty over the feudal system, and the regulation and centralization of justice had in the formation of the French monarchy. You must read, in reference to this matter, his *Particular Remarks*, at the end of the third race.

XVII.

VAUVENARGUES.

1715–1747.

THERE are two books in French literature lying in ruins. Singular ruins! There are materials laid down in the very place, whence they should rise into colonnades, vaulted roofs, and cupolas. The materials are brought from far, some of them hewn, others continue in their rude state; disorder is everywhere, but everywhere a great idea is manifest, or a great design is revealed. I speak of the *Thoughts* of Pascal, and of the work which Vauvenargues has left us, under the title of *Introduction to the Knowledge of the Human Mind*. A wandering star in the age in which he was born, Vauvenargues was really a being by himself. The relations which he exhibits to Pascal, his life of suffering, his premature death, and his works left imperfect, are very striking, so that he may be called the Pascal of the eighteenth century. But if a more regular work was intended by Pascal, and if there was nothing to prevent him from accomplishing it, Vauvenargues never thought of doing any thing else than he did. The title of his book clearly shows the unity of his design, and even exaggerates it; and, perhaps, if he had lived, scattered ideas would have been brought together, as he extended his works, and he might have discovered their secret relations, and have seen the somewhat lax unity of his book drawn around a central idea, the materials spontaneously put in order, and the rubbish become a palace. I have some difficulty in believing that this did not take place, for these stones lying about are so well prepared for one another, and the form so well indicates their place and destination, that the attentive reader makes out with almost no difficulty what Vauvenargues has not attempted. And yet he would be a bold man who would undertake the office of architect for the designs of Vauvenargues and Pascal. The finishing of the work requires a master's hand; but there is less rashness in classing these materials, in bringing together those which correspond, and in conceiving from a comparison of them the general idea of the form, proportions, and character of the edifice, which remains, as it were, buried in the graves of these two thinkers. This is what we have elsewhere attempted to do for Pascal,[1] assisted by the indications of Pascal himself; and this is what we shall immediately undertake for Vauvenargues, assisted by the very nature of his thoughts, and by the transparency of his mind.

But when we bring Vauvenargues and Pascal together, an essential feature, which should be common to both, is wanting. Vauvenargues was not a Christian, and, besides, he has neither the depth, nor energy, nor passion of Pascal. His education, indeed, bore some analogy to that of Pascal, or rather Vauvenargues received no other education than that which he gave to himself. Both were little indebted to reading, and were rather taught directly by things than by means of the exposition of them, which the distinguished minds of all ages have given. Both were deficient in erudition. Solitary thinkers, they lis-

---

[1] Voir les Etudes sur Blaise Pascal, par M. Vinet.

tenced to the voice within much more than to the voice without. By this they probably gained in candour, originality, and independence. Vauvenargues himself has highly extolled these advantages, and has perhaps rather too much depreciated learning. But, in point of simplicity and truth, both in thought and style, Pascal is only equalled by Vauvenargues.

The life of Vauvenargues was singularly distressing. Born in Provence of an ancient family, at the very time when Louis XIV. died, by his position he was destined for the military service. He entered it when very young, and engaged in warlike operations with bravery, but without distinction. His constitution, naturally feeble, was unable to endure fatigue, and the campaign in Bohemia ruined at once his health and fortune. Eager to be engaged in active life, and perhaps, too, pressed by pecuniary necessity, he endeavoured in vain to obtain employment in diplomacy. Twice he made direct application to the government, and to the king himself. One of his letters to Amelot, at that time minister of foreign affairs, has been preserved:

"Monseigneur, I am exceedingly sorry that the letter which I had the honour of writing to you, and the one which I took the liberty of addressing to you for the king, should not have attracted your attention. It is not surprising, perhaps, that a minister so occupied should not find time to examine such letters; but, Monseigneur, you will permit me to tell you, that it is this moral impossibility, in which a gentleman, anxious to approach his master, is placed, which produces that discouragement so generally observed among the nobility of the provinces, and which extinguishes all emulation. I have spent all my youth, Monseigneur, far from the amusements of the world, in endeavouring to render myself capable of performing duties to which I believed my character called me; and I ventured to hope, that a will so disposed for active exertion would have at least placed me on a level with those who expect all their fortune from their intrigues and pleasures. I am sorry, Monseigneur, that a confidence, which I had principally founded on the love of my duty, should have completely deceived me. My health does not allow me any longer to continue my military services, and I have written to M. le Duc de Biron, requesting him to put another in my place. In my unfortunate circumstances, I could not avoid acquainting you with my despair. Pardon me, Monseigneur,

if it has dictated any expression not sufficiently moderate.—
I am, etc."

In answer to this letter, Vauvenargues received flattering
words and promises, but nothing more. He expected something
farther, and retired to his family with the rank of captain. A little
after, he was attacked with small-pox, which loaded him with
infirmities, and ended by depriving him of sight. He passed the
last years of his life at Paris—a time of suffering and meditation,
of which the solitude was interrupted by illustrious friends, whom
his character inspired, notwithstanding his youth, with a sort of
filial veneration. The most illustrious was Voltaire. Voltaire,
so touching in verse, is seldom so in prose, and was never so
much so as when he spoke of Vauvenargues:—

" Thou art no more, sweet hope of the remainder of my days!
Loaded with sufferings from within and from without, deprived of
sight, and losing every day a part of thyself, it was only from
excess of virtue that thou wast not unhappy, and that this virtue
cost thee no effort. I have always seen thee the most unfortunate
of men, and the most tranquil. How wonderful was it, that at
the age of twenty-five thou hadst attained true philosophy and
true eloquence, without any other study than the assistance of
some good books! How didst thou take a flight so high in an
age of little things? How did the simplicity of a timid child
cover that depth and that strength of genius? I will long feel
with bitterness the value of thy friendship. I have scarcely
tasted its charms."[1]

We are tempted to think, that when Voltaire lost Vauvenargues, he lost his good genius. If Vauvenargues had lived,
Voltaire, it appears, would not have gone so far astray. Vauvenargues had no passion but for truth; he was, consequently,
serious, as every man is who is deeply imbued with truth. He
was moderate, too; and Voltaire might have learned from him
that moderation in which he became more and more deficient.
The career of Voltaire is divided into two periods, by no means
strange to one another, but of which the death of Vauvenargues
seems to mark the point of separation, and of which the second,
worse than the first, has not as an excuse the passions of youth.
Indeed, with advancing age Voltaire's rashness is redoubled.

Fifty years after the loss of Vauvenargues, Marmontel speaks

---

[1] Voltaire, Eloge des Officiers morts dans la Campagne de Bohême.

still of him with the enthusiasm of youth. Neither the progress of time nor of thought could efface him from his heart. When he became a Christian, after having shared in the errors of the sect called philosophical, Marmontel gives a characteristic trait of the society which surrounded Vauvenargues : " Those who were capable of appreciating so rare merit, conceived for him such tender veneration, that I have heard some give to him the venerable name of *father*." [1]

The works of Vauvenargues are included in one little volume. [2] We have already mentioned the *Introduction to the Knowledge of the Human Mind*, published in 1746, a year before his death. In the plan of the work, he reviews, first, the faculties of the mind; second, the passions; and lastly, the virtues and vices, not in their forms but in their principles. At the same time he published a collection of *Reflections and Maxims*, to the number of six hundred and twenty-three. The second half appears to be the first effort of the author, and are often the mere sweepings of his study; the first part is his definitive work. Many maxims of this first part are disadvantageously introduced into the second.

Without separating these two works, both more or less fragmentary, we shall endeavour to draw from them the author's real opinions. It is quite clear that Vauvenargues had made no summary, and had no distinct idea of his system. He seems not to have been very anxious to form one, and it may be asked whether he was in a condition to do so? He might not perhaps disown our analysis ; but assuredly we would think it strange if he did not.

His object is to know man, in order to know every thing which it is of importance to learn : morality, religion, and politics. " Men," he says in his preliminary discourse, " are the only end of my actions and the object of my whole life." Farther, " what do we not find in the knowledge of mankind? The duties of men united together in society, that is morality; the reciprocal interests of these societies, that is politics; their obligations towards God, that is religion."

We may observe, that Vauvenargues does not contemplate his morality in the depths of the soul, but makes it go forth in the

[1] Memoires de Marmontel, tome i.

[2] More recently they are published in three volumes, in the edition of Brière, Paris 1821, which is at once the best and most complete edition.

social relations. He forgets, like so many others, that if man is a
member of society, it is not in the sense that my foot is one of
the members of my body. Bringing men together and forming
a society, we admit, completes the man. Alone, he would have
been incapable of finding language, and therefore thought, and
especially the highest of all thoughts. But to conclude from
this, that the knowledge of religion exists only in society, is an
idea eminently false. Individuality is inalienable, and once developed in contact with his equals the individual remains a moral
being, who by himself has relations to the law of duty, to the
infinite and to God. We are tempted to express our astonishment when we see such errors still continuing. And yet this
view pervades the theories of our days, which present to us man
as an animal purely social, without ulterior relations, and almost
without being an individual.[1]

But Vauvenargues makes no account of human nature. He
pronounces upon it no summary and absolute judgment, and
does not generalize. He has a number of partial judgments, but
no definitive sentence. He does not inquire whether man is or
is not in an ordinary and regular condition. He does not set
out with his fall like Christianity, nor with his original goodness
as the moralists of another school—he says, " There are no contradictions in nature,"[2] which in another sense we also say, while
we acknowledge that its powers and their arrangement have not
changed, but that their object is changed. As to the worth of
man he appears to judge of it as moderate. In his opinion, there
is no being quite virtuous or quite vicious.[3] He laments over the
pollution of our virtues, and agrees " that there is no soul so
strong as to be exempted from littleness."[4] He has even here
and there very sharp remarks on human nature—sayings which
almost surpass La Rochefoucauld :—

" Those who think that they have no need of others become
intractable."[5]

" The most part of men at the bottom of their heart despise
virtue, few glory."[6]

" Men have the wish to be serviceable, so far as they have it in
their power."[7]

[1] This was written in 1833.—*Editors.*   [2] Maxime, 289.
[3] Introduction. Livre iii., § xliv.   [4] Ibid. Livre iii., § xlv.
[5] Maxime, 83.   [6] Ibid. 353.   [7] Ibid. 81.

He even believes that the world grows worse:—

"The world is like an old man, who preserves all the desires of youth, but who is ashamed of them, and lets no one know, either because he is undeceived about the worth of many things, or because he wishes to appear so."[1]

Vauvenargues, then, cares little about balancing the account of human nature, he wishes, apart from anything else, to go forward and take advantage of whatever resources remain to him. He establishes the reality of virtue, but without inquiring what it is, and declares, that whether it be referred to interest, to reason or to the heart, it is no more possible to confound it with vice, than health with sickness; "Virtue," says he, "consists principally in goodness and in vigour of mind."[2] But it is in the middle of a paragraph, and in a manner almost accidental, that he threw out this definition. He even goes so far as to demonstrate that virtue is the end of man's destiny.[3] But he takes away all the force of this principle, by abolishing conscience. Without denying it formally, he treats it with so much contempt, that it would be much better not to acknowledge it—"Conscience is the most changeable rule."[4] "Conscience is presumptuous in the strong, timid in the weak and unfortunate, restless in the indecisive, etc., an instrument of the feeling which rules us, and of the opinions which govern us."[5]

Vauvenargues places the seat of virtue in the heart, and in the good and beneficent affections.[6] It is a very creditable notion, but false, because it is incomplete. Beneficent affections are not virtue. *Virtue* signifies *force, resistance;* a man is not virtuous because he has good feelings; he is virtuous when, in the performance of duty, he succeeds in combating his irregular desires. Obedience alone constitutes moral *good* and morality.

On this subject two observations present themselves.

The first is, that man, whatever he may say or do, cannot deny the notion of duty. Vauvenargues himself occasionally acknowledged it. But establish the existence of the duty in relation to a single point, acknowledge that you owe something to another, or that another owes something to you, instantly the duty becomes the sovereign principle. If the idea of duty exists

---

[1] Maxime, 327.   [2] Ibid. 296.
[3] Pratiquons la vertu ; c'est tout. Premier discours sur la gloire.
[4] Maxime, 133.   [5] Ibid. 135.   [6] Introduction. Livre iii , § xliii.

anywhere, it is that which is the foundation of morality. For this purpose, we may refer you to a book, and to a passage in that book, which manifests this truth with more authority and vigour than any man could do. On opening the Bible we see a single law and a single prohibition expressed by the simplest of emblems. But it is always a *law* and a *prohibition*, and it required the mean and scoffing spirit of the last century to turn into ridicule the most striking symbol of the most profound truths— it is that it has not pleased God to be worshipped without being obeyed. God furnishes to the obedience of man a single exercise, but by this one rule duty enters into the world. In the second place, we remark, that if virtue consisted in feeling, it would have no peculiar essence, but would evaporate, so to speak, in the clashing of interests and individualities. Feeling belongs to an individual; it urges each of us singly to certain acts; each of us has his good or bad affections, or rather, each has some good or bad affections. In the midst of this conflict, where will be the identity, were the rule of duty once removed?

But if virtue does not exist without obedience, it does not consist entirely in obedience. There is a rule which we must first know, as it is imposed from without, and which we must then observe in love; in other words, virtue must end in being absorbed in affection. " Moral truth is only realized and completed in the man, who by the road to the good arrives at the beautiful, that is to say, by the feeling of duty arrives at the feeling of love. Love, which only desires to elevate itself, and only obeys itself, instinctive love, which has not crossed the defile of conscience, love which comes before duty, does not constitute, as a whole, a moral being; not more, at least, than the duty which is not resolved into love. These two elements are necessary, and in the order which I have mentioned." [1]

It is very rare, moreover, for man to arrive at a point in which virtue is not to him more than a pleasure. It was so in his state of innocence before his will was detached from the divine will. It may be, that he who on entering upon his Christian career only performed his duty with reluctance, comes at a later period to fulfil it with love, but it is also possible, and most fre-

---

[1] M. Vinet here quotes from himself. See the Studies of French Literature in the Nineteenth Century. Tome ii., p. 507.—*Editors*.

quently happens, that even to the last, duty is painful in itself, although rendered agreeable by the feeling of gratitude towards God. Before the Fall, there was no obedience, properly so called, no obedience at least which had any selfish feeling; love absorbed all, and the human soul exerted itself in communion with God. Now, the idea and the feeling, the duty and the affection, are two distinct things. But the great end of Christianity is to unite us to God anew, to transform duty into feeling, and to teach us to love what we ought to do, and to do what we ought to love. Perfect harmony supposes two distinct beings, but so united, that there is no longer any separation. Man by himself could not recover the harmony that was lost between duty and affection, and it was the work of Jesus Christ to re-establish it. His life and death have accomplished the mysterious marriage between law and feeling. By his example, He has, no doubt, rendered the law more majestic; but it is not only for the promulgation of a new law that He appeared in the world. He came to present God to man in a new aspect, and to make him understand and feel that God is the true name of happiness, and that to love God is to love happiness. According to the beautiful expression of Scripture, Jesus has rendered the law of God "good, acceptable, and perfect."[1] *Good* and *perfect*, reason tells us so, *acceptable* (*agrèable*), it is love alone that makes it such. When I meet with a mind which gratitude urges to fulfil the divine will, a mind that acts, because it loves, I repeat it, for this soul the law is not abolished. Obedience, though easy and spontaneous, does not the less on that account remain the fundamental element of virtue.

But among moralists, some reject the feelings of the heart, and are satisfied with mere obedience, while others resolve all morality into the feeling of love, and reject obedience. Both are equally wrong—both have only reached the half of the truth, agreeable, no doubt, but still only the half, and in morality, errors are so much the more dangerous as they come nearer the truth. A mind somewhat honest does not easily allow itself to be abused by gross errors, it is more likely to be seduced by such as are agreeable.

We may observe this matter in its progress. Man was originally

---

[1] Rom. xii. 2.

subject to God, but he murmured at his dependance, and cast off God, yet conscience remained, and with the view of being entirely sovereign, he cast off conscience, and made virtue consist in feeling. Feeling is still *we*, but conscience is no longer *we*, it is absent from us.

What follows is still more true. Vauvenargues defends the reality of virtue against those who refer it to custom ; he refers it to nature. He does not mean that we see in nature a mere version of custom. He gets this thought in Pascal, that what we take for nature is often nothing else than a primary custom.[1] " A maxim very true," observes Vauvenargues, " yet before there was a primary custom, our souls existed and had their inclinations, which laid the foundation of their nature ; and those who reduce every thing to opinion and habit, do not understand what they say; every custom previously implies nature, and every error truth."[2]

He sees in nature a guide—if not absolutely a sure guide to morality, at least surer than reason—to which, in this view, he only attributes very subordinate functions: " Reason deceives us more frequently than nature."[3] " The mind does not discover to us virtue."[4]

He observes, however, that " reason and feeling take counsel together, and supply each other's defects. Whosoever only consults one of the two, and renounces the other, inconsiderately deprives himself of a part of the assistance which has been given to us for the direction of our conduct."[5]

He points out more particularly the feeling in which virtue ought to consist. In his opinion, " the preference of general to personal interest is the only definition worthy of virtue, and fitted to fix its meaning."[6] " In order that a thing may be regarded as good by society as a whole, it must tend to the advantage of society as a whole; and that it may be regarded as an evil, it must tend to its ruin. This is the grand characteristic of moral good and evil."[7] Vauvenargues here confounds the result with the end. The principle which he lays down is no doubt beautiful in theory, but I do not know whether it is easy to apply it in prac-

---

[1] I much fear that this nature is itself only a primary custom, as custom is a second nature. (Pascal, Pensées, partie i. Art. vi., § xix.)

[2] Reflexions sur divers sujets, ii.   [3] Maxime, 123.   [4] Ibid. 516.

[5] Maxime, 150.   [6] Introduction. Livre iii., § xliii.   [7] Ibid.

tice. In one sense, every act of virtue contributes to the common
good; but how many virtuous actions are suggested and performed without any thought of the general interest!

On this account, it will be asked, May not vices contribute to
the general interest? Vauvenargues foresaw the objection, and
this is his answer:—

" In one sense, that is very true; but we must allow that the
good produced by vice is always mixed with great evils. . . . In
truth, virtue does not completely satisfy all our passions; but if
we had no vice, we would not have these passions to satisfy, and
we would do from duty what we do from ambition, pride, and
avarice. . . . When vice wishes to procure some great advantage
for the world, in order to take admiration by surprise, it acts like
virtue, because that is the true and natural means of doing good;
but that good which vice performs is neither its object nor its
end." [1]

After such remarks, we are surprised to find in Vauvenargues
a maxim of this sort: " Let us take the aid of bad motives to
strengthen ourselves for great designs," a contradiction arising
from the absence of Christianity. The *virtue* of Vauvenargues
has no relation but to society, and has no other sphere than this
present state. Christians, on the contrary, know that the end of
living is not merely the production of external good, but the
goodness of the inner man—that goodness which is realized by
the condition of a soul truly good. The good done by us derives
its highest value from the fact, that it is the testimony of the
goodness existing within us. Society esteems us according to
our actions; another judge will form an estimate of what we are;
the condition of our moral being renders us capable of holding
communion with God.

Vauvenargues concluded, that in this preference of general
interest, personal interest is not really sacrificed—it is always
found entire in the performance of duty. He is not, however,
by any means a utilitarian; the idea of virtue in relation to self-
interest was very far from his mind—he censures a convenient
morality: " Some authors treat of morality as men treat of the
new architecture, in which they particularly require convenience." [2] " Let us do generously, and without calculation, all

¹ Introduction. Livre iii., § xliii.   ² Maxime, 29.

the good to which our hearts are attracted, we cannot be the dupe of any virtue." [1]

We may observe in passing, the beauty of this expression *tenter*,[2] commonly used in a bad sense, when it is appropriated to what is good. We may here apply to Vauvenargues one of his own most celebrated sayings : " Great thoughts come from the heart." [3] Never, indeed, will true virtue become a mere matter of calculation, in which the expense of to-day must be carried to the account of to-morrow. The Christian knows that he will be abundantly repaid, but he seeks only a recompense in his heart, if God dwells there and re-establishes its harmony by His presence.

Vauvenargues crowns the fine reflections now quoted with this admirable thought : " It is a proof of littleness of mind, when a distinction is always made between what is estimable and what is amiable. Great minds naturally love what is worthy of their esteem." [4]

Man was born for action. In all positions, and with all opinions, it matters not, he must act. It is our destiny and our happiness. In the view of Vauvenargues, virtue essentially consists in action : " The falsest of all philosophy is that which, under pretext of delivering men from the entanglement of passion, advises them to indulge in idleness, carelessness, and forgetfulness of themselves." [5] " Man can only have enjoyment in activity, and only loves it." [6] " Fire, air, spirit, light—all live by action. Hence the intercourse and connection of all beings—hence the unity and harmony in the universe ; yet we find that this very fruitful law of nature is a vice in man ; and because he is obliged to obey it, and is unable to subsist in a state of repose, we conclude that he is out of his place." [7]

Vauvenargues alludes to Pascal and his chapter on the *Misery of Man*. We have elsewhere discussed the opinion of Pascal ; [8] we may here again admit that this great genius has not sufficiently shared in the impulse which urges man to act, and in the necessity of action for the development of his powers. It is still a portion of truth becoming an error, and detached from the gene-

---

[1] Reflexions sur divers sujets, xix.
[2] The author here refers to the phrase *qui tente nos coeurs,* in the preceding paragraph ; but the English idiom does not admit of a literal translation.
[3] Maxime, 127.　　　[4] Ibid. 43.　　　[5] Ibid. 145.　　　[6] Ibid. 199.
[7] Maxime, 198.　　　[8] Etudes sur Blaise Pascal.

ral aspect in which Christianity presents it. To wish to prove, according to it, that contemplation takes the place of action, is to impute to it an extreme opinion, which it never maintained. Christianity may be compared to atmospheric air, composed of several elements, of which each, by itself, kills, but which, united, gives us life. It is from the centre of the Gospel that we must draw our life, and by a single effort seize upon all truth.

It is action, according to Vauvenargues, that we must oppose to discouragement : " Do not amuse yourself with complaining —nothing is less useful; but, first of all, look around you—you have sometimes resources at hand of which you are ignorant. If you discover none, instead of losing time in vain lamentation, venture to take a greater flight—a turn of fancy somewhat bold often opens up to us paths on which the light is fully shed. . . . Let those believe who wish to believe it, that men are miserable amid the perplexities of great designs—it is from idleness and meanness that virtue suffers."[1]

In a higher sphere, religion gives the same recommendations. It does not aim at an idle humility.

Vauvenargues does not understand that the fear of committing faults should keep us from acting : " We must not be afraid of committing faults, the greatest fault of all is to deprive ourselves of experience. . . . . . He who would train his mind for great achievements, should risk the committing of faults, and not let himself be discouraged, or fear discovery."[2]

Action, and consequently virtue, does not pass away with the breath of passion. According to Vauvenargues, it is the wind which will swell our sails. The passions must play a great part in a well ordered life : " We owe, perhaps, to the passions the greatest advantages of the mind."[3] " The passions have taught men reason."[4] " Would we have cultivated the arts without the passions ?"[5] " The mind is the eye of the soul, not its power. Its power is in the heart; that is to say, in the passions. The most enlightened reason does not give us the power of acting and willing. Is it enough to have good sight to walk ? must we not also have feet, and the will, along with the power, of moving them ?"[6]

This is an idea very philosophical in all its simplicity of ex-

[1] Reflexions sur divers sujets, xxiii. § 10.   [2] Ibid. xviii.   [3] Maxime, 151.
[4] Maxime, 154.   [5] Ibid. 153.   [6] Ibid. 149.

pression. All that, however, is perfectly true and lucid; the term *passions* only is badly chosen, as its popular sense involuntarily refers to the mind, and, in the case of many readers, disturbs the clearness of their thoughts. Vauvenargues, besides, who does not always sufficiently weigh his terms, and does not avoid a little confusion, speaks also, as we have seen, of passions in the popular sense, and thus appears to contradict the good that he has said of them. He even doubts the nature of the passions, and almost recalls the praise which he had given :—

" Is it power in man to have passions, or is it insufficiency and weakness ? Is it greatness of soul to be exempt from passion, or mediocrity of genius ? or is every thing mixed with weakness, and power with greatness and littleness ?"[1]

If, peradventure, these passions, which Vauvenargues has shown to be the source of all greatness in man, were in themselves a weakness, how would the author defend what he said so positively, " that there is no contradiction in nature ?[2]" and he speaks here of human nature. Instead of *passion*, he should have said *affection*, any affection whatever—the prevailing affection—and all would have been clear. We even go farther than Vauvenargues ; we regard a strong affection as the life of the soul, which does not live without emotion. Taken in this sense, this emotion is perfectly consistent with Christianity, which absorbs the law in love, and tends to rule the entire life, by a feeling at once imperious and calm, because it is from heaven. The love of God is the only passion formed to suit the perfection of our soul, and the only feeling with respect to which it is permitted to be exclusive and unlimited. Life has only unity from the feeling which regulates it, and entirely enters into it, as heat penetrates the bodies subjected to its influence. Every man, who thinks of his life as based on one thought ; every man, whose system has only one idea for its root, will have always something stiff, cold, and incomplete. But, when love gains the mastery over the life of the Christian, then it is elevated and developed, with the majestic unity of a temple consecrated to the Lord.

Among all the passions, that which is most strongly recommended by Vauvenargues is the love of glory : " What are the virtues of those who despise glory ?"[3] " Have they deserved

---

[1] Maxime, 340.   [2] Ibid. 289.   [3] Introduction. Livre ii., § xxvi.

it ?" He sometimes makes glory and virtue entirely one: "It is a strange thing that so many distrust virtue and glory."[1] "If men had not loved glory, they would not have had sufficient spirit nor virtue to deserve it."[2]

We conceive that he has raised to a high degree the passion for glory. He does not bestow upon man the approbation of God, and it was therefore necessary to supply it with something else. Take away the satisfaction arising from the senses, and from interest, and there only remains the approbation of our equals. Glory, indeed, that primary and essential feeling of our nature, is only vicious, because we have turned it away from its true object. Pascal himself remarks, in the desire of the approbation of our equals, some remains of that glory with which man was crowned before the fall.

But, when we come to the application—when we see, as Vauvenargues says, that "those who despise glory pique themselves on dancing well,"[3] and when we think how many approve what is evil, and how many wicked actions may be committed to please them, we may perceive how far this motive may lead them. There are individual and general errors. A whole nation may be the dupe of a great sophism, and there the man of the strongest and most enlightened mind is nationally a fool.

On the other hand, it is pretended that the internal testimony, the approbation of conscience, might suffice to conduct man to virtue. 1 scarcely believe it, if at the bottom of his conscience; if behind it, man, a butt to calumny, does not discern a being superior to him—God—I do not think that the consolations of this conscience can satisfy him. In a matter of this sort, it seems strange to quote Voltaire; and yet he says, " My avenger is in heaven."

Yes, we must have approbation beyond ourselves—we must have the approbation of God. Harmony between the divine will and ours, sympathy between God and us, is the glory which comes from Him, and which will have a good effect on our virtue. Three thoughts constantly accompany it : God is perfect, and only approves in us what tends to perfection ; God sees every thing, and judges without mistake ; He penetrates into the inmost part of our being, and lays bare our real worth.

[1] Reflexions sur divers sujets, xvi.   [2] Maxime, 152.
[3] Introduction. Livre ii., § xxvii.

In short, God is a jealous God; He desires all glory to return to himself. He refuses every thing of His to any one whatever, that determines it in His own favour, and appropriates the least portion of the good which it has been given Him to do. Humility is the only garb which He admits in His presence. Men praise modesty; but, when modesty is sincere, it is humility. It is thus, at bottom, humility which they praise and love; and where is this humility, if not with him who seeks the glory that comes from God?

Can it be discovered by evidence whether Vauvenargues attaches his morality to any other thing than to nature and society? As to that point, we must hear him speak concerning death. He does not express himself on this subject lightly, or with affected indifference. He says: "The necessity of dying is the bitterest of our afflictions,"[1] an avowal more simple, and perhaps more energetic in its expressions than the well-known saying of Rochefoucauld :—" Neither the sun nor death can be steadily looked at." Vauvenargues does not believe in the contempt of death, and censures those who wish to persuade us that the thought of death does not excite terror. " Restless men, trembling for the most trifling concerns, affect to brave death."[2] Yet he does not wish that the thought of death should any way influence our life, whence, without meaning it, he confesses a contradiction in the condition of mankind. If death be a necessity, how can it be to us an object of affliction and terror, so far as we are in the harmony of our being? He has not attempted to answer this question; the remedy which he advises, is not to think of death.

"To achieve great things, we must live, as if we should never die."[3] By *great things*, we apparently understand things different from Vauvenargues. " The thought of death deceives us, for it makes us forget how to live."[4] No; but to live in a certain way. The thought of Vauvenargues is true of the view of death without any view beyond it. It appears, at least, that we should live differently, if we judge of it by the distress which the approach of that moment produces in the mind. Vauvenargues explains this distress by physical causes, by the failure of the senses, and by the weakness of the nerves, and declares

[1] Maxime, 524.   [2] Ibid. 603.   [3] Ibid. 142.   [4] Ibid. 143.

"that the conscience of the dying is a calumny on their life."[1]
A new contradiction, for he understands by this a distress
different from that of the senses. But these contradictions are
proofs of his candour. Why, indeed, should dying men be distressed if they had no reason for being so? It is much more
natural to think that at that moment, conscience accuses justly.
Vauvenargues himself understood how unbelievers may be
troubled. "The intrepidity of a dying unbeliever may not
secure him from some *distress* if he reasons thus: I have been
deceived a thousand times respecting my plainest interests, and
may have been deceived too regarding religion. Now, I have
neither time nor strength to investigate it, and I die."[2]

I say that it is not this speculative uncertainty which should
trouble him, if he had the inner consciousness of being before
God what he ought to be. The real ground of his distress is in
his conscience, which tells him that if religion be true, he is not
secure.

This brings us to the religion of Vauvenargues—he was a
deist. In his works, there are many indirect attacks against
Christianity. "Men distrust the customs and traditions of their
ancestors less than their reason."[3]

"The strength or weakness of our belief depends more on our
courage than on our knowledge. All those who scoff at augurs
have not always more understanding than those who believe in
them."[4] "It is easy to deceive the ablest men if you propose
to them things which surpass their understanding, and interest
their heart."[5] "There is nothing of which fear and hope may
not convince men."[6]

How did La Harpe, who ranks Vauvenargues among Christian moralists, not observe such sayings? He quotes with complacency the following passages:—

"If every thing terminated with death, it would be extravagance not to apply ourselves entirely to make the most of life,
since we should only have the present; but we believe in a
future, and leave it to chance, a thing quite inconceivable."[7]
"Our passions are not distinct from ourselves. There are some
which are altogether the foundation and substance of the soul.
. . . That does not excuse a man from resisting his habits,

[1] Maxime, 136. [2] Ibid. 322. [3] Ibid. 317. [4] Ibid. 318.
[5] Maxime, 319. [6] Ibid. 320. [7] Reflexions sur divers sujets.

and none ought to be either discouraged or grieved. *God is Almighty.* Sincere virtue does not abandon its votaries, the very vices of a man well-born may be turned to his glory."[1]

The whole of Vauvenargues' book, abounding in thoughts, which amount to the denial of revelation, protests against the advantage that some would take of these passages, in which I can only see the language of accommodation well suited to the prudence of the author. I believe that he speaks there on the principles of Christians, unless we be disposed to impute to him moments of inconclusive reasoning, to which I willingly agree. He was, however, more just than the deists of his time, and censured and despised the arrogance of unbelief, and the jests of which Christianity was the object :—

" We must not cast ridicule on opinions that are respected, for by this we offend their adherents without confuting them."[2] " Unbelief has its enthusiasts as well as superstition."[3] " Those who combat the prejudices of the people, think that they do not belong to the people. He who framed at Rome an argument against the sacred chickens, regarded himself perhaps as a philosopher."[4] " M. de Turenne, the wisest and bravest among men, respected religion ; and a vast number of obscure men rank themselves as persons of genius and of strong minds, merely because they despise it."[5]

This is a kind of homage paid to religion. Vauvenargues' book contains some instances of it still more direct :—" The public good requires great sacrifices, and cannot be equally diffused among all men. Religion, which supplies the defects of human affairs, secures enviable indemnities to those who seem to us aggrieved."[6]

" Newton, Pascal, Bossuet, Racine, Fenelon—that is to say, the most illustrious men in the most philosophic age, and in the power of their spirit and their time, believed in Jesus Christ, and the great Condé, when he was dying, repeated these noble words : Yes, we shall see God as he is, *sicuti est, facie ad faciem.*"[7]

We cannot help speaking here of a remarkable piece of Vauvenargues, his *Meditation on Faith*, and of the prayer, which follows it. This piece has given rise to different suppositions or

[1] Introduction. Livre ii., § xli. [2] Maxime, 535. [3] Ibid. 537. [4] Ibid. 325.
[5] Maxime, 538. [6] Introduction. Livre iii., § xliii. [7] Maxime, 605.

explanations. According to the first, Vauvenargues might have been willing to show how men can write eloquently on religion without being convinced of its truth. According to the second, he might have chosen a religious subject to exercise himself in a form of diction, for which he had a fancy, the introduction of verses of different measures into prose. Always when his style is elevated, it takes this form, thus in the *Eulogy* on the young de Seytres, and in ccii. of his *Reflexions*. According to the third explanation, this piece would prove that Vauvenargues was a Christian. According to a fourth, which we have adopted, there is a play of wit, and, at the same time, in some respects, real sentiment. He may have been caught at his sport, and drawn on by the beauty of his subject, may have felt that lively regret which he has so eloquently depicted : " August religion ! sweet and noble belief, how can men live without thee ? Is it not quite clear that something is wanting to men, when their pride rejects thee?"[1]

More than one philosopher, perhaps, partakes in his heart of the regret of Vauvenargues; all those, at least, who have become Christians, would willingly take up his language. But a Christian who—a thing unheard of—would leave the faith which gives peace, to return to philosophical doubts, would never exclaim, " August philosophy ! sweet and noble belief, how can men live without thee ? "

Thus, then, in the whole work of Vauvenargues, there is no system nor proportion, but a number of contradictions, which do not prove the want of sincerity, far from it, but the want of arrangement in the mode of thinking. This makes him more evidently resort to the necessity of going back to the first principle of all things. We may remark, that no morality from man's hand has any consistency, harmony, or proportion. We should not think it strange that all such is faulty in its principle ; but as the logical faculty furnishes a middle term, by which we may easily reach consistency and proportion, we ask how it happens that these qualities are wanting in so many different theories, and that Christianity presents the only system of morality well connected and consistent with itself ?

Among all the others, the morality of Vauvenargues is remark-

[1] Meditation sur la foi.

able for its inconsistency. But this perpetual vacillation forms, in my opinion, the principal merit of his book, and this is precisely the reason why I like it. His sincerity does not fail before any of the inconsistencies of his thoughts; he is conscious of it, and adds more to it. He has a number of valuable observations, tangents to the circle of truth. He has only sentiments, but some of them are admirable. He diminishes and often contradicts his thoughts. The idea fails him, because the first principle is wanting. Sometimes he denies it and sometimes affirms it. The perfect consistency of a book would lead me to suspect the sincerity of an author, because there are subjects on which it is either impossible or artificial, and especially when the first principle is wanting.

The candour of Vauvenargues has an inexpressible charm—it is the characteristic feature of his individuality—he may be called the *candid Vauvenargues*. He has candour of mind as well as of character, and this furnishes the key to his excellencies and defects. His mind knows imperfectly, but is always sincere.

Vauvenargues was not well informed, which means two things: first, that he had little knowledge, and, secondly, that his knowledge was by no means organized, and he was deficient in philosophical training. He had very little acquaintance with men or books; his knowledge was almost intuitive, and in that way it was admirable. He had thought for himself; and for certain minds this is an advantage. He says somewhere, " Things which we know best are those which we have never learned;" [1] and elsewhere, " Experience in the world enables us to think naturally, and acquaintance with the sciences to think profoundly." [2]

Vauvenargues had properly neither the one nor the other, but was acquainted with himself. La Motte said, he was new, because he was natural. Candour is to the soul what nature is to the understanding; when a man is candid he cannot fail to be profound. The sayings of children are often the most profound. It is certain that, to an upright mind, all things present themselves more purely when they are not perplexed with set forms, provided that these minds join strength to uprightness. Men such as Vauvenargues are children in the republic of letters; question them, the truth readily proceeds from their lips.

[1] Maxime 488.   [2] Introduction. Livre ii., § xxviii.

It is remarkable that the greater part of the men of talents, who have given a lively impulse to human thought, had little taste for science. They are somewhat irregular and adventurous; they are not troops of the line, but light troops and sharp-shooters, and they must be sent forward to make discoveries. On the other hand, it must be admitted that their discoveries are sometimes imaginary. Without doubt, it occasionally happens to them as to the child in *Moses saved :*—" There, the sprightly child, to the first comer, displays, as something precious, the strange pebble which he picks up at his feet—he takes up a shell, and, transported with joy, artlessly presents it to his mother." And then there is always in such minds a little incoherence and confusion. They are full to overflowing, and yet they have empty spaces. They furnish materials for building. They scarcely construct a perfect edifice. Vauvenargues was deficient in scientific analysis for arriving at precise results. The real point of difficulty sometimes escapes him. His fundamental views are somewhat enveloped in clouds; his particular views sometimes terminate badly, without our being able to say whether their fault is in the expression or in the idea : " We must not easily believe that what nature has made amiable is vicious."[1] " How many virtues and vices are of no consequence."[2] " Inevitable abuses are laws of nature."[3]

In short, the book of Vauvenargues is valuable for a number of plain confessions ; we hear in it a faithful testimony and a clear voice. On the whole, he has not reached the truth ; but no moralist, who is not a Christian, touches it at so many points. Such an author of morality setting out from fixed principles is in general much less true, and much less instructive and even edifying, how strange soever this saying may appear. It is not objective truth which edifies in a work ; it is also subjective truth which resides in the mind of the author. We do not merely read the book of Vauvenargues, we read also his mind.

As a writer, the principles of Vauvenargues are reduced to two. He was convinced that a man must first think for himself :—

" What makes the most part of books on morality so insipid and their authors insincere, is that, weak echoes of one another, they would not venture to bring forward their own maxims and

---

[1] Maxime 122.   [2] Ibid. 555.   [3] Ibid. 26.

their secret sentiments. Thus not only in morality, but on any subject whatever, almost all men pass their lives in speaking and writing what they do not think."[1] "All that we have only thought in regard to others is commonly unnatural."[2]

Many others have said that it was necessary to think *by themselves*, Vauvenargues alone said, *for himself*. The one is the means of the other, but the idea of Vauvenargues is the most profound. He gives elsewhere the example with the rule. It is a point of view quite as dangerous as that in which the author places himself. It is very difficult to remain in the exact line of his own thought in the presence of dispositions which are supposed to be natural to his readers.

In the second place, Vauvenargues recommends men to think with the heart : "Great thoughts come from the heart,"[3] a principle singularly true on all subjects in which sentiment can have any part to play. The heart does not think, but in many cases it determines the point of view from which we think; an elevated sentiment is like a high mountain, from which we take in a wider horizon. And how many great thoughts are only great sentiments of which the mind takes account? How many talents have been expanded by sentiment, how many sprightly spirits by a lively affection! We see how much Vauvenargues thought with his heart.

The chief commendation of Pascal's style may be transferred to Vauvenargues. It is a true style. It is Pascal without his strength and passion. Both have a degree of truth which few literary men have been able to reach. Vauvenargues, indeed, is occasionally somewhat obscure and deficient in correctness, and he has some antiquated expressions. These old forms naturally occurred to his mind from the daily reading of the ancient French authors. But the beauty of his style is that the expression with him is the faithful image of the thought. Each thought, strictly speaking, has only a single expression perfectly adequate to itself, every other errs by too much or too little, or like a picture badly placed, presents only a part of its surface to the light. The single form, necessary to thought, is most beautiful without the assistance of figures or turns of expression; sometimes the writer falls into it at once, when the thought instantaneously

---

[1] Maxime 300.   [2] Ibid. 371.   [3] Ibid. 127.

conceived and quickly apprehended, is immediately seized by its form, and springs forth, so to speak, with it. At other times, the discovery of this pure form only occurs after several attempts, and the rejection of several forms less perfect. We meet with traces of this labour in Rochefoucauld, and also in Vauvenargues. Sometimes the latter arrives, with full spring, at his expression, sometimes he only reaches it by degrees. He wished to be simple, and is only satisfied when he is simple. He says, "when a thought is too weak to bear a simple expression, it is a sign that it should be rejected."[1] He thought that "clearness is the good faith of philosophers,"[2] that the reception which errors obtain, is only due to the artifices of language; "that there are no errors, which do not disappear of themselves when distinctly expressed;"[3] that truth is beautiful in itself, and, in short, that "clearness adorns profound thoughts."[4] We might add to this: and simplicity adorns great thoughts.

Often, indeed, the thought passes away in turns of expression and figures, but these are at times necessary on account of the sterility of language. In the beginning, the primitive and typical language expressed every thing by images; ours, such as it is, contains still a number of images or figures, which long use has transformed into proper expressions. The terms which mark out metaphysical objects, are figures taken from the material world, thus the word (*âme*), the soul, signifies breath or wind.

Vauvenargues has few figures, but he is not entirely deprived of their assistance, and his, from their rarity, are so happy, that we think it impossible to express his ideas otherwise:—"Affable looks adorn the countenances of kings."[5] "The brightness of the morning is not so sweet as the first rays of glory."[6] "The counsels of old age give light without heat, like the wintry sun."[7]

Vauvenargues at times surprises his readers, but in general this feeling is the opposite of that which La Bruyère makes us experience. The latter employs unexpected and singular phraseology to arrive at a common thought. Vauvenargues, on the contrary, often veils under a common expression a thought of high value. Yet the manner of La Bruyère is not absolutely

[1] Maxime 3.   [2] Ibid. 372.   [3] Ibid. 6.   [4] Ibid. 4.
[5] Ibid. 394.   [6] Ibid. 382.   [7] Ibid. 159.

strange to him. We recognise the imitation, or at least the analogous style in such thoughts as these:—" Those who make us buy their honesty, commonly sell to us only their honour."[1] " The man who dresses himself in the morning before eight o'clock to hear a pleading before the judges, or to see pictures exposed at the Louvre, or to be present at the recitation of a play ready to appear, and who piques himself on judging in every department on the works of others, is a person often deficient in judgment and taste."[2] Vauvenargues is not only a distinguished moralist, but a critic, too, of the first order, so much the more interesting as he is simple. He has the boldness of childhood, and ventures to hold his own opinion. Two things especially keep us under subjection, too great distrust of ourselves, and too great pretension to appear independent. Vauvenargues avoids these two extremes, and has an humble courage. This should be the feeling of every author who sets himself to judge of others. In the writings of Vauvenargues, the pieces of criticism are exquisite.

Here are some choice thoughts and profound observations, on which we are happy to rest:—" To punish without necessity is to encroach on the clemency of God."[3] " We quarrel with the unfortunate to excuse ourselves from pitying them."[4] " We have no right to render those miserable whom we cannot render good."[5] " Magnanimity owes no account of its motives to prudence."[6] " A man cannot be just, if he is not humane."[7] " When we feel that we have not wherewithal to make ourselves esteemed by any one, we are very near hating him."[8] " There is only moderate ability in making dupes."[9] " Those who have merely ability, hold in no place the first rank."[10] " No one is subject to more faults than those who act only from reflection."[11] " It is a great sign of mediocrity always to praise moderately."[12] " Those who have not the courage to search for truth amid the rude trials (of familiarity), are far below anything that is great; it is especially base to fear raillery, which helps us to tread under foot our self-love, and blunts, by the habit of suffering, its bashful delicacy."[13] " We ought to console ourselves because

---

[1] Maxime 49.   [2] Ibid. 64.   [3] Ibid. 165.   [4] Ibid. 172.
[5] Ibid. 27.   [6] Ibid. 130.   [7] Ibid. 28.   [8] Ibid. 45.
[9] Ibid. 97.   [10] Ibid. 94.   [11] Ibid. 131.   [12] Ibid. 12.
[13] Reflexions sur divers sujets, xvii.

we have not great talents, as we console ourselves because we have not great places. At heart, we may be above both the one and the other." [1]

XVIII.

MONTESQUIEU.

1689—1755.

I COME now, gentlemen, to a man whom all approach with respect and sympathy—the only one perhaps among the great minds of the eighteenth century, to which I feel a powerful attraction.

Montesquieu is a noble and worthy person, one of those men difficult to be met with amid the loss of our original advantages and the corruption of our civilisation—men, whom it does us good to contemplate, and especially to find in the eighteenth century. His life does not abound in events. Descended from a noble family, Montesquieu prepared himself by hard study for the magistracy; but the natural laws of the heart and mind of man occupied him still more than positive law, and if he studied the codes of nations, it was less as a jurist than as a philosopher. At an early period he was president of the parliament of Bordeaux, but resigned that office afterwards, and was anxious to spend his life in the improvement of his mind. For this purpose he travelled, a thing which the great authors of the seventeenth century scarcely ever did; a spirit of universal benevolence began to be introduced among men of letters. He went through Italy, Germany, and England, which was at that time to make the tour of the world. He gained by it a rich fund of observation, and a breadth of view very superior to his contemporaries. He studied the working of the social machine, which will always continue to be a great mystery. On his return to France, he divided his time between Paris and his chateau de la Brède. At

1 Maxime 68.

Paris he was able to keep himself free, and to resist the allurements of the coteries and of the philosophical movement. It was from the solitude of La Brède that his best works issued—*Reflections on the Causes of the Greatness of the Romans, and of their Decline*, and the *Spirit of Laws*.

His works, at their appearance, procured for him celebrity, consideration, and respect, in the widest sense of the term, in France, and even in Europe. At a later period, however, his death was little felt and scarcely observed. That sun set, without any one condescending to take notice of it: Voltaire was in his apogee, and the philosophical movement in its greatest effervescence.

When you speak to children of a celebrated man, they begin with asking, whether he is *good*. Happy the man, who on this point remains always a child. We cannot withstand a curiosity so natural. So far as it has been granted to our fallen nature to realize this divine character, let us inquire, if Montesquieu was good.

He is depicted in his actions, his whole life bears his portrait, but his death has given to this picture the last stroke of the pencil by revealing the conversations of the man with himself. Every evening he was in the habit of writing his reflections and remarks on his own character, and the freedom and negligence of these confessions show, that they were only intended for himself, or, at most, for his son. After his death this manuscript was printed under the title of *Thoughts*. From the most remarkable of these thoughts, we shall see the faithful representation of his nature. In my opinion, autobiographies of this sort, when they are sincere, are better than a treatise on morals, and here the outline of the author's natural disposition is so much the more interesting as it is confirmed by his works. From the first, we are struck with the feelings which he particularly notes: " I awaken in the morning with a secret joy at seeing the light; I look upon the light with a kind of rapture, and all the rest of the day I am contented ; I pass the night without wakening, and in the evening when I go to bed, a kind of torpor prevents me from reflecting."[1]

He was, according to his own statement, *born happy* and endowed by Providence with a perfect organization. He possessed

---

[1] Pensées diverses: Portrait de Montesquieu par lui-même.

a constant serenity of mind, with the rare, perhaps singular, privilege of joining to lively enjoyment and to moderate desires a very weak susceptibility of pain, which proves the constitution to be the most pleasant and the best regulated :—

"I have the ambition necessary to make me take part in the things of this life, and have nothing to disgust me with the position which has been assigned to me by nature." "When I enjoy a pleasure, I am delighted with it, and always wonder at my having sought it with so much indifference." "I have never almost felt vexation, and still less weariness." "I have never felt any annoyance, which an hour's reading did not dispel."[1]

Indignation, with him, is entirely intellectual; he is very indignant, but is never irritated. Pity, a feeling which he possesses in a high degree, produces a lively emotion without ever depressing him. "I have never," he says, "seen tears shed without a feeling of compassion."[2] His life was an admirable commentary on these words, but he buried his acts of generosity in the most profound secrecy. The grave has revealed several of them. A passage in his Persian Letters appears to express well the natural tenderness of his heart:—

"I have the feelings of humanity for the unhappy as if none but they were men; and even the great, towards whom I find my heart as stone, while they are in prosperity, I love when they are fallen. And indeed during their prosperity, what need have they of tenderness? It looks too much like equality. They are fonder of respect, which requires no return. But as soon as they are fallen from their high station, nothing but our lamentations can make them recall the idea of their greatness."[3]

How rare is it to see in the same individual so much sympathy for human nature, and never an emotion which implies mental distress!

Montesquieu has little taste for glory and little need to shine; he is perhaps the only writer that could have said of himself: "I am, I believe, the only man, who has published books without having obtained the reputation of wit."[4]

He joins to it anxiety for fortune : " I have greatly improved my lands ; but I felt that it was rather from a certain idea of

[1] Pensées diverses : Portrait de Montesquieu par lui-même.   [2] Ibid.
[3] Lettres Persannes.   Lettre cxxvi.   [4] Pensées diverses : Portrait.

skill, which that gave me, than from the idea of becoming richer."[1] "To investigate our interests too strictly is to apply a sponge to all the virtues." "We must look upon our fortune as our slave, but we must not destroy our slave."[2] "I am," he says elsewhere, "much attached to friendship;"[3] and he adds, in another place, that he never lost a friend.[4]

He pardons easily, but expresses contempt strongly : "I pardon readily, for this reason, that I feel no hatred; in my opinion hatred is painful."[5] "I have always despised those whom I did not esteem."[6]

A mind so lofty would naturally have little taste for raillery, that little exercise of little minds. Montesquieu had an aversion to it, and, with the mind that he possessed, as a Frenchman, that is no small matter. La Bruyère calls banter, *poverty of understanding.*[7] Montesquieu defines raillery to be "an exercise of the mind contrary to one's good nature ;"[8] and he says of himself, "I never had any pleasure in ridiculing others."[9]

He engaged in no quarrel, but, when attacked, he defends himself with dignity.

To this individual benevolence he joins attachment to the public good. He has the mind of a citizen in the highest degree. This love of country, which in so many men is artificial, and in many others is transmitted by tradition or example—an instinct frequently mechanical, and not spontaneous—in Montesquieu exists full of life : "I had a natural love for the good and the honour of my country. I always felt a secret joy when any regulation was made which tended to the common good."[10]

But Montesquieu goes farther; his zeal for his country is without that egoism which would willingly sacrifice the rest of the world to his native land. The universal benevolence which others have in the mind, he had in the heart : "When I travelled in foreign countries, I attached myself to them as to mine own; I took part in their fortune, and would have wished them to be in a flourishing condition."[11] "If I knew any thing that would be useful to me, and hurtful to my family, I would reject it with all my heart. If I knew any thing that would be useful to my

[1] Pensées diverses : Portrait.   [2] Pensées diverses varietés.
[3] Pensées diverses : Portrait.   [4] Ibid.   [5] Ibid.   [6] Ibid.
[7] La Bruyère, Les Caractères, chap. v.   De la societé et de la conversation.
[8] Pensées diverses varietés.   [9] Pensées diverses : Portrait.   [10] Ibid.   [11] Ibid.

family, but prejudicial to my country, I would strive to forget
it. If I knew anything useful to my country, and injurious
to Europe and the human race, I would look upon it as a
crime."[1]

In short, Montesquieu knew himself well. Every thing in these
confessions reveals a character pacific, equitable, and indulgent,
and a benevolent, and even tender heart, without impatience or
violent desires, and open to all that is great. There is no littleness, except a little weakness for his name, and he avows it :
" I am making a very foolish thing be drawn out, that is, my
genealogy."[2] " Although my name is neither good nor bad, as
it has only about a hundred and fifty years of proved nobility,
yet I cling to it, and would be the man to make entails."[3]

His serenity is very remarkable. I wish I could affirm that
all the minds of the first order have been serene ; but the most
part, and these, too, the greatest, have possessed this high quality.
Greatness is serene, sublime, and peaceful. As in the atmosphere there is a clear zone, to which clouds never come, so, in
the moral world, there is a region which storms cannot trouble,
and, when they enter into it, then it is an exception to the rule.

One trait more : Montesquieu, who loved at once the world
and retirement, enjoyed society, though, in one sense, he was not
suited to it : " When I was in the world I loved it, as if I could
not endure retirement ; and, when I was at my estate, I never
thought of the world."[4] He enjoyed it in a passive way, for he
was deficient in the gift of conversation. Several men of genius
of the eighteenth century suffered from the same defect ; neither
Buffon nor Rousseau were eloquent or agreeable in common
conversation. Among all these master spirits, Voltaire alone in
that showed himself powerful. This is a mystery which, in
reference to each of them, had different causes. Too many
ideas presented themselves at once to Rousseau, and, in combining them, he lost the moment for repartee. To Voltaire, on
the contrary, ideas came in sufficient number, but without confusion, and the expression of them was clear, lively, and rapid.
Buffon, on his part, only showed his power in reflection ; his
first view was not extensive. There was another thing in Montesquieu's character—he was timid. Society annoyed him. Was

[1] Pensées diverses : Portrait.   [2] Ibid.   [3] Ibid.   [4] Ibid.

it self-love, vanity, or modesty? This is what he says of himself:—

" Timidity has been the scourge of my whole life ; it seemed to blunt my senses, tie my tongue, cloud my thoughts, and disorder my expressions. I was less subject to this weakness in the company of men of ability than in the presence of fools, because I had the hope that they would understand me, and this gave me some confidence."[1]

According to this statement, his timidity was not, it appears to me, so much a feature in his character as a defect in the form of his understanding. He was almost destitute of the power of connecting his thoughts, when a somewhat extended development was necessary. What he wrote, too, was fragmentary ; the gift of seizing and representing a vast whole may give great assurance to those who write, and, above all, to those who speak. Montesquieu, in conversation, had brilliant thoughts, but they stood alone ; they rushed to his lips, and there they often remained.

The moral doctrine of Montesquieu differs little from the ancient stoicism, but he has not laid it down in a systematic form. His own nature was his true system. Nevertheless, he loses no opportunity of boasting of stoicism in general :—

" No philosopher has ever made men feel the sweetness of virtue, and the dignity of their being better, than Marcus Antoninus ; he affects the heart, enlarges the soul, and elevates the mind."[2] " If I could for a moment cease to think that I am a Christian, I could not possibly avoid ranking the destruction of the sect of Zeno among the misfortunes that have befallen the human race."[3]

Stoicism is that high and stern doctrine, of which the peculiarity is to consider duty and virtue as the only spring of human conduct, and to make no mention of pleasure and pain. It pursues its end without deviating either to the right or left, and holds difficulties and dangers to have no existence. To a certain extent this doctrine is true—absolute obedience to the rule of duty is in itself excellent. It would be the half of Christianity, if Christianity were capable of being divided into fractions. But it is not to God that this obedience is rendered ; it is, in prin-

[1] Pensées diverses : Portrait.   [2] Pensées diverses : Des Anciens.
[3] Esprit des Lois. Livre xxiv., chap. x.

ciple, merely obedience to the man himself. In this system, man somehow becomes his own god. Humility is banished from his mind; stoicism commands man to do what he ought, but it does not point out either what is deficient, or how it should be supplied. By leaving him ignorant of his weakness, it deprives him of the help which he would have obtained from God.

Men have been true stoics from constitution. Strong minds, in certain relations, were able to make very high attainments; but yet they had some weaknesses, of which they were ignorant, or which they cherished, and their virtues were counteracted by pride. Without doing any injustice, we may repeat what Descartes said of them : " Frequently, that which they call by the beautiful name of virtue, is only insensibility, or pride, or despair, or parricide." Voltaire says of stoicism : " It swells the soul, but does not feed it."

If Christianity did not exist, the stoics would furnish some fine specimens of the human race ; but how much more would their doctrine leave men unhappy? Instead of help in their weakness, and consolation in their sufferings, they would only hear a voice constantly crying to them, Go forward! go forward!—But I am infirm, wounded, paralysed.—It is of no consequence; go forward—*it is your duty!* This is the only moving power presented by stoicism. Christianity tells us also to go forward, but it stretches out its hand to him who is weary, and supports him who cannot walk ; it alone terminates and unites that circle which is always left half open, and which no human doctrine is capable of completing.

On this subject we may remember, once for all, first, that we apply the term *spring,* or *motive* (*mobile*), to whatever gives to the soul the impulse and the power to act ; in the second place, that there is in the morality of men two classes of motives. The first refers to fear and hope—gross motives, no doubt—but their importance must be acknowledged in the actual state of society. From a more elevated point of view, however, we could not found a morality worthy of the name merely on fear and hope, since we would only make from these slaves or egoists. Man necessarily, in his quality of a moral individual, requires a profound interest, an interest of long continuance, which takes possession of the whole heart. This is what all true doctrine should furnish to him—all religion deserving the name. This living power is only complete in love—love on the part of him who demands, love on the part of him who renders obedience. Sovereign love in God, pure love in man, such is in itself and in its essence the only motive worthy of religion, and worthy of man, if man had remained in his primitive condition. God is not like a human legislator, He is the spiritual Being who requires the worship of the heart—a worship in spirit and truth, produced and supported by love. It is for this end that Jesus Christ restored to man the divine image, effaced by sin, and reinstated by love alone. Fear and hope, no doubt, concur in this work, as needful and preparatory levers; but they almost only act— the first at least—provisionally, in the absence or in the failure of the great motive, love, which, however, will only be perfected in man under a new dispensation.

The stoicism of Montesquieu is softened and restrained by a certain feeling of religion. Stoicism alone could not satisfy this loving mind. In the picture which he draws of human virtues, the idea of God constantly returns, not as what is useless, but as its necessary completion. He several times took the opportunity of expressing the very lively aversion that he felt to atheism : " The pious man and atheist always talk of religion ; the one speaks of what he loves, and the other of what he fears." [1]

This aversion, which had its principle in the uprightness of his mind, was strengthened by his acquaintance with the real necessities and true condition of society.

He defends with no less warmth the immortality of the soul :—

" Although the immortality of the soul were an error, I should be sorry not to believe it; I confess I am not so humble as the atheists. I know not how they think, but, for myself, I would not exchange the idea of my immortality for the happiness of a day. I delight in believing that I am immortal as God himself. Independently of revelation, metaphysics give me a very strong hope of my *eternal happiness*, which I would not willingly renounce." [2]

" Indifference about a future life leads us to be soft and easy with regard to the present, and renders us insensible and incapable of every thing which implies an effort." [3]

---

[1] Esprit des Lois. Livre xxv., chap. i.   [2] Pensées diverses de la religion.
[3] Pensées diverses varietés.

Montesquieu knew that all religion is social, while atheism is eminently anti-social. The first effect of any religion whatever is to bind men to one another, for it is impossible to ascribe to their gods any good qualities, and not believe themselves bound to imitate them.

Frequently they transfer to their gods the virtues, whose existence is necessary to society, and thus render them sacred—as Jupiter is the god of hospitality. And their social practices, which the conscience, left entirely to itself, would not have sufficiently secured, are sealed by the most powerful motive. In like manner, vices, whose existence threaten society, receive a stronger check than any which nature would attempt to impose on them. Montesquieu felt this, and more than once expressed it. Not only does he admit that " all religions contain precepts useful to society,"[1] but he declares that " religion is always the best guarantee that we can have for the morals of mankind ;"[2] and he goes so far as to say that " all societies require a religion."[3]

No one has shown better than he the intimate relation between religion and social life ; and it is interesting to observe, that it is in the Persian Letters, namely, in the work into which he has introduced the rashest statements, and in which he has conceded most to the ideas and manners of his time, that we find this remarkable passage, which explains so well what we have merely indicated :—

" In any religion which we profess, the observance of laws, love to men, devotedness to parents, are always the first religious acts. . . . . For, whatever religion a man professes, the moment any religion is supposed, it must also necessarily be supposed that God loves mankind, since He establishes a religion to render them happy ; that, if He loves men, we are certain of pleasing Him in loving them also ; that is, in exercising toward them all the duties of charity and humanity, and not breaking the laws under which they live."[4]

In the *Spirit of Laws* and in the *Thoughts* we meet with passages much stronger in favour of Christianity: they prove that Montesquieu understood it much better than the moralists of his time, at least in the philosophical view. Here and there he

---

[1] Lettres Persannes. Lettre lxxxv.   [2] Grandeur de Romains, chap. x.
[3] Dissertation sur la politique des Romains dans la religion.
[4] Lettres Persannes. Lettre xlvi.

abuses devotion, at which he sometimes shoots the arrows of his satire. Thus when he says: " Devotion is a belief that we are much better than any one else."¹ Yet he adds soon after, "I call devotion a disease of the heart, which gives to the soul a folly whose character is the most amiable of all."²

The unfortunate age in which Montesquieu lived, afforded few examples of humble, firm, and sensible piety, and the sickly and presumptuous tint, which even in our days devotion so easily contracts, explains this judgment, at least in part. However, the defect of this noble character was stoicism—the absence of humility. Not that he was disposed to vanity, we have just seen the contrary; nor was he even very proud in reference to men, but he was proud before God. His readiness in expressing contempt is certainly connected with this fund of pride. Besides this thought already quoted, " I have always despised those whom I did not esteem."³ This natural character betrays itself in what follows: " I had at first, for the most part of the great, a childish fear; so soon as I became acquainted with them, I passed almost without any medium to contempt."⁴ If he acknowledged weaknesses in himself, he did not acknowledge all, and yet he had several, which his writings show. Licentious descriptions are found in the Persian Letters, in which the author evidently took pleasure, and it cannot be concealed that he was not very strict in his conduct.

In taking a general view of the character and career of Montesquieu, we must add this: Montesquieu belongs to his age; but the longer he lived the less did he belong to it. He does not detach himself from it to become the man of former or future times, but to be the man of all times. It was necessary at the time to belong to the eighteenth century, and to have the mastery over it to write what he did. *The Spirit of Laws* is throughout in the style of Montesquieu—it existed already in the Persian Letters. This was the work of his life. In the seventeenth century he could not have written this book, because he could not have thought as he did. But had he belonged to the eighteenth century only, there is reason to believe that he would not have written a serious book. Are not all his great productions subject to this double condition—to belong to his own time to a

---

¹ Pensées diverses de la religion.   ² Ibid.   ³ Pensées diverses: Portrait.   ⁴ Ibid.

certain point, and beyond that to become free. Every age has its individuality, which is at the same time its limit and its power. A man must come to the level of his age, and from this to start for a higher flight.

The three principal works of Montesquieu are the *Persian Letters*, *Reflections on the Causes of the Greatness of the Romans and of their Decline*, and the *Spirit of Laws*.

The *Persian Letters*, published in 1721, may serve to fill up the portrait, which we have just sketched. They were composed, it is said, at very long intervals, and in some sort as an amusement after the labours of the day. Montesquieu pours out the numerous ideas which flow upon him. He puts every thing into them, metaphysics, theology, politics, morality, and literature. He throws into them every thing regarding his own early conduct, all the first efforts of his genius, and all his foam, like a young fiery steed. He did not, however, enter very early on his literary career, for he was thirty years of age. Several parts of his book prove it, and evince a real maturity of understanding; in other respects, there is in the Persian Letters something of a very young man. The author has two ages, and touches on two ages; the victory is not gained, this is precisely the hour of the crisis.

The form of the book is not new. The author makes himself a Persian, that he may see things better, as he looks at them from a greater distance. This proceeding served his purpose. It made him perceive particulars, which, without it, would have escaped his notice, it allowed him to put in the mouth of a Persian remarks which a Frenchman could not have uttered. The astonishment of the foreigner is communicated to the reader, who, for the first time, lays aside the prejudices in favour of his country, and learns to look upon it with a kind of independence.

This book has two parts mixed together, although they are distinct. It is very serious and very frivolous, and the frivolous part is more than frivolous, it is quite imbued with the licentious manners of the regency. If you examine it in this point of view, you will be struck with three contrasts—the difference between the profession of the author and his book; the difference in the nature of the numerous subjects which he treats; and, finally, the contrast between the licentiousness of his ideas and the power which he knows when necessary to exercise over them. When Montesquieu is frivolous, he is

resolved to be so. Such a letter of this collection would never
have been written by a man of strict morals. Elsewhere he
wishes to be serious. Read the two letters on suicide;[1] you there
discover the man, who knows how to gain the mastery over himself. He advances with a spring into the midst of the rashness
of his age, but we conjecture that he will not be slow in taking
the position which suits him:—

"These are valuable days, indeed, which lead us to expiate our
offences. It is the time of prosperity which ought to be shortened. What end does all our impatience serve, but to make us
see that we would be happy, independently of him who bestows
happiness, because he is happiness itself. If a being is composed
of two parts, and the necessity of preserving their union is the
greatest mark of submission to the decrees of the Creator, this
then may be made a religious law; if this necessity of preserving
that union is a better security of human actions, it may be made
a civil law."[2]

The Montesquieu of the *Spirit of Laws* was already almost
entirely in the *Persian Letters;* he has a moderate and conservative spirit joined to a spirit of liberty, and a serious feeling of
the social compact, otherwise called the state. He is one of the
men for whom the state is not merely an idea, but a sentiment—
men in whom the sense of patriotism, doubly developed, gives
to every thing which relates to the government of the country
a characteristic vigour and importance. Montesquieu is of this
number. "The sanctuary of honour, reputation, and virtue,
seems," he says, "to be seated in republics, and in those states
where the word *country* may be pronounced."[3] The same
sentiment was energetically declared by L'Hôpital, had been
effaced by the age of Louis XIV., and was restored, as we have
seen, by D'Aguesseau. Some emotion may be perceived in the
mind of the latter at the mention of these old words *country*,
and even *republic*, to which he gives, so to speak, a new meaning. This single emotion would be sufficient to make an impression of seriousness on the work of Montesquieu. I have
quoted a passage relating to religion. Here are some remarks on
the observance of laws :—"It is sometimes necessary to change
certain laws. But it is an uncommon case; and when it hap-

---

[1] Lettres lxxvi. and lxxvii.   [2] Ibid. lxxvii.   [3] Ibid. lxxxix.

pens, it should be touched with a trembling hand : they ought to observe much solemnity in doing it, and conduct it with such precautions that the people may naturally conceive that the laws are very sacred, since so many formalities are necessary to be observed in repealing them. . . . Be the laws of what nature they may, they must be always punctually adhered to, and considered as the conscience of the public, to which that of individuals should always be conformable." [1]

But the seriousness of the Persian Letters is not confined to politics. The same man who seems anxious to excite illicit desires, and who sketches pictures bordering on lasciviousness, speaks a little after of the different family relations with gravity, and with a kind of unction. This gravity has nothing affected. Montesquieu, composed and solemn, appears then to take up his natural feeling. See what he says on paternal authority :— " Some legislators have, by one regulation, discovered great prudence ; they have given fathers a great share of authority over their children. Nothing contributes more to the ease of the magistrates—nothing more surely prevents the courts of justice from being crowded—nothing more firmly establishes tranquillity in a state, where morality always makes better citizens, than laws can make. Of all sorts of authority, this is less frequently abused. This is the most sacred sort of magistracy ; it is the only one which does not owe its origin to any contrast, but has even preceded all contrasts. It has been observed that in the countries where the greatest share of power is lodged in the hands of parents, the families are always best regulated ; fathers are representatives of the Creator of the universe, who, though He might bind men to serve Him through love alone, has thought proper to attach them to Him still more by the motives of hope and fear." [2]

What exquisite moral sentiments, what nobleness of expression in the following passages :—

" I have known some people to whom virtue was so natural, that they themselves were scarcely sensible of it. They applied themselves to their duty without any constraint, and were carried to it as by instinct ; far from extolling in their conversation their own great qualities, it seemed as if they themselves were not

---

[1] Lettre cxxix. [2] Ibid.

aware of their existence. Such are the men I love, not those virtuous persons who appear surprised at their being so, and who consider a good action as a prodigy, the report of which ought to astonish everybody."[1] "I everywhere meet with people whose conversation is continually about themselves; their discourse is a mirror, which always presents their own impertinent figure; they will talk of the most trifling things which have happened to themselves, and think their interest in them must make them of consequence in your sight; they have done every thing, seen every thing, thought every thing; they are a universal model, an inexhaustible subject of comparison, a spring of examples never to be dried up. Oh! how despicable is praise, when it bounds back from whence it comes!"[2] "Modest men, approach that I may embrace you! From you spring all the charms of society. You think yourselves destitute of all sorts of merit, but I cannot help saying that every merit is yours. You think you humble nobody, though you humble all the world. And when, I in idea, compare you to those assuming persons whom I meet with everywhere, I immediately pull them from their tribunal, and make them fall prostrate at your feet."[3]

Admirable observations, which ought to be engraven for ever on our memory.

It would be necessary to multiply quotations in order to become acquainted with all the passages which breathe a generous love of justice and liberty, a generous hatred of despotism and tyranny, and their power is still increased by the calmness and moderation of the language. Montesquieu never declaims, he rarely even jests on these subjects; he takes the trouble to reason and to prove, but in a manner clear, brief, and unanswerable. Read letters cii. and ciii. on despotism, and on questions of political morality, and letter xcv. on the rights of the people. See farther, on the liberty of conscience, letter lxxxv. There is much more calmness in the *Persian Letters* than in the other works of Montesquieu, written at a riper age. Thus in speaking of religious liberty, he demands it with a coolness almost overwhelming, as if he wished to compel tyrants to feel that in regard to simple logic, they are the greatest fools in the world. At a

---

[1] Lettre, l.   [2] Ibid.   [3] Ibid. cxliv.

later period, he will be found to express himself on these subjects with remarkable freedom and sensibility. We should carefully mark the following passage on the truth due to princes :—

" It is a grievous burden when we are obliged to carry truth into the presence of princes ; they should therefore consider that those who undertake the office, are constrained to it, and that they would never have resolved to take a step so invidious and ungrateful if they had not been forced to it by their duty, their respect, and even their love."[1]

Finally, is there any thing more beautiful and more ancient in antiquity than the history of the *Troglodytes?* Montesquieu, if he had only written this episode, would be reckoned among the greatest writers, and the most profound philosophers. Had Fenelon, in like manner, only written the *Adventures of Aristonoüs* he would have been placed among our best writers.

The history of the *Troglodytes* should not be confounded with what has been usually called Utopia, viz., the dream of a tender and benevolent imagination, which flatters itself by thus inspiring men with a taste for virtue. It is not *Salente* nor *Betique*, in spite of the charm and merit of these pieces, especially the last. When we read them we experience a pleasant, perhaps a salutary, impression; but we have no distinct idea, and no precise instruction. It is not thus with the episode of the *Troglodytes* hazardous as it appears, and, at the first glance, more hazardous than *Betique*. Undoubtedly, Montesquieu only thought of a people such as might exist; but when the allegory is once admitted, we must not be deceived by it—the story contains moral and social ideas much less remote from application. The more Montesquieu has outdone the Utopia, the farther has he removed error and illusion. He only meant, and we perceive it, to furnish a case for a lesson. And what beauty in the conclusion of his history :—

" I very well perceive what is the cause. O ye Troglodytes, your virtue begins to be too heavy for you. In the state you are, without a head, you are constrained to be virtuous, in spite of yourselves, or you cannot subsist, but must sink into the miseries of your ancestors. But this seems too hard a yoke for you ; you like better to be subject to a king, and obey his laws less

[1] Lettre cxl.

rigid than your morals. You know that then you may gratify your ambition, gain riches, and languish in slothful luxury; and, provided you avoid falling into great crimes, you will have no want of virtue." [1]

Such thoughts carry back the mind to one of those expressions whose profound and manifold signification affects it in one relation. " The perfect law," says St James, " is the law of liberty." [2]

There is much, then, in the *Persian Letters* for serious minds, but much also for the frivolous and malignant. What constituted their most considerable ornament was undoubtedly appreciated, but was not more so than the philosophical boldness of the work. To certain people, indeed, its licentiousness would have been sufficient. It was the time of reaction. After the last years of Louis XIV., and the influence of Father le Tellier, and of Madame de Maintenon, the liberty of the French mind shook off the restraint of a devotion that had been imposed upon them. The most grievous licentiousness was not only admitted, but eagerly welcomed. With what avidity was that book perused, which described all the voluptuousness of the East, and all that is ridiculous in the West, which defied, with unusual freedom, and with overwhelming coolness, ancient idols, and which represented the pope as a " magician, who makes men believe that the bread which they eat is not bread, or that the wine which they drink is not wine, and a thousand other things of the same nature." [3] And it is added, that this same pope is " an old idol, whom they reverence through custom ;" [4] that, in the present state of Europe, " it is not possible the Catholic religion should subsist there five hundred years ;" [5] that there are in France " men who are continually disputing about religion ; but it seems as if they contended, at the same time, who should least observe it ;" [6] that " the king of France has more wealth than the king of Spain, for he derives it from the vanity of his subjects, more inexhaustible than mines." [7] We are pleased to see ourselves so well ridiculed, and this pleasure every one enjoys when he is not the only butt.

What gave so lively pleasure, and continues to do so in our times, is the small scenes contained in the form of a brief letter—those portraits so picturesque, those shafts of satire so piercing, with which sublime and affecting traits are inter-

[1] Lettre xiv.   [2] James i. 25.   [3] Lettre xxiv.   [4] Ibid. xxix.
[5] Lettre cxvii.   [6] Ibid. xlvi.   [7] Ibid. xxiv.

mingled, or which they succeed. There is some resemblance between this style of writing and that of La Bruyère—both have the lively and dashing style, the satirical and witty manner; in both the mode of writing aims at surprising, but internal force belongs to Montesquieu. He has the intellectual power and moral intention, which gives seriousness even to raillery. See, among others, that charming letter on the Persian dress;[1] letter lxxxiv., on the Hospital of Invalides, so full of noble sentiments; letter lxxii., on the *decider*, or the man who cuts short all questions; read the dispute between the geometer and the philologer,[2] and the portrait of the eminently sociable man.[3] The perfection of each of these pictures is very striking. Here is the portrait of the man who supports his dignity :—

"Sometime ago, a man of my acquaintance said to me, I promised to bring you to the best house in Paris; I will take you now to a great lord, who supports his dignity better than any man in the kingdom. What do you mean, sir? Is it that his behaviour is more polite, more affable than that of others? No, said he. Ah! I understand; he takes all opportunities to make everybody who comes near him sensible of his superiority : if it be so, I have no business to go thither. I allow him his whole demand, and acquiesce in the inferiority to which he condemns me. Yet it was necessary to go, and I saw a little man so lofty; he took a pinch of snuff with so much dignity; he blew his nose so unmercifully; he spat with so much phlegm, and caressed his dogs in a manner so offensive to the company, that I could not but wonder at him. Ah! said I to myself, if, when I was at the court of Persia, I behaved so, I behaved like a great fool! We must, Rica, have been naturally very bad, to have practised a hundred little insults towards those people, who came every day to show their good will to us. They knew very well our superiority over them; and if they had been ignorant of it, the favours we every day conferred on them must have convinced them of it. Having no need to do anything to make ourselves respected, we did all to render ourselves beloved: we were accessible to the meanest: amidst those honours, which commonly harden the heart, they experienced the sensibility of ours; they found only

---

[1] Lettre xxx.   [2] Ibid. cxxviii.   [3] Ibid. lxxxvii.

our souls superior to them ; we condescended to supply their
wants. But when it was necessary to support the dignity of our
prince in public ceremonies; when it was proper to make our
nation respectable to strangers; or, lastly, when in cases of
danger, it was necessary to animate our soldiers, we ascended a
hundred times higher than we had before descended ; recalled
all our dignity into our looks, and it was found that we sometimes
properly supported our dignity." [1]

This letter, which breathes a sentiment not unsuitably characterized by the term unction, shows that the serious is· at the
bottom of all Montesquieu's thoughts. He cannot be absolutely
frivolous. In his mind, thought is always joined to every thing
—to sentiment, to agreeable trifling, and to licentiousness. Even
in his loose and voluptuous pictures there are strong ideas and
reflections, and much more in his raillery. This raillery is not
only bitter and cutting—the satisfaction or revenge of good sense
outraged by irregularities—it is something still more profound—
it is thought and principles which obey the necessity of appearing
in public, and, if it be possible, of rendering themselves acceptable.
Everywhere Montesquieu aims at inculcating some truth. In
short, if the Persian Letters were without the youthful extravagance, which the author himself at a later period regretted, they
would be reduced to almost a half; but what would remain of
them would furnish very attractive reading from a mind very
elevated, and calculated to make a salutary impression on those
who give it their attention. I do not here speak of political
views, but especially of those that refer to morality.

The style of the Persian Letters was a bold and singular
novelty—a little hard and knotty at times, very often defying
harmony, blunt, very irregular, sparkling, individual, and masculine, in which the subject is crowded and condensed, and, by
the energy of the expression, less resembles a painting than a
bas-relief. It is neither simple nor plain, it has more sallies than
ease and freedom, it spouts rather than flows, it abounds in picturesque phraseology, worthy of Montaigne the compatriot of
the author, and noble besides. The seventeenth century had
entirely disappeared. As the style is the man, as a century is a
collective individuality, so a style is a century. The style of
Montesquieu is the eighteenth century itself.

[1] Lettre lxxiv.

The splendour of the style, its vivacity and animation, the depth of the thoughts, the richness and intellectual ability which, in its light form, this work displayed to the public, fixed their attention. Its beauties and defects were, consequently, observed; and Montesquieu appears at the first to have taken his proper place, which does not always happen to great men. Nevertheless, if we speak of the Persian Letters in relation to literature, their appearance cannot be said to have been altogether a fortunate event; nothing acted so powerfully in authorizing the abandonment of the beautiful and graceful simplicity of the seventeenth century. In this respect, we may observe that the *Persian* were historically as important as the *Provincial Letters*; they determined the literary language of their century, as the work of Pascal determined that of his time. But this style, so brilliant and yet unaffected—for this perpetual sparkling of ideas appears to have been the natural growth of Montesquieu's mind—was not in itself of a nature absolutely sound, and it therefore became one of the causes of the deterioration of the language. Montesquieu was only admitted into the Academy seven years after the publication of the *Persian Letters* in 1728. Without doubt, if the merit of his book secured his entrance, the boldness of its contents retarded his admission.

Montesquieu was forty-five when he published, in 1734, *Reflections on the Causes of the Grandeur of the Romans, and their Decline.* Two writers had preceded him in this path—Saint-Evremond, in the first place, an author not well qualified for such a task, who yields to the ordinary temptation of second-rate minds, in disparaging great events, and in carrying the critical spirit to calumny. This satirical taste may procure a moment of satisfaction, but there is always poverty concealed under this appearance of superiority.

Montesquieu had, especially, for his rival and predecessor, the great Bossuet, who, in his *Universal History*, treated this subject in a few pages. Bossuet examines with rare sagacity the influence of institutions on events; he puts, so to speak, Providence at the head of history. He is the first philosophic historian; and although, in several respects, Montesquieu was his superior, we must not forget that Bossuet preceded him. On some points, Montesquieu repeats what he says, but as a Montesquieu could repeat; he reproduces by renewing and joining his own ideas to those of Bossuet; he thinks, in his turn, of the same things, but in his own way. The inevitable coincidence is here only the recurrence of the same subjects. Yet, Montesquieu is more particular, more complete, and more learned; while Bossuet guides us perhaps less surely, but takes a more vigorous hold of the imagination. Besides, Bossuet presents, in the first place, general reflections, and then the story; Montesquieu makes both go side by side, and distributes his reflections in due proportion—a method unquestionably preferable. As to the style, both are models for study, and both are the greatest in French literature. Bossuet has more images, more fancy, an easier mode of exciting emotion—something broader, more simple, less concentrated, and more copious, without ever ceasing to be animated; animation is Bossuet's characteristic. Montesquieu wrote his book quite differently from his usual method—no wit, no brilliant strokes, nothing sharp or pointed, no sparkling, a light uniformly expanded, a simple and powerful style, and something Roman and stoical in the language. The stoicism natural to the author has here passed into his mode of expression. Montesquieu bears a greater resemblance to himself than in any other of his writings. If he used research in his other writings, it was rather a habit of mind than a weakness of heart; in himself he was simple, and he has found his true style in this book—the diction is so grave, simple, and nervous, and is like a statue of the Roman people cast in bronze; and yet, concise as this style is, it is not narrow nor contracted: Napoleon said it was the only history of which there was nothing to retrench. In every case—it is a fact to be noticed —a great author, writing one of his books in a manner quite different from that which he uses everywhere else! This peculiarity appears also in the *Social Contract*. Rousseau is a rhetorician—the first of rhetoricians—a sublime rhetorician, if you choose; but in the *Social Contract* he could not be so—a very unerring tact made him understand that such a book could not be written like the *New Eloise*.

The composition of Montesquieu's work is very simple, it is only the enumeration of the causes which produced the greatness of Rome, and then those of its decline—a natural plan, which has no need of a more sensible unity, because then it would be artificial. Montesquieu had not the capricious wish to create, beyond the unity of his subject, a forced and chimerical unity.

The affectation of the necessity of unity is the disease of our age; to collect into a single category analogous facts is real unity. Montesquieu goes no farther.

He follows the chronological order; he begins with showing the republic hatched in the monarchy, as the eagle in his egg, the powerful genius of conquests already preparing itself under those kings, who were almost all great men, without excepting Tarquin. Montesquieu in speaking of the last says: "The places which posterity assigns are subject, like other things, to the caprices of fortune. Wo to the reputation of any prince who is oppressed by a party which becomes predominant, or who has attempted to destroy a prejudice that survives him!"[1]

Freed from monarchy, the republic settled down on its own basis, and here the author brings forward certain facts, even then little observed, whose influence is vital, such as the equal division of the lands and of the booty, which interested each citizen in the war:. "It was the equal division of the lands which enabled Rome to rise from its low condition."[2] "As Rome was a city without commerce, and almost without arts, pillage was the only means of enriching individuals."[3]

Thus the future state of Rome depended on the equality which was established at the beginning of its history—the first cause of its aggrandizement.

The second cause was the sacredness of an oath: "The plunder was set out in public, and was distributed among the soldiers; nothing was lost, because, before he set out, every one had sworn that he would turn nothing to his own advantage. Now, the Romans were the most scrupulous people in the world respecting an oath, which was always the strength of their military discipline."[4]

This inviolability, this sort of social religion, in a great measure explains the success of the Roman arms. Although at bottom, religion at Rome, as among all pagans, was merely a social institution; there, however, it was much less subordinate to politics than at Sparta. The idea of country there had assumed the character of infinitude, so much of a religious life as there is naturally in the human mind had passed into patriotism; Rome itself was a divinity; it was the voice of the gods

---

[1] Chap. i.   [2] Ibid. iii.   [3] Ibid. i.   [4] Ibid. i.

which spoke from the summit of the capitol, and announced the future empire of Rome over the world. Hence that firmness of purpose; that prophetic anticipation of victory, that obstinate courage in reverses, that love of country, which rose even to fanaticism, and that enthusiastic devotedness which smothers the strongest feelings of nature, and even imposes silence on factions. Too frequently, alas! our country is only our opinion, our sect, or our party; many persons have only a patriotism of faction. Factions were not wanting at Rome, but the good of their country kept them silent; they loved their country with as much eagerness as men elsewhere love their party. It was this, in spite of the prodigious increase of the republic, which procured for it so long duration. "There was joined to the wisdom of good government all the strength which a faction could possess."[1]

As a consequence of this feeling, obedience to the laws, the third source of Roman grandeur, was not only respectful, but fervent and impassioned.

Another element of success was the constant and enlightened care in reference to the art of war, that power of selection with which this people so exclusive knew how to appropriate, in this respect, all that they found good in other nations: "What has most contributed to render the Romans masters of the world was, that after they had contended successively with all nations, they always gave up their own customs so soon as they found better."[2]

With the same practical good sense, they did not impose on the vanquished people manners and customs, which would have been revolting to their habits, without better securing their submission. In this sense, they avoided the desire of empire.

But it is not only in the heroic strength and in the wisdom of Rome that Montesquieu places the causes of its aggrandizement, he ascribes a part of it to its very vices. He describes the terror which its name inspired, the Machiavelism of its politics, the complication of tricks and intrigues, and the art of everywhere sowing division, and, at the same time, of rendering its arbitration necessary, with a view to arrive gradually at the subjugation of the whole world: "What is surprising is, that this people (the Gauls), whom the Romans encountered in almost all places, and at almost all times, allowed themselves to be destroyed one after another without ever knowing, examining, or preventing the cause of their misfortunes."[1] " Kings who lived amid luxury and pleasures durst not fix their eyes on the Roman people, and, losing their courage, they expected by their patience and baseness, to suspend for a time the miseries with which they were threatened."[2]

Among the enemies of Rome, Montesquieu depicts with a master's hand two great personages, Annibal and Mithridates, especially the last, who never allowed himself to be vanquished through fear : " A magnanimous king, who, in adversity, like the lion looking at his wounds, was only the more indignant. . . . In the abyss in which he was plunged, he formed the plan of carrying the war into Italy, and of going to Rome with the same nations which subdued it some centuries afterwards, and by the same road which they travelled."[3]

The last cause of the grandeur of Rome was the civil wars :— " There is no state which threatens others with conquest so much as that which is involved in the horrors of civil war. Every one, noble, citizen, artisan, labourer, become soldiers, and when their forces are united by peace, this state has great advantages over others which have only citizens. Besides, in civil wars great men are formed, because amid the confusion, those who have merit come forth, each takes his place, and assumes his rank, instead of being placed as at other times, and almost always wrong."[4]

These were the principal causes of Rome's decline ; first of all, the immense increase of the city and of the empire. By the enlargement of the city, and the extension of the right of citizenship, a considerable number of strangers settled in the ancient part of the town, and the old notion of citizen was considerably shorn of its former energy. By the enlargement of the empire, the soldiers, kept at a distance from Rome, were attached to their generals, and detached from the republic.

Secondly, the corruption of manners, the consequence of an increasing and unparalleled prosperity. When a people naturally hardy are corrupted, this corruption becomes frightful, of which Sparta and Rome furnish proofs.

---

[1] Chap. iv.   [2] Ibid. vi.   [3] Ibid. vii.   [4] Ibid. xi.

"The Romans, accustomed to sport with human nature in the persons of their children and slaves, could scarcely know that virtue which we call humanity.   Whence can proceed that ferocity found among the inhabitants of our colonies, but from that continued practice of chastising an unfortunate part of the human race ?   When men are cruel in the condition of citizens, how can mildness and natural justice be expected ?"[1]

Montesquieu follows out the picture of this period.   After the death of Cæsar, he shows us that liberty had become impossible : "There happened what had never been seen before—no tyrant and no liberty, for the causes which had destroyed liberty, still remained."[2]

Men were seen at that time arriving at power, assisted by the very defects, which at other times would have prevented their success.   Thus, Octavius was preferred for his cowardice. "This, even perhaps, was in his favour, that he was less feared.   It is not impossible that the things which dishonoured him most were those which served him best."[3]

After Augustus, Tiberius, Caligula, Claudius, Nero, and others followed. "Here we must take a view of human affairs. Let any one look into the history of Rome, so many wars undertaken, so much blood shed, so many nations destroyed, so many great actions, so many triumphs, such policy, wisdom, prudence, firmness, and courage ; the scheme of usurping every thing so well planned, so well supported, and so well executed, in what did it all end, but in glutting with prosperity five or six monsters !"[4]

When the author has once crossed this bloody marsh of the empire, he runs over the vicissitudes of its two great divisions, the East and West ; he shows us the avenging armies of the barbarians, and the causes which first precipitated them on the West, and afterwards on the East, till the moment when "the empire, reduced to the suburbs of Constantinople, ended like the Rhine, which is no more but a small stream before it is lost in the ocean."[5]

Montesquieu had the advantage of writing his book during a time of peace when no important event occurred.   It was when Cardinal Fleury was minister.   We may sometimes

---

[1] Chap. xv.   [2] Ibid. xii.   [3] Ibid. xiii.   [4] Ibid. xv.   [5] Ibid. xxiii.

imagine that a season of political storms is better adapted for the composition of history, but this is a mistake. The narrative will be more animated, but less true; an undisturbed light enables us better to distinguish objects than the blue gleam of the lightning. In like manner, the writer, who labours at a time of political stagnation, has a much better chance to lay hold of the reasons of the past, and the probabilities of the future.

Connected narratives, gentlemen, are not history. The man who only looks at external facts and their date, is not acquainted with true history, which displays the springs of action concealed under the variety and succession of external facts. The serious task of the historian is to dig below the surface with a view to discover the secret meaning of those changes, and the real laws, by which external events are directed. For there are many laws, and an attentive observation discovers the permanent and analogous characters under which, in the same conditions, the same facts are reproduced. In this respect, the history of human nature belongs to the grand department of natural history; that is, from the analysis of particular facts, the general law which unites and explains them, may be deduced. But the integrity of historical judgments has been often altered by the inevitable influence of success. Fortune is a great corrupter of truth, so that actions reckoned highly illustrious, have only become so by the help of this delusion, and what a different colouring would they have received from a different result! True, success is the proof of a plan fitted to reach a certain end; it is no proof of the value of that end, and yet the proof is not absolutely in favour of fitness, since personal success is always complicated by various circumstances and different wills. There is often nothing more difficult than to form a correct judgment of the man who is successful. How much fame, perpetuated for many ages, must have crumbled before the simple good sense of a judgment on men, and their deeds founded on better reasons! This has been carried to excess, and some have recently attempted to challenge one of those types, which for two thousand years have possessed the right of attracting admiration—they have pretended to strip Cæsar of his greatness. How far paradox and prejudice have had any share in this attempt, I will not decide; I merely use this illustration as a proof of the power of the analytic mind directed to historical facts when it is once raised above the false glare of good fortune.

Of all the laws of nature, those respecting history are, beyond contradiction, the most difficult to determine. But if you succeed in them, you obtain a sort of historical psychology, a science of the phenomena of the social mind, a real enlargement of the domain of individual psychology, since they exhibit and prove certain facts which cannot be studied in an isolated mind.

The eighteenth century took little notice of the influence of general causes in history; and it was asked at the time whether Montesquieu had not committed the fault of conceding too much to them, and of not sufficiently taking into account contingent and particular facts. But, although Montesquieu, it must be admitted, has enlarged, after Bossuet, a path, which our age has immeasurably extended, he has much less than others allowed himself to commit the fault, into which we so frequently and so willingly fall. More than many writers, he has foreseen and recounted accidental circumstances. Indeed, the double influence of ideas and personalities constitutes history, and each of these elements is necessary for the discharge of its functions. At one time, history only rose above romance by the reality of the facts. Thus Vertot, in his *History of the Knights of Malta*, and Saint Real in the *Conspiracy of Venice*. There is even a kind of history, of which we can form no other idea, such as Charles XII., which is only the account of the adventures of an eccentric person.

Reflections on the Greatness and Decay of the Romans abound in political maxims and moral observations of high value; they show the utmost sagacity, and a sort of instinctive divination in the art of referring facts to their causes: it may be truly said that the glance of the author embraces at once the past and the future. They contain a number of portraits, sketched with rare vigour, in the manner of Tacitus, or rather in the manner of Montesquieu; for Montesquieu is a type. Tacitus is impassioned and gloomy, Montesquieu vehement but serene. He has a deep feeling of indignation, but he is not swayed by the impression which he experiences. Everywhere his morality is elevated; it breathes love and respect for human nature; and he unites the sentiment of social progress to that of stability. We say stability, and not stagnation; Montesquieu means that we may correct without blunting or breaking anything. His mode of thinking is clearly brought out in the following passages :—

" When government has a form long established, and things have been put in a certain situation, it is almost always matter of prudence to leave them there, because reasons, often complicated and unknown, which formerly required such a condition, still require its continuance; but, when the whole system is changed, inconveniences, which present themselves in theory, cannot be remedied, and others are left, which practice alone can discover." [1]

" A free government, that is, one always in agitation, could not subsist, were it not capable of correction by its own laws." [2] " To ask, in a free state, men to be bold in war and timid in peace, is to wish for things impossible ; and, as a general rule, always when you see every body calm in a state which is called a republic, you may be assured liberty is not there." [3]

Montesquieu powerfully attacks legal tyranny :—

" The lives of the emperors, therefore, began to be more secure ; they might die in their beds, and that seems to have somewhat softened .their manners—they no longer shed blood with so great ferocity. But, as this immense power must have an outlet somewhere, another kind of tyranny arose, but more silent—there were no longer massacres, but unjust decisions and forms of justice, which appear to keep off death with the view of withering life. The court governed, and was governed by more artifices, by more exquisite refinements, and in greater silence ; in short, instead of that boldness in conceiving a bad action, and of that impetuosity in committing it, we see no longer anything but the prevalence of vices arising from weak minds and languid crimes." [4] " There is no more deliberate tyranny, than that which is exercised under shelter of the laws, and under colour of justice, when you go, so to speak, to drown the unfortunate on the very plank by which they were saved." [5]

Montesquieu rises above traditional admiration ; he judges these Romans who " conquered all to destroy all ;" he shows them great but odious. He fills us at once with admiration and hatred. It is rare to find in any other author more indepen-

---

[1] Chap. xvii.   [2] Ibid. viii.   [3] Ibid. ix.   [4] Ibid. xvii.   [5] Ibid. xiv.

dence of spirit. It is worthy of remark, that Montesquieu, the man of liberal thought, has allowed himself to be less prejudiced in favour of the republicans of Rome than the high priest Bossuet. In the sublime genius of the latter, some emotion was produced by the sight of grandeur, whether despotic or republican; and the false glare of fortune shut his eyes on many points, which Montesquieu blames, and which, with stronger reason, the Christianity of Bossuet should have condemned.

We may take up, in passing, the admirable judgment which Montesquieu passes on liberty of conscience. His expressions could not be placed on a level with what was said on this subject at a later period; but, for the time, we cannot overlook the importance of such principles and such statements:—

" The greatest error in the political state of the government was the scheme of reducing all men to one opinion on matters of religion, in circumstances which rendered the emperor's zeal very indiscreet. . . . . . He believed that he had increased the number of the faithful—he had only diminished the number of men."[1]

Going back to the origin of such tyranny, Montesquieu perceived it in the confusion of temporal and spiritual things : " The most pernicious source of all the misfortunes of the Greeks is, that they never knew the nature nor the boundaries of ecclesiastical and secular power, which made them fall, in both cases, into perpetual errors. This great distinction, the basis on which the tranquillity of the people rests, is founded, not only on religion, but still more on reason and nature—which shows that things really separate, and that can only exist separately, should never be confounded."[2]

Montesquieu manifests great respect for human nature, because man is worthy of respect. But we regret to meet, in this excellent work, a sort of apology for suicide, which the author had so successfully combated in the *Persian Letters*. Allured to it by the greatness of certain persons, such as Cato and Brutus, Montesquieu cannot resist, but lets himself be subdued; and, after some correctives, tells us : " It is certain that men have become less free, less courageous, and less disposed for great undertakings than they were, when by this power,

[1] Chap. xx.   [2] Ibid. xxii.

which they took upon themselves, they were able at any moment to escape from every other power."[1]

Undoubtedly, the less man is free the less courageous he is; and, indeed, according to the notions of mankind, there is something great in the liberty of disposing of themselves, independently of all power. It is of suicide committed from this one motive, of which Montesquieu pretends to speak, and not of suicide from despair; and it must be acknowledged that several of the great actions of antiquity were backed by this liberty. But men dispose of themselves in two ways; they may take away their life by suicide to escape the acts of a tyrant, or they may withdraw their spiritual being from errors and attacks by religion. Under Christian influence spring up an unalterable courage and devotedness, the fruits of calm resignation, which submits to the shock of events, because there is a conviction that God directs them, and also of the power which braves dangers, because God knows their limits.

In the work, with which our attention has been occupied, Montesquieu was called to consider, in the history of a celebrated people, the reciprocal influence of circumstances upon the laws, and of the laws upon events. By turns the laws were presented to him as the concentrated expression of the state of the nation, and as one of the causes of that state. This double aspect was attached to his prevailing thought, that of contemplating legislation less as an object of erudition than as a philosophical subject. As a magistrate, he must have occupied himself with the letter of the laws; as a writer, he studied them in their general appearance, and in their spirit. The *Spirit of Laws*, published in 1749, is an historical and practical examination of the relation which the laws bear to places, times, the form of government, the different ends of society, climate, religion, and manners. This work, to which Montesquieu devoted twenty years of his life, appeared six years before his death. He had founded on this publication great hopes, better than those of fame. The *Spirit of Laws* is divided into thirty-one books. The first is a general introduction. In those which follow (ii. to viii.), the author inquires how legislation is, or ought to be, influenced by the *form of government*. The government is always, according to him, monarchical, despotic, or republican. This last form comprehends two forms quite distinct, democracy and aristocracy. Now, in each of these governments, there are two things which we must not confound, and to each of which legislation should have respect, the nature of the government, that is the elements of which it is composed, or the system on which it is established, and the principle of the government, that is the idea, or rather the sentiment, which animates this form. Montesquieu successively directs his attention to these two points of view, but much more to the last, which is properly the prevailing thought in this part of his work. The principle of monarchy is, in his opinion, *honour*, that of despotism, *fear*, and, lastly, that of the republic, *virtue*, that is the love of equality, the principle which, in the aristocratic form, is modified, and takes the name of *moderation*. These different principles have necessary consequences in relation to every thing with which legislation is called to occupy itself, *education, courts of law, luxury*, the *condition* of *women*—all things, which must vary in different countries, according to the form of government which is established there, and especially according to the generating principle of that form. We learn afterwards how each of these governments perishes in consequence of corruption, or the excess of its principle, which returns to the same point. The author, in the progress of his work, is frequently led to the object of these first books, I mean the different forms of government; yet in setting out from book ix., this distinction ceases to be the direct object of his inquiries, and it is under other points of view that he studies the spirit of laws. The relations of these to the *defensive power of the state*, and then to the *offensive power* or war, are taken up in books ix. and x., the second of which traces to some extent the rules of what may be called the *right of the people*.

Passing to other objects, Montesquieu inquires by what combinations political liberty may be best secured to the whole of the citizens, book xi. It is chiefly by the distinction and separation of the three principal powers which exist in every state, the power of making laws, the application of them in decisions, and their execution in the administration of public affairs. It is on this occasion that Montesquieu first gives scope to his admiration of the English government, which seems to him to have fully solved the great problem of political science.

But as the liberty of the whole of the citizens would be of little value without the *liberty of individuals*, we must farther examine the laws in this last respect, and inquire by what system the rights of the citizen find the surest guarantee. This is the object of book xii. The same question of liberty again appears in book xiii., combined with the *levying of taxes*, of which the author discusses the sources and the mode of collection. The following books, xiv. to xvii., treat of *climate*, whose influence on the manners and ideas of the citizens he clearly brings out—a cause of the difficulties of a legislator, on whom Montesquieu imposes the task of counterbalancing this influence by wise institutions.

The author refers the origin of slavery to the power of climate, which he sets himself to demolish in three books, viewing it under the three forms of *civil slavery*, which is the state of one man possessed by another; *domestic slavery*, which is the state of woman in certain countries; and, lastly, *political slavery*, in which a whole people is held by a despot. The nature of the soil, book xviii., as barren or productive, as cultivated or uncultivated, is the cause of important differences in the condition of a people, and determines their degree of fitness for liberty and the laws by which they ought to be governed.

So far the author has only, it appears, shown the laws in connection with external circumstances, but they have more delicate relations; there are in every nation a *general spirit*, *manners*, and *customs*, against which the laws can do nothing directly: to influence them they must first be respected, and to gain the mastery over them they must first be followed. This is the subject of book xix.

The four following books, xx. to xxiii., treat of laws in relation to *commerce*, *money*, and *population*. On this last object Montesquieu returns to the ideas which he had already broached in the *Persian Letters*; he inquires into the causes of depopulation, and reviews the principal laws by which men, at different times, have endeavoured to remedy it; he regards this depopulation as in itself an evil.

But every legislator, unless he has himself imposed a religion on the people, finds a religion in possession of the people, for whom it is necessarily the first of the laws. The law cannot possibly pass by the public religion without taking notice of it, nor can it adopt as a rule of the state all the precepts of religion.

Another difficulty arises—Ought the religion of the country to tolerate any other? Is persecution the right of the legislator, and the interest of the public, and of the prevailing religion? The author recommends toleration. He also gives different rules respecting the conduct which a wise government ought to pursue in regard to sacred things and to the clergy.[1]

In book xxvi., Montesquieu distinguishes different orders of laws, shows the relation of each to an order of particular facts, and points out the inconvenience and the danger of a false application, viz., the judging of facts of a certain order by the principles of another order. Thus the facts of the religious order cannot be judged by the laws of the civil order, nor the facts of the civil order by the laws of the religious.

The rest of the work is historical. The history of the right of succession among the Romans and Franks, and of the feudal laws, almost occupy the whole of the last books. Of these questions, many are now common, which, at the appearance of Montesquieu's work, were quite new. Among these historical discussions, he throws out, without much apparent connection, book xxix., on *the manner of composing laws.*

This analysis justifies and makes us understand the title of the work. It is neither the law of laws, nor the rule of laws, nor the guide of the legislator, it is the *spirit of laws;* this is the explanation of what it is; and the definition of the design is found entirely in this expression—" Each nation will find here the reasons on which its maxims are founded."[2] This design, the only one which Montesquieu announces and avows, constitutes the novelty of his undertaking. The works of Plato and Cicero in ancient times, of Bodin and Algernon Sidney among the moderns, furnish plans of government. The work of Montesquieu is not even avowedly a criticism on this and the other form of government; it is the study of the social forms, and of the principal political institutions, considered by turns in their principles and consequences. Farther, Montesquieu defends himself from having had any other design; and, far from deserving the epithet revolutionary, he seems to have disdained or declined to be called a reformer. This is the reproach cast upon him by his contemporaries; and, indeed, the following statement is not what a revolutionist or a reformer would have made :—

---

[1] Livres xxiv., xxv.   [2] Preface.

" Could I but succeed, so as to afford new reasons to every man, to love his duty, his sovereign, his country, his laws; new reasons to render him more sensible, in every nation and government, of the blessings he enjoys, I should think myself the happiest of men."[1]

But these words were spoken neither by a man without sensibility nor by a slave; and the end which the author proposes to himself, and the view which he announces is such that every true friend of man and of virtue may attain it. Montesquieu would wish men to be contented—others seem to believe it sufficient to be happy. Yet let us not forget that he who is contented is at the same time happy, and this is the reason why the art of rendering men contented is worthy of being mentioned. Ages most or least happy, taking these words in their ordinary sense, are not the most contented; and we must remark that, in general, the more a people are discontented, the less cause have they to be so. Their complaints, then, are more determined, and they know better what is deficient. We may regard contentment as an element in human happiness, and we may learn to perceive in it a part not only of that happiness, but of the moral disposition, in which society ought to be found.

Montesquieu, however, does not mean to say that it is sufficient for a government to render men contented—he joins to it also the obligation of rendering them happy. This ought to be, in his opinion, the end of the legislator; it is, especially, on the writer on public law that he imposes the duty of rendering people contented. But whatever he may have meant by this thought, his book should have a different effect from that of obliging all people to congratulate themselves on their condition; for they cannot ascend from effects to causes, or descend from causes to effects, without praise or blame; we can scarcely explain without judging. This was well understood by Montesquieu. He made it his duty to instruct. " It is in seeking to instruct men that we can practise that general virtue which comprehends the love of all."[2] Now, he who speaks of instruction, speaks of enlightening and disabusing men, not only respecting the nature of things, but their value; otherwise, we do not see how instruction would have any relation to that *general virtue* of which Montesquieu

---

[1] Preface.　　　　　　　[2] Ibid.

speaks. To instruct the public, is not to present to it a nomenclature; it is to set before it disorders and abuses, and this is not
the way to render it contented.

How ought we, then, to understand the passages which we
have now quoted? The author no doubt meant to say that his
book, in pointing out abuses and disorders, would also take up
what was good in existing institutions, would bring out some of
their advantages less appreciated or less known, would give a
reason for things which seemed to have none, and would attach
to each inconvenience its natural compensations; in a word, it
would establish such a balance between good and evil, that there
would result from it, in the mind of the reader, a feeling of satisfaction, or at least a disposition to patience, and a horror for
violent changes.

Montesquieu perhaps thought that the best and most useful
reforms are always dearly purchased by the troubles of a revolution; that care must be taken not to excite men's minds by too
lively a picture of the public disorders, and by too vehement
complaints; that truths of this order must be presented in such
a way as to make them welcomed by men in power as willingly
as by the public; that the authorities must not be all at once
embroiled with the citizens, but, on the contrary, a rupture must
be prevented, which too much knowledge on one side, and too
great obstinacy on the other, would render inevitable; that for
all this, fundamental questions should be more avoided than
sought after; and that, in order to attain to what is best, we
should set out from what exists, and not go bluntly to the point
of view, which pure reason, separated from all historical consideration, would indicate.

" In a time of ignorance men have committed even the greatest evils without the least scruple; but in an enlightened age
they tremble while conferring the greatest blessings. They perceive the ancient abuses; they see how they must be reformed;
but they are likewise sensible of the abuses of a reformation." [1]—
" To propose alterations, belongs only to those who are so happy
as to be born with a genius capable of penetrating into the entire
constitution of a state." [2]

This is a plausible thought. We may believe, that if it had

----

[1] Preface.   [2] Ibid.

been adopted and followed out by all the writers who, in the same age, were interested in social reform, it would have facilitated, without precipitating the movement, which was preparing in the state. But this is perhaps to ask a thing impossible; few minds know how to restrain themselves; it is difficult to pass over in silence one part of the truth when the whole is known; self-love leads writers to value some more than others; boldness is excited by danger; impatience is provoked by inactivity; and moderation disconcerted by indignation. Abuses appear greater in proportion as knowledge increases; they are in fact more intolerable, when they injure not only interests and rights, but offend public conviction; in short, it might be said, that towards the end of their reign their poison becomes more sharp, and their pretensions more exorbitant, whether it really is so, or whether the contrast makes us judge of them in this way.

However this may be, if we take account of Montesquieu's principles and motives, we will not judge severely of what others have called in him timid silence, or a compromise with prejudices. In acknowledging that, on many points, his censure should have been more direct and cutting, we shall not make it an object of reproach. We shall observe, besides, that the author of the *Spirit of Laws* has shown no indulgence to any institution, which is really contrary to the laws of nature and humanity; and if we find him timid, it is rather in his judgment of certain political forms, which may be bad, without our being struck with their faults at first sight, and without its appearing possible suitably to replace them. Montesquieu undoubtedly did not appear entirely free from prejudice when he spoke of the nobility, and when he exaggerated the importance and usefulness of the intermediate classes; but these errors are more than balanced by all the truths spread over his work, of which several, at the time when it appeared, were new, bold, and liberal.

Here we may observe the contrast, which two classes of prejudices, very different in their nature and origin, form in the mind of Montesquieu. You see him, on the one hand, much prejudiced in favour of the institutions of his country, and, on the other, in favour of the democratic institutions of antiquity; the very wanderings of a jealous and tyrannical liberty, too, often take his admiration by surprise :—" I am strongly confirmed in my opinions

when I have the Romans on my side." [1]   He allows himself to
praise, among the ancients, institutions which natural equity and
true patriotism condemn.   Thus, in reference to the Ostracism,
and an analogous institution at Rome, he says :—" I must confess, notwithstanding, that the practice of the freest nation that
ever existed induces me to think, that there are cases in which a
veil should be drawn for a while over liberty, as it was customary
to cover the statues of the gods." [2]   We perceive here the man
of imagination, the poet excited by every species of grandeur,
and presenting his homage at the most different altars, provided
that he sees, under any form whatever, in all its brilliancy, the
perfection of human nature; and as a throne, surrounded with
a valiant aristocracy, has also its poetical grandeur, and as this
form of government was that of his country, he pays to it his
tribute of admiration.   It is not even despotism, embellished by
virtue, that has obtained any praise from this proud and sensible
man; and the painter of the liberty of the Troglodytes, has delineated, with no less sympathy, the happiness of the people under
Arsace and *Ismenie*. [3]   The preference, however, of his mind and
heart is not equivocal; liberty is at the foundation of the idea
which he forms of social happiness and political perfection.

With these reservations, I freely confess that there is in the
point of departure taken by Montesquieu, in the conception, and,
so to speak in the spirit of the *Spirit of Laws*, something uncertain and doubtful.   Sometimes, by a voluntary and systematic
indifference, he sets himself in opposition to his own form, which
is not strictly systematic.   Sometimes, by bursts of indignation
or sympathy, he escapes from the circle, in which he seemed
willing to be enclosed; and one would be tempted to apply to
him this saying :—" A double-minded man is unstable in all
his ways." [4]   In short, sincerity in the tone and manner appears to be wanting in the conception, or in the form of the
work, and, in spite of the high morality, and of the liberality of a number of Montesquieu's thoughts, it has appeared
to a number of readers that he opened the way to fatalism,
to political atheism, and to Machiavelism.   Philosophers and historians complained of it, religious men reproached him with it;
men were constrained, they said, to come to this inevitable con-

---

[1] Book vi., chap. xv.   [2] Ibid. xii., chap. xix.
[3] Arsace et Ismenie.   Histoire Orientale.   [4] James i. 8.

clusion, so soon as they were obliged to show the connection of effects and causes, without reference to morality. But what Montesquieu wished to do, and what he really did, in my opinion, was to write the natural history of the laws. This was a new and original undertaking. The history, morality, and theology of laws had been already written. Montesquieu wrote their philosophy. Some were preoccupied with doctrine, others passionately devoted to their ideas of politics or humanity; all were surprised at this careful and scientific manner of treating the laws. This was the crime of Montesquieu.

We must confess, however, that he has sometimes the appearance of Machiavelism. He seems to counsel tyranny. It is not necessary either to do this or to seem to do it, but the true meaning of Montesquieu is clear under these appearances. Not to be direct, the censure in the *Spirit of Laws* has not less force, when he shows us what are the necessary consequences of a system, and to what extent we are invincibly impelled when we set out from a certain point, and he gives judgment, while he has the appearance of explaining. Something, no doubt, at first astonishes the mind in the cool condescension with which, setting himself to contemplate despotism, he teaches it what is best to be done to maintain it, but this is only a matter of form; he sets in its true light the spirit of despotism as of any other institution—he unfolds this spirit, and the result of his teaching is to inspire us as much with contempt as aversion for this form of government.

In reflecting on this matter, we shall, perhaps, see that the relative point of view in which Montesquieu places himself, as he sets out from what is granted, and refers every thing to that, coincides as to results with the absolute point of view, or the point of view of what is absolutely good and true. In setting out from this point, he should have written not the *Spirit of Laws*, but the *Law of Laws*. He does not write, but supposes it, and if after all we cannot entirely acquit him respecting the form of his book, we may say, if we consider the whole work and all the effects which it has produced, that Montesquieu has succeeded in directing the movements of modern nations towards justice, liberty, and civilization.

This is our first criticism. We would have wished, and would still wish, that at the time when Montesquieu wrote, he had frankly and directly urged the people towards liberty. I leave you to form your own judgment on this point; in general, from the time of the appearance of the book, blame has appeared to be greater than praise. The *Social Contract* made him be regarded as a friend of liberty rather lukewarm, and before its publication, the *Spirit of Laws* had been subjected to criticism. We are astonished at it, especially if we reflect that the real beauties of that book have lost somewhat of their relish by the progress of political ideas, and for the same reason the errors and defects have been more keenly perceived. But it would be very unjust to reproach Montesquieu with not knowing what we know, and more unjust still to treat as commonplace what became so from his time, and, perhaps, entirely originated with him. What it was vain to think of saying in the time of Louis XV., has now become extremely common, and the errors of 1750 must appear gross in 1846, without proceeding, however, from an unpolished mind. The times are changed. In the present day, for example, a state is not formed and constituted independently of other states; a sort of mutual security prevails among them all, and in consequence of the same principle, there is in reality only the same government wherever the idea of liberty is found. The civilized world is, so to speak, merely one great nation, of which each state is a province, and whatever may be the diversities of form, there is at bottom much more uniformity of opinion, interests, and political principles, than at first sight appears. We have come to see that civil law has at least as much influence over political as political law has over civil. The material element introduced into law by political economy plays a more decided part than formerly in political ideas. General views respecting population are no longer, and can be no longer the same. .

To be just, criticism ought not therefore to blame, or at least ought not to charge Montesquieu with faults, which at that time he could not have committed. The most serious criticism, of which the Spirit of Laws was the object, refers to the classification of the governments according to each of their forms, and according to the leading principle in that form. According to Montesquieu, there are three principal forms of political government, *monarchy*, *despotism*, and *a republic*. In his opinion, *aristocracy* is only a variety of the republican form. Now, this classification, according to all that we have been able to see in history, appears very superficial, and has, perhaps, more appearance than reality. In order that a classification may be truly useful, it must rest on something else than form. Things very unlike in form may conceal a very great resemblance in reality, and things greatly resembling each other in form may hide differences, nay, contrarieties quite fundamental.

To give only one proof of it, it is not quite clear that there are more republican elements in the English monarchy, such as Montesquieu knew and celebrated it, than in the aristocracy of Venice, to whose decrepitude he lent his assistance. This fact alone might have sufficiently informed him that the division which he chose was unsound and fallacious. In each of these principal forms, which, to say the truth, are only names, it would have at least been necessary to distinguish and define particular forms, which alone present realities.

In this way, Montesquieu has only distinguished aristocracy; and, as if to bind the knot harder, and to render it incapable of being loosed, he has made of each of his three forms a psychological fact, by attaching to it a principle by which he makes it exist; to monarchy, *honour;* to despotism, *fear;* to a republic, *virtue.* In each kind of government, he refers every thing without exception to one of these sentiments, not permitting it to quit its post, and go to exercise its influence in the two others, although he defends himself from this imputation in the advertisement to his second edition. He cannot, in fact, permit it to them, so soon as he has resolved to characterize each form by one of these motives, and to deduce every thing from it. But what embarrassments and inconsistencies does he prepare for himself, to what quibbling and subtilties has he recourse, and how difficult is it to understand that he could say in his preface, " when I had discovered my principles, every thing I sought for appeared!"

What is the vital principle of a government? "It is," said he, " the human passion, which sets it in motion;" by which he understands a feeling which, spread over the masses governed, corresponds to the form of government, and maintains it. But if, in monarchy, *honour* is the principal guide and motive of the nobles, what remains to guide the rest of the nation? And when all the rest of the nation, besides, should be interested in its affairs,

what principle will be applied to them? There will remain nothing else than *fear*. Again, what is this honour, which is made
the soul of monarchy? If you believe Montesquieu, it is very frequently the reverse of true honour :—" Ambition in the midst of
idleness, meanness mixed with pride; a desire of riches without industry; aversion to truth, flattery, perfidy, treason, violation of engagements, contempt of civil duties, fear of the prince's virtue, hope
from his weakness, but, above all, a continual ridicule cast upon
virtue, are, I think, the characteristics by which most courtiers, in
all ages and countries, have been constantly distinguished. Now,
it is exceedingly difficult for the leading men of the nation to be
knaves, and the inferior sort to be honest ; for the former to be
cheats, and the latter to be content with being only dupes." [1]

After all these deductions, what remains for the notion of honour? The author teaches it to us in the chapter on *Education
in Monarchies :*—" Here it is that we constantly hear three rules
or maxims, viz., that we should have a certain nobleness in our
virtues, a kind of freedom in our morals, and a particular politeness in our behaviour." [2] I believe the public happiness very
badly guarded by all this—it leaves the field free and open to
oppression, to tyranny, and to contempt for humanity ; the members of an aristocracy, which only carries to the foot of the throne
such honour, may be considered as the hundred hands of despotism. In that case, what Montesquieu calls monarchy, would be
merely the combination of despotism and aristocracy, and the real
motive of that kind of government would be fear. If, on the
contrary, the nobility exercises in a state effective political privileges, the motive of honour may be joined to that of virtue. The
working of this political influence among the English nobility is
remarkable.

As to *fear*, which Montesquieu makes the principle of despotic
government—that is, as it appears to me, monarchy without any
intermediate body—it is not, and cannot, be exclusively the principle of any government. No state in Christendom, nor perhaps
anywhere else, can rest entirely on the motive of fear. Something
better is required, and is always to be found. In all cases there
is no absolute despotism conceivable without the intervention of
religion, and whatever this religion may be, that alone ennobles

---

[1] Livre iii., chap. v.   [2] Ibid. iv., chap. ii.

and transforms slavery, since the principle of fear is modified and restrained by the free element of faith.

There remains the republican form; and, first of all, democracy, whose principle, in the author's opinion, is *virtue*. He defines it, in the first place, to be the *love of equality*. On this point we have two remarks to make. First, the love of equality is not a virtue; it is an instinct, and even of an inferior order. Secondly, it would have been much better to have said more generally, that it is the love of government and of country, in which men enjoy the advantage of equality; in a word, the love of a system in which men are something, and may do something. This love is so natural, and so easily excited, that you will often meet with it in countries where what we call *liberty* does not exist, and where the individual is politically nothing. It is sufficient, that he be happy there, that his habits be respected, that his slavery be ennobled by ideas of religion, and softened by the moderate exercise of power, or by family relations between the sovereign and his subjects. But this love assumes a far more energetic character when every one feels himself a part of the state, and exercises in it his own share of influence, or at least feels that he may exercise it. Without profoundly analyzing this feeling, we may say that it is a love; that as such it does not calculate, and that it is much less the republican virtue in itself than the soul of that virtue and its point of departure. The author well understood it, for he elsewhere defines virtue to be a " self-renunciation;" and adds, " it is in a republican government that all the power of education is required." [1]

This definition is good: it remains to be known whether the republic—that is democracy—is eminently fitted to develop that disposition or that virtue; but it is certain that there it is most required, and that in democracy nothing can supply its place.

Besides, whatever Montesquieu's commentators may have said, political, as well as all other virtue, has this character. You may say as much as you please, and we will not contradict you—that in this renunciation the mind knows how to find its account; and it is sufficient for us that it reimburses itself independently of matter for the material sacrifices, which it imposes on itself. You will never go farther; but virtue goes so far, and without

---

[1] Livre iv., chap. v.

this noble imprudence, and this renunciation of the grossest part of our *self* (*moi*), there is really nothing great in human life. Every exalted mind, in this sense, is a bad calculator, or rather it does not calculate. Those critics of Montesquieu, who were ignorant of these truths, have incurred the reproach which he himself addressed to certain authors, who, according to him, speak to the understanding and not to the heart.

Thus, in making an abstract of human nature, Helvetius, in his Notes on the *Spirit of Laws*, takes Montesquieu to task for having spoken of one's country as an object of duty and service. " Country is only citizens; to make it a real being is to give rise to much false reasoning." [1]   I do not know, gentlemen, what these *false reasonings* are. Community of origin, of habitation, of remembrances, of laws, of interests, and of duties, has always given, and will always give, a reality to the idea of country ; this idea excites a natural feeling, like family affections ; this feeling may become egoistical and exclusive, like other feelings ; but in itself it is innocent and useful ; and when it is made consistent with the love of humanity, and is subordinate to the love of God, it is certainly one of the beauties of the human mind.

In the other form of a republic, aristocracy, the vital principle, is still *virtue ;* but this is not the love of equality, it is *moderation*. It is no longer the virtue of all, but only of men in power, when they abstain from desiring all that they might. We may say, that this is another form of *self-renunciation*, which Montesquieu has now made the soul of democracy. For he who keeps himself under restraint exercises self-renunciation ; and the author himself says of moderation :—" I understand that which is founded on virtue, not that which proceeds from indolence and pusillanimity." [2]   Of these two renunciations, however, the one is energetic and impassioned, the other has not that character ; and I can scarcely call the moderation, which Montesquieu prescribes to aristocracies, a *virtue ;* on the other hand, I believe them to be capable of higher virtues, more real, too, and more capable of exciting passion. I intentionally use this last word, remembering that he has defined the vital principle of each government, " the human passion, which sets it in motion ;"[3] now moderation is not a passion.

---

[1] Livre v., chap. iii., note 3.   [2] Ibid. iii., chap. iv.   [3] Ibid., chap. i.

These observations are very important. The defects which they take up are such as injure perspicuity, and diminish information, but we must not exaggerate their extent. Those critics pass over many things in the first nine books, because the general ideas which are found there, are not so faulty in being false as in their being incomplete, inaccurate, and, by no means proportioned to the author's design. There are in these first books a number of sound views, observations which denote rare sagacity, and which are particularly explanatory of social phenomena, and of the working of different governments, in which we must perceive a very great knowledge of the human heart, and of human affairs. Few authors, it appears to me, have discovered with so much sagacity, through many obscure media, what ought to be the most remote consequences of a certain system of government, or, if you choose, in what relation such and such a fact appears to be totally isolated from politics, and yet is found connected with them. Here surely is *judgment*, and in this sense we would say that Montesquieu showed his *judgment on the laws*, which a lady more witty than considerate, applied in another sense.

The very foundation of the ideas in the work has been severely criticised, especially in later times. Montesquieu referred too many things to the influence of climate; on this subject, he has been too minute and too rigorous ; we can scarcely help smiling when we see introduced into the *Spirit of Laws*, the detailed account of experiments, to which he had subjected a calf's tongue. Let us not forget, however, that after he has ascribed much to the influence of climate upon manners, he concedes to the laws, that is to man, a decisive power over climate, and makes it the legislator's duty to resist the operation of this physical fact.

But the progress of all the sciences, and of political economy in particular, has rendered, it must be allowed, several parts of the *Spirit of Laws* of little intrinsic value. There, the author on the subject of population repeats the very erroneous ideas which he had already put forth in the *Persian Letters*. Population in itself is not an element of prosperity, it is not even a sign of it, therefore the legislator ought not to strive to increase it; for where is the advantage in multiplying wretchedness, but his aim should be to increase to such an extent the public resources, that they may be sufficient for a larger population. And as to

the prudence of preventing early marriages, and of withdrawing
years and whole lives from reproduction, it is not the business of
the legislator to command it, but it should be inculcated by
moralists and philanthropists, and suggested by education.

On the subject of luxury and commerce, Montesquieu was
deficient in the knowledge, which we have acquired during the
century that has terminated since his death. Never did the
genius of one man arrive at the knowledge of a whole science,
and never was genius able absolutely to supply the place of
observation and experience.

To continue our criticism, we may say, gentlemen, that the
distribution of Montesquieu's work is not the most convenient.
Analogous subjects are separated by great distances ; some topics
are attached to others by the use of the same terms, rather than
by the force of the thought. When uniformity is not in the
things, it must not be put in the words. We are surprised to
find a great number of general observations on criminal legislation, placed in a book which treats of the particular character
of legislation in monarchies, then observations of the same sort
repeated somewhat farther on under a very different title. See,
for example, book xii. on the *Liberty of the Citizen*. Sometimes the titles of books do not exactly announce their subject.
Often chapters have but little connection with one another.
We cannot tell whither the author means to conduct his reader,
and are sometimes disposed to say, that, embarrassed by a great
number of facts, anecdotes, and historical events, which he has
collected, he knows not very well to what general idea to refer each of them, and gets out of the difficulty by bringing forward, whether good or bad, a general idea of the fact which he
relates. The nature of the work, attention to perspicuity, and
perhaps, even the interest in reading it were opposed to the
cutting up of the subject, so to speak, into so many small pieces
under the name of chapters. There is something contrary to
the gravity of the subject, and to the very mode of thinking of
Montesquieu—something like mockery in writing what follows :
" Chapter xv., *Sure methods of preserving the three principles*.
I shall not be able to make myself rightly understood till the
reader has perused the four subsequent chapters." Chapter
xvi.

Voltaire, sometimes unjust to Montesquieu, was not so when

he called him the *skipping Montesquieu;* and Buffon was not more unjust in the indirect criticism, which *the discourse at his admission to the French Academy contains:—*

"The interruptions, pauses, and sections should only be used when a person treats of different subjects, or when, having to speak of great, difficult, and incongruous topics, the progress of genius is interrupted by a multiplicity of obstacles, and constrained by the necessity of circumstances, otherwise the great number of divisions, far from rendering a work more compact, destroys its unity; the book appears clearer to the eye, but the design of the author remains obscure—he can make no impression on the mind of the reader; he cannot even make himself understood, but by the continuity of the thread, by the harmonious dependence of ideas, and by a successive development, a sustained gradation, and a uniform movement, which every interruption destroys or weakens."

The severity of form, with which Montesquieu could invest his *Reflexions on the Causes of the Grandeur and Decline of the Romans,* is a proof of the deliberate choice, by which he meant to give to the *Spirit of Laws* a character by no means consistent with the gravity of his subject. Austere in his former work, he had sacrificed that poetic element, which is so easily found in his mind by the side of the philosophical. In the *Spirit of Laws* he thought he could, nay ought, to remove the interdict, which he had placed on his fine imagination. He desired, and no doubt expected, a more extensive circle of readers; he wished in one sense to be popular; this was the position in which he was placed in this respect, that at the beginning of his work he commenced with an invocation to the muses. Guided by the advice of a man of letters, he suppressed it. We think that if his imagination could have been kept within bounds, it might without inconvenience have coloured, like the rays of the rising sun, the lofty summits of his subject, but Montesquieu's imagination has sometimes abused its liberty by exercising itself on the foundation of things.

In short, it is impossible to clear him entirely of contradictions and incongruities. We do not certainly agree, that he deserved the saying of Madame du Deffand, to which we have just alluded, still less the unjust and indecent criticism of Voltaire, who reproaches him with "making diversion in a book on universal

jurisprudence." Would any one call diverting, the chapter entitled, *Idea of Despotism*? Here it is entire: "When the
savages of Louisiana are desirous of fruit, they cut the tree at
the root, and gather the fruit. This is an emblem of despotic
government."[1]

Nothing in all the book contributes to the reproach so much
as this. And where is the harm? Where is the ridicule of
having summed up in this image the whole character of despotism?
There is no doubt wit in the *Spirit of Laws;* there is perhaps too
much, but there is no drollery. The irony to which Montesquieu
has sometimes recourse, in his despair to prove things too clear,
is an irony by no means droll but poignant, and most seriously
intended. I will give, as an example of it, chapter v. of book
xv. The author in the preceding chapters pretended to search
for a valid reason for slavery; the more he seeks the less he
finds it, and the reasons which he imagines are a bitter satire
on this pretended right. He continues in this tone on the subject of negro slavery:—

"Were I to vindicate our right to make slaves of the negroes,
these should be my arguments:—The Europeans, having extir-
pated the Americans, were obliged to make slaves of the Africans,
for clearing such vast tracts of land. Sugar would be too dear,
if the plants which produce it were cultivated by any other
than slaves. These creatures are all over black, and with such a
flat nose, that they can scarcely be pitied. It is hardly to be
believed that God, who is a wise Being, should place a soul,
especially a good soul, in such a black ugly body. The colour
of the skin may be determined by that of the hair, which among
the Egyptians,—the best philosophers in the world, was of such
importance, that they put to death all the red haired men who
fell into their hands. The negroes prefer a glass necklace to
that of gold, which polite nations so highly value; can there be
a greater proof of their wanting common sense? It is impossible
for us to suppose these creatures to be men, because allowing
them to be men, a suspicion would follow, that we ourselves are
not Christians. Weak minds exaggerate too much the wrong
done to the Africans; for, were the case as they state it, would
the European powers, who make so many needless conventions

---

[1] Livre v., chap. xiii.

among themselves, have failed to enter into a general one, in behalf of humanity and compassion?"

When we read this chapter we feel a sort of comfort, humanity appears to be half avenged.

One of the characteristics of Montesquieu's style is the taste, perhaps excessive, but yet the admirable talent of throwing out, like flashes of lightning, a number of very profound thoughts, of which a single one might be sufficient to arrest the attention of the reader. It is often a defect—it is the sacrifice of the whole to the detail—but it is a defect of which very few minds would be capable. See the *Very Humble Remonstrance to the Inquisitors of Spain and Portugal:*—

" A Jewess of ten years of age, who was burned at Lisbon at the last auto-da-fé, gave occasion to the following little piece— the most idle, I believe, that ever was written. When we attempt to prove things so evident, we are certain never to convince. The author declares that, though a Jew, he has a respect for the Christian religion, and that he should be glad to take away from the princes, who are not Christians, a plausible pretence for persecuting this religion. ' You complain,' says he, ' to the Inquisitors that the Emperor of Japan caused all the Christians in his dominions to be burned by a slow fire. But he will answer, We treat you, who do not believe like us, as you yourselves treat those who do not believe like you; you can only complain of your weakness, which has prevented you from exterminating us, and which has enabled us to exterminate you. But it must be confessed that you are much more cruel than this emperor. You put us to death, who believe only what you believe, because we do not believe *all* that you believe. We follow a religion, which you yourselves know to have been formerly dear to God. We think that God loves it still, and you think He does not; and because you judge thus, you make those suffer by sword and fire who hold an error so pardonable, as to believe that God still loves what He once loved. . . . . . We entreat you, not by the God whom both you and we serve, but by that Christ who, you tell us, took upon himself the human form, to propose himself for an example for you to follow ; we entreat you to behave to us as He himself would behave were He upon earth. You would have us be Christians, and you will not be so yourselves. But, if you will not be Christians, be at least men : treat us as you would, if, having only the weak light of justice which nature bestows, you had not a religion to conduct, and a revelation to enlighten you. If heaven has had so great a love for you, as to make you see the truth, you have received a singular favour; but is it for children, who have received the inheritance of their father, to hate those who have not ? If you have this truth, conceal it not from us, by the manner in which you propose it. The characteristic of truth is its triumph over hearts and minds, and not that impotency which you confess, when you would force us to receive it by tortures. . . . . You live in an age in which the light of nature shines brighter than it has ever done—in which philosophy has enlightened human understandings—in which the morality of your gospel has been more known—in which the respective rights of mankind, with respect to each other and the empire— which one conscience has over another—are best understood. If you do not shake off your ancient prejudices, which, whilst unguarded, mingle with your passions, it must be confessed that you are incorrigible—incapable of any degree of light or instruction ; and a nation must be very unhappy that gives authority to such men as you. . . . . It is necessary that we should inform you of one thing, that is, if any one, in time to come, shall presume to assert that, in the age in which we live, the people of Europe were civilized, you will be quoted as a proof that they were barbarians ; and the idea they will have of you will be such as will dishonour your age, and spread hatred over all your contemporaries.' "[1]

I do not complain, gentlemen, that the *Spirit of Laws* has been too much blamed ; I merely complain that it has not been sufficiently praised. What author, in the eighteenth century, abounds in ideas so grand, ingenious, copious, and striking ? What author, with so great vigour, and in so many ways, stimulated the public thought ? What author has furnished to political writers more quotations and comparisons ? What book, during the agitation of the French revolution, and during the times which followed it, could have appeared more prophetic ? And, if the *Spirit of Laws* is not a body of regular and complete doctrine, what a treasure of elevated, useful, and practical truths has it not opened up to us ?

[1] Livre xxv., chap. xiii.

The virtue which Montesquieu enjoins on aristocracies is, if we dare say so, that which shines in his book—*moderation;* but his moderation, in the same way as that which he recommends to aristocratic governments, is not cowardice or weakness of mind. He is moderate because he is strong. Young minds are apt to think that there is more force in being absolute—they forget that the question here is respecting a science and a sphere in which every thing, with the exception of the principles of eternal justice, is essentially relative. Thus Montesquieu judges of it. He wishes neither mathematical rigour nor the absolute character of morality. Politics, indeed, hold only as absolute what touches on morality. We would not, however, say with Pope :—

> " For forms of government let fools contest,
> Whate'er is best administered is best."

If anything appears clear in Montesquieu's book, it is the necessity of uniting, in the best possible proportions, the leading distinctive elements in each form of government. This is a kind of creative eclecticism, by which he has gone beyond his own time, and has come to the knowledge of ours. The political opinions of the nineteenth century are his; if he is deceived, so are we.

The views of Montesquieu are the loftiest, because they are the most comprehensive. But it is very extraordinary in the domain of minds, as in the kingdom of heaven—the violent take it by force. Man is naturally sectarian, if men truly great are not so. The human mind wishes only one thing at once : it is at the mercy of men of vehement and exclusive genius; we take two steps forward and one backward, and this is the progress of the human mind. We must not think, however, that calm and moderate men of genius lose their time and trouble. Their day comes, or rather, their day is eternal. Let them console themselves, for not receiving popular applause reserved for minds more under the influence of passion, and more narrow.

We may still further commend Montesquieu's respect for human nature ; his love for justice and truth ; his true philanthropy ; his reverence for all the virtues which ennoble man and his destiny; and, in short, his attachment to the principles which form the basis of human society. In regard to this last point, we must quote what he has written on public continence :—

" There are so many imperfections attending the loss of virtue in women, and so greatly are their minds depraved, when this principal guard is removed, that, in a popular state, public incontinence may be considered as the last of miseries, and as a certain forerunner of a change in the constitution. Hence it is that the sage legislators of republican states have ever required of women a particular gravity of manners. They have proscribed, not only vice in their republics, but the very appearance of it. They have banished all gallantry—a species of intercourse that produces idleness; that renders the women corrupters even before they are corrupted; that gives a value to trifles, and debases things of importance; in a word, an intercourse that makes people act entirely on the maxims of ridicule, in which the women are so perfectly skilled." [1]

It is no longer the author of the *Persian Letters*, nor the man of his own age, who is speaking. He sets himself to strengthen what the most part of the moralists of his time sought to weaken and destroy. There is in that passage a little more social philosophy than in this remark of an editor of Voltaire, who gives, in a few words, what Voltaire himself had said or insinuated in a hundred places: " There is more reason, innocence, and happiness in a pleasant and voluptuous life, than in a life spent in intrigues, ambition, avarice, and hypocrisy. . . . . Seek over the whole globe for a country where austerity of manners is in great repute, you will be sure to meet there with all vices and all crimes." [2] This is the favourite doctrine of the eighteenth century. Not only Voltaire, but many other great minds, gave to it the weight of their authority; for example, Rousseau and Condorcet. We have no desire to see all this true—that corruption of manners is closely connected with this levity of conduct, and that one vice opens the door to all. Especially, we have no desire to see what had struck Montesquieu, and what La Rochefoucauld had seen before him, that woman, in losing her modesty, loses all at once. Yet, in the present day, the miseries of France,

---

[1] Livre vii., chap. viii.
[2] Avertissement des Editeurs de Kehl, en tête de la Pucelle.

and the imperfection of its civilization, are in a great measure explained by this circumstance.

On several points, we shall listen to Montesquieu himself, and, in the first place, on moderation of punishments :—" Mankind must not be governed with too much severity ; we ought to make a prudent use of the means which nature has given us to conduct them. If we inquire into the occasion of all human corruptions, we shall find that they proceed from the impunity of criminals, and not from the moderation of punishments."[1]

" There are two kinds of corruption—one, when the people do not observe the laws; the other, when they are corrupted by the laws—an incurable evil, because it is in the very remedy itself."[2] " The excessive severity of the laws therefore prevents their execution : when the punishment surpasses all measure, they are often obliged to prefer impunity to it."[3]

Elsewhere, on penal laws in their relation to offences against religion, Montesquieu expresses himself thus : " In things that prejudice the tranquillity or security of the state, secret actions are subject to human jurisdiction. But in those which offend the Deity, where there is no public act there can be no criminal matter; the whole passes between man and God, who knows the measure and time of his vengeance. Now, if magistrates, confounding things, should inquire also into hidden sacrileges, this inquisition would be directed to a kind of action that does not at all require it; the liberty of the subjects would be subverted by arming the zeal of timorous, as well as of presumptuous, consciences against them. The mischief arises from a notion which some people have entertained of revenging the cause of the Deity. But we must honour the Deity, and leave Him to avenge His own cause. And, indeed, were we to be directed by such a notion, where would be the end of punishments? If human laws are to avenge the cause of an infinite Being, they will be directed by His infinity, and not by the weakness, ignorance, and caprice of man."[4] " Penal laws ought to be avoided, with regard to religion ; they imprint fear, it is true, but as religion has likewise penal laws which inspire the same passion, the one is effaced by the other ; and, between these two different kinds of fear, the mind becomes hardened."[5]

---

[1] Livre vi., chap. xii.   [2] Ibid.   [3] Ibid. vi., chap. xiii.
[4] Livre xii., chap. iv.   [5] Ibid. xxv., chap. xii.

On the evidence of morality :—

" It is much easier to prove that religion ought to humanize the manners of men, than that any particular religion is true."[1] " In order to raise an attachment to religion, it is necessary that it should inculcate pure morals. Men who are knaves in detail are very honest in the gross—they love morality. And, were I not treating of so grave a subject, I should say that this appears remarkably evident in our theatres : we are sure of pleasing the people by sentiments avowed by morality—we are sure of shocking them by those which it disapproves."[2]

Montesquieu is not a theologian, nor even a good Christian ; nor can we say that he makes any such pretension ; but among the laymen of the eighteenth century, no one has spoken so admirably of Christianity. " How admirable the Christian religion, which, while it seems only to have in view the felicity of the other life, constitutes the happiness of this !"[3]

" Mr Bayle, after having abused all religions, endeavours to sully Christianity. He boldly asserts that true Christians cannot form a government of any duration. Why not? Citizens of this profession, being infinitely enlightened with regard to the various duties of life, and having the warmest zeal to fulfil them, must be perfectly sensible of the rights of natural defence. The more they think themselves indebted to religion, the more they would imagine due to their country. The principles of Christianity, deeply engraved on the heart, would be far more powerful than the false honour of monarchies, than the humane virtues of republics, or the servile fear of despotic states."[4]

This is what Montesquieu says on the subject of inexpiable crimes : " From a passage of the books of the pontiffs, quoted by Cicero, it appears that they had among the Romans inexpiable crimes. . . . . The pagan religion, indeed, which prohibited only some of the grosser crimes, and which stopped the hand, but meddled not with the heart, might have crimes that were inexpiable, but a religion which bridles all the passions, which is not more jealous of actions than of thoughts and desires, which holds us not by a few chains, but by a vast number of threads; which, laying human justice aside, establishes another kind of justice; which is so ordered, as to lead us perpetually from repentance to

[1] Livre xxiv., chap. iv.   [2] Ibid. xv., chap. ii.
[3] Livre xxiv., chap. iii.   [4] Ibid. xxiv., chap. vi.

love, and from love to repentance; which puts between the judge
and the criminal a great Mediator, between justice and the Mediator a great Judge; a religion like this ought not to have inexpiable crimes. But, while it gives fear and hope to all, it makes
us sufficiently sensible, that though there is no crime in its own
nature inexpiable, yet a whole criminal life may be so; that it is
very dangerous to affront mercy, by new crimes and new expia-
tions; that an uneasiness on account of ancient debts, from which
we are never quite free, ought to make us afraid of contracting
new ones, of filling up the measure, and going even to that point
where paternal goodness is limited."[1]

Has Montesquieu, with all the moderation of his language,
impressed on the forehead of all tyrants a mark of disgrace less
deep than the impassioned declamations of some other writers of
the same period? Is any one of them equal to him in equity
and impartiality, and does any one go to the investigation of every
subject with a mind so unprejudiced? This equity shows a fine
mind or a lofty spirit; and I think, in the case of Montesquieu,
it is both. Voltaire said: "Humanity had lost its title-deeds;
Montesquieu recovered and restored them to it." This time
Voltaire was magnificently just.

We shall only say a few words on the other works of Montesquieu. It will be quite sufficient for us only to mention the *Defence of the Spirit of Laws* (1750). Against those who taxed it
with irreligion, Montesquieu quotes in his own justification several
passages of his book, and adds: "These passages are clear, you
see in them a writer who not only believes the Christian religion,
but who loves it."[2] As to the spirit and tone of this defence,
they are excellent. It was worthy of Montesquieu to write these
words: "Those who give us information are the companions of
our labours. If the critic and the author seek truth, they have
the same interest, for truth is an advantage to all men; they
will be confederates, not enemies."[3]

The *Temple of Gnidus* appeared in 1725. It is surprising to
see this work come from the same pen as the *Spirit of Laws*.
It is the morality or the casuistry of love, and this love is not
the mysticism of a profound and delicate sentiment, nor is it that
mysticism of another kind which falls into extravagance, and still

---

[1] Livre xxiv., chap. xiii.   [2] Première partie.   [3] Troisième partie.

maintains its intelligence; it is a cool love and a sport of the
mind, in which sentiment goes for nothing. We find in it brilliant pages, and a rapid and prominent style, but freedom and
grace are wanting. Montesquieu could not get rid of his massive
thoughts, and of his nervous style. In general, his sentiments
were easily expressed, they were condensed like the steam which
is attached to the lid, and as the drops fall again as water, so
they came under his pen as thoughts. It is, as has been said,
the eagle that takes to flight in a thicket, and breaks the branches
as he expands his wings. He cannot help being sublime : " A
man adores in secret the caprices of his mistress, as he adores
the decrees of the gods, which become more just when he ventures to complain of them." [1]

Lysimachus is an admirable little story full of sublimity; it is
the history of the philosopher Callisthenes, mutilated by Alexander, and of Lysimachus his general, and afterwards his successor.

" Lysimachus," says he to me (it is Callisthenes who is speaking to him), " when I am in a situation which requires strength
and courage, I think I am almost in my own place. Indeed, if
the gods had placed me on the earth merely to lead a voluptuous
life, I should think that they would have given me in vain a great
and immortal soul. To enjoy the pleasures of sense is a thing
of which all men are quite capable; and if the gods have made
us only for this purpose, they have performed a work more perfect than they intended, and the execution is better than the
undertaking." " Prexapes, to whose care I was entrusted,
brought me this answer : Lysimachus, if the gods have resolved
that you should reign, Alexander cannot take away your life,
for men cannot resist the will of the gods." " This letter
encouraged me, and reflecting that the happiest and most unhappy men are surrounded by divine power, I resolved to conduct
myself, not by my hopes, but by my courage, and to defend to
the last a life respecting which there were so great promises."

The Dialogue of Sylla and Eucrates is the development of the
thought, which Montesquieu had expressed in the *Reflexions on
the Causes of the Grandeur and Decline of the Romans :* " In
the whole life of Sylla, and amid all his violence, we see a republican spirit; all his regulations, though tyrannically executed,

tend always to a certain republican form. Sylla, a passionate man, violently leads the Romans to liberty."[1]

The Essay on Taste consists only of a few pages, which are still read with interest, and which contain very ingenious thoughts. Unfortunately this *Essay* is incomplete.

We have already spoken of Montesquieu as a writer. We may add in conclusion, that he leaves us dissatisfied in respect of sweetness, harmony, fluency, elegance, and even correctness. The great prose writers of the seventeenth century were simple ; Montesquieu is not. He is even affected, but he is so in his manner as a genius who sports with his power. He blunts the French idiom, subdues it, and makes it entirely break its habits. He scarcely lets all his thought escape, as if he were afraid to degrade himself by being too lavish. He is close, concise, detached, and epigrammatic. He goes to his subject in lively and impetuous sallies. It is in order and connection that the style of Montesquieu is faulty, and it is precisely these qualities which constitute the perfection of style in the seventeenth century. In this respect, the eighteenth was conscious of its deficiency, and sometimes could supply it.

With Montesquieu, the character of the expression is that of a power which is condensed or concentrated. All his poetry or his rhetoric is summed up, in my opinion, in his admiration of Florus, and in that passage in his *Essay on Taste :* " What commonly constitutes a great thought is, when a thing is said which suggests a number of others, and when we discover at once what we could only hope to obtain after much reading."

Montesquieu is brilliant, but not effeminate ; what shines upon his person is the polish of steel armour, not the gold embroidery of Asiatic purple.

Bossuet and Montesquieu are the two sublimest of our prose writers. Certainly the style of Bossuet is much purer and more classical than that of Montesquieu, but there are in both the same bursts of thought, and the same extent and rapidity of view.

[1] Chap. xiii.

XIX.

VOLTAIRE.

1694–1778.

FIRST PART.

VOLTAIRE! we have not yet, gentlemen, in the course of our studies, met with his equal. He is, for the time, the personification of the eighteenth century. His life even is divided according to that great period. The year 1750, or rather 1746, marks the turning point in the career of Voltaire, and in the tendency of the age.

It would be highly interesting to obtain a thorough knowledge of the individuality of that unhappy genius, whose appearance is a fact in the history of human nature. We are well acquainted with the character of Montesquieu from the confessions which we have secretly drawn from him, but which are not less explicit and authentic. With perhaps a single exception, the seventy volumes of Voltaire's works, do not contain a single line to this effect;[1] and yet every thing, even to the most trifling note, has been collected.

Voltaire never knew himself, nor was he anxious that he should. Well, this is the first feature in his character; he was social, worldly-minded, restless, constantly going from place to place, not given to reflection or meditation, and no anchorite; he had a lively sensibility, and an irritability, which does not work on his peculiar impressions, and which is unsuitable to the general conduct, but quite sufficient for talent. He is always satisfied with the first thought and sentiment, and in his case, there is but one great effort—he is instinct personified; and even in his literary criticism, instinct still prevails. Among the men presented to us in literary and political history, there is none in whom this character existed to the same degree.

---

[1] Except when he speaks as a poet, and especially in the theatre by the mouth of an actor. The poet is not quite the man, nor the true man, it is not by the understanding, but by the heart that a man shows himself.

Never had any living man merely impressions without any change. Voltaire had not the internal mirror from which the man is reflected, he never knew repentance, which is the reflection of one's own character; he persevered in his long career without self-consciousness. He was a natural man without resistance or counterpoise—a natural man elevated, so to speak, to the second place of authority, equally a stranger to the renewing of the mind, which Christianity produces, and to that internal work, by which certain men have in some measure renewed themselves.

This feature must first of all be carefully observed. Might there not be in it weakness, or a cause of weakness? When to this disposition is joined much talent and genius, and when we have to do with an impressible and impetuous people, when impatience and the necessity of all kinds of novelties work in all minds, then what we might be tempted to call weakness becomes power. But, here we are only making a profile, the full face portrait must be taken from the whole life.

Voltaire has another power. Among all the writers of the first half of the eighteenth century, among all the authors who figure in that intellectual and animated drama, he is the only one who was, I do not say *universal*, much less do I say *extensive*, but the only one who was so flexible and brilliant, even where he is less strong and less solid than any other. The mind of Montesquieu is more enlarged, but he is deficient in flexibility, while the most distinctive character of Voltaire is the power of going over every point, and of taking up all positions; in short, his extraordinary facility of conception and execution. No where, perhaps, is he the first, unless it be in fugitive poetry, where he remains without a rival; but he is every where, and every where he is sparkling. His peculiarity is not to be peculiar. An obscure poet of the last century said of him : " He is never below his subject ; but he is not what he supposes himself to be— original ; every where he finds his master." This is true, but it is defective. Into all the subjects which Voltaire treated, he introduced a new element—his manner of comprehending life. At bottom, his philosophy is perhaps only that. Every where, indeed, if we view him in connection with art, any one may be called his master, but still he possesses that indescribable thing called Voltaire, with which he succeeded in characterizing his age. Every where second, and every where himself. His personality and flexibility were two conditions of the part which he had to perform. Without them, he would have simply shared in the brilliant aristocracy of men of letters of the sixteenth century, but the republic would have never become a monarchy.

Farther, he must have been a poet. Without poetry, the greatest genius cannot aspire to royalty. Poetry is addressed to the public at large, and to the most sensible portions of every public. The sonorous vibrations of this universal organ, penetrate deeper and re-echo longer than any other.

Voltaire began with poetry; by it he laid the foundation of his fame, and directed attention to himself. He was almost the only poet of his time. Neither Louis Racine, approved by some, but devoid of the power of rousing the public, nor J. B. Rousseau, then as it were forgotten and buried alive in the century in which he was born; nor Crebillon, a man capable of communicating very strong emotions, but of a talent quite peculiar, and related, besides, to the age of Louis XIV., could have maintained poetry against an age which the blasphemies of La Motte did not revolt, and which took for poetry the eclogues of Fontenelle. Voltaire took up the golden thread, which was beginning to be dragged along the ground, and renewed the tradition, which was about to be interrupted.

He was then a poet! Yes; but although he more than any other has made the muse subservient to certain purposes, the poet, in his case, was not intimately united to the man. There is here opened up a field of discussion, in which we shall not engage. What follows, is nearly a summary of what might have been said.

From simplicity and want of reflection, men love to believe that the poet and the man are sureties for one another. This is an illusion, which they willingly indulge, but it is an illusion. With the most part of men, poetry is more and less than a talent, it is an inner life. An existence without poetry is a light without the bright halo around the head, and no one is deprived of this crown without being disgraced by nature. It is more than a talent, for it is a life; it is less than a talent, for it is not realized, and is deprived of the power of creating. But among that select party, who are called poets, poetry is a talent. With some even, poetry is merely that; in themselves, they have no more poetic life than a man who has never made verses.

Would it be possible then, gentlemen, that there should be no communication between the life and the talent? No, for it is necessary that the poet should interrogate the man, but these are, so to speak, two concentric existences; the poet envelopes the man as the pulp envelopes the stone, or the pellicle the seed. Poetry, in many cases, does not compromise their position in life, they write it on their way to the country, in the evening, or on Sunday. This way of being a poet is not inferior to the other; the greatest, perhaps, belong to this category. The contrast, which I have now particularly observed, is striking in Voltaire. In him, although there exist great relations between the ideas of the poet and the man, contemplated in connection with society, the two beings by no means correspond, and their mutual independence may be seen at every step. But how was Voltaire a poet, and what was the distinctive character of his poetry?

In the seventeenth century, poetry had man for its subject, since poetry derives its principle only from human nature. But with this admission, we must perceive that this vowel takes different accents. At certain periods, poetry is more generally devoted to human nature, and is, therefore, of a loftier description. At other times, it becomes more particularly social, that is, it attaches itself to man such as society has made him. Then it degrades him by turning his view from the depths of his being, and from the greatness of his destiny. In becoming more social, it has less of human nature. In the seventeenth century, poetry was particularly social, taking this term in the sense which we have now given to it, and not in its actual meaning.

This century had only two characters—it was social, or it might even be called worldly, and sacerdotal. Poetry followed the current of these two ideas. The worldly character is found more in some, the sacerdotal in others, both, perhaps, in all. But these two ideas are under the direction of the idea of humanity. A century under the expansive feeling of human nature would be much greater than the seventeenth century. If the eighteenth had completed the idea of humanity with the idea of religion, it would have been far greater than its predecessor. The idea of humanity, considered in itself, was evidently peculiar to the eighteenth century, which is clearly brought out in its literature and philosophy. It was badly conceived, indeed, but it was not less the idea of humanity.

Voltaire was ignorant of the mysteries of existence, these high conditions of poetry; he remained a stranger to the greatness of the infinite, but he understood human nature, and brought clearly to light an element lost in the majestic shadow which was cast by the social edifice of the seventeenth century. This century took notice neither of individuals nor humanity—it was unacquainted with nature. Although the sentiment of nature was not profound in Voltaire, still he was not deficient in it. All these conditions were indispensable to the part which he had to perform.

There was yet need of boldness and activity. His activity was not the profound and intense labour of certain men, it was real activity, that is, incessant and determined motion. As to boldness, no man in that age carried it so far as he. At a later period, Diderot and D'Alembert went, perhaps, beyond him, but Voltaire had made the road, for them. To be convinced of it, we may open his *Letters on the English*, referring them to their date in 1726. Voltaire carried on the agitation—he feared neither noise nor scandal. He united in an equal degree fickleness and perseverance. His was a wandering and rambling life, but constant as a river, which, through all its windings, steadily maintains its progress towards the sea. A single thought pervaded the whole—it was the design to *crush that which was branded with infamy*, and was that superstition or Christianity? " You will labour in vain, sir, you will never destroy Christianity," said the magistrate to him, who was passing sentence on one of his youthful pamphlets. " We shall see !" replied Voltaire.

In short, it became necessary for him frankly to take the part of his age, and to be subject to it, in order to carry it along with him. The power of Voltaire, we shall not say his greatness, consists in drawing his age along with him, and in being himself drawn along with it. This is like the chain which confines the horse to his chariot. But this is only true of the writer, who wishes to improve his age, and not of him who aspires at reigning over posterity. Montesquieu belonged to his age, and ruled over it, and this was his glory. Voltaire was a man who concentrated in himself, without mixture, all the essential elements of the French character and of the eighteenth century, and who gave himself entirely to new tendencies. Voltaire, in surpassing his age, wonderfully resembled it—the elder or twin brother of his people, who acknowledge in this man another and better self: "He was the spoiled child of an age that he spoiled." He was born at a period in which he could be in all its fulness what he was, and could fulfil his destiny. He was one of those destructive men of genius, whom Providence throws headlong on the old age of empires. At any other time, would he have been such as we have seen him in the eighteenth century? In one sense, no, and in another, yes, and here the yes and no are identical. At any time he would have quickly seized the spirit of his age, or he would have been quickly seized by it, and he would have exhibited it with wonderful vivacity; he would, however, have remained always himself, at least in a negative sense; to him the inward feelings would have been always wanting. But his time showed him as he is. In no other age could he have been displayed in such breadth. His happiness, unfortunate happiness, consisted in loving what his age loved, and in hating what it hated. They were quite agreed, but not always so, nor on every point. A century composed of men is renewed by generations, and becomes young from one generation to another. Voltaire was a slave, and did not cease to feel it. The reverse of the Pope, who called himself servant, he, a servant, called himself Pope. This part is, perhaps, incompatible with originality. We have already said, Voltaire had rather the originality of character than of mind.

We meet everywhere with details in the life of Voltaire so dramatic and so various, we are here only anxious to show their spirit. He was the son of a notary; that is to say, he was born among French and Parisian citizens, who are naturally sprightly, bustling, passionate, whenever they can, and boil over so soon as the pressure is removed. What is noise and bustle in one age would have been tragedy and passion in another. This depends on circumstances. The passions of the multitude are only roused for an idea. Thus, in the time of the Fronde, an idea was wanting. At a later period they meet with the idea—it is terror. These citizens had always an independent and caustic character, and were opposed to government. An intellectual and speculative people are consoled for the loss of their liberties by liberty of mind, and this is what the French have always maintained. But at this period the citizens came forth, so to speak, when a signal was given; they began to feel that they might become some-

thing, and showed it by raising themselves towards the aristocracy.

Voltaire was educated among the Jesuits, and long gave to
his masters proofs of his respect and gratitude. We may remark
in passing, that the career of Voltaire, and his education among
the Jesuits, which was worldly, light, elegant, and more literary
than learned and philosophical, and which consisted of a literature
more agreeable than substantial, are very far from being uncon-
formable.

His early years gave ample tokens of his future career. On
the boundary line between two centuries, when the hypocrisy of
the one saw itself replaced by the licentiousness of the other, Voltaire ardently assumed the bold spirit of this reaction, and, at
school, was already distinguished as the Coryphœus of deism. Introduced, when still a child, into the house of Ninon de Lenclos ;
meeting there with such men as Chaulieu and Vendome, and
mentioned in the will of the celebrated courtezan, Voltaire in
some measure received the baptism of unbelief, and was initiated
into the part which he was to perform. Comedians, it is said,
should be reared on the knees of queens. His wit soon placed
him in the most depraved and most brilliant society. Certain
pages of his works cast a fearful light on the manners of the time.
He courted the great lords, but he could do it without meanness ; and we wonder how, amid so great familiarity, he never
offended them, and how his flattery, when he was in their company, never descended to adulation. He cultivated with particular care, the friendship of the Duke de Richelieu. These two
men were types, and were the complement of each other, and
mutual protectors. This intimacy was uninterrupted. D'Alembert in vain reproached Voltaire with his fondness for the Duke.
He wrote to him, " You will labour to no purpose, my dear philosopher ; you will never make anything of him but an old prig."

Voltaire soon felt the necessity of rendering himself independent. He employed himself in acquiring a fortune, and speedily
amassed a very considerable sum for the time, about eighty thousand livres of annual income (L.3200 sterling). With most
men the choice lies between pleasure, business, and study. Voltaire acted differently—he engaged in all at once. He passed his
youth in the midst of storms, which his self-love rendered more
furious. His audacity threw him into a thousand dangers. Al-

ready, at this period, literary controversy occupied a great part of his life. We must do him justice; he does not make the first attack, but when once attacked he never pardons. He does not despise small enemies nor petty offences. No one criticised his productions without drawing upon himself implacable vengeance. Thus, for a pointed saying, he pursued J. B. Rousseau beyond the grave. He said, in speaking of himself—and this is the single confession, to which we have alluded : " I am of a character which nothing can bend, firm in friendship and in feeling, and fearing nothing, either in this world or in the world to come." [1]

He sometimes rushes violently forward, but never loses courage. The troubles of his youth were rather derived from the boldness of his opinions than from the vivacity of his disputes. As he never knew himself, he was never subjected to restraint; but he could keep within bounds. His anger had some moderation, even in its excesses. He required persecution to make himself the subject of conversation. Twice in the Bastille, and twice or thrice banished, once for an affair with the Duke de Sully, but in general for the boldness of his writings, yet he made all these occurrences the means of his success. During one of his exiles he was led to visit England, and returned loaded with spoils, better armed and more courageous than before. Nothing could be done to him; he was marked with a seal. It might be said that the god of this world has also his chosen ones, and that he says, like the God of heaven,—" Touch not mine anointed." [2] This is fully and naturally explained; the world acknowledged him as its representative, and protected his person from the troubles arising from the exercise of authority.

He was master of all questions, of all subjects, and of every mode of writing. He enters with the *Minerva of France* (Madame du Chatelet) into the domain of the exact sciences. He introduced Newton and Locke to his countrymen, and was very eager to take a part in politics. His was a singular position; he was suspected by the government, and yet Cardinal de Fleury, who was anxious to annihilate his influence, employed him as chargé d'affaires at the court of Frederic. On his first journey to Prussia, a strong friendship was formed between Voltaire and Frederic, which continued till the period of Voltaire's second visit.

[1] A. M. Formey, 1752.   [2] Psalm cv. 15.

In 1746, Voltaire was admitted into the French Academy, from which the Cardinal de Fleury had kept him till that time. This event, at first sight insignificant, was in fact of considerable importance. Montesquieu was admitted very young, in spite of the *Persian Letters*, and on their account. His nomination was delayed, but only for a few years—Voltaire waited for his, twenty-five years. He did not gain his election till he was fifty-two. This was the first instance of so great talent being so long kept by its tendency at the door of this association.

Precisely at this period, in 1747, Voltaire lost Vauvenargues, whose influence, though insufficient, appeared so far to restrain him. Although Vauvenargues was the only man, perhaps, that inspired him with a feeling of respect, we cannot, however, affirm that, if he had lived, Voltaire would not have shown himself in the way he did more and more. The convictions of that moralist were not of a nature so precise as to sway the mind of Voltaire; and we have seen that, long before this time, he had clearly conceived the design, to which his whole life was subservient. He was long its chief, its soul, and its centre. *La Pucelle*, that foul deed, which lasted thirty years, was begun in 1730, and, though it was not published till near 1760, fragments of it were circulated, and passed from hand to hand, which were often disavowed by their author. But although this poem contains as much venom as any other of Voltaire's works, we may say that his second journey to Berlin marks in his life a new period. As he became old he became depraved. So far, in his avowed writings, he observes some moderation : in the theatre and in history he was already the champion of deism, but he still keeps within certain limits; the balance is equally poised; and, in his different works, he will be found to be as much the enemy of abuses as the adversary of creeds.

This first period of Voltaire's life is the most literary, and presents him to us almost entirely as a poet. We have already remarked that he began with poetry. He never abandoned it, and almost always kept by the theatre. He was only faithless to the latter during six years of his life, from 1736 to 1742.

At a very early period, when yet a child, Voltaire formed the plan of an epic poem. The poem appeared in London in 1723, in nine cantos, entitled, *The League, or Henry the Great*. He was then twenty-nine. Its success had crowned it with a parody,

Le Lutrin. The end was, men no longer believed in epic poetry. It was vanity, more than enthusiasm, which made Voltaire undertake the *Henriade.* Anticipations of a lofty description were wanting to him, in a style of writing the most exalted of all. He appears not to have had one more serious than to attach to his name a glory, which had been refused to so many others. Nothing, in this respect, is more significant than the pitiful vengeance, in memory of his quarrel with the Duke de Sully, of having substituted, in a new edition, for this historical name the far less famous name De Mornay. This circumstance recalls to us Holbein and his *Lais Corinthiaca.* Farther, you may observe the hurry in which the work was written. The important changes made by Voltaire in his first plan do him honour, but the necessity for these changes is by no means honourable; and no one can read the poem of *The League* without feeling surprise at the levity of the poet. Voltaire undertook his work without enthusiasm, and without faith in epic poetry, and repeated to himself that the French have no head for the effusions of the epic muse. That was especially true of the French of the eighteenth century, and, above all, of the Frenchman Voltaire. He merely wished to show that he was capable of doing every thing.

Epic poetry, in truth, is nothing else than the explanation of what is on earth by what is in heaven. Of all modes of writing, it is most essentially religious. History is a chain, which trails along the ground, so long as it is not bound to its first ring—the ring fixed to the Rock of Ages. It is incomplete, and has all its philosophy only on this condition. The manner in which Bossuet has connected historical events with the divine will cannot be approved; but all the criticisms on his book do not reach the foundation of the question. Apart from this there may, no doubt, remain to history, contemplated in itself, a certain sense and a certain philosophy; but the epic poem, which is only history idealized, loses all its value without the intervention of the Deity. It is not purely conventional, but the result of profound reasoning. It does not depend on a man to make an epic poem, because it is his wish. If a religious heart be wanting, there must at least be a religious imagination. An epic poem must farther be animated with some great fact referring to human nature. But, in such a work—and there the limit of individuality is found—there is need of support from the whole people—from the whole world.

If the religious element be taken away, you must entirely give up writing an epic poem, or you must merely make an historic poem, which would succeed according to circumstances. But, above all, you must not affect an inspiration which you do not feel, and write a hypocritical work. Still less, in a poem on the conversion of Henry IV., should you declaim against intolerance, or satirize the Holy See. People were so little deceived by it, that *The League* was very soon reprinted at Geneva by *John Mokpap*, an assumed name, which wonderfully characterized the true meaning of the poem. In spite of Voltaire's wit, and the beauties in detail, in which his work abounds, we may be permitted to say that, on the whole, it is deficient in spirit, and even in common sense :—

" Fortunate priests, with tranquil foot, trample on the graves of the Catos, and on the ashes of Emilius. The throne is on the altar, and absolute power puts into the same hands the sceptre and the censer. There God himself has founded His rising church, sometimes persecuted, and sometimes triumphant. There candour and simplicity, along with truth, guided His first apostle. His happy successors for some time imitated him ; so much the more respected, the more humble they were. Their brows were not invested with vain splendour ; poverty supported their stern virtue ; and, eager to obtain the only good which a true Christian desires, from their lowly cottage, thatched with straw, they took their flight to the martyrs' grave. Time, which corrupts every thing, soon changed their manners : heaven, to punish us, gave them greatness. Since that time Rome, powerful and profaned, saw itself abandoned to the counsels of the wicked ; treason, murder, and poisoning were the fearful foundations of its power. The successors of Christ, within the sanctuary, and without a blush, committed incest and adultery ; and Rome, which their hateful empire oppressed under these sacred tyrants, regretted her false gods."[1]

All, or almost all, that refers to religion is taken from the negative point of view. Abuses in religion, fanaticism, intolerance, and superstition, are constantly recurring : " It is religion,

[1] Canto iv.

whose inhuman zeal puts arms in the hands of all Frenchmen."[1]
With the exception of a few verses devoted to propriety, religion
is scarcely ever brought forward, but as the occasion or the
source of evil. Moreover, as the author becomes deficient in
frankness, and wishes to pass himself off for what he is not, the
result is something weak and equivocal ; indeed, the whole poem
is equivocal, false, and consequently cold. In the way of poetry,
Voltaire would have done better if he had been openly satirical
or openly licentious. How much more valuable would fanaticism have been? He is only straightforward and eloquent on
the side of natural religion. When he acts the Christian, he
becomes flat, and almost ridiculous. He forgets himself so far,
as to put in the mouth of Saint-Louis—addressing God—verses
such as these : " Father of the universe, if thine eyes *sometimes*
honour with a look people and their kings !"[2]

But if Voltaire's character was not adapted to epic poetry any
more than the taste of the times, the subject selected was scarcely
more suitable. We understand that, in the eighteenth century,
Henry IV. had become popular ; but that does not imply a character for epic poetry. Even in taking up this subject in the point
of view in which Voltaire apprehended it, we find that it is very
vague in its conception. It wants the precision which the great
poets know how to give to their subjects : for example, the *Iliad*
and *Æneid*. This poem is a rag of the history of Henry IV.
against the League. We see in it an embassy without importance,
a battle, the states of Paris, the assault, the famine, and the conversion of Henry de Bourbon. The arrangement is defective,
and the parts are not well connected. There is no real unity,
nor the philosophical unity of history, nor even poetical unity.
We are the more surprised at this, as it is the very fault with
which Voltaire himself reproached Camöens.

In what consists the real turning-point of the poem? Is it
Gabrielle? is it heresy? Here are two, and the two are not so
good as one. Gabrielle reminds us of the Armida of Tasso ; but
it would be mockery to regard Gabrielle as the real point of interest. Observe, she comes after the vision of Henry and his

---

[1] Canto iv.
[2] Canto x. See Psalm xxxiii. 13, 14 : " The Lord looketh from heaven ; He be-
holdeth all the sons of men. From the place of His habitation He looketh upon all
the inhabitants of the earth."

journey to heaven. Then Mornay arrives as a truly troublesome guest, to recall Henry to his duty. Voltaire was always deficient in a feeling of gravity respecting divine things.

Is it the abjuration of Henry IV.? What interest can be taken in the conversion of a man who says, like a petty student of philosophy in the eighteenth century, in the third rank under Voltaire and Diderot : " I do not decide between Geneva and Rome" ?[1] This is the paraphrase of the famous saying : " Paris is well worth a mass."

The little ability in the beginning shows the absence of the epic character. What a difference in the *Æneid!* Troy is destroyed; but this calamity is to be the source of the greatest destinies. Æneas goes forth to found an empire, which is to be the ruler of the world. It is worth while to set to work all the gods of Olympus. Nothing, on the contrary, can be colder or more vulgar than the meeting of Henry and Elizabeth, with which the *Henriade* opens.

We are struck with the author's want of invention. Virgil imitated Homer ; Voltaire imitates Virgil ; Tasso, every body ; in the imitation he becomes weak, and invents nothing, if it be not a few episodes, whose execution is the only merit. We have said a word on the distance which separates Gabrielle from Armida, an immortal creation, and the real turning-point of the *Jerusalem.* Again, compare Elizabeth with Dido, the walk in the other world which Saint-Louis takes with Henry IV., with the descent of Æneas into hell, and that of Telemachus.

There are no characters drawn. The poem, viewed as a whole, produces the effect of a vast landscape without water—that is to say, without life. There are found in it some portraits—that of the Duke de Guise is a happy one, but there is nothing in it dramatic. In the great epic poems we meet with few portraits —the characters must be made to speak and act, and must not be described. Voltaire was ignorant of the proverb— " Speak, that I may see thee." His characters fight and say nothing. But for a few words from Henry IV., which he versifies, his features would not be better brought out than any of the others.

As to the marvellous allegory of the *Henriade*, an opinion has

---

[1] Canto ii.

long ago been pronounced. The gods of Homer were no doubt at one time allegories; but the Greeks were too intelligent to be satisfied with allegory. Then the allegories of the *Henriade* are often, according to the principles of reasoning, utterly false : thus Discord, which is only the result of a passion, and not the passion itself. In a poem pretending to be religious, what are we to say of a personage entitled *Religion?* The marvellous, with Voltaire, is only the discharge of a vain form ; while in the great epic poems, every thing rests on the marvellous. It is like love in tragedy : it should be every thing or nothing.

The style is injured by its vagueness, the impropriety of the terms, and the abuse of antithesis, and it is prosaic withal. It was Voltaire who gave, in the *Henriade*, the first example of careless rhymes. He makes *humains* rhyme with *inhumains*. He indulges in such verses as these :—

> Et par droit de conquête et par droit de naissance.[1]
> —— Tous ces évenements leur semblaient incroyables.[2]

But if, in spite of all this, the *Henriade* be reckoned among its author's titles to glory—if many verses, and even many pieces of this work are remembered by its admirers—there is no doubt a reason for it. This may be found in a certain number of interesting and pathetic fragments, in the eloquence of certain passages, and in the elegance of a few others. Philosophical discourse was really the tendency of Voltaire's mind. The *Henriade* is not a poem, but a series of little poems, some of which are charming. See, among others, *Fanaticism* (canto v.), *Sleep* and *Hope* (canto vii.), *Envy* (canto vii.) ; and, after the murder of Coligny, the piece so frequently quoted : " The Medicis received it with indifference,"[3] etc. ; and, in general, the whole description of Saint-Bartholomew. We should also notice the famine (canto x.), the prophetic history of France (canto vii.), the anecdote of D'Ailly (canto viii). There are a great number of fine verses standing alone, which are easily taken up. Voltaire is the man for fine verses—verses which contain a beautiful thought, set off by the graceful turn of the phrase, or by the elegance of the expression : " A name too soon famous is a heavy weight,"[4] etc.

Then his colouring was poetical, his versification harmonious,

---

[1] Canto i.   [2] Ibid. x.   [3] Ibid. ii.   [4] Ibid. iii.

his touch bold and easy; in short, his comparisons were admirable. In this last manner of writing Voltaire has no equal; his comparisons are new, striking, ingenious, and always set off by the execution : " Thus, in a vessel, which the waves have tossed, when the air is no longer struck by the cries of the sailors, we only hear the noise of the foaming prow, which cleaves, in its prosperous course, the obedient sea."[1]

"Thus when the winds, unruly tyrants of the waters, have raised the waves of the Seine or the Rhone, the mud, that had lain long in their deep grottoes, is raised boiling on the face of the billows. Thus in the fury of those conflagrations, which change cities into desolate plains, iron, brass, and lead which the fires melt are mingled in the flame, with the gold which they darken."[2]

" So from the brow of Caucasus or from the summit of Athos, whence the eye takes in afar the air, the earth, and the seas; the eagles and vultures with extended wings and with hurried flight cut the vast clouds, and go into the fields of air to seize the birds, and in the woods and on the meadows tear the flocks, and into the horrid sides of their bloody rocks carry with loud cries these living spoils."[3]

I daresay this style and these beauties were new. We recognise Voltaire in such strokes as these, almost as easily as skilful judges distinguish a Rembrandt or a Claude Lorraine.

Horace supposes, without saying so, that an epic poem should be a moral work. He particularly notices this character in the *Iliad.* No doubt, this trait should be found more or less in every other kind of writing. But the epic poem is by its nature, as we have already said, the only poem which has remained essentially religious, and hence also moral. All ages have been anxious to sum up the wisdom of their own time in great national poems, of which the form has little varied. The people do not merely require stories, but also lessons; the memory of the human race has always been at the service of their reason. Epic poems are true human bibles : the commemoration of a great event in them serves to consecrate a great truth. It is in an idea that the human race demands the conclusion of each of the historical revolutions.

---

[1] Canto vi. [2] Ibid. iv. [3] Ibid. iv.

Do we find this idea in the *Henriade?* To a certain extent. The *Henriade* is not exclusively sceptical, for the terms scepticism and epic poetry are contradictory; it is a protest against fanaticism, it endeavours to establish the superiority of moral over religious virtues; in a word, it is rather an attempt to substitute moral instinct for religious feeling.

After Corneille and Racine the theatre had remained vacant. The *Manlius* of La Fosse, and the *Rhadamiste* of Crebillon had undoubtedly deserved admiration. The very name of Crebillon preserved a very high rank, and it was long attempted to make him the heir of the two great tragic poets. But if Crebillon and La Fosse published tragedies more or less beautiful, they displayed no new art; neither they nor any one else had opened up to men of wit and talent a new world of poetry. Now in the history of the arts, men are only great on condition of being new, not only of saying or doing something new, but of being new in their whole manner of thinking. Every great poet is a Columbus, who discovers an America; every great poet is armed with Moses' rod. Where the people only saw arid rocks, Moses made fresh streams gush out. At every new epoch, the people exclaim, " every thing has been said," and at each time some one is raised up, who finds still something to say. Such is the fertility of nature and the human mind—such are the riches of God. When, at the age of twenty-four, Voltaire puts forth *Œdipus*, which he had written at nineteen, La Motte, a better critic than a good poet, immediately declared that Corneille and Racine had found a successor. He must, therefore, have been new—men only succeed on condition that they are not like others.

But in what was Voltaire new? Did he introduce upon the stage a different system from his predecessors? We cannot generally say of system what Buffon says of style. System, to a certain extent, is apart from the man, especially the system adopted; the system is not the man, although at the moment of its formation a system may be a man.

Voltaire left standing, what he found standing, unities, the sustained pomp of language, theatrical manners—all remain. Voltaire maintains even the long speech uttered by a single actor (*tirade*), that distinctive mark of French tragedy, which is only a series of discourses. Strangers are struck with this last character, from which our great tragic poets, to begin with

Corneille and Racine, are not free.   In an inferior degree, Sedaine suppressed the *tirade;* he had read Shakspeare, and felt the necessity of realizing on the French stage the new idea of theatrical action substituted for the speech.   But this prevailing feature in our tragedy remained with Voltaire absolutely the same.   Moreover, we cannot help remarking that great geniuses more easily consecrate evil than good.   Good can only be imitated by their equals, but when their example has consecrated an inferior art contrary to nature, they set their seal to it, and this contraband article gets into circulation.   Genius is not transferable, but systems and conventions pass from one generation to another.   In point of art, Voltaire was not endowed with a revolutionary genius—it may be boldly asserted that he changed nothing in the established system of his time.

Voltaire comes far short of Corneille in dramatic invention and sublimity, and is inferior to Racine in the judicious management of the action, in justness of thought, and in perfect execution. His maxim is to strike vigorously rather than justly, and to comprehend every thing in emotion.   He falls into the inexcusable error of substituting himself for his characters, which Racine, and even Corneille, never do; if the characters of Corneille reason much, they reason for themselves and in their own place. Voltaire does not rise above his predecessors in truly representing manners.   His diction wants purity, but in this respect Corneille is not superior to him, for he is vague.   Voltaire's style is inflated with improper and superfluous words, it is declamatory and often incorrect.   There is no appearance of deep reflection, and thus nothing is profound; a first effort, more or less happy, is sufficient for the author, and he never occupied himself in correction. Racine required years to finish *Phedre*, Voltaire devoted fifteen days to the composition of *Zaire*.   He does not fill the soul like Corneille, nor engage the understanding like Racine.   Racine is not the most affecting nor the most pathetic of the dramatic poets, but he most of all interests the understanding.

Here the author is passive, when the duties of criticism are performed.   We now proceed to the other part of his character. In the first place, Voltaire extended the domain of the tragic affections.   Till his time, ambition and love were almost the only occupants of the stage.   He was the first, or nearly the first, who composed tragedies without love—such as *Merope, La*

Mort de César. He said to himself: " Tragedies which can subsist without this passion are the finest of all." [1]

He has, at the same time, extended the field of ideas peculiar to tragedy. Corneille and Racine have merely represented man in society, and man at court. Voltaire goes farther : man, with him, is superior to the prince ; the man of nature prevails over the man in society, and the idea of humanity is introduced into tragedy. Voltaire farther brings to it philosophical interest. No doubt he abused it, and is justly reproached with the spirit of system, in whose favour he was prejudiced, and with the sententious character of his style ; but we cannot call in question his just and liberal ideas, which give to his tragedies a much greater interest than to those of his predecessors. Racine, for example, though an admirable moralist, is not, perhaps, very philosophical. In Voltaire, I prefer the philosophy of the poet to that of the philosopher.

It is a pity that he did not venture on the popular topics of Shakspeare, or of the ancients, or on the mixture of the familiar with the noble ; and still less did he mix laughter with tears, and comedy with tragedy. The people whom these introduce upon the stage are much more men than princes. We must compare, with the scene of Anthony in the *Julius Cæsar of Shakspeare,* the imitation of Voltaire, to see how little he dared to attempt. At the origin of the French stage, comedy and tragedy go in quest of each other, and are almost united. This character is found in several of Corneille's plays, and traces of it are discovered in the first tragedies of Racine ; but, from that time, Racine carefully avoided it. It would have appeared very natural that the philosophical ideas of Voltaire should have led him to this fusion.

He first consecrated the tragic stage to national remembrances ; he brought to it the middle age, and France. It does not follow that he is superior to Corneille and Racine in the true representation of manners. Orosmanes says to his mistress : " Condescend, beautiful Zaire . . . worthy and charming object of my unchangeable fidelity ;" [2] and is he anything else than a Frenchman of the eighteenth century? To lose the nature of one, it is not sufficient to bear the name of Ottoman or American ; but

---

[1] Epitre dedicatoire de Zulime.   [2] Zaire, acte iii., scène vi.

what is certain is, that Voltaire knew how to get rid of Greeks and Romans.

In short, he has restored to the eyes their legitimate office; he has not gone beyond what is proper; and yet he has made of the theatrical representation a true representation. In proof of this, we refer to the senate in *Brutus*, the knights in *Tancréde*, and the dead body of Cæsar in *La Mort de César*.

But all this could be done without genius; and there are few novelties which have not been formerly attempted. The most part of the germs of romance subsisted in concealment during the seventeenth century; many bolder attempts had been made in the sixteenth. The changes which appear the most important are brought about by the course of time, and are suggested by the general feeling. That which is the property of genius, and the triumph of individual feeling, is to put to them the seal of eloquence. In the eighteenth century, some authors attempted bolder novelties than Voltaire. Henault composed a national tragedy; Mercier was the author of some dramas, in which may be discerned the dawning of romance. But it was the merit of Voltaire that he conscientiously wished what others would have liked, but without any feeling of conscience. They attempted more than Voltaire, but it was unseasonable; Voltaire joined the clear and lively view of certain innovations to the power of form and to the gift of eloquence. In *Œdipus*, for example, there is no innovation as to system. This bold spirit does there, in one sense, the work of a slave, who extravagantly praises the mode in which his patrons act; he made love enter into the subject which suited it least. At that time Voltaire suspected little ridicule of that love which, at a later period, he himself turned into a jest. But the scene of the double confidence alone justified the prophecy of La Motte. It revealed the great writer; and never was a great writer a person of ordinary thought.

The style of Voltaire, defective as it may be, is admirable for its copiousness, freedom, and easy and noble manner. Its rhythm is by no means skilful, and its harmony little studied, but attractive. There is brilliant fancy, an easy and rapid progress, and the magic of colouring—real magic, for all in it is not sincere, there is trickery and dazzling. The sketch is not clearly marked, but nothing can surpass the splendour and richness of the colouring. No one has carried this ease farther; and he calls it the *grace of genius*. Lamartine alone has equalled him. Voltaire has a number of verses produced without effort, which found at once their sense and their form. We meet with these verses in Racine, but they are abundant in Voltaire : " No one can desire what is unknown."[1] " At the Ganges I would have been the slave of false gods, a Christian at Paris, a Mussulman in this country."[2] " Our country is where the soul is captivated."[3] " Stained with my blood, thou pretendest to my heart."[4]

The foundation of all this is an admirable sensibility, in which he trusts, and which he must obey. He draws men along with him, provided that he himself be drawn. He may say, what Orosmanes said to Zaire : " Art was not made for thee, thou hast no need of it."[5] Not only has he no need of it, but he would lose something by giving to it too much attention. He knew this, and improperly made it a general rule. The well known saying, " You must have the devil in your body to act tragedy and to write it," and other sayings of the same kind, riveted in his mind this prejudice. The public was subdued by this poetry ; it tells Voltaire, by the mouth of Gresset : " If my mind objects to it, my heart has tears in its behalf." It appears to me, that in pathos which penetrates the heart, and is painful even to the feelings, and in a free and flowing eloquence, Voltaire has few rivals. Who could have written better the speech of the aged Lusignan ?[6] In my opinion, he succeeded better than any other in inspiring sympathy for his characters. In this point he perhaps surpasses Racine himself. Voltaire appears to me to possess in perfection the gift of drawing from its greatest depths the feeling of pity. He not merely rouses your interest, but produces a feeling of desolation.

We shall not enter into any detailed examination of Voltaire's tragedies. Here especially, coming after so many others, a particular literary study of them might appear superfluous ; and yet from one age to another, we may form new judgments without contradicting what has been already said. Every age, every individual, brings new light. This is especially the inheritance

---

[1] Zaire, acte i., scène i.   [2] Ibid.   [3] Mahomet, acte i., scène ii.
[4] Mahomet, acte v., scène ii.   [5] Zaire, acte iv., scène ii.
[6] Zaire, acte ii., scène iii.

of certain epochs. Every judgment is subject to revision, not to be reversed, but to be better explained, and, in some respects, to acquire a new meaning. Thus, we may adopt the judgments of La Harpe, and yet we no longer see the objects under his point of view, and we may perceive slight differences, and even characteristics, which have escaped his notice. This consideration might be sufficient to authorize a very long commentary, we shall only take the advantage of it to add a few words.

Œdipus (1718) was written by Voltaire, when he was nineteen years of age. We have already spoken of it.

Brutus (1730), a composition really new, was neither the first political nor the first Roman tragedy, and yet Voltaire developed in it ideas, which had escaped the notice both of Corneille and Racine. Its pathos is remarkably true; the scene in which Brutus receives the confessions of his son, is eminently tragical.

In *La Mort de Cæsar* (1735), the innovation may be said to be complete. This is quite the political tragedy; love is excluded from it, but the interests of mankind are still superior to the political interest. *Brutus* and *The Death of Cæsar*, are two corresponding subjects, very similar, and yet they are treated in a manner very different. *The Death of Cæsar* is of a great and noble simplicity; he does not mix up with it any strange or superfluous element. Its conception is extensive, and the style elevated and appropriate to the subject. It is one of the finest tragedies of Voltaire. He gets over a difficulty in it, which has, perhaps, not been taken into account, and that is, bringing on the stage the companions of Brutus, without any change in his countenance. Let any one read the principal scene of the conspirators, he will perceive that Brutus says in the main the same things as the others, but in an original manner. This merit is worth the trouble of being carefully noticed.

Zaire (1732) long passed for Voltaire's masterpiece. He said: "*Zaire* was the first play in which I gave myself up to all the sensibility of my heart." Indeed a passionate sensibility, which disguises the gross faults of the subject, is the merit of *Zaire*. These faults have been long acknowledged, and severely criticised. Voltaire had succeeded in spite of these defects, and it cost him little to acknowledge them. Under this confession, he concealed a refinement of self-love; the tears shed were, as it were, the absolution from these faults. He has given a good account of the charm of this production: "Every thing," says he, "is not undoubtedly what it should be, but she loves with so good faith."

This play has been called a *Christian tragedy*. But the struggle between the duty of fidelity to the worship of her fathers, and the passion of love, is not sufficient to impress on a theatrical piece the Christian character, especially when the interest rests, not upon religion, but upon a feeling which religion condemns.

The description of Orosmanes' jealousy was borrowed, as you know, from the Othello of Shakspeare. But the barbarian (it is thus Voltaire speaks of Shakspeare) is more profound and delicate than the gentleman. It is precisely in expressing this jealousy, that Voltaire is feeble. Zaire herself is perhaps as interesting as Desdemona; she is much more virtuous, since she struggles against her love. But Desdemona is conceived with an ideal grace, and a poetical charm, which is not to the same extent the portion of Zaire. The French tragic poets are more eloquent, and have more taste, but they are less poets. Pure poetry abounds more in the theatre of other nations. The characters in the English plays do not speak as they ought, and spoil their part by an insupportable mixture of the cynical, the grotesque, and the ridiculous. But the gift of the ideal and fertility of creation have been bestowed upon the English.

Alzire (1736) is truly the Christian play of Voltaire, and M. de Chateaubriand might justly say on this subject, that Voltaire was very ungrateful in persecuting a religion to which he had so many obligations. The meeting of the Peruvian Alzire and of Zamore, formerly betrothed to her, at the very moment when she had married the Spanish Gusman, is exceedingly noble, and the pardon of Gusman is truly sublime.

Mahomet (1741) was at first entitled *Fanaticism*. Voltaire, already raised to the rank of authority, found a pleasure in dedicating to the Pope this satire on the Catholic religion. What would have been said seventy years before, if Molière had dedicated *Tartufe* to Bossuet? But the most extraordinary thing was, that Benedict XIV. accepted the dedication of this new *Tartufe;* and between the pontiff and Voltaire, there was established a sort of literary correspondence. We may judge from this of the change of manners that had taken place during these years. It has been repeatedly said that, in this play, as a continuation of Molière, who had only aimed at hypocrisy, Voltaire had only attacked fanaticism. But it is wrong to attempt to acquit him; in spite of this excuse, which he has brought forward, the attack is really directed against the Catholic religion. This play, however, has overshot the mark; Voltaire heaps on the character of Mahomet so many atrocities, that historic truth revolts at them, and the moral and literary sense is equally offended. The stage does not admit gratuitous horrors. Yet the character of Seide is so well drawn, that this name has become a type, and a new word in the language. The character of Zopire is one of the finest creations of the theatre; Voltaire, who knew no family ties, and who in spite of his grey hairs, remained young under the worst relations, generally excels in describing old men and fathers. Besides, in Zopire, we do not merely find the tender and devoted father, but the citizen and the patriot unaffectedly represented. The winding up of the piece is finished pathos, and the moment when the old man, dying, embraces his children, is unparalleled on the stage.

Merope (1743) is a tragedy without love, and this is "a merit moreover," says its author. No doubt, we must not reject love, but it must be said the ancients did not know it. What we call by that name has undoubtedly its principle in nature, but is developed by civilization. Thus this sentiment does not exist in the ancient tragedy, which runs entirely on the affections of father, wife, child; and in this respect Voltaire again discovered the vein that had been abandoned. The interest of *Merope* only rests on maternal love. Here he was most simple, most true, and most judicious; the philosopher and the eighteenth century disappeared. He is not an ancient, but he is a man. It is nature. The points of interest are perfect, naturally brought in, and executed with superior talent; the action is conducted with taste and simplicity, the style is pure, clear, and animated. There are some admirable stories, among others, that of the fifth act.

Semiramis, Rome Sauvée, L'Orphelin de la Chine, Tancrede, belong to the second period of Voltaire's life; we shall find them there.

Our age has too closely followed the imprudent counsel of Voltaire, to strike vigorously rather than justly, a counsel doubly imprudent, since it tends on the one hand to render art unnatural, and on the other to make the artist be forgotten. Voltaire has been condemned for his carelessness about posterity—posterity only listens to correct and moderate strains. The mighty blows, which stirred up our emotions and appeared destined to a very long re-echo, will not reach our children; not that weakness and indifference are conditions of success, but what is within the bounds of art and truth is alone endowed with vital power. Why then does that which is false deceive us to-day, which will not deceive us to-morrow? Because a certain form of the false corresponds to each period, which appears at the time to be true. Afterwards that which is false is scarcely noticed, and is therefore treated with the utmost indifference. At present the people have nothing to receive from Voltaire, who appears to them timid and superannuated, and good judges prefer to him the author of *Iphigenie*. Racine's laurels are still fresh and green, while Voltaire's are withered; he is neglected and unknown. We would seek in vain, however, for his superior among those, who, since his death, have in their turn written for the stage, and we must confess that in our opinion the fine scenes in *Œdipus*, *Merope*, and in *The Death of Cæsar*, did not deserve to become antiquated. They will always remain in the memory of the lovers of poetry, of the beautiful and of the pathetic.

Voltaire created the tragi-comedy in its most agreeable form in *l'Enfant Prodigue* (1736), and in *Nanine* (1749), in which he is always perfect, when he does not think of being comic. He wished to introduce into comedy the sentimental element, and he even wrote the theory of this new art in the preface to *Nanine*:—

"The transition from compassion to laughter, difficult as it is to deal with it in comedy, is nevertheless natural to men. . . . . A regiment in the battle of Spire was forbidden to give quarter ; a German officer begs his life from one of our officers, and he gives him this answer:—*Ask of me, sir, anything else, but as to your life, it is not in my power.* This artless speech passed from mouth to mouth, and there was laughter in the midst of carnage. With how much greater reason may laughter follow affecting sentiments in comedy? Do we not weep with Alcmena and laugh with Sosia?"

But if Voltaire admits the comedy that moves our pity, provided that love alone makes us shed tears, he does not mean that comedy should degenerate into tragedy for the masses:—"The

art of extending its limits, without confounding them with those
of tragedy, is a great art," he says, " which it would be well to
encourage, and shameful to wish to destroy."[1]

There are fine verses and charming passages in the *Prodigal
Son*, and in *Nanine*, and yet Voltaire was wrong perhaps in
using in them verse of ten syllables.   No one manages it better
than he, but this verse is in reality less adapted to the stage than
the Alexandrian.

If Voltaire had not written comedies, it would never have been
known, gentlemen, to what extent he exceeded true comedy or
fell below it.   This first of satirists is the last of comedians.   His
comedy is merely grotesque and of the grossest description.   The
genius of satire seems to exclude comedy.

He has, if possible, been less successful in the ode.   He has
neither the principle nor the form of this style of writing.   The
principle must be wanting, counterfeit enthusiasm gives counterfeit poetry, and Voltaire never rose to enthusiasm—a contemplation simple, full and ravishing, the most noble condition, in which
the human soul can be found.   He could not cherish within him
personal poetry, his is altogether objective; it is, we repeat it,
merely a talent.   This talent may be sufficient for many kinds
of writing but never for the ode; the satiric vein, the true vein
of Voltaire, is quite opposed to lyric poetry.   And as to the form,
lyric poetry, most easy for the concatenation of thoughts, is in
this respect the most inflexible; it requires a sustained perfection,
which the nature of Voltaire's talent excluded.   All its grace
consists in negligence and perfect liberty.

There remains the philosophic poetry, which comprehends a
very great number of Voltaire's productions.   Many of his so-
called *fugitive* pieces are nothing else; and perhaps nothing is
more suited to Voltaire, than the talent of throwing out in all his
poetical compositions with the happiest negligence, a number of
natural, judicious, accessible, and agreeable thoughts, clothed in
a very striking and easy style, which engraves them indelibly on
the memory.   In this kind of writing he has no rivals, it is his
peculiar gift.   His light poetry is not merely trifling, but most
frequently sustained by some thought.   Gresset, usually so
graceful, does not possess this philosophical merit.   The philo-

---

[1] Conseils à un journaliste.

sophy of Voltaire is assuredly not good, it is even scarcely philosophy, it is sometimes an elevated good sense, that moderate wisdom of honest persons in all ages, of cultivated men and of those who know the world, which takes its place between stoicism and epicurism, undoubtedly much nearer the second than the first, but never entirely giving way to it; it never affirms too strongly, nor pushes to extremes the results, which it maintains and avoids above all the pretension to dogmatism and the tone of speculation. If Voltaire enervates the doctrines of the seventeenth century, he mitigates those of the eighteenth, to which he always seems to say: " Do not go so far:" or, "Do not go so fast." His philosophy is not materialism in the proper sense of the term, it is rather involuntarily than intentionally that it becomes so. It expresses modern civilization not in its pride, but in that which it has most agreeable and most acceptable.

What Voltaire has written most complete and consistent in this way, is contained in the *Discourses on Man*, and in the *Poem on Natural Law*. Verse was the language he preferred, and that in which he found himself most at ease.

The *Discourses*, seven in number, appeared from 1734 to 1737. M. de Fontanes has estimated them with elegance and correctness. " Voltaire, in general," he says, " wishes to be read amid the noise and bustle of great cities, amid the pomp of courts, and amid all the decorations of accomplished and corrupt society."[1] These *Discourses* present no new or striking idea, but they are a good summary of the feeling of their author. Their charm and real value are the diction, the colouring, the grace, a new and easy manner, the *sermo pedestris* of Horace; sometimes, however, the style falls below that measure. Prosaic verses abound; and we have here an example of the degree to which Voltaire can descend:—

.Tu ne veux pas, grand roi, dans tu juste indulgence,
Que cette liberté degénére en license
Et c'est aussi le vœu de tous les gens sensés.[2]

But the number of these verses is greatly exceeded by those that

[1] Fontanes, traduction de l'Essai sur l'Homme de Pope. Discours preliminaire.
[2] Thou dost not wish, great king, in thy just indulgence, that this liberty should degenerate into licentiousness, and this is the wish of all sensible people.

are brilliant and graceful; the author passes without an effort
from the most ordinary forms of expression to the most poetical
and the most ornate language, and, above all, he has a talent for
easy and harmonious description.

The first discourse has for its subject *Equality of Conditions.*
It is elegant, poetical, but superficial; it has less philosophy
than some pieces of Fontenelle, for example, contain. Voltaire
attempts to show that fortune and rank go for nothing in the
estimate of happiness, notwithstanding that account which, when
finally summed up, and, with its apparent disproportion of situations, gives almost in every case the same result:—" Happiness
is the haven for which all men are bound; the quicksands are
numerous, and the winds are uncertain. To make this unknown
shore, Heaven has given to mortals a slight bark: as the help, so
also the dangers are equal. What avails it, when the storm has
raised the waves, that thy mast displays a purple sail and silken
ropes. The wind is no respecter of persons—it overturns at the
same time the boats of the fishers and the yachts of kings. If
any happy pilot has escaped the storm, has approached the harbour, or at least gained the shore, his more fortunate vessel was
not better constructed, but the management was judicious, and
God was his guide. . . . . . Alas! where, then, are we to seek,
where are we to find happiness? In all places, at all times,
through all nature, nowhere perfect, everywhere in moderation,
and everywhere transitory, except in its Author alone. It is
like the fire, whose pleasant heat secretly insinuates itself into
every other element; it descends into the rocks, it rises to the
clouds; it goes to redden the coral in the sand of the sea; it exists in the ice, which winter has hardened."

With respect to Voltaire, happiness consists entirely in circumstances; he neither knows nor imagines that happiness
which springs from the internal disposition of the soul. We
may remark, in passing, that, in almost all languages, the words
employed to convey the idea of happiness bear this external and
superficial character. The German is an exception: the word
seligkeit expresses the condition of the soul itself.

The second discourse, *Moral Liberty,* aims shortly at establishing the point, that we feel ourselves to be free, and are so,
notwithstanding all the systems which endeavour to deny that
liberty.

The third, on *Envy*, has for its principal idea: "Endeavour to surpass, or at least to equal those by whom your success is obstructed"—a remedy not within the reach of every one.

Moderation forms the subject of the fourth discourse, the most beautiful and the most eloquent of the whole. We should be moderate, says Voltaire, in every thing—in curiosity, in ambition, in pleasure: "Reason guides thee—proceed by its light; advance still some steps, but set bounds to thy career: on the borders of the infinite, thy course must be stopped; there an abyss begins, which must be respected. . . . . Ask of Sylva by what secret mystery this bread and this meat digest in my body, and are transformed into a sweetly prepared milk? How, always filtered in its unerring course, does it run in long purple streams to swell my veins? How does it give to my languishing body a new power, and make my heart beat, and my brain think? He raises his eyes to heaven, he bows down, and exclaims—Inquire at that God who gave us life."

Well! these verses are preceded by the following: "To discover a little what is passing within me, I am going to consult the king's physician; no doubt he knows more about it than his learned brethren." We read a little farther on: "O you, who bring within the walls of Paris all the shameful excesses of the manners of the Sybarites, who, plunged in luxury and enervated with effeminacy, cherish in your soul a perpetual excitement, learn, ye fools, who seek pleasure, and the art of knowing and enjoying it, pleasures are flowers which our divine Master causes to spring around us, amid the thorns and briars of the world, each in its season; and, with prudent care, we may preserve them for the winter of our years; but if we must gather them, let it be with a light hand—their passing beauty speedily fades. Do not offer to your senses, overpowered with delicacy, all the perfumes of Flora, at once exhaled. There is no need to see, feel, and hear every thing: we should leave pleasures, to be able to take them up again. . . . . Labour is often the father of pleasure. I pity the man loaded with the weight of his own leisure; happiness is a good which nature sells us. There are here below no harvests without cultivation. Every thing undoubtedly requires care, and every thing is bought."

It is a pity that, in a theme so noble, and so well fitted for calming the passions, Voltaire was unable to restrain himself from attacking his enemies, and from low personalities. This malicious feeling, under whose influence he constantly acted, produced here the effect of rags thrown upon a purple robe.

We may sum up the fifth discourse, *On the Nature of Pleasure*, with these two maxims, that pleasure reveals a God, and that we must enjoy without excess : " Use, abuse not ; so the wise man directs." This encroaches on the subject of the preceding discourse.

In the sixth, *The Nature of Man*, Voltaire concludes that man is not the centre of creation. Every thing is not subordinate to him ; he should content himself with his rank and lot. Here the author slides into the burlesque : " One day some mice said to one another, What a charming world this is ! what an empire we have ! This palace, so magnificent, was erected for us ; from all eternity God made for us these large holes. Dost thou see these fat gammons of bacon under this dark vault ? they were created there by nature's hands. These mountains of lard, perpetual food, are here for our use till the end of time. Yes, great God, if we believe our wise men, we are the masterpiece, the aim and the end of Thy works ! The cats are dangerous, and ready to devour us, but this is for our instruction and correction !"

How far Voltaire may be right in his leading idea, we shall not take upon ourselves to decide. We shall merely say that we are the creatures of God, provided by Him with reason and sensibility, and thus rendered capable of knowing and adoring Him, and of becoming, for His praise, the voice of this dumb world. The glory of God is our true end, and our supreme destination ; but the beautiful, the great, and the human in this idea, which is still more metaphysical than moral, has entirely escaped the observation of Voltaire. He goes so far as to say that, when men suppose God to take pleasure in their giving to Him glory, they treat Him as a coxcomb.

Contempt for mankind is at the bottom of every thing which Voltaire has written on man and human affairs. He does not say, like Lamartine : " Man is a fallen god, who remembers heaven." [1] At the sight of the odious counterfeit which he is pleased to display to us, he compels us to exclaim with Athalie : " But I found nothing more than a horrible mixture of bones

---

[1] Lamartine, Meditations poetiques. Med. ii., l'Homme.

and mangled flesh dragged in the mire."[1]   At a later period, in his *Tales*, and *Philosophical Dictionary*, we again find the pitiless sarcasm with which Voltaire pursues human nature.

The seventh discourse turns on *True Virtue*. According to the author, it consists essentially in beneficence : " Love God, said he to him, *but* love men." This *but* has more meaning than size. It shows clearly that, with Voltaire, the idea of morality was quite detached from religion. He calls the love of God a *dogma*. To love God is not, in his view, a state of the soul—a psychological act, resulting from this, that God is worthy of our love—it is only an appendix, which is more or less a hindrance to the love of our neighbour. Voltaire never intended to comprehend the necessities which he never felt, or which education had stifled in his bosom. Besides, does not morality rest on a *dogma*—on an article of faith ? Was he not obliged to defend his dogma against materialists and utilitarians ? Is not the belief of moral obligation the beginning of religion ? What would Voltaire answer, if he were to hear conscience and the sentiment of duty treated as mysticism ? This was scarcely as yet admitted ; but the doctrines of Voltaire must lead to this conclusion. So soon as the idea of God is withdrawn from morality, we must necessarily arrive at utilitarianism, or, in other words, at egoism.

After this, I ask him how the love of God is inconsistent with morality ? Upon what is morality founded, if not on natural relations, whence certain obligations flow? Are there no natural relations between God and us ? Certainly, there are not only the most profound and the most natural relations, but also the first of obligations. Some put themselves on the side of conscience, and think to render God useless by making of it a god. But what does conscience do, if it be not in us God's representative ? The conscience is not *we*, it is *against us ;* it is, then, *other than we.* If it be other than we, it can only be God. If, then, it be God, we must treat that God as He deserves, and not respect the king less than the ambassador. If God has assigned us an end, that end cannot be beyond himself.[2]

---

[1] Racine, Athalie, acte ii., scène v.

[2] A few words of Chancellor Bacon will render this fundamental truth more distinct : " Man becomes guilty of total rebellion against God, and carries his presumption so far, as to imagine that the commandments and prohibitions of God were not the rules of good and evil, but that good and evil had a principle and an origin peculiar to themselves. He was ardently desirous to acquire the knowledge of those

One of the characters of Voltaire's morality is, that he does not consider man in himself, but man in the social relation, only as a being associated with other beings like himself. It must be said, by the sentiment of the social relations, man is led to the idea of duty, and by it to religion. Entirely isolated, and never coming in contact with his fellows, he would remain a stranger to God, and would be classed with brutes. If Providence has brought men together, it is not merely to favour the progress of their material condition, but also, and above all, with a view to their moral development.

But, because the relations of man with society have been the occasion of the knowledge of his duty to God, to conclude that we are only moral and religious in virtue of society, is to fall from truth into falsehood. The thought of God once known and perceived by His word—God, so to speak, once created by the conscience—it is evident that this great idea becomes the first in man, and that, upon this divine relation—not anterior, but superior to all the others—all the others should be regulated.

The *Poem on Natural Law*, dedicated to the King of Prussia, should be referred, by its date (1756), to the second period of Voltaire's life ; but we place it here because its morality is absolutely the same with the *Discourses on Man*, and the same observations apply to these two works. M. de Fontaine finds the latter by no means profound, and adds :—" It is a fine subject, but is it fully treated ? Was it necessary to destroy its gravity by that jeering and satirical tone, which Voltaire too often uses improperly in his most serious compositions ? The conversation of a simple man, the *Vicar of Savoy*, is more poetical than his verses, when he writes to Frederic. The *Poem on Natural Law* is inferior to the *Discourses*, not only in gravity of tone, but also the charms of poetry. It is divided into four parts. The first establishes the existence and universality of this law. In short, God has only spoken by conscience, but he has really spoken in this manner :—

" Morality, uniform at all times, and in all places, has ever spoken in the name of this God. It is the law of Trajan and Socrates, and it is yours. Nature is the apostle of this eternal

principles, and of that origin, with the sole view of being no longer dependent upon the will of God, who was known to him, and of having only obligations to himself, and to his own understanding, as if he also were God—a design the most diametrically opposed to the law of his Creator."

worship; good sense receives it, and avenging remorse, produced by conscience, is its defender; its formidable voice makes itself everywhere be heard. . . . . This law, sovereign in China and Japan, inspired Zoroaster and enlightened Solon. From one end of the world to the other, it speaks, it cries,—Adore one God, be just, and love thy country."

The second part is devoted to the solution of some difficulties. Many causes may obscure this natural light, especially the passions; but " the fatal tempest of our impetuous desires leaves at the bottom of our hearts morality and its rules. The source is pure; in vain the contagious winds have troubled its waters in their channels; in vain on its surface a strange mud boiling bears a slime, which alters it ; man, most unjust, and the least regulated, is there easily contemplated when the storm passes away."

He refutes, in like manner, the objection derived from the diversity of manners and customs; he shows that, amid a variety of applications, the principle remains invariably the same.

The third part includes complaints against intolerance of opinions, and the provocation to persecute those which we do not approve. As morality is everywhere the same, no one should condemn his neighbour for mysterious, and, according to Voltaire, incomprehensible dogmas. Under the cover of this idea, he sets himself anew against the pretension of adding the dogma to morality. We shall not return to a point of which we have already spoken above. At the foundation, what else is religion than morality?

" Discreetly faithful to religion, be gentle, compassionate, wise, and indulgent, like her, and think of gaining the harbour without drowning others : clemency is right, and anger is wrong. In our transitory day of pains and miseries, children of the same God, let us live at least as brethren; let us assist one another in carrying our burdens. We advance, quite bent under the weight of our evils. . . . . I think I see galley-slaves in a fatal prison, able to assist each other, but mutually provoked to fight with the fetters with which they are chained."

In the fourth part, Voltaire examines the functions of governments in relation to religion and decides, that they ought to settle the disputes, which trouble society. It is, in a word, religion put into the hands of the prince :—

" Unfortunate the nations, whose opposite laws entangle the

divided reins of the state. The Roman senate, that council of conquerors, *presided over the altars,* and governed the manners, wisely restricted the number of the vestals, and regulated the bachanals of an extravagant people."

He developed this doctrine in his *Philosophical Dictionary :—* " In a religion, of which God is represented as the author, the functions of ministers, their persons, their goods, their pretensions, *the mode of teaching morality, of preaching doctrine, of performing ceremonies, spiritual punishments, every thing,* in a word, *which is of importance to civil order,* ought to be subjected to the authority of the prince, and to the inspection of the magistrates." [1]

The summary of the morality of these two works may be included in these four verses :—" Be just, beneficent, avoiding every extreme, indulgent to thy brother and thyself; make no inquiry, whence thou hast come and whither thou art going ; and proceed towards the end without fear and without hope."

We are struck with the vacillation which this morality presents. It is by turns a piece from all systems ; but from all the rags of truth, which hang at all errors, we do not make truth. It is like our Lord's coat, it has no seam.

But the great inconsistency of Voltaire, the uncertainty of his opinions, the finished quackery of his doctrines, if so be that he has doctrines, are explained by the extreme frivolity of his character. He was naturally and systematically frivolous; he has even eulogised frivolity :—" What convinces me most that there is a Providence, said the profound author of *Bacha Bilboquet,* is, that, to console us amid our innumerable miseries, nature has made us frivolous. If we were not frivolous, what man could remain without trembling in a city, where a high-titled lady of honour to the queen was burnt, under the pretext that she had made a white cock be killed by moonlight." [2]

Of modern poets, Voltaire most resembles Horace ; although the character of their talent is different, their philosophy is the same, a mitigated epicurism. There is also a resemblance in their manner. Both have a graceful and witty carelessness, a negligence, which never descends to trifling ; but although a more finished writer, Horace is less brilliant, and has less than Voltaire the charm of an expansive sensibility.

---

[1] Dictionnaire Philosophique : Article Droit Canonique.
[2] Ibid. : Article Frivolité.

The subject of the *Discourses on Man* is analogous to that of Boileau's Epistles. But, for Voltaire, truth is a matter of impression; he represents it as useful, beautiful, amiable, never as true. With Boileau, truth is more objective, and at the same time has more dignity. Yet Boileau, more true and more moral, has less breadth and originality; in general, he knows less than Voltaire how to appropriate that truth which he believes; his is less intimately united to him, it is a little that of every one. Sometimes, however, he is superior to Voltaire in the depth of his thoughts; as in his Epistle on *Truth*, where he believes truth for its own sake. But he rarely rises to this height, and he wants the charm of Voltaire.

Pope, the author of the *Essay on Man*, is superior to Voltaire, whether in the elevation of his thoughts or in the sustained merit of his manner. He has conciseness elegant and exact, nobleness, force and grandeur, but grace and ease remain as Voltaire's portion. From the moment at which you are withdrawn from the moral point of view, where, in respect of literature, you wish to judge less than you seek to enjoy, you feel yourself always attracted to the side of Voltaire, while strictly, he would rather deserve the last rank among the poets whom we have now named. Horace, Pope, Boileau, are much more equal, they keep at a height from which Voltaire often descends. The other philosophical poems belong to another period.

There remains a cloud of light and fugitive poems, and small philosophical discourses, which have the satirical form, without, however, being satires. They are, in general, poems of very loose morality. We notice *le Mondain*, a true apology for luxury and sensual pleasure; *le Temple de l'Amitié*, a small interesting poem; *le Pour et le Contre*, or *l'Epitre à Uranie*. This sceptical piece, in which Voltaire appears at first to present the eulogiums of Christianity, to make on it afterwards a merciless satire, was followed by the exile of its author. We should farther mention *l'Epitre à Madame du Chatelet*, an explanation of the discoveries of Newton; it was a kind of poetry then unknown, and really created by Voltaire; *l'Epitre à Rosalie*, addressed to Madame Denis, the author's niece, a classical piece, and a masterpiece of the kind; *les Vous et les Tu*, a delightful play, but its morality was by no means strict; in short, the charming strophes, which begin with these words : " If you wish that I should still love !"

On the whole, we must conclude, that into the fugitive poetry, Voltaire put more poetry and more thought than any of those who preceded him.

The prose of Voltaire was at once elevated and debased beyond its just value. On the whole, he has not bestowed upon the French prose any forms absolutely new; he has added nothing to the language of the seventeenth century, of which he has preserved, if not all the grace, at least the clearness, the flow, and the simplicity, while he gives to it a quicker motion, and more lively turns. His prose remained the same till the end of his career without being in any way superannuated.

Voltaire the prose writer, and Voltaire the poet, are two men, or rather gentlemen; it is the prose writer who is the truer man, the accomplished Voltaire. There is something conventional in Voltaire, the poet, the talent is there more than the personality. Still the poet has much of the eighteenth century, he is less pure and less chastened; his style on serious subjects is not exempted from redundancies, and from time to time sounds hollow. The prose writer never falls into these defects, his simplicity is unalterable. If he has permitted the diction of prose to enter too often into his poetry, it was because the latter tended to practise real life, but he never allowed poetry to invade his prose.

His prose is animated, easy, brilliant, always exciting, and exceedingly attractive. It gave wings to the ideas, to which it was perfectly adapted, and of all prose, it is the most purely French. Its turn and animation are new, although it is substantially the same as that of the seventeenth century. The same tendencies had not hitherto assumed this form. Hamilton and Saint-Evremond have something of it, but they have not applied this form of expression to subjects so varied. On serious subjects in the seventeenth century, they were either more grave or more poetical. Voltaire is neither the one nor the other; his prose furnishes light armour to a very light philosophy, it supplies strength by its rapid movement, and depth by its clearness.

But is there anything in Voltaire's mode of thinking truly philosophical? This must be admitted. Yes, it includes an element of philosophy. To substitute nature for convention, and good sense for authority, to prefer moral to outward acts, things to words, deeds to persons, and generals to particulars, to bring together what the vulgar separate, and to distinguish what they confound; all this is philosophy, but this is all that Voltaire possesses. He rises no higher. He lays no claim to the noblest elements of human nature, faith, the infinite, providence; he only knows the soul in its lower and middle regions; he was only acquainted with man in his social capacity; he does not know man in the presence of himself, much less in the presence of the Infinite; he is deficient in true morality. With respect to morality, he has instincts, prejudices, and habits, but no prin ciples.

This mode of thinking stamps the character of his style. His light, lively, and brilliant prose wants, if we may say so, body. It is delicate and easy, but slender, thin, and meagre—it is never majestic. "Light, and in a short dress, it moves along with large steps."[1] But we feel not the earth tremble under it, and each shake give forth the sound of armour. It has the vivacity which comes from the understanding, rarely the heat which issues from the soul. It abridges, but does not concentrate; it does not make us feel much more than it expresses, and it never goes into the interior of things like the style of Montesquieu. In me it always produces the effect such as a piece of wood does which you wish to sink in water, but which always rises to the surface. It has no defects, but it wants some essential qualities.

After all, the type and ideal of French prose have been given by Bossuet and Fenelon. The sceptre of this prose remains in the hands of the seventeenth century. If the prose of Voltaire resembles in several respects that of his predecessors, if we may apply to it what he himself said of something else—" ever surprised, and always enchanted," at bottom it differs from it still farther. It has less substance, harmony, and colouring. We have already shown this; in theory, and especially in practice, no writer has established a boundary so decided between prose and poetry. These two modes of writing and these two men never meet. Voltaire, the prose writer, does not remember that he is a poet; he does not require to watch over himself in this respect, nowhere does he permit the least breath of poetry to penetrate into his prose. There is, in French literature, no similar ex-

[1] La Fontaine, Fables. Livre vii., fable 10.

ample. No doubt, prose, which is called poetical, is in itself false; but it does not follow that the prose writer and the poet should have nothing in common. Poetry and prose are not two substances, but two languages peculiar to man. Ought a man, or is he always able, to distinguish the precise point, so that, in his prose, the least image should never betray the impressions and language of the poet? Fenelon, Bossuet, Montaigne, and J. J. Rousseau, have often mixed their prose with poetry. Voltaire found even the prose of Massillon too poetical.

I confess, gentlemen, that in the prose of Voltaire, this last method, as well as the distant and profound, are wanting. I am kept near the shore, I long to reach the bank. Voltaire is elegant and luminous, and leads us forward pleasantly, but he does not reach the inner part of our nature. This is not merely the defect of language, but of thought.

If we agree with Montesquieu, Voltaire *is only pretty.*[1] This saying betrays Montesquieu's mode of thinking. Rightly understood, it has, no doubt, a fund of truth. Voltaire deserved this sentence. When his philosophy is not remarkably defective, it may be called pretty.

Voltaire, during the first period of his life, applied himself to all kinds of subjects. I pass over several scientific works, especially intended, for the most part, to render science popular. Voltaire's genius was suited to the common people; he is not one of those to whom inferior minds and more popular understandings come to borrow strong ideas, which they afterwards attempt to crumble down to the multitude. He discovered the fund of his ideas, and alone invents their popular form; he then sets them forth, and puts them at once in circulation. His manner is superior to that of Fontenelle; he does not beautify science, he does not seek to render it imposing by the use of technical terms, nor attractive by excluding them.

In 1726, the *Letters on the English* appeared, written from England, and at first circulated secretly, and in manuscript. So soon as Voltaire thought he could do it without danger, he collected and published them, with the title of *Philosophical Letters.* We may remark, in passing, what influence was exercised over the times in which they saw the light, by three works published in the form of letters. In the seventeenth century, there were

[1] Montesquieu, Pensées diverses: des Modernes.

the *Provincial Letters*, still less a theological discussion and a struggle against the Jesuits than a manifestation of the liberty of thought; in the eighteenth, the *Persian Letters*, 1721; and, ten years later, the *Philosophical Letters* closely related to them.

Montesquieu's object was simple—he wished to make France known to the French. Voltaire had a double aim—it was at once France and England that he wished to bring before the public. Montesquieu had revealed France, so to speak, by using the eyes of an Asiatic. Voltaire uses his own eyes—the eyes of a Frenchman—in opening up England. Their mode of procedure is in reality the same. Montesquieu takes his point of view in Persia, to judge from that quarter of France and Europe. Voltaire is, in fact, transported into England; but it is almost enough for him to speak of England in order to judge of France, although he does not affect to put England above France, and although he does not directly speak of the latter. Beyond Montesquieu, however, he boasted of the English government. Voltaire, still young, was bolder on these subjects, and showed himself more prejudiced, than he afterwards appeared at a maturer age. He applied himself to all kinds of subjects: the church, philosophy, literature, Bacon, Locke, Shakspeare, inoculation; in short, Voltaire was the first that revealed England to France, and the undertaking was more daring and more important than it appears. These two neighbouring nations, rivals and related, were contented to give themselves up to mutual hatred, without knowing one another.

The *Philosophical Letters* appeared to have greater boldness than the *Persian*. They really had so, although on the surface it did not appear. Montesquieu's mode of expression is more lively; but Voltaire's, more circumspect in the form, is much less so in the main. Neither the public nor the government were deceived by them. The *Persian Letters* made the authorities start, but that was all; for, a little after, Montesquieu obtained a seat in the Academy. Now, it was there that literature received political approbation or acquittal. The work of Montesquieu, considered as a work of art and·imagination, was taken less seriously than Voltaire's, though it was perhaps more so. The work of Voltaire appeared what it was, a pamphlet; it was truly the *pamphlet of pamphlets*. At a time when the double despotism of government and fashion reigned, when the govern-

ment took the side of fashion, and when even music was directed
by the public offices, Voltaire was bold to a degree which we can
scarcely now understand. No people submits more willingly to
the yoke of fashion than the French—to obey the fashion is a
duty in France. Voltaire boldly attacked these two despotisms,
and united them against him. Afterwards, his political independence underwent a course of diminution, but his intellectual independence continued the same.

Voltaire is witty in quite a different manner from Montesquieu,
who has as much wit as any one else, but he is wrong in using
it. Without making a parade of his superiority, he lets it too
much appear. Voltaire conceals his : he translates his wit into
good sense, while so many others endeavour to translate their
good sense into wit. He is the man of the world who had most
wit, but who uses it least. This circumstance ensures the success
of a great number of his works ; he has the tact to make us believe that we have intelligence, and even as much of it as he
himself.

The *Persian Letters* rest upon a fiction, which the author
renewed ; the *Philosophical Letters* have no framework, not
even that of the epistolary form, notwithstanding their title, and
they are not less pointed. Their style has fewer beauties and
defects than that of the *Persian Letters*. As to the subjects
treated, if they have become soon old, it is because the talent of
the author soon rendered them common. Great men work
against their own glory, by making common and trivial what
was before their time extremely rare.

The *History of Charles XII.* (1728), is the history of a soldier,
who by chance was a king. " He did not direct his conduct
according to the actual disposition of things, but according to a
certain model which he had taken, though he followed it very
badly. He was not Alexander, but he would have been Alexander's best soldier."[1] It is a biography, an epic poem—nay, it
is only a long anecdote, which is detached from history without
leaving a void. Voltaire lets us scarcely see in it the new spirit
and the new idea, with which he intended to endow history. It
has not the tint of irony and fatalism which prevails in his other
historical writings. This narrative is animated, luminous, elegant,

---

[1] Montesquieu, Esprit des Lois. Livre x. chap. xiii.

and written with remarkable good sense, and is a sort of masterpiece; and yet I cannot admire it, I confess, quite so much as many do. It is undoubtedly a classical work, but there is perhaps something a little conventional in the rank which is assigned to it. Here, more than elsewhere, the defect arises from the depth and the prospect of future events. We have at once every thing which we can have, a second reading gives us nothing more. Voltaire wrote this work without feeling and without warmth; he only wrote it with his intellect. I wish authors were either largely objective, or freely subjective. Often in a work we like as well to meet with the author as with the subject. It is, perhaps, a defect in a book, but it is very pleasant. The *History of Charles XII.* has, for me, neither great attraction nor much value.

Literary Criticism. Counsels to a Journalist. Voltaire wrote literary criticism well, and he thought it good. He is not profound, nor has he extended the boundaries of this kind of criticism, but he has great good sense. It is especially in the domain of theoretical criticism, that good sense is rare. Here the great models become posthumous tyrants, we must imitate them in every thing, and adopt their excellencies and defects. In literature, France is the country of routine. When a man is allowed to have good sense, by that very thing he becomes original and powerful. Good sense is always original, for convention and tradition constantly tend to substitute themselves for it. Voltaire had the originality and the power of good sense.

But he has the folly to make himself the personification of his literary theories, the type of the good and the beautiful. He has the appearance of terminating every thing by repeating: You have merely to study how I escaped. There is in it a want of delicacy, an impudence, which are revolting. He reminds us of the fable of the *Bee and the Fly :* " The bee spoke to her of the honey which she had made, it was exquisite and perfect in her view, preferable to the honey of Hymettus. I must send you some, said she—I must, for your complaints in the breast; it will be a sovereign remedy. . . . Vapour! Ah, my sister! should you be subject to them, I have for that complaint an excellent recipe, and which you would in vain seek elsewhere. . . . Form an extract of my honey. . . ."

SECOND PART.

WHEN we compare, gentlemen, the first half of the century, which now occupies our attention with the period of Louis XIV., it seems as if we were already in the very heart of the eighteenth century. But when we pass to the second half of this great period, we feel that the first was only the prologue and the explanation of the drama. The explosion has not yet taken place. " Voltaire and Montesquieu," as I have said in another place, "fill with their glory and their influence the first half of the eighteenth century ; but the action of Voltaire is more immediate and extensive, and better felt. By all his talents, he corresponds with every department of the national mind, he sums up in himself all the lively tendencies, and all the impatience of his age. This age he wishes to instruct and amuse by turns, and to occupy it without relaxation. The writers whose names pervade his universal fame, dispose each only of a part of the public, of an opinion, and of a particular world ; Voltaire has rights over them all ; Rollin, Louis Racine, D'Aguesseau, Massillon, Dubos, Fontenelle, La Motte, Destouches, Le Sage, Prevost, share unequally with him public attention, but do not dispute it. He has something new, which none of them possesses, and among them all he alone appears to belong to the eighteenth century. What he composed from 1718 to 1750, is sufficient to put him, in reference to influence and celebrity, above all comparison. When the second half of the century was opened and exhibited, a new generation of talents, of which several were of the first order, and altogether a powerful school, Voltaire was already the author of almost all that is more solid in his literary fortune. To set out from 1750, he was still the most popular and powerful of writers ; the talents which his example had, more or less, called forth, and which his lessons had prepared, had a peculiar value, and an independent existence ; and the second period of the eighteenth century owed to them a character in which Voltaire did not always perceive that of his personal opinions, nor the impulse of his mind."[1]

---

[1] Vinet, Discours sur la Literature Française, pp. 47, 48.

The political events, even in 1780, are not unconnected with the literary and philosophical progress of the age. Literature had undoubtedly a share in the expulsion of the Jesuits. The exile of the Parliament was an internal revolution in itself important. The humiliating conclusion of the seven years' war (1756–1762) gave a new impulse to philosophy and literature. They alone emerged from the tarnished principles which led to this political condition, and on their ground France was still the conqueror. At a later period, the division of Poland and the American war exercised a lively influence over men's minds. All these circumstances, no doubt, contributed to the prodigious number of intellectual productions during that time; but what is especially worthy of remark, is the suddenness of the explosion, and the accumulation, within a very limited space, of all the elements whose presence must characterize the eighteenth century. There are times when every thing seems to burst forth at once, and when men of genius of every description seem to have appointed a place of general resort.

Ten or twelve years in the middle of the eighteenth century saw the display of more varied talents, the accomplishment of more literary destinies, and the consummation of a literary revolution more important than perhaps was ever seen in any country, and in a much longer period. A simple biographical notice would render this fact quite clear.[1]

In setting out from this point, all the doubtful or intermediate shades disappear, and the eighteenth century takes all its character—the time is come to characterize it. This is the true eighteenth century; this is properly the epoch or reign of philosophy.

[1] See le Discours de M. Vinet sur la Literature Française, p. 48. To omit nothing important, we may refer merely to a few years within the point of departure indicated, and may mention in succession :—1746, Introduction à la Connaissance de l'Esprit Humain, par Vauvenargues. Essai sur l'Origine des Connaissances Humaines, par Condillac. Pensées Philosophiques de Diderot. 1749, De l'Esprit des Lois, par Montesquieu. Les Premiers volumes de l'Histoire Naturelle de Buffon. Lettre sur les Aveugles, par Diderot. 1750, Discours sur les Sciences, par J. J. Rousseau. 1751, Considerations sur les Moeurs, par Duclos. Discours Preliminaire de l'Encyclopedie, par D'Alembert. Siécle de Louis XIV., par Voltaire. 1753, Discours de Reception de Buffon a l'Académie Française. Discours de J. J. Rousseau, sur l'Inégaleté des Conditions. 1754, Traité des Sensations, par Condillac. 1755, Discours de l'Esprit Philosophique, par Guénard. 1756, Essai sur les Moeurs des Nations, par Voltaire. 1759, De l'Esprit, par Helvetius. This nomenclature and these dates appear to us not to be wanting in eloquence.

The seventeenth century, which Vauvenargues called " the most philosophical of all ages," had undoubtedly philosophized, but it was under a glass. The philosophy of that time was not a reaction, or at least it did not seem to be so; in fact, it was more so than it was aware, but not intentionally. We do not see it breaking the bands which attach it to public belief—it seeks only to lengthen them; it applies and explains—it neither destroys nor creates. It does not build a new house, it is suffi- cient for it to lodge in the old one with the greatest possible convenience. If a few miners dig under the foundations of the edifice, the dull noise of the digging, either within or without, is scarcely heard.

The philosophy of the eighteenth century is a reaction. It repairs and supports the foundations; it sweeps away all that had been formerly built; it removes all traditions and all autho- rities. It wishes to build a new dwelling, but it would rather prefer living in the open air, exposed to rain and wind, than enter into the old house. It is more employed in destruction than in creation. What age ever wished two things at once ? Its character is essentially negative.

It is negative, but it assumes the appearance of being positive. It professes to inquire into the origin of thought, and reduces man to an organism—thought, sentiment, and virtue are only sensations. By inevitable consequence, the disinterested prin- ciple is abolished in man, who, having nothing more but the senses, has nothing more than interests; happiness, which is, in this philosophy, only pleasure on a great scale, becomes the universal rule and measure. Locke produced Condillac, Con- dillac inspired Helvetius, and, at a later period, Cabanis.

With respect to every thing which, in science, belongs to the domain of purely sensible facts, this is not an inconvenience. An epoch, animated with this spirit, should love, and may suc- cessfully study, this order of facts. Thus we see the eighteenth century ardently devote itself to the study of physics, natural science, and political economy—a mixed science between natural and moral philosophy. We begin to speak of the sect of the *Economists*, Locke is not more appealed to than Bacon. There was formed at that time, according to this great man, the design of *organizing human knowledge*—a premature scheme ; but its conception may characterize an age. Hence this great work of the *Encyclopedie,* an enormous pamphlet, at once a magazine and a plan of war.

Divided on so many points, there is one on which the philosophers are agreed—that is the destruction of Christianity, unjustly involved in the just hatred, of which the priesthood is the object. I cannot conceal from myself that there was, on every side of a blind hatred, the lawful necessity of disinterring from the mass of theocratic elements the human element, which was found hidden there, like those monuments of Egypt that had almost entirely disappeared under heaps of sand. This necessity corresponded to other necessities—to that of discovering nature under convention, and justice under a mass of positive laws. Man inquired into his own nature, and threw off, with some effort, that great old tyranny—official truth. Unhappily, at that time, it was by degrading him that he was restored; at the very moment that you snatch him from the priest, you take him away from God. The times did not permit another and more real deliverance. They passed from Egypt to Egypt, and from one slavery to another; and such was the violence of the reaction, that, by the same blow, suppressing God and the soul, they gave up man to his senses, whose insolence henceforth was no longer expressed, but by the calculations of egoism. " Gorge yourselves with pleasures ; as for me, I can do no more, I have finished my time," said Voltaire. Thus spoke the guides of humanity. Wo to the age which pretends to shake off prejudices without strengthening morals in the same proportion !

A nation less intellectual and social, which should have adopted such maxims, would have sunk in the mire. The taste for mental enjoyments, sociality, perhaps vanity—some instincts difficult to be destroyed, and some traditions which are only slowly effaced—prevented the utmost excesses.

The hatred of religions did not extend to political institutions ; at least the second was less vehement and unanimous. Among those enemies of the old religion there were many conservatives, by character, position, and the love of an easy, soft, and elegant life. Look at Voltaire at the feet of Madame de Pompadour, and of Madame du Barry. Nevertheless the reaction operated also on that side. A few persons of exalted rank went into that view, as far as it was possible, showing the truth of the famous saying of Diderot : " And my hands would twist the bowels of the priest for want of a cord to strangle kings!" This is, however, the violent throe of a disordered imagination, to which we must not attach too much importance.

The power of the literature of the eighteenth century clung to the new spirit, which, directing every thing toward one end, made for the first time sciences, letters, and arts a homogeneous and compact mass, and all the writers, under the name of philosophers, a close phalanx. Every miscreant was admitted into this league. Its public sittings were long so many festivals of the reigning philosophy, by the intercourse which it opened up for its benefit, and by the object which it continued to present to the ambition of literary men. Internally divided into two camps, and restrained by the suitableness of an official position, it was not less a splendid theatre, on which the thought of the age might be displayed, and might triumph in the public view.

The ladies, whom French manners mix up with every thing, were not useless in the maintenance of this league. The saloons of Mesdames Geoffrin, du Deffand, de Lespinasse, were its principal centres; but the general place of meeting was the house of Baron d'Holbach. They were anxious to gain the favour of the great lords and princes; they tried to persecute their opponents; and they sometimes succeeded in arming power against them. Saint-Lambert, who never forgot that he was a marquis, made Clement, the *inclement*, be imprisoned, to teach him to form a better estimate of the poem on the *Seasons*. They succeeded in turning Freron into ridicule in a crowded theatre. Voltaire allows himself, without compunction, to do to his opponents what he found frightful on the part of J. B. Rousseau; we may judge of it by this passage in one of his prefaces: " A very contemptible pride, a base self-interest, more contemptible still, are the sources of all those criticisms with which we are inundated. A man of genius will undertake a play for the theatre, or any other poem, to acquire some renown; a Freron will rail at it to gain a crown. A man, who does infinite honour to literature, enriched France with the beautiful poem of the *Seasons*. What happens? A young pedant from college, ignorant and hotheaded, urged by pride and hunger, wrote a gross libel against the author and his work; he pretends, etc.

" A man of this sort, named Sabatier, a native of Castres, wrote a literary dictionary, and praises a few individuals in order to get bread. He met another beggar: 'My friend, you write eulogies, you will die of hunger, make a satirical dictionary, if you would have wherewithal to live.' The unfortunate man laboured, and became still poorer.

" Such was the rabble of literature in the time of Corneille, such is it now, and such will it be seen at all times. There will always be in an army officers and blackguards, and in a great city magistrates and thieves."[1]

The ancient law has few courageous and able defenders. Living, evangelical Christianity, more philosophical than the philosophy of the eighteenth century, should have kept up its head, but where was it? Besides, on that side, it would have been necessary to act, and they wrote.

You must see in France and in Europe the state of society such as the philosophers found it, and such as they made it.

In France, at first, " this comparison brings to view two contemporaneous, and, no doubt, corelative facts, the weakness and disorganization of the social institution, and at least the comparative vigour of literature ; every thing in the first order of facts is shown to be false, contradictory, and precarious. All appears to have a tendency to go out from its position and course. There is not a power nor an order in the state, which, like a door with broken hinge, is not lifted out of its place. There is no system which does not bear in itself its own negation. On the threshold of a revolution, despotism is without bounds and discretion, and also without energy and foresight; it gnaws the last remains of ancient liberties, while a new and young liberty is at hand. Deprived of the decorations of glory, it is also deprived of that trust in itself, which is a power and an excuse, and of that trust in the multitude, which is the only right of absolute power. Amid liberality of opinions and of manners, it is no more than a scandalous and stupid opposition. The great, whose haughtiness has turned into effrontery, and who have made for themselves a liberty for the splendour of their vices, affect the knowledge of the citizens, and laugh publicly at the prejudices which make them what they are. Those among them who would wish to maintain the institutions of the kingdom, puff irreligion, and applaud the undertakings of impiety, without suspecting that all

---

[1] Avertissement de Voltaire en tête de son édition de Corneille.

things which have constantly existed together, end by adhering, and become reciprocally united, and that one part of the edifice cannot be overturned without the others falling into ruins along with it. Religion itself, betrayed by its ministers, makes advances to philosophy, whose constant practice is never to use it. Parliaments, ignorant of the times, were unacquainted with themselves, but sometimes, we may believe, going out of their course from patriotism, make a revolutionary opposition, and lend, like the horse in the fable, their shoulders to their future enemy. Were men of letters, whom these false inferences should at least have profited, more sound in their reasonings? In our opinion they were not, when to the maxims of Sparta they united the manners of Sybaris, to the lofty contempt of the Portico the flexibility of Aristippus, to the declamation of the forum the adulations of the court; when they were anxiously dressing up the image of a revolution, of which they must all one day detest the reality, and when they opened up to their contemporaries the foolish prospect of a society without belief, and of a liberty without morals. The public uniting the most extravagant tastes, obeying the most varied impulses, smitten with the savage life, and refining on all the enjoyments of civilization, ironical with Voltaire, and misanthropical with Rousseau, attached to France, and fond of the foreigner, eager for positive knowledge, and attempting the sentimental reverie, affecting great passions in unfeeling hearts; the public uniting in itself elements of power and symptoms of decrepitude, was, like each of the classes and of the authorities of society, only chaos and contradiction. A torrent swept away all wills, as it happens, whenever thought, under lively excitement, finds not its complement and counterpoise in morals. Thus all the orders of society pushed each other towards an unknown termination; and this progress, which appeared dictated by fatality, was revealed in French literature from the year 1750 to the year 1780, an epoch, in which the complete publication of the work of Raynal, is like the last blaze of a fire when nothing remains to be consumed."[1]

We may add that authority, half-inimical, half-conniving, opposes to philosophers only weak barriers, and offers only to their adversaries weaker encouragements. You must see Male-

---

[1] Vinet, Discours sur la Literature Française, pp. 52-54.

sherbes concurring in the publication of the *Emile*. You must hear that same Malesherbes, the day of his reception into the French Academy in 1775, acknowledge, and in some sort consecrate the empire of public opinion : " The public feel an eager curiosity about things which were once most indifferent to them. They have raised a tribunal independent of all power, and which all power respects, this tribunal appreciates all talents, and pronounces on all kinds of merit, and in an enlightened age, in an age in which each citizen may speak to the entire nation in the way of impression, those who have the talent of instructing men, and the gift of rousing their feelings, in a word, men of letters, dispersed among the public, are what the orators of Rome and Athens were in the midst of the assemblies of the people. This truth, which I now set forth in a meeting of men of letters, has been presented to magistrates, and no one has refused to acknowledge this tribunal of the public as the sovereign judge of all the judges of the earth."[1]

But this idea of the sovereignty of public opinion has been too lightly adopted. They establish as a right what is only a fact. The duty of the statesman is not only to listen to public opinion, but to put it right according as it requires correction ; nothing is done without it, but he must not let it do all. This soon began to be observed. We may compare with the discourse of Malesherbes, the no less remarkable discourse of Rulhière delivered thirteen years later :—

" It was at that time, there was set up among us what we call *the empire of public opinion*. Men of letters were soon ambitious to be its organs, and almost its arbiters. A more serious taste prevailed in intellectual productions ; the desire to instruct was shown more than the desire to please. The dignity of *men of letters*, an expression just and new, soon became a phrase generally acknowledged, and received into common use.

" But if in the former period, the inevitable abuse of wit had been that barren profuseness, and that vain subtility of thoughts and expressions, sometimes even servile complaisance and degrading flatteries, the abuse in this new period was a kind of magisterial affectation, an imprudent boldness, a sort of fanaticism in opinion, a tone of affirmation and dogmatism, which made

[1] Choix de Discours de Reception, tome ii., pp. 68, 69.

Fontenelle say, then in his hundredth year, and still a witness of this revolution : ' I am afraid of the horrible certainty which I now meet with everywhere.' "[1]

In Europe, the credit of philosophers was immense : " The age was disposed to listen to truths, which the novelty of their aspect made appear new, and which their suitableness rendered bold. The French philosophy found disciples among kings, who had all at once become more philosophers than their subjects. Several princes had at Paris literary correspondents. The King of Prussia and the Empress of Russia disputed the possession of D'Alembert. Diderot, loaded with benefits by Catherine, was invited to her court. The northern sovereigns travelled into France, and seemed to have come merely for the philosophers. True, with the most part of these sovereigns, this admiration led to no result, but elsewhere the philosophical principles wrought out important reforms; in Spain and Portugal, they appeared to guide two celebrated ministers, La Ensenada and the Marquis de Pombal. At this time, when the greater part of the European nations had no literature of their own, foreign writers did scarcely anything else than imitate or translate French works."[2] Such was the state of minds and things.

But all the remarkable writers neither belonged to the philosophical sect or party, nor did they unite with it. Those who entirely belonged to it were Voltaire, D'Alembert, Diderot, Helvetius, Raynal, D'Holbach, and Grimm. Those who marched under other banners, or who made their exceptions, were Buffon, Duclos, Mably, Rousseau, Bossuet, and Condillac.

We left Voltaire at Cirey, at the house of the Marchioness du Chatelet, where he passed the time which was not devoted to Stanislaus, King of Poland. At the death of this lady, for whom Voltaire appeared to have experienced the only deep feeling of his life, he yielded to the urgency of the King of Prussia, and resolved to set out for Berlin. It was not, however, without some apprehensions : " I have been given up, my dear child, in due form to the King of Prussia," he writes to his niece. " My marriage is then made, will it be happy? I cannot tell. I could not help saying, *yes*. It was necessary to end well with this

¹ Choix de Discours de Reception, tome i., p. 375.
² Vinet, Discours sur la Literature Française, pp. l.-li.

marriage, after the flirtations of so many years. My heart beat at the altar."[1]

Admiration seems to have been sincere on the part of Frederic, who never ceased to praise the genius of Voltaire. Was it equally so on Voltaire's side, who already called Frederic *the Marcus Aurelius of Germany*, when he was only a royal prince, and had hitherto done nothing, and who wrote : " In regard to verse, I defy all Germany, and almost all France, to produce anything better than this fine epistle : ' O you, in whom my tender heart, filled with the desire of home, still cherishes the parentage which gave it birth ?' This word *encore* (*still*) appears to me one of the greatest niceties in art and language ; it says very energetically in two syllables, that a man's parents are loved a second time in his brother."[2] Is not this *speaking at random?*

The first enchantment of this honeymoon is not unknown to you : " This prince appears to resemble Marcus Aurelius in every thing, except that the Roman did not make verses, and that he makes excellent ones. . . . . He had good courtiers, who told him that every thing was perfect, but his perfection consists in the love and in the perception of truth. He must be perfect in every thing. . . . . Know still that he is the best of all men, or rather I am the greatest fool."[3]

In spite of the warnings of Frederic against quarrels ("Make no more quarrels about reports—a report is the gazette of fools"), mutual offences were not slow in manifesting themselves. Frederic had the fault of using improperly, in the presence of others, the superiority of his rank and intelligence. Voltaire reproaches him with it : " The unfortunate pleasure which you have always taken," he writes to him, " in wishing to humble other men, in saying and writing to them sharp things, a pleasure unworthy of you, and so much the more, as you are far elevated above them by your rank and singular talents."

On the other hand, the character of Voltaire was truly that of a spoiled child. His life is a series of great works and of low tricks. The author of *La Henriade* disputes with the King of Prussia about the most worthless trifles. We do not repeat the anecdotes about the wax candles, the linen to be bleached, and

---

[1] A Madame Denis, October 13, 1750. [2] 1er Janiver 1739.
[3] A M. D'Argental, Aout. 20, 1750.

the purpose attributed to Frederic respecting the orange, whose skin was thrown away after the juice was squeezed out. Voltaire was generous, but he had the passions of a miser, and he was devoid of that self-respect which shuts the eyes upon things which we ought to have the appearance of disregarding. His more serious quarrels with Maupertuis, his severe criticism on *Akakia*, the part which Frederic took in making this pamphlet be burnt by the hands of the common hangman, determined the violent rupture which followed. You are acquainted with Voltaire's flight to Frankfort, his arrest, and the humiliations to which he was subjected there. He spent two years in Alsace, then he went into Switzerland, and established himself first near Lausanne, at Monriond, then at Delices by the gate of Geneva, and, finally, at Ferney. In seeing him wander from place to place, Montesquieu cannot help saying: "There now is Voltaire, who does not know where to lay his head!—sound judgment is better than wit."[1]

At Ferney, a new era in Voltaire's life really commences, in which he must be carefully studied. He is no longer the man of hope, but of action, who wishes to reap what he has sown. We have seen him; from the beginning of his career he had proposed to himself an end which had in view the interests of society and human nature (*humanitaire*), to use a term of the present day. He expected, in order to treat with severity the *infamous*, that God would bestow upon him a sure and tranquil position. He found it at Ferney. In this château, which has become the Mecca of unbelievers—a pilgrimage frequently taken by great personages—Voltaire, an exile in fact, though not banished in form, is constantly present at Paris by his immense correspondence, and by the influence of his great abilities. He is the undisputed chief of the sect, who sometimes murmur, and whom he cajoles in order to secure them. In every sense his activity redoubles, he is the Briareus of the fable, whose hundred hands reach every thing. He employs all sorts of means, good or bad, shameful or honourable, to strengthen his authority, flatteries, controversy, defence of the oppressed, and merciless war against his opponents; we may see him everywhere at work. He could not have chosen for the execution of his design a posi-

---

[1] Montesquieu, Lettre à l'Abbé de Guasco, Sept. 28, 1753.

tion more distinguished or more dazzling. But for him, as for Madame de Staël, Paris alone was his country, Paris alone was France, and so long as Louis XV. lived, a weak, but clear-sighted prince, Voltaire could not obtain permission to return to it. There could not be two kings in France, any more than there could be two suns in the heavens.

The other object of his care was the securing of his fortune. Very considerable for that age, it served him, in every sense, for living in great style. He founded at Ferney a sort of colony, and displayed towards the workmen, whom he attracted thither, a liberality which must be acknowledged. By the side of good public works, there are in his life some good secret deeds.

There is almost no question that he was excited; twenty times he returns to the same subject. The pamphlets and small treatises accumulated, but he did not intermeddle with politics. His maxim was to manage kings. He wrote to Damilaville: "The priests, it is true, are hateful in this book, but kings are so too. . . . Nothing is more dangerous or more awkward; brothers ought always to respect morality and the throne." Absolute monarchy pleased him better than any other form of government, and revolutionists are quite wrong in reckoning him in the number of their chiefs. We have here and there in his works a few polite expressions addressed to free states, but they lead to no result. He is by no means friendly to parliaments in general, and to intermediate authorities : " We are treating here of parliaments; which do you prefer? None of them, I swear to you. I have no law-suit, and in my obscure life, I leave to the king my master, as a poor citizen, the care of his kingdom, to which I make no pretension." [1]

He is constantly anxious to obtain his return to favour with the king. He writes to the Duke de Richelieu: " Whoever may be the author of this book (*the System of Nature*), he must be unknown, but it was of the greatest importance to me in present circumstances to let it be known, that I do not approve of its principles. I would be greatly obliged to my hero, and he would do a very meritorious action if, in his merry moods with the king, he were gaily to drop a hint in his usual way, that I have refuted this book which makes so great noise."

[1] Cabales.

Another time he said to him : " Could you not have the kindness to represent to Madame de Pompadour that I have precisely the same enemies as she has, and that I have only quitted France, because I am persecuted by those who hate her." After Madame de Pompadour, he equally flatters Madame du Barry. He lavishes flattery on foreign sovereigns; he goes even so far as to do to them the honours of France. We have seen what he is in regard to Frederic, here he is with respect to Catherine :—

" Madame, is it quite true ? Am I sufficiently happy, because I am not deceived ? Fifteen thousand Turks killed or taken prisoners on the Danube ! This news comes from Vienna ; can I reckon upon it ? Is my happiness certain ? I wish also, madame, to tell you the exploits of my country. We have for some months an excellent dancer at the Opera in Paris. The last comic opera has not had great success, but one is preparing, which will become the admiration of the *universe;* it will be performed in the first city of the *universe,* and by the first actors in the *universe.* Our comptroller-general, who has not the money of the *universe* in his coffers, is engaged in operations, which draw down upon him some remonstrances, and a few curses. Our fleet is preparing to row from Paris to Saint Cloud. We have a regiment, which has been reviewed; politicians presage some great event. It is pretended that a detachment of Jesuits was seen towards Avignon, but they were dispersed by a corps of Jansenists, which was very superior—no one was killed."[1]

Elsewhere : " I did not think a month ago that I should be still living on the globe, which you astonish. I thank nature, which has, perhaps, wished me to live till you be established in the country of Orpheus and Mars, that is some months hence ; but do not make me wait longer. I must absolutely set out for annihilation. I shall die, preserving for you the worship which I have vowed to your Imperial Majesty."

At the same time he wrote to Madame de Choiseul : " With respect to Cato, I refer you, madame, to the Turkish history, and leave you to decide, if the Sultans have not done a hundred times worse. Ask especially M. l'Abbé Barthelemy, if the Greek language be not preferable to the Turkish."

As to the division of Poland, he says to Catherine : " The con

---

[1] August 1771.

federates of Poland are another plague. I flatter myself that your Majesty will cure them of their contagious malady."[1] "Certainly," says he, in another place, speaking of Catherine and Maria Theresa, " since these two brave ladies have so well understood how to change the face of Poland, they will still better understand how to change that of Turkey."[2]

With these two ideas, Voltaire would not be popular among his fellow-countrymen in the present day. The actual arrangement of his correspondence produces the most singular effect— one page belies the praises of another. He has for men of letters charming cajoleries, which are turned into satires with other interlocutors. In 1757, Frederic, discouraged by the bad state of his affairs, wished to put himself to death. Voltaire wrote to him, to divert him from his purpose. Frederic did not kill himself, and fortune smiled on him anew. Voltaire apologises for this good action: " Could any one possibly imagine that I feel any interest in the King of Prussia ? I am, indeed, very far from any such feeling."[3]

Elsewhere he takes advantage of it : " I am not sorry that the Solomon of the North has a few partizans in Paris, and that it has been seen that I have not praised a fool. I feel an interest in his glory, from self-love ; and I am happy, at the same time, from reason and equity, that he has been a little punished. I wish to see whether adversity will bring him back to philosophy. I swear to you that a month ago he was scarcely a philosopher : despair got the better of him ; and it is not a disagreeable part for me to have given him on that occasion some very paternal counsels."[4] " Luc is always Luc, greatly embarrassed and not less embarrassing others, astonishing Europe, impoverishing it, filling it with blood, making verses, and writing to me the most singular things in the world. The Duke de Choiseul, who has more wit than he, and a better spirit, always did me the honour to show me marks of kindness, of which I am more sensible than of my intercourse with Luc."[5]

We must, however, say, to his praise, Voltaire continued faithful to M. de Choiseul, notwithstanding that minister's disgrace. " I hope," he writes to the Duke de la Vrillière, " that you will carefully protect my colony, as the Duke de Choiseul protected

---

[1] 1st Jan. 1772.
[3] A M. d'Argental. 2d Dec. 1757.
[5] A Madame de Fontaine. Nov. 1757.

[2] 2d Nov. 1772.
[4] Ibid. 8th Nov. 1757.

it. I owe every thing to him. I shall feel till the end of my
life the respectful gratitude which is his due, and the admiration
with which the nobleness of his character has always inspired
me."[1]

He honoured Turgot, and dedicated to him his *Epitre à un
Homme.* Has he made any declaration against conquests and
unjust wars, except in his poetry ? This has been denied ; but
M. Destutt de Tracy has taken up this allegation too lightly.
Here, among others, is a letter from Frederic, and Voltaire's
answer :—

. . . . " Were I to tell you that we are preparing with great
care to destroy some walls raised at great expense, that we are
reaping a harvest which we have not sown, and that we have
become masters where no one was at the gates to resist us, you
would exclaim : ' Ah ! barbarians ! ah ! robbers ! inhuman that
you are ! the unrighteous shall not inherit the kingdom of heaven.
Since I foresee all that you will say on this subject, I will not
speak to you about it.'"—(23d March 1742). " I have only,"
replied Voltaire, " placed one foot on the bank of the Styx ; but
I am much distressed, sire, at the number of poor wretches whom
I have seen pass. Will not you and your brother kings cease to
ravage this earth, which you have, you say, so great desire to
render happy ?"—(April 1742).

After a representation of the *Clemency of Titus,* he addressed
to Frederic the following verses, in behalf of some Frenchmen
imprisoned at Spandau : " Universal genius, with a soul at once
endowed with feeling and firmness, what ! when you reign, there
are unhappy persons ! You must put an end to the torments of
a culprit, and never impute it to your generous cares. Behold
around you prayers offered with trembling lips ; daughters of
repentance, mistresses of great hearts, astonished at watering
with helpless tears the hands which ought to dry up the tears of
the whole earth. Ah ! why show me with magnificence this
brilliant spectacle, in which Titus triumphs ? To finish the festival, equal his clemency, and imitate him in all things, or boast
of him no more." " The request was somewhat hard, but one has
the privilege of saying what one chooses in verse," adds Voltaire
in his *historical* commentary.

---

[1] A M le Duc de la Vrillière. Mai 1771.

What, indisputably, does most honour to Voltaire's memory, was his defence of the oppressed, and his efforts against religious persecution. We know all that he did in the affairs of the Calas, of the Sirvens, and of the chevalier de Labarre. Pamphlets without end, indefatigable proceedings, and enormous correspondence, cost him nothing. All this, no doubt, was subservient, in one sense, to his great design—and he knew it; but he was urged to it by an imperative sense of humanity and justice. Who does not acknowledge here the accent of sincerity? "What horrors, just Heaven! They take a girl from her father and mother, they apply to her the whip, and, when she is covered with blood, they set about making her a Catholic; she is cast into a dungeon, and her father, mother, and sisters are condemned to the last punishment! I am ashamed, I blush to be a man, when I see, on one hand, the comic opera performed, and, on the other, fanaticism arming the executioners. I live at the extremity of France, but I am still too near so great abominations."[1] He took, it is said, every year a fever at the anniversary of Saint-Bartholomew.

At the same time, he set himself against the barbarity of the laws, both in his great works and in his occasional writings. In the *Summary of the Age of Louis XV.*, and in the *Conspiracies against the People*, there are beautiful passages. We shall be able to judge of them by these two quotations :—

"If one day in France humane laws soften some practices at present too severe, without, however, affording facilities to crime, we may believe that a reformation will take place in the procedure, on points respecting which those who arranged the laws have apparently given themselves up to too great zeal. Should not the criminal law be as favourable as it is terrible to the culprit? In England, a single false imprisonment is repaired by the minister who ordered it; but in France the innocent man, who has been cast into a dungeon, and who has been subjected to torture, has no consolation to hope for, and no damages to seek, since it is the public minister who prosecuted him; he is blasted for ever in society. The innocent blasted! and why? because his bones are broken! He should only excite pity and respect. Inquiry into crimes demands severity; it is a war which human justice

[1] 23d March 1765.

wages against wickedness, but there are generosity and compassion even in war. The brave man is compassionate—must the lawyer be a barbarian?"[1] "Is it the history of serpents and tigers that I have written? No: it is the history of men. Tigers and serpents do not treat in this manner their own species. It was, however, in the age of Cicero, Pollio, Atticus, Varius, Tibullus, Virgil, and Horace, that Augustus made his proscriptions. The philosophers de Thou and Montaigne, and the chancellor de L'Hôpital, lived at the time of Saint-Bartholomew, and the massacres of the Cevennes were in the most flourishing period of the French monarchy. Never were the minds of men more cultivated, talents more abundant, and politeness more general. What contrasts! what a chaos! what horrible inconsistencies are found in this unhappy world! Men speak of pestilence, earthquakes, conflagrations, and deluges which have desolated the globe; happy, they say, are those who have not lived in the time of these disorders! We say rather: happy those who have not been eye-witnesses of the crimes which I describe! How were barbarians found to order them, and so many other barbarians to execute them? How are there still inquisitors and familiars of the Inquisition?"[2]

We remember de Morangiés, de Montbailly, the serfs in mortmain of the Pays-de-Gex, whose deliverance Voltaire succeeded in accomplishing. When he learned the restoration of M. de Lally, the father, he wrote to the son: "The dying man revives on hearing this great news; he embraces very tenderly M. de Lally; he sees that the king is the defender of justice; he will die content."[3]

But if he was easily accessible to humane and generous sentiments, no one was more merciless to his opponents. He constantly treats them as enemies. See what he does with J. J. Rousseau, La Beaumelle, Freron, Lefranc de Pompignan, and how many others! He renders them ridiculous and odious; he loads them with gross injuries, and imputes to them the most horrible crimes; and yet men have privileges even in controversy:—

"The *Social Contract* was burned at Geneva in the same pile as the silly romance of *Emilius*. This *Social*—or unsocial—*Contract*

1 Siecle de Louis XV., chap. xlii.   2 Conspirations contre les Peuples.
3 1778.

is only remarkable for a few injurious sayings against kings, by a citizen of the Burgh of Geneva, and for four insipid pages against the Christian religion."[1] "I should not have attributed to Jean-Jacques genius and eloquence. I find in him no genius. His detestible romance, *Heloise*, is absolutely devoid of it. *Emilius*, in like manner, and all his other works, are those of an empty declaimer."[2] "He thought that he resembled Diogenes, and he has scarcely the honour of resembling his dog."[3]

It must be admitted, gentlemen, that a sort of natural antipathy must have existed between Voltaire and Rousseau. The sentimental taste for religion exhibited by Jean-Jacques and his theories, in point of politics and society, must have rendered him unsuitable to the jeering levity, and even to the good sense of Voltaire; but if nothing obliged him to admire his rival, nothing excuses his unworthy mode of proceeding. The worst was the part which he made Rousseau play in the poem, *The War of Geneva*.

Voltaire descends so low, as to reproach his opponents with their name and profession : " How can you complain," said he to Nonotte, " of my having made it known that thy father was a porter, when thy style so clearly shows the profession of thy dear father?" And of Sabatier : " He has merely the property of being a good wig-maker like his father !" So of a thousand others : " When I see a dark and frowning visage, a hideous brow, the starched air of a pedant, a yellow neck upon a bent stump, a hog's eye fixed on the earth (the mirror of a mind a prey to remorse, always dim with the fear of being seen), I distinctly tell you, without hesitation, that this baboon is Tartufe or Vernet !"[4] And Jacob Vernet was very respectable !

Voltaire at length made, in one of his letters, this tardy confession : " I was wrong, but these gentlemen attacked me during forty years, and I lost my patience for ten years in succession."

He replied to D'Alembert, who wrote on the subject of Clement, sent to Fort l'Eveque to form his taste : " Dissuade M. de Neufchâteau from the design of entering a process, which would be very ridiculous. It may be very well for Freron and La Beaumelle to have made a better *Henriade* than mine— nothing is more easy. There is no way of presenting a request

---

[1] A Damilaville, 25th June 1762.   [2] A Bordes, 19th Nov. 1766.
[3] A Cideville, March 1765.   [4] L'Hypocrisie.

to the Council to obtain a decree that my *Henriade* should be preferred to Freron's; this proceeding, besides, would be contrary to the principles of M. de Turgot, who gives all liberty to booksellers, as well as to grain dealers."[1] This moderation came too late. His opponents entertained a prejudice against him, which still continues; their obscure names are embalmed in the ridicule, as embryos in the spirit of wine. Freron, whose name has become celebrated for the war of thirty years which he waged with Voltaire, was treated by him with unexampled indignity. In the face of all Paris, Voltaire brought him on the comic stage in his play *l'Ecossaise* (the Scotchwoman), in a way not to be misunderstood, either as to the name, or in other respects, and gave him the most detestable part.

But how could he have properly treated the dry wood, when he did not care about the green? In general, he has been accused of being jealous of his rivals, and of aiming at Montesquieu and Buffon in his attacks. The case was little better with his friends, such as Henault and Thibonville, who were abominably treated in the *Pucelle*. It is true he had recourse to disavowals: " I beg, as a favour, that I may never be considered the author of the *Portatif*. The Frerons and Pompignans cry out that it is mine, and consequently honest men should cry out that it is not."[2] " I have read at length *Candide*. You must have lost your senses, to attribute such a piece of baseness to me."[3] " I am much interested in this play (*Le Droit du Seigneur*); I know that it is attributed to me; but I swear to you, it is by an academician of Dijon. Look on me as a dishonest man if I lie to you."[4]

See, farther, the *official*—one may say the *solemn*—disavowal of the *History of the Parliament*, in his letter of the 5th July 1769 to M. Morin, secretary of the library.

In this chosen position, with the weight of his popularity, present everywhere by his immense correspondence, and receiving the homage which the greatest lords came to render in person to the king of public opinion, Voltaire was incessantly troubled with the desire of gaining the good graces of the court, and of obtaining permission to return to Paris. On this subject he shows how wit often helps to do foolish things boldly.

[1] A D'Alembert, 24th Aout 1775.   [2] Ibid. 2d Octobre 1764.
[3] A M. Vernes, 1758.   [4] A Thibonville, 26th Janvier 1762.

In the hope of being restored to favour, he affected the appearance of returning to religion, and that, too, at a time when he launched forth against Christianity his most audacious pamphlets. He states the circumstances himself in his *Commentary on the Life of the Author of the Henriade.*

The recluse of Ferney was sick (it was in 1769), and having nothing to do, wished only to avenge himself on this slight illness, by the pleasure of making extreme unction be administered to him by a regular summons. He made it known by a verger to his rector, that the said rector would have to anoint him in his chamber without fail on the 1st of April. The rector came, and showed him that it was necessary to commence first with the communion, and that afterwards he would bring as many holy oils as he chose. The sick man accepted the proposal; he made the communion be carried into his chamber the 1st of April, and then, in presence of witnesses, he declared before a notary, that he pardoned his calumniators who had tried to destroy him, and who had not been able to succeed.

Here are the reasons which he gives to Saurin: "I was at the point of death some days ago. In the tenth fit of the ague, I performed all the duties of an officer of the chamber of the most Christian king, and of a citizen who should die in the religion of his country."[1]

He wrote also to Madame du Deffand: "I am an old invalid in a very delicate position, and there are no glisters nor pills which I do not take every month, in order that the faculty may let me live and die in peace." It was on his part the last outrage, and it was committed in vain. Nobody paid attention to these reasons: this parody horrified the devout, excited the pity of the philosophers, and the mass of unbelievers laughed at it as a new insult. D'Alembert formally reproached him with it: "I cannot approve of this ceremony in the situation in which you are. Have you reflected well on this proceeding? Did you think to deceive the devout by the part which you have taken? They only regard your Easter devotion as one scandal more. . . . What will they say to the king of the kind of profanation which they attribute to you? I am much afraid, my dear friend, that you have gained nothing by this comedy, which may, perhaps, involve you in danger."

[1] Avril 1769.

It was only in 1778, under the government of Louis XVI., that Voltaire was able to obtain what he had so long desired. The day of his entrance into Paris displayed his intellectual royalty, and the triumph of philosophy. On that day the most scandalous of his works was loaded with general homage! One of the shouts of applause, which re-echoed on that occasion, announced that the people had given up to their idol the last treasure of a nation, public decency. This outcry, *" Long live the author of the Pucelle,"* had a self-consciousness. Morals, religion, patriotic memorials—all were involved in disgrace by that exclamation. Such an apotheosis was never seen, and we do not think that this literary enthusiasm is ever likely to be renewed. The eighteenth century was more ingenuous than it is usually represented, many points were new to it, which are no longer new to us.

Voltaire survived this ovation but a short time. He died that same year some months before the author of *Emilius.* I know nothing more frightful than that triumph followed by that death. He renewed the scene which he had exhibited at Ferney in 1769. This is his last confession : " I, the undersigned, declare, that being attacked four days since with a vomiting of blood, at the age of eighty-four, as I was unable to crawl to church, the rector of Saint-Sulpice wished to add to his good works by sending to me the Abbé Gauthier, a priest. I confessed myself to him, and if I die, I die in the holy Catholic religion in which I was born, hoping, in the mercy of God, that He will pardon all my faults, and if I have scandalized the Church, I ask pardon for it from God and from her."

The two periods of Voltaire's life are marked, as we have already shown, by a different character. The first is more literary, and especially more poetical—his masterpieces are crowded into it. The second has particular reference to prose, that is to practice. Here the quantity far surpasses the quality. Short productions and small pieces abound. The work of Voltaire was not a book, it was a library. This collection was long the only library of a great number of men ; it was much more, it was their bible. This measures the colossal importance of Voltaire's literary activity.

To set out from this period, Voltaire appears to have devoted himself to his great object ; every thing that he publishes bears the impress of this prepossession. Still we perceive in it the artist, or at least the intention of the artist; but gradually the latter retires behind the man. Voltaire, however, wrote for the stage till his death; one of the motives of his ardent desire to return to Paris was to assist at the representation of his last theatrical pieces. *Rome Sauvée*, a tragedy without love, appeared in 1752. *Semiramis* had appeared in 1748, and the tragi-comedy of *Nanine*, which has been mentioned before, in 1749. *L'Orphelin de la Chine* in 1755. It contains touching beauties; and each of these plays is remarkable for a true philosophical interest.

In 1760 appeared *Tancrede*, carelessly written, it is true, but one of the most melting plays of the French stage. Goëthe translated it, which is a mark of true homage. *Tancrede* possesses a merit and an attraction, which has been generally felt; these were the lively colours by which Voltaire revived the middle age, then so little known. It is a picture somewhat arbitrary and fantastic, but which continues to be attractive, even at present, when the truth respecting that time is somewhat better understood. No doubt, a part of the charm, which the author knew how to spread over it, has vanished, its freshness is tarnished, but there always remains to Voltaire the merit of having felt the chivalrous attraction of the middle age, and of having fixed its brilliant colours in his poetry. *Tancrede* will remain one of the productions of its author most agreeable to read. *L'Ecossaise* is also of the same date, 1760.

La Loi Naturelle and *le Disastre de Lisbonne* belong to 1756. Of the former we have already spoken. The author is much more a poet in *le Disastre de Lisbonne*. Fontanes calls this poem " an elegy sometimes sublime on the misfortunes of the human race."[1] Voltaire was really under the power of a profound impression before this catastrophe at which all Europe trembled; he took this occasion to develope his ideas on the mixture of good and evil among men. It is the great question, which, lulled asleep, every one awakens. Between what is worst and what is best, the choice was embarrassing. Voltaire at first professed optimism, for he professed every thing. But when other authors, Pope among the rest, had given credit to this system, he passed to the

---

[1] Fontanes, Traduction de l'Essai sur l'Homme de Pope. Discours Preliminaire.

opposite extreme, *pessimism*, a little heedlessly, perhaps, and described the disaster of Lisbon, asking *if all was good*. According to his former plan, he finished thus : " O mortals, what is to be done ? Mortals, you must suffer, submit in silence, adore, and die." Voltaire soon saw that it was necessary to terminate his work in a different strain, he replaced this conclusion with the following : " The present is fearful, if there be no future, if the night of the grave destroys the thinking being ; *one day all will be well*, this is our hope ; *all is well now* is our mistake."

It would have been too extraordinary to make people despair at the end of a poem inspired by pity. Besides, to end thus was to let the optimists gain their cause. It was to say, according to them, that individual misfortunes are the elements, the means of general good ; or it was to say that the universe is not governed by any law, and that all is given up to the caprices of chance. Now as the two verses quoted say the one or the other of these two things, it was quite necessary that he should change them, and that he should enter good and bad, into the Christian system. For between this system and that of the optimists there is only absurdity.

The optimists are only strong or only appear to be so, when they remove God from the government of created things, and when they substitute for Him indifferent and insensible nature. They say that nature cares for species and not for individuals. And according to this, partial or individual misfortunes ought not to astonish us, for these misfortunes never reach species for which *all is good*. Even though we were to adopt the point with which these philosophers set out, we will not find their system unassailable. And first of all, what do they understand by *species*? It is very possible that some species of animals may disappear one day from the surface of the globe, exterminated by another species, which nature herself has interested in this extermination. Will they then say, that nature has been wanting to herself? But let us leave this objection and go to the principal defect in the system.

This defect is in the name, which they give to it. It should not be called *optimism*, for it establishes the principle, that every thing is necessary, not that every thing is good. It will be vain to show us that by dating from the point of departure, the chain of effects is necessary and continuous ; does it follow from this, that every thing is good? It is singular that these philosophers reproach their opponents with an arbitrary application of the term *evil*, while they in like manner apply the term *good*. Where do they find the measure of that good? By what rule do they compare the whole of creation in order to pronounce that this whole is good? What is good is that which is conformable to the end or views of any being whatever, and this notion is necessarily subjective. In order that an object may be called *good*, there must be some one who finds it good, that is, corresponding to its end and desires. Now, has nature an end or does it form desires? All that can be said is, that the chain of effects which it produces is conformable to its first hypothesis, but with what justice and on what ground can we say that this primary hypothesis is good? I confess to you, I think it more natural to do like the *pessimistes*, make individual sensibility the touchstone of the order of things and say : Beings suffer, then every thing is not good.

The optimists should lay down their borrowed name and content themselves with saying : So far as we can see, every thing is necessary—a desolating doctrine which we neither answer nor refute by a long deed of accusation against nature, which would not regard it and would not even listen to it, and whose chariot incessantly running in an unbending orbit, will crush under the same wheel its accuser and defender. But if the idea of God drawn from the depth of the human conscience, if the idea of God, the invincible belief and unalienable attribute of our nature, if the idea of God, the first of our ideas in logical order, comes to be substituted, living and sensible, for the dead idea of nature, if the *good* pleasure of God becomes the supreme necessity of the world, every thing assumes a new aspect. What does it signify, that effects appear to us connected with causes, and the details bound to the whole by an adamantine chain? All this necessity is absorbed in the will of God, and blended with it. Before this eternal Being, in respect to whom all is simultaneous; before this immense Being, to whom all is present, and before this infinite Being, to whom all is one, would we refuse to admit, that every event is at once the necessary consequence of a cause, which He has pre-ordained, and the immediate result of an immediate act of His will, so that the thing which he has commanded for ages, He commands still at the moment that it comes to pass? In a word, shall we dare to deny that a special, nay, the most special providence is compatible with a general providence? No, God has prepared from eternity, or rather He has embraced in a single act of His thought the infinite chain of successive causes combined and interwoven, which make at this moment a hair fall from my head, or a sigh escape from my breast; but it is by His express and immediate will that these two events come to pass; it was His will from eternity, that this hair should fall, and that this sigh should be heaved; He is free and sovereign every moment, as if at every moment He was beginning anew the work 'of creation, and as if in place of general and fixed laws, He himself without interruption treated every particular case, having bestowed a constitution on the universe, and who is, nevertheless, its absolute Monarch. Equally independent in the government of moral creatures, he applies to each of them, every moment, the arrangement and government suitable to them; treats them day by day as if he followed this maxim—that for every day his pains were sufficient; prepares trial for the soul, and prepares prayer in the soul, which must overcome ; and prepares Himself to hear and answer them; when once God, the God of eternity and the God of the present moment, is thus put in the place of necessity, we say no more with the optimists : *all is good*, nor with the *pessimistes*, *all is bad*, but we say, God reigneth. We suffer, but we have sinned; we suffer, but eternity, which is God's, is also ours; the world groans, every creature sighs, there is much suffering in the world, but God, who has not made sin, has not made suffering; there is here a mystery, which He will one day explain to us. What we know is, that all things work together for good to those who love God. Let us gain the mastery by this word, and, giving up all unprofitable researches, let us proceed to the end which He has marked out.

In this second period, between 1760 and 1774, the satires also appeared. Voltaire has only put into them his one nature. Satirical genius was his peculiar genius ; his tragedies are his only works in which he does not indulge this taste. Less perfect than Regnier, less correct than Boileau, Voltaire exercises a joyous wickedness. That of others is scarcely so, but his is always laughing ; he is happy in pouring out his satirical bile— the opening of this vein relieves him, as tears relieve the afflicted. It is not merely with him that esthetic malice which is remarked in others; he gives way to all his hatred and all his contempt. He does not aim in particular at mediocrity of talent, he attacks his enemies. If he falls in with peaceful mediocrity he passes it by; but wo to those who have criticised his work, and who have not sufficiently praised him, whatever may be in other respects the degree of their talent. He is the reverse of Boileau, who spares no mediocrity, but who never mixes with his satires personal rancour. The immortal satire of the *Poor Devil* involves in it the same contempt of men of very different merit. Other satires refer to literature in general, as that of the *Russian in Paris*. *Vanity, Cabals, Systems, Pegasus, Tactics*, may be distinguished: "'I have,' said he, 'by good luck, a new work, necessary to mankind, and judicious as beautiful; they must apply themselves to the study of it—it is *Tactics*.' ' Tactics!' said I to him; alas! at the moment I was ignorant of the meaning of a word so learned. This noun, he replied, comes from Greece into France, and means the great art, or the art which is superior to every other; it satisfies all the desires of the most noble minds. I bought his *Tactics*, and I thought myself happy. I hoped to discover the method of prolonging my life, of soothing the sorrows with which it is troubled, of cultivating my taste, of being without passion, of subjecting my desires to the yoke of reason, and of being just to all without ever being a dupe. I shut myself up, I read, and only employed myself in committing to memory a book so divine. My friend, it was the art of cutting our neighbours' throats!" The *Marseillais and the Lion* is a satire on human nature : " The lion, that laughs little, began, however, to laugh, and wishing, for the sake of sport, to know this empire, by two great blows of his paw strips quite naked the absolute monarch of the whole universe : he sees that this great king concealed under his shirt a weak body mounted on an ape's two *legs*, two large feet attached to two small heels, and hindered in their progress by five superfluous toes. . . . . . A narrow and hollow skull, covering a flat countenance, sadly impoverished with the tissue of hair, with which the hand of a barber dressed his greasy forehead. Such was, indeed, this king without a crown, deprived of his dress, and reduced to what he really is. He perceived that he indeed owed his grandeur to the thread of the wig-maker, and to the scissors of the tailor."

This *pessimism* of Voltaire, this contempt for man, which goes so far as to deteriorate his figure, has a visible object. He only degrades man so profoundly and universally, to prevent him from imagining that he can have any relation to God; but there is also this result from it, that such a creature ought not to pride himself on a very high moral ambition. The point of departure is placed too low for him to think that he can raise himself very high.

All these satires are remarkable for their natural composition. Their plan is always ingenious, and the diction incomparably easy, although, perhaps, too near prose. Horace has, no doubt, prosaic passages also, but he is borne. up by the rhythm of his beautiful language. As to Voltaire, he has so much wit and nature, that we pardon the negligent form of his verses. His particular distinction, besides, we have already remarked, is to introduce every where general ideas. Without philosophy there is no true poetry; without philosophy you may make pretty verses; but, to be truly a poet, you must, to a certain extent, be a philosopher.

Voltaire's *Tales* in verse are in some respects inferior, and in others superior, to those of La Fontaine. The same spirit prevails there. As dangerous as La Fontaine in the principle, he is in general under more restraint in the details. The tale of the *Three Ways* is charming—they are three tales on a different measure. The *Daughters of Minée* may be also noticed. He managed the verse of ten syllables as no one did since the sixteenth century.

The *Pucelle* was given to the public in 1755. It is peculiarly the work of Voltaire, and the summary of his philosophy: it is there that he is found in every view bad. Thirty years, we repeat it, he caressed the monster. The favour which welcomed this poem corresponded to the care which the author had bestowed upon it—a frightful sign of the spirit of the times, which were eager to possess this infamous book. Wit and fancy abound in it, and yet, in a literary point of view, it is a very imperfect work; or rather, it is not a finished work—it is a badly sewed patchwork of obscenity, impudence, and impiety; even its style is to the last degree negligent. We have sufficiently explained the disgrace with which Voltaire was not afraid to brand the memory of Joan of Arc, so that we may dispense with any farther reference to it. To choose such an episode, in order to make it the framework of licentiousness and impiety, is a characteristic feature. This poem is, moreover, a satire. Voltaire by it crushes his enemies, and does not even spare his friends. He writes to D'Alembert : " By the bye, do you always hate M. de Ximenes ? There will be always room in the *Pucelle* for the people whom you shall recommend to me."[1] Now, here is a specimen of what he calls *making room* in his book : " Thibouville and Villars, imitators of the first of the Cæsars;" and, after having made room in this way, Voltaire writes to this same Thibouville : " I slip into it scandalous verses against persons to whom I am most attached;"[2] and, at a later period : " Some one wrote to me that you were thrust into this rhapsody, but I did not see how it could concern you; it is an abomination that must be forgotten ; it would make me die of grief."[3]

We pass on to the prose writings of the second period. *The Age of Louis XIV.* appeared from 1751 to 1752. The French language does not possess any historical writing more brilliant. Under the double relation of general composition and diction, it is eminently distinguished for grace, elegance, rapidity, and attractive ease. Such is the merit of this work, but the book is not sincere. The first element of sincerity, loyalty and truth, is wanting. It is the panegyric, not of a man, but of an age. Voltaire, the apostle of humanity in the eighteenth century, sacrificed it to art and literature. The relations of man to God are unnoticed ; for example, his account of the religious wars. Delighted with the cultivation of mind, and elegance of manners, he pardons every thing in a prince who plunged France into an abyss of evils.

The *Essay on the Spirit and Manners of Nations* (1756) indicates a new mode of writing history. It is the philosophy of the age applied to human events. It is not a history, properly so called, but a discourse. The historical narration is not unfolded in large and sustained proportions. Some generous acts are illustrated by anecdotes. There are entire parts of human nature which he has not taken in, and which he preferred to make ridiculous. He seeks the ridiculous in what is serious, instead of seeking the serious in what is ridiculous. Hence the irony with which his history is always sprinkled.

[1] A D'Alembert.   20th April 1761.   [2] A Thibouville.   21st Mai 1755.
[3] A Thibouville.   21st Nov. 1755.

" Voltaire is like the monks," said Montesquieu—" he writes for his convent."[1] The prophecy has been accomplished—posterity did not accept history in the spirit of Voltaire—he acted the counterpart of Bossuet ; he abases what Bossuet had elevated, and elevates what Bossuet had abased, the human causes of events. He is a fatalist. He excludes the element of Providence, enthrones chance, and suppresses the connection of facts—all is detached ; he exhibits immediate causes, but the causes of causes do not appear. In no sense under his hand is history concentrated in unity. It is a series of episodes, in which it might be said that he seeks to astonish us by two things, the extravagance of events and of the human mind.

But when he is not blinded by passion his judgment of persons and things is exquisite. He shook off the yoke of many prejudices. What interests him in the mind of man is man himself. In this sense he formed a new mode of writing history ; he wrote the memoirs of the human mind. As far as it is possible to know man without knowing God, he knew him ; he has a number of pointed observations and brilliant strokes; his condition is less faulty than you would think. Few things that you read are more agreeable or more easy.

A great work without an idea and without passion is a failure. The soul, the sentiment, the passion of the *Essay on Manners* is the passion of human nature. Voltaire had just brought humanity from below its ruins ; he withdraws it from them, little, pitiful, degraded, it is true, but still it is humanity, and, besides, the fault does not lie with him alone. Drawn on by anti-sacerdotal reaction, he does not stop at indignation, he goes as far as hatred, which is always unjust. Humanity disparaged by Voltaire appeared at that time great. By abasing it in one sense, he raises it in another.

Voltaire's *Romances and Tales*, in prose, are only a slight canvas, on which he embroiders his favourite ideas. They have almost no plan ; in beginning each of his stories, the author is scarcely less ignorant than the reader of what is to follow. They are really little connected. This form is so natural to him, that he every moment glides into it ; even in pieces essentially didactic he unexpectedly introduces a scene, a character, or a fact.

---

[1] Montesquieu, Pensées diverses des Modernes.

But he interests no one; his characters are not ridiculous, but extravagant; he has no allegory, and almost nothing marvellous, but there is something fantastic in his manner of describing life —he makes an abstract of two or three of its principal conditions. The action of his tales could never have passed in any age or in any part of the world. Still, he has an end in view; he has always an idea, but he does not keep by it. He constantly leaves it behind him. He ventures so far, that he at length comes to support theories different from his own. His fictions are not romances, in this sense, that, contrary to the practice of ordinary romance writers, he is only desirous to take away from life all its enchantment. His is properly the satirical romance, in the sense of Rabelais and Swift. But Voltaire's satire goes directly to man; it is not precisely an age or a party that he attacks—it is altogether man that he wishes to unmask. There is still the same contrast; he who sought with so much care the lost rights of human nature, is he who has done every thing to force it to despise itself.

The gaiety of these tales is bitter, or rather insulting. We are ashamed to be gay with Voltaire; even when he smiles, the heart is locked; nothing is at once more gay or more sad than the most part of these little works—there is hell in that smile. Sometimes this gaiety is of a different character—it is that of a man foolish or tipsy—but this is rare. We have an example of it at the beginning of the Ingenu: " One day Saint Dunstan, an Irishman by nation and a saint by profession, set out from Ireland on a small mountain, which moved towards the coast of France, and arrived by this conveyance in the Bay of St Malo. When he landed, he gave his blessing to his mountain, which made him a profound bow, and returned to Ireland by the same road that it came."

In the Ingenu, Voltaire opposes the savage to the civilized state, and judges of the latter by the former. In Micromegas, he transports us to another planet. He sets out with the principle that to see a thing well, we must see it at a distance. It is an artifice like the construction of geometers, a proceeding of which the first idea is ingenious and philosophical, although the practice of it may become childish.

Zadig is almost the only one of the tales whose romantic interest is anything worth. It is not susceptible of analysis. The

author also entitled it *Destiny*. He brings out in it the caprices
of fate; he points out how much we are the dupes of appearances, and, what is astonishing, he shows himself there to be an
optimist. It may be read without disgust, as well as *Memnon*
and *Babouc*. As to the style of these tales, nothing can be more
light, pointed, and rapid, or more animated. Of the productions
of Voltaire, the tales must, in a literary point of view, be ranked
as the most finished.

In the poem on the *Disaster of Lisbon*, we have seen Voltaire
attempt a kind of reputation of optimism, and fall at length into
the Christian idea. But in *Candide* (1758) there is no longer
any restriction. He speaks no more of *bowing in silence and
adoring*, nor of an antidote to the poison which he pours into
the soul. If the philosophy of *Zadig, Memnon*, and *Babouc* be
worldly, it is at least human; if that of the *Ingenu* be the same
with which Voltaire has so often reproached J. J. Rousseau; if
he joins in this work irreligion to false reasoning, at least he does
not show himself to be an atheist. But an atheism badly disguised is the doctrine of the impure *Candide*—an insolent satire
on man, an insult, which is directed even against God. The
work is aimed at the optimism of Pope, and perhaps of Leibnitz,
and refutes error by blasphemy. It is a contrast between the
idea of the best possible world and what is most worthless and
most disgusting in the vices and sufferings of mankind, for any
one who judges of them, like Voltaire, by sight and not by faith.
The commentary on Corneille was published in 1764, for the
benefit of his grand-daughter, whom Voltaire thought it to be
due to his glory to treat with kindness. We may easily conceive
the education which a young girl must have received in such a
house. Moreover, he married her very badly. The irreverent
injustice of this *Commentary* reminds us of the exclamation:
" Ah! thou spoilest to me the saying, *Be friends, Cinna.*" Yet,
in spite of his want of respect for the great man whom he calls
his *general*, this work contains a number of interesting remarks
on the French language, and on the dramatic art. When Voltaire admires, it is as a man of genius; he does not, however,
. anywhere rise above received theories.

We shall not stop at other works of less importance, such as
the *Summary of the Age of Louis XV.* (1757). The *Annals of
the Empire*, a work bespoken and very carelessly executed (1754),

the *History of the Czar Peter*, inferior to *Charles XII.*, and innumerable small treatises or pamphlets, which succeeded each other at less than an interval of fifteen days. The author had a double end; to keep himself before the public, and to remove every thing calculated to obstruct or obscure his fame. Sometimes, however, there are occasional writings, such as the defence of the oppressed, or questions in philosophy or politics; or, still farther, defences of his own works, published under a different name, to teach the reader to admire beauties too little noticed, such as the *Eulogy of Crebillon*, the *Commentary on the works of the author of the Henriade.* Voltaire never forgets himself, the point, the cadence, and the accent are always the eulogy of M. de Voltaire. Yet his most trifling jokes are full of fancy, but vengeance and hatred, as well as pride, have given rise to the most part of his works. To these feelings may be ascribed satires, libels, and something still worse. Nothing is more extravagant than his memoir of the *King of Prussia.* " Voltaire, as we have seen, has philosophized in all his works, and under all forms. He comes nearest to the forms of discussion, properly so called, in his *Philosophical Dictionary*, begun in 1760, and afterwards much increased; a work, or rather a collection of several works, full of wit and interesting views, but in it there prevails in the ideas an obstinate prejudice, and in the tone a malignant and cynical gaiety. Metaphysics, morals, history of religions, politics, and literature, are all met with in this collection, of which it might be said that he achieves for his own amusement what has been the torment of the most exalted understandings of all ages. And what amusement!"[1]

With the people, even with those who have not read his writings, Voltaire passes for the leader of impiety. Blamed by some, praised by others, the part of destroyer is every where attributed to him. As to the learned, they are divided between the anathema and the apotheosis. An angel of darkness in the eyes of many, he is for some an angel at once of extermination and of light.

" The unrestrained admiration, with which too many people surround Voltaire," says M. de Maistre, " is the infallible sign of a corrupted mind. Let them not deceive themselves; if any one

<hr/>

[1] Vinet, Discours sur la Literature Française, p. 57.

going through his library feels himself attracted to the *works of Ferney*, God does not love him. . . . He has pronounced against himself, without perceiving it, a terrible sentence, for it is he who said, ' A corrupt mind was never sublime.' Nothing is more true, and this is the reason why Voltaire with his hundred volumes was never more than *pretty*.[1] I except his tragedies, in which the nature of the work forced him to express noble sentiments foreign to his character. . . . Have you never observed that the divine curse was written on his forehead? After so many years, it is still time to prove it. Go and look at his statue in the palace of the Hermitage. Never do I behold it without congratulating myself on this, that it has not been transmitted by any one who has inherited the chisel of the Greek, and who might have been able perhaps to send it abroad as a kind of beau ideal. Here all is natural. There is as much truth in this head as there would have been in a cast taken from the corpse. See that abject forehead, which the blush of modesty never coloured, these two extinct craters from which luxury and hatred still seem to gush forth ; that mouth (I speak badly, but it is not my fault), that frightful *rictus* (scornful opening of the mouth) extending from ear to ear, and these lips pinched by cruel malice, like a spring ready to unbend, in order to dart blasphemy or sarcasm. Do not speak to me of this man, I cannot bear the idea of him. Ah! what evil he has done to us! Like the insect, the scourge of the gardens, that only applies his bites to the root of the most precious plants, Voltaire with his sting, does not cease to prick the two roots of society—women and young people ; they imbibe his poison, which he thus transmits from one generation to another. He cannot allege, like so many others, youth, inconsideration, the impulse of passion, and to sum up all, the sad weakness of our nature. There is no excuse ; his depravity is such as only belongs to himself—it is rooted in the inmost fibres of his heart, and is strengthened by all the power of his understanding. Always allied to sacrilege, it braves God by destroying men. With a fury that has no example, this insolent blasphemer goes on to declare himself the personal enemy of the

---

[1] M. de Maistre, perhaps without knowing it, repeats the saying of Montesquieu in his Thoughts : " Voltaire is not beautiful, he is only pretty." (Pensées Diverses des Modernes).

Saviour of men ; he ventures from the bottom of his nothingness to give him a ridiculous name, and that adorable law, which the God-man brought into the world, he calls *infamous*. Abandoned by God, who punishes by withdrawing himself, he knows no more restraint. Other cynics astonished virtue, Voltaire astonishes vice. He plunges into the mire, he rolls in it, he drenches himself with it, he gives up his imagination to the enthusiasm of hell, which lends him all its force to drag him to the utmost extremities of evil. He invents prodigies and monsters, which make men turn pale. Paris crowned him, Sodom would have banished him. Impudent profaner of the universal language, and of its greatest names, the last of the men who came after those who loved it. How should I describe to you what he makes me feel ? When I see what he might have done, and what he has done, his inimitable talents only the more inspire me with a holy rage, which has no name. Suspended between admiration and horror, I would sometimes wish to make a statue be raised to him . . . . . by the hand of the executioner."[1]

After this estimate, here is a very different one :—

" At the beginning of the last century, the spirit of philosophy, which meditated the conquest of society, required to associate with the gravity of Montesquieu something more active and lively ; and I imagine that, at the foot of the throne of the Author of things, it bowed low one day, to ask the coming of a representative suitable to its designs. Descartes, Malebranche, Spinosa, Locke, appeared ; Leibnitz displayed a peaceful and profound universality ; but the time claims another, ardent, warlike, and insurrectional. God will grant it to the genius of philosophy. Oh, my God ! since this young man, who came forth to the world in 1718, is not hot-headed, or a forlorn hope —since he must not miscarry in an expedition which Thou thyself hast decreed, load him with all gifts, arm him from head to foot for what works and toils await him ! He runs the risk, so long as he has not hurried the world away with him, of being crushed by it. But God does not abandon him, without having fortified him with an invincible ability for the undertaking for which He sends him."[2]

[1] J. de Maistre, Soirées de St Petersbourg, tome i.
[2] Lerminier Philosophie du dix huitième siècle, p. 53.

We do not wish, gentlemen, to follow the example of men without any opinion, and form our judgment by beating one against another, and by blunting one by another, the most extravagant strokes of a panegyric, and the severest censures of a violent animadversion. Fear, mixed with hatred, cannot command injustice in regard to Voltaire.

If we had only here to sum up his moral character, our task would be easy. What renders him terrible, and what exaggerates his wickedness, is his genius; there is in this an optical illusion. But we ought not to take, as the measure of a man's wickedness, the evil which he has produced. If any one were desirous to estimate Voltaire as a man, he must keep out of view his talent and his works; take him merely in his personal relations; in a word, make the distinction between the writer and the individual. It would then be seen that he was not more wicked than many others, but that, in his case, all was prominent and freely developed. His life received no guidance from the law of God, or from his conscience—he had only instincts. Some were decidedly bad, others were not. Had he been reduced to the condition of a citizen or artizan, Voltaire would have been, like so many others, impassioned, unbridled, very vain, very irritable, capable of sympathy, and of many things which the most vulgar morality quickly repels; formidable, hateful, and one to whom there would have been granted some interest and affection. His talent and his age have impressed on his existence something monstrous, without being able to call him a monster.

The character of Voltaire does not present the dignity of harmonious existence; but he has the power, which is joined to the irregularity of a nature in lively contrast. No man was made up of antitheses more frequently repeated. Extravagancies multiply; this disposition is like a thicket, whose branches, crossing one another, stop your progress in every direction. As a man of art, in the ideal sense of the term, Voltaire would have known internal peace and harmony. In philosophy and literature men of system are encountered. They may be so in two ways: some embrace their circle of ideas with a breadth which allows them to comprehend those of other men; others are exclusively attached to their own ideas, but their exclusiveness is quite consistent with themselves. Unity always prevails. But in all ages men of action have been a series of contrasts, and, so far from weakening them, these contrasts were a condition of their strength. The power of a scientific, synthetic, benevolent, and peaceful genius, is much more beneficent and profound; but it acts only at a distance—the force near at hand was exercised by men deficient in internal harmony.

It is difficult to refuse to Voltaire the epithet great; his destiny pronounced him " to be of an entire age the thought and the life ;" this is to be great, and this is his greatness. *Tu regere imperio populos.*[1] But this greatness is not personal; true greatness cannot be conceived without generosity, and without a certain degree of goodness, otherwise the devil himself would be great. " We see here," said Lavater, " a personage greater and more energetic than we. We feel our weakness in his presence, but without his making us great; instead of each being, who is at once great and good, not merely awakening in us the feeling of our weakness, but, by a secret charm, elevating us above ourselves, and communicating to us something of its greatness."[2] There is nothing sublime in Voltaire—nothing to inspire respect for human nature. He has not one great thought. That of the destruction of Christianity is not great—an abstraction made from our faith to the divinity of our belief. Hatred, according to its object, may make a man great, but that of Voltaire was not high-minded and not honest. Besides, to strip, without any indemnity, the human species of the future state and of God, and consequently of their dignity, is not greatness. Strange and primary antithesis, he has for human nature an ardent love, but it is without respect; he loves her as a mistress, not as a lawful wife.

Conservative from disposition and interest, Voltaire, in his hatred of Christianity, spends his long life in destroying it. He aims at improvements in the social government, but he rejects with anger every thing which might reach the root of the evils against which he complains. To overturn the positive religion of his age and country, and to maintain almost every thing else, was his wish and the end of his efforts. Irreverence, violence, and treachery signalized the war which he declared against Christianity, or at least what he took for Christianity. The

---

[1] Virgil, Æneid, vi. 52. [2] Lavater sur Voltaire.

gross indecency of his attacks became proverbial; there was no
want of any trick; if he required authorities, he had no hesitation in referring to books which did not exist. He continually
appealed to prejudices, instead of raising the mind to generali-
ties, at which he himself might have arrived. He brings forward
the perpetual sophisms of the evils produced by Christianity.
To superficial understandings this argument is irresistible; to
persons of cultivated minds it is very weak. The true statement
of the question is this: "Does the Gospel contain any doctrine
intended to authorize the horrors, of which the Christian religion has been the occasion?" Let us suppose that Socrates,
for example, had been a witness of the life of Jesus Christ, of
His miracles, of His doctrine, and of the conduct of His first
disciples, he would undoubtedly have said: "There is a religion
about to banish oppression, injustice, and wars; it will render
the world happy." He would have spoken as a wise man of the
world. God alone could say: "I have come to send fire on
earth. Suppose ye that I am come to give peace on earth? I
tell you, Nay; but rather division."[1] A sublime paradox, which
God alone could utter! God alone knew that He was going to
create upon the earth two worlds at enmity with each other.
He saw all vices and all hypocrisies taking refuge under the
robe of Christianity. He knew that the worst of corruptions is
that of excellent things, and the worst of persecutions that of
false against true Christians. Yes, the Gospel has brought out
human nature in all its wickedness. Will it be said, on this
account, that Christianity has been hostile to society? One
word is sufficient: do we live for time or for eternity? Is the
direct object of Christianity better to organize the society of the
earth, or to prepare the society of heaven? Do we consider
Jesus Christ merely as the author of the principle of social
equality and fraternity? Let us reject, then, a religion which
becomes to society the occasion of unquestionable evils, or let us
accept it as training the soul for heaven; and, in that case, let
us hold it as absolved from all the scandals with which men have
been pleased to weigh it down.

Voltaire always favoured theism. He pleaded the cause of
God against Diderot and the sect of Holbach; he defended it in

<hr>

[1] Luc. xii. 49-51.

prose and verse.[1] But he makes little account of the necessary relations of this great truth. All the ideas which complete the idea of God, without which it would remain inactive in the soul, he utterly disregards. He withdraws from this notion every thing which constitutes its substance. He does not trouble himself about the question, whether his God be personal or impersonal. Is there a future reward? He knows nothing about it. Frederic writes to him, "that a certain philosopher of his acquaintance is quite persuaded that this Intelligence is no more embarrassed with Moustapha than with the greatest Christian, and that what happens to men disquiets him as little as that which may happen to an anthill, which the foot of the traveller crushes without perceiving it." Voltaire answers him: "Your abominable fellow, who is so sure that every thing dies with us, may be quite right."[2] He said somewhere: "If God did not exist, it would be necessary to contrive one." Robespierre was charged with paraphrasing this verse. Truly the God of Voltaire is a God invented, a God imagined for the necessities of society. People cannot give up this belief; it appeared to Voltaire reasonable and specious; the idea of God was important—let us preserve the idea of God. This theism is an affair of good sense; and it is the good sense of Voltaire, and not his soul, which demands a God. When he gets Him, he does not know what to do with Him. He wants the materials to be a pantheist. Nevertheless, this theism, meagre as it was, could not be borne by the philosophers; they took it amiss that he wished to defend God, and he required courage to persist in it.

But, through all these contrasts, is there no unity in Voltaire? Two features prevail, and go through the whole:—

First, common sense, the genius of good sense. This genius is quite sufficient to destroy. His philosophy does not rise above it, and hence he has even denied philosophy, for philosophy consists in leaning on common sense, that it may go beyond it. Voltaire made the leaning point the end; he was the apostle of

---

[1] If a clock proves a clockmaker, if a palace proclaims an architect, how does not the universe indeed demonstrate a supreme Intelligence? What plant, animal, element, or star does not bear the impress of Him whom Plato calls the eternal Geometer? It appears to me that the body of the smallest animal shows a depth and a unity of design which must at once delight and overwhelm the mind, etc.— (*Note on the satire respecting Cabals*).

[2] Lettre au roi de Prusse. 21st Nov. 1770.

that circle of received ideas, and sometimes of prejudices, which
is commonly honoured with the title of good sense. The power
of Voltaire consisted in presenting passion as the interpreter of
good sense. As to his work, we meet with an admirable conformity to what he was and to what he did. He descends instead of rising; the form of his mind puts him within reach of
the vulgar. He is not speculative; he appeals constantly to the
current notions. He collects facts, and this is his characteristic.
Voltaire was not learned, but well informed. On the surface of
all the sciences he was well provided with curious facts. Never
does he reason without alleging facts, always ingeniously related;
and it is thus he renders his discussions interesting. He repeats
facts and ideas; men like him, animated with an ardent desire to
make proselytes, are led by habit to say over and over the same
things; but no one has done it more frequently than Voltaire,
and at the same time in such a variety of forms. In his case
this repetition is not tedious. He was eminently a pamphleteer,
and this word exactly expresses what he was. Epic, tragic, comic,
and satiric poet, he was, above all, a pamphleteer.

In the second place, Voltaire had the feeling of social justice,
and, more generally, the instinct of civilization. There is, no
doubt, a more noble civilization than his, but it is civilization
which is his divinity. His morality is incomplete, and by no
means elevated; it is reduced to justice and benevolence, and yet
it is morality. Moreover, he reasoned little: he did what was
better, he opened his heart, he appealed, not to abstract principles, but to instincts. "He does not demonstrate," says M. de
Barante, "he sympathizes."

If ever Voltaire, who is not naturally an orator, rises to eloquence, it is when he attacks, as we have seen, the abuses of the
law, and especially of the criminal law. This is perhaps the
greatest service that he has rendered to human nature. Montesquieu and Rousseau directed their efforts to the same point, but
Voltaire knew better how to bring his ideas within reach of all.
Nothing certainly is more universally welcomed than good sense
and civilization. By these two things, and by the last especially,
Voltaire was popular. Men are not so, even in the worst times,
without appealing to some truth or honourable sentiment. But
this popularity has also foundations less noble—scepticism and
irony. In spite of his prodigious intelligence, Voltaire's reason

continued to be of a middling description, if we understand by reason the faculty by which man embraces truth. He judges with marvellous sagacity the man of society; he does not even apprehend man in his primitive condition. The grand features of humanity escape his observation; there is nothing artless in him—he is not even in a state to comprehend artlessness. La Fontaine was always to him inexplicable.

With his incomparable intelligence, and deprived of the superiority of reason, which might have served as a guide to his intelligence, he ought naturally to be a scoffer. Irony abounds in France; Voltaire was the prince of irony and the banterer of the age. His irony bears upon every thing—it blasts, withers, burns, it is eminently profane wit. He scoffs at humanity as a whole. " Our dignity is unknown to him, our miseries impress his mind and divert him, he delights in their enumeration, and adds some that are imaginary; man only appears in his eyes a defective beast, as the produce of a *foolish joke* of the Creator, and he greets with a loud and cruel laugh that shameful parody on his own nature. So disposed, how would he have reached the utmost depths of philosophical questions? On every subject of this order, his specific lightness keeps him near the surface. He comprehended every thing, which is comprehended by the understanding; and when he meets with truth, no one falls into it, we must say, more perpendicularly; but what is comprehended by the soul—that is to say, every subject which is more profound and sublime, has almost always escaped his notice. The prejudices of civilization, and the appearances of common sense, are his arguments on questions which refer to the Infinite; these are sufficient to convince and subject light minds, already vanquished by materialism. But with one gift besides, with the philosophy of the soul, Voltaire was no longer Voltaire; he was as well as others strong in what he possessed, and strong in what he was deficient."[1]

A better philosopher and a more finished writer he would perhaps have had less authority over his age. We have seen nothing more superficial and more hazardous than his philosophy of history. Man is an adventurer, a Gil Blas, whose memoirs, it was his duty to digest, and yet it was, perhaps, on this side that

[1] Vinet, Discours sur la Literature Française, p. 57.

he did most wrong to religion. Had he been more deeply learned, he would not have engaged with Buffon in a ridiculous controversy on the formation of the globe. Buffon's system was inconvenient for him, probably on account of some points of contact with the Bible. He covered it over with jokes, which succeeded better with the multitude than with serious minds.

The popularity of Voltaire has still another cause—the licentiousness of his pictures and of his stories. The French nation always loved trifling on these matters ; in other respects they look upon vice more seriously. Nothing better marks the weakness of power than the indulgence of it in this respect; it is a forced compensation by which a practised government is anxious to replace the exercise of liberty of thought. Impunity was granted to the author of *la Pucelle*, and a young man was condemned to death, because he had shown himself irreverent to the crucifix. Napoleon did not allow a fourth of such things as Louis XV. tolerated.

In short, a part of this popularity should be attributed to the unequalled activity of Voltaire. Nothing is more popular than perseverance and rapidity of labour. This constitutes the illusion of power ; a man is present in several places at once, he never relaxes his attention, and fills with his name space and time. Perfection is much less popular ; the vulgar do not understand studied, conscientious, and solitary exertion. Voltaire is not perfect, but his manner is easy, broad, prompt, and yet always correct.

Armed with all these instruments, Voltaire did the work for which perhaps he *had been sent.*[1] Voltaire destroyed. He reminds us of those who ravage nations, and who receive, like Genseric, this word of command : *Go to the peoples against whom the wind of God's wrath blows.* He destroyed the evil and the good. In this world they are entwined ; we cannot destroy the one without cutting down the other. Besides, they honoured Voltaire for all this destruction, but they did not observe that all was perishing, and that he only killed the dying. In the way of gangrene, this would have lasted longer and ended in the same way ; he only hastened the times and transformed into an acute disease, a chronic malady, which was incurable.

---

[1] Allusion au mot de M. Lerminier cite plus haut. Voir page 327.

An infallible symptom of the evil was the weakness of the good. It is said Voltaire destroyed faith, morality, and Christianity. But where were faith and Christianity? Had not this blow been struck in the time of Louis XIV.? Must we see in this deficiency the effect of the divine will? But God has never refused an agent to a firm faith. We may look at the condition of the party, which Voltaire beat into the breach. The whole Gallican, the whole Reformed Church were unable to oppose a man to him. There had been no revival of theological science since the time of Bossuet; philosophy was wanting to the defenders of the Gospel, which is itself a philosophy; above all, life was wanting. It is the *virtutem videant*,[1] which is important. Writings would not have changed the age, the energy of action was necessary. The life of an Oberlin would have spoken in a higher tone than a hundred volumes of polemics. After all, there was a vengeance to be inflicted, a justice to be executed, whole ages to be expiated. Christianity in exercising power over the earth, had received into itself the element of corruption, and had borne its own sentence. It was necessary to send it to the wilderness. All Voltaire's work was a necessity and a preparation.

Whatever may be the talent of Voltaire as a man of art and of literature, and although he may have excelled in certain kinds of writing, it is less as an artist than as a political or historical personage that he should be viewed. Without being a magistrate officially, he was the true tribune of the people—more than any other he rendered literature popular. But he invented neither in literature nor philosophy; and as an artist, it may be said that his track is effaced. Beyond the age of the empire, in which he had some imitators in satire and tragedy, Voltaire, as a man of literature, no longer exists but in literary history. The age, in point of art, claims no acquaintance with him, no one supports him or appeals to his authority. Corneille and Racine, his predecessors, are much more alive, and much more known at present than he. Five and twenty or thirty years ago a new edition of Voltaire's works[2] was factiously undertaken, but it was not to the writer but to the pamphleteer that the appeal was made. Against the return of the enemies that he had van-

---

[1] Perseus, Sat. iii. 38.   [2] Allusion au Voltaire. Tonquet (Editeurs).

quished, they called forth his shade. It was the carcass of the Cid still gaining a battle. Now even his unbelief excited the pity of the learned unbelief of our age,—it was necessary to dig deeper.

The disappearance of Voltaire's literary influence naturally suggests some reflections. Art is not incompatible with the pursuit of a moral and social end. The period most devoted to literature was also the most social and the most effective. I speak of the delightful times of Greece. But what is not true, is that art in its purity may be compatible with designs too particular, and with an end too near, and, above all, with the spirit of party. Voltaire might have been an artist, his critical labours prove it; but by his prejudices he took away the rank, which he might have occupied in art. Shall we blame him for having so acted? I would be tempted to praise him. Previously occupied as he was with social reforms, and even, in despite of appearances, with moral reform, we cannot withhold from him honour for having preferred such ideas to the exclusive idea of art.

The feeling which remains after all this is sad: we must exclude from it hatred and only preserve pity. No man has better served the cause of the Prince of Darkness than Voltaire, but if we enter into the interior of his being, we still say, gentlemen, we only find there a man like many other men.

XX.

D'ALEMBERT.

1717–1783.

WE have now come to what may be called *Voltaire's band*. This numerous group includes eminent men, true leaders of the philosophical faction, of which they were the founders, men of activity, unceasingly in the breach, who only aimed at pulling down, and in whom the speculative faculties remained completely subordinate to the practical end. The most illustrious are D'Alem-

bert, Diderot, Helvetius, Raynal, and two Germans, Baron
d'Hólbach and Baron de Grimm.

A judgment has been formed of this whole school by M. de
Barante, he has spoken of it with justice; these men were not so
much the causes of the movements of the age and of the fatal
revolutions, which terminated it, as they are the sign and the
effect of the spirit of this memorable epoch. M. de Barante was
the first to acknowledge this truth. Their work was no doubt
fatal, but they were only the secondary causes, the primary
existed long before. They followed and perhaps accelerated the
current of the ideas of their contemporaries; possibly, without
them, those, whose circulation they earnestly promoted, would
not have assumed an identical character, but this point of view
is accessary. What was done with them would have been done
without them, the reverence for the seventeenth century had
perished before their time, and the only point was to remove the
carcass. This was the work of the eighteenth century.

Besides, with the exception of Voltaire, D'Alembert, and perhaps Diderot, the chiefs in this movement were men of moderate
intellectual power. Voltaire was the king. At a great distance
we find Diderot. D'Alembert was a distinguished mathematician,
but as a literary man, he does not occupy a very high place.
The number of the party constituted its strength; by their works,
their conversation, and their influence, they altogether contributed to the work of demolition. Destruction entirely by itself
does not require so much power.

The seventeenth century reckoned many more superior men,
who were necessary to the labour of construction then in progress. In the eighteenth, however, some thinkers wished to
construct. Montesquieu was a builder, Rousseau fell foul of the
philosophers to preserve some important matters. Buffon was a
man of science attached to his own erection, and he never engaged in the business of destruction. In his own way, too,
Condillac was anxious to build up. There are many more men
of genius on the side of those who build, protect, and preserve.
To destroy, indeed, requires no genius—talent is sufficient. But
it is a good thing to manage appearances, and a man must pride
himself in building. This is what the great destroyers of the
last age did, and we ourselves pretend to be an age of organization. At bottom, all these men with their different tendencies

were little else than Voltaire divided into small portions—the small change of the golden coin.

D'Alembert, of illegitimate and shameful birth, but belonging both by father and mother to the higher classes of society, was from his earliest age abandoned to the care of a glazier's wife, for whom he always maintained a tender veneration. At a later period, when he had become illustrious by success, he was acknowledged by his real mother, but refused to go near her, and answered: " The glazier's wife is my mother."

From this situation there resulted in his case a certain misanthropy, a sharpness, so to speak, of thought and language. He possessed otherwise estimable qualities, disinterestedness and simplicity of manners, he was sincere and faithful in his friendships, and appears to have had an affectionate and even an impassioned heart. Endowed with powerful talent for the mathematics, and already celebrated at twenty years of age, he was successively a member of all the academies in Europe. Although less illustrious as a man of literature, D'Alembert came near to the great writers in his *Preliminary Discourse to the Encyclopedia.* This discourse is ranked among the masterpieces of the age, and among them all in the eighteenth century, perhaps he alone was capable of writing it. He has neither the fancy of Buffon nor the passion of Rousseau, but he is lucid, grave, and in admirable possession of his subject. " He traces the genealogical order of human knowledge, points out the limits of each branch and its relation to others, and the characters which distinguish them in our mind, and he raises the encyclopedical tree of the sciences distinct from the historical order of their development, after which he unfolds the history of intellectual culture in Europe since the revival of letters. This discourse is written in a style severe without stiffness, and noble with simplicity; and without ever departing from the peculiar language which philosophy claims, the author renders perfectly clear and we may say palpable, the most abstract ideas."[1] There existed at that time a class of literary men, to whom there was nothing analogous in the reign of Louis XIV. The seventeenth century had poets, philosophers, scholars, critics, but not a man, who was all these at once. In the relation of intellectual eminence, the Bossuets, the Fene-

[1] Vinet, Discours sur la Literature Française, p. 56.

lons, and others, are far from being surpassed by the men of the eighteenth century, but among all these great minds, the most part applied themselves to some special study and generalized little; the others generalized without having any precise or peculiar object. This is the difference in the manners and in the age. In the seventeenth century, the different branches of culture remain isolated or are only looked at in passing; we only glance here and there at some men, whose minds bear in themselves something universal, but the idea of connecting all the forms of human study happens to nobody. This will be one of the ideas peculiar to the new era, to the era which will realize the views of Bacon.

In ancient times, at the beginning of science, there was a kind of universality, easy, because superficial. Eminent minds were then more or less encyclopedists; but each of their chapters is short, and the necessity of special study was speedily felt. At a later period, the tendency to universality reappears, but it is enriched with the acquirements of ages. With some men, science may be compared to an archipelago, the assemblage of a vast number of islets brought close together, but quite separate. With others, it resembles a continent, through which there is full communication. It is no longer knowledge, properly so called, it is the knowledge of knowledge, it is truly *science*, an aspiration at that unity which is only manifested in God, but towards which man is constantly gravitating. D'Alembert had the idea of this universal science; he already conceived the hope of reaching that one principle, and in this point of view he was, perhaps, the man of his time most fitted to write the *Preliminary Discourse to the Encyclopedia*.

This *Discourse* is, indeed, his true title to glory, but besides, he has published several works which are valuable; among others his *Elements of Philosophy*, where each science is characterized by its object and by its spirit, and where the rules which direct their study are traced with a firm and a prudent hand. This book, in which every page reveals a very great mind, and the only ornament of whose style is its clearness, but a clearness so lively as to be brilliant, deserves for D'Alembert, too little appreciated by literary men, a distinguished place amongst them. The *Essay on Men of Letters*, full of striking observations, and of pointed passages, may appear written with a little rudeness, but it shows in the author an independence of character, whose example was not then sufficiently common not to render it somewhat meritorious in the case of D'Alembert.[1]

In his *Eulogies on the Members of the French Academy*, of which he was perpetual secretary, D'Alembert gave scope to his caustic humour. Irony, idle talk, too many anecdotes, a certain dryness of style, diminish the pleasure of the reader. Nevertheless, the book continues to be amusing and instructive; you may draw from it several thoughts of great value. What wears us out is the fixed idea of the author. He is not so desirous to do justice to his heroes as to overthrow received ideas and traditions. He has, however, pieces truly serious and exquisite, as the eulogies on Bossuet, Fenelon, and Massillon, which are quite classical. On the whole, D'Alembert is a man of distinguished attainments, and a remarkable writer, but he still remains in the second rank.

His influence over the eighteenth century was considerable. A bachelor, without family connections, poor, and sober, D'Alembert gave to the service of the philosophy of his time a real power, but he did less by his talents than by his character. A lieutenant of Voltaire, the boldest propagator of his master's thoughts, in whose absence he represented him at Paris; and under him he was, in fact, the most influential person in the philosophical movement. It is marvellous to see that mind, otherwise so independent, obeying the impulses of Voltaire. He had refused the most attractive offers of foreign princes; to all these brilliant fetters, he preferred his poverty and his freedom. He was afraid neither of public opinion nor of disgrace, but he was afraid of two things, sufferings and death. This fear gave to his last moments a colouring quite opposite to his life, abandoning the colours under which he served, he sincerely implored the succours of religion.

[1] Vinet, Discours sur la Literature Française, p. 56.

XXI.

DIDEROT.

1713–1784.

DIDEROT was the attendant of D'Alembert. Indeed, what is the thing which Diderot was not? A kind of *logogriphe*, or enigma personified, writing less, as it appears, to teach his readers something than to lead them astray, sentimental and cynical, an enthusiast and a materialist, mixing with pathetic exclamations the oaths of the populace, passionately urging social reforms, and the impudent apologist of the torture, carrying great zeal into atheism, speaking of virtue with unheard-of ardour, and enriching literature with nameless horrors and turpitudes, a mind in a constant state of heat, a man whose word would have moved a world, if he had had only what Archimedes asked for, a point of support, but who had no support either in reason or conscience. Diderot is a phenomenon to study rather than an author to analyse.

As well as D'Alembert, he partook of universality. His science immense, and on certain subjects profound, is almost in no case superficial. Diderot was capable of serving as an auxiliary to a number of writers. If, on any occasion, a bold, burning, and paradoxical paper were required, it was asked from Diderot. It is not yet known in how many works he had a share. Nearly a third of the *Philosophical History* of Raynal belongs to him. He co-operated in the *System of Nature*, and in the book *On the Mind*. He was also the principal author of the *Encyclopedia;* the general conception of the work, the spirit which animates it, a considerable number of important articles, are all referred to Diderot. A new and original critic, a writer of romance, a dramatic poet, a philosopher; in short, he is all these together, and ought to be studied under all these relations.

As a critic, he laboured much, but his influence was not in proportion to his efforts. In his examination of the works of poetry and the fine arts, he is himself a creator; he not merely sees faults, but the absence of beauties. His literary theories made a sensation, but nothing more—none went so far as to admit them. They were better suited to the views of our age than his. He was romantic, but his ideas were neither very clear nor very finished, nor even very just. He wished to shake off the yoke of conventions, and bring art to nature, but to what nature? Diderot did not know reality, it was especially for him a reality of convention, as well as the poetry of convention against which he revolted. Besides, he wished with all his might to introduce morality into literature. But here again, what morality? For him it was the natural development of the human will, and it was by saturating with this sort of morality all the branches of literature, that he pretended to regulate manners. He himself never succeeded in his compositions, but when he forgot his theories, to be purely and simply an artist. Among his writings on literary criticism, we should notice his *Letters on the Deaf and Dumb, addressed to those who Hear and Speak,* and his *Philosophical Inquiries into the Origin and Nature of Beauty.* On painting, we have from his pen the *Saloons* of 1765 *and* 1767.

As a dramatic poet, Diderot was one of the promoters and models of a style of writing almost new in his time, although introduced by Voltaire and La Chaussée. It was the great changes and the great passions of the drama brought under the roof of a family of citizens. The idea of the family beset Diderot, and yet—flagrant contradiction—he was neither a good husband nor a good father. But he had the deep feeling of what a family might be ; and it was to restore it that he consecrated his dramatic works, *The Father of a Family,* and *The Natural Son.* These dramas are conceived with genius, rather than composed with talent. Talent is the paper-money of genius : genius alone is not a bill easy to negotiate. Everywhere, and especially in France, talent is necessary to genius. M. de Chateaubriand remarks somewhere, that in foreign countries we meet with a very great number of these men of genius who have passed without inquiry. With Diderot, talent is not proportioned to genius : with the talent of Racine, he would have been the first writer of the eighteenth century ; but his plays are faulty in the execution ; he becomes dull ; he leaves too little air and space around his characters. Even in *The Father of a Family,* the better of his two dramas, we feel that the author is mastered by his subject much more than he is its master.

As a writer of romance, Diderot has shown himself much

more of an artist; but his two romances, *The Nun*, and *James the Fatalist*, are pernicious, and therefore to be. condemned—the author dwells with a criminal complacency on the most dangerous images. When this is well understood, and when we occupy ourselves with these. books merely in reference to art, we must admit that they are written with real talent. Rousseau could have written nothing so true and so objective as *The Nun*. It is the veil lifted from the most odious mysteries of the monastic life. Diderot spared nothing, and went to the extreme boundaries of the hideous. A nun, who had escaped from her convent, relates her own history ; another man would have thought it his duty to give to this personage an interesting countenance —something at least marked. Diderot did nothing of the kind ; his nun is quite an ordinary character, and so much the more true. But, once for all, we must be plain—the book deserves the epithet of infamous.

James the Fatalist, as immoral as *The Nun*, is a series of episodes, in which are found sublime passages ; among others, we may notice the story of Madame de La Pommeraie. This book, however, is written in the spirit of Voltaire's romances.

The tales of Diderot are well known ; they are to be met with everywhere, and particularly at the end of an edition of Gesner's poetry. Admirably written, they are easily read ; and the piece entitled, *The Danger of Setting Ourselves Above the Laws*, deserves particular notice.

We may now consider him as a philosopher. It is in this department that Diderot is known, and yet it is as a philosopher that we have most difficulty in characterizing him, as he was so variable and inconsistent.

The *Essay on Merit and Virtue*, freely translated into English, or rather imitated, by Lord Shaftesbury, appeared in 1745 ; he expresses some sentiments which may be called religious. In his preliminary discourse, he speaks in the following terms :— "The end of this work is to show that virtue is almost indivisibly attached to the knowledge of God, and that man's temporal happiness is inseparable from virtue. There is no virtue without believing in God, and no happiness without virtue : these, he adds, are the two propositions of the illustrious philosopher, whose ideas I am now to explain." In the course of the work, we find in a note this thought : " True piety, a quality almost

essential to heroism, enlarges the heart and the mind."[1]   And,
farther on, also in a note : " Atheism leaves probity without
support ; it does worse, it indirectly urges men forward to depravity."[2]

The *Philosophical Thoughts* (1746) have already a character
more decided. They were condemned, and afterwards reprinted,
under the title of *Presents to Strong Minds.* Here follow some
specimens :—

" Moderate passions make common men."[3]   " There are
people, of whom we must not say that they fear God, but rather
that they are afraid of Him."[4]   " Superstition is more injurious
to God than atheism."[5]   " The deist alone can face the atheist ;
the superstitious man is powerless."[6]

Disguised atheism is betrayed in thought xxi., on the various
chances in the origin and beautiful arrangement of the universe,
on the supposition that motion is once granted to matter. In
the following thought, we meet with this saying : " I pity those
who are really atheists ; with respect to them all consolation
appears to me lost." And, farther on, thought xxvi. :—

" We do not sufficiently insist on the presence of God. Men
have banished the Divinity from the midst of them ; they have
confined Him in a sanctuary ; the walls of a temple bound His
view ; He does not exist beyond it. Fools that you are ! destroy these enclosures, which narrow your ideas ; set God free ;
look at Him wherever He is, or say that He is not. If I had a
child to train, I would make the presence of the Divinity so real,
that he would, perhaps, have less regret to become an atheist
than to separate himself from it. . . . I would multiply around
him the signs that indicate the Divine presence. If, for example,
he made for himself a circle in my house, I would mark in it a
place for God, and would accustom my pupil to say : We are
four—God, my friend, my tutor, and myself."

Some pages after this, we find an indirect attack on miracles.
The question is on the return of Elijah : " Elijah may return
from the other world when he chooses ; men are such, that he
will perform great miracles, if he be well received in this world."
—(Thought xli). And, farther : " All Paris might assure me
that a dead man had come to life at Passy, I would not believe

---

[1] Œuvres, edition Naigeon, tome i. p. 85.   [2] Tome i. p. 96.
[3] Tome i. p. 220.   [4] Ibid. i. p. 223.   [5] Ibid. i. p. 224.   [6] Ibid. i. p. 225.

it. An historian may impose upon us, a whole people may be deceived, this is nothing wonderful."—(Thought xlvii.)

We perceive that a great number of Diderot's thoughts, which were at the time strong or specious, are far from being either the one or the other in the present day ; and it is entirely owing to himself. His attacks, and those of his friends, have made us have recourse to proofs more solid, and to notions more precise.

That which is derived from the *Philosophical Thoughts*, notwithstanding their incoherence, is scepticism considered as the superior state of human reason. In the *Additions to the Thoughts*, the author goes one step farther, and declares himself against Christianity. He calls the Christians *atrocious*. He began by saying: "To prove the Gospel by a miracle, is to prove an absurdity by a thing contrary to nature."—(Thought xxi.) In another thought (lxviii.), while he denies the truth, he very nearly touches it: "If man is unhappy without being born guilty, might it not be that he is destined to enjoy eternal happiness without being ever able by his nature to render himself worthy of it ?"[1]

Three years after, in 1749, Diderot maintained, in his *Letter on the Blind, for the use of those who See*, that our moral ideas are only produced by our organization. In consequence of this letter, he was imprisoned at Vincennes.

In 1751, the two first volumes of the *Encyclopedia* appeared ; the idea of the work was suggested by Diderot and D'Alembert. Diderot managed several parts of it, almost alone, such as the history of the ancient philosophy. The *Letter to my Brother*, contained in the first volume of his works, became the article *Intolerance*. After the publication of the first seven volumes of the *Encyclopedia*, the privilege was revoked, D'Alembert withdrew, and Diderot continued the undertaking alone. The work was from that time bolder, and more carelessly managed.

In the *Supplement to the Voyage of Bougainville*,[2] Diderot annihilates moral ideas, and invites man, as a social being, to take

---

[1] Greater development would have been desirable for the reputation of the Thoughts of Diderot, but time failed M. Vinet at the end of the course on the moralists; and although he had prepared notes, from which a part of these pages are taken, he could only mention this philosopher. At Lausanne, in 1846, the literary point of view must naturally prevail. The Thoughts were only matter of inquiry in passing, and there was only time to name them.— (Editors).

[2] Œuvres de Diderot. Tome iii.

the liberty of the brutes; he sets free from all rule the commerce of the two sexes, and proscribes marriage. He exclaims, "that the code of nations would be short, if it was strictly conformed to that of nature!" And elsewhere : "Do you wish to know the abridged history of almost all our misery? Man existed a natural being—within that man an artificial man was introduced, and he has raised in the cavern a civil war, which lasts all his life."[1]

The *Thoughts on the Interpretation of Nature* (1754), present, along with extravagant passages, fine turns of style, abundance of ideas, and admirable bursts of imagination. This book is dedicated to young people, and begins with these words : "Young man, take and read." Here follow some remarkable sayings :—

"The great habit of acquiring experience, gives to the grossest seamen a foresight, which has the character of inspiration. . . . This may be called the art of proceeding from what is not known to what is still less known. It is this habit of acting without reasoning, which those possess in a surprising degree who have acquired or who hold from nature the genius of experimental philosophy; to this kind of dreams we owe several discoveries. . . . . . The most important service which they have to render to those whom they initiate in experimental philosophy, is much less to instruct them in the mode of proceeding, and in the result, as to introduce into them that spirit of divination, by which they *smell afar*, so to speak, unknown proceedings, new experiments, and unknown results."[2]

Diderot gives example along with precept ; he himself at times developes this spirit of divination. In 1765, the Empress Catherine bought Diderot's library. In 1773, he went with her to Petersburg. He returned to Paris, and there died in 1784.

Diderot was an atheist—if not convinced, at least zealous. He ardently and enthusiastically preached atheism. Atheism and enthusiasm ! It is truly a contradiction in the object and in the terms. But the atheism of Diderot is not ordinary atheism—it is not purely negative—it is rather a sort of worship of nature, a matter, in his case, of temperament still more than of system. Indeed *naturism*, in the true sense of that word, coined in our times, suited the robust constitution, the broad shoulders, and the

---

[1] The dull and systematic collection of Diderot's monstrous principles may be seen in the system of Fourier.—(Editors).

[2] Tome iii. p. 285-291.

round back of Diderot. This constitution rendered him more sensible of the powers of nature, and put him, so to speak, in harmony with it, considered as an active and creative power. With respect to him, nature was a divinity; he believed in the eternity of matter, and this matter, imperishable, and, according to him, always acting, inspired him with a kind of adoration.

But the enthusiasm of Diderot is neither the serious nor calm enthusiasm of conviction, nor the tender enthusiasm of the heart, it is rather the intoxication, we may even say the cynicism of a thought, which nothing fixes nor keeps together, and of a wandering imagination, which knows no restraint. The peculiarity of Diderot is to express boldly every thing which passes through his mind. He said himself : " I have spoken enough of absurdities in my life to know well how to judge of myself by them." He says truly, he rolled down a real torrent of mud and pebbles. And yet all his enthusiasm does not affect us, it might be said to be coolly meditated ; his exaggeration of subjects, which are not worth the pains, approaches to the ridiculous. Thus he says some where, that he will curse his own children if they have no taste for the reading of Clarissa Harlowe. He thus celebrates the author of that romance :—

" O Richardson ! Richardson ! a singular man in my eyes ; thou wilt be read by me at all times. ' Forced by urgent necessity, if my friend falls into poverty, if my moderate fortune be not sufficient to give my children the care necessary for their education, I will sell my books, but thou wilt remain to me on the same shelf with Moses, Homer, Euripides, and Sophocles, and I will read you one after another."[1]

Without any regulation in his progress, his books, even the most serious, are not books ; they are only, by his own confession, a simple conversation : " I do not compose, I am not an author, I read or converse, I question or answer."[2]

In these unpremeditated thoughts put on paper, he is at times full of fancy, copious and original, but that does not prevent the method from being bad. We should not write as we speak. Diderot has no doubt many ideas, many ideas too in the germ; but these ideas do not form a chain, they are not terminated, they are fruits that have perished in the bud. Some say to them-

---

[1] Œuvres, tome ix.   [2] Essai sur les Regnes de Claude et de Neron.

selves this man might have been a philosopher, he has the beginning, but not the end of a philosopher's ideas. Certain minds
seem doomed to miscarriage. Diderot was a bad steward of a
great intellectual fortune.

As a writer, he has fine phrases and beautiful pages, but, at
the same time, he is not one of the great writers of the language,
except in his fictitious narratives, in which he is excellent and
truly classical. In his didactic works, he is below his reputation,
he is devoid of that didactic eloquence, the glory and triumph of
French literature. Gilbert, in his *Satire on the Eighteenth
Century*, said of him: " And this dull Diderot, a doctor with a
harsh style, who passes for sublime, in consequence of being
obscure."

In the present day, what remains of Diderot? Merely his
name and a vague remembrance. This name and Voltaire's are
joined together, and in him the most extravagant tendencies of
materialism are summed up. He is no longer read. Who would
read, for example, the *Essay on the Reigns of Claudius and Nero?*
two thick volumes of a paradoxical apology, in which he endeavours to make Seneca a kind of pagan saint. The want of
truth in the attempt produces impatience, which rises to irritation in spite of the abundance of the ideas, and of the real
beauties of several passages.

We have said that Diderot had more genius than talent! Yes,
if genius is the abundance of intelligence, no doubt Diderot was
endowed with a very abundant intelligence. But if we understand by genius, a decided peculiarity of mind and a particular
aptitude, which far surpasses the usual degree, we cannot call
him a man of genius; we repeat it, genius builds, men of genius
are, above all, called to construct. I say *build* and not *preserve.*
In order to build, it is often necessary to overturn what exists.
To destroy, talent alone may be sufficient. As a man, I can
neither love nor hate Diderot. Compared to Voltaire, he is at
once not so good and not so wicked. He is all body and understanding; a powerful head united to a strong piece of timber; the
heart is wanting. Frequently, we must confess, he is affecting
in his works, but it is when he invents as an artist.

XXII.

HELVETIUS.

1715–1771.

HELVETIUS was descended from a Dutch family, which in all probability was originally from Switzerland, for the German name of his great-grandfather was *Schweizer*. He was born in France and acquired there a considerable fortune as a farmer-general. Thus, this philosopher derived profit from the very abuses against which he afterwards inveighed, a thing not uncommon in that age. Of a robust constitution, and with the prospect of long life, he shortened his days by his excesses. A man of the world and a wit, living among philosophers, and enriching himself with their ideas, by means of listening to them, he came to write a book, and thus to acquire that of which he was ambitious—his share of celebrity.

The treatise *On the Mind* appeared in 1759. It is an analysis of the nature of man, in which all the intellectual and moral phenomena are referred to the action of the humours, and to the play of the organs. "His object is to prove that physical sensibility is the source of all our thoughts, that interest is the principle of all our judgments, and of all our actions, that the intellectual powers are the same in all men properly organized, and that the passions are the only means of all development; whence it follows, according to Helvetius, that to educate a man is to cultivate his passions."[1]

It is surprising that he has given the title *On the Mind* to a book which only treats of matter. It was the first time in France that materialism was openly professed. As a whole, this work has no value, it is not conceived in the spirit of true philosophy, and yet some parts of it are philosophical. "It contains enlarged views, which to be useful and salutary, would only require to be separated from the basis, on which the author has placed them. The *fourth discourse* presents an analysis of the different forms or

[1] Vinet, Discours sur la Literature Française, p. 55.

faculties of the mind, methodical and very judicious. The style of Helvetius is ingenious and brilliant, but generally without warmth, except in the description of sensations. The ornaments of his language are almost always borrowed from this order of ideas, and there is a remarkable connection between the doctrine of Helvetius and his style. Perhaps the treatise *On the Mind* owed a part of its success to the great number of pointed anecdotes well brought in, and still better told, which the author has scattered over his work."[1]

Helvetius has undoubtedly borrowed a great deal; he was greatly assisted by the talents and attainments of others, but it must be allowed that he had talents and acquirements himself, and turned them to use.

When his treatise appeared, it caused great scandal. The author wished to make a noise, and he attained and went beyond his object; he even incurred the blame of the moderate portion of his own party. Voltaire was displeased with him; he was unwilling that they should go too quickly or too far. In short, the result of the work was a series of annoyances and troubles to Helvetius. In the present day, when others have gone beyond him in point of materialism and of cynical boldness, it would no longer excite any emotion; his book would be found quite naturally ranked among works of mediocrity.

Helvetius published other works conceived in the same spirit, but they are not worth the trouble of being mentioned.

XXIII.

RAYNAL.

1713–1796.

RAYNAL was one of the most passionate destroyers that the eighteenth century produced; to boldness of thought, he joined

---

[1] Vinet, Discours sur la Literature Française, p. 55.

that of character. Born poor, this abbé, who did not believe
in the existence of God, and who attacked the church and
religion without measure, and with a brutal eagerness, drew
from the religious establishment of his time fifty or sixty thousand
livres of annual income (L.2000 or L.2400). When he saw
before him the revolution which his writings helped to precipitate, and when ruin reached this rich possessor of abbeys, he
opened his eyes and began to doubt a philosophy, which treated
so cruelly him and so many others. He had survived all his
friends. What would they have done if, like him, they had
witnessed the reign of Terror ! Probably, like him, they would
have abjured their opinions ; who knows but Voltaire would
have gone so far as to make his throat be cut ?

Raynal employed himself in historical pursuits. His first
work was a history of the Stadtholdership, in which he showed
much erudition, and patient and laborious research, but little
talent for style.

His important work is the *History of Commerce, and of the
French Establishment in the East and West Indies.* The complete edition is that of 1780. This book is esteemed for the
number of facts, and for the abundance of information, but it is
very badly executed. Its most precious documents are buried
under a mass of impassioned, diffuse and rambling declamation,
without any relation to the subject. Raynal made his work the
theme of his attacks against the order of things then existing,
and he invited to this festival several of his philosophical brethren
—among others, Diderot. " Insert," said he to them—" insert
into my book every thing that you choose against God, against
Religion, and against Government." Thus this work of many
colours is a receptacle of all the obscenity and impiety of the
eighteenth century—a true literary monster, on whatever side
you take it. In fact, Raynal constituted himself the responsible
editor of his friends. At present this work is completely despised, unless it be used as a document to be consulted.

XXIV.

D'HOLBACH AND GRIMM.

1723–1789.   1723–1809.

WE join under one head these two men, both of German origin and born in the same year. The one died on the eve of great storms; the other prolonged his career long enough, so that he passed through the four seasons of life, and saw the seed that he helped to sow become fruit.

Baron d'Holbach was brought to France at twelve years of age, and remained there till his death. Possessed of a large fortune, he employed his time in the study of science, and was successful in it. He developed his ideas in his intercourse with the philosophers, whose place of meeting was his house. The suppers at which they met constituted his real importance; they consolidated the position of the party, by furnishing to them an occasion for meeting. D'Holbach was not contented with this celebrity; he wished to write; and, accordingly, he published numerous works, either anonymously, or under the veil of a false name. The profession of authorship was according to the custom of the times; to be in the fashion, every one wished to write his book. The most celebrated of Baron d'Holbach's productions—the *System of Nature*—appeared in 1770, under the name of Mirabaud. This work is the most scandalous, but, at the same time, the most open and complete manifesto of the philosophy of the eighteenth century. There is no veil, no circumlocution, no going about the bush; materialism, atheism, and cynicism are professed, not with enthusiasm, but with a dull coldness and a heavy dogmatism. The sternest author could not have assumed a more serious tone. A long and tiresome pleading against all the truths which raise man above the brutes, this book is the crime of high treason against humanity. It excited lively displeasure among the moderate portion of the philosophers; Voltaire, in his correspondence, does not cease to complain of it. This time, at least, we see Voltaire forgetting his own attacks, to take up at length the defence of outraged humanity. It is true, the odiousness of the doctrines attracted great attention.

Baron de Grimm was originally from Bavaria, but descended from a poor and unknown family. In Germany he made excellent progress in his studies; then he came to France, where he took up his abode. He appeared there as tutor to a young German lord connected with the philosophers; he obtained a small diplomatic office; then he became the literary correspondent of several foreign princes—of the court of Gotha, among others, and even of the Empress of Russia. This correspondence lasted nearly forty years, and only terminated in 1791. Grimm had the largest share of it, but he was assisted by Diderot, and by a native of Zurich called Henry Meister. It is to this last individual that we must attribute almost the third part of that collection, composed of fifteen volumes, recovered and published in 1812. Without this correspondence, which has cast so much light on the eighteenth century, we should scarcely have known Baron de Grimm, but from the *Confessions* of J. J. Rousseau, who, after having lived with him in a sort of intimacy, at last quarrelled with him. These letters reveal to us the influence which Grimm must have exercised in the circle, of which he formed a part; they furnish us with a number of events and important details for attaining a philosophical and literary knowledge of the reign of Louis XV.

In them we see also a very distinguished critic, eminent for his learning, for the force of his wit, and for the independence of his judgments. In forming part of the philosophical club, Grimm estimates his friends with severity and justice. Even Voltaire is not spared. Grimm had too much mind, and too solid knowledge, to acquiesce in all the extravagances of the party. As a critic, he has remarkable observations on esthetics and the theory of art. On the whole, this correspondence, although at times disgusting to read, is a precious document of that period.

XXV.

BUFFON.

1707–1788.

IT remains for us now, gentlemen, to speak, in the first place, of the writers who, in following the negative tendency of the age, only gave themselves up to it with moderation ; afterwards, of those who set themselves against it.[1]

Buffon, an imposing subject, on account of his labours, the character of his mind, and the greatness of his talent, died on the eve of the revolution. " One of the four great prose writers of the eighteenth century, he rises, by his whole height, above the rest of the writers of his time, without being able to equal, in point of influence, the three men of genius whose honours he shares. He had all the power which talent without passion can possess, and which can only reign by intelligence, and over men of intelligence. He was not, however, a stranger to the tendencies of his age, since he willingly made the speculations of science aim at the interests of life, and at the necessities of society ; he was, still farther, a man of his age, by applying to science the results of philosophy, and the resources of eloquence."[2]

Born at Montbard, not far from Dijon, of a family connected with the law, in easy circumstances, ancient and honoured, Buffon soon found himself master as to the choice of his future career. In spite of paternal traditions, he devoted himself, without hesitation, to science, and at first to the mathematics and general physics. After having accompanied into Italy, and then into England, a young Englishman, his tutor, he began to make himself known by the translation of two scientific works—the *Statics of Vegetables*, by Hales (1735), and the *Treatise on Fluxions*, by Newton (1740). In 1739, appointed overseer of the King's Garden, he had scarcely, till that time, cultivated the natural

---

[1] This plan could not be entirely executed by M. Vinet, as his course was interrupted, as we have mentioned in the advertisement, by the aggravation of the disease, to which he yielded the 4th May 1847.—*Editors.*

[2] M. Vinet, Discours sur la Literature Française, p. 59.

sciences; it was then for the occasion, and in some sort officially, that Buffon became a naturalist.

In 1749, appeared the first volumes of his *General Natural History*, which seems to be beyond the strength of a single man. Buffon, who applied himself to it with indefatigable perseverance, got the help of different fellow-labourers, among others, of Daubenton, for the anatomical part, and his choice was so fortunate, that several pieces by their help are found worthy of their master. In fact, a superior writer may be equalled in his manner by writers possessed of talent far inferior to his. The great matter is to create a new style; any imitation whatever is never very difficult. But if the style be borrowed, the diction, properly so called, is not; the original always possesses a grace, a colouring, and a freshness of novelty, which no imitation can equal.[1]

The work of Buffon consists, in the first place, of a *Theory of the Earth* and of a *History of Minerals;* he comes next to mammalia, beginning with man; and lastly, to birds, which he has completely discussed, though in a manner less prominent. Some, however, of his finest passages belong to this series. His plan embraced the finished picture of our globe from the mass to the minutest details, but he was unable to accomplish the gigantic task which he had prescribed to himself. In 1776, after the publication of the greatest number of his volumes, he takes up, so to speak, his work at the beginning, and writes the *Epochs of Nature*, a magnificent book : " Of all the books of the eighteenth century, this is the one which has, perhaps, most elevated the imagination of men," says M. Flourens.

The first volume of the *General Natural History* contributed to the character of a great epoch, it appeared at the same time as the *Spirit of Laws*. Forty years of a perseverance, which nothing could distract, were consecrated to the compilation of this illustrious work. " Genius," said Buffon, " is labour." Labour in his case knew, but without any pain, less what it cost than what it was worth.

The career of Buffon presents few events, it was peaceful, respectable, and glorious; his time was divided between the

---

[1] We might say of the difference between *style* and *diction*, that the one consists rather in the arrangement of the words, a matter of habit, judgment, and taste ; the other, in the invention of terms, a work especially of the imagination, and necessarily spontaneous.—*Editors.*

king's garden and his estate at Montbard; no literary age exhibits such a life. There have been men of science, whose lives
have been as calm, and have been adorned with as much, or,
perhaps, more glory, such as Newton; but Buffon was a man of
literature as well as of science, with a strong chance of trouble
and agitation. Yet careful at once of his repose and of his dignity, he knew how to avoid every conflict. He had two passions,
science and glory, the consciousness of his talents placed him
above vanity. He had few enemies, although Le Brun speaks
of some; he was, no doubt, criticised, but not torn in pieces.
The object of universal homage, kings became his tributaries;
his statue was set up in his lifetime, with this inscription : " Ma-
jestati naturæ par ingenium" (a genius suited to the majesty of
nature). Created count by letters patent, he was received into
the French Academy in 1753. It will be difficult to find a career
more enviable. Nevertheless, representation is not reality; the
care of his glory and his peace, doubtless, cost him trouble, and
in this respect he is set in opposition to D'Alembert, who was
surnamed the slave of liberty. Moreover, a single blot spoils
this noble tranquillity; he could not conceal the jealousy with
which the glory of Linnæus inspired him.

His book is faulty in consequence of his immoderate love of
hypotheses. Hypothesis, indeed, is a scientific instrument, a
manner of searching into nature, by which many things are discovered. Buffon has beyond all doubt often abused this method;
he compels facts to arrange themselves under his hypotheses,
which of themselves would not be ranked there, and hence transforms them into propositions and systems. But in his very errors
his genius bursts forth, and that greatness of imagination, which
at times leads him astray, has also been the occasion of his making beautiful discoveries. Truths have been guessed at by him
with the aid of a small number of data; and science, which from
that time has rectified a portion of the results at which Buffon
had arrived, has done justice to several of his theories.

He is liable to a graver reproach, and that is his contempt for
method. His method is that of the people, and is properly the
absence of method; for example, in his classification of animals,
he divides them into *wild* and *tame*. This want of method is an
essential error, which we have neither the right nor the wish to
extenuate, but we cannot help asking sometimes, if it be always

a good thing to despise the popular point of view, which from that very circumstance is more synthetic, and if some truths be not concealed at the foundation of certain prejudices, and under the irrational form with which the instinct of the masses has invested them?

Buffon, first among the moderns, united natural history with eloquence. Linnæus is, no doubt, eloquent, and he proves that regard for method does not exclude eloquence, but Buffon's aim is much more literary; science presented itself to him under a synthetic aspect. The naturalists, who are friends of method, are analytical, and their work is a sort of anatomy. The work of Buffon is truly philosophical; the character of his mind is the capability of seizing the greatest relations, of analysing the smallest, and of ennobling the most vulgar details by the grandeur of the views which he habitually attaches to them. His most particular articles are filled with general considerations, and he rises in science to a height which nothing can equal. Buffon exhibits nature in all its magnificence, it appears greater after we have read his work; but it is on general subjects that he is in all his beauty. The whole of Buffon's talent is brought together in the piece entitled *First View of Nature*. We must also point out the *History of Man*, and in particular the passages in which he treats of his primary functions.

As to the character of Buffon's eloquence, he has himself traced its rules in the *Discourse at his admission into the French Academy*. " The tone of the philosopher will become sublime when he speaks of the laws of nature, of beings in general, of space, of matter, of motion, and of time, of the soul, of the human mind, of sentiments, and of passions; as to the rest, it will be sufficient for him to be noble and elevated."

Buffon seems to have been inspired by his subject with this noble and elevated tone :—" The tone," he says, " is only the suitableness of the style to the nature of the subject ;" the tone especially results from the impression which the mind receives from the subject. The most striking feature in Buffon's style is its fulness, a copiousness of expression corresponding to the copiousness of things, he appears everywhere inspired with the majesty of nature.

This sustained majesty has made it be remarked that Buffon had not a natural style. The criticism is unjust; it is evident, that criticism is important to the world, provided it be not false. Buffon is natural, but not simple. His style is dignified; in reading his writings, we are somewhat astonished to learn that he only wrote in full dress, with ruffles at his wrist-band, and sword at his side. He, who in conversation, remained vulgar, and even trifling, and who expelled dignity from ordinary life, became majestic when quite alone. He felt for himself profound respect; in his style he would not have permitted the slightest negligence to be seen.

To this majesty Buffon joined an extraordinary power of description. This talent, at that time new, is magical. He penetrates to such an extent into the character of objects, that no one brought out the idea of them like him. There is, however, nothing minute and nothing isolated; he unites the three kinds of description — the first representing the object, the second its character, the third the impression excited by it in the mind of him who describes it. With others, observation, reflection, and imagination act each by itself; with him all go on together, all are harmonious. This character is due to profound meditation. What is meditation, that slow and eager brooding over an idea? This is always the closest identification of the writer with his subject, especially for the purpose of uniting all its parts, and of placing them in a general point of view. Buffon generalises at once for the eye, and for the thought, but in this last respect, he pushed his taste for generalization to excess; he pretends, that in description, we should only employ general terms, which is manifestly false.

It has been said, not without reason, that Buffon was deficient in passion and sensibility. In regard to sensibility, however, he possessed it on the great scale, without which he would not have been able to attain to eloquence. But he had scarcely that sensibility of detail, by means of which we find ourselves suddenly moved by the presence of the object. Once, indeed, about the close of his career, Buffon showed himself affected by a particular subject—he mourned over the affecting fable of the swan's song :—

" Now the ancients were not content with making the swan a marvellous singer ; among all the beings that tremble at the view of their destruction, he alone still sang at the moment of his agony, and uttered harmonious sounds as a prelude to his last sigh. It was, they said, when he was ready to expire, and bidding a sad and tender adieu to life, that the swan put forth these accents so sweet and touching, which, like the light and doleful murmur of a low, plaintive, and mournful voice, formed his funeral song. This song was heard, when at morning dawn, the winds and the waves were calm, and swans had even been seen expiring in the midst of music, and singing their funeral hymns. No fiction in natural history, no fable among the ancients has been more celebrated, more frequently repeated, or more generally believed; it took possession of the nice and lively imagination of the Greeks; poets, orators, even philosophers adopted it as a truth too agreeable for them to wish to doubt it. We must pardon them their fables, they were amiable and affecting, they were far more valuable than sad and dry truths, they were sweet emblems for sensitive minds. Undoubtedly swans do not sing at their death, but always when we speak of the last flight, and of the final transports of a fine genius about to be extinguished, we shall recal with feeling this touching expression—*It is the swan's song.*"[1]

Buffon had investigated the theory of the art of writing, and felt more than any other all its importance. There is, perhaps, no style more profound than his. You may read the *Discourse at his admission into the French Academy,* and reflect on thoughts such as these :—

"Nothing is more opposite to warmth than the desire of bringing in every where brilliant touches; and nothing is more contrary to light, which ought to form a body, and spread itself uniformly over a writing, than those sparks which are elicited by forcibly dashing words one against another, and which dazzle our eyes for some moments, only to leave us afterwards in the dark."

"To write well, you must be in full possession of your subject; you must reflect on it sufficiently to see the order of your thoughts, to form a sequence, a continuous chain, of which each link represents an idea, and when you take up the pen, it will be necessary to conduct it successively over this first point, without permitting it to wander away from it, without bearing upon it too unequally, and without giving to it any other motion than that which will be determined by the space that it ought to

---

[1] Histoire Naturelle des Oiseaux : le Cygne.

traverse." " Knowledge, facts, and discoveries are easily taken
away and transferred to others, and they even gain by being put
into operation by abler hands. These things are beyond the
man, but style is the man himself. Style cannot then be removed, transferred, or altered; if it be elevated, noble, and sublime, the author will be equally admired at all times, for it is only
truth which is durable and everlasting. Now, a beautiful style
is only such, in fact, by the infinite number of truths which it
presents." " The extreme attention which Buffon gave to his
style was not precisely grammatical; we are surprised to find in
one of our most finished writers more imperfect constructions
than in any other—his attention was directed to the relation of
the expression to the idea. The articulations of the phrase were
less regarded than the logical connection of its parts, and its
substantial correctness. The phraseology of Buffon, rich and
trim, seems to have increased from a single mental effort, so
much are the details set against the principal idea, so much does
the principal idea embrace forcibly those that are accessory to it,
and so perceptible is the unity of thought and effect. This
character of Buffon's style is not bounded by the phraseology;
the same unity binds the phrases in the paragraph, and the para-
graphs in the discourse. No writer is more compact, none, however, is less harsh or more copious. The grammatical impro-
prieties, which he here and there presents, are, perhaps, a proof
of his preference for a full and solid style; the writer prefers
breaking down his phrase rather than his thought, or rather
without perceiving it, the large wave of his phrase carries away
or surmounts the rules of a common syntax. Madame Necker,
who has preserved precious traditions respecting the proceedings
of this great artist, observes, " That he could not give an account
of any of the rules of the French language, but that he has not
put into his works a word of which he could not render an
account."[1]

In the philosophical point of view, Buffon is quite a man of
his own time; he is not of the seventeenth century; he searches
after truth, without embarrassing himself with authority. He is
not descended from Malebranche. The theocracy, in this matter,
was not deceived; and, prudent as he was, he quarrelled with the

[1] Vinet, Chrestomthie Française, tome ii. p. 165.

Sorbonne. His *Natural History* incurred censure; several of his propositions were condemned, and he himself was summoned to defend himself. He showed some condescension, but it was ironical.

The real place of Buffon is in the second group, that of moderate men. He intentionally avoided all co-operation with those that pulled down; if he connived at the sect, it was involuntary. Hence he very frequently encounters Cóndillac. He entered into a field, in which you come to nothing, if you are not set at full liberty. On several points, on the contrary, he clearly separated himself from the miners of the eighteenth century, and often shows himself openly opposed to materialism.

As to his religious views, it would be rash to pronounce upon what Buffon understood by the word *God*, which so often falls from his pen. He received from his subject the impression, which the presence of a mysterious power, continually and universally felt, ought to produce—the hidden principle of life and order. Was this for him a personal God? or did he only give that great name in the way of accommodation? But nature is only majestic to him, who ackowledges its author; and may we not say, that in the case in which the mind of Buffon might have excluded God, his soul involuntarily perceived him? It was a kind of intellectual adoration. Let us, gentlemen, draw the conclusion, that Buffon was far from being a materialist, like a number of his contemporaries.

XXVI.

DUCLOS.

1704–1772.

DUCLOS was a native of Brittany, and went to Paris, like many others, to seek his fortune by the exercise of his talents. He was a moralist, quite different from Vauvenargues—a man of the world and a man of wit, especially that wit which is suitable for

society. " No man," said D'Alembert, " had more of it in a
given time." In fact, he possessed that ready wit so well fitted
to advance his interest, and he joined to it an honesty truly estimable. Rousseau loved him, and, amid his universal distrust,
seemed to make an exception in his favour. His was a character,
he said, upright and dexterous. Duclos realized in his life what
he reduced to a maxim : " Much ability may be joined to much
uprightness."[1] " There is a delicate intelligence, as much opposed
to falsehood as to imprudence."[2]

As to his general tendency, we may call him a philosopher of
a mean temperature. He framed no system, and did not attack
the systems of others. He saw with displeasure his friends, the
philosophers, sap the foundations of morality by denying religion,
yet he does not set himself strongly against their philosophy, but
rather attacks their manner of acting than their theories. He said :
" They will go so far as to make me go to mass." If he regards
the religion of the church as a prejudice, he at least respects it
as a salutary prejudice.

" Prejudices hurtful to society can only be errors, and cannot
be too much combated. . . . In regard to prejudices which
tend to the good of society, and which are germs of virtues, we
may be sure that they are truths, which we should respect and
follow."[3] " I cannot help blaming writers who, under the pretext, or with the honest desire of attacking superstition, sap the
foundations of morality, and aim a blow at the bonds of social
life, as much more foolish as it would be dangerous for themselves
to make proselytes. The fatal effect which they produce upon
their readers is, to make them in youth bad citizens and scandalous criminals, and, in old age, utterly wretched ; for few of
them at that period of life have the miserable privilege of being
sufficiently perverted to be tranquil. The eagerness with which
this species of writing is read should not flatter the authors, who
may otherwise be men of merit. They should not be ignorant,
that the most miserable writers of this sort almost equally divide
this honour with them. Satire, licentiousness, and impiety, have
never of themselves been considered as a proof of understanding.
The most contemptible, on account of these topics, may be read
once ; without their excesses they would never have been men-

---

[1] Considerations sur les Mœurs, chap. iii.   [2] Ibid. chap. v.   [3] Ibid. chap. ii.

tioned, like those wretches, whose mode of life condemned them to darkness, and whose names the public only learn by their crimes and their punishment."[1]

Duclos attempted different kinds of writings: he was a grammarian, a writer of romances, an historian, and traveller; and in all of them he was a nice observer, and a steady, precise, and pointed writer. He possesses a great talent for analysis, but he is deficient in what constitutes the life of talent, sensibility.

Sensibility and goodness should not be confounded. M. de Gerando, an author of merit, in his book, on the *Improvement of One's-self*, has clearly established this distinction. Duclos, who had little natural sensibility, and who said, in speaking of tragedy, that " here his skin thrilled," possessed real goodness of heart. His acts of beneficence were only known after his death, and afforded reason for thinking, that when a benefactor has no other confidant but the person obliged, his secret is commonly quite secure.

The work of which we have to speak was entitled by Duclos, *Reflections on the Manners of this Age.* [2] Precept is there mixed with description, and this description is more an analysis than a painting, but a very just analysis. The author sets out on all his subjects with a very rigorous definition. His are true models in that way, as well as his synonyms. He was born to define. He proposed to himself " to discern, by men's conduct, what are their principles, and perhaps to reconcile their contradictions." [3]

He does not show moral facts in external deeds; he inquires into their inward motives. Notwithstanding this, we cannot say that he has revealed to us the depths of our being. It was less, he said, *man* than *men*, whom he wished to make known; that is to say, less the mind by itself than the mind in contact with other minds. The titles of his different chapters, with a few exceptions, show this :—*Manners, Education and Prejudices; Politeness and Praise ; Honesty, Virtue, and Honour ; Reputation, Celebrity, Renown, and Consideration ; the Great Lords ; Credit ; People of Fashion ; Ridicule, Singularity, and Affectation ; People of Fortune, Men of Letters ; the Madness of Wit ; the Relation of Mind and Character ; Esteem and Respect ; the Real Value of Things ; Gratitude and Ingratitude.*

---

[1] Considerations sur les Mœurs, chap. ii.

[2] This lecture is taken from the Course on the Moralists, in which M. Vinet was not called to take up other works of Duclos.—*Editors.*

[3] Introduction.

Duclos indeed knew *men* better than *man*. On this last subject his views are vague and wavering. He says, for example :
" In wishing too much to enlighten certain men, you only inspire
them at times with dangerous presumption. Ah ! why undertake
to make them practise by reasoning, what they were following
from feeling, and by an honest prejudice ? These guides are
quite as sure as reasoning. Let men be first formed to the practice of virtue, it will be so much the more easy to point out to
them principles, if that be necessary."[1]

Elsewhere, on the contrary : " To render men better, it is only
necessary to enlighten them ; crime is always a false judgment."[2]

We repeat, on our side, that crime does not proceed merely
from a judgment more or less false, that if in vice the judgment
takes part, still evil has its root in the heart, that the heart has
seduced the understanding, and that it is the absence, or the false
direction of the moral sense, which determines false reasoning.
Man has not his principle in reasoning, but in feeling. The
most part of crimes are committed without judgment, or contrary
to the judgment of the culprit.

The distinction which Duclos makes : " There is a great difference between the knowledge of man and the knowledge of
men," is followed by these words : " To know man, it is sufficient
to study one's-self ; to know men, one must converse with them."[3]
I neither admit the first of these propositions nor the second. I
believe that at bottom these two pieces of knowledge are not so
distinct. The one is necessary to the other, the one completes the
other, and I cannot better maintain what I here say, than by
reminding you of this maxim of Vauvenargues : " We discover
in ourselves what others conceal from us, and we perceive in
others what we conceal from ourselves."[4]

On the contrary, here follow beautiful thoughts, this one is
even exceedingly noble : " There is nobody who has not sometimes occasion to do an honest and courageous action, and yet
without danger. The fool lets it pass without perceiving it, the
man of understanding perceives and seizes it. Experience proves,
however, that mind alone is not sufficient for it, and that a noble
heart is necessary to practise this happy art."[5] And again : " In
matters in which we have an interest, ideas are not sufficient for

---

[1] Considerations sur les Mœurs, chap. ii.   [2] Ibid. i.   [3] Introduction.
[4] Vauvenargues, Maxime 106.   [5] Considerations sur les Mœurs, chap. v.

the justness of our judgments. The accuracy of the mind depends in this case on the uprightness of the heart, and on the calmness of the passions."[1]

The *Book of Reflexions* is a brief collection of the finest observations. Every phrase is a sentence, which stands alone without support. No man has included more thought in less space; and in general these ideas are as just as their expression is prominent. In other writers, the style is painting, in Duclos, it is bas-relief. This is its merit and defect. This merit is not for nothing.

We may divide these thoughts into two classes, psychological and moral. Let us consider some of the first :—

" There reigns at Paris (in the great world) a certain general indifference, which multiplies passing tastes, which takes place of connection, and which makes nobody one too many in society, and nobody necessary to it; every one suits his own convenience, and no one is missed."[2]

In the chapter on *Politeness :* "Self-love grossly persuades every man, that what he does from decency, is rendered to him from justice."[3] In the same chapter on the subject of praise: " There is scarcely a eulogy, whose hero could be guessed, if his name was not at its head."[4]

In the chapter on *Reputation :* " Pride makes as many base things be done as interest."[5] In that of credit: " We only acknowledge merit with regret, this bears too great resemblance to justice, and self-love is more flattered by doing favours."[6] In the chapter on *Ridicule :* " The childish fear of ridicule stifles ideas, narrows the powers of the mind, and forms them on a single model, and suggests the same topics by no means interesting in their nature, and tedious from their repetition. It appears that a single spring gives to different machines an equal motion, and in the same direction. I see only fools who can gain by an irregularity, that brings down to their level superior men, since they are all at once subject to a common measure, which the most ordinary persons may reach."[7]

In the chapter on the *Mind and Character :* " The greatest advantage for happiness is a kind of equilibrium between the ideas and the affections, between the mind and the character."[8] In the chapter on *Education :* " We form men of science and

---

[1] Considerations sur les Mœurs, chap. xiv. [2] Ibid. i. [3] Ibid. iii. [4] Ibid. iii.
[5] Chap. v. [6] Ibid. vii. [7] Ibid. ix. [8] Ibid. xiii.

artists of all kinds; we have not yet thought of forming men, that is, to educate them in relation to one another."[1]

"We should in all states inspire men with the feelings of citizens, and should form Frenchmen among us; and to make them Frenchmen, we should labour to make them men."[2] This idea, as sound as beautiful, was developed by M. Jouffroy. Duclos, is not, however, exempt from national prejudices. He is very strongly attached to France, of which his brethren said less good. He greatly commends the French character, of which he mentions elsewhere some things very true : " The Frenchman is the child of Europe."[3]

But see again : " The virtues of this nation set out from the heart, its vices are only attached to the mind."[4] Here the author forgets what he stated in another place, that the faults of the mind are very often attached to those of the character.[5] " They are the only people whose morals may be depraved without the whole heart being corrupted."[6] " A very enlightened, and very estimable people, in many respects, complains that corruption among them has come to such a pitch, that there are no longer principles of honour, that every action is valued, that they are in exact proportion to their interest, and that a *scale of honesty* might be made. Happily it is not so among us."[7]

A man of great good sense[8] had before my time made the following note on this passage : " If the form of government presented to the royal authority in France the same necessity, and the same means of bribing as in England, who can doubt that a scale of honesty might be also made there?"

The observation, which will occur to those who study the history of the two states, is that in England honour has never had the same influence as in France. Among the English, we see on one side an exhibition of grossness and impudence in wickedness, and on the other, we admire their strictness and lofty eminence in that which is good. In that country, interest and conscience measure every thing. There is nothing intermediate between the two motives.

---

[1] Considerations sur les Mœurs, chap. ii.   [2] Ibid.   [3] Ibid. i.
[4] Chap. viii.   [5] Ibid. xiii.   [6] Ibid. i.
[7] Chap. i.   It was the English minister, Sir Robert Walpole, who boasted that he had this scale in his pocket.—*Editors.*
[8] The father of M. Vinet.—*Editors.*

In France, on the contrary, the gap between interest and conscience is admirably filled. up by honour. We must say, this principle may lead to consequences both fatal and wicked; nevertheless, in its origin, honour had for its office to take the place of conscience. Where it was deficient, honour presented itself the heir, the distant relation of conscience. Then morality was separated from conscience, virtue withdrew, and honour was almost left alone. But honour itself is becoming weak; Duclos complains that already in his time it was no longer what it was in the seventeenth century, and we may in our turn remark, since that period, in this motive a diminution of vigour. If this progress continues, it will end by being extinguished. But which will then become the heir of honour? Will it be interest or conscience?

The moral reflections are remarkable in the book of Duclos; and the justness and fineness of the observations are not its only merit. This work breathes integrity, the love of what is good, and virtue. To convince yourselves of this, you may read the chapters on *Politeness*, on *Honesty and Virtue*, and on *Gratitude*. This last subject inspires Duclos with thoughts peculiarly elevated: " Ingratitude distresses more than it exasperates generous hearts."[1] " Noble minds pardon their inferiors from pity, their equals from generosity."[2] And again: " We ought neither to offend nor deceive men."[3] " The people ought to be favoured by a king."[4] " The great, who keep men at a distance by means of politeness without kindness, are only good by being kept at a distance by respect without attachment."[5] " It might be said that the heart has ideas which are peculiar to itself.... that there are ideas inaccessible to those whose feelings are cold."[6] " We have some consideration in the present day, even without any view to interest, for the man most decried. One says to you, I have no ground of complaint personally, I will not go to make myself a redresser of wrongs. What weakness! It is very difficult to understand the interests of society, and consequently one's own. Why should dishonest men blush at being what they are, when people do not blush to welcome them? If honest men were to think of making common cause, their league would be very strong. When men of spirit and honour shall understand one

---

[1] Considerations sur les Mœurs, chap. xvi.   [2] Ibid.   [3] Ibid. iii.
[4] Chap. v.   [5] Ibid. iii.   [6] Ibid. iv.

another, fools and rogues will play a very inconsiderable part. Unhappily it is only rogues who form leagues, honest men keep themselves isolated. But honesty without courage is unworthy of any consideration ; it resembles the contrition which has only for its principle servile fear."[1]

Duclos combats, with all the force of a just and elevated judgment, that idle talk, that affected turn of mind, and that fashionable wickedness, of which *le Mechant* of Gresset furnishes the most complete idea. This irregularity, so peculiar to the French society of the time, that Frederic the Great, an unmerciful joker, confessed he did not understand the comedy of Gresset, has disappeared in our days. We happily no longer know—a thing very important—of wickedness considered as the fashion of society :—

" Wickedness is only at present the fashion. In former times, the most eminent qualities could not have excused it, because they can never return as much to society as wickedness makes it lose, since it saps its foundations, and is, in consequence, if not the union, at least the result of vices. In the present day wickedness is reduced to an art ; it takes the place of merit with those who have no other, and often gives them consideration. This is what produces such a crowd of petty subalterns and imitators in this kind of wickedness, and of malicious weaklings, among whom are found some quite innocent ; their character is so much opposed to it, they would have been good people, if they had followed the dictates of their heart, so much does it cost them to do evil. Thus we see some abandoning their part as too painful; others persevering, flattered and corrupted by the progress which they make."[2]

It has been remarked that, in this book on the manners of the eighteenth century, the word *woman* does not once occur. La Harpe made this remark. The word *woman*, however, is found in the chapter on *Reputation*,[3] and in the chapter on *Esteem;*[4] there is a question about love, which is an allusion to women. But, in spite of this, it is certain that this great element of the social life of the eighteenth century may be considered as passed over in silence by Duclos, although women at that time possessed an influence which they had not previously obtained—a

[1] Considerations sur le Mœurs, chap. iv.   [2] Ibid. viii.   [3] Ibid. v.
[4] Chap. xiv.

woman governed France. This silence cannot have been involuntary.

Still, as to Duclos' book, it is a farther proof that to do well is not all, but that it is especially necessary to come to the point, as Voltaire said. The *Reflexions on Morals* appeared in 1750, the same year that the ardent genius of J. J. Rousseau produced a strong sensation, and the work of the thinker, who was only intellectual, calm, and delicate, was naturally thrown aside.

XXVII.

J. J. ROUSSEAU.

1711–1778.

FIRST PART.

" THE eighteenth century had reached its middle, the philosophical school was in all its strength, and the minds of men were in all the fervour of a new protestantism, when a man, forty years of age, unknown till then, the sport of all vicissitudes, a deserter from all employments, after a life inconsistent, disorderly, and sometimes shameful, but whose storms had enlarged his thought and inflamed his genius, darts into this arena, into which combatants crowd, and, by some eloquent passages, announces a rival to the great writers of his age."[1]

J. J. Rousseau gained such *eclat*, that Voltaire alone could stand before him : and even he felt himself to be in danger, for Rousseau became the object of his special hatred. Was the irritation which he experienced directed against the pretended faults of Rousseau, against the defects of his system, or against his fame ? In all these cases, it must be confessed, nothing so much resembles envy.

The universal mind of Voltaire had mastered the most pro-

[1] Vinet, Discours sur la Literature Française, p. 61.

minent elements of the eighteenth century; but he had left
many vast domains uncultivated in dark and deep valleys, which
his eye never reached.   A man of his age, suited to civilization,
and even to corrupt civilization—pathetic only in fiction—he was
not the person for collected, spiritual, and melancholy minds,
smitten with nature, returning to it in consequence of their regret for losing it—constantly seeking the enigma connected with
themselves, and the interpreter who will explain it.   This interpreter was Rousseau.   A whole class of men, for whom the
sources of the inner grave emotions had been dried up with
Christianity, asked for something which would restore to them
what unbelief had taken away; the withdrawal of the sap, and
the dryness of the social tree, constrained them to seek another
soil.   The social idea, with Voltaire, and men of his school,
tyrannically ruled and absorbed morality; the individual man—
the inner man—claimed his rights; the religious instinct, which
was denied, and rejected from human life with disgrace, required
food.   Rousseau reached the depths of the soul; he opened up
new sources of enjoyment; he was pathetic in speaking of man—
of himself, indeed—but of man in his inmost relations; beyond
social interests, he raised our views towards another sphere, still
more worthy of our thoughts—which society shuts to us, because
it draws us away from ourselves.   He perceived the necessity of
a God, and Voltaire's dull and artificial gap of deism; but he
deceived rather than satisfied the religious necessity, by his affectionate and sentimental deism.   He took up morality, but rendered it unnatural, by the substitution of vague sentiments for
the positive idea of duty.

Voltaire, and even Montesquieu, had left in politics a gap still
more astonishing.   Voltaire takes society as he finds it, and it is
not for us to blame him for not having touched the foundations
on which it rests; but when the foundations of religion were
once sapped, it was easy to foresee that society would be shaken;
it is even inconceivable how certain delicate and dangerous questions had not yet been raised.   Rousseau first developed them
with all the impetuosity of his eloquence.   He found the soil
prepared; the germ of the insurrection against society, in reference to its dissolution, was at the bottom of all ardent minds,
the time was come to protest against it.   We may understand,
gentlemen, that this time never came, for such a protest is fool-

ish, but the state of men's minds must make it welcome. It was believed that there was no choice but between society and nature ; but where was this nature to be found ? The world threw itself with ardour into the way, in which it thought its traces had been discovered ; they dug under society to find what ? human nature and the springs of society corrupted. Unable to arrive at the nature of man, either divine or made divine, they cried up the savage state.

You see how many different necessities appealed to Rousseau. In satisfying them, he was not less than Voltaire, the man of his age. What could be done, in a certain sense, by the voices of Voltaire, Montesquieu, and Buffon, issuing from their castles? The voice of Rousseau came from a garret. He was as great in one direction as Voltaire was in another. But in filling up the void, he gave the first impulse to the movement, which was necessary to precipitate society into the abyss. His part, a part not chosen, for men only acquit themselves well in parts which they do not choose, is composed of all the elements which we have now mentioned. It is to appreciate this part, and to let you understand the man to whom it fell, that we shall now apply ourselves.

Before we pass to the study of Rousseau's morality, let us glance at his life. Its importance is great, it gives an interest to his writings, and they again give it back to his life. Here the man excites interest, at least as much as the writer. It is not all in all to come from the desert, with leathern girdle about his loins, and a garment of camel's hair ; " he must have truth for his girdle,"[1] and " be clothed with the new man."[2] With what was Jean Jacques bound and clothed? This is what his life will teach us.

Apologists and detractors have been occupied by turns in raising and throwing down the statue of Rousseau. We are first of all anxious to be just, and then to derive some profit as to the knowledge of the man from the increasing mirror of this life. We may say with Bossuet : " I desire in a single misfortune to deplore all the calamities of the human race."[3] And we shall willingly add: " May the immortals who guide my tongue, grant that I say nothing that should be unsaid."[4]

1 Eph. vi. 14. 2 Colos. iii. 10. 3 Bossuet, Oraison Funebre de Henriette d'Angleterre.
4 La Fontaine, Fables. Livre xi., fable vii.

Rousseau did not know his mother, a circumstance which was
not without influence on his life.   He describes his father as a
man of an elevated mind, and of an enthusiastic spirit.   Almost
entirely left to himself, Jean Jacques grew up without instruction ; the fictions, which were the only food of his early years,
developed the sentimental and romantic tendency of his mind.
The *illustrious men* of Plutarch, a book which came afterwards
into his hands, made a great impression upon him.   He says in
his *Confessions :* " My childhood did not belong to a child, I felt
and thought always as a man.   It was only when I grew up that
I entered into the class of ordinary men ; when I was born I went
out of it."[1]   And in his correspondence : " At twelve years of
age, I was a Roman ; at twenty, I had run over the world, and
was nothing more than a blackguard."[2]

The antithesis is not so great as Rousseau fancies.   Enthusiasm
for what is great, is at the foundation of our nature, and never
makes itself be felt so lively as in childhood.   It is the flower and
the poetry of virtue which fills the imagination of children, and
gives them delight.   At a later period, the flower falls to make
way for the fruit, poetry becomes prose.   The fine dreams of
virtue are like these high mountains, whose bold forms attract
our notice, and to whose summit the imagination rises without
effort.   But when we are required to climb them in reality,
slowly and painfully we ascend, and are speedily discouraged.
Life is not spent on heights, where great and sublime deeds are
accomplished ; virtue consists of a long and uninterrupted succession of petty sacrifices, and demands this calm and firm
resolution, which runs not after duty, but holds itself ready for
every thing which God will impose.   I think that even when
Rousseau had not run over the world, he would have undergone
the experience of all, and would have felt in himself the same
transition.

A theft of small value committed in his master's house, an
act by no means consistent with the enthusiasm of his youthful
romances, obliged him to quit Geneva.   This flight was the commencement of the wandering life, to which he attributes the most
part of his faults ; and it must be allowed that the necessity of
this adventurous career became so imperious in his case, that

---

[1] Confessions. Livre ii.   [2] A M. Tronchin, 27th Nov. 1758.

afterwards, when he might have enjoyed a tranquil existence, it was impossible to carry it into practice. I believe that this instability in his habits was more attached to his character than to what he called *the fatality of his life.* He might have said with more reason, *the fatality of my character,* for if there exists fatality, it is here.

The youthful fugitive was met in Savoy by a rector, and was recommended by him to Madame de Warens, who adopted and educated him. He assures us in his *Confessions,* that this lady formed his mind and heart, and he rewards her by giving her up to a sad and shameful celebrity. After he had quitted her, his life continued to be as unsettled as his mind. He devotes himself to different studies, and passes from one condition to another. Employed as servant in several houses, his *Confessions* reveal to us shameful acts, the abandonment of his friend Le Maître, at the very time when a severe indisposition seized him in a street in Lyon; the theft of a riband, which he allowed to be imputed to a young girl, who was ignominiously dismissed from her place. The remembrance of this action always harassed him. At a later period, he was placed as tutor in the family of M. de Mably, brother of the abbé of that name, and of the celebrated Condillac, there he was still guilty of dishonesty. This inclination to steal seems strange to us in a man like Rousseau, and yet it ought not to be a motive for us to place him higher or lower than the mass of men. Many among them undoubtedly are not tempted to acts so vile, but, for all that, we will not decide, that in themselves they are less perverse than others. We usually judge of the faults or vices, which are directly hurtful to society, with much more severity than those from which individuals alone seem to be obliged to suffer, because we set out with the general interest in which our own is comprised. The most part of men in this narrow portion, which is in principle that of their ego, do not reflect that in the view of the Gospel, a simple act of egoism may be found to be a graver matter than a theft, for it contains the germ of all crimes, and it has not for excuse material necessity.

Nevertheless, at this period of his life, which was by no means brilliant, he began to reflect on his own conduct, and to draw from his observations rules for his guidance, which show a reach of mind very remarkable.

"I have inferred from it," he is speaking in reference to an observation on the conduct of his father, "this great maxim of morality, to avoid situations which place our duties in opposition to our interests, and show us our own advantage in injury done to others, assured that in such situations, however sincerely the love of virtue may be felt, it is sooner or later weakened without our being aware of it, and in practice we become unjust and wicked, and yet in the mind we have not ceased to be just and good."[1]

And, he adds, because he continued faithful to this maxim, he appeared fantastical, and was accused of wishing to be original and to act differently from others. This maxim, generalized in his mind, led him to an idea, which he proposed afterwards to make the subject of a book, *Sensitive Morality*.[2] In his opinion, the just temperature of the soul may be found in the wisdom, which renders virtue superfluous, because it restores the being to his equilibrium :—

"Virtue is only troublesome to us by our own fault; and if we would be always wise, we would rarely require to be virtuous."[3] " Virtue is only the power of doing one's duty on difficult occasions; and wisdom, on the contrary, is to remove the difficulty of doing our duties. Happy the man who is contented with being good, and has placed himself in a position in which he never needs to be virtuous."[4]

Passing from the principle to its actual practice, Rousseau felt convinced, from numerous observations, "that we might avoid many deviations from reason, and prevent many vices from springing up, if we knew how to force the animal economy to favour moral order, which it so often throws into confusion. Climates, seasons, sounds, colours, darkness, light, the elements, food, noise, silence, motion and rest act upon our machine, and consequently upon our soul; they all offer to us a thousand means almost unerring for governing, in their origin, the sentiments, which we allow to rule over us."[5]

After he had left M. de Mably, he went to Paris with a memoir on a new method of marking music. He read it at the Academy,

[1] Confessions. Livre ii.
[2] The MS. of this book is lost. See Confessions. Livre xii.
[3] Confessions. Livre ii. [4] M. L'Abbè de . . . 6th Jan. 1764.
[5] Confessions. Livre ix.

but that was all. He was successively a music-master, a clerk, a copyist, and an editor of a journal; his life is a real labyrinth, in the midst of which is placed the episode of his sojourn at Venice, as secretary to the ambassador. But this office was of short duration; and on his return to Paris, he was principally occupied in composing operas, and found himself cast into the bosom of a brilliant and vicious society, whose ideas were as corrupt as their manners. From this period, 1745, or about this time, is dated his meeting with a woman, who was unworthy of him. The difficulties, in which his relations to her placed him, do not excuse his conduct, of which the avowal ought to be to him most painful, the abandonment of his five children, whom he put into the Foundling Hospital.

Such acts require no commentary, but it is instructive to stand by and contemplate the strange combat which takes place in the soul of Jean Jacques on the subject of this *crime*, for this is the proper term. Sometimes he seeks to palliate his fault:—

"Never for a single moment of his life, could Jean Jacques be a man without feeling and compassion, and an unnatural father. I might have been deceived, but could not have been hard-hearted. My fault is great, but it is an error."[1] "What advantage the barbarians have taken of my conduct! With what skill have they put it in the most odious light! How have they the more described me as an unnatural father, because I complained! How have they sought to draw from the foundation of my character a fault, which was the fruit of my misfortune!"[2] He even congratulates himself that he is unknown to his children: "I prefer that they should live by the work of their hands without knowing me, than that I should see them debased and fed by the treacherous generosity of my enemies, who might instruct them to hate and perhaps betray their father."[3] "What Mahomet did with Seide is nothing to what would have been done with them in regard to me."[4]

But all these extravagant suppositions are a useless attempt to satisfy his remorse. This wound never heals; his heart remained stronger than his sophisms. A little farther on, he adds:

---

[1] Confessions, Livre viii.   [2] A M. de Saint-Germain, 26th Feb. 1770.
[3] A M. de Saint-Germain. The same words occur in the letter to Madame B., 17th Jan. 1770.
[4] Les Reveries du promeneur solitaire. Neavieme promenade.

" When my reason tells me that I have done in my situation, what I ought to have done, I believe it less than my heart, which groans and gives it the lie."[1]

If his heart be not tranquil, his conscience is still less so; it is perpetually scared by allusions real or pretended; the slightest prick makes it bleed afresh :—

" The longest and most curious article in the *Eulogy of Madame Geoffrin* turned upon the pleasure which she took in seeing children, and in making them prattle: the author (D'Alembert) justly drew from this disposition a proof of good nature; but he did not stop there, and decidedly accused of ill-nature and wickedness all those who had not the same taste—nay, he went so far as to say, that if any one should ask about those who were brought to the gibbet or the wheel, all would agree that they had not loved children. . . . I easily understood the motive of this vile affectation."[2]

On other occasions, conscience becomes master, and demands satisfaction: " In thinking over my *Treatise on Education*, I felt that I had neglected duties which could not be dispensed with. Remorse at last became so lively, that it almost forced from me the public acknowledgment of my fault at the beginning of *Emilius*, and the act itself is so clear, that after such a passage, it is surprising that any one has had the courage to reproach me with it."[3]

Here is the passage: " Neither poverty, nor labour, nor respect for mankind can dispense with a father supporting his children, and educating them himself. Readers, you may believe me. I predict to any one that has feeling and neglects his holy duties, that he will long continue to shed bitter tears over his fault, and will never obtain consolation."[4] Till the age of thirty-eight, Jean Jacques did not know his powers; before this period, and it is a great psychological phenomenon, no one could anticipate what he would be afterwards. It was in 1750 that he burst forth suddenly, and that France knew one great writer more.

There was something accidental in the direction of his talent. The Academy of Dijon had at their meeting put this question :

---

[1] A Madame B., 17th Jan. 1770.   [2] Reveries, neavieme promenade.
[3] Confessions. Livre xii.   [4] Emile. Livre i.

Whether the establishment of arts and sciences has contributed to the purity of manners? This programme fell accidentally under the eyes of Rousseau, and his mind was suddenly enlightened. He lay down on the grass, he tells us, and instantly conceived a portion of the work which laid the foundation of his renown. This circumstance has been disputed, and the origin of the *Discourse on the Sciences* has been explained in a different manner. Diderot pretends that Rousseau was going to decide in the affirmative, and that he pointed out to him the negative as a new idea and a means of attracting attention.

There is so little apparent relation between the previous life of Jean Jacques and his *Discourse*, that we are at first tempted to regard as arbitrary the part which he took in this question. But if this supposition, by no means worthy of the character of Rousseau, appears to be favoured by his history before his *conversion* (he does not furnish us with this term, but he suggests to us the idea of it), his life, setting out from this period, is better calculated to contradict than confirm it; for it is quite certain that, in spite of all his extravagances, of which the most part are shocking, this life habitually and distinctly reflects the same idea; and I find it difficult to admit that an idea entirely artificial can rule a whole life, and that, from a simple point of honour, a man should bind himself to persevere in a career to which he is not led either by conviction or by nature. It is more probable that, like many other men of genius, J. J. Rousseau, who was in possession of a powerful idea, was not conscious of it till very late, and after long groping. Those who have never known the transports of imagination, and the joys of the understanding, when it thinks it has laid hold of a great truth, can comprehend nothing of the simple enthusiasm and revelations of Jean Jacques. But let us remember that we are dealing here with a man who never approached any question coolly; and it will appear to us natural that, at the moment when an accidental circumstance laid the train for the explosion of this thought, he experienced all that he described— a terrible shaking, a transport mixed with consternation, a tumult among all his faculties, bringing together all the parts of his soul at that powerful and unexpected call, and bearing with impetuosity towards a single point, to lighten the star of his destiny and the pharos of his life.

Already this first work contains implicitly his whole thought.

He only speaks there of arts and sciences, and of their influence on the morality and happiness of the people; but the arts and sciences, being themselves only a social development—a result of society, as it is constituted—it is, properly speaking, against society that the bad humour of Rousseau is directed. He does not say it, but it is in his thoughts: in attacking the outer-work of a fortress, his efforts are turned against the fortress itself; already his whole doctrine is formed, already his part is taken. *Man is born good, society depraves him;* this maxim becomes the ruling thought of his life, and if occasions are wanting entirely to develop it, he calls for them, and knows how to create them. Three years after appeared the *Treatise on Inequality.*

It is asked how such an idea could find a place to support it in a head otherwise sound, well organized, and powerful; but we are less surprised at it when we consider the vehemence of Rousseau's sentiments. It is true the world presents to all men, and especially to those who diligently observe and deeply feel, numerous subjects of scandal and affliction. All the world agrees with the friend of Alcestes, that we see " a hundred things every day, which might have gone better if they had taken a different course."[1] But after this confession, which unites almost all men, two opinions or two sentiments divide them. One party, whether gaily or not, take their side, and repeat, after Philinte : " I take quite pleasantly men as they are."[2] There are others, on the contrary, who cannot come to this resolution. Human perversity does not leave them at rest—it is a mystery, which persecutes them; they wish to have their heart pure, and they will only be satisfied with a system which, good or bad, will give them the key of that moral disorder of which they are at once the witnesses, the victims, and the accomplices. We know what solution Christianity presents; and this solution comes not alone—it brings in its train the reparation of the evil which it explains. As to those who do not accept it, and who yet want a solution, there is scarcely a choice; and the necessity of the means of explanation drives them almost inevitably towards the system of Rousseau: Nature has created man good, society depraves him; we must, then, as much as possible, return to nature.

This system dictated to Jean Jacques strange assertions, and even strange counsels. He wished to maintain it by his conduct, and has frequently pushed it to extravagance. Men have laughed at him—they have laughed at his system; perhaps there was some ground for it; but it would be necessary to know if the doctrine of the laughers was much less ridiculous. The system of Philinte will only appear to me specious when its partizans will practically prove all the resignation which their theory boasts, and when, wounded by one of the thousand stings of human wickedness, their countenance will show "*that their* mind, in short, is not more offended at seeing a deceitful, unjust, or interested man, than at seeing vultures greedy of carnage, apes mischievous, and wolves full of rage."[1] There is certainly more depth and more humanity in the system of Rousseau, though it conduct us to extravagances, than in this frivolous and often immoral optimism which is adorned with the name of *practical philosophy*, when even the practical side is that of which it has least to boast.

But it will be said, Could Rousseau be an upright judge? Was he well enough with society, to speak well of it? In his continued hostility against his age, and against that society, was there not, as has been thought, less indignation than personal feeling? Was not this feeling itself soured by the secret struggle between the inclinations of the man and the principles of the writer? All this is far beyond demonstration; but in regard to ourselves, we are led to believe in the sincerity of Rousseau, so far as his system is concerned.

However this may be, in this first work he laid down a creed, and considered it his honour and his duty to render his external conduct consistent with his faith. He felt that it was not sufficient to maintain a proposition, that the book and the man should be one, and that it was necessary for his conduct to become the faithful delineation of his opinion. The austerity of his life should correspond to the austerity of his maxims. Poor as he was, it appears that he must have a few things to reform; he found their subject in the superfluities of his indigence. His mode of dressing informed others, his frugal table informed himself that he had become another man. Had he become so?

No, the system had entirely engrossed his mind, but his heart

---

[1] Molière, Le Misanthrope, acte i., scène i.

was unaffected. He had reformed the external part, a reformation, of which the beginnings may appear easy, but the internal portion remained the same. There was no proportion between his affections and his thoughts, consequently there was no unity in his life, and the more he professed elevated maxims, the more the want of unity shone forth. In adopting, and especially in setting off his system, he had condemned himself to inconsistency.

Everybody in the same circumstances is inconsistent, because every one has principles which are very high, and a conduct which is much less so. Every one suffers in his own mind from this incongruity, and each has a remedy for it, whether by raising his conduct to his principles, or by lowering his principles to his conduct, which is much easier, and, therefore, much more common. The two terms, however, of which we are now speaking as approaching each other, never come in actual contact; inconsistency is the permanent, we should even suppose it the regular, condition of all men who have principles; but in general, it occasions only slight surprise with regard to the most part of men, either because the latter proceeding is the most useful, and the distance between profession and practice is commonly not very great, or because the most part of people do not publish their maxims.

But when Rousseau raised his standard, the man who bore it was sought for under its folds. In spite of his laudable intention of being one with his book, it was seen that the book and the man were two; it was known that " a double-minded man is unstable in all his ways."[1] It was observed that he was unable equally to distribute his powers over all the points of his life; sometimes he descended to a level with the men whom he censured, sometimes, as a counterbalance, he dashed his forehead, in the name of virtue, against the most reasonable proprieties, and even against the most positive duties. His very tastes were not in harmony with them—a new source of inconsistencies. Thus the love of solitude and need of the world, contempt for men, and an immense value attached to their opinion, the feeling of moral beauty, and no principle of conduct. He was blunt with the great, and lived under their patronage; he blamed the theatre,

[1] James i. 8.

and wrote for it; a preceptor of the human race, the Hercules of virtue, he abased himself, alas! to the most extraordinary vices. This character struck every one, they did not understand it, they did not honour, as perhaps they ought, these blunt efforts to gain an ideal, which the mind of Rousseau continually pursued, and they could only see in this great moral phenomenon the singularities of a man of genius. How great would have been the difference, if J. J. Rousseau had taken hold with his heart of what he conceived by the understanding, if his system had risen to affection, and if he had loved what he believed! This is, indeed, all the secret of moral unity, and for this the divine Founder of Christianity set himself, by means entirely His own, to make us love what He wished to make us believe.

And it is not merely unity which is wanting in the moral position, in which we believe Rousseau to be placed; it is also moderation and discernment. In the subject of morals, our soul is our eye; by it we only see and measure objects. By artificial means a voice may be given to the deaf and dumb; but as they do not hear, and do not know the effect of the action of the organ which they have been taught, their voice is without accent, and its inflexions are without precision. So it is with the application of a system to moral conduct. Deprived of the information derived from the moral sense, and of the delicate suggestions of the heart, we have recourse to reasoning and induction, a rough and dangerous guide; we grope, we every moment hurt ourselves; we have modes of acting without any nice distinction; by turns we are active, and abstain from action, we are silent, or speak away from the purpose; we are never informed by the voice from within of the quicksand which we are approaching, we are never sure of the value of what has been said, or of the bearing of what has been done; we are like a geometrical figure, divided into triangles and squares, which we endeavour to apply to a piece of ground with soft undulations, and sometimes we leave an empty space between it and the soil, and sometimes its pointed angles sink firmly and deeply into it. The sentiment by itself is quite flexible and lively, so as to touch equally all the points, and to cover all the parts of this unequal surface which human nature subjects to its pressure.

The tone which Rousseau assumed in his two first works, it was necessary to maintain in the world. When this tone was

taken up, it soon became natural and true by the continual•
impression made by a false position, by domestic discontentment;
and, in short, by the sad trials through which the conduct of the
world made Jean Jacques pass. And yet he does not conceal
from us that in principle, his misanthropy had something affected.
His *Confessions* confirm all that we have said:—

" Cast against my will into the world without having its tone,
and without being in a condition to assume its manners, and
without being able to submit to it, I thought of adopting one
which would dispense with it. My foolish and ungraceful timidity,
which I could not conquer, having for its principle the fear of
failing in propriety, I took, in order to become bold, the part of
treading it under my feet. I made myself cynical and caustic
from shame; I affected to despise the politeness, which I knew
not how to practise. It is true, this bitterness, suited to my new
principles, was ennobled in my mind, and took thence the intrepidity of virtue, and it is, I daresay, on this august basis, that
it has been better and longer maintained than might have been
expected from an effort so contrary to my nature."[1]

Do you observe, gentlemen, this defect, which it was impossible
to avoid, and which, for want of knowing how to correct, it has
been determined to transform into virtue? Are these, yea or
nay, the ingenious tricks of human pride?

But what, then, is that foolish and disagreeable timidity which,
by a strange counteraction, produces its opposite extreme, coarse-
ness and cynicism? " Perfect love casteth out fear."[2] It ought
also to cast out shame, which is merely a species of fear. If
J. J. Rousseau had loved his system he would not have been
timid, or his timidity would not have been so great. Love would
have overcome obstacles; love would have produced a sweet and
tranquil boldness, exempted at once from softness and hardihood.
But a man is always ill at ease in a borrowed part; it must either
be rejected or overdone, and he only saves himself from inconsistency by exaggeration; he remains immovable, or only moves by
a violent effort; it is in vain that the system is true; he is always
in a false position. This reminds us of the young German, whom
his friends reproached with his excessive phlegm and indolence.
They surprised him one day preparing to jump out at the window—" I am making myself lively," said he to them.

[1] Confessions. Livre viii.   [2] 1 John iv. 18.

M. de Fontaine formed a correct judgment of Rousseau, when he said:—" Let a man open the *Confessions* of J. J. Rousseau; all the faults of which he is accused spring from false shame."[1] I add faults, in appearance the most opposite. When, from timidity, he had violated the truth, then, to balance it, he was guilty of some preposterous brutality. If we wish examples of these consequences of false shame, Rousseau will amply supply them. The facts are not important, but they are characteristic.

The Abbé, afterwards Chevalier de Boufflers, had painted a portrait of Madame de Luxembourg:—" This portrait was horrible. She maintained, Rousseau tells us, that it did not at all resemble her, which was the truth. The treacherous abbé consulted me, and I, like a fool and a liar, said that the portrait was a resemblance."[2]

Will any one say, that almost everybody would have done the same thing? Perhaps; but Jean Jacques was not free to do as every one did; he was bound to be more inflexibly true than everybody else.

On another occasion, he says:—" I had a dog, which had been given to me quite young, about the time that I came to the Hermitage, and at that time I called him *Duke*. This dog, not beautiful, but of a rare species, that I had made my companion and friend, and certainly he deserved that title better than the most of those who took it to themselves, had become celebrated at the Castle of Montmorency for his affectionate sensible disposition, and for the attachment which we had for one another; but from a pusillanimity, very foolish, I changed his name to Turk, as if there were not multitudes of dogs called *Marquis*, without any Marquis giving himself any trouble about it. The Marquis de Villeroy, who knew this change of name, annoyed me so much about it, that I was obliged to tell before the whole company at table what I had done. In this story, what was offensive in regard to the name of duke did not consist so much in my having given it to him as in having taken it from him. The worst of it was, that several dukes were there—M. de Luxembourg and his son had that title."[3]

Ashamed of his weakness, which may seem trifling, but which

---

[1] Fontaine's Traduction de l'Essai sur l'Homme de Pope. Discours Preliminaire.
[2] Confessions. Livre xi.
[3] Ibid. Livre xi. Rousseau lived near M. de Luxembourg, and was protected by him.

must have appeared to him very great, his virtue longed to take
its revenge; but he had not always the patience to wait for the
opportunity, and was not always happy in choosing it; for
example, his conduct to the Prince de Conti, the most powerful and the most generous of his friends. This prince, while
Rousseau dwelt on his estate, had twice sent him baskets of game :
" Sometime after he made another be sent to me, and one of his
principal gamekeepers wrote, by his orders, that his highness was in
the field, and the game was shot by his own hand. I received it,
but wrote to Madame de Boufflers that I would receive no more.
This letter was generally blamed, and deserved to be so. I have
never read it in my collection without blushing at it, and reproaching myself for having written it."[1] Here are some fragments of this letter :—

" Listen, Madame, to my just complaints : I have received, on
the part of the Prince de Conti, a second present of game, of which
assuredly you are an accomplice. . . . . I will not again infringe
my maxims, even for him. I perhaps partly owe to them the
honour which he has done me, and this is a farther reason that
they should be always dear to me. If I had thought as another
man, would he have deigned to come to see me? These gifts
are only game, I admit, but what matters it? They are of a
higher value on that account, and I only see the more in them
the constraint which has been used to make me accept them."[2]

Sometimes, however, he was more happy in finding the middle
point, between complacency and rudeness. Here is an interesting example of it :—

" The Prince of Conti wished that I should have the honour
of making one of his party at chess. I knew that he beat the
Chevalier de Lorenzy, who was a better player than I; still, in
spite of signs and grimaces from the chevalier and the assistants,
which I did not appear to see, I gained the two games, which we
played. At the end, I said to him, in a respectful but grave
tone : Monseigneur, I honour too much your most serene Highness not to beat you always at chess."[3]

A circumstance, which the biographers of Rousseau have not
perhaps taken sufficiently into account, must have augmented the
pain and difficulty of the part which he had imposed on himself.

[1] Confessions. Livre x.   [2] A Madame de Boufflers, 7th Octobre 1760.
[3] Ibid. Livre x.

The gift of speaking was almost wanting to this great writer. He tells us himself: " Two things, which can scarcely be united, are united in me, without my being able to conceive the manner of their union—a temperament very ardent, lively and impetuous passions, and ideas, which are slow in springing up, and which only present themselves in a state of confusion, and when it is too late. It might be said that my heart and my mind do not belong to the same individual. Sentiment, more prompt than clear, fills my soul, but, instead of enlightening, it burns and dazzles me. . . . You may judge of what I must be in conversation, in which, to speak to the purpose I must think at once, and, at the moment, of a thousand things. The single idea of so many suitable topics, of which I am sure to forget at least some one, is sufficient to intimidate me. I cannot even comprehend how any one dares to speak in company."[1] How should one conduct himself, when stripped of all power of extempore speaking? If I force myself to speak to the people whom I meet, I infallibly talk nonsense: If I say nothing, I am a misanthrope, a strange animal, a bear. Total imbecility would have been much more favourable, but the talents in which I have been deficient in the world have been made the instrument of my loss of the talents which I had in myself."[2]

To mention it in passing, there are important exceptions to the axiom of Madame de Staël, who is of opinion that all men of genius can speak. This gift, we have already said, seems to have been wanting in Buffon, Montesquieu, and Rousseau. I would be tempted to explain to myself the incapacity of the two last, not only from their natural timidity, but from the very qualities of their mind. It is easy to make a stick pass through a hedge, but not a bundle of sticks. Now, every thought in these two writers is a bundle of thoughts, with this difference, that in the case of Montesquieu there prevails the necessity of reducing them to a single one, and often to squeeze them into a word; and, in the case of Rousseau, there was the necessity of grouping them around the idea which gave them birth, with the determination to express them all. I fancy to myself both these men stopped in their way by an abundance of ideas, and they strive to distribute and put them in order, and seek their centre, and have no rest till they have found it. This produces in the writer a sparkling

---

[1] Confessions. Livre iii.   [2] Ibid. Livre x.

style, nervous, and full; but this laborious habit of the mind, if it is present at the moment of conversation, is more painful than advantageous; it comes always too late; it is still preparing itself, when all is said; it cannot, embarrassed as it is with all its wealth, march in front with the mind of others; this is the business of a Voltaire, whose thought, always eager to come, is not loaded with any accessories, and less substantial, less strong, and lightly armed, is, for that very reason, more prompt and more nimble.

Perhaps, also, the condescension which very great minds have known and practised was wanting to these two writers. It might cost them something to lend themselves to the caprices of conversation, and to ramble in *this immense hall*, in company with frivolous talkers; but, in France, at Paris, in the eighteenth century, a person without this talent was exposed to serious evils; and you may represent to yourselves what Rousseau must have suffered, when this incapacity prevented him from bringing out some of the thoughts which oppressed him; and what irritation gathered in his heart, when the silence to which he saw himself reduced had let his true opinion be doubted on some subject on which he was not permitted to express himself:—

" Long did I abuse myself on account of the cause of this invincible disgust, which I have always experienced in my intercourse with men. I attributed it to regret, because I had not sufficient presence of mind to show, in conversation, the little that I have, and, consequently, to the fact that I did not occupy in the world the place that I thought I deserved." [1]

Afterwards, he changed this opinion, and tells us that he discovered another source of his disgust for society, but it is still true that this incapacity rendered him unhappy, that it would not contribute to make him enjoy society, and that he loved solitude better, in which this kind of mortification could not reach him, and in which glory, in exchange for it, knew well where to find him.

If we are to believe the explanation which he gives us of the motives of his conduct in his remarkable letters to M. de Malesherbes, it would not be what he calls misanthropy, still less affectation, which made him seek solitude, but an indomitable love of liberty—the fear which the pretended duties of society produced in reference to his leisure, and the experience which he had ac-

---

[1] Première Lettre à M. de Malesherbes.   4th Jan. 1762.

quired, that his *pretended friends* did not love him as he wished to be loved, or rather did not love him at all.

But let us not forget, that if these letters, which were written in one of the most lucid moments of Rousseau's life, describe with much vivacity and freshness the impressions under whose charm he then was, it is very doubtful whether they give a faithful account of the foundation of his character. , He says : " Passing my life by myself, I ought to know myself."[1] This is far from being a reason ; to be ignorant of one's-self, it is not necessary to live in the world. Besides, a man who tells you that *he always thought himself the best of men*,[2] and that, *in spite of the consciousness of his vices, he has for himself a high esteem*,[3] is assuredly possessed of extraordinary pride. And what guarantee is there that this pride does not enter into the judgments pronounced upon himself?

Would not the letters, then, to M. de Malesherbes, be a fine hypothesis, a pleasure of the imagination, of which the power, acting on the past, transforms the motives of our actions, and tells us, according to fancy, the history of our feelings? Still there is too much truth and heartiness in the picture which Jean Jacques sketches to us of his contemplative pleasures in the bosom of nature, to make us doubt that he was born, as he says, " with a natural love for solitude,"[4] and that the attraction of nature determined his retreat, as much as his dissatisfaction with social life. His style, which, in consequence of its fulness, is sometimes strained, is quite different in these admirable letters— it possesses the utmost grace and nature. In them the author fully enjoys himself, and the objects around him ; he plunges entirely into them, and suffers no third party to come in between nature and himself. We may quote some of these fine passages :—

" Oh ! that the lot which I have enjoyed were known throughout the universe, every person would wish to make a similar one for himself ; peace would reign upon the earth ; men would think no more of hurting one another, and there would be no more wicked men, when no man would have any interest in being so. But, in truth, what was my enjoyment, when I was alone ? My-

---

[1] Première Lettre à M. de Malesherbes. 4th Jan. 1762.   [2] Confessions. Livre x.
[3] Quatrième Lettre à M. de Malesherbes. 28th Jan. 1762.
[4] Première Lettre à M. de Malesherbes. 4th Jan. 1762.

self, the whole universe, every thing which exists, or may exist, every thing beautiful which the sensible world possesses, and every thing which the intellectual world can imagine; I gathered around me all that could flatter my heart; my desires were the measure of my pleasures. No, never have the most voluptuous known such delights, and I have a hundred times more enjoyed my chimeras than they do realities.

" When my pains make me sadly count the tedious hours of the night, and when the restlessness of the fever prevents me from enjoying a moment's sleep, often do I withdraw myself from my present condition, in thinking over the different events of my life, and repentance, sweet remembrances, regrets and tender feelings, divide among themselves the care of making me forget my sufferings. What time, sir, do you think that I recall most frequently and most willingly in my dreams? It is not the pleasures of my youth—they were too few, too much mixed with bitterness, and are already too far from me. It is those of my retreat, my solitary walks, the swiftly passing but delightful days which I spent, entirely alone, with my good and simple housekeeper, with my well-beloved dog, with my old cat, with the birds of the field and the hinds of the forest—with all nature—and its incomprehensible Author. When I rose at early dawn, to go and contemplate in my garden the rising sun; and when I saw the commencement of a beautiful day, my first wish was that neither letters nor visits should come to dissolve the charm. After having devoted the morning to various cares, all of which I attended to with pleasure, because I might have put them off till another time, I hastened to dinner, to escape importunity, and to procure for myself a longer afternoon. In an hour, even in the warmest weather, and when the sun was high in the heavens, I set out with my faithful Achates, quickening my pace, lest any one should come and lay hold of me before I had it in my power to give him the slip; but when once I had turned a certain corner, with what a beating heart and sparkling joy I began to breathe when I felt myself safe, saying to myself: Here am I master of my time for the rest of the day! I then went with more tranquil step to seek some wild place in the forest, some desert spot, where nothing shows the hand of man, and announces slavery and tyranny; some asylum, which I might suppose myself the first to penetrate, and to which no third person comes with his importunities to interpose between nature and myself. It was there that nature seemed to display in my eyes a magnificence always new. The golden broom and the purple heath struck my sight with a luxuriance which affected my heart ; the majesty of the trees which covered me with their shade, the delicacy of the shrubs which surrounded me, and the astonishing variety of the herbs and flowers which I trampled under my feet, kept my mind in a constant alternation of observation and wonder.

" . . . . My imagination did not allow the earth, so adorned, to be long a desert. I soon peopled it with beings according to my own heart, and I drove far away opinions, prejudices, and all artificial passions, and transported into the retreats of nature men worthy of inhabiting them. I formed to myself a charming society, of which I considered myself not unworthy. I framed to myself a golden age, according to my fancy, and, filling up these beautiful days with all the scenes of my life which had left any sweet memorial, and with all those which my heart might yet desire, 1 was softened, even to tears, as 1 contemplated the true pleasures of humanity—pleasures so delicious, so pure, and yet so far from men. Oh, if in these moments any idea of Paris, of my own age, and of my trifling glory as an author, came to trouble my reveries, with what disdain did I drive them away at the moment, to give myself up, without distraction, to the exquisite sentiments with which my soul was filled ! And yet, in the midst of all this, I confess the nothingness of my chimeras sometimes appeared to cast a gloom over my spirit. Though all my dreams had been turned into realities, they would not have satisfied me ; I would all the more have imagined, dreamed, and desired. I found in myself an inexplicable void, which nothing could have filled up—some violent tendency of heart towards another kind of enjoyment, of which I had no idea, and of which, however, I felt the necessity. Well, sir, that itself was enjoyment, since I was affected with a very lively feeling of it, and with an attractive sadness, which I would not have wished not to have.

" From the surface of the earth I soon raised my ideas to all the beings of nature, to the universal system of things, and to the incomprehensible Being, who embraces all things. Then my mind was lost in this immensity, and I neither thought, nor reasoned, nor philosophized. With a kind of pleasure, I felt myself overwhelmed with the weight of this universe, gave myself up with delight to the confusion of these grand ideas, and, in imagination, loved to lose myself in space ; my heart, shut up within the bounds of existence, felt itself straitened ; I was stifled in the universe, and would have wished to dart into the infinite. I believed that, if I had unveiled all the mysteries of nature, I would have been in a less delightful situation than in this stunning ecstasy, to which my spirit was given up without restraint, and which, in the restlessness of my transports, made me sometimes exclaim : O great Being! O great Being! without the power of saying or thinking more."[1]

But we draw near the period when sentiments—certainly different from those of which we have now read the description— take possession of Rousseau's soul ; when his distrust, more and more gloomy, will render him prejudiced against the human race ; when his most devoted friends will appear to him implicated in a vast plot, whose end is to destroy him, by exposing him to dishonour ; when he will connect every thing with this prevailing idea ; when he will seek those who avoid him, and flee from those who seek him, because the former will alone be sheltered from his suspicions ; the period, in short, which will furnish a proof of what he wrote to M. de Malesherbes, " that he had a disordered imagination, ready to become wild on every occasion, and to push every thing to extremes."[2]

Formerly he had given proofs of it. Suspicions had early impoisoned his relations to his friends. Very long before the letters to M. de Malesherbes were written, his memoirs show him to us quick in interpreting the most trifling proceedings, and even looks and gestures. He was born of a confiding nature, and, during his youth, he had lived in an illusion ; he had arranged in his thoughts an imaginary world, and, suited to this fine nature, which he required to people with beings worthy of it, he found himself all at once thrown from this warm and soft atmosphere into an icy sea ; his heart was shut to the same extent as it had been opened ; he was distrustful in proportion to his former confidence ; and, always devoured by the necessity of sympathy, he constantly repelled it ; and the heart, the most

---

[1] Troisième lettre à M. de Malesherbes. 26th Jan. 1762.
[2] Première lettre à M. de Malesherbes. 4th Jan. 1762.

naturally affectionate, became the most savage. With a heart like his, the man must be a Christian to look on the world as it is, without a feeling of desolation.

And into what a world had he fallen? I mean that, in principle, Rousseau was not better than his new friends; but if he was as bad, it was at least in another way. He had the vices of nature ; the men of the Holbach club had those of society. They were cunning and intriguing, Rousseau was simple and straightforward. In short, they rejected all the doctrines which constitute the dignity of man ; Rousseau was naturally religious. If he had learned their art, and had inured himself to their manners, his genius would have been ruined, for he could never write but under the dictate of emotion ; he would have figured at most among the literary men of the age of moderate talents, and would not have written the *New Heloise.*

His retreat saved his genius, but not his happiness. In solitude he got the advantage of that world which had injured him. To immense moral necessities he had only to offer his own substance, which, in truth, he multiplied, so to speak, by pride, but without succeeding in satisfying the hunger of a soul which God alone could suffice. His pride had been in vain made a counterpoise to the remembrance of his faults ; he had in vain said to himself : " My life is full of errors, for I am a man ; but this is what distinguishes me from the men that I know—in the midst of all my faults I have always reproached myself with them."[1] These very reproaches, this remorse, well suited to open up the heart, are not well calculated to fill it. Besides, this simple and natural happiness, of which Jean Jacques had dreamed from his youth, wanted several elements through his own fault. He had corrupted, to his sorrow, all the pleasures of existence ; he had not formed his heart so as to satisfy himself. " He dragged everywhere," says one of his biographers, " the most cruel enemy of his repose ;" and although, in the end, he made her his wife, with whom he had formed an unlawful connection, he might experience that, if respect for public morality is not sufficient to give happiness, contempt for that same morality rarely fails to take it away.

We must not believe his word when he tells us that all his

---

[1] A Madame Houdetot. 25th Mars 1758.

misfortunes were derived from that ardent "hatred of injustice, which he could never subdue."[1]

When he said so, he no doubt believed it, but I think that he would have had some difficulty in proving it. The wrongs which his friends had done to him, have no relation to this explanation, and these wrongs themselves were much exaggerated in his imagination. He was persecuted for the doctrines of one of his works, and in this persecution there were circumstances which must have rendered him indignant; but all his misfortunes did not flow from this persecution, which would have left many ways of happiness to any other character than his. When the *Emilius*, on account of the *Profession of Faith of the Savoyard Vicar*, was burnt by order of Parliament, its author was ordered by a decree to be apprehended and imprisoned at Paris and Geneva, and he was forced to quit that sweet solitude of Montmorency, where the most generous friendship might have constrained him to be happy; he might, no doubt, be grieved, and some bitterness might be mixed with the grief of the writer, who believed that this blow had been struck, because he had served the cause of humanity, " he was the defender, he said, of the cause of God, of the laws, and of virtue."[2]

But this very idea must have consoled him, and if he had always found at the bottom of his heart the beautiful words, which one day fell from his pen: "I have rendered glory to God, I have spoken for the good of men; my friend! for so great a cause, neither thou nor I will ever refuse to suffer;"[3] the injustice of men would have involuntarily become the happiness of his life.

Several of my auditors, on hearing these last words will ask, whether Rousseau could be sincere, when he uttered them. For my own part, I believe it. If the Vicar of Savoy attacks revelation, on the other hand he defends natural religion, and Jean Jacques was much more struck with the second fact than the first. Nay, farther, he even believed, as we shall see afterwards, that he served the cause of Christianity, by relieving it from some arbitrary formulæ. As to theism, he defended it with the double warmth of a profound conviction, and of an advantage gained by long disputes which he has delineated to us in his

[1] A M. de Mirabeau. 31st Jan. 1767.   [2] A M. de Gingins. 22nd Juin 1762.
[3] A M. Moultou. 7th Juin 1762.

Reveries. He thought he was much more culpable with regard to the Holbach club than with regard to the Christian Church; and indeed, the *Vicar's Profession of Faith,* which made him be taxed with impiety by some, made him be treated as a bigot by others.

Under the inspiration of these thoughts, his first impressions, on quitting his asylum, were mixed with much sweetness. There was not even in his heart room for anything but joy, when he arrived at the frontiers of Switzerland : " When I entered the territory of Berne, I stopped, I came down from the carriage, I prostrated myself on the ground, I embraced, I kissed the earth, and exclaimed in my transport, Heaven, protector of virtue, I praise thee, I touch a land of liberty!"[1] This enthusiasm was not destined to last long. Scarcely had he touched that land of liberty, when the senate of Berne sent him an order to quit it. At that very time, Geneva, his native place, sent him a summons to appear and answer for a crime committed at a great distance from it, and which on the same ground might have been taken up by all the governments in Europe. We must recal to memory a little, those times, to bear patiently the present.

This last blow overwhelmed Rousseau. He tenderly loved his country. He endeavoured to do it honour by his writings, of which one of the most celebrated had been dedicated to the Genevese government; it was published with this on the title page, *Citizen of Geneva;* he had written his most finished work, his *Letter to D'Alembert* to save his country from the dangers, with which it seemed to be threatened by the establishment of a theatre. All these recollections aggravated his grief. In this disposition of mind, he fixed his residence at Motiers-Travers, and perhaps felt a bitter satisfaction in obtaining under a monarchy the asylum which the republics refused to the apostle of equality. You must read here the noble letter by which, on his arrival, he made a favourable impression on the King of Prussia, and begged his hospitality: "I have said much ill of you, I will perhaps say still more, but driven from France, Geneva, and Berne, I now seek an asylum in your states. It was perhaps my mistake that I did not at first take this step; this is one of the eulogies of which you are worthy. Sire, I

---

[1] Confessions. Livre xi.

have not deserved any favour at your hands, and I ask none; but I thought it my duty to declare to your Majesty, that I was in your power, and that I wished to be so : you may dispose of me as you please." [1]

I cannot deprive myself of the pleasure of communicating, by way of following up this letter, the one which a short time after he wrote to the king, who seemed to him by no means in earnest to let his subjects enjoy the benefits of peace after so many wars. It must not be forgotten, that Frederic made offer of a pension to J. J. Rousseau:—

" Sire, you are my protector and benefactor; and I have a heart formed for gratitude; I shall now discharge this debt, if I can.

" You wish to give me bread; is there any of your subjects who wants it? Remove from my sight that sword which dazzles and offends me, it has only too well done its duty, and the sceptre is abandoned. It is a great career for kings of your condition, and you are still far from its termination; yet time presses and there is not a moment to lose, in order that you may make an end. Sound well the depth of your own heart, Frederic! Can you resolve to die without having been the greatest of men?

" May I see Frederic, the just and the feared, at length fill his states with a happy people, of which he is the father, and Jean Jacques Rousseau, the enemy of kings, will go to die at the foot of his throne." [2]

Established at Motiers in the midst of a Protestant population, J. J. Rousseau felt the necessity of binding himself to them, by uniting with them in their worship. We omitted to say, that during his stay in Savoy, he became Catholic. At this period of his life, his belief was opposed by his reason, but he made it up with good will; he formed for himself a faith more than childish; he informs us himself that the fear of damnation often agitated his mind, and he had recourse to singular expedients to escape from uncertainty respecting his future destiny : " One day, as I was meditating on this serious subject, I employed my-self mechanically in throwing stones at the trunks of trees, and with my usual dexterity too, that is to say, without ever touch-ing one of them. In the midst of this fine exercise, I thought of

[1] Au Roi de Prusse. Juillet 1762. [2] Au Roi de Prusse. 30th Oct. 1762.

forming from it a kind of prognostic to calm the restlessness of my mind. I said to myself: I am going to cast this stone at the tree opposite to me, if I hit it, then this is a sign of salvation; if I miss, it is a sign of damnation. In saying so, I threw the stone with a trembling hand and with a fearfully beating heart, but so successfully, that it struck the very middle of the tree, which really was not difficult, for I took care to choose one very thick and very near. From that time I no longer doubted," adds Rousseau, " of my salvation."[1]

In the days of his glory, he made a sojourn at Geneva, and formally returned to the bosom of the Protestant religion. I express myself thus to mark in what sense Rousseau understood Protestant Christianity. At Motiers he remembers it :—

" After my solemn reunion with the reformed church, living in a reformed country, I could not, without failing in my engagements, and in my duty as a citizen, neglect the public profession of the worship, to which I had returned. . . . Always to live alone upon the earth, appeared to me a very sad destiny, especially in adversity. In the midst of so many proscriptions and persecutions, I felt the utmost pleasure in being able to say to myself: At least I am among my brethren, and I went to communicate with an emotion of heart and tears of tenderness, which were perhaps the most agreeable preparation to God that could be made."[2]

I pray my hearers to remember the communion of Voltaire : this comparison may be used in drawing a parallel between these two men. The communion of Rousseau had many defects, but it was not an impious farce ; it was done with great gravity and feeling. " Reverence disappears," was the profound remark of a woman of understanding in the eighteenth century ; Rousseau, amid much error and weakness, knew how to show reverence.

They thought it was in their power, without any difficulty or previous examination, to grant the communion to the author of the *Vicar of Savoy;* they considered it their duty to refuse it to the author of the *Letters from the Mountain,* written by him during his abode at Motiers. He might have complained of it as an inconsistency ; but that was not enough for his genius, he was the friend of exaggeration, and fond of sophisms. In the *Letters*

---

[1] Confessions. Livre vi.   [2] Ibid. xii.

from the Mountain, he exclaims, that "he was the defender of the Protestant religion;" that if they had not refused to him the communion after the *Emilius*, they had far less right to refuse it after these *letters*. Then they might have taken the communion from me, but at present they ought to give it to me again."[1]

Now, you must know that in the *Letters from the Mountain*, J. J. Rousseau overturns the principal doctrines of our confessions of faith. It is true he pretends to do this by means of passages from the Gospel, but if a partisan of polytheism claimed the Christian communion, and founded his claim upon this—that the books of the Christians contain this passage—*there are Gods many and Lords many*, I very much doubt that any Christian community would receive him into its bosom. Rousseau forgot that Protestantism, taking this term in its proper sense, is not a religion; that a man has not one religion from the simple fact that he has abjured another, and that by the side of the negative principle, which separated us from the Roman Church, there is a positive principle which unites us to one another; that this positive principle is nothing else than a common belief; that it is in virtue of this principle that we form churches, since a church, which would believe nothing, would be a thing absurd and contradictory. Around what do we meet, if not around a belief or a common idea?

The *Letters written from the Mountain* had raised against J. J. Rousseau not only men in authority, but also the masses of the people. He was soon made to experience it. He was attacked in his house by his new fellow-townsmen. There has been much reasoning on this occurrence, and it has been extenuated till it has been reduced to nothing. Rousseau's imagination might have exaggerated, but it did not create what took place; and, all fear laid aside, we have no farther need to have recourse to inconsistency and caprice to explain the new removal of Jean Jacques. He found, in the island of St Peter, the most cherished of his retreats, and the foretaste of perfect happiness. We taste it with him, when we read the description which he has twice given of it in his *Confessions* and in his *Reveries*. And when a decree by the authorities expelled him, within twenty-four hours, from this charming solitude, we feel

---

[1] Au Consistoire de Motiers. 29th Mars 1765.

ourselves, so to speak, struck with the same blow, and we understand that this unexpected and inconceivable violence gave the last and fatal stroke to his reason, which was already shaken.

From that moment, indeed, it is impossible not to perceive in Rousseau the heir of the misfortune of Tasso. And it may be doubted if the circumstances which followed this last exile, did not accelerate the progress of this intellectual aberration, or if this aberration alone has not given to these circumstances their unfortunate character. The unhappy Rousseau, who should have been always on his guard against the Holbach society, accepted the offers of services and hospitality from one of the trusty members of that club, David Hume, the celebrated English historian. He set out with him to England, and scarcely had he arrived in that country, full of his admirers, when he believed himself to be given up by his friend to public hatred and derision. Scandal followed on both sides, and France soon learned, from J. J. Rousseau, that Hume was treacherous; from Hume that Jean Jacques was a villain. We may dispense with following the distressing and almost incredible details of a rupture, in which Rousseau showed on his side the most extravagant susceptibility, and the strangest wanderings of the imagination, but in which his host was not distinguished for delicacy and generosity.

Always pursued by the thought that he was the central point of a vast conspiracy against his honour, Rousseau then took the part of disconcerting his enemies, by saying of himself more evil than they knew of him, or could imagine.[1] But his design, you perceive, was not to degrade himself. He thought that the evil which he said of himself with unexampled sincerity, would force them to believe the good that he proposed to speak of himself too; and he was persuaded that the good so far surpassed the evil, as that the clear product of his confessions in the mind of his readers would be admiration and sympathy. This is the prevailing and perhaps the single idea of the *Confessions*, if any other hope more disinterested was joined to his principal design, his mind rested on it for a little. If he said once, " The history of a man who will have the courage to show himself within and without, may give some instruction to his equals;"[2] he twenty

---

[1] It appears by a letter from Rousseau of 30th Jan. 1763, to M. Moulton that this plan had been long formed.   [2] A M. Moulton. 30th Jan. 1763.

times points out the interest of his reputation as the real object
of his undertaking : " I will say every thing, good, bad, in short,
all.   I feel that I am one who can show himself."[1]   "Feeling
that the good exceeded the evil, it was my interest to say every
thing, and I did so."[2]   But the most remarkable passage is at
the very beginning of his book.   We shall still quote it, though
it be well known:—"Let the trumpet of the last judgment
sound when it will, I will go with this book in my hand and
present myself before the sovereign Judge.   I will say aloud :
There is what I have done, what I have thought, and what I
have been.   I have shown myself what I was—contemptible and
vile when I was so, good, generous, and elevated, when I was so ;
I have unveiled the inner man, such as Thou, O eternal God,
hast seen him thyself.   Gather around me the innumerable
multitude of my equals to listen to my confessions."[3]

Represent to yourselves, gentlemen, the human race sitting
before the throne of the Eternal, and in expectation of their
sentences, to listen to the harsh recital which J. J. Rousseau
spins out in his *Confessions*, with too visible complacence.   Certainly the time and place are well chosen :—

" Let them groan at my indignities, let them blush at my
miseries.   Let each of them in his turn lay open his heart at the
foot of thy throne with the same sincerity, and then let a single
one say, if he dare, I was better than that man."[4]

It will be none of us, gentlemen, I dare promise for it—of us,
educated in the school of that apostle, who, only bearing in his
conscience remembrances honourable in the eye of the world, did
not less regard himself as *the chief of sinners.*[5]   The Christian
has forgotten to treat men with contempt : the Christian scarcely
thinks of putting himself on a parallel with his brother, and, by
comparison, of making to himself a subject of glory from the
shame of his neighbour.   A fundamental equality of misery and
sin does not permit him to give much attention to the inequalities
which other eyes may perceive, and of which we ourselves, in one
sense, do not deny the reality.   J. J. Rousseau, who thinks to
astonish us by a bold apostrophe, has missed his mark in reference
to us.   Without a moment's hesitation, we reject his defiance,
and consent not to pass for better than he.

---

[1] A Milord Maréchal.   20th Juillet 1766.   [2] Reveries, Quatrième Promenade.
[3] Confessions.   Livre i.   [4] Ibid.   [5] 1 Timothy i. 15.

However this may be, gentlemen, Rousseau spares us the trouble of choosing between the suppositions respecting the true end of his book. This book, entitled *Confessions*, is quite an apology for, one might almost say a monument to, his moral glory. That he has said of himself all the ill that he knew, I make no doubt; I do not know what confession would have been painful after those which he has made. He has confessed not only what is *criminal*, but what is *ridiculous* and *shameful*, and he justly observes that "this is most painful to tell."[1] Besides this, the vice most difficult to acknowledge is perhaps envy, a feeling which Rousseau does not seem to have experienced. Pride, which, according to Pascal, is a counterpoise to all our miseries, counteracts also all our confessions, even the confession of what is ridiculous and shameful.

Besides, what occasion was there at the end of the *Confessions* for the detail of so many follies and so many wanderings, of which a mere summary would have been sufficient? What could be the design of the author in these descriptions of gallantry, more worthy of an amatory poet than of a philosopher and moralist? Is it thus that, in the decline of life, the apostle of a stern doctrine ought to occupy his leisure, he who boasts of having formed " a scheme, the greatest, perhaps, or at least the most useful to virtue, which mortal ever conceived"?[2]

In the next place, if there was the right, under certain reservations, to make one's confessions, was there equally the right to make those of others? Yes, perhaps, when the defence of one's own honour rendered it necessary, and when self-justification required the accusation of others. But when this motive cannot be pleaded, there is no right to accuse others, even when a man accuses himself, how much less to accuse his benefactors, and to blast their character. Now, every one knows the place which the unfortunate Madame de Warens occupies in the memoirs of J. J. Rousseau. There has been a wish to palliate this wrong, but this very attempt itself is a wrong. Charity cannot be alleged; how could there be charity in justifying the most serious infraction of the laws of charity? Rousseau, in speaking as he did of his benefactress, was very ungrateful, or very senseless. His memoirs, it is said, should only have been published in 1800,

---

[1] Confessions. Livre i.   [2] Ibid. viii.

a time at which there would not have been one of the family of Madame de Warens in existence; but what security was there that they would not appear long before? and this actually happened.

From this time we can only follow the course of Rousseau's life, and mention the different places where he dwelt to collect the marks, and exhibit the symptoms of the malady which consumed his old age, and of which, astonishing to say, he had the consciousness without being in a condition to cure it. In 1770 he wrote to Du Belloy: "My suspicion is so much the more deplorable, as being almost always well founded (and I add *almost* on your account); it is always boundless, because every thing which is beyond nature no longer regards it."[1] It may be judged of by a few circumstances.

In 1750, he had maintained a controversy, of an entirely literary character, with M. Bordes of Lyon. The latter made a voyage to England ten years after, and Rousseau, without examination, has no doubt that M. Bordes had gone to London for the express purpose of doing him an injury.[2]

Du Belloy himself sends him a tragedy—the *Siege of Calais.* This is his answer: "In my second reading I fell in with a couplet which had escaped me in my first, and which, on reflection, has lacerated my feelings—' How much virtue shone in his false repentance! Can any one describe it so well and not feel it?' In this I discovered, not, thanks to Heaven, the heart of Jean Jacques, but the men with whom I have to do, and whom, to my misfortune, I know too well."[3] He wrote to M. de Saint-Germain: "In short, no attention has been wanting to misrepresent me in every way, even beyond what could be imagined, by withdrawing from public view the portraits which resemble me, and by sending abroad in the most ostentatious manner one which gives me a fierce appearance and the look of one of the Cyclops."[4]

Listen still to this circumstance related in his *Reveries*, a work written in the last year of his life, a monument of vigorous talent and of a bruised mind. He met in one of his walks with a child whose face interested him: "I asked the child, who was his father, and he pointed out to me a man who was putting hoops on casks. I was about to quit the child to go to speak to him,

---

[1] A M. Du Belloy. 12th Mars 1779.   [2] Confessions. Livre viii.
[3] A M. Du Belloy. 19th Fev. 1770.   [4] A M. de Saint-Germain. 26th Fev. 1770.

when I saw that a man of a bad look had got before me, who appeared to be one of those flies who never quit me ; while this man was whispering in his ear, I observed the looks of the cooper attentively fixed upon me with an air which was by no means friendly. This object shut my heart, and I quitted the father and the child with greater speed than I had shown in my walk."[1]

It is well known that at one time,[2] he accompanied the date of each of his letters with the four following verses : " Poor blind creatures that we are ! O Heaven unmask the impostors, and force their barbarous hearts to open themselves to the eyes of men !" But what is more striking is his opinion on the subject of a strophe of Tasso, whose case his so sadly resembled. He firmly believed that, in the seventy-seventh strophe of the twelfth canto of the *Jerusalem Delivered*, Tasso had thought of him, or at least had, without intending it, predicted his lot. The strophe, but for this, would, in his view, be an inexplicable excrescence— mere nonsense. Here follows its translation : " Alone with my thoughts, implacable furies, I drag everywhere their detested train. I fear the night ; its unfriendly shades represent my fault to my lacerated heart. I fear the sun ; his perfidious light reveals my destiny by my looks. I fear myself, and always, wretch that I am, chained to myself, I flee, but in vain."

After having read these verses, do we not know, gentlemen, the true name of the phantoms which haunted Rousseau ? Was it not, under a thousand false names, old and incurable remorse ? Were not his life and his previous troubles at perpetual war with his conscience ? Was it not with the view of appeasing or vin- dicating it that he wrote his *Confessions* ? Are not this employ- ment of his moral courage, this care to establish a balance be- tween his virtues and vices, this anticipated appeal to the supreme judgment, symptoms of that inward trouble, to which the verses of Tasso give an expression so terrible ? We do not mean to determine these points.

Rousseau seemed to have preserved all the vigour of his un- derstanding only to render it subservient to his fixed idea. He has himself, without thinking, given an account of this singular state of his mind when he falls in with an occurrence of an older

---

[1] Reveries, Neuvième promenade.　　　　[2] En 1770, 1771.

date. I do not know what extraordinary idea he had in his head. He says on this subject : " It is astonishing what a number of facts and circumstances came into my mind to imitate this folly, and to give to it an air of probability, what do I say! to show me its evidence and demonstration."[1]

It would have been very difficult, if we looked at him in any other sphere, to perceive or suspect in him the slightest symptom of this cruel distemper. On the contrary, to this period is referred the most interesting part of his correspondence. There is even a sounder morality, more moderate wisdom, and a juster estimate of life and of society in his letters at that time than in the most part of his works; in them he shows himself, especially for young people, a man of excellent counsel; a fool for himself, he is admirably wise for others.

In the midst of this dark delirium, he returned to Paris, threw himself again into the world, showed himself everywhere, and then withdrew to Ermenonville in 1776. He looked upon his literary career as terminated, and had formed the determination to write nothing more for the public. We have no farther information about him than some anecdotes, and many marks of alienation are mentioned at this period. It was at that time, nevertheless, that with bruised mind, but with unbroken pride, he wrote his *Reveries*, a monument of the most admirable talent, and of the strangest perversion of ideas. Here is a remarkable passage of a letter written by Rousseau a few months before his death : " The swallow is naturally familiar and confiding, but this is a folly, for which she is punished too well not to correct it. By patience, she is accustomed to live in confined apartments, so long as she does not perceive the intention of keeping her captive there, but so soon as this confidence is abused (and they never fail to do so), it is lost for ever. From that time she eats no more, she never ceases to struggle, and ends with killing herself."[2]

Men wished to see a suicide in the death of Rousseau. Without discussing this question, we shall observe, that the evidence furnished in support of this fact has little weight in itself, so that apart from the disposition of Rousseau's mind, the thought would not have arisen. It is right to mention, in connection with this matter, a letter which he wrote to his wife a few years before :

---

[1] Confessions. Livre xi.   [2] A Madame de C. 9th Jan. 1778.—*Note.*

" I am not going to make a very long or a very perilous voyage; still nature disposes of us at the moment when we are thinking least about it. You know too well my real sentiments to fear that, whatever degree my misfortunes may reach, I am the man ever to dispose of my life before the time that nature or men may have pointed out. If any accident should terminate my career, be very sure, whatever may be said, that my will has not had the smallest share in it."[1]

Jean Jacques Rousseau died at Ermenonville, the 4th of July 1778, two months after Voltaire. These two deaths so near each other present a striking contrast; Rousseau ended his days in solitude, in abandonment, and almost in indigence; Voltaire died amid all the parade of renown, "and, as it were, buried under his own triumph." Both still live by the powerful influence which they exercise over the minds of men.

Although in this rapid view of Rousseau's life we have especially endeavoured to bring out what characterised him, it is scarcely possible, in this respect, to arrive at positive conclusions. It would, however, be well worth our pains, whether on account of the light, which, when better known, the character of the writer would spread over his works, or because for man, there is no study more interesting than man. A book is always produced by art; a man is the work of nature and of circumstances, and the light which comes from him is with respect to us nearer and surer than that of books.

It is not, however, easy with all materials in our hands rightly to determine a character. A character is the collective product, the moral unity resulting from a meeting of dispositions in the same subject, humanity, nation, and individual. I know well that the most common idea is to fix the character according to the actions; it seems natural at first sight to discover the tree by its fruit; yet this method cannot lead to truth, so considerable is the influence of external circumstances over our actions. The character can only be immediately concluded from actions by means of certain reservations and rules. The whole of a man's actions—life, in short, is like an ample drapery cast over a statue; it indicates in a general way its form, and yet there would be great need of reflection and art to mark out exactly the

---

[1] A Madame Rousseau. 12th Aout. 1769.

body which it covers. But, it will be said, cannot vices and virtues make us determine character? Well, not absolutely. Considered barely, and by themselves alone, they are not the character, vices may have been contracted, and virtues, too, by influences, which do not merely flow from character.

The character is composed of distinct features, prominent and permanent, which are revealed during the whole continuance of a life, and which determine and explain the whole of it. These features are affections, simple and elementary, which are neither compounded nor derived. To discover these primary elements, it would be necessary, I think, to study them, and take them up from the life among little children. How much by what follows does life change these natural propensities? To lay hold of the nearest example, suspicion was not with Rousseau a disposition of his youth; at that time, on the contrary, we have seen him excessively confiding. Suspicion belongs to one period of his life, confidence to another; we must then necessarily suppose, between the two, something primary, a quality to which we are compelled to go back.

The intensity, the combination, and the proportion of these natural affections, are sufficient to explain all the immense variety of individual characters. But we do not conceive nor represent a character when we only see the features which compose it in juxtaposition; there is mutual attraction and repulsion as in the system of Newton. Things the most independent tend to organize themselves, when they are brought close together, at the same time the natural powers are modified, and penetrate one another; often one of them becomes dominant, and subjugates those which were primarily associated with it. The character is an organism of affections, which act one upon another, in such a way that the whole together, the unity which springs from their being brought near, is not a sum but a result. It is the same as in chemistry, whose elements are reduced to a very small number of simple substances, which, by their mixture, form other substances, new and individual, but which are no longer elementary. We shall better understand the mode of mixing up individual characters by observing national character, such as the English, for example. In them, we undoubtedly find many traces of the particular character of the different races of which that people is composed; but this amalgamation has produced a new race. A character could not consist of the primitive powers of being; this is what renders the unfolding of a character difficult. Suppose the elements given, we have not for all that the result; suppose the result given, it is not easy to go back to the elements. To these general observations, we must add some, more particular.

Mind does not constitute character; but the form and degree of intelligence has so great an influence on the tenor of a man's life, that it is impossible not to reckon intellectual qualities among the elements of character.

Opinions are not character. Some are even opposed to it; education, society, and interest come in and form in the mind of an individual, opinions contrary to his natural dispositions, and when these continue, we must search in some corner of the character for the explanation of their presence in the mind.

Certain events develop in excess certain principles of character. We must then take into account external circumstances; but when events appear to change one or more of these elements, we must not be in haste to believe in a change of nature. We must believe that the character was capable of giving to the soul two opposite directions.

The character may include in itself contradictory elements, and it is this which embarrasses us most in the estimate of different individualities. We do not say that nature has placed at their beginning *yes* and *no* beside one another, but we say that it sometimes unites qualities whose results lead to formal contradictions. If the combat lasts to the end; if, for example, the mind be in contradiction to the moral qualities, man is in himself a perpetual storm, and to others, he is an enigma. I say nothing of storms from without, which may leave the soul entirely calm.

But sometimes the character is overpowered, and neutralized in certain points by means of the character itself. It may be so also by the influence of a fact which produces a prevailing affection. This may be applied to the phenomenon of conversion. I do not speak here of the conversion of the mind, but of real conversion—the conversion of the heart, the result of an affection which gives to the soul a new life. This conversion can only be accomplished by a fact, not by an idea. The pardon of God received into the heart, can alone produce such a revolution.

The primary powers of the moral being, however, subsist as far as this affection allows. If the idea absorbed the man, and identified itself with him, there would be no more individual character. A creature perfectly holy would have no character in the ordinary sense of the word. His whole soul would tend to God, and his whole being would be disposed to be identified with the divine nature. Holiness is the character even of God; Jesus Christ has no character, His individuality, if I dare employ this term, does not exist out of the perfections which we attribute to the divinity. It is no longer so with the apostles ; we discover in their case individuality. It is, I think, less decisive in John. In one sense, perhaps, he is not nearer perfect holiness than his colleagues ; in another, however, his individual character is, as it were, lost, absorbed, and annihilated in the living impression of Jesus Christ. But this is a personal sentiment, which others will not be able to share.

If a new affection be capable of modifying so powerfully the character, we will understand how far the action of early education and first impressions can go. They do not constitute the character, but they have an influence on the materials, which come in their way, and when they produce any effect on the character, they throw into it elements which are never lost. Rousseau will furnish us with a proof of this fact.

In this point of view, the accurate analysis of a character would give an appearance of necessity to all the facts which prevail in a life, even to those which appear to be a deviation from nature, so far as they could be withdrawn from the operation of external circumstances. All the great features of life correspond to the great features of character. But the extreme difficulty of such an analysis, combined with the just estimate of external influence, the condition of prominent individualities, is that which renders it so difficult for poets to create a true character. This creation, however, is the end of poetry; it alone gives life and reality to ideas and sentiments which, without it, would slumber in the region of abstraction. The poet must succeed in combining, not only characters generally human, but also persons perfectly individual. In this way the truest individualities often appear not at all probable ; and, to return to Rousseau, with what reproaches of improbability would such a character as his be received, if it were the fruit of a poetical conception !

According to these general indications, when we investigate the principal features of J. J. Rousseau's character, we find at first in him, as a primary and principal element, " an irregular imagination,"[1] sometimes active and sometimes dreaming. Let us remember that it is from himself that we have borrowed this epithet, which has been already quoted. This imagination at times is exceedingly devoted to events; it exaggerates and changes them, and renders them unnatural; at other times, when no event tempts it, then it gives full scope to reverie, which the mind of Rousseau, naturally indolent, always preferred to the regular labour of thought. It was agreeable to himself that " this spirit of liberty was derived, less from pride than from indolence; but, he adds, this indolence is incredible; every thing startles it; the least duties of civil life are insupportable to it; a word to be spoken, a letter to be written, and a visit to be paid, so soon as they become necessary, are to me punishments." [2]—" Reverie refreshes and amuses me," he says in another place; " reflection fatigues and makes me sad. Thinking was always to me a painful and disagreeable occupation." [3]

This imagination habitually retained him beyond the bounds of reality; he early formed a world for himself—a world of romance:—" Soon forced, against my will, to occupy myself with my sad situation, I could only very seldom call up these dear ecstasies, which, for fifty years, had been to me instead of fortune and of glory. . . . . Sometimes my reveries end in meditation, but more frequently my meditations end in reverie: and, during these wanderings my soul roams and flutters over the universe on the wings of imagination, in ecstasies, which surpass every other enjoyment." [4]

This imagination, which had so greatly embellished his life, prodigiously darkened it, after he had acquired some experience. Incapable, on its account, of continuing in reality, it at last drove him to that distrust, which was proportioned to the confidence of his early years. The same principle produced directly opposite results; he formed to himself that ideal world, which, in his youth, he thought to find beyond himself; and, at a later period, he exaggerated the vices and dangers of the real world. He had

[1] Première Lettre à M. de Malesherbes. 4th Jan. 1762.
[2] Ibid. See also Confessions. Livre xii.   [3] Reveries, Septième promenade.
[4] Reveries, ibid.

only seen friends; he now only sees enemies. Notwithstanding,
this fantastic disposition allayed the wounds which it had made :
" Feeling that I could not obtain among my contemporaries a
situation which could satisfy my heart, I gradually detached myself
from the society of men, and formed another for myself in my
imagination." [1]—" The comparison of what is with what ought
to be, has given me a romantic spirit, and has always kept me
far from every thing practical." [2]

This dreaming and irregular temper was cherished by the disorderly youth of Rousseau. Nothing regulates the mind like a
life regulated from within, however troubled, events may render
it from without. The soul may maintain its level amid checks
and crosses, but it infallibly loses it in a wandering existence,
without any object, on which education has placed no restraint,
and whose irregularities have given full scope to the caprices of
imagination.

When the imagination of Rousseau is attached to a given
object, it finds a powerful auxiliary in the dialectic habits of his
mind. A second element of his nature, his dialectics are always
perfect, on whatever subject they are exercised. The basis
may be erroneous, nay, even fallacious, and only resting upon
that burning brain; but if the first point be conceded, his
vigorous reasoning renders every thing possible, or rather absolutely necessary. This is the reason why J. J. Rousseau requires
to be read with extreme caution; he is, perhaps, the most dangerous of sophists, because he is honestly a sophist. He says
to himself: " If my principles are true, all is true ; if they are
false, all is false, for I have only deduced rigorous and necessary
consequences." [3] Indeed, a trifling examination demonstrates,
that most frequently he has set out from a principle quite gratuitous. Of an independent spirit, he never sees but one thing at
a time, and he only looks at every thing in its abstract idea, that
is in an artificial reality. To Rousseau especially may the saying
of Benjamin Constant be applied :—" Nothing is so fearful as
logic without reason."

The third characteristic feature is the connection of his powerful imagination with an impassioned nature :—" I have," he says,

[1] Deuxième Lettre, à M. de Malesherbes. 12th Jan. 1762.
[2] Au Prince de Wirtemberg. 10th Nov. 1763.
[3] A M. Moultou. 4th Juin 1763.

" very ardent passions, and whilst they agitate my mind, nothing equals my impetuosity. I know neither discretion, nor respect, nor fear, nor propriety: I am cynical, impudent, violent, and intrepid; no shame arrests my progress; no danger frightens me, beyond the one object which occupies my attention; the universe is to me nothing." [1]

Without the ardour of his passions, his indolence would perhaps have gained the mastery over his genius. He only wrote constrained, so to speak, by the force of inspiration; he was fully stirred up to it, though almost disinclined: " I have thought sometimes very profoundly, but rarely with pleasure, almost always against my will, and, as it were, by force." [2] Passion, then, made him an author, but an impassioned author—less a writer than an orator—and paradoxical, because we scarcely look at truth through the eyes of passion without exaggeration.

Still, if in the case of Rousseau, we see passion and imagination united, let us remember that it is not always so. The most general opinion willingly admits the simultaneous existence of these two elements, and the power which they lend to each other; for my part, I think, on the contrary, that impassioned people exist, who are almost entirely devoid of imagination, and that their passions are only the more frightful on that account. The imagination, it will be said, unceasingly furnishes to passion a renewal of combustible materials; but I consider less dangerous the passions cherished by imaginary elements than those which, from want of ideas, are brought to turn upon themselves, or to seek their food in real life.

Contrasted with this impetuosity of passion, we must show in Rousseau a contemplative disposition very decisive. Let us take care not to confound contemplation with observation. The latter is an activity, which lays hold on its object, and which analyzes and dissects it; in contemplation, on the contrary, it may be said that the object itself lays hold of the soul, and modifies it. The contemplative faculty rules Rousseau; nature penetrates his soul, and in some measure mixes itself with it; he is in love with its harmonies, and this sentiment rises even to religion: " I feel ecstasies and inexpressible delight in my being dissolved, so to speak, in the system of beings, and in identifying myself

---

[1] Confessions. Livre i.   [2] Reveries, Septième promenade.

with the whole of nature."[1] But this religion, which is nothing more than the contemplation of nature, very much resembles pantheism. By adding to it the worship of moral beauty, we shall have, I think, all the ingredients of the religion of Jean Jacques; and who among us would presume to say, that such a religion might be sufficient for the eternal necessities of man ?

Pursuing our analysis, and keeping close to these contemplative faculties, we shall find in our subject a reflected sensibility, a pleasure in the inward sentiments which, under the somewhat discreditable name of sentimentality, has given rise to a whole department of literature. To Rousseau we owe the first expression of this inner life of the heart, which requires a careful investigation of one's-self; he knows the poetry of little objects, and of domestic life. If the passions lay hold on life on a great scale, sentimentality is attached to the little incidents of every day ; it cultivates them with love, and invests them with poetry. New for France in this respect, Rousseau remained a long time alone. No one formerly had so well comprehended nature, and no one had plunged so deep into certain mysteries of the heart ; he was naturally, what others endeavoured to appear. If, in his artlessness, and with most sagacious attraction, he has done justice to a whole world, which no one had either described or perceived, it is because he had for this merely to describe his own tastes, and to relate the operations of his own mind. His poverty even may have had an influence on his intimate acquaintance with nature ; it was, I think, very favourable to his poetical character. Had he been rich, he would not have been able to dream in his castle, as he did in a cottage in the middle of a meadow. Instead of his delightful descriptions of fields and woods, he would, perhaps, have left to us the description of his park. Read, for example, the account of his sojourn in the Isle of St Peter, and the charming episode of the rabbits, and endeavour to represent to yourselves Voltaire in a similar situation.

We discover this passion for nature even in what is peculiar in the manner in which Rousseau studied botany. The scientific spirit entered into it in a small degree. He tells us himself: " It is the chain of accessory ideas which attaches me to botany. It joins together, and recals to my imagination all the ideas which flatter it still—the meadows, the streams, the woods, the solitude, the peace, especially, and the repose which are found in the midst of all this, are continually delineated by it on my memory." [1]

Two essential qualities of Rousseau remain to be particularly noticed.

The one is the sentiment of moral beauty. This sentiment is not virtue ; one would even be astonished at the weak dose of virtue which may be sufficient for this admiration. It may appear strange—it is, however, certain—that the same disposition which urges us to admire, sometimes relaxes in us the active power which would furnish us with the means of deserving admiration. The man most dazzled and charmed with the splendour of a diamond, is not on that account most inclined to bury himself, with a pick-axe in his hand, in the mine from which this treasure is derived. The diamond is beautiful, but the mine is gloomy. The sentiment of moral beauty is only the imagination applied to the poetical face of virtue. It may exist by the side of the most shameful deviations.[2] Rousseau gave proof, among a thousand, that sensibility is not virtue. No one, however, better felt, or more tenderly adored, moral beauty. With what veneration has he not surrounded those whom he esteemed its accomplished types, Abauzit, Milord Maréchal ! He, as it were, bowed before them, as he says in one of his letters.

And, if he loved moral beauty, he also loved justice : he felt it profoundly ; for example, his eloquent appeals in favour of the victims of injustice, even when that did not reach him, or when he did not love those who were its objects.

But his life ! Let us look at his life, though it be not strictly the portrait of his character. It was not without virtues, any more than that character was not without good elements. Rousseau was disinterested. His conduct might give him the right to say : " Nothing vigorous, nothing great, can come from a pen quite venal."[3] In his poverty he was beneficent ; he often bestowed charity out of his necessity ; he long continued a pension to an aged relative. His sincerity also, which was not always rudeness, was sometimes not without merit, if we consider the personages to whom he addressed himself, and especi-

---

[1] Reveries, Septième promenade.
[2] See Mackintosh's History of Moral Philosophy, pp. 278 and 433.
[3] Confessions. Livre ix.

ally when he could speak the truth in that tone, which also marks the intention of doing good. When he returned truths for compliments, he thinks he gave more than he received.[1]

But how he transgressed the rule of duty! What gross stains in the immorality of that life! Without recalling to memory his faults, we may say that he loved the chosen rule, not that which was imposed. ·Now, virtue consists in taking the rule, which we do not give to ourselves; it is an act of submission of the conscience, in the first place, and of the heart, in the second. A virtue chosen is not a virtue.

In a letter to M. de Malesherbes, we find an ingenuous confession of that in which Rousseau felt himself to be deficient: " Intimate friendship is so dear to me, because it is no longer a mere duty; one follows the suggestion of his heart, and all is done. This is the reason why I have always been so greatly afraid of benefits, for every benefit requires gratitude; and I feel my heart ungrateful, from this circumstance alone, that gratitude is a duty."[2] These words are characteristic. They are intended to make each one of us reflect. This is still one way of rejecting conscience. Rousseau has, however, spoken much of conscience; but, under this name, he understands either the internal mirror, in which every man may see himself, or the moral sentiment, but not the acknowledgment of a rule. This gap makes a great difference; conscience, in this case, is no longer the adamantine chain which binds man to his duty.

Rousseau confesses that he was ungrateful, and he has, alas! given too many proofs of it. He was so in many ways, and to many persons. We may remind you of Madame de Warens alone, and the remorse, which that ingratitude produced in the heart of Jean Jacques. After twenty years' separation, he discovers her in a state of wretchedness, even of degradation, and he makes no effort to rescue her from it. " Ah! that was the time to discharge my debt. I should then have left every thing to follow her, to continue with her till her last hour, and to share her fate, whatever it might be.' I did nothing of the sort. Drawn away by another attachment, I felt my affection for her diminish in despair of rendering it useful to her. I sighed over her distress, but did not follow her. Of all the remorse that I

---

[1] See the letter to Mlle. D. M. 7th Mai 1764.
[2] Première lettre à M. de Malesherbes. 4th Jan. 1762.

have felt in my life, this was the most lively and the most permanent. In consequence, I deserved terrible punishments, which have not ceased ever since to overwhelm me. O that they could expiate my ingratitude! It was in my conduct; but it has too much torn my heart, for that heart ever to have belonged to an ungrateful man." [1]

We have already mentioned, in reference to his children, the determination of Rousseau to believe a fault effaced or annihilated, when he reproached himself with it. Every moment of his life have we heard him say, according to this opinion, "Jean Jacques could not be a man without feeling and compassion, nor could he be an unnatural father." [2] But was this less a fault committed by him? Is it blotted out on that account? Can it make what was as if it had not been? No; man cannot take away from the offence which he deplores, all its reality nor even all its power. He who commits an act of ingratitude, may not be always ungrateful, but, however, his heart must privately feel the share which it took in the circumstances which urged him to this act. We seek in vain, by such sophisms, completely to detach man from his actions; they form part of ourselves, and although they have not always the same value when set in opposition to the foundation of nature which they express, we cannot yet abstract them from it.

Moreover, Madame de Warens did not know that Jean Jacques returned to her what he had received from her. It was in her house, and under her inspiration, that he imbibed the notion that sentiment is every thing, and a rule nothing.

The last words that we have quoted, must awaken several other sayings of the same kind, inspired by a lofty pride; they lead us to notice this last feature in his character.

This pride, which he naturally possessed, having been long restrained, burst forth with so much greater force from his first success as a writer. It surpassed, I believe, all ordinary bounds. His pretension to be a pattern apart from humanity, is an instance of it. We do not speak of the admiration of his own works. Among superior men, he is not certainly the only one who has estimated or over-estimated his genius; several among them know alone what they are worth, and we do not pretend

---

[1] Confessions. Livre viii.   [2] Ibid.

here to reproach them, but what distinguishes the pride of Rousseau is the high opinion which he cherished of the excellence of his moral nature: "Oh, Moultou, Providence has been deceived; why was I born among men, and yet formed of a species different from them?"[1] He said bluntly: "I, who always believed myself, and who still believe myself, all things considered, the best of men."[2] And again: "You have done me the favour to set a high value on my writings. You would do me a still greater favour by setting a high value on my life, if it was known to you, and still farther on my heart, if it was open to your view; there never was one more tender, more excellent, or more just, neither wickedness nor hatred ever approached it."[3]

This pride showed itself, from the publication of his first work, in his pretension to take an extraordinary part, analogous to that of the founder of an empire or of a religion, and in the imperious and peremptory tone of his writings. From the very first, what contempt for his adversaries! How he treats, from the height of his greatness, the criticisms which are presented to him, though they were serious! He forgets that sincere and earnest criticism is complaisant, according to the remark that we made upon it the other day.

Pride was found in his harsh speeches, which spared nobody, and which he especially reserved for his best friends, who were constantly worn out with his rudeness and gloomy temper. His correspondence with Madame de la Tour Franqueville is an example of it; we feel shocked with the manner in which he treats the most obliging and the most amiable of women.

This pride, truly intoxicating, had its foundation in egoism. Egoism may take a thousand different directions. With men who want elevated ideas, it endeavours to satisfy itself with puerile matters, it turns to sensuality, and is changed into vanity. With Rousseau, it becomes pride. He wished, and it is the principal object of his *Confessions*, to create for himself a society, especially formed to admire him; hence, his perpetual imprecations against society as it is. Pride breathes in his extraordinary paradoxes, and in his disease of speaking constantly about him-

---

[1] A M. Moultou. 15th Juin 1762.   [2] Confessions. Livre x.
[3] A Madame B. 16th Mars 1770.

self, and of referring every thing to himself—the true enthusiasm of egoism. Other great writers also, Montaigne, for example, spoke of themselves without moderation ; but no one has carried this excess so far as Rousseau. He is the discoverer of the genus *egotist*, unfortunately so common in our times. Each of his works is a eulogy, a description and a defence of his person, and even contains the evil which he is pleased to speak of it. Often, it is well known, we love better to speak evil than not to speak at all of ourselves, and this refinement is even mixed with our humility. Yes, humility itself, till God has purified it, is properly no more than an egotism of good taste.

In short, Rousseau's belief in a universal plot directed against him, that folly which rendered desolate the last period of his life, was only the delirium of pride. It merely manifested the supreme degree of that importance attached to every thing that affected his person,—it burst forth every where, even in his extraordinary maxims regarding honour, and in the excessive care of his reputation.

Nevertheless, to this pride we must refer two good effects. The one, that he was unacquainted with envy, which we have already mentioned. No trace of it is found in his works. He has done justice with perfect sincerity to all the great men of his time, even to those of whom he had some right to complain. The other is, that he carried into controversy a dignity and elevation in which so many others were deficient. Here is the end of a letter on this subject to Voltaire : —

"I do not love you, sir; you have done to me, your pupil, and enthusiastic admirer, the most painful evils that you possibly could. You have injured Geneva, as the reward of the asylum which you found there. You have alienated from me my fellow-citizens as a reward for the applauses which I lavished upon you, when I was with them. It is you who renders my stay in my native country insupportable: it is you who will make me die in a foreign land, deprived of all the consolations of the dying, and cast, as all my honour, into a dung-hill; while all the honours that a man can expect will accompany you in my country. I hate you at last since you wish it, but I hate you as a man still more worthy to love you, had it been your desire. Of all the sentiments which my heart entertained for you, there only remain admiration, which cannot be refused to your fine genius, and the love of your writings. If I can honour in you nothing but your talents, it is no fault of mine. I shall never be wanting in the respect that is due to them, nor in the conduct which that respect requires."[1]

After all this, it will be natural to return to the religious disposition of J. J. Rousseau, of which we have mentioned two sources, the love of nature, and the feeling of moral beauty, and to ask ourselves what influence this religion obtained over his life. We cannot do better than quote here the saying of M. de Barante : "On examining Rousseau, we see that there is some analogy between a religion without worship, and a morality without practice."[2]

We have now come to the end of our analysis. We have proved the different elements of this character—an irregular imagination, sometimes active and sometimes dreaming, ardent and imperious passions, logical habits of mind, a contemplative disposition, tender and deep sensibility, a lively feeling of moral beauty, and a lofty pride even to intoxication. I think, in studying the works of J. J. Rousseau, we will easily take up these different features. But it is much more difficult to construct in one's thought the being in whom they meet. The elements remain scattered, and new life does not circulate from the one to the other. The poet, after a laborious and powerful creation, and with the fictitious being before him that his genius has produced, resembles the woman in the Gospel, who remembers no more the anguish, for joy that a man is born into the world.[3] The analyst, devoted to dissection, could not pretend to withdraw, from his cruel work, a living and palpitating creature.

It remains to speak of Rousseau's works. Time fails us ; and we are afraid lest the biography and the criticism should not be in proportion.

SECOND PART.

Rousseau had formed himself, by his own exertions and without assistance, for his profession of authorship ; this was his strength and his weakness ; hence his originality ; and hence too, in part,

---

[1] A Voltaire, 17th Juin 1760. Confession. Livre x.
[2] Barante, Tableau de la Literature Française, au dix-huitième siècle.
[3] John xvi. 21.

the false direction of his system, and the outrageous contempt for facts, which characterised him. He placed at the head of his works this device, *Vitam impendere vero*, a saying of which he gives us the translation himself at the beginning of his *Discourse on the Origin and Foundation of Inequality among Men*, " Let us begin by taking out of the way all facts."

The *Discourse on Arts and Sciences* (1750) is divided into two parts. In the first, the author applies himself to the proof by facts, which he chose and established as seemed good to him. In the second, abandoning facts and setting out from one philosophical idea, he begins and pursues a process of reasoning, which will lead to the conclusion : that what is, ought to be.

The prelude of this rhetorician is a declamation against rhetoricians. We have, at first, difficulty in comprehending how the sophist, who had contested with society the results of his natural development, was so feebly refuted. But from the point at which we looked at the author and his doctrines, it was scarcely possible to combat them with success. Very little attention was paid to criticisms, which Rousseau held very cheap ; the imagination was charmed with his prose at once magnificent and impassioned. To say the truth, the first moment was badly chosen for the defence ; this lava should have been left to cool before touching it. See for example the prosopopœia of Fabricius : "O Fabricius, what would your great soul have thought, if, for your misfortune, you had been restored to life and had seen the pompous appearance of that Rome which was saved by your arm, and which your venerable name had rendered more illustrious than all its conquests ? Gods ! you would have said, what has become of those thatched cottages and of those rustic hearths where moderation and virtue formerly dwelt ? What fatal splendour has succeeded Roman simplicity ? What a strange language is this ? What effeminate manners are here ? What mean these statues, pictures, and edifices ? Fools, what have you done ? You, who are the masters of nations, have rendered yourselves the slaves of the frivolous men whom you have vanquished ! It is rhetoricians who govern you ! It is to enrich architects, painters, statuaries, and players, that you have watered with your blood Greece and Asia ! The spoils of Carthage are the prey of a flute-player ! Romans, hasten to throw down these amphitheatres, break these marbles, burn these pictures, and drive away these slaves, who bring you under their yoke, and whose fatal arts corrupt you. Let other hands become illustrious by vain talents; the only talent worthy of Rome is to conquer the world, and to make virtue reign there. When Cyneas took our senate for an assembly of kings, he was neither dazzled by vain pomp nor by affected elegance; he did not hear there that frivolous eloquence—the study and the charm of silly men. What then did Cyneas see so majestic? O citizens! he saw a spectacle which neither your wealth nor all your arts will ever produce, the finest spectacle which has ever appeared under heaven, the assembly of two hundred virtuous men worthy to command at Rome, and to govern the whole earth!

"But let us get rid of the distance of time and place, and let us see what has passed in our own countries and under our own eyes; or rather let us remove the odious pictures, which would offend our delicacy, and let us spare ourselves the trouble of repeating the same things, under different names. It was not in vain that I called forth the shade of Fabricius; and what did I make this great man say, which I might not have put into the mouth of Louis XII. or Henry IV.? Among us, it is true, Socrates would not have drunk the hemlock; but he would have drunk, in a cup still more bitter, the insulting raillery and the contempt a hundred times worse than death."[1]

Rousseau begins with establishing a fact without proof, the greater happiness of barbarous nations. We might have denied both the fact and the principle. The fact, by defying him to establish the moral superiority of ignorant people; the principle, by denying that this superiority, if it occurs, is the effect of ignorance.

And, although it might be conceded to him, that the sciences corrupt society, he might be asked, why? You are not going to the root of the evil, might some one say to him. What you give as its cause is only one of its effects. Here Rousseau must face an inevitable dilemma. It is impossible for him to show how science, in so far as it is science, could corrupt the mind, if it was not already corrupted, or in the course of being corrupted. There is one of two things—either the desire of knowledge is sinful, or it is not. If it is a sin, say so; if it is not, how could it become

---

[1] Première partie.

sinful? To render us wicked, science must find us already wicked. Could man be pushed to evil by an external cause, if there was not within him a correspondence, a secret principle, which corrupts him? "An unclean vessel sours the sweetest liquor." No, man is virtually, before he is actually, corrupted; if civilization makes us bad, it finds that we ourselves are the accomplices. But we already know Rousseau's opinion on the original goodness of human nature. We have here, on other questions, some very curious passages in the *Discourse on the Sciences* :—

"The thick veil with which Eternal Wisdom has covered all His operations, seemed to be a sufficient intimation that He has not destined us for vain researches. All the secrets which He conceals from us are so many evils from which He secures us."[1] "Until that time, the Romans were contented with practising virtue; all was lost when they began to study it."[2] "Astronomy arose from superstition; eloquence from ambition, hatred, flattery, and falsehood; geometry from avarice; natural philosophy from vain curiosity; all, even morality, from human pride."[3]   .

When we first read this work, we could not help feeling a kind of indignation against such an insolent abuse of thought, and it increased at the second reading.

The *Treatise on the Origin and Foundation of Inequality among Men* appeared in 1753. When he had once entered upon this road, in which opposition led him always farther forward, he pursued the development of his idea.

This *Treatise*, admirable for its style, is divided into two parts. The first is the description of the state of man before the establishment of inequality. Inequality! read, society, for it is rather that which the author attacks, under the name of inequality.

This first state, which is no other than the state of brutality, but of a brutality which bears in itself the germ of progress, appears to Rousseau to be the regular condition of humanity, from which it should never have emerged. I really do not know where he found this type; he acknowledges, at least, that he never discovered it in history. We speak of man in the antediluvian state, but this is man before the creation of Adam. Here, especially, paradoxes abound. We have seen that he begins

---

[1] Première partie.   [2] Ibid.   [3] Deuxième partie.

with putting all facts aside, and this sets him quite at ease; so we shall not be astonished at any thing, even when the author shall tell us: " I dare almost maintain that the state of reflection is contrary to nature, and that the man who meditates is a depraved animal;"[1] we shall merely ask him what is the use of this *almost*, without which the phrase would be more beautiful. We might also ask him, What is Nature? Will he prove to us that an acorn is more in nature than an oak? The proof would be pleasant; the one, nature developed; the other, the germ of development. The description of this state of nature is the most lugubrious romance that can be imagined: " The first, who made for himself clothes and a lodging, in doing so procured for himself things not at all necessary, since he was not without them even at that time."[2] He must, then, have been born with clothes: " There must be an immense space between the pure state of nature and the necessity of language."[3] " The mother at first gave suck to her children because she felt its necessity; then habit rendered them dear to her, and she nursed them afterwards because it was necessary for them."[4] " It is reason which engenders self-love." Others have said, with as little truth, that self-love engenders reason: " It would be sad for us to be forced to admit that this destructive and almost unlimited quality (perfectibility) is the source of all the misfortunes of man; that it is this quality that forcibly draws him at times from this original condition, in which he might spend his days in tranquillity and innocence; that hatches for ages his knowledge and his errors, his vices and his virtues, and renders him at length a tyrant over himself and over nature."[6]

At length we emerge from this happy state of nature; and how? We say, that we come out of it, because we ought to come, or rather because we have never been there. He (Rousseau) asserts that man has come out of it by chance, by fortuitous circumstances:—

" After having shown that *perfectibility*—the social virtues, and the other faculties, which man, in a state of nature, had received in all their power—could never have been developed by themselves, that they required for that purpose the fortuitous concurrence of several foreign causes, which might never arise,

---

[1] Première partie.   [2] Ibid.   [3] Ibid.   [4] Ibid.   [5] Ibid.   [6] Ibid.

and without which he would have for ever remained in his primitive condition, it remains for me to consider and compare the different chances which might have perfected human reason by deteriorating the species, might have rendered a being wicked by rendering him social, and, from a time so remote, might have at length conducted man and the world to the point at which we now see them."[1]

Deteriorate the species! But what could it at that time lose? It had nothing. I am wrong: with every moral attribute it had sympathy, and society made it lose that feeling. As to religious principle, it had none. Man is born without religion; he only gets religion along with corruption; it is apparently in him one of the bad results of society. Man without God is, according to the *Treatise on Inequality*, man regular and perfect

The great power of Rousseau in this discussion consists in only viewing and showing man as an individual, a being of reason, which never existed. The Bible, on the contrary, from the world's early morning points out to us the family. "It is not good for man to be alone,"[2] said Eternal Wisdom, when He gave to him a companion. Never was man found in the state of complete isolation which Rousseau describes; he finds, when he is born, a family, a society, and a country. What a contrast between the noble and simple tradition of the Bible and the dark and cold fiction of Rousseau! His is a world without God; for it is not God, who, after He has put into the heart of man the germ and the conditions of society, meant at the same time that society should corrupt and degrade him. For ourselves we say with the Bible, with Montesquieu, with good sense, that man born into a family is born a social being. And this will serve us afterwards to maintain against this same Rousseau,[3] that in one sense government is anterior to society. Now, the whole pitiful fiction of Rousseau crumbles into ruins as a necessary consequence.

In the second part, Rousseau describes the origin and progress of the state which follows the period of pure nature. He fixes on property as the point at which inequality sets out. But this property, which, he says, has ruined the human species, and which, in his opinion, has been accidentally brought in, has been

---

[1] Première partie.　　[2] Gen. ii. 13.　　[3] See the Contrat Social. Livre i., chap. v.

only able to establish itself after a long series of facts, which, I think, suppose its existence. Husbands, wives, and children living together in a common dwelling, the assembling of different families in front of their houses for songs and dances, already some value attached to the delicate enjoyments of opinion ;—and after all this comes property! Would all this have existed, if the fruit of men's labours had not been more or less secure? This series of facts proves, besides, contrary to what the first part established, that the social development is not owing to accidental circumstances. If the author intended to refute himself, he could not have better chosen his arguments.

There is still a singular contradiction. After all these facts, you find a period of transition, which is that of the greatest happiness of human nature, and yet this happiness is the result of a development, of which the principle was vicious. Why did not humanity stop at this happiness? What accident made men depart from it? The author says nothing of these things. Nowhere have I been able to discover the occasion of this mistake.

But here is the decisive moment :—

" From the moment that one man required assistance from another, and so soon as it was perceived to be useful for one to have provisions for two, equality vanished, property was introduced, labour became necessary, and the vast forests were changed into smiling plains, which it was necessary to water with the sweat of men, among whom were soon seen slavery and misery springing up, and increasing with the harvests. With the poet it was gold and silver, but with the philosopher it was iron and grain, which civilized men, and ruined the human race."[1]

And we say that it is much more natural to admit that man is the proper cause of his own corruption. It is sin which turns every thing, even the best things, to its own profit, and to the injury of humanity, and which has dragged our species into the miseries into which they are plunged. Admit this once for all.

No, Rousseau prefers saying : *Man is good, men are bad;* which means that man has merely to come in contact with his equal, that sin may be immediately produced. And how would it be produced from the contact of two men, if its germ did not exist in each? Men are wicked, because man is wicked.

[1] Deuxième partie.

Rousseau pursued the progress of inequality, which has, according to him, three epochs; the institution of property, the institution of the magistracy, and the change of legitimate into absolute power. Then the mischief was consummated.

Amid the general errors with which this book is filled, there are many particular truths, and judicious observations. For example, the author says, in reference to pleasures: "The will still speaks when nature is silent."[1]

In another place: "The most expert politician would not succeed in subjecting men who only wished to be free."[2]

Lastly: "Frightful discussions, and infinite disorders, which this dangerous power (the right of the people to renounce dependence) would necessarily bring along with it, show more than anything else how much human governments required a more solid basis than reason alone, and how much it was necessary for the public peace, that the divine will should interfere to give to sovereign authority a sacred and inviolable character, which might remove from subjects the fatal right of disposing of it. Although religion should have only done this good to men, it would have been sufficient to induce them to cherish and support it, even with all its abuses, since it spares still more blood than fanaticism sheds."[3]

The *Social Contract* (1760) forms the natural complement of the preceding work. It was published two years before the *Emilius*. The author begins thus: "I mean to inquire, if, in civil order, there can be any sure and legitimate rule of administration, by taking men as they are, and the laws as they may be."[4]

That we may not judge of the *Social Contract* too severely, we must remember the time at which it appeared. Royalty had long been comparatively popular. It had become so especially by overturning a power more unpopular than itself. When the aristocracy was overthrown, and the part of royalty was performed, the latter was found without any popularity connected with itself. Far from labouring to make a popularity for itself, it appropriated all the errors of the nobility, and oppressed the people as the nobility had done. All, or at least the greatest, misfortunes of the people came from royalty, as from an au-

---

[1] Première partie.   [2] Deuxième partie.   [3] Ibid.   [4] Livre i. Introduction.

thentic source, and there was no longer any way of deceiving themselves. They knew that royalty had not so much removed the scourges of the people as its own competitors, and that it had not so much corrected an evil as replaced it. Tradition, remembrances, and the necessity of an acknowledged power maintained it some time longer, but these supports wore out, or rather it destroyed them itself. Contempt began its part when a poet could say, without fear of contradiction, " absolute monarchy is a prey to the people,"[1] and when honest men could ask, if the quality of a good subject was not incompatible with that of a good citizen. At that time royalty, which was entirely undermined by destroying or degrading the intermediate bodies; royalty having no longer any hold of the ground but by its weight, and no longer any reason, so to speak, for its existence, fell at the first blast of the popular tempest. J. J. Rousseau foresaw its downfal. It was then clear to sagacious minds that the state was a baseless fabric. A foundation was sought for. Hence the *Social Contract*, which may be defined in two words, *the gospel of the sovereignty of the people*.

The system, as a whole, is especially the weak part of the work. Break down this system, and you will see that one-half of these grains of dust are diamonds. In this work we meet with admirable passages, very sound opinions, and very beautiful thoughts; I acknowledge it beforehand, so much the more willingly, as the time will fail us to appreciate in detail these fragments worthy of our sympathy, and as the criticism which I feel myself bound to give will, perhaps, appear to be severe.

In reference to this expression, *sovereignty of the people*, we must take this circumstance into account: every abstract noun, and every noun expressive of relation, signify something else, according to circumstances, and borrow from the intentions and character of those who utter them, another meaning. It is not the thing itself that we see, it is the men who give it a name. Neither Algernon Sidney, nor Rousseau himself, saw attached to their theories all the impressions which the mere name of these doctrines awakens in the present day. Men of talent of their time were comparatively very little moved by them.

At a later period, these same ideas appearing anew, amid a

Gilbert, Sat. i. Le dix-huitième siècle.

mass of extraordinary facts, make quite a different impression on the mind. We only see and judge them through these facts; they are adorned or polluted by them; rarely can a sound idea, which has given rise to any abuse, be looked upon with impartiality. The doctrines tainted with blood assume an untoward aspect; like the hands of Lady Macbeth, they cannot get rid of their stains. In our days the principles of Rousseau have acquired a very important meaning. Whether they involved their consequences or not, we do not the less repeat that, in the eyes of their author, and of the men of his time, they did not present the sense which we attach to them at present.

It is not less certain, and more singular, that, in the one case, the phrase was preferred to the thing; while, in the other, the thing is admitted, and the phrase rejected. Is it not strange that the phrase, sovereignty of the people, should be in great disfavour with a people who exercise this right in all its fulness and reality, and that it should be in every mouth and ear among a people who esteem as an equal privilege the creed and the pantomime? Without entering into a discussion, which would be dangerous, if it produced any effect, and idle, if it produced none, let us advance some truths beyond all dispute.

The first is, that individuals united, and living under the same laws, form together a society, in this sense, that none of them can exist merely for others, nor merely for himself. *One for all, all for one*—this device of our confederation should be in reality the device of all civil society. Whether written or not, the social act is found in the conscience.

The second is, that, in any state whatever, the governed are bound to obedience, and the governors to justice. This truth may be considered under two aspects. First, in connection with religion; for the accomplishment of these obligations each party is answerable to God, the Master of subjects, and the Master of masters; and the infringement of the one of these two things does not authorize the infringement of the other. If they be well observed by both parties, this principle should protect the people from tyranny, and the authorities from seditions. It is always expressly *by the grace of God* that sovereigns reign, and this saying should serve as a guarantee to governors and governed. If it was especially intended for the benefit of the first, it was so because, between the two evils of anarchy and despotism, it was necessary to choose the least, because any form of government was judged preferable to anarchy, and because the sacred character of governors is the only proper security against it. In a civil point of view, government and people are bound to one another. This second contract is sometimes written; but though it should not, it would be neither less real nor less to be respected. Though it has neither sanction nor arbiter on the earth, it finds its conditions in the necessities of society. It is tacitly agreed between the two parties, that if they go beyond a certain limit—which is, on the part of the people, patience, and, on the part of the authorities, necessity—there will infallibly be a conflict and a rupture. In both cases it is society which, at all times careful of its preservation, provides for it by a violent check, and thus rescues itself from its dangers, from whatever quarter they come.

So much for the principle; now for the fact. A people—a term which includes the governors and the governed—may be compared to the alphabet, which contains some vowels and many consonants. The vowels are the governors, the consonants are the governed. And, as human speech, with its power and its life, only springs from the close union and constant intertwining of vowels and consonants, so the life of a people only results from the active and real concourse, and from the organic union of the governed with those who direct them. Although we might have the strongest desire to deny these truths, it appears to be totally impossible.

But Rousseau goes farther. He is truly the father of the modern system, which has produced the revolutions of our age. The world took at first the spirit of its doctrines; it afterwards had recourse to the letter.

This, then, is the theory, such as it is developed in the *Social Contract*. Its contradictions will not escape us.

A state, according to Rousseau, regularly and legitimately exists only by the voluntary association of all the individuals who compose it. At least, there must have been at one time unanimity. Those whom the clauses of the contract did not suit, should have withdrawn.

But in a society already formed, how will the exercise of the people's sovereignty be introduced without anarchy? Almost everywhere the people find the government already formed.

Must not the constituted or provisional authorities summon the first meetings? And here we have at the outset a vicious circle.

In the next place, what are the clauses of this contract? Rousseau says nothing of them, which proves that in this primary contract nothing has been determined about the constitution; and the author acknowledges "that a blind multitude, which often does not know its own intentions, because it seldom knows what is good for it, cannot execute of itself an undertaking so great and so difficult as a system of legislation;"[1] and summons a legislator—that is, a wise man, to execute, in his single person, the office of a constituent assembly.

When the work of the wise man is accomplished, and the form of government chosen, the people take up again, or rather enter upon the exercise of sovereignty. For all their acts, a plurality of votes is sufficient, and represents the general will. Rousseau says, however : " What generalizes the will is not so much the number of votes as the common interest which unites them."[2] This is a remarkable confession; but if we prove that the addition of individual interests does not necessarily form the common interest, what will remain of Rousseau's system? How will this common interest be apprehended by the majority of a multitude, which at the moment was quite blind, and which rarely knows what is good for it? The author does not answer this objection. On the question—*whether the general will can err*—he is contented to say: " They always wish their own good, but they do not always see it."[3] But if the general will does not always see what is good, it may then err; it does err, and Rousseau's distinction only rests on a play of words.

Let us proceed—the chiefs elected by this majority, make primary laws, which must be, one after another, submitted to the ratification of the people in assemblies met for the choice of electors, of which all the votes are counted ; yet in this case, as in all others, the author declares that a law is only really a law, when each citizen has given his individual opinion. This would be good in theory, but impossible in practice.[4] Often the principles of Rousseau are not so much errors as lame truths. Give

---

[1] Livre ii. chap. vi.   [2] Ibid. iv.   [3] Ibid. iii.
[4] We have seen it done, however ; let us not forget that this was written in 1833.—
Editors.

them the foot that they want, and they will walk marvellously.

We have said nothing of the form of government. The author declares that such a form of government, the best in certain cases, is the worst in others. (He does not seem to doubt that this observation may be applied also to the direct exercise of the sovereignty of the people). He is not by any means favourable to a pure democracy ; he almost absolutely condemns monarchy, which he judges nevertheless to be inevitable in great states, and prefers it to elective aristocracy, which must not be confounded with representative democracy, such as exists in the greater part of the cantons of Switzerland. Rousseau is the sworn enemy of all representation ; it would inevitably lead, according to him, to the overthrow of liberty. He wishes nothing to come in between the people and the authorities. And then, " when every thing is well examined, it does not seem to be possible, after all, for the sovereign—that is, for the people, to preserve the exercise of their rights, unless the city be very small."[1]   Thus, then, this universal and inalienable principle, the sovereignty of the people, is only applicable to small states. From the dignity of absolute truth, we see it brought down to the humble condition of relative truth. Thus, Rousseau only means, in fact, very few people. But as such states would be in danger of being conquered, he collects them into associations or confederations, whence it follows that the federative system is the only regular position of political societies.

We cannot help repeating here the well-known saying of Voltaire : " It is good to come at the proper time." The ashes of Voltaire and Rousseau were transported in pomp to the Pantheon. Had the revolution, which canonized them after their death, found them alive, it would have brought them both to the guillotine—the one as an aristocrat, and the other as a federalist.

I pass to the *Emilius* (1762). This book is Rousseau himself. It is an addition to the two works of which we have now spoken, and is naturally co-ordinate with them. The author wished to regenerate society ; now, a society is composed of men, and derives its character from them. It was necessary to form men.

---

[1] Livre iii. chap. xv.

The times required a reform in education. All that was spontaneous and natural was suppressed, they did not draw from the child himself the education of the child, it was imposed on him from without; it was not truly *education*. The precepts of Fenelon and Locke were forgotten.

But it may be asked, was Rousseau called to this task? More perhaps than any other he was called to bring out the faults and unreasonableness of the system pursued. He knew to a certain extent what nature required. He repeated with passion, and often with eloquence, what Montaigne, Locke, and Fenelon had said before him; and as the true means of making others feel is to have strong feelings ourselves, Rousseau had a much greater influence on public opinion than those writers had exercised. He had the satisfaction of seeing the public in France, and even in foreign countries, in a great measure, welcome his views. The form of his book, slightly dramatic and romantic, added to the interest of his ideas. To learn where he failed, we have only to analyze *Emilius*.

We may first of all inform those, who from the title of the work, might be tempted to draw from it directions for the education of their children, that this book is not intended for every one. We may tell them for whom it is not, they will tell us if they can, for whom it may be intended.

If they are poor or only in moderate circumstances, then the book is not for them. The author has chosen for his pupil a rich person, and he informs us that "the poor have no need of education, the education of men in their condition is forced, and they could have no other."[1] Such a thought condemns itself: we will not do our hearers the injustice to refute it. Have they any profession, civil duties or a work to perform, the book is not for them : " Neither poverty, nor toil, nor respect for the opinion of mankind can dispense with a father educating his children. What does that rich man do, that father of a family so engaged in business, and forced, in his view, to leave his children without proper attention? He pays another man to bestow that care, which is peculiarly his charge. Venal soul! dost thou think to give to thy son another father for money? Do not deceive thyself; it is not even a master that thou givest to him, but a

---

[1] Livre i.

servant. He will soon form a second."[1]   But we have public
education, these parents will say.   No, you have not, replies
Rousseau: "Public instruction no longer exists, nor can it
exist."[2]

What, then, is to be done, if, for one reason or another, it is
impossible for a man to educate his child himself? Rousseau
provides for it.   He makes a tutor come out of the earth or fall
from heaven, like the legislator in the *Social Contract.* What! a
tutor? that means a servant; did he not say so a little ago?   It
is of no importance; but as a good tutor is a *prodigy,* "you will
be at more trouble in getting him than in becoming one yourself."[3]   Whence it clearly follows, in my opinion, that you will
not find one, and that, according to Rousseau, your son will
remain without education.   You see, then, that this book is not
intended for you.

And observe well, that in this system of education very thing is
necessary, every fault irreparable, and every evil without remedy:
you must never make a mistake.   This is what the author informs
you by his everlasting repetition, *all is lost,* applied to every purpose.   Madame Necker de Saussure, who draws from another
source, does not speak in this manner.   She thinks, on the contrary, that in education few errors are beyond the reach of the
remedy, which a Providence truly paternal most frequently provides for them.   This is not all; the indispensable condition of the
success of the system is during several years an absolute isolation.

"Where shall we place this child?" asks Rousseau.   "Shall we
keep him in the globe of the moon or in a desert island?   Shall
we remove him from all things human?   Will he not continually
have in the world the sight and the example of others' passions?
Will he never see children of his own age?   Will he not see
his parents, his neighbours, his nurse, his governess, his footman,
and even his tutor, who, after all, will not be an angel?   This
objection, he continues, is strong and solid.   But did I tell you
that a natural education would be an easy undertaking?   Men,
is it my fault, if you have rendered difficult all that is good?   I
feel these difficulties, I grant them; perhaps they are insur-
mountable; but it is always certain, that, in applying ourselves
to prevent them, we prevent them to a certain extent.   I show

[1] Livre i.   [2] Ibid.   [3] Ibid.

the end that we must propose; I do not say that we can arrive at it, but I say that he who shall come nearest to it will have best succeeded."[1] But then we must not, through the whole four or five pages, be overwhelmed with this utterance of despair, *all is lost*. Besides, the system of Rousseau does not permit us easily to enter upon it: it is easier to refuse or concede to him every thing than to refuse to him something.

In short, have you to educate a sickly child, the book is not intended for you : " I would not take the charge of a sickly and ill-conditioned child were he to live for eighty years. Let another, instead of me, take charge of this weakly creature; I consent to it, and approve his charity, but my talent does not lie in that way; I cannot teach to live, a person who is only thinking how to prevent himself from dying."[2]

After all this, we may conclude that Rousseau's work is the romance of education, if you do not wish to see in it the indirect demonstration of the utter impossibility of any other education than that of chance. To suppose alone true, and exclusively good, a system applicable to an exceedingly limited number of cases, would be to calumniate the divine wisdom, which does not intend that the impossible road should be the only good one.

We shall now give an idea of the book, or rather of the system. Education is a work for the future—a preparation. But Rousseau does not wish the present to be sacrificed to the future. The present has its rights as well as the future. Every one in preparing himself to live must live ; but the preparation varies according to the end, and it is thus Rousseau understands it. You must choose between making a man or a citizen, for we cannot make both at once."[3] Reconcile this if you can with what he says elsewhere, that every father " owes social men to society and citizens to the state."[4]

A child, too, is educated with a view to some particular profession for which he is destined. But " my pupil may be intended for the army, the church, the bar—it matters not. Before the calling chosen by his parents, nature calls him to human life. To live is the business that I wish to teach him. When he goes out of my hands he will not be, I admit, either magistrate, or soldier, or priest, he will be first of all a man."[5] A sounding term,

---

[1] Livre ii. [2] Ibid. i. [3] Ibid. [4] Ibid. [5] Ibid.

no doubt, which involves a truth too much neglected; but a person may be formed for human life in general, without being inattentive to the various forms which this life assumes. The future calling of the child is one of these. To forget it would be to treat the child as we would treat the globe of the earth, if we should call in question one of its motions.

He then divides man into two portions, general and special, but that is not sufficient for Rousseau; he goes on to cut down man general into three successive beings, the sensitive, the intellectual, and the moral. Here, then, are three modes of education for three men placed over, or enclosed within, one another. A twofold idea pervades to its full extent this triple work; according to the author man is born good, and at his birth he is without individual character; it is society which at once depraves and individualizes him. Till his fifteenth year, Rousseau only sees the species. At this point (between his fifteenth and eighteenth year) the infinite division of character begins."[1]

Thus, then, it will only be necessary to let nature work, and to remove all the influences which might interfere with her operations. The task of education in the first period will be essentially "negative," and the principal rule will be to know how "to kill time."[2]

It is the natural man that we educate at first, we educate the senses. Let us avoid any anticipation and any desire to educate a child by reason : " The principal point of a good education is to make a man reasonable, and yet we pretend to educate a child by reason! This is to begin at the end, and to wish to make the instrument of the work."[3]

There is truth in the exclamation of Rousseau; this is undoubtedly a vicious circle, but life is full of them, and Rousseau is hourly dashing his head against them. He falls into this one, when he sets himself to maintain his pupil in exclusive dependence on some things, rejecting all others, and only endeavouring to inculcate on him a single principle,—the proportion of his desires to his powers. Hence he will become a free man; for " a man really free, only aims at what he can do, and does what he pleases. . . . . Your child ought to do nothing from obedience, but from necessity; the words *obey* and *command* will be blotted

---

[1] Livre iv.   [2] Ibid. ii.   [3] Ibid.

out of his dictionary. Never command him to do any thing, although it be absolutely of no importance. Do not let him even imagine that you pretend to have any authority over him. Let him only know that he is weak and that you are strong."[1] But this is reasoning, and how will the child do it, unless he uses his reason? Take away authority, and it will be very necessary that the child obey his own reason.

Rousseau goes still farther on the point of independence, and adds, "We may be sure that the child will treat with obstinacy every will contrary to his own."[2] That is not true. The child, before you have deprived him of his natural feelings, believes his parents and is not disposed to think badly of every will contrary to his own. By cutting the ties which bind a son to his father, you cut the roots of morality. This relation of filial affection so noble, so sweet, and so holy, does not exist for Rousseau; nature, in what she holds most sacred, is trampled under foot. It is truly marvellous, truly senseless to educate for twenty years a human being in ignorance of all the moral relations with a view to make them, after this age, known and loved by him. Would Providence have given to the child that delightful instinct of confidence, that education might apply itself to the destruction of those relations, which are most natural as well as first in point of date?

In such an education, he goes on without saying that there can be no question about punishments. The child ought only to be chastised for the bad success of his attempts. He should not "know what it is to be in fault."[3] "He will never intend to injure any one; as he only does what nature requires, he will do nothing but what is good."[4] Interest is his only guide, I was going to say his only master. Rousseau expressly declares it. "Present interest, that is the grand motive, and the only one, which conducts us with unerring certainty, and to a great distance."[5]

But as the lessons of experience would not be in themselves very frequent nor very distinct, it is the duty of the tutor to bring them out, and, so to speak, to give them utterance, and, as he is not allowed to show himself on the side of experience, he must have recourse to a number of tricks, pretences, and

---

[1] Livre ii.   [2] Ibid.   [3] Ibid.   [4] Ibid.   [5] Ibid.

falsehoods. See, for example, the history of Robert the gardener,[1] and of the juggler,[2] and a fit of passion as the crisis of a disease,[3] and many others besides. All this is entirely contrary to the spirit of Christianity. But will you be less surprised than I am, on reading, after such episodes, what follows: "We cannot teach children the danger of lying to men, without feeling, on the part of men, the greater danger of lying to children. A single lie told by the master to his pupil would destroy for ever all the benefit of education."[4]

Present interest, then, will be the only motive for this first period of education. It is only materialism and egoism combined. An excellent preparation for forming man intellectual and man moral, whose turn must at last come. Rousseau is very anxious that, till twelve years of age, "the child should not exert his mind," because, according to him, he should make no exertion "till the mind is in possession of all its faculties."[5] Be not astonished at what happens at twelve years of age, Emilius scarcely knows what a book is.[7] And, if it were possible, he never would know one, for his Mentor hates books: "They only teach men to speak of what they do not know."[7] Still, as Emilius is not a savage to send into the wilderness, but a savage formed for inhabiting cities, he must be brought from the forest and must develop the faculties which man in his social capacity uses. He will be instructed since it is necessary; but Rousseau dispenses with it: "You give science early, I employ myself with the proper instrument for acquiring science."[8] How much more happy is his pupil than any other! How much all others have to complain. Examine one of them at the moment, when study comes to snatch him away from his sports:—

"The hour strikes, what a change! His eye becomes dull and his gaiety vanishes; farewell to joy, farewell to wanton sport. A stern and angry man takes him by the hand and says to him harshly, *Let us go, sir,* and leads him away. In the room, into which they enter, I saw books. Books! what miserable furniture for his age (ten or twelve years). The poor child lets himself be dragged along, turns an eye of regret upon every thing which surrounds him, is silent and goes away, his eyes swim with tears which he dares not shed, and his heart is big

---

[1] Livre ii.   [2] Ibid. iii.   [3] Ibid. ii.   [4] Ibid. iv.   [5] Ibid. ii.   [6] Ibid.   [7] Ibid. iv.   [8] Ibid ii.

with sighs which he dares not breathe. O thou who hast no such thing to fear, come, my happy, my amiable pupil, and console us by thy presence for the departure of this unfortunate boy."[1]

Knowledge is the avowed end of the most part of education. Rousseau would rather teach his pupil to be ignorant; but at least what he believes to be the principal object of intellectual culture, is to teach him not to be deceived : " Though he should know nothing, it is of no importance to me, provided that he is not deceived."[2]

In other systems of education, science is exhibited as it is already formed; in his, the pupil is taught to acquire it for himself. The author goes very far in his applications; it would be necessary to hear him, for Emilius to perform anew the whole work of the human race : " He will be found to be ignorant of the microscope and telescope, and your learned pupils will scoff at his ignorance. They will not be wrong, for, before he uses these instruments, I mean that he should invent them, and you may well suspect that this will not so soon happen."[3]

What will be the motives of intellectual education at this period ? Almost the same. At the age of fifteen, Emilius " is considered without respect to others;"[4] and, to use the author's expression, he is only yet " a natural being; we must then treat him as such."[5]

The only difference, says his Mentor, and it is not essential, is, that, instead of our only having known till now the law of necessity, we hereafter have respect to what is useful : " *What is the advantage of this?* For the future, this is the sacred saying that determines between him and me in all the actions of our life."[6]

The teacher ought always to have an answer ready for this question ; if he has not, he must obtain it. But the example which Rousseau gives of it is again an incursion into the domain of morality, and is in effect one inconsistency more.

We pass over the detail of the cultivation of different faculties. This part of the *Emilius* contains interesting points. As to the direction in which the author pretends that these faculties should be exercised, we shall merely add a single word. He has discovered, " that, with the habit of bodily exercise and manual

---

[1] Livre ii.   [2] Ibid. iii.   [3] Ibid.   [4] Ibid.   [5] Ibid.   [6] Ibid.

labour, you insensibly give to your pupil a taste for reflection and meditation."[1] For this reason, and still more for another, namely, the possible vicissitudes of fortune, he wishes that Emilius should learn a trade, and he chooses that of a joiner. If, however, there was a marked aptitude in the pupil for the mathematical sciences, he might become a manufacturer of telescopes. We think, on the contrary, that experience contradicts this favourable influence of material labour on the superior faculties of the mind; and, besides, we do not understand very well how Rousseau combines and accumulates all these occupations at the same time, nor how there could be joined to it the indispensable preparation for a future calling; and we pointedly ask what Emilius will be good for?

Are you not waiting with a certain impatience till this new Prometheus finishes the work of his creation, and till he breathes into it a living soul? God set himself to it less slowly; but, pardon the expression, the whole of Rousseau's book appears to have for its intention, to prove that God was in too great haste. Should not the Heavenly Artizan, after the creation of man, "have begun by exercising the body, and then the intellectual faculties, and, finally, should He not have completed His work by giving to him the moral sense, which makes of him an affectionate and sensible being?" It is thus, at least, that Rousseau begins, in proceeding to what he calls the "second birth" of his pupil.[2]

Before this time, Emilius knew neither benevolence nor affection, but nothing is more easy than to produce them—the elements and powers are given; from self-love, well understood, springs love. Besides, nature provides it at the suitable time. From the need of a wife arises the need of a friend. "All his relations to his species, and all the affections of his soul, spring from that one feeling."[3]

What! from the moment that Emilius will think of marriage, it will come into his mind to love his father, mother, and tutor! This tutor will be obliged to wait till his pupil has attained his eighteenth year, before he can reap any fruit from his cares! Till then, every sentiment of gratitude, and even the word itself, must remain unknown to Emilius.

---

[1] Livre iii.　　　　[2] Ibid. iv.　　　　[3] Ibid.

After this, can we be astonished that there has not been hitherto any inquiry about a higher and juster gratitude? The name of God has not been uttered in the presence of Emilius for eighteen years—this idea remains unknown to him; for Rousseau says, "every child who believes in God is necessarily an idolater;" then he adds, "or at least attributes to God a human form."[1] But he forgets that this is also the case with every man, and in a certain sense must be. Every man supposes in the supreme Being the moral qualities of which he perceives the germ in himself, or in the moral beings with whom he is surrounded; he merely adds to each of them the idea and the brilliancy of perfection. It is not that, we think, which changes the nature of the worship of the eternal God. How should we be capable of conceiving His goodness, love, and even holiness, if the reflections of these divine attributes did not shine among men? Yes, in this sense, we make God in our image, but it is because He began by making us in His.

However this may be, if the moral being takes root in the feeling formerly mentioned, I do not see at least how religion flows from it—religion, which is also an affection of the soul. As to Emilius, if once his existence were completed by the idea of God, as he has formed all his ideas for himself, he will also form his own religion. All the care of his guide will be "to put him in a condition to choose it."[2] There is truth in this thought—it is a pitiful and meagre faith, which is not the result of our own examination. But Rousseau pretends to more than this. As he wished to make his pupil discover the arts and sciences, and thus cause this poor individual to recommence the work of the human race, the work of six thousand years, so he imposes on him farther the work of sixty centuries for the religion which he must discover or invent. This is what the *Profession of Faith of the Vicar of Savoy* reveals to us.

This remarkable fiction, whose foundation is an episode in the life of J. J. Rousseau, contains the finest passages in his book, and perhaps in all his writings. It is an axe with a double edge, of which the one is turned against the materialists and atheists, the other against the Christians. In the first division of this piece, Rousseau defends against impious denials the most noble

---

[1] Livre iv.　　　[2] Ibid.

part of our nature and the existence of God. In the second, he attacks the principle of revelation in general, and the authority of Christianity in particular.

The first part forms a singular contrast to the whole of the work ; it is quite a different philosophy. True, lofty, and sound, it is like a line of obliteration drawn through all the rest. I need not say that there are in it sublime passages :—

" The more I examine myself, the more I deliberate, and read these words written in my soul : *Be just and thou wilt be happy.* It is nothing, however, to consider the present state of things ; the wicked prosper and the just continue to be oppressed. See also what indignation is kindled within us when this expectation is disappointed ! Conscience is roused and murmurs against its author ; it cries with groans : Thou hast deceived me. I have deceived thee, rash man ! and who told thee that ? Is thy soul annihilated ? Hast thou ceased to exist ? O Brutus ! my son ! do not stain thy noble life by self-murder : leave not thy hope and thy glory with thy body on the plains of Philippi. Why sayest thou *virtue is nothing,* when thou art going to enjoy the reward of thy own ? Thou thinkest thou art about to die ; no, thou art about to live, and then I will perform what I have promised."

" Every one, it is said, contributes to the public good for his own interest. But how does it come that the just contributes to it to his own prejudice ? What is dying for one's own advantage ? Undoubtedly no one acts but for his own good ; but if there is not a moral good, of which we must take account, we will never explain by self-interest the actions of the wicked ; it may indeed be believed, that we shall not attempt to go farther. This philosophy would be truly detestable, in which we would be embarrassed with virtuous actions, in which we could not extricate ourselves from our difficulties, but by inventing for them base intentions and motives without virtue, and in which we would be compelled to vilify Socrates and calumniate Regulus." " Conscience ! conscience ! divine instinct, immortal and heavenly voice, sure guide of a being ignorant and finite, but intelligent and free ; infallible judge of good and evil, thou renderest man like God ! It is thou that constitutest the excellence of his nature and the morality of his actions ; without thee I feel nothing in myself which raises me above the brutes, but the sad privilege of wandering from error to error by the help of an understanding without rule, and of reason without principle."[1]

Such passages prove that Rousseau really occupies a place by himself—a singular position among the philosophers of his age. We have no longer the slender sophisms and jokes of Voltaire, and of so many others; he speaks of the great interests of man with feeling and cordiality. A certain degree of religion may be found at the bottom of Rousseau's soul. The remembrance of the worship of his childhood was, perhaps, no stranger there.

A remarkable vacillation is to be noticed in the second part of the *Vicar of Savoy*. The author disputes positive Christianity, miracles, and the testimony of the apostles. His reasonings have in them, at first sight, something specious, but when we examine them we discover their weakness. What is extraordinary cannot be rejected according to mere probability; it is not necessarily reduced to absurdity. No doubt supernatural facts ought not to be lightly admitted; but the denial of the principle of supernatural facts is in itself unreasonable. The only legitimate way is to go straight to the fact itself, and to assure ourselves whether it took place—yea or nay.

It is striking, moreover, to observe how much the author is divided between his heart and his understanding. The understanding cannot take the side of Christianity, the heart constantly returns to it—a mysterious attraction leads him back to it, at the moment that his system drives him from it. It is too well known for me to quote at full length the famous passage : " The majesty of the Scriptures astonishes me, the holiness of the Gospel speaks to my heart." But, when we have read it, and meditated on these words : " Yes, if the life and death of Socrates manifest the wise man, the life and death of Jesus manifest God. . . . . . My friend, men do not so invent; and the deeds of Socrates, of which no one doubts, are less attested than those of Jesus Christ,"—we have difficulty in believing that Rousseau was not a Christian. He does not, any more than Voltaire, attack Christianity at its centre. He has indirectly done this, by maintaining that man was born good, and by snapping in every direction at the idea of redemption; but, directly, he scarcely touches what constitutes the strength of Christianity. All the unbelievers of the last age were contented with turning their arms against the authenticity of the Christian religion, and I conceive that the veracity of the apostles is a great means of proving it; but a more direct proof of the truth of the Gospel is furnished by the Gospel itself. The great fact of the Gospel is God-man—God manifest in the flesh—God assuming our nature to exalt and sanctify it. We are only Christians when we have acknowledged with the heart this truth, which was at all times a stumbling-block to the Jews, and to the Greeks foolishness. It is remarkable that the eighteenth century has neither attacked nor defended Christianity on this fundamental point; while, in the present day, it is there that friends and enemies press one another.

Till the *Vicar of Savoy*, however, Christianity had not been exposed to so sharp an attack; it also gave rise to the persecution of its author. We have seen how, in consequence of the publication of the *Emilius*, Rousseau was obliged to quit France, and then the canton of Berne. It was at Motiers-Travers, in the country of Neufchatel, that Rousseau received the mandate of the Archbishop of Paris against the *Emilius*,[1] and that he replied to it by the letter entitled : *Jean Jacques Rousseau, citizen of Geneva, to Christopher de Beaumont, Archbishop of Paris*.[2] This letter is a masterpiece of reasoning, eloquence, and sophistry. But let us return to the *Emilius*, and endeavour to form a definitive judgment of this work.

In the first place, the *Emilius* is a work purely abstract, without any possible practical consequences, as no place has been reserved in it for man in particular. In this point of view, it may be arranged among the writings of humorists. Farther, this book is the work of unrestrained rationalism. I do not take this word in its theological, but in its most general sense. By it I understand the abuse of reason in all things. Rationalism, whose legitimate office would be to give an account of facts, is ignorant of them, renders them unnatural, isolates them, and distributes them differently from nature. The *Emilius* divides man—changes into reality and applies to life the artificial classifications of science. By taking literally man, *physical, intellec-*

---

[1] Mandement du. 20th Aout 1762.   [2] Motiers. 18th Nov. 1762.

tual, and *moral,* as if there were three men in each individual, and by forgetting that their formation is parallel and reciprocal, by perpetual action and reaction, and by insensible measures, and that the cultivation of each cannot be carried on without the two others, Rousseau has taken three faculties for three essences. He did not see that, by this successive cultivation, and by this arbitrary delay of the development of faculties, which appear from the cradle, and for whose education, under the severest penalty, there is only the proper time, he killed his men, the one by means of the others, and the last especially by the first. He did not see that his system, extensively and completely applied, denies, overthrows, and annihilates the family relation, and hence it is necessarily false and pernicious. He did not see the absurdity and impossibility of educating men without society, since it is for society that he is destined.

Rousseau denied the great principle of duty and obedience. He denied the element of faith. The child only lives by faith, and faith is in itself opposed to reason; and, strange to say, by suppressing faith, and making the child a rationalist, Rousseau wishes to give to man, in all circumstances, sentiment as his only guide. But to make sentiment the rule of life, is to abandon life to every wind of emotion.

He did not see, in short, that his system,—a web wrought with so much art and skill,—only depends on a fiction, and that if a living Emilius, of real flesh and blood, were capable of proving something, an Emilius written, an Emilius in a book, proves nothing.

The idea of Rousseau, the general idea of all his books, is to bring us back to nature. But let us be at one about the word. If by nature is understood the moral state of man as he comes into the world, we must not return to it, for that is a bad condition. And who proves it? J. J. Rousseau himself, when he endeavours to establish the contrary. That his pupil may be good, he removes him from all men, but what is the goodness which the least contact changes into wickedness? What sort of a being is he who cannot obey one of the laws of his nature, love of society, without failing in another law, which is goodness? Is this being good? I say that he is bad, and instead of leading him back to nature, we must remove him from it, and educate him above it. It is on this account, that the Gospel speaks of regeneration or the new birth, and it does more than speak of it, it furnishes us with its elements and conditions. If it had merely told us that we are bad, and that we should come out of the state of nature, it would have done nothing more than the ancient philosophy. But whence comes it, that neither Plato nor Socrates ever regenerated the heart of any man? Because to convert a soul, that is to say, to change its direction, a new career must be opened up to it, another destination must be pointed out, and the heaven above the earth must be perceived. That is the reason why Jesus Christ alone converts, and why Socrates does not. Facts alone act upon the heart of man; never will the same power be given to ideas. Now, the Gospel is a fact, a fact which undoubtedly clearly shows us our misery, but which goes much farther than that. It is alone capable of regenerating our hearts, and it alone leads us back to nature.

This will become evident to us, if we understand by nature the true relations of things. Then assuredly we must return to it. But Rousseau removes us from it. He forces every thing, he makes every thing void; he overturns not only the institutions, but that same nature, to which he pretends to bring us back. Where is this more unworthily violated than in the state of nature, as it calls itself, of which he thought he was giving us the history. There remains, indeed, the other extreme, the extreme with which his mind was still struck, the extreme of civilization. Here still it is the Gospel which places us again in nature. Those who have been able to lay hold of the true spirit of Christianity are of all men those who live most reasonably.

Let us not be surprised at this; and let us remember that the nature against which the Gospel protests, is the moral condition in which we were born in consequence of the Fall. But there exists another nature, a primitive nature, to which the Gospel renders homage, and of which it deplores the extinction by the mouth of St Paul, when he speaks of men *without natural affection*.[1] This nature is the true relations of things. It should be found when the first of all relations is known and respected; and this is the effect of Christianity; a life, accordingly, animated with the spirit of the Gospel will be the most natural of all.

[1] Rom. i. 31. 2 Tim. iii. 3.

I will ask, for example, if the work of Madame Necker de Saussure,[1] who is a Christian, does not lead us in every thing to nature, but quite differently from J. J. Rousseau? And to pass from books to men, and from systems to facts, I will ask, if an education quite contrary to that of Rousseau may not be productive of excellent results? There is a great man, of whom we spoke last year, the Chancellor de l'Hôpital. He was, I think, an accomplished man, as much distinguished by his character as by the powers of his mind. His education was the opposite of the system of Emilius, as strict and severe as any one of his time; nevertheless, this great man continued as liberal in his views as he was firm and solid in his faith. Let us dwell a little on this studious and Christian youth :—

"This city (Toulouse) contained a well-frequented school, in which the youth applied themselves under a severe discipline to those classical studies, which at that time were not aided either by exactness or easy methods, and had therefore all the laborious slowness of erudition. At four o'clock in the morning, in winter, they rose for prayers, and then went to the schools till eleven o'clock; they then returned from them to discuss texts, to verify passages, and, as all their amusement, to read Aristophanes, the Greek tragic poets, Plautus and Cicero."[2]

In short, we may conclude that Emilius did more ill than good. The principles attacked by the author are in themselves more important than the errors which they overturned were prejudicial. At the foundation of this work, what is invented is erroneous. What is found to be just, sound, and solid, had been said before the time of Rousseau. Nevertheless, let us be just, and render to him what is really his. His error was not very far from the truth. On some points, indeed, he led us back to nature, and rendered some precious ideas popular.

It is well known that we owe to him the suckling of the child by the mother in the wealthy class, and in all cases the presence of the little child in the house, and his participation in the cares and caresses of the mother. Another benefit was his getting rid of swathing the child, which confined his limbs, and injured his development. In reference to physical education, he gave other

---

[1] De l'Education Progressive, par Madame Necker de Saussure.
[2] Villemain, vie de l'Hôpital, dans les Melanges Litteraires, tome ii.

precepts, salutary when they are applied with discernment, hurtful when they are improperly and too literally used.

He showed that education has no other commencement than life, and that we cannot begin too soon to give good habits to children. This is undoubtedly one contradiction more, between the maker of systems and the man; but it is not less a truth, and we listen willingly to Rousseau, when he tells us: " In an age when the heart no longer feels any thing, we must make children imitate the actions, of which we wish to give them the habit, expecting that they may do them from discernment, and the love of good."[1]

After he had proscribed all obedience, and after he had banished its very name, is it not curious to see imitation recommended? What is it to imitate, if it is not to obey in act, if not in word? What is it to *accustom one's-self*, an expression which Rousseau uses elsewhere, if it is not to obey his own deeds, and to bind himself to his past life? But this passage, which in principle overturns the system of Emilius, is not, in reference to us, an error. As well as the author, we find man so weak, that we acknowledge the necessity of strengthening his principles by the repetition of the same acts. It is the same with society; how weak soever for a nation may be the restraint of habits, they add, however, a certain weight to institutions. Man is in one sense a bundle of habits, but this expression must be explained. Without a counterpoise, it is certain that habit crushes intelligence and moral liberty. It is necessary, above all, for man to possess principles, virtues, and affections. Habit in itself is not the full ear of corn, it is only the band which unites the sheaf, and prevents it from being scattered.

Rousseau has undoubtedly pushed too far the principle of making his pupil devote himself to the discoveries of science; we have shown its extravagance and absurdity, but this idea applied in moderation, may become very useful, and may improve in a high degree the minds of children.

A happy influence, too, on the whole of education, may be exercised by manual labour. The revolutions of our times have been the means of demonstrating the direct advantage of this resource; we shall not return to the subject. But another

[1] Livre ii.

view, in reference to rich young men, is the extreme facility with which they procure their enjoyments, and their general ignorance of what they cost others. Bodily labour brings nature closer to them, and our dependence upon her; it establishes a sort of intercourse between rich and poor, and furnishes them with a common ground of meeting necessity.

In our opinion, nevertheless, it is much more necessary to educate the poor towards the rich, than to make the rich descend towards the poor. The essential point of intercourse consists, not in the manual labours of the rich nor in the community of physical necessities, but in the community of one idea. At the foot of the cross, at the threshold of the Bible, the rich and poor meet together in a way most salutary to both. A single book presenting the same interest to all classes of men, and to all degrees of intelligence, how very wonderful! The marvellous things to which we are accustomed, no longer strike us; but if you carefully consider them, you will be astonished, as I lately was myself, in reflecting, that a book filled with the sublimest ideas of morality and metaphysics, can satisfy the black slave in the midst of his master's plantation, and the man of genius in the highest state of mental improvement. Permit me to suppose,—I know well it is impossible—but in short, be pleased to admit for a moment, that the Bible does not exist, and that, notwithstanding, man has arrived at the degree of civilization, which he has actually attained. In the meantime, what would we say, if there should appear somewhere, in India if you will, a book suited at once to the intellectual and moral necessities of the different classes of which human society entirely consists? Would you believe this phenomenon, this result scarcely possible in all that could be met with in the largest library? It is, nevertheless, this common ground which the Word of God has put within the reach of the poor.

In finishing the analysis of the *Emilius*, we have attached the last link to the chain of works, which are but the development of one and the same idea.[1] A single work interrupts this con-

---

[1] " All that I have been able to retain of that number of great truths, which in a quarter of an hour flashed upon my mind under that tree, have been very feebly scattered in my three principal works, namely, *The First Discourse, On Inequality,* and the *Treatise on Education,* and these three works are inseparable, and together form a whole."—*Second Letter to Malesherbes.* M. Vinet has added to these three works the *Social Contract,* as a development of the same idea.—*Editors.*

tinuous series; it is the *Letter to D'Alembert on Public Shows* (1758). It arose from an article in the *Encyclopedie* on Geneva, or rather on the establishment of a theatre at Geneva. This article, of an interest so entirely local as to make a strange figure in the *Encyclopedie*, was suggested by Voltaire to D'Alembert, who was settled in the neighbourhood of Geneva, and was passionately desirous to have his works performed in that city. Rousseau was afraid of the effect of this innovation on the manners of his country, and replied by a direct address to D'Alembert.

The style of none of Rousseau's writings is more natural or more true; none of them bears the seal of a more thorough conviction. And yet this letter, admirable as it is, leaves many things to be desired; it is not exempt from paradoxes; its ideas, as everywhere in this author, are taken in a sense too absolute. We will find this by and by.

Rousseau begins with this just observation :—" It is yet quite a problem, respecting the true effects of the theatre, because the disputes which it occasions only divide the church and the world, and each looks at it through prejudices." Indeed, how are we to vanquish an enemy whom we do not meet? Theologians describe authors and actors as poisoning the public. Racine himself, since his conversion, accused himself of having deserved that epithet. But let us remember, that we must be really out of the world to succeed, when we wish to induce others to come out of it too. We are not out of the world, because we have abandoned its noisy pleasures, we have merely passed from one hemisphere to another, and have entered into the domain of purer and more elevated enjoyments. A whole life is sometimes necessary to prove that we are not of the world any longer, and to exercise in this respect some influence over others.

Let us not forget especially, that if we wish to induce any one to give up a gratification, we must present him with another in return for it, and that other must be so superior as that hesitation shall be no longer possible. Simple reasonings never induced any one to quit the world. Though they should be incontestably clear, this evidence would only tend to provoke men. It is labour lost to tell them, that the joys of the world pass away, or even that they are injurious to their salvation, we must have something to present to them as a compensation for what we take from them. Without this condition, all arguments sound hollow. When God wished to snatch man from the dominion of sin, he did not merely promulgate his law, but he manifested his grace, and the hearts affected with this divine attraction were disengaged from worldly joys. First of all, make true Christians, and you will easily obtain afterwards the abandonment of certain pleasures.

Setting out from the point of natural morality, Rousseau could make himself understood by a superior number of hearers. The love of the public good, and the religious worship of their country, were motives addressed to many minds incapable at the time of reaching the measure of Christian renunciation. Rousseau is in possession of the truth, when he asks, whether all kinds of amusements are equally salutary : "If it be true that man must have amusements, you will at least agree that they are only permitted as far as they are necessary, and that every useless amusement is mischievous to a being whose life is so short, and whose time is so precious." And at first sight it is a bad sign and an evil to be obliged to go in search of pleasures so far from his natural sphere; a life well employed ought itself to be the source of true pleasures. As much as possible, these ought to be attached to our condition and brought close to our duties; for example, the joys of domestic life, the best of all terrestrial enjoyments.

Some one says : " I am going to the theatre to obtain instruction." Precious confession ! he involuntarily proves the necessity that man feels of attributing a certain degree of utility to his diversions. As to the reality of that supposed utility of the theatre, that is another question. To be really salutary to public morality, it would be necessary for the theatre to teach those who have need of being taught. Now, no one can teach without reproof, and if the theatre sets itself exclusively to correct, it will be no longer a diversion. Preaching would then be as much prized. No doubt, it treats as infamous great crimes and notorious vices, against which the general conscience revolts, but how does it speak against favourite passions, and the secret inclinations of the heart ? It connives at them ; it inflames and fosters them ; and for its own ends, it must do so. To please the people, it is necessary to furnish spectacles suited to their inclinations. " Let no one attribute to the theatre the power of changing sentiments or manners, which it can only follow and embellish."

But, it will be said, "the theatre as it may and ought to be directed, renders virtue amiable and vice odious. It works a great miracle in doing what nature and reason have done before it! Wicked men are hated on the stage." Are they loved in society, when they are known as such? Some object that the theatre disposes the heart to compassion. "I hear it said," replies Rousseau, "that tragedy leads to pity by terror; it may be so. But what is that pity? a passing and vain emotion, which lasts no longer than the illusion which produced it . . . . when we shed tears over these fictions, we have satisfied all the rights of humanity, without requiring to give farther assistance, instead of by our cares, our soothings, our consolations, and our exertions, assisting the personally unfortunate."

There is truth in this remark. At the theatre, we gradually feel the necessity of looking at misfortune in a poetic light. Now, as the streets are not filled with dramatic characters, are we quite sure that the emotion produced by the elegant and picturesque grief of the stage, will better dispose us to look at, and succour real misfortunes reduced to their real proportions, and rendered prosaic, and often seasoned with flatness, vice, and disgust? If dramatic pity made the heart more sensible to realities, the theatre would be a nursery of philanthropists. I doubt, however, whether Wilberforce and Oberlin were formed in this school.

Nevertheless, it must not be said that every emotion of pity or benevolence, produced by the representation of imaginary events, is a thing prejudicial to the mind, and subtracts in some measure from the interest which we owe to real misfortunes. This would be going too far, no doubt, and Rousseau falls here into the error of pushing his ideas to extremes.

What is necessary to say is, first of all, that that soul frequently softened by theatrical misfortunes, does not become more tender on that account; and, in the second place, that there is a false pity, or a false benevolence too often excited by dramatic writers, which do to the mind more harm than good.

Rousseau disputes the importance of the catastrophe, virtue triumphant and vice punished, in relation to the moral impression; and in this view we are of his opinion. Aristotle himself thinks that the plays in which the hero is overcome, produce the greatest effect. The moral impression results from the whole of the piece, and from the development of the characters, much more than from the catastrophe. If that be attached purely to circumstances, it is a great defect; it has only a value when it is closely connected with the character of the victim.

Rousseau has treated tragedy very badly, perhaps for want of knowing any other than French literature, and for want of conceiving tragedy otherwise than as the nation conceives it. The Frenchman, a practical person and a man of application and effect even in the fine arts, has declared that tragedy is an instrument, a machine destined to produce in the soul, emotions of terror and pity; a definition, which if it rest there, appears to me unworthy of tragedy. But the French genius, being much more oratorical than poetical, examines the action, and scarcely knows contemplation. To tickle and stimulate the mind is in general the end of French tragic poets. This gives to their works a character of fixedness, from which other nations have succeeded better by withdrawing. There is in tragedy a speculative element which they have been able to feel and seize, and which is attached to the highest faculties of the mind. Tragedy does not expound a proposition; it realizes an idea, and this is its principal interest, not only for professional philosophers, but for every serious man. The interest of *Macbeth*, for example, is entirely of this nature; there the spectator contemplates, so to speak, the fatal crime invading the soul, step by step, from the germ originating in a bad thought, to the horrors which precede the final event. Like that of *Macbeth*, the philosophy of *Hamlet* and *Julius Cæsar*, is in each of these plays, a severe and powerful charm, by which the common people allow themselves to be no less captivated than the highly cultivated mind. Without knowing English literature, Rousseau might have found in French tragedy some examples of this contemplative poetry. *Britannicus* derives decidedly its principal interest from its psychological part. If the serpent will issue from the egg, if a monster is about to be hatched, if nature will gain the mastery over education, if Nero will become Nero—the march of crime, in short, insinuating itself into that mind, as into any human mind, such is the true plot of the *Britannicus* of Racine, which is one of the most philosophical works, with the least pretension of being so. *Cinna* is another example of the same sort of interest; this tragedy is not a mere machine for emotion. This kind of play requires a public suited to it, but it is capable of forming one for itself.

Still, the speculative element, dear to the great poets, prevails more than one would think in Corneille, and should restore to many of his tragedies the rank which is refused to them in other respects. This perhaps constitutes the dramatic weakness of some of his works. In all cases, and without any consideration of this point of view, Rousseau should exempt from his proscription not only *Britannicus* and *Cinna*, but *Horace*, *Polyeucte*, *Rodogune*, *Nicomede*, and *Merope*.

Rousseau passes next to comedy, and begins with attacking Molière, whose theatrical writings appear to him a school of vices and bad manners. We think the example badly chosen in reference to the most part of the works of that great genius; we do not enlarge, as we had occasion to unfold them elsewhere. As to Regnard, we entirely agree with Rousseau. *Le Legataire Universal* and, even to return to Molière, *George Dandin* are filled with scenes which make us at once blush and shudder. It is idle talk, some will say, but under favour, why choose such jests? We smile at them, it is true, but have we asked ourselves, whence proceeds that complacency at seeing things represented, which would horrify us if they passed in our neighbourhood? Can it be that, worn out with the fetters of morality and society, and weary of avoiding in our houses things which in our hearts do not displease us, we love to indemnify ourselves for these things by the illusions of the theatre? I leave this point to your reflections.

But Rousseau is too well contented with himself to quote examples. It would have been necessary to go back to the principle in order to establish the point, that ridicule is only good as the accompaniment and modification of the imagination and of contempt, and it is even then a very delicate instrument to manage. *L'Avare* and le *Tartufe* may be a proof of it. In the first of these two comedies, the idea of the paternity is turned into ridicule at a point, which does mischief, whatever may be the truth of the picture. In the second, the description of hypocrisy in all its depth requires the counterfeiting of sentiments and the use of expressions, which are certainly out of place on the stage.

Another principal element of comedy is love intrigue, on which the plot of the play usually turns. Rousseau objects to the part which women are made to perform, a part in general calculated to weaken the respect with which society ought to surround them. The dignity of women is inseparable from the respect which it becomes them to maintain. And which of us would wish to have a daughter or sister, a heroine of comedy. Comedy is, then, pernicious in this respect, that it presents a series of pictures calculated to soften the heart and to incline it to the most attractive passion; it deceives youth, especially women, by holding up, as the great business of life, what only occupies a very short period of it. This misrepresentation has an influence on the character, which is too often imputed on the stage to the old age of both sexes; it tends to render age contemptible, and the duties of a father hateful. In all this we agree with Rousseau. We may only add, that these faults are not peculiar to the theatre, they equally refer to literature and especially to romance. Romance is the theatre transferred to the house.

But is the theatre condemned without reference to its immorality? A difficult question. Rousseau has only taken his examples from the French stage, and, I confess, that the other theatres known to him were not calculated to modify his opinion. There exist, however, in French, some moral pieces; the characters which excite our interest in *les Deux Gendres*, in *l'Avocat*, in several plays of Picard and in some other ancient dramas, are worthy of our sympathy. There are also in German some moral plays, which are indeed seldom acted. Nevertheless, between the excellencies and defects of the theatre, it is perhaps very difficult to make a choice.

If Rousseau had farther generalized his thoughts, he would not have so exclusively censured the theatre, but would have gone back to literature in general, and from literature to life. He would have discovered in both the first principle of the inconsistencies with which he reproaches the theatre alone. Ideas, which quietly circulate in the world, and more or less pervade all the branches of literature, make a loud explosion on the stage; the theatre gives them a charm, a power, and an effect, which they would not have beyond it, but it does not give them their character, and much less does it create them. It is not, then, to the stage that we must ascribe them; it is not there that they are produced, it is, on the contrary, these ideas which have produced the theatre.

In the next place, Rousseau has been too arbitrary in considering the theatre and not dramatic literature in itself; or rather he has confounded the two things. Now dramatic poetry is not in itself worse than any other kind of poetry. To make war against it, is to make war against every species of poetry, and even against life, which is itself also full of fictions. Not only is man without poetry a being incomplete, but moreover, the necessity, not of the theatre but of public shows, is rooted in human nature; it has, in one sense, been sanctioned by divine authority, and to blame absolutely what is done to satisfy this necessity, would be at once unjust and inconsiderate.[1] We may say in acquittal of Rousseau, and in support of truth, that he admitted the need which men have for public shows, and that he endeavours on his side to provide for that necessity.

We do not touch upon the second part of the work of Rousseau, which treats on the effects of frequenting the theatre taken by itself, and of the immoral lives of the actors. Nothing, we think, can be opposed to this part of his argument.

But before concluding, I have a word to say in order to make myself quite understood. I do not absolutely condemn the theatre and those who frequent it, I only take leave to remark, that a true Christian will scarcely indulge the taste for the theatre, or feel its necessity, and that there exists no harmony between Christianity and the theatre in its present condition; and always in the religious point of view, I infer that those who have for the theatre a decided taste are under a delusion, which is not without danger. If the theatre devotes its performers to immorality, and sometimes to infamy, by the task which it imposes on them, how could we be allowed to encourage such an amusement?

Rousseau has been too absolute in his condemnation, but it was partly because the matter in dispute referred to a new establishment, and that he did not believe it possible to go too far in preserving his country from what he regarded as a public misfortune. Persuaded that in certain places, and in certain cases, the theatre may become a necessity and take the place of a greater evil; he did, in his view, honour to Geneva, by supposing

---

[1] M. Vinet has developed these last thoughts in a piece entitled *Theatrical Inclination*, inserted in his essays on moral philosophy and on religious morality.

that it had not yet reached the position of having nothing to lose in point of morality. If a theatre had existed at Geneva, and if the frequenting of that theatre had appeared one of those moral necessities which are acknowledged in deploring them, even then he would have written, but his work would have changed its object. He would have satisfied himself with counsels on the manner of rendering public shows as little pernicious as possible. He would only have permitted comedy to attack the vices, which all the world detests, and let the rest alone; but he would have asked them to reject the works by which bad passions are decidedly flattered. He would have insisted on the men, who had the direction of the theatre, removing from their table all works which directly tend to relax family bonds. He would have even solicited the exclusion of those plays in which the homage of love is presented in a manner equally degrading to the sex which pays and the sex which receives that homage. He would have required the prohibition of all those works in which poetry, music, and dancing are combined, with the evident design of lulling asleep the superior part of our being in the momentary intoxication of the least noble part of ourselves. I know not all that he would have demanded, and still more, I do not know all that he would have obtained; it would be necessary rather to know to whom he addressed himself. He would not have failed if he had made his voice be heard amid an energetic population, ripened by experience, and formed at once by a serious education and serious recollections,—a population which must have derived the greatest part of its prosperity from the purity and simplicity of domestic manners, and to whom, moreover, grave events would have occasioned the conception of anticipations still more grave. To make himself understood by such a people, Rousseau would have had no need of all his talent; the reflections of his fellow-citizens would have taken the lead and have probably left little for his eloquence to accomplish.

The *New Heloise* appeared in 1757–1759. It bears the title of a romance, and in one sense it deserves it, since it is a fiction —the story of a young girl seduced by her tutor; but it is also a didactic and philosophical work, and, in truth, we do not know which of the two elements most prevails. These lovers, in their correspondence, open their minds more than their hearts. Each, in this book, gives dissertations, and sometimes they are masterpieces; for instance, the letter against suicide, addressed by Lord Edward to Saint-Preux, who endeavoured to prove to his friend that they could do nothing better than that both of them should terminate their sufferings by death. We shall quote a few lines of it :—

" Young man, a blind transport leads thee astray ; be more discreet ; do not give advice, while thou requirest it for thyself. . . . . What have I found in the reasonings of this letter, with which thou seemest so satisfied ? A miserable and perpetual sophistry, which, in the wanderings of thy reason, marks the observations of thy heart. . . . . To overturn all this, in a word, I will only put one question : Thou, who believest in the existence of God, in the immortality of the soul, and in the liberty of man, dost thou believe that an intelligent being receives a body, and is placed on the earth by chance, only to live, suffer, and die ? There is, perhaps, in human life an aim, an end, and a moral object ? I entreat thee to answer me clearly on this point, after which we will take up thy letter, line by line, and thou wilt blush at having written it.

" . . . . Art thou, then, permitted, in thine own opinion, to cease to live ? The proof of it is singular—it is because thou hast a desire to die. This is certainly a very convenient argument for villains; they should be much obliged to thee for the arms with which thou furnishest them ; there will be no more offences, which they may not justify by the temptation to commit them ; and, so soon as the violence of passion will prevail over the horror of crime, in the desire they will also find the right to do evil. Is it, then, permitted to thee to cease to live ? I should like to know if thou hast begun to live. What ! wast thou placed on the earth to do nothing ? Along with life, did not Heaven impose on thee a task to perform ? If thou hast finished thy journey before the evening, rest the remainder of the day ; thou can'st do it, but let us see thy work. . . . . Unfortunate man ! find me that just person, who boasts that he has lived long enough, that I may learn from him how one must have borne life to obtain the right of quitting it.

" Thou reckonest up the evils of humanity ; thou dost not blush to wear us out with common-places a hundred times refuted, and thou sayest, life is an evil. . . . . . Life is an evil to the wicked who prosper, and a good to the honest man, though unfortunate. . . . . Dost thou think that I have not discovered, under thy feigned impartiality in the enumeration of the evils of this life, the shame of speaking of thy own ? . . . . Thou art tired of living, and thou sayest life is an evil. Sooner or later thou wilt be comforted, and thou wilt say, life is a good. Thou wilt speak more truly, without reasoning better, for nothing will have changed but thyself. Change, then, from this day ; and, since it is in the bad disposition of thy soul that all the mischief lies, correct thy irregular affections, and do not burn thy house that thou mayest not have the trouble of putting it in order."[1]

This passage is certainly beautiful; but, altogether, the work is spoiled, because it is defective. What a mockery the *New Heloise!* " A monster in literature, and especially in morality ; a book, in which one must see the effect of the most extraordinary prejudice, not to say the most refined perverseness ; a book, in which the good and the bad are mixed, and identified in a manner the most perfidious, or with the most fatal honesty ; but in which passion, although it always reasons, and reasons constantly under the influence of passion, make streams of eloquence flow ; in which sophistry commands, and absurdity makes itself be believed ; in which the purity of the style, like water resting on a bed of marble, is never disturbed by the most tumultuous agitations of the writer ; a book, besides, much too subjective to be good of its kind ; a book more filled with its author than with its subject ; a false work, deficient as a fiction and romance—which assigns to its author, if you will, a place by the side of the true poets, but at a distance from them, if disinterestedness of thought is the first condition of all poetry."[2]

The composition of the *New Heloise* coincides with a sort of crisis in the life of J. J. Rousseau,—the love which he felt for Madame d'Houdetot. He himself informs us that his work was the means of disclosing and expressing his passion.[3]

The feeling might, indeed, light up his genius, but could not furnish the idea of his book ; the personal passions are not the materials for a work of art. This would be to confound reality and truth. Rousseau himself is a proof of it, in spite of the defects of his work. He confides to us the fact, that to succeed in painting his heroine, he was led to create for himself a Julia

[1] Partie, iii. Lettre xxii.
[2] Vinet, Discours sur la Literature Française, p. 70, 71.   [3] Confessions. Livre ix.

purely ideal, and that he himself was enchanted with his own creation.

Some are disposed to compare the *New Heloise* with the *Clarissa* of Richardson. We reject this parallel with indignation; *Clarissa* is a masterpiece of true and simple art, and simplicity is the thing particularly wanting in Rousseau.

Rousseau was the reverse of Diderot; he had more talent than genius; he did not so much strike out new ideas as he had an immense power of execution. We cannot, however, refuse to him the interest which is attached to the obstinate pursuit of one idea. His is no other than the grand idea of the Gospel—regeneration. He seeks it where it is not; but he seeks it, and that is a great matter. To bring back the human race to the moral law, and to re-establish man in his true relations, especially in connection with his equals, is also the end of Rousseau. Unhappily, he could not lay hold on the means. He fell into the error common to so many thinkers, and took possession of it with a brilliant effect; he professed that man is born good, and that society depraves him. In consequence, he wished to begin with the regeneration of society, that he might afterwards arrive at that of the individual. The contrary mode of proceeding strikes us as evident; we think, if society is to be changed, it can only be done by changing individuals. Unless we are ignorant of our primitive dignity, we are forced to confess that, in his present state, man is neither what he ought to be, nor what he was when he came from the hands of his Creator. For want of this point of departure, the whole system of Rousseau is erroneous and vicious; for the more rigorous the logic, the more important are the consequences of a false principle.

It is not less true that Rousseau, who appeared to destroy, and who has perhaps destroyed much, continues to be one of the most synthetic geniuses of his time—that is to say, one of those whose mode of thinking endeavours to construct, to edify, and not to overthrow, especially if he be compared with Voltaire. With his conservative appearance, Voltaire has in fact demolished more. I do not say that Rousseau has not, like Voltaire, furnished arms to those who attacked received ideas; but, I repeat it, that his prevailing idea was positive and constructive. He himself remarks, in his preface to the *Emilius*, that " the literature and science of the age tended much more to destroy than to build up."

It is easy to see that he is sometimes frightened at the consequences of his own system. He seeks to avoid them, and retreats before them. He shows that there are in him two men, who fight against each other; in the front rank the free thinker, the man educated above his age ; then the individual historical man, J. J. Rousseau, a citizen of Geneva, a member of a republic, and a representation of his own age. Nothing can be more flagrant than the contradictions in which these two points of view by turns involve him. The reasoner, the framer of abstractions, is on a thousand occasions contradicted by the historical man. Sometimes even Rousseau, who had less cause to be satisfied with society than Voltaire, defends it against his own boldness. We may remember, in particular, the contrast between the dedication of his *Treatise on Inequality* and the contents of the work. It is the same with respect to the *Social Contract*. See farther his frequent protestations against violent revolutions :—

" For myself, I declare to you that I would not wish for any thing in the world to have taken part in the most lawful conspiracy, because such undertakings cannot be executed without troubles, disorders, and violence, and sometimes not without bloodshed ; and, in my opinion, the blood of a single man is of greater value than the liberty of the whole human race. Those who love liberty sincerely have no need, in order to find it, of so many machines ; and, without causing either revolutions or troubles, whosoever wishes to be free is so in fact." [1]

By another contradiction, Rousseau sometimes regards conscience as an inviolable sanctuary, and faith as an individual sentiment, of which the state can demand no reason ; sometimes he advances a doctrine quite the reverse.

He said in the *Social Contract :* " The right, which the social agreement gives to the sovereign over his subjects, does not pass the bounds of public utility. The subjects are not bound to give to the sovereign any account of their opinions, except in so far as these opinions have a bearing on the community. Now it is of much importance to the state that each citizen should have a religion, which will make him love his duties ; but the doctrines of this religion do not concern either the state or its members, except in as far as these doctrines relate to morality and to the

---

[1] A Madame . . . 27th Sept. 1766.

duties, which he who professes them, is bound to perform to others." [1]

But here is a passage quite different, in his letter to Christopher de Beaumont: " I do not think that strange religions can be lawfully introduced into any country without the permission of the sovereign; for if it be not direct disobedience to God, it is disobedience to the laws; and he who disobeys the laws, disobeys God . . . . It is quite different to embrace a new religion and to live according to that in which we were born; the first case alone is punishable. We should neither allow a diversity of worships to be established, nor proscribe those which have been once settled."

Would disobedience to the laws, then, constitute in itself the falsehood of a religion? Would truth only depend on the state? Religions, true when they continue for a long time, would be false from this very thing that they appear new. How does the apostle of liberty set himself to dogmatize in behalf of these syllogisms?

Such contradictions show, that if Rousseau is more conservative than Voltaire, he is at bottom quite as superficial. His sophisms have not the same character of levity, but the style of these two may draw us into error. That of Rousseau, so full, so strong, and so rich, makes him appear to us more profound than Voltaire, whose phraseology is deficient in fulness and vigour. I repeat it, let us not be seduced by appearances; Rousseau is quite as superficial, but in our estimate of these two men, both formidable instruments of a mysterious will, let us not forget the times in which they lived, and the reality of many of their good intentions.

In the whole of his works, Rousseau strongly inclines to the description of man ·as a solitary individual; he makes this idea prevail over that of man modified by the proprieties of social life. He was the first who placed man in presence of himself. He leads man to the desert and to the bosom of creation, isolated from all others; and while formerly the model of the portrait was always a multitude of heads, it was all nature that served as a model for that which Rousseau delineates. It cannot, however, be said, that Jean Jacques is properly the founder of the

---

[1] Contrat Social. Livre iv. chap. 8.

style called descriptive, of which our time was destined to experience the excess and the abuse. Rousseau knows where to stop, he is wise in point of description; man is to him the living and sensible mirror of the physical world, and what he gives us is much more his own impressions than the wonders of nature. Bernardin de Saint-Pierre has gone one step farther; he had studied nature with greater care and attention, and he describes more. Here I am led to return in part to what I lately advanced. After having, in some measure, disputed the genius of Rousseau, I must still admit that the proper function of genius is the introduction of a new idea. Montesquieu is a man of genius, because he has given as the basis of the *Spirit of Laws* one or two great and fruitful ideas. Although an esthetic cannot be so clearly defined as a scientific idea, it is not less an idea. Rousseau has endowed the imagination with a new world, by the invention of the sentimental style; he expressed, in a manner till then unknown, the mysterious harmonies of the human soul with nature. Rousseau placed in opposition to each other, primitive and social man, and regards the second as degenerate. True or false, this notion was by no means peculiar to his age. The philosophers of that time were struck with certain abuses and certain peculiar defects of society; but this society itself was fully admitted by them.

Rousseau has in like manner opposed sentiment to reason. The eighteenth century is the age of reason, or rather of reasoning, and Rousseau protested against this tendency. If he ever put forth an idea containing an equal mixture of truth and error it was this. On the one side he could perceive that reasoning is not the only source of human knowledge; on the other, he could not see that sentiment is only the impression of the moment, and to hold it as the only basis for the direction of life is to give up life to the mercy of all the passions. Idea alone is without date, it alone escapes the conditions of space and time; it alone maintains in man the element of stability and perseverance. When Rousseau, however, returns to reason, he does what the philosophers of his time did, he opposes it to tradition and authority.

Rousseau is the orator of the eighteenth century; he has transferred the eloquence of the tribune into his books. His prose is not more perfect than that of Buffon, but he had passion, which the other had not. Buffon had little liking for passion, and did not hold in high esteem the style of Rousseau. " He has only," he said, " exclamations and interjections; he is a man badly educated."

Rousseau has given to the language of the eighteenth century all the force of which it is susceptible without altering its essential forms; and I here declare, that my admiration for him as a writer is boundless ; and that I know nothing more impetuous than the fine parts of his *Treatise on Inequality,* of his *Emilius,* of his *Letter to the Archbishop of Paris,* and of his *Heloise.* His eloquence is overflowing, and is not less energetic. The developments which he gives to the same idea, the reasonings with which he supports it, the proofs with which he surrounds it, and the warmth which he circulates through it, all, in proportion as we advance, goes on increasing, with a view to produce in the end a strong inward conviction, even when he is establishing an error, unless we are defended by great accuracy of reasoning. I think that on reflection, and at a later period, he would himself have rejected many of his paradoxes, but it is impossible for me to believe, that at the time at which he is establishing them, he is not perfectly convinced; we do not persuade in this manner without being ourselves persuaded.

What is deficient in Rousseau, then, is neither force, nor proportion, nor animation, nor originality, nor warmth. He wants that calmness which arises from the consciousness of truth, that candour of an upright and simple mind, that peace which makes itself be felt in works of an order quite superior, and which is necessary even to the most impassioned writings. I consider Rousseau inferior to the great prose writers of the seventeenth century in this that he is a rhetorician, a rhetorician above all others, a sophist convinced of his sophisms; but still a rhetorician and a sophist. It is the counterpart of all the wonders of his style. Bossuet is never a rhetorician, so his prose is superior to that of Rousseau. He would have more analogy to Massillon. The latter is constantly seeking a perfect form for his thought; but while the one aims at elegant simplicity, the other unceasingly aspires at redoubled energy. Rousseau is Massillon cased in iron.

Such as he is, Rousseau has exercised vast influence both in politics and literature. It partly depended, no doubt, on this, that more than any one else, he was the apostle of independent ideas, and that he brought them into the domain of social questions. Independent opinions are favourable to a certain kind of eloquence; but this influence is attached, too, to the serious appearance which the nature of Rousseau impressed on his words. Man, at the bottom of his heart, remains a serious being; whosoever speaks to him in a serious way has a better chance of being listened to with attention. This remark applies to the labouring classes, where the primitive characters of humanity are better distinguished. The people, when men laugh with them, think they laugh at them. The masses are serious.

Rousseau was, then, the most powerful writer of his age. In one point, however, this power found its limits. He undertook to give a religion to France; he pretended to substitute for the dry and dull deism of Voltaire an attractive deism, heightened with fancy and sentiment, but it only tended to prove the insufficiency of deism for the consolation and support of humanity. By the mouth of Rousseau, deism has spoken its last word. The world will never go into deism. It will either become Christian, or it will become something which I am reluctant to express.

APPENDIX.

I.

THE FRENCH MORALISTS OF THE EIGHTEENTH CENTURY.

FRAGMENTS OF A COURSE DELIVERED AT BÂLE IN 1833.

FIRST LECTURE.

GENTLEMEN,—The most part of the writers, whom I shall have occasion to bring under your notice, have taught a morality, which is justly revolting to minds accustomed from their infancy to the pure instructions of the Gospel. It would be necessary to search very far back into the history of ages, and perhaps we would not find the period at which the teaching of morality has been so generally altered in its principles. Perhaps by no moralist of antiquity has this science been treated with so little dignity, and polluted with so many indecencies. Perhaps no-where had moralists less call, personally, to this serious office. Besides, we think, the life of a moralist—an instructor of the people—should be, at least, grave. Among the moralists, who will be the object of this second review, gravity is generally wanting both in their lives and discourses. It is wanting in these to such a degree, that it will be sometimes difficult for me to give a complete account of their character. Judging of your disgust by my own, I must pass over important facts, which are decidedly improper both for this place and this auditory, and I shall feel myself obliged either to acquit them in appearance or to accuse them without proof. A serious inconvenience, if the object of this course was not much less a discussion respecting the merit of certain authors, than the comparative estimate of their principal theories, and of those of the Gospel; much less the case of certain individuals than the case of certain ideas. You have anticipated this since the opening of my course last winter, and even from the summary of thàt first course. If, in spite of this anti-cipated remedy, our discussions carry us from time to time to any distressing subject, I shall use another resource. I shall put, in opposition to such a painful passage, some extract of a different origin from an ancient or modern moralist, or better still, the instructions of evangelical wisdom ; this contrast alone will spare me sometimes the fatigue or the disgust of a refutation, and you, and I will be able in this way, without separating with difficulty the lion's jaws, to draw the sweet from the bitter and the pure from the impure.[1]

Before we enter upon the particular examination of each of the moralists of the eighteenth century, let us attempt shortly to characterize the tendency, and the moral doctrines of the period proposed for our study.

The first characteristic which strikes us is, that morality per-vades all the branches of literature. Literature at this period is only a subordinate of morality, taking this last term in its most extensive sense, that is to say, as the art of regulating all the re-lations of man in society. "To correct," said La Bruyère, "is the only end which we ought to propose to ourselves in writing."[2] All the literature of the eighteenth century seems to be founded on this maxim. Few think of correcting themselves, but each one strives to correct others. From the academic discourse to the pamphlet, from the massive quarto to the small sheet, from the eipc poem to the ballad, from the ode to the couplet, all is connected with morality. Literature loses its literary character, the art is no longer cultivated for itself, its form has only value in so far as it may concur in giving authority to a doctrine or some practical view, this is the termination of all the roads ; phi-losophers, historians, poets, economists, artists, men of science, all preach—they preach in prose and in verse ; they preach at their amusements, and when they are weary ; they preach in the black gown, and in harlequin's dress ; they preach at the bar, at the academy, in the theatre, in the drawing-rooms, everywhere, except perhaps in the pulpit ; all the literature of the eighteenth century is only a long sermon. The sole branches of literature, which have not been altered by this universal tendency are those into which instruction enters of itself, and of which it is

---

[1] Allusion to the enigma of Samson. Judges xiv.—*Ed.*
[2] La Bruyère, Les Caractères. Introduction.

the avowed reason and object, the others, as you may imagine, have suffered much from it. The eighteenth century, so brilliant, so rich in writers, so powerful in language, is one of the least literary periods in history, but what is more astonishing, at the first glance, is that this literature has not gained on the scientific side what it has lost in the literary relation.

A scientific character was wanting to the morality of the eighteenth century, and such could not fail to be the case. An object can only be scientifically treated in so far as the design of the researches, which is known beforehand, is not too directly influenced by the will; in other words, in so far as an internal impulse does not decidedly urge more towards one end than towards another. Even in the studies, which have essentially no connection with human interests and passions, this purely scientific character is difficult to attain; in the moral and religious sciences, it is constantly compromised, and is only rarely preserved quite entire. The cultivation of science, as such, may sometimes preserve it; it is a passion which suppresses the rest, but this antidote failed the moralists of the eighteenth century. They did not rise up to the idea of cultivating science for itself, and of making it an object, contenting themselves with gathering up in its footsteps the practical results, which it might let fall from its hand. Science was in their case a means as well as literature; the end was marked; they laboured in the view of certain predetermined results, but they did not inquire. Besides, how could this morality have been scientific, when their minds were not calm? It is not so much at ideas that men wish to arrive as at facts, and at these they wish to arrive by the shortest possible road; it is not study, it is a struggle, it is war; in objections obstacles are especially seen, instruction becomes a keen controversy, not a slow and peaceful elucidation of questions laid down by the human mind or raised by the life. These philosophers are men of action; their philosophy is a business, their school is a league, their mode of speaking a harangue—they do not merely reason, they conspire.

Every thing which at any time has been stamped with the seal of science, elaborated at first among adepts, and included by them in abstract formulæ, has long ripened into these formulæ; then, afterwards, from translation to translation, it has come to the vulgar tongue, and has been placed within the reach and use of all.

Such is not in general the science of the eighteenth century; urged to appear, it is at first set forth in the popular formula : it has a vulgar origin, so to speak, because the thinker himself is vulgar ; this kind of science is not a translation, but an original, the true original is wanting,—I mean to say, the scientific thought. We are clear on the first point, we did not begin by being obscure, because we do not come to the people from a higher ground than they have themselves occupied. The point of departure is common sense, that is, on many subjects, appearance and prejudice. Yes, prejudice, the great object of hatred in the eighteenth century ; prejudice, a word in which the philosophers of the times have so often summed up all the opinions which they did not share ; prejudice is the original sin of the philosophy of the eighteenth century. It is by means of a prejudice, common sense, instinct, appearance, and vulgar opinions, that they have killed all other prejudices. The same causes which deprived the morality of the eighteenth century of a character truly scientific, have imprinted on it a negative character. It came into the world to destroy, this was its mission ; it could not accomplish any other ; the same period cannot demolish and build up.[1] It is not that morality pretended to give to the world any thing positive. It said, it is only getting rid of old rubbish ; Herculaneum is standing under redoubled layers of ashes and lava from Vesuvius, and is ready to be examined, inhabited, and made valuable. A morality should be found entire and well preserved under the cover of old errors. But let these moralists be read with attention ; there is nothing positive in them but destruction ; some vigour and agreement in destroying, but no clear and uniform doctrine comes from this long work ; at the termination of the demolition, the workmen disperse ; and to find them again united, we must seek them near the ruins, where something still remains to be thrown down, and near the rubbish, which must be still reduced to powder. Divided among one another, and each divided in his own mind, you see them, from one book to another, and often in the same book, oscillating from the doctrine of obligation to the theory of pure egoism. There have been

---

[1] This has not escaped all the writers of the time. " The time of building," says one of them, " is perhaps not far off. It appears to me that it is only by combating errors that we establish truths, and that the best books only enlighten, because they undeceive."—(Saint-Lambert. Notes on the poem of the *Seasons*.)

some .efforts towards a determined end, some attempts of consequence, and these make us almost tremble; but it may be said that this philosophy, during sixty years of labour to obtain morality, has produced none, unless a medley of instinct and reason, of conscience and self-interest well understood, of cynicism and sentimentality, of immateriality and materialism, may pass for morality.

Still for want of a settled system, bound to the rule of human actions,· some common tendencies characterize the moralists of the eighteenth century.

Their morality is irreligious, and this is its first and most prominent character. This had never, so far as we know, been communicated to morality, by means of pure science. When morality ceases to be religious, it is the effect of a psychological, not a logical cause. This rupture has for its principle passion rather than reason. Morality every where began with being religious; when it ceased to be so, the discovery was not made by a process of reflection, that the connection of these two things was not logically necessary, and was not essential; but from different causes, this connection was false, and, for that reason, weak. Things came to the point that morality and religion contradict each other, and it became necessary to choose, and then they commonly kept by morality, which altered as it might be, was still more valuable than their religion. Then they were occupied in separating morality and faith, in making the one adhere to conscience, and the other to an indescribable faculty, which is neither conscience nor reason. This crisis took place among almost all civilized people, at the time when public religion was no longer of any value, and when morality was still worth something. It is proved in the psychological history of Athens in the *Euthyphron* of Plato, in which Socrates endeavours to give to conscience an existence by itself independent of God. But in certain countries, and at certain periods, the eagerness of hatred controls this dangerous operation, and aggravates its consequences. It is when the religion of the country has become at once ridiculous and hateful. Such it must have appeared to many at the end of the reign of Louis XIV. We must recall all that, under this unfortunate prince, it seemed to sanction, atone for, and advise. Religion sanctioned the conquest of Holland, the burning of the Palatinate, absolute power, and the oppression of the people.

It expiated adultery, and advised persecution. This last fact, more than all the rest perhaps, awakened hatred against the religion of the prince. Bacon has said somewhere, that if Lucretius had been a witness of Saint Bartholomew, he would have become a hundred times more an atheist than he was before. We may be assured that the revocation of the edict of Nantes would have been equivalent in his eyes to Saint Bartholomew. This cause, more than any other, gave a terrible blow to the influence of religion. It introduced unbelief into the heart, before reasoning had made it enter into the mind. A school of free thinkers was formed secretly during the last years of Louis XIV. With less frankness and plainness than Montaigne and Charron, the very bitter fruit of more ancient abuses, these new unbelievers, artificial, subtile, and ironically respectful, pushed forward to much more important conclusions. Atheism was exhaled from their writings; and who does not know how short the road is from deism to atheism? Voltaire has explained it in his own way, which is not quite ours, but it deserves to be known :—

"Too many persons," he says, "who wish to be informed, and who have no time to acquire sufficient information, say : The masters of my religion have deceived me; there is no religion then, it is far better to cast one's-self into the arms of nature than into those of error; I prefer dependence on natural law rather than on the inventions of men. Others have the misfortune to go still farther, they see that imposture has put a restraint upon them, and they do not even wish the restraint of truth; they incline to atheism. Some become depraved because others have been crafty and cruel.

"These are certainly the consequences of all pious frauds and all superstitions. Men commonly reason by halves ; it is a very bad argument to say : Vovagine, the author of the *Golden Legend*, and the Jesuit Ribadenéira, the compiler of the *Flower of the Saints*, have said only foolish things, therefore there is no God. The Catholics have cut the throats of a certain number of Huguenots, and the Huguenots in their turn have assassinated a certain number of Catholics, therefore there is no God. Some have used confession, communion, and all the sacraments, in order to commit the most horrible crimes, therefore there is no God. I would draw the contrary conclusion, therefore there is a God, who, after this transitory life in which we have been so very ignorant, and have committed so many crimes in His name, will deign to console us for so many horrible misfortunes."[1]

A secondary cause favoured the progress of atheism, the comparative tranquillity which France enjoyed during almost the whole of the eighteenth century. Bacon has said somewhere, with too good reason, that periods of study and improvement, and at the same time of peace and prosperity, are particularly favourable to the development of that fatal doctrine, while public calamities give to the mind a strong impulse towards religion.[2] The eighteenth century has now confirmed the observation of the English philosopher, and has furnished a new justification of our wretched morality.

It was quite necessary that atheistic philosophers should by all means seek some new ring to which they may hang this chain of precepts or advices which they are pleased still to call morality. But what is worthy of remark is, that the others, I mean the deists, are not less bound to do the same thing. They do not see that one among them has seriously connected the principle of morality with the notion of God. This grand idea has remained quite useless in their hands. The contrary, indeed, might have formed an exception in the history of the philosophy of the human race, since it is not generally observed that the followers of natural religion have never made of their God any thing else than an idea. From time to time we hear them strongly recommending to us " the consoling doctrine," the " necessary doctrine" of the existence of God, but they neglect to show us what sorrow it soothes and what gap it fills up. The system of duties, nay, the idea of duty, is neither enforced nor modified, so that we must generally affirm that the morality of the eighteenth century was irreligious.

What the greater part of the deists see most positive and most applicable in the idea of God, is the idea of a restraint on the bursts of wild passions, which, in every civilized society, tremble under the yoke of laws and manners. To reduce religion to the state of acting merely as a restraint, is to degrade

---

[1] Voltaire, Traité de la Tolerance, § x. Du danger de fausses legendes et de la persecution.

[2] Postremo pomutur (sicut causa atheismi) secula erudita praesertim cum pace et rebus prosperis conjuncta. Etenim calamitatis et adversa animos hominum ad religionem fortius flectunt.—*Sermones Fideles* xvi.

it. It ought to do something else than prevent and restrain; it must urge, animate, and create. Fear is only the beginning of wisdom.

If we now become acquainted with the contents of the morality of the eighteenth century, and with what it has particularly taught, we shall remember what we have already said, that it was essentially negative, and that, if we look at it positively, we can scarcely demand anything else than rough drafts of systems. It was almost entirely deficient in what referred to the heart—a part so rich among Christian moralists. Neither in description nor in precept has it reached, in this respect, some of the moralists of whom we have spoken. Above all, it passes over what constitutes the inner man, to go at once to his external and visible relations. It is man as a member of society which it immediately proceeds to consider, and this is not astonishing, since the heart of man is only something in his relations to God, and since God is excluded from it.

The favourite idea of the morality of this time, is to reinstate nature in all its privileges. Nature, and nothing short of it, and nothing beyond it, is the theme of all the moralists. Nothing short—that is, nothing which curtails it; nothing beyond—that is, nothing which raises it above itself; for every thing which was above nature appeared to them to be contrary to nature. Often have they proclaimed, that the only virtues worthy of esteem are natural virtues; that every thing which the soul acquires by an effort is false and dangerous, and that man is only perfect in the sense of a direct development, provided that his principles are positively good, and that he is only vicious from defect. As we enter into the social relations—the only object, to say the truth, of its instructions—it has endeavoured to do honour, under the name of humanity, to one of the lessons of Christian charity. It has recommended man to man, by insisting upon the natural relations which bind together the members of the human race, whatever be their difference and their distance. Setting out with this simple idea, or with this instinct, it sets itself strongly against the usages and laws, which contradict such indisputable relations. It accuses society of its gratuitous barbarities, and of its abuse of power with regard to its members. It strives with all its might to make morality enter into law. It casts disgrace on religious persecution and intolerance. It treats roughly the odious vestiges of feudalism.[1] It condemns slavery, and the infamous traffic of human flesh, known by the name of exportation of the blacks. It claims the abolition of infamous punishments, modified inflictions, and examination by the torture. It brings out, in legislation and in manners, traces of barbarism unworthy of a civilized age. We must neither deny nor disparage any of these services, neither should they be exaggerated.

In giving to the language some new words—*humanité, philanthropie, bienfaisance*—the moralists of the eighteenth century presented it with small portions of the term charity. Charity is all these things at once; it had existed already eighteen centuries, but it was unknown before Christianity. Consequently philosophy did not invent it, but it has given a new edition of it. When Christianity appeared dead in the hearts of man, it was in vain for philosophy to gather together the remnants of its patrimony, which was without an heir, and abandoned, and to do what—I do not say Christianity, always the same, and always faithful to its heavenly traditions, but what those who arrogated to themselves the administration of the divine legacy of Jesus Christ should have done. Why did those, who called themselves Christians, abandon to philosophy some of the appearances, and many of the works of Christianity? Why do we so often see the followers of positive religion among the opponents of the reforms for which philosophy was anxious? Some were not Christians, and others were reluctant, from mistaken prudence, to appear to make common cause in anything whatever, with men whose designs appeared to them dangerous, and whose intentions seemed suspicious.

We must confess that these intentions excited their distrust. For our part, we do not call in question the sincerity of Voltaire, when he defended Calas, Sirven, and Labarre. To feel indignation at the atrocious stupidity, of which these three men had been the victims, it was only necessary to be a man. But it must also be admitted, that the confederation of the philosophical writers of this time too much resembled a league; that their attacks against the social order of the age was greatly deficient in moderation and charity; that their manners and their lan-

---

[1] Such as the right of hunting.

guage were too often wanting in dignity; that, for an end apparently good, they employed means too immoral; and that there was, in a word, too evident an inconsistency between their lives and their office as moralists, between some of their opinions and others, for sincere men not to fear to join in works, whose end otherwise seemed to be lawful and praiseworthy.

Morality is one; we cannot take one part of it and leave the other; duties that differ most in their object are bound to one another by a common tie; we cannot be moral on one point and immoral on another, because we cannot be at once moral and immoral. Man has the inward consciousness of this truth; he is constrained, from his very nature, to demand uniformity in his own life and in the life of others; he must be nothing, or all; he can no more conceive obedience on one side and disobedience on the other, than he can conceive a sphere with a single pole. The absence of one pole makes him deny the reality of the other; the voluntary, systematic, and radical absence of one virtue does not permit him to believe in any other; he only sees their artificial imitations or pure instincts. Thus when moralists, in preaching justice, tread modesty under their feet; when in taking up the natural relations, they vilify others, which, conventional as they may be, are not less the source of the sacredness of the first; when, in boasting of general society, they degrade family society, I know not what within us urges us to doubt their sincerity in what they affirm, since what they deny is its pledge, complement, or dependence.

I have spoken of the value which they have attached to the natural relations: I mean the relations of father, son, and brother. To hear them speak, they were the restorers of a whole side of our moral constitution, which had fallen into ruins. The simple or inattentive are deceived by these things. The enthusiasm, and the kind of mysticism, with which they speak of them, may make it be believed at first sight, that in point of fact all this part of the social relations was uncultivated before their time. In that case they would have very badly succeeded, since no age saw these sacred ties more relaxed. We have every reason to believe that they were much stronger and more respected, when they were less spoken of. The moralists of the eighteenth century spoke much of them, because it was a subject hitherto untouched, popular in itself, and calculated to render them popular. They have spoken much of them, because in their pretension to lead their age to nature, it suited them to insist upon the relations nearest to nature ; but in place of being necessarily satisfied with them, we must call them to account for the discredit, into which, under their own eyes, the relations, which they have so much recommended, have fallen.

In short, we must say that they have preached duty, but none of them has preached morality. No one has gone back to the centre of duty, because no one knew it. By repeated touches, they have made the surface of the human heart quiver; they have appealed to natural sentiments, which had still sufficient life to respond to it; they have ably played on this fine-toned harpsichord, but no one has opened it to regulate it within. The government of the heart, its relations not only to what is without, but to itself, its internal harmony, its unity, its reference to the invisible world, the whole of human destiny—not one of all these things has seriously occupied their minds. They have introduced useful reforms; they have operated upon things, not upon men; they have not brought into the world a single new principle of internal government ; they have not retarded for a moment, nor weakened in the slightest degree, the dissolute principles which tormented the social body ; they have not made the state avoid the profound crisis, the fatal rock, to which the corruption of manners and the overthrow of creeds, were driving it. On the contrary, they have added to the power of the principle of decomposition; they have driven on towards the rock, and if one might say that something good in their work still remains, this something good is entirely as I have said in reference to things, and by no means to man's heart.

I might add, that those men, who show in their writings so much zeal, have not shown so much in their life, and they have written much more than they have performed. But I would not be unjust. Doing was at this time more difficult than speaking, and speaking is also an action. Yet few, very few facts, in the history of the philosophy of the eighteenth century present a clear and unexceptionable character for devotedness. They wanted the circumstances fitted to make their disinterestedness and self-denial more clearly appear. A similar situation, if they have desired it, has always been refused to them. By a singular fatality, pain and sacrifice were always more than compensated;

and martyrdom, even in the smallest degree, was impossible. Suddenly changed at its fall, the storm became a pleasant dew ; the lightning a halo, and censure a triumph. Disgrace was the utmost boundary of a writer's ambition. Persecution, mild, and not continued, was at first disreputable in general opinion ; it came forth with hissing, but retired with shouting. It procured public favour for him, who perhaps would have had none ; and a court for the writer who was already in favour with the public. This was a misfortune for these writers ; their glory at that time may be inferred from their glory at present, and we must subtract heroism from all their qualities. They had no occasion to be heroes, and we shall know by and by whether they had any desire to possess this quality.

It will be natural to inquire, what sort of philosophy prevailed at that time parallel with this morality, for the appearance of a new philosophy always coincides with the appearance of a new morality, and the reverse. The only question which it may be difficult to answer is this : Is it philosophy which produces morality, or morality which determines philosophy ? Without at first answering this question directly, let us remember how rare it is for intellectual speculations to be under the shelter of moral influences ; how many psychological researches especially are subjected to them, how far the ascendancy of the will is acknowledged to be above opinion ; in short, how rare it is for thought to go forth from itself,[1] and only consult itself alone, and imperturbably trace for itself a road through the suggestions and attractions of the moral being, which is constantly by its side. Those who will reflect on these perpetual attempts of the will to usurp the province of thought, will be disposed not to reject as absurd the supposition of a philosophy produced, or at least, if we dare say so, *conditionated*[2] by morality.

Those who inquire, in the next place, which has the greatest power in man,—sentiment or thought ; which more imperiously sways his determinations,—desire, or conviction, which more irresistibly governs his life ; in other words, which has more influence in making him be what he is,—sentiment or thought ; those who will remark, too, that all social theories, and all institutions, did

[1] According to Pascal the will is one of the principal organs of belief.—*Thoughts*, part i., art. vi. § 3.
[2] It is the German word, *bedingt*, which M. Vinet translates here.—*Editors*.

not commence from speculation, but from affection and necessity, will not be far from preferring the supposition which subordinates philosophy to morality. I believe it is much more easy to admit that a certain direction of the will leads to a certain theory respecting the soul, the world, and life, than to admit that such a theory, deduced from pure intellectual speculations, has impressed on the will a certain direction. But if you object that morality itself flows from certain speculative principles, and that philosophy is at its basis, I answer: What are these principles themselves, if not moral facts, facts of the inner man—in other words, sentiments discovered at the bottom of the soul, the first materials, the substance of all farther speculation? Would you pretend that this coincidence, or this proportion between philosophy and morality is an accidental occurrence, to which each doctrine has independently proceeded; a kind of pre-established harmony. No, certainly; we must then admit the influence of one of these authorities over the other, and if this be laid down, it appears to me difficult to hesitate as to the choice.

The son of the celebrated Fichte, writing the life of his father, cannot conceal how much the philosophy which he adopted introduced unity into his conduct, on account of its striking conformity to his moral character, and that moral character had directly led him to the generative hypotheses of his system. Now, we perceive that hypotheses are the point where science and the will meet.[1] Why should not that which happens to a philosopher, happen in a like manner to an age?

In fact, the relation of the philosophy of the eighteenth century to the morality of the same period is very striking. This morality made God an abstract being, and so did the philosophy. This philosophy was sensualism, the morality was equally so. This philosophy was only founded on some appearances; this morality had nothing profound, and drew all its instructions from the surface of the soul. The influence of moral sentiments on metaphysical doctrines is so remarkable in this philosophy, that it has excited in many the species of disgust or aversion which is attached to dishonest acts. They speak in the same way of a responsible action, and of an involuntary opinion, which is of course irresponsible. They apply to it epithets, which are natu-

---

[1] See Buchez. Introduction to the Science of History, page 189.

rally applied to a moral action. All proofs and discussions set aside, they prefer to it, as more elevated and more worthy, the opposite doctrines. They cannot help judging by conscience. Thus M. Frederic Schlegel explains himself in his *Lectures on Literature* :—

" This material philosophy, if the name of philosophy may be so misapplied, which explains all by the body, and refers every thing to sensation, as the one principle, is an error even below humanity. It is probable that a nation or generation will have no sooner seen in all their extent the moral consequences of this philosophy of the senses, than they will turn from it with horror." [1]

M. de Barante expresses himself in this manner respecting the opposite doctrines, in his work on French literature in the eighteenth century :—

" The science of mind was the noble study of Descartes, Pascal, Malebranche, and Leibnitz. This kind of metaphysics led them directly to all the questions which bear most on human destiny. Perhaps they occasionally lost themselves among the clouds of those lofty regions to which they had taken their flight, perhaps their labours were not quite practical, but, at least, they followed an elevated direction. . . . . . This road necessarily conducted them to the noblest of sciences, religion and morality." [2]

We do not at all hesitate to think that the inclination of a whole age to the doctrines of sensualism—that eagerness for a doctrine whose consequences are by no means favourable to the dignity of man and to morality, that desire of being reduced to dust, that longing after death—did not indicate in the heart a very elevated tendency ; and the philosophy of the eighteenth century, in so far as it was prevalent and popular, as it appears to us, might have been justly classed among the moral phenomena of that celebrated age.

We do not farther prosecute these general observations on the morality of the last century. Though insufficient to paint it, we hope they sketch it with some fidelity. The discourses that follow are intended to fill up the sketch which we have now traced.

We have only a single word to add to this introduction. We have more than once, on the occasion of studies of a different

---

[1] Tome ii., p. 235.
[2] Barante, Picture of French Literature in the Eighteenth Century.

kind, traversed in every direction the eighteenth century, on which we are about to enter anew. We have never done so without disgust. This age of inconsistency, exaggeration, imposture, and irreligion, repels, instead of attracting, our attention. We are, then, prejudiced, and we feel it; and we are obliged to arm ourselves against our own prejudices. We are not indisposed, we think, to put an end, within ourselves, to unfair disgust and all excessive aversion. At least we are very firmly convinced that the good cause which we have embraced has no need of our injustice. We may, as the case requires, approve, praise, and excuse our opponents. Truth is a generous enemy. Every thing which may be to the honour of those whom we assail, or to the shame of those who were their adversaries before us, we may and ought to tell. To act otherwise would be to do injury to the truth which we preach. Why dissemble or conceal any thing? Truth has nothing to fear from truth.

END OF THE SECOND LECTURE.

I stop here, because I must stop; the task which was imposed upon me is not accomplished; *pendent opera interrupta.*

We may, however, say that the principal and most influential moralists of the eighteenth century have been brought under our view; and without wishing, when it is too late, to accommodate our design to our circumstances, we may say that the writers who remain to us only deserve, in comparison with the first, a very short consideration, which does not prevent us regretting our inability to give more than a few words to each of them.

Mably occupied himself much with the science of morals, in its relations to government and politics, and assigned, under a soft name, self-interest as the foundation of morality. This tendency began to show itself. We see this observation, which I have made, verified, that when the religious element is withdrawn from morality, it strives with all its might to become utilitarian.

Some traces of it are found in Voltaire, and even in Rousseau; and it is very striking in Helvetius, who, more frankly than any of his time, professes that true morality can only flow from self-interest, properly regulated. This is the leading idea of his book *On Mind,* an expression of unveiled materialism.

This idea receives very extensive developments in the writings of Saint-Lambert, and a rigorous and scientific form in Volney, who, in his *Catechism of the French Citizen*, or *Morality referred to Natural Philosophy*, will teach you to place on the same level, and to treat with the same esteem, cleanliness and gratitude.

Let us now rest for a little with Bernardin de Saint-Pierre, in whom you find once more Montaigne, Fenelon, J. J. Rousseau—all three weakened or softened—and, in short, Bernardin himself, a peculiar and distinct individual. He abused society, like Jean Jacques, but with more discretion. He claimed, like him, the privileges of nature, so often outraged, or unknown in extreme civilization; but, above all, he endeavoured to make Providence be acknowledged and adored in every part of His magnificent creation.

It might now be necessary to draw conclusions from this course, but all that I can do is to retrace my steps, with a view to gather up the ears of corn which here and there in this vast field we have left on the ground. To each of the writers whom we have criticised, we are indebted for some truths. They have instructed us especially by their errors, their defects have enriched us, they had each their beginning in some truth, the Gospel has supplied their deficiencies, and has enabled us to rectify their errors or to solve their enigmas.

J. J. Rousseau, in endeavouring to draw the conclusion that man is good, has proved to us the contrary; man is bad in this sense, that a vicious power constantly tends to remove him from the law of his being, which is obedience and love, and goes even so far as to render him ignorant of that law.

Duclos has given us the opportunity of establishing the fact, that the moral restoration of man can only take place from the heart to the understanding, and not from the understanding to the heart, and that the heart can only be modified by facts—these are principal truths.

Vauvenargues, in excluding conscience, has provoked us to re-establish it in all its privileges, and to show, according to our best ability, that virtue is compounded of obedience and affection.

Voltaire, in referring all our duties to society, has warned us to lay down and to establish this truth, that the existence of God and the immortality of the soul once admitted, these two ideas must be the centre and life of our morality, and that it is on our relations to God that the exactness and solidity of all our other relations depend.

Vauvenargues, farther, in showing that man must have passions, has made us admit that one is necessary to him, which has a holy object, and which acknowledges that object. Several of these philosophers have led us by different roads to the imposing revelations of the first chapters of Genesis ; it is there that we have found the clearest instructions respecting the human heart, the destiny of man, and human society.

All in commencing, each in his own way, an edifice of morality which they were unable to finish, and an arch which they could not close, have sent us back to the workman, who alone can lay the key-stone of the arch—Jesus Christ, " who of God is made unto us wisdom and righteousness, and sanctification and redemption."[1]

All in attempting systems of morality, which are at best only good for men of thought, and not for men in general, have led us to this reflection, that if truth be anywhere, it will have the character of gathering around it, if not all minds, at least minds of every capacity and of every form, the extremes of intellectual culture. Now Christianity alone is the doctrine suited to all, imparting the same ideas, communicating the same affections, and inspiring with the same hopes Schleiermacher and the patient of Planchamp.[2]

If we have succeeded in rendering these conclusions evident to each of you, if you have seen as we have, Christianity finishing, explaining and reforming all systems, and completing by the greatest simplicity of means, and by a single fact, the work often begun by philosophers, we would not believe that we had laboured in vain, and we might console ourselves for all the imperfections of our labours. These are important and numerous, and it is not merely to-day that they strike me ; I have never once come into this hall without bringing into it the oppressive feeling of my own weakness ; I have never once gone out of it without the conviction of having in some way failed in my subject, my task, and my position. But I confess, that now at the end of this course

---

[1] 1 Cor. i. 30.

[2] The paralytic of Planchamp is known in French Switzerland, for the Christian resignation with which he supported his long-sufferings till his death.—*Editors.*

my faults and mistakes are brought together before me, and frighten me by their number. A man is never so rich as when he is removing his goods. My imperfect analyses, lengthened out by so many digressions, the want of precision in my language, the unmerciful length and diffuseness of my developments, wearisome repetitions, the weakness of my expressions, their familiarity sometimes perhaps unsuitable, the too frequent use of irony, too great want also of that charity which for the Christian is only simple justice, and—what do I know? many other defects which I was aware of beforehand, make me at once wonder at my own rashness and at your indulgence.

There is only one testimony which will perhaps be granted to me, and which after strict self-examination, I cannot refuse to myself —it is, that from the beginning to the end of my course, I was a lover of truth. I do not think it possible to reproach me with having even once knowingly led this assembly into error respecting the character and thoughts of the authors whom I analysed, nor respecting any question of morality or philosophy; and when there came before us questions of a delicate character, which I neither could nor should avoid in treating of them, I neither passed them over in silence nor attempted concealment. Independently of the general rule of duty, which I acknowledge, the time in which we live, warned me and kept me on my guard. In the midst of the great agitations of life, the mind is like a lake, the surface of which is ruffled by the wind; so that the images of objects can only appear uncertain and broken. The emotion which great events produce is by no means favourable to the soundness of our judgments, and we have sometimes much difficulty in the time of trouble to remember what we thought and held as true during a period of peace and order. I ought to be on my guard against impressions which had affected me in a more lively manner than many others, and I hope that none of these involuntary impressions has transpired in my discourse.

My interest in this respect was met by my duty. Devoid of the talents which embellish truth, or which make its absence endurable, truth was my only resource. I knew that, if anything could attract you towards me, it was the confidence that, if the man who was speaking to you was scarcely in a condition to say fine things to you, he had it, at least, at heart to tell you the truth; and that, if he erred—a thing to which he is more subject than any other—it would not be with his will. Besides, what motive would have prevented me from telling the truth? Did you not wish it? Were you not come to seek it? Did I not know, long ago, that you were able to hear it? Gentlemen, I have also said it : I have fostered no opinion; I have parleyed with no prejudice ; I have avoided, I confess, some very exciting questions ; but, when the plan of this course imperatively led me to controverted points, far from avoiding them, I went straight to them. In vain an insidious voice whispered in my ear that I risked the loss of your kindness : how highly soever I may value your kindness, I did not wish it separated from your esteem. Truth, gentlemen, your interest and mine, your end and mine, your salvation and mine! To some is the task of speaking it, to others the obligation of hearing it, and to all the duty of loving it. What purpose would it serve to be ignorant now of that which, one day, must come forth with a blaze of evidence? To-day we proceed amid a tumultuous concert of voices, shouts, and murmurs, some pretending to regulate, others to judge, our conduct : they will be one day silent ; we shall scarcely remember having heard them ; a single voice will fill that universal silence —the voice of truth—the voice of God himself. At that penetrating voice, which will vibrate even in the marrow of our bones, and will make the utmost depths of our being start, it will be necessary to join ours. . . . . Shall we be capable of doing this? Shall we ourselves be a lie or a truth before the Lord? Shall we bring to Him hearts in communion or disagreement with His?

II.

STATISTICS OF MORAL IDEAS.

[At the very time when M. Vinet was preparing his course of lectures on the French Moralists, to the end of the eighteenth century, of which several important fragments have been collected in these volumes, he was deeply impressed with the necessity of giving an exact account of the contemporaneous moral ideas. This second study was, in his view, indispensable to the accomplishment of the first. Hence we thought that it would be interesting to compare, with the fragments which we have just given, the following piece, written in 1831, which will show them, we think, in a new light, and which was intended by M. Vinet to be followed by other works, of which the study of the moral ideas of our age was to form one of the essential bases.— *Editors.*]

Statistics, a modern science, has endeavoured to estimate, by means of material facts, the absolute morality of each nation, and the comparative morality of different people. While we do justice to its efforts, and admit that its calculations go much farther than the circumscribed sphere within which it appears to be confined, we regret that it cannot pass certain boundaries, and lend us aid in an important research, which we would willingly attempt, if it could afford us assistance. The morality, of which we would desire to be able to draw up an inventory, is not that gross and legal kind which the tables of M. Dupin show us in a report, so astonishingly consistent with certain given circumstances; nor is it even the morality of the heart—morality in the truest and most extensive acceptation of the term. What we would wish to have is an inventory—a statement, of moral ideas in modern society. We readily perceive that society is not without moral ideas; we see even some of them detached with much force from the midst of all the rest. It is the same with such as are peculiar, so that their designation is almost that of man; but, after all, the view of the whole is confused; the very details are marked with indecision; several ideas are insensibly mingled with strange notions; and the general list, if a person desired to take account of every thing, would be, perhaps, as much more confused as it would be exact.

It would be the duty of a philosophic spirit to class all the particular observations according to their analogies, to blot out apparent differences, to bring out concealed resemblances, and to reduce to a common denominator many different fractions; in a word, to readjust masses, no longer arbitrary and badly connected, as a first look had seized them, but natural and compact, in such a way as to teach us what are the few ideas which, in reality, and in spite of all denials, rule and guide society.

Whatever may be the difficulties of this kind of research, it should nevertheless be attempted; the principal elements of the question would be gradually disengaged, and the work begun by some, and continued by others, would give some general results, which would, perhaps, excite astonishment. Whenever these ideas are produced under the form of scientific systems, it would be found that the work was almost quite finished; but that would not be sufficient. A moral *theory*, whatever relation it may have to generally received ideas, of which it bears always the mark, has yet something free and individual, which does not allow it unreservedly to enter into the public domain, nor consequently into that general inventory, of which we conceive the idea. · It is not merely from theory, but from the life, not merely from philosophers, but from the people, that we must demand an account of the moral ideas which govern society. We must then listen to the people, look at their conduct, seize in its flight their inmost thoughts as they escape from their bosoms less as maxims 'han as deeds. We must not merely collect with care the adages in circulation, but observe private and public life; we must take up its principal and characteristic features, take advantage of artless confessions, which are derived, no doubt, from conversation, but especially of the conduct, manners, and institutions, and enter in every way into society, in order to press out its sap, and to learn what is, in short, not only its morality, but what are its moral principles.

I say, with sorrow, without anticipating the results of this research, that never were principles more rare than precisely at this time of theories; that the multitude of theories is only perhaps a proof of the greater need of principles, and that never perhaps did mankind live more by chance than at this rational period, when every one pretends to know wherefore he obeys, acts, and loves!

Still, there are moral ideas under the various appearances of principles, prejudices, and systems, but they are fragmentary, and consequently false. Men have truths, not the truth. The truth of each idea is only in its combination with other ideas. From its contact with them, and from its modification by them, it receives the absolute and incontestable character of truth. A particular isolated truth, to which you refer the direction of the whole life, is necessarily extended over the whole life, bursts its bounds, so to speak, and improperly applied, ceases to be truth. Isolated, it has no intelligence and disposition of itself; a simple word preserved in a phrase that has been effaced, it has no meaning, and gives no information. It is because in morality truth is one. Before we have taken hold of the central point, to which all particular truths converge, we do not possess even these truths, at least we cannot make any sure and lawful use of them. Before we know why life has been given, what is the condition of the soul, what it wishes, and what it can do, we could do nothing truly useful with these remains of truth, which we still possess; at least, we could not suit our whole life to them; the disproportion is too great between an object so vast and truths so narrow, a rag does not cover a man. It is the same with these ideas as with the brilliant lustre of a broken glass, none of the pieces reflects the whole man; bring them together, fix them carefully, you have not yet a mirror; you will only get one, when you have exposed these broken pieces to the heat of one fire, and when you will have made of it a new one mass. It is the same with moral ideas, one will not be sufficient, nor all these truths in juxtaposition will form the truth; of all the systems, united in connection, you will not make a system of truth. We must go to the very centre of human nature and human life; it is primeval truth that we must find, that will conduct us to all the rest, and will also procure them all for us.

There are many errors in morality; if we would look closely into it, we will see, I believe, that there are many stray truths which require, like stray children, to be led back to their mother. It is not in man's power to invent a pure error, but in possession of a truth, he deranges, isolates, exaggerates, and tortures it till he makes it a lie. The state of the *disjointing* of moral ideas has been always since the fall of man; it is striking in our days among all those who live without Christianity. Christianity appeals to it, collects in its bosom all these ideas, arranges them, fits them, balances them, and makes truths of them, but till they have been elaborated in its crucible, they deceive more than they enlighten. It would be interesting to apply this view to some of the moral, political, and even purely philosophical theories, which are now in favour, or which aspire to the government of the human will. We wish it were in our power to take them one by one, to show their strength and weakness, to determine the point at which they are true, and the point at which they cease to be true, and to prove, with the Gospel in our hand, the facts before our eyes, that Christianity would give them the truths they want, that Christianity knows well what to make of them, if men would allow it to govern them, and that it is in its bosom that all theories are regulated, all excesses moderated, all disorders rectified, and all contradictions melted into harmony, and all truths become true.

THE END.